PREDICTING HEALTH
BEHAVIOUR

Second edition

PREDICTING HEALTH BEHAVIOUR:
RESEARCH AND PRACTICE WITH SOCIAL COGNITION MODELS

Second edition

Edited by
**Mark Conner and
Paul Norman**

Open University Press

Open University Press
McGraw-Hill Education
McGraw-Hill House
Shoppenhangers Road
Maidenhead
Berkshire
England
SL6 2QL

email: enquiries@openup.co.uk
world wide web: www.openup.co.uk

and Two Penn Plaza, New York, NY 10121–2289, USA

First published 2005

A catalogue record of this book is available from the British Library

ISBN–13 978 0335 21176 0 (pb) 978 0335 21177 7 (hb)
ISBN–10 0335 21176 3 (pb) 0335 21177 1 (hb)

Library of Congress Cataloging-in-Publication Data
CIP data applied for

Typeset by YHT Ltd, London
Printed in the UK by Bell & Bain Ltd, Glasgow

Chomolungma

CONTENTS

CONTRIBUTORS

Professor Charles Abraham is Professor of Psychology at the Department of Psychology, University of Sussex, UK.

Dr Henk Boer is Associate-Professor of Health Communication at the Department of Communication Studies, University of Twente, The Netherlands.

Dr Mark Conner is Reader in Applied Social Psychology at the Institute of Psychological Sciences, University of Leeds, UK.

Professor Peter M. Gollwitzer is Professor of Social Psychology and Motivation at the University of Konstanz, Germany and New York University, Psychology Department, New York, USA.

Dr Aleksandra Luszczynska is Senior Lecturer at the Department of Psychology, University of Sussex, UK.

Dr Sarah Milne is Area Prison Psychologist, London Area Office, HM Prison Service, London.

Dr Paul Norman is Reader in Health Psychology at the Department of Psychology, University of Sheffield, UK.

Professor Ralf Schwarzer is Professor of Psychology at the Institut für Psychologie, Freie Universität Berlin, Germany.

Professor Erwin R. Seydel is Professor of Organizational and Health Communication at the Department of Communication Studies, University of Twente, The Netherlands.

Professor Paschal Sheeran is Professor of Psychology at the Department of Psychology, University of Sheffield, UK.

Dr Paul Sparks is Senior Lecturer at the Department of Psychology, University of Sussex, UK.

Professor Stephen Sutton is Professor of Psychology at the University of Cambridge, Institute of Public Health, UK.

Dr Thomas L. Webb is a Lecturer in Social Psychology at the Department of Psychology, University of Manchester, UK.

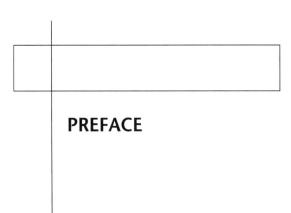

PREFACE

The study of behaviours that influence health and the factors determining which individuals will and will not perform such behaviours has become a key area of research within health psychology. As the second edition of this book testifies, there is a considerable and impressive body of research in this area. The purpose of this book is to provide in a single source an overview of current research and practical details of how to apply the most widely used social cognition models to the prediction of the performance of health behaviours. Social cognition models start from the assumption that an individual's behaviour is best understood in terms of his or her perceptions of the social environment. Such an approach has been widely and successfully used by psychologists to help understand a range of human behaviours, and by health psychologists to understand health behaviours in particular.

The chapters in this book bring together detailed reviews and descriptions of the most common social cognition models and their application to the understanding of health behaviours. It is hoped that this will provide a useful resource to those interested in work in this area and make the described approaches to understanding health behaviours more accessible and more appropriately applied. Moreover, by bringing together these models, similarities and differences between approaches can be examined and the whole approach critically evaluated. Chapters provide the relevant theoretical background, practical examples of how to apply each social cognition model, and details of intervention studies conducted with the model. The chapters focus on a range of different health behaviours and describe the particular problems of using particular social cognition models.

The introductory chapter was prepared by the editors, and examines the concept of health behaviour and briefly reviews epidemiological work on the variation in who performs the different health behaviours. It then outlines the general social cognitive approach taken to understanding and predicting health behaviour. The key features of the social cognition models described in the subsequent chapters are then outlined. Similarities, differences and the potential for integration among these models are then discussed. Finally, the potential for using social cognition models to change health behaviours are outlined.

Following the introductory chapter are six individual chapters describing the most widely applied social cognition models. Each chapter has been produced by prominent researchers in the area and generally follows a common structure. The first section of each 'model' chapter outlines the background to and origins of the model. This is followed by a description of the model, including full details of each of its components, in the second section. The third section contains a summary of research using the model and the findings with a range of health behaviours. The fourth section examines recent developments and expansions to the model. Sections 5 and 6 are intended to provide a clear demonstration of how the model might be applied to a particular health behaviour. First, a detailed consideration of the procedures for developing appropriate measures for each component of the model is presented; and then an application of the model to a specific health behaviour is described and specific problems highlighted. Section 7 reviews intervention studies that have been conducted using the model to change health behaviours. The final section reviews potential future directions for research with the model.

Chapter 2, by Abraham and Sheeran, looks at the most widely used social cognition model in the health domain, the health belief model. Chapter 3, by Norman, Boer and Seydel, reviews protection motivation theory. Both these models were specifically developed in the health domain. Chapter 4, by Luszcynska and Schwarzer, examines social cognitive theory, while Chapter 5, by Conner and Sparks, reviews a model developed in the social psychology domain, the theory of planned behaviour. The next two chapters have been added to the second edition. These new chapters focus on two more recent approaches and employ a slightly different structure. Chapter 6, by Sutton, reviews a group of models known as stage models. These describe the process by which behaviour change occurs and have been widely applied in relation to health behaviours in recent years. Chapter 7, by Sheeran, Milne, Webb and Gollwitzer, examines work on implementation intentions and its application to health behaviours.

In following a common structure, the chapters provide a clear introduction to the background, operationalization, current findings and developments within each model. Each chapter provides a general review of the research, an overview of applying that model to a variety of health behaviours, a description of intervention studies using the model, and discusses the particular problems with applying that model. Each chapter also provides an extended example of the application of the model to a health behaviour and discusses the particular problems with such an application. In the final chapter of the book, the editors review a number of unresolved issues in this area, discuss some future directions for research, and evaluate intervention research based on the social cognition approach.

The book is not intended to be a 'cookbook' of how to apply social cognition models to predicting health behaviours. Rather, the intention is to introduce readers to the general social cognitive approach to the understanding of such behaviours, to describe the most commonly used social cognition models, their differences and similarities, advantages and disadvantages, to enable researchers to apply each model appropriately to their own area of interest, and adequately to analyse and report the results. Useful directions for future research within this paradigm are described both in the model chapters and final chapter of the book.

The common format of the 'model' chapters is intended to help readers access specific aspects of each approach and to aid comparison between approaches. Such comparisons are also drawn out in the first and final chapters of the book. The 'common' coverage should allow readers more easily to use the book as a 'user manual'. It also makes clear distinct features of each model and how each might be applied to specific health behaviours. The book should allow readers to see the advantages and disadvantages of each model and allow them to apply each model appropriately to the health behaviour of interest.

We would like to thank the authors of the chapters for all their hard work in producing such clear descriptions of these models and extensive reviews of the relevant literature. We would also like to thank Open University Press for its help and encouragement during the preparation of the second edition of this book.

Mark Conner and Paul Norman

ABBREVIATIONS

A	attitude towards behaviour
AIDS	acquired immune deficiency syndrome
BB	behavioural beliefs
BI	behavioural intention
BSE	breast self-examination
CB	control beliefs
CHD	coronary heart disease
ELM	elaboration likelihood model
HAPA	health action process approach
HBM	health belief model
HIV	human immunodeficiency virus
HLC	health locus of control
HSM	heuristic-systematic model
IAT	implicit association test
IUD	intra-uterine device
LCR	ligase chain reaction
MAP	model of action phases
MDA	model of dual attitudes
MHLC	multidimensional health locus of control
NB	normal beliefs
PAP	precaution adoption process
PBC	perceived behavioural control
PMAC	proxy measure of actual control
PMT	protection motivation theory
PWM	prototype/willingness model
RCT	randomized controlled trial
RPM	relapse prevention model
SCM	social cognition model

SCT	social cognitive theory
SDT	self-determination theory
SES	socioeconomic status
SET	self-efficacy theory
SEU	subjective expected utility
SN	subjective norm
SRHI	self-report habit index
SRT	self-regulation theory
STD	sexually transmitted disease
TIB	theory of interpersonal behaviour
TPB	theory of planned behaviour
TRA	theory of reasoned action
TSE	testicular self-examination
TTM	transtheoretical model

PREDICTING HEALTH BEHAVIOUR: A SOCIAL COGNITION APPROACH

1 Introduction

A considerable body of research has examined the role of social cognitive factors in predicting health behaviour (see Conner and Norman 1995; Norman *et al.* 2000). This chapter overviews the social cognition approach to understanding health behaviours; introduces key theories employed; compares theories; considers theory integration; and, finally, examines the potential of the approach for changing health behaviour.

Justification for the study of health behaviours is based on two assumptions: that in industrialized countries a substantial proportion of the mortality from the leading causes of death is due to particular behaviour patterns, and that these behaviour patterns are modifiable. It has been increasingly recognized that individuals can make contributions to their own health and well-being through adopting particular health-enhancing behaviours (e.g. exercise) and avoiding other health-compromising behaviours (e.g. smoking). Identification of the factors which underlie such 'health behaviours' has become a focus of research in psychology and other health-related disciplines since the mid-1980s (e.g. Winett 1985; Adler and Matthews 1994; Conner and Norman 1995; Baum and Posluszny 1999; Norman *et al.* 2000). This research has been motivated by a desire to: design interventions to change the prevalence of such behaviours and so produce improvements in individuals' and populations' health; and gain an understanding of the reasons why individuals perform a variety of behaviours.

The health behaviours focused on have been extremely varied, running from health-enhancing behaviours such as exercise participation and healthy eating, through health-protective behaviours such as health screening clinic attendance, vaccination against disease, and condom use in response to the threat of AIDS, to avoidance of health-harming behaviours such as smoking and excessive alcohol consumption, and sick-role behaviours such as compliance with medical regimens. A unifying theme has been that they each have immediate or long-term effects upon the individual's health and are at least partially within the individual's control. Epidemiological studies reveal considerable variation in who performs these behaviours. Approaches taken to understanding factors underlying this variation have been many and varied. A broad distinction can be made between factors intrinsic to the individual (e.g. sociodemographic factors, personality, social support, cognitions) and factors extrinsic to the individual, which can be further divided into incentive structures (e.g. taxing tobacco and alcohol, subsidizing sporting facilities) and legal restrictions (e.g. banning dangerous substances, fining individuals for not wearing seatbelts). The first has received most attention from psychologists, and within these intrinsic factors, cognitive factors have been focused on as the most important proximal determinants. Models of how such cognitive factors produce various 'social' behaviours are commonly referred to as social cognition models (SCMs) and have been widely used by health psychologists. They are recognized to have provided a contribution to the greater understanding of who performs health behaviours (Marteau 1989) and how extrinsic factors may produce behaviour change (e.g. Rutter *et al.* 1993). Justification for focusing on social cognitive determinants in SCMs is twofold. First, they are assumed to be important causes of behaviour which mediate the effects of other determinants (e.g. social class). Second, they are assumed to be more open to change than other factors (e.g. personality). These justifications imply that effective interventions should be based on manipulations of cognitive factors shown to determine health behaviours.

2 Understanding health behaviours

Health behaviours have been defined as 'Any activity undertaken by a person believing himself to be healthy for the purpose of preventing disease or detecting it at an asymptomatic stage' (Kasl and Cobb 1966: 246). There are limitations to this conception including the omission of lay or self-defined health behaviours and the exclusion of activities carried out by people with recognized illnesses that are directed at self-management, delaying disease progression, or improving general well-being. This definition limits the range of behaviours considered to fall under this heading. Gochman (1997) in the *Handbook of Health Behavior Research* defines health behaviours as '... overt behavioral patterns, actions and habits that relate to health maintenance, to health restoration and to health improvement' (Volume 1: 3). A useful broad definition would include any activity undertaken for the purpose of preventing or detecting disease or for improving health and well-being. A variety of behaviours fall within such a definition including medical service usage (e.g. physician visits, vaccination, screening), compliance with medical regimens (e.g. dietary, diabetic, antihypertensive regimens), and self-directed health behaviours (e.g. diet, exercise, smoking). In this section we look at the role of such behaviours in health outcomes, and the range of factors predictive of the performance of such behaviours.

2.1 The role of health behaviours in health outcomes

A number of studies have looked at the relationship between the performance of health behaviours and a variety of health outcomes (e.g. Whitehead 1988; Blaxter 1990). Such studies have demonstrated the importance of a variety of behaviours for both morbidity and mortality. For example, studies in Alameda County identified seven features of lifestyle: not smoking, moderate alcohol intake, sleeping 7–8 hours per night, exercising regularly, maintaining a desirable body weight, avoiding snacks, and eating breakfast regularly, which together were associated with lower morbidity and higher subsequent long-term survival (Belloc and Breslow 1972; Belloc 1973; Breslow and Enstrom 1980). In addition, research into the major causes of premature death in the Western world (e.g. cardiovascular diseases and cancer) has emphasized the importance for prevention of behaviours such as smoking, alcohol consumption, dietary choice, sexual behaviours and physical exercise (e.g. Smith and Jacobson 1988). Studies of premature deaths attributable to lifestyle factors also confirm smoking, alcohol consumption, exercise and diet as major precursors together with gaps in primary prevention and screening uptake (Amler and Eddins 1987). Finally, several authors have pointed out (e.g. Conner and Norman 1995) that health behaviours may have a positive impact on quality of life via delaying the onset of chronic disease and extending active lifespan.

2.2 Predicting the performance of health behaviours

Can we predict and understand who performs health behaviours? This would enable us to make a contribution to the understanding of the variation in the distribution of health across society. It might also indicate targets for interventions designed to change health behaviours. As one might expect, a variety of factors account for individual differences in the propensity to undertake health behaviours, including demographic factors, social factors, emotional factors, perceived symptoms, factors relating to access to medical care, personality factors and cognitive factors (Rosenstock 1974; Taylor 1991; Adler and Matthews 1994; Baum and Posluszny 1999).

Demographic variables such as age, gender, socioeconomic and ethnic status show reliable associations with the performance of health behaviours. Generally, younger, wealthier, better educated individuals under low levels of stress with high levels of social support are more likely to practise health-enhancing behaviours. Higher levels of stress and/or fewer resources are associated with health-compromising behaviours such as smoking and alcohol abuse (Taylor 1991; Adler and Matthews 1994).

Social factors such as parental models seem important in instilling health behaviours early in life. Peer influences are also important, for example in the initiation of smoking (e.g. McNeil *et al.* 1988). Cultural values also appear to be influential, for instance in determining the number of women exercising in a particular culture (e.g. Wardle and Steptoe 1991). Emotional factors play an important role in the practice of some health habits. For example, overeating is linked to stress in some obese people (e.g. Greeno and Wing 1994). Self-esteem also appears to be an important influence in the practice of health behaviours by some (e.g. Royal College of Physicians 1992). Perceived symptoms will control health habits when, for example, a smoker regulates his/her smoking on the basis of sensations in the throat. Accessibility of medical care services has been found to influence the use of such health services (e.g. Whitehead 1988).

Personality theory proposes that traits or combinations of traits are fundamental determinants of behaviour and there is considerable evidence linking personality and behaviour (see Furnham and Heaven 1999, for a general review). Personality factors have been either positively (e.g. optimism) or negatively (e.g. negative affectivity) associated with the practice of health behaviours (Adler and Matthews 1994; Steptoe *et al.* 1994; see Norman and Conner, Chapter 8 in this volume, for a discussion).

Finally, cognitive factors also determine whether or not an individual practises health behaviours. For example, knowledge about behaviour–health links (or risk awareness) is an essential factor in an informed choice concerning a healthy lifestyle. The reduction of smoking over the past 20–30 years in the Western world can be attributed to a growing awareness of the serious health risks posed by tobacco use brought about by widespread publicity. A variety of other cognitive variables have been studied. These factors include perceptions of health risk, potential efficacy of behaviours in reducing this risk, perceived social pressures to perform the behaviour, and control over performance of the behaviour.

A large range of variables, from different models, have been related to the performance of health behaviours (e.g. for reviews see Cummings *et al.* 1980; Becker and Maiman 1983; Mullen *et al.* 1987; Weinstein 1993). For example, Cummings *et al.* (1980) had experts sort 109 variables derived from 14 different health behaviour models. On the basis of non-metric multidimensional scaling six distinct factors were derived:

1   Accessibility of health care services
2   Attitudes to health care (beliefs about quality and benefits of treatment)
3   Perceptions of disease threat
4   Knowledge about disease
5   Social network characteristics
6   Demographic factors

Factors 2 to 5 represent social cognitive factors (beliefs, attitudes, knowledge). Such factors have been central to a number of models of the determinants of health behaviours for several reasons. These factors are enduring characteristics of the individual which shape behaviour and are acquired through socialization processes. They differentiate between individuals from the same background in terms of their propensity to perform health behaviours. They are also open to change and hence represent one route to influencing the performance of health behaviours. Cognitive factors have thus formed a particular area of study in the area of health promotion because they may mediate the effects of many of the other factors discussed earlier and because they are believed to be a good focus in attempting to change health behaviours. These cognitive factors constitute the focus of a small number of widely used models of health behaviour. Such models have been labelled social cognition models because of their use of a number of cognitive variables to understanding individual social (including health) behaviours.

3 Social cognition approach to health behaviour

Social cognition is concerned with how individuals make sense of social situations. The approach focuses on individual cognitions or thoughts as processes which intervene between observable stimuli and responses in specific real world situations (Fiske and Taylor 1991). A significant proportion of social psychology over the past quarter century has started from this assumption that social behaviour is best understood as a function of people's perceptions of reality, rather than as a function of an objective description of the stimulus environment. The question of which cognitions are important in predicting behaviour has been the focus of a great deal of research. This 'social cognitive' approach to the person as a thinking organism has been dominant in social psychology for the past decade or more (Schneider 1991). The vast majority of the work in social cognition can be broadly split into how people make sense of others (person perception) and themselves (self-regulation) (Fiske and Taylor 1991: 14). The focus here is on self-regulation processes and how various social cognitive processes relate to behaviour.

Self-regulation processes can be defined as those '... mental and behavioral processes by which people enact their self-conceptions, revise their behavior, or alter the environment so as to bring about outcomes in it in line with their self-perceptions and personal goals' (Fiske and Taylor 1991: 181). As such, self-regulation can be seen as emerging from a clinical tradition in psychology which sees the individual as involved in behaviour change efforts designed to eliminate dysfunctional patterns of thinking or behaviour (Turk and Salovey 1986). Models of the cognitive determinants of health behaviour can be seen as part of this tradition. Self-regulation involves the setting of goals, cognitive preparations, and the ongoing monitoring and evaluating of goal-directed activities. Two phases are commonly distinguished: motivational and volitional (Gollwitzer 1993). The motivational phase involves the deliberation of incentives and expectations in order to choose between goals and implied actions. This phase ends with a decision concerning the goal to be pursued. The second, volitional phase involves planning and action toward achieving the set goal.

Research concerned with developing models which explain the role of cognitive variables in the motivational phase still dominates the area, although increasingly research has sought to redress this balance by developing models of the role of cognitive variables in the volitional phase (e.g. Kuhl 1984; Kuhl and Beckmann 1985, 1994; Weinstein 1988; Heckhausen 1991; Bagozzi 1992, 1993; Gollwitzer 1993) with increasing applications to health behaviours (e.g. Schwarzer 1992; Sheeran *et al.*, Chapter 7 in this volume).

Social cognition models (SCMs) describing the key cognitions and their inter-relationships in the regulation of behaviour have been developed and extensively applied to the understanding of health behaviours. Two broad types of SCMs have been applied in health psychology, predominantly to explain health-related behaviours and response to treatment (Conner 1993). The first type are attribution models concerned with individuals' causal explanations of health-related events (e.g. King 1982). However, most research within this tradition has focused on how people respond to a range of serious illnesses including cancer (Taylor *et al.* 1984), coronary heart disease (Affleck *et al.* 1987), diabetes (Tennen *et al.* 1984) and end stage renal failure (Witenberg *et al.* 1983) rather than the health-enhancing and compromising behaviours of otherwise healthy individuals. Recent work on illness representations (Petrie and Weinman 1997; Moss-Morris *et al.* 2002; Hagger and Orbell 2003), based on Leventhal's self-regulation model (Leventhal *et al.* 1984), also falls into this category. This work seeks to examine individuals' reactions to a disease (or disease threat). In particular, the model delineates three stages. In the first stage the individual forms an illness representation along five main dimensions, these being disease identity (i.e. the symptoms experienced as part of the condition), consequences (i.e. the perceived range and severity of the consequences of the disease), causes (i.e. the perceived causes of the disease), time-line (i.e. the extent to which the disease is perceived to be acute or chronic in nature), and control/cure (i.e. the extent to which the patient and others can manage the disease). In the second stage, the illness representation is used to guide the choice of coping efforts and, in the third stage, the outcomes of coping efforts are appraised and used to adjust the illness representation. Thus in this model, individuals' perceptions of their illness are seen to have a central role in determining coping efforts and subsequent adaptation. However, a recent meta-analysis conducted by Hagger and Orbell (2003) of studies on illness representations only revealed evidence for a weak correlation between the control/cure dimension and specific problem-focused coping efforts (e.g. medication adherence). In contrast, stronger correlations were found between illness representations and various measures of physical and psychological well-being.

The second type of SCM examines various aspects of an individual's cognitions in order to predict future health-related behaviours and outcomes. The SCMs commonly used to predict health behaviours include the health belief model (HBM; e.g. Becker 1974; Janz and Becker 1984; Abraham and Sheeran, Chapter 2 in this volume); protection motivation theory (PMT; e.g. Maddux and Rogers 1983; Van der Velde and Van der Pligt 1991; Norman *et al.*, Chapter 3 in this volume), theory of reasoned action/theory of planned behaviour (TRA/TPB; e.g. Ajzen and Fishbein 1980; Ajzen 1991; Conner and Sparks, Chapter 5 in this volume); social cognitive theory (SCT; e.g. Bandura 1982, 2000; Schwarzer 1992; Luszczynska and Schwarzer, Chapter 4 in this volume); and health locus of control (Wallston 1992; Norman and Bennett 1995). Another set of models focus on the idea that behaviour change occurs through a series of qualitatively different stages. These so-called 'stage' models (Sutton, Chapter 6 in this volume) include the transtheoretical model of change (Prochaska and DiClemente 1984), the precaution-adoption process (Weinstein 1988), and the health action process approach (Schwarzer and Fuchs 1995). Finally, some recent work examining health behaviours has focused on specific volitional variables (e.g. Kuhl 1984; Gollwitzer 1993, 1999; Abraham *et al.* 1999) In particular, implementation intentions (Gollwitzer 1993) have emerged as a useful technique for changing health behaviours (Sheeran *et al.*, Chapter 7 in this volume).

These SCMs provide a basis for understanding the determinants of behaviour and behaviour change. They also provide a list of important targets which interventions designed to change behaviour might focus upon if they are to be successful. Each of these models emphasize the rationality of human behaviour. Thus, the health behaviours to be predicted are considered to be the end result of a rational decision-making process based upon deliberative, systematic processing of the available information. Most assume that behaviour and decisions are based upon an elaborate, but subjective, cost/benefit analysis of the likely outcomes of differing courses of action. As such they have roots going back to expectancy-value theory (Peak 1955) and subjective expected utility theory (SEU; Edwards 1954). It is assumed that individuals generally aim to maximize utility and so prefer behaviours which are associated with the highest expected utility.

The overall utility or desirability of a behaviour is assumed to be based upon the summed products of the probability (expectancy) and utility (value) of specific, salient outcomes or consequences. This can be represented as:

$$SEU_j = \sum_{i=1}^{i=m} P_{ij}.U_{ij}$$

where SEU_j is the subjective expected utility of behaviour $_j$, P_{ij} is the perceived probability of outcome $_i$ of action $_j$, U_{ij} is the subjective utility or value of outcome $_i$ of action $_j$, and $_m$ is the number of salient outcomes. Each behaviour may have differing subjective expected utilities because of the value of the different outcomes associated with each behaviour and the probability of each behaviour being associated with each outcome. Whilst such a model allows for subjective assessments of both probability and utility, it is assumed that these assessments are combined in a rational, consistent way.

Such judgements underlie many of the widely used SCMs, including the health belief model, protection motivation theory, theory of reasoned action/planned behaviour, and social cognitive theory (Weinstein 1993, 2000; Van der Pligt 1994). Whilst such considerations may well provide good predictions of which behaviours are selected, it has been noted by several authors that they do not provide an adequate description of the way in which individuals make decisions (e.g. Jonas 1993; Frisch and Clemen 1994). For example, except for the most important decisions it is unlikely that individuals integrate information in this way (Van der Pligt *et al.* 2000).

4 Overview of commonly used social cognition models

In this section we outline the different SCMs which form the focus of this volume. We briefly describe how each model conceptualizes the social cognitive variables important in determining behaviour and the way in which these variables are combined to predict behaviour (see other chapters in this volume for a detailed review of key SCMs).

4.1 Health belief model

The health belief model (HBM) is perhaps the oldest and most widely used social cognition model in health psychology (Rosenstock 1966; Becker 1974; Abraham and Sheeran, Chapter 2 in this volume). The HBM has been considered more a loose association of variables that have been found to predict behaviour than a formal model (Conner 1993).

The HBM uses two aspects of individuals' representations of health behaviour in response to threat of illness: perceptions of illness threat and evaluation of behaviours to counteract this threat. Threat perceptions are seen to depend upon two beliefs: the perceived susceptibility to the illness and the perceived severity of the consequences of the illness. Together these two variables are believed to determine the likelihood of the individual following a health-related action, although their effect is modified by individual differences in demographic variables, social pressure and personality. The particular action taken is believed to be determined by the evaluation of the available alternatives, focusing on the benefits or efficacy of the health behaviour and the perceived costs or barriers to performing the behaviour. So, individuals are likely to follow a particular health action if they believe themselves to be susceptible to a particular condition which they also consider to be serious, and believe that the benefits of the action taken to counteract the health threat outweigh the costs.

Two other variables commonly included in the model are cues to action and health motivation. Cues to action are assumed to include a diverse range of triggers to the individual taking action which may be internal (e.g. physical symptom) or external (e.g. mass media campaign, advice from others) to the individual (Janz and Becker 1984). Furthermore, as Becker (1974) has argued, certain individuals may be predisposed to respond to such cues because of the value they place on their health (i.e. health motivation).

4.2 Protection motivation theory

Protection motivation theory (PMT; Rogers 1975) was originally proposed to provide conceptual clarity to the understanding of fear appeals. The theory has been revised on a number of occasions (Norman *et al.*, Chapter 3 in this volume). As typically applied (Maddux and Rogers 1983; Rogers 1983), PMT describes adaptive and maladaptive responses to a health threat as the result of two appraisal processes: threat appraisal and coping appraisal. Threat appraisal is based upon a consideration of perceptions of susceptibility to, and severity of, a health threat. Coping appraisal involves the process of assessing the behavioural alternatives which might diminish the threat. This process is assumed to be based on the individual's expectancy that carrying out a behaviour can remove the threat (response efficacy) and a belief in one's capability successfully to execute the recommended courses of action (self-efficacy).

Together these two appraisal processes result in the intention to perform adaptive (protection motivation) or maladaptive responses. Adaptive responses are held to be more likely if the individual perceives him or herself to be facing a health threat to which he or she is susceptible and which is perceived to be severe. Fear arousal is assumed to operate via increasing perceptions of susceptibility and severity. Adaptive responses are also more likely if the individual perceives such responses to be effective in reducing the threat and believes that he or she can successfully perform the adaptive response. These two cognitive appraisals feed into protection motivation which is an intervening variable that arouses, sustains and directs activity to protect the self from danger. Protection motivation is typically operationalized as intention to perform the health-protective behaviour or avoid the health-compromising behaviour. Actual behaviour is assumed to be a function of intentions.

The theory has appeared in a number of different forms, originally being developed as a way to understand the response to fear appeals. In the revised theory (Maddux and Rogers 1983), described here, it can be seen as a hybrid theory (Prentice-Dunn and Rogers 1986) with susceptibility, severity and response-efficacy components all originating from the HBM, and self-efficacy originating from Bandura's self-efficacy theory (Bandura 1982).

4.3 Theory of planned behaviour

The theory of planned behaviour (TPB) represents a model developed by social psychologists which has been widely applied to the understanding of a variety of behaviours (Ajzen 1991; Armitage and Conner 2001; Conner and Sparks, Chapter 5 in this volume). The TPB outlines the factors that determine an individual's decision to follow a particular behaviour. This theory is itself an extension of the widely applied theory of reasoned action (Fishbein and Ajzen 1975; Ajzen and Fishbein 1980).

The TPB proposes that the proximal determinants of behaviour are intention to engage in that behaviour and perceptions of control over that behaviour. Intentions represent a person's motivation in the sense of her or his conscious plan or decision to exert effort to perform the behaviour. Perceived behavioural control is a person's expectancy that performance of the behaviour is within his/her control. The concept is similar to Bandura's (1982) concept of self-efficacy (see Trafimow *et al.* 2002). Control is seen as a continuum with easily executed behaviours at one end and behavioural goals demanding resources, opportunities, and specialized skills at the other.

Intention is itself determined by three sets of factors: attitudes, which are the overall evaluations of the behaviour by the individual; subjective norms, which consist of a person's beliefs about whether significant others think he/she should engage in the behaviour; and perceived behavioural control, which is the individual's perception of the extent to which performance of the behaviour is easy or difficult. Each of the attitude, subjective norm and perceived behavioural control components are also held to have prior determinants. Attitudes are a function of beliefs about the perceived consequences of the behaviour based upon two perceptions: the likelihood of an outcome occurring as a result of performing the behaviour and the evaluation of that outcome. Subjective norm is a function of normative beliefs, which represent perceptions of specific significant others' preferences about whether one should or should not engage in a behaviour. This is quantified as the subjective likelihood that specific salient groups or individuals (referents) think the person should perform the behaviour, multiplied by the person's motivation to comply with that referent's expectation. Judgements of perceived behavioural control are influenced by beliefs concerning whether one has access to the necessary resources and opportunities to perform the behaviour successfully, weighted by the perceived power of each factor to facilitate or inhibit the execution of the behaviour. These factors include both internal control factors (information, personal deficiencies, skills, abilities, emotions) and external control factors (opportunities, dependence on others, barriers).

4.4 Social cognitive theory

Social cognitive theory (Bandura 1982) forms the basis of a further model of the determinants of health behaviour. In this approach human motivation and action are assumed to be based upon three types of expectancies: situation-outcome, action-outcome and perceived self-efficacy. Situation-outcome expectancies represent beliefs about which consequences will occur without interfering personal action. Susceptibility to a health threat represents one such situation-outcome expectancy. Action-outcome expectancy is the belief that a given behaviour will or will not lead to a given outcome. For example, the belief that quitting smoking will lead to a reduced risk of lung cancer would represent an action-outcome expectancy. Self-efficacy expectancy is the belief that a behaviour is or is not within an individual's control. An individual's belief that he or she is or is not capable of performing a particular behaviour, such as exercising regularly, would constitute such a self-efficacy expectancy.

There is also a clear causal ordering amongst these three types of expectancies (Schwarzer 1992). Situation-outcome expectancies are assumed to operate as distal determinants of behaviour and to influence behaviour principally via their impact on action-outcome expectancies. For example, perceptions of the threat from a health risk to which the individual perceives him or herself to be susceptible motivates the individual to consider different actions to minimize this risk. Action-outcome expectancies in turn are assumed to impact upon behaviour via their influence upon goals or intentions to engage in the behaviour, and upon self-efficacy expectancies. Situation-outcome expectancies in conjunction with consideration of action-outcome expectancies lead to the formation of intentions to take specific actions. Behaviours perceived to be efficacious in reducing a perceived risk lead to intentions to engage in such behaviours. Action-outcome expectancies impact upon self-efficacy expectancies because individuals believe they can produce the responses necessary to produce desired outcomes. Self-efficacy expectancies are assumed to have a direct impact upon behaviour and an indirect effect via their influence upon intentions. The first link is attributable to the fact that optimistic self-beliefs predict actual behavioural performance. The second link reflects the fact that individuals typically intend to perform behaviours they perceive to be within their control (Schwarzer 1992; Bandura 2000; Luszczynska and Schwarzer, Chapter 4 in this volume).

4.5 Health locus of control

A final model worthy of comment here, which is not covered in this edition of the book, is the health locus of control (HLC) construct, which has been extensively applied in health psychology (Wallston 1992; Norman and Bennett 1995). The HLC construct has its origins in Rotter's (1954) social learning theory. The main tenet of social learning theory is that the likelihood of a behaviour occurring in a given situation is a joint function of the individual's expectancy that the behaviour will lead to a particular reinforcement and the extent to which the reinforcement is valued. Rotter (1966) later developed the locus of control construct as a generalized expectancy, making the distinction between internal and external locus of control orientations: internals are seen to believe that events are a consequence of their own actions, whereas externals are seen to believe that events are unrelated to their actions and thereby determined by factors beyond their control. Wallston *et al.* (1978) built on Rotter's earlier work by developing the multidimensional health locus of control (MHLC) scale which measures expectancy beliefs with respect to health along three dimensions: the extent to which individuals believe their health is under the influence of their own actions (i.e. internal HLC), powerful others and chance. The main prediction from HLC theory is that internals on the MHLC scale should be more likely to engage in health-promoting activities. The HLC construct has been applied to a wide range of behaviours (for a review see Norman and Bennett 1995). However, studies linking internal HLC control beliefs to the performance of preventive health behaviours have produced a mixed set of results, with some studies reporting a positive relationship (e.g. Duffy 1987) and others reporting a non-significant relationship (e.g. Brown *et al.* 1983). A number of researchers, though, have commented that tests of the HLC construct have been inadequate because they have failed to consider the role of health value (Wallston 1992; Norman and Bennett 1995). It is argued that HLC beliefs should only predict health behaviour when people value their own health; no relationship is expected for individuals who place a low value on their health. Studies which have tested for the predicted interaction between internal HLC and health value have generally produced positive results (e.g. Lau *et al.* 1986; Weiss and Larsen 1990), although some studies have failed to find such an interaction (e.g. Wurtele *et al.* 1985; Norman *et al.* 1997).

Overall, the HLC construct has been found to be a relatively weak predictor of health behaviour, accounting for only small amounts of the variance in health behaviour, even when considered in conjunction with health value (Wallston 1992; see Norman and Bennett 1995 for a review). Currently, as a result, there is not a great deal of research interest in the HLC construct as a predictor of health behaviour (but see Steptoe and Wardle 2001 for an alternative view). However, a couple of developments in HLC work are worth noting. First, a number of researchers have attempted to construct more behaviour-specific locus of control scales. For example, Saltzer (1982) has developed a weight locus of control scale to predict weight reduction behaviour. In general, these scales have been found to be more predictive of behaviour than the more general MHLC scales (Lefcourt 1991). Second, Wallston (1992) has attempted to incorporate the HLC construct into a more general theory of health behaviour, which he has labelled as modified social learning theory. In this theory, health behaviour is seen to be a function of health value, health locus of control and self-efficacy such that self-efficacy should only predict health behaviour when the individual values his/her health and has an internal HLC orientation. This modified model not only incorporates one of the most powerful predictors of health behaviour, self-efficacy, but also outlines a role for HLC as a more distal predictor of health behaviour. However, as yet, modified social learning theory has seen little application in the health behaviour field.

4.6 Stage models of health behaviour

A number of researchers have suggested that there may be qualitatively different stages in the initiation and maintenance of health behaviour, and that to obtain a full understanding of the determinants of health behaviour it is necessary to conduct a detailed analysis of the nature of these stages (see Sutton, Chapter 6 in this volume, for a review). From a social cognitive perspective, an important implication of this position is that different cognitions may be important at different stages in promoting health behaviour.

One of the first stage models was put forward by Prochaska and DiClemente (1984) in their transtheoretical model of change (TMC). Their model has been widely applied to analyse the process of change in alcoholism treatment (DiClemente and Hughes 1990) and smoking cessation (DiClemente *et al.* 1991). In one recent form, DiClemente *et al.* (1991) identify five stages of change: pre-contemplation, contemplation, preparation, action and maintenance. Individuals are seen to progress through each stage to achieve successful maintenance of a new behaviour. Taking the example of smoking cessation, it is argued that in the pre-contemplation stage the smoker is unaware that his/her behaviour constitutes a problem and has no intention to quit. In the contemplation stage, the smoker starts to think about changing his/her behaviour, but is not committed to try to quit. In the preparation stage, the smoker has an intention to quit and starts to make plans about how to quit. The action stage is characterized by active attempts to quit, and after six months of successful abstinence the individual moves into the maintenance stage, characterized by attempts to prevent relapse and to consolidate the newly acquired non-smoking status.

Other stage models have recently been developed including the health action process approach (Schwarzer 1992; Schwarzer and Fuchs 1995); the precaution-adoption process (Weinstein 1988, Weinstein and Sandman 1992); goal achievement theory (Bagozzi 1992, 1993), and the model of action phases (Heckhausen 1991; Gollwitzer 1993). Whilst relative widely applied, the evidence in support of stage models and different stages is at present relatively weak (see Weinstein *et al.* 2000; Bridle *et al.* 2005; Sutton, Chapter 6 in this volume). In addition, as yet there is limited evidence that interventions matched to individuals' stage of change are more effective than unmatched interventions.

4.7 Implementation intentions

The main social cognition models of health behaviour can be seen to be primarily concerned with people's motivations to perform a health behaviour and, as such, can be considered to provide strong predictions of behavioural intentions (i.e. the end of a motivational phase). However, strong intentions do not always lead to corresponding actions. In his meta-analysis of meta-analyses, Sheeran (2002) reported an average intention–behaviour correlation of 0.53. However, the major social cognition models do not directly address the issue of translating intentions into action. A construct that appears important to the translation of intentions into actions is implementation intentions (Gollwitzer 1993, 1999; for a review in relation to health behaviours see Sheeran *et al.*, Chapter 7 in this volume).

Gollwitzer (1993) made the distinction between goal intentions and implementation intentions. While the former is concerned with intentions to perform a behaviour or achieve a goal (i.e. 'I intend to achieve x'), the latter is concerned with plans as to when, where and how the goal intention is to be translated into behaviour (i.e. 'I intend to initiate the goal-directed behaviour x when situation y is encountered'). The important point about implementation intentions is that they commit the individual to a specific course of action when certain environmental conditions are met; in so doing they help translate goal intentions into action. Take the example of going swimming; an individual may have the intention to go swimming, but this may not be translated into behaviour if he/she does not have an implementation intention which specifies when, where and how he/she will go swimming. Gollwitzer (1993) argues that by making implementation intentions individuals pass over control to the environment. The environment therefore acts as a cue to action, such that when certain conditions are met, the performance of the intended behaviour follows.

Sheeran *et al.* (Chapter 7 in this volume) provide an in-depth review of both basic and applied research with implementation intentions. In particular, implementation intentions are shown to increase the performance of a range of behaviours with, on average, a medium effect size. Factors which promote or inhibit the effectiveness of implementation intentions in relation to health behaviours have become an important focus of research attention.

5 Comparison and integration of key social cognition models

5.1 Empirical comparisons

Despite a substantial volume of empirical work using the main social cognition models to predict a range of health behaviours, there has been little empirical work comparing the predictive power of the different models. As Weinstein (1993) notes, the lack of comparison studies means that there is little consensus on whether some variables are more influential than others and whether some models of health behaviour are more predictive than others. However, while this criticism of research with social cognition models is clearly valid, it is also evident that those studies which have attempted to compare different models have been important in helping to identify the key predictors of health behaviour. A number of these studies for the key SCMs are reviewed below (see also Bagozzi 1992; Bagozzi and Kimmel 1995; Hunter *et al.* 2003). It is also worth noting that the increasing number of meta-analyses of the major SCMs provide another basis on which to make comparisons.

Hill *et al.* (1985) compared the HBM (i.e. susceptibility, severity, benefits, barriers, health motivation) with the TRA (i.e. attitude, subjective norm) in their study on the determinants of womens' intentions to perform breast self-examination and to have a Pap test (cervical smear). Both models were found to predict intentions, explaining 17–20 per cent of the variance in breast self-examination intentions and 26–32 per cent of the variance in Pap test intentions. The HBM was found to predict slightly more of the variance in each case but, as Hill *et al.* (1985) point out, this may be due to the greater number of constructs measured in the HBM.

Similar results have been reported by Mullen *et al.* (1987). They examined the ability of the TRA and the HBM to predict changes in a range of health behaviours over an eight-month period. Again, both models were found to produce significant predictions of changes in the health behaviours, with the HBM explaining slightly more of the variance. Mullen *et al.* (1987) also reported that the HBM was more economical in predicting behaviour change in that it only required an average of 23 items to measure its constructs, compared with the 32 needed to measure the constructs of the TRA. However, it should be noted that Mullen *et al.* (1987) used both direct and indirect measures of the attitude and subjective norm components of the TRA. While the above studies show the HBM to be a slightly superior model when compared with the TRA, a couple of further studies have suggested the opposite conclusion. For example, Oliver and Berger (1979) found the TRA to be a superior predictor of inoculation behaviour, as did Rutter (1989) in relation to AIDS-preventive behaviour. More recently, a couple of studies have compared the TPB and the HBM. Conner and Norman (1994) examined the determinants of attendance at a health check and found the models to predict intentions and behaviour to a similar level, while Bakker *et al.* (1994) found the TPB to be more predictive of condom use among heterosexuals.

A number of studies have examined the role of self-efficacy in relation to the main social cognition models and have identified it as a key social cognitive variable. For example, Seydel *et al.* (1990) compared a restricted HBM (susceptibility, severity, outcome expectancies) with the PMT (susceptibility, severity, outcome expectancies, self-efficacy) and found outcome expectancies and self-efficacy to be the most important predictors of cancer-related preventive intentions and behaviour. Dzewaltowski (1989) has also highlighted the importance of self-efficacy in a study comparing the TRA and SCT. The study examined the predictors of exercise behaviour measured seven weeks later, and found SCT to provide a better prediction of exercise behaviour than the TRA (R^2 = 0.14 vs 0.06), with self-efficacy emerging as the most important single predictor. Ajzen (1991) added the concept of perceived behavioural control to the TRA with good effect (see Conner and Sparks, Chapter 5 in this volume). However, given the close similarity between perceived behavioural control and self-efficacy, Schwarzer (1992) has suggested that perceived behavioural control be replaced with the self-efficacy construct. A number of researchers have followed this suggestion, producing encouraging results (e.g. DeVries *et al.* 1988). However, recent studies (e.g. Trafimow *et al.* 2002) have distinguished two components of perceived behavioural control: a self-efficacy component and a control component (see also Ajzen 2002). Whilst meta-analytical evidence appears to support the greater power of self-efficacy as a predictor of both intentions and behaviour (Trafimow *et al.* 2002) further research is required to further disentangle the effects of these two variables (see Conner and Sparks, Chapter 5 in this volume).

On the basis of the above review of work, which has sought to compare the predictive power of the social cognition models, it is possible to draw two main conclusions. First, many of the comparisons have shown the models to perform to a similar level, suggesting that there may be little to choose between them. Second, the self-efficacy construct appears to be a key predictor of health behaviour, providing a strong case for its inclusion in social cognition models of health behaviour.

5.2 Theoretical comparisons

A number of authors have commented on the considerable overlap between constructs contained in the main social cognition models of health behaviour (Kirscht 1982; Armitage and Conner 2000; Gebhardt and Maes 2001; Norman and Conner, Chapter 8 in this volume). Moreover, as Cummings *et al.* (1980) note, where differences do appear they tend to represent differences in labelling rather than differences in underlying constructs. This suggests that there might be some benefit in developing integrated social cognition models of health behaviour. In this section we consider some of the main constructs outlined in social cognition models of health behaviour and the extent to which they may overlap. Seven main areas of overlap are identified.

First, models that have been developed specifically to predict health behaviour (i.e. HBM, PMT) focus on the notion of threat as measured by perceived susceptibility and perceived severity. In addition, SCT focuses on expectancies about environmental cues (i.e. risk perception) (Rosenstock *et al.* 1988). In contrast, the TPB does not explicitly cater for emotional or arousal variables, leading some authors to suggest that the TPB may be limited to the rational part of a health decision (Oliver and Berger 1979). Weinstein (1993) argues against this viewpoint, pointing out that perceptions of severity may be tapped indirectly by the evaluation component of behavioural beliefs, while perceptions of susceptibility may be tapped by belief strength. For example, a behavioural belief may focus on the perceived likelihood that continued smoking may lead to lung cancer (i.e. perceived susceptibility) and an evaluation of this consequence (i.e. perceived severity). However, while perceptions of susceptibility and severity may be tapped by a consideration of behavioural beliefs, it may be advantageous to maintain the distinction between threat perception and behavioural beliefs (see Norman *et al.* 1999).

Second, most social cognition models of health behaviour focus on the perceived consequences of performing a health behaviour (Rosenstock *et al.* 1988; Weinstein 1993; Conner and Norman 1994; Van der Pligt 1994). For example, in the TPB the focus is on behavioural beliefs, in the HBM it is on the benefits and costs of performing a health behaviour, while in SCT it is on outcome expectancies and in PMT it is on response-efficacy.

Third, as noted earlier, there is considerable overlap between the perceived behavioural control component of the TPB and self-efficacy (Ajzen 1991). A number of the models also focus on specific control issues or barriers to the performance of health behaviour. Thus, a similarity can be noted between control beliefs in the TPB, the perceived barriers dimension of the HBM and response costs in the PMT (Conner and Norman 1994; van der Pligt 1994). Rosenstock *et al.* (1988) have further considered the overlap between the perceived barriers dimension of the HBM and self-efficacy. They consider the perceived barriers dimension to be a 'catch-all' term for all the potential barriers to action, both internal and external. As a result, they argue for the inclusion of self-efficacy as a separate construct within the HBM, highlighting two important consequences; first, it would help delimit the scope of the barriers dimension and second, it would add to the predictive power of the HBM.

Fourth, normative influences on behaviour are not explicitly covered by social cognition models of health behaviour (Conner and Norman 1994), with the exception of the TPB which includes the subjective norm construct and underlying normative beliefs. In the HBM, normative influences are simply listed as one of many potential cues to action. In SCT, normative influences may be covered by outcome expectancies that focus on the perceived social consequences of behaviour. However, Schwarzer (1992) has questioned the extent to which it is necessary to differentiate between social outcome expectancies and other expectancies in SCT (see Bandura 2000). Weinstein (1993) has put forward a similar argument in relation to normative beliefs and behavioural beliefs in the TPB. Nevertheless, there may be some merit in limiting the scope of outcome expectancies or behavioural beliefs so that the independent influence of normative influences can be considered in more detail (Trafimow and Fishbein 1995).

Fifth, the TPB, SCT and PMT include an intervening variable which is seen to mediate the relationship between other social cognitive variables and behaviour (Weinstein 1993). In the TPB this variable is behavioural intention, while in PMT it is labelled protection motivation, although Prentice-Dunn and Rogers (1986) state that protection motivation is most appropriately assessed by behavioural intention measures. The other social cognition models considered here do not include a measure of behavioural intention, although a number of researchers have called for the addition of behavioural intention to the HBM to act as a mediating variable between the HBM variables and behaviour (e.g. Becker *et al.* 1977; King 1982; Calnan 1984). Sixth, the TPB and SCT also postulate a direct relationship between self-efficacy (or perceived behavioural control) and behaviour in addition to the one between intention and behaviour.

Finally, there are a number of similarities in more recent models that have sought to outline the variables that are important in the volitional phase of health behaviour (e.g. Weinstein 1988; Heckhausen 1991; Bagozzi 1992; Schwarzer 1992; Gollwitzer 1993; Kuhl and Beckman 1994). In particular, these models emphasize the need for individuals to deploy a range of self-regulatory skills and strategies to ensure that strong intentions are translated into behaviour. For example, Kuhl (1984) details a wide range of action control processes that can be used to strengthen and protect intentions from alternative action tendencies, whereas both Schwarzer (1992) and Gollwitzer (1993) emphasize the importance of formulating action plans specifying where, when and how an intended behaviour is to be performed.

Five main conclusions can be drawn from the above comparisons. First, there is considerable overlap between the constructs included in the models. For example, most focus on outcome expectancies or the consequences of performing a behaviour. Second, some of the models may usefully be expanded to consider normative influences and perceived threat. Third, there is a strong case for including self-efficacy in all models of health behaviour. Fourth, behavioural intention should be included in all models as a mediating variable between other social cognitive variables and behaviour. Not only does intention typically emerge as the strongest predictor of behaviour but it also marks the end of a motivational phase of decision making that many SCMs focus upon. Fifth, models need to consider post-intentional influences on behaviour.

5.3 Integration

Given the considerable overlap between constructs it is not surprising that some researchers have attempted to produce integrated social cognition models of health behaviour (Norman and Conner 1995; Armitage and Conner 2000; Fishbein *et al.* 2001). Most prominent among these attempts is the work of a number of major theorists who attended a workshop organised by the National Institute of Mental Health in response to the need to promote HIV-preventive behaviours. The workshop was attended by Bandura (SCT), Becker (HBM), Fishbein (TRA), Kanfer (self-regulation) and Triandis (theory of interpersonal behaviour; see Norman and Conner, Chapter 8 in this volume) and they sought to 'identify a finite set of variables to be considered in any behavioral analysis' (Fishbein *et al.* 2001: 3). They identified eight variables which, they argued, should account for most of the variance in any (deliberative) behaviour (Figure 1.1). These were organized into two sets. First were those variables which they viewed as necessary and sufficient determinants of behaviour. Thus, for behaviour to occur an individual must (i) have a strong intention, (ii) have the necessary skills to perform the behaviour and (iii) experience an absence of environmental constraints that could prevent behaviour. The second set of variables were seen primarily to influence intention, although it was noted that some of the variables may also have a direct effect on behaviour. Thus, a strong intention is likely to occur when an individual (iv) perceives the advantages (or benefits) of performing the behaviour to outweigh the perceived disadvantages (or costs), (v) perceives the social (normative) pressure to perform the behaviour to be greater than that not to perform the behaviour, (vi) believes that the behaviour is consistent with his or her self-image, (vii) anticipates the emotional reaction to performing the

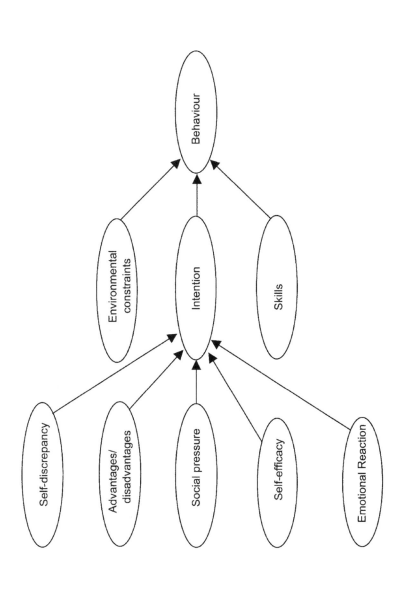

Figure 1.1 Major theorists' model of behaviour

behaviour to be more positive than negative, and (viii) has high levels of self-efficacy.

This 'major theorists' model has a number of positive features. In particular, it is both logical and parsimonious and incorporates many of the key constructs included in the main social cognition models. Nonetheless, there are a number of observations that can made about this model. First, it includes a number of constructs that do not feature in the main social cognition models. For example, although some researchers have suggested that self-identity should be included as an additional predictor in the TPB (e.g. Charng *et al.* 1988), subsequent research has shown that it explains little additional variance (Conner and Armitage 1998). Similarly, anticipated affect has also been put forward as an additional predictor (e.g. Conner and Armitage 1998), although Ajzen and Fishbein (in press) have argued that anticipated emotions should be considered as a subset of behavioural beliefs. Second, it is noteworthy that the integrated model fails to include perceptions of susceptibility and severity, that are key constructs in the HBM and PMT. Third, the model lacks detail regarding the relationships between its constructs. In fact, Fishbein *et al.* (2001) noted that the major theorists were unable to agree on the likely nature of these relationships. Fourth, to date, there have been no empirical tests of the model. Finally, the model is fairly mute on the post-intentional (i.e. volitional) phase of health behaviour, simply stating that in addition to a strong intention, an individual must also possess the necessary skills to perform the behaviour and not encounter any environmental constraints that could prevent performance of the behaviour. However, recently developed volitional models identify a wide range of variables that might be important in translating intentions into action (e.g. Weinstein 1988; Heckhausen 1991; Bagozzi 1992; Schwarzer 1992; Gollwitzer 1993; Kuhl and Beckman 1994).

6 Using social cognition models to change health behaviour

One important development in recent years has been the increased use of SCMs to develop interventions to change health behaviours (e.g. Rutter and Quine 2002). The chapters in this volume provide reviews of applications of the major SCMs to health behaviour change: HBM (Abraham and Sheeran, Chapter 2), PMT (Norman *et al.*, Chapter 3), SCT (Luszczynska and Schwarzer, Chapter 4), TPB (Conner and Sparks, Chapter 5), implementation intentions (Sheeran *et al.*, Chapter 7), and stage models (Sutton, Chapter 6). Norman and Conner (Chapter 8) also provide an overview of the use of SCMs for changing health behaviour and highlight a number of unresolved issues (see also Sutton 2002). This development is welcome for two reasons. First, appropriate intervention studies can provide strong tests of SCMs. In particular, where interventions appropriately target and successfully manipulate components of an SCM they can provide good tests of the proposed causal relationships within the SCM. Second, if a key justification for the SCM approach to health behaviours is their ability to produce more effective interventions then this assumption needs to be tested.

7 Conclusions: using social cognition models to predict and change health behaviour

The present chapter has set out the rationale for the interest in understanding health behaviours, particularly as a basis for attempting to change their occurrence in order to increase both length and quality of life. SCMs provide an important and increasingly widely used approach to understanding health behaviour in describing the important social cognitive variables predicting such behaviours. As such, these models provide an important basis for achieving the aim of changing health behaviour by providing a means for identifying appropriate targets for intervention work. Intervention work is now proceeding to test the causal role of these variables, as identified in SCMs, as a means to change health behaviour and promote health outcomes.

References

Abraham, C., Sheeran, P., Norman, P., Conner, M., De Vries, N. and Otten, W. (1999) When good intentions are not enough: modeling postdecisional cognitive correlates of condom use, *Journal of Applied Social Psychology*, 29, 2591–612.

Adler, N. and Matthews, K. (1994) Health psychology: why do some people get sick and some stay well?, *Annual Review of Psychology*, 45, 229–59.

Affleck, G., Tennen, H., Croog, S. and Levine, S. (1987) Causal attribution, perceived control, and recovery from a heart attack, *Journal of Social and Clinical Psychology*, 5, 356–64.

Ajzen, I. (1991) The theory of planned behavior, *Organizational Behavior and Human Decision Processes*, 50, 179–211.

Ajzen, I. (2002) Perceived behavioural control, self-efficacy, locus of control, and the theory of planned behaviour, *Journal of Applied Social Psychology*, 32, 1–20.

Ajzen, I. and Fishbein, M. (1980) *Understanding Attitudes and Predicting Social Behavior*. Englewood-Cliff, NJ: Prentice-Hall.

Ajzen, I. and Fishbein, M. (in press) The influence of attitudes on behavior. In D. Albarracin, B.T. Johnson, and M.P. Zanna (eds) *Handbook of Attitudes and Attitude Change: Basic Principles*. Mahwah, NJ: Erlbaum.

Amler, R.W. and Eddins, D.L. (1987) Cross-sectional analysis: precursors of premature death in the U.S., in R.W. Amler and H.B. Dull (eds) *Closing the Gap*. New York: Oxford University Press, 54–87.

Armitage, C. J. and Conner, M. (2000) Social cognition models and health behaviour: a structured review, *Psychology and Health*, 15, 173–89.

Armitage, C. J. and Conner, M. (2001) Efficacy of the theory of planned behaviour: a meta-analytic review, *British Journal of Social Psychology*, 40, 471–99.

Bagozzi, R.P. (1992) The self-regulation of attitudes, intentions and behavior, *Social Psychology Quarterly*, 55, 178–204.

Bagozzi, R.P. (1993) On the neglect of volition in consumer research: a critique and proposal, *Psychology and Marketing*, 10, 215–37.

Bagozzi, R.P. and Kimmel, S.K. (1995) A comparison of leading theories for the prediction of goal-directed behaviours, *British Journal of Social Psychology*, 34, 437–61.

Bakker, A.B., Buunk, A.P. and Siero, F.W. (1994) Condom use of heterosexuals: a comparison of the theory of planned behavior, the health belief model and protection motivation theory. Unpublished Manuscript.

Bandura, A. (1982) Self-efficacy mechanism in human agency, *American Psychologist*, **37**, 122–47.

Bandura, A. (2000) Health promotion from the perspective of social cognitive theory, in P. Norman, C. Abraham and M. Conner (eds) *Understanding and Changing Health Behaviour: From Health Beliefs to Self-regulation.* Amsterdam: Harwood Academic, 229–42.

Baum, A. and Posluszny, D.M. (1999) Health psychology: mapping biobehavioral contributions to health and illness, *Annual Review of Psychology*, **50**, 137–63.

Becker, M.H. (1974) The health belief model and sick role behavior, *Health Education Monographs*, **2**, 409–19.

Becker, M.H. and Maiman, L.A. (1983) Models of health-related behavior, in D. Mechanic (ed.) *Handbook of Health, Health Care and the Health Professions.* New York: Free Press, 539–68.

Becker, M.H. Haefner, D.P., Kasl, S.V., Kirscht, J.P., Maiman, L.A. and Rosenstock, I.M. (1977) Selected psychosocial models and correlates of individual health-related behaviors, *Medical Care*, **15**, 27–46.

Belloc, N.B. (1973) Relationship of health practices to mortality, *Preventive Medicine*, **2**, 67–81.

Belloc, N.B. and Breslow, L. (1972) Relationship of physical health status and health practices, *Preventive Medicine*, **9**, 469–21.

Blaxter, M. (1990) *Health and Lifestyles.* London: Tavistock.

Breslow, L. and Enstrom, J.E. (1980) Persistence of health habits and their relationship to mortality, *Preventive Medicine*, **9**, 469–83.

Bridle, C., Riemsma, R.P., Pattenden, J., Soeden, A.J., Watt, I.S. and Walker, A. (2005) Systematic review of the effectiveness of health behaviour interventions based on the transtheoretical model, *Psychology and Health* (in press).

Brown, N., Muhlenkamp, A., Fox, L. and Osborn, M. (1983) The relationship among health beliefs, health values, and health promotion activity, *Western Journal of Nursing Research*, **5**, 155–63.

Calnan, M. (1984) The health belief model and participation in programmes for the early detection of breast cancer, *Social Science and Medicine*, **19**, 823–30.

Charng, H. -W., Piliavin, J. A. and Callero, P. L. (1988) Role identity and reasoned action in the prediction of repeated behavior, *Social Psychology Quarterly*, **51**, 303–17.

Conner, M.T. (1993) Pros and cons of social cognition models in health behaviour, *Health Psychology Update*, **14**, 24–31.

Conner, M. and Armitage, C.J. (1998) Extending the theory of planned behavior: a review and avenues for further research, *Journal of Applied Social Psychology*, **28**, 1430–64.

Conner, M. and Norman, P. (1994) Comparing the health belief model and the theory of planned behaviour in health screening. In D.R. Rutter and L. Quine (eds) *Social Psychology and Health: European Perspectives.* Aldershot: Avebury, 1–24.

Conner, M. and Norman, P. (1995) *Predicting Health Behaviour: Research and Practice with Social Cognition Models.* Buckingham: Open University Press.

Cummings, M.K., Becker, M.H. and Maile, M.C. (1980) Bringing models together: an empirical approach to combining variables used to explain health actions, *Journal of Behavioral Medicine*, **3**, 123–45.

DeVries, H., Dijkstra, M. and Kuhlman, P. (1988) Self-efficacy: the third factor besides attitude and subjective norm as a predictor of behavioural intentions, *Health Education Research*, **3**, 273–82.

DiClemente, C.C. and Hughes, S.O. (1990) Stages of change profiles in outpatient alcoholism treatment, *Journal of Substance Abuse*, 2, 217–35.

DiClemente, C.C., Prochaska, J.O., Fairhurst, S.K., Velicer, W.F., Velasquez, M.M. and Rossi, J.S. (1991) The process of smoking cessation: an analysis of precontemplation, contemplation, and preparation stages of change, *Journal of Consulting and Clinical Psychology*, 59, 295–304.

Duffy, M.E. (1987) Determinants of health promotion in midlife women, *Nursing Research*, 37, 358–62.

Dzewaltowski, D.A. (1989) Toward a model of exercise motivation, *Journal of Sport and Exercise Psychology*, 32, 11–28.

Edwards, W. (1954) The theory of decision making, *Psychological Bulletin*, 51, 380–417.

Fishbein, M. and Ajzen, I. (1975) *Belief, Attitude, Intention, and Behavior*. New York: Wiley.

Fishbein, M. Triandis, H. C., Kanfer, F. H., Becker M., Middlestadt, S. E. and Eichler, A. (2001) Factors influencing behavior and behavior change, in A. Baum, T. A. Revenson and J. E. Singer (eds) *Handbook of Health Psychology*. Mahwah, NJ: Lawerence Erlbaum Associates, 3–17.

Fiske, S.T. and Taylor, S.E. (1991) *Social Cognition* (2nd edition). New York: McGraw-Hill.

Frisch, D. and Clemen, R.T. (1994) Beyond expected utility: rethinking behavioral decision making, *Psychological Bulletin*, 116, 46–54.

Furnham, A. and Heaven, P. (1999) *Personality and Social Behaviour*. London: Arnold.

Gebhardt, W.A. and Maes, S. (2001) Integrating social-psychological frameworks for health behaviour research, *American Journal of Health Behavior*, 25, 528–36.

Gochman, D.S. (ed.) (1997) *Handbook of Health Behavior Research* (Vols 1–4). New York: Plenum.

Gollwitzer, P.M. (1993) Goal achievement: the role of intentions, *European Review of Social Psychology*, 4, 142–85.

Gollwitzer, P. M. (1999) Implementation intentions: strong effects of simple plans, *American Psychologist*, 54, 493–503.

Greeno, C.G. and Wing, R.R. (1994) Stress-induced eating, *Psychological Bulletin*, 115, 444–64.

Hagger, M. and Orbell, S. (2003) A meta-analytic review of the common-sense model of illness representations, *Psychology and Health*, 18, 141–84.

Heckhausen, H. (1991) *Motivation and Action*. Berlin: Springer-Verlag.

Hill, D., Gardner, G. and Rassaby, J. (1985) Factors predisposing women to take precautions against breast and cervix cancer, *Journal of Applied Social Psychology*, 15, 59–79.

Hunter, M.S., Grunfeld, E.A. and Ramirez, A.J. (2003) Help-seeking intentions for breast-cancer symptoms: a comparison of the self-regulation model and the theory of planned behaviour, *British Journal of Health Psychology*, 8, 319–33.

Janz, N.K. and Becker, M.H. (1984) The health belief model: a decade later, *Health Education Quarterly*, 11, 1–47.

Jonas, K. (1993) Expectancy-value models of health behaviour: an analysis by conjoint measurement, *European Journal of Social Psychology*, 23, 167–83.

Kasl, S.V. and Cobb, S. (1966) Health behavior, illness behavior and sick role behavior, *Archives of Environmental Health*, 12, 246–66.

King, J. (1982) The impact of patients' perceptions of high blood pressure on attendance at screening, *Social Science and Medicine*, 16, 1079–91.

Kirscht, J.P. (1982) Preventive health behaviour: a review of research and issues, *Health Psychology*, **2**, 277–301.

Kuhl, J. (1984) Volitional aspects of achievement motivation and learned helplessness: toward a comprehensive theory of action control, *Progress in Experimental Personality Research*, **13**, 99–171.

Kuhl, J. and Beckmann, J. (eds) (1985) *Action Control: From Cognition to Behavior*. Berlin: Springer-Verlag.

Kuhl, J. and Beckmann, J. (eds) (1994) *Volition and Personality: Action Versus State Orientation*. Gottingen: Springer-Verlag.

Lau, R.R., Hartmam, K.A. and Ware, J.E. (1986) Health as value: methodological and theoretical considerations, *Health Psychology*, **5**, 25–43.

Lefcourt, H.M. (1991) Locus of control. In J.P. Robinson, P.R. Shaver and L.S. Wrightsman (eds) *Measures of Personality and Social Psychological Attitudes*. New York: Academic Press, 661–753.

Leventhal, H., Nerenz, D.R. and Steele, D.F. (1984) Illness representations and coping with health threats. In A. Baum and J. Singer (eds) *A Handbook of Psychology and Health*. Hillsdale, NJ: Erlbaum, 219–52.

McNeil, A.D., Jarvis, M.J., Stapleton, J.A., Russell, M.A.H., Eiser, J.R., Gammage, P. and Gray, E.M. (1988) Prospective study of factors predicting uptake of smoking in adolescents, *Journal of Epidemiology and Community Health*, **43**, 72–8.

Maddux, J.E. and Rogers, R.W. (1983) Protection motivation and self-efficacy: a revised theory of fear appeals and attitude change, *Journal of Experimental Social Psychology*, **19**, 469–79.

Marteau, T.M. (1989) Health beliefs and attributions. In A.K. Broome (ed.) *Health Psychology: Processes and Applications*. London: Chapman Hall, 1–23.

Moss-Morris, R., Weinman, J., Petrie, K.J., Horne, R., Cameron, L.D. and Buick, D. (2002) The revised illness perception questionnaire (IPQ-R), *Psychology and Health*, **17**, 1–16.

Mullen, P.D., Hersey, J.C. and Iverson, D.C. (1987) Health behaviour models compared, *Social Science and Medicine*, **24**, 973–81.

Norman, P., Abraham, C. and Conner, M. (2000) *Understanding and Changing Health Behaviour: From Health Beliefs to Self-regulation*. Amsterdam: Harwood Academic.

Norman, P. and Bennett, P. (1995) Health locus of control and health behaviours. In M. Conner and P. Norman (eds) *Predicting Health Behaviour: Research and Practice with Social Cognition Models*. Buckingham: Open University Press, 62–94.

Norman, P., Bennett, P., Smith, C. and Murphy, S. (1997) Health locus of control and leisure-time exercise, *Personality and Individual Differences*, **23**, 769–74.

Norman, P. and Conner, M. (1995) The role of social cognition models in predicting health behaviours: future directions. In M. Conner and P. Norman (eds) *Predicting Health Behaviour: Research and Practice with Social Cognition Models*. Milton Keynes: Open University Press, 197–225.

Norman, P., Conner, M. and Bell, R. (1999) The theory of planned behavior and smoking cessation, *Health Psychology*, **18**, 89–94.

Oliver, R.L. and Berger, P.K. (1979) A path analysis of preventive health care decision models, *Journal of Consumer Research*, **6**, 113–22.

Peak, H. (1955) Attitude and motivation. In M.R. Jones (ed) *Nebraska Symposium on Motivation* (Vol. 3, pp. 149–88). Lincoln: University of Nebraska Press.

Petrie, K.J. and Weinman, J. (1997) *Perceptions of Health and Illness: Current Research and Applications*. Amsterdam: Harwood Academic.

Prentice-Dunn, S. and Rogers, R.W. (1986) Protection motivation theory and preventive health: beyond the health belief model, *Health Education Research*, 1, 153–61.

Prochaska, J.O. and DiClemente, C.C. (1984) *The Transtheoretical Approach: Crossing Traditional Boundaries of Therapy*. Homewood, IL: Dow Jones Irwin.

Rogers, R.W. (1975) A protection motivation theory of fear appeals and attitude change, *Journal of Psychology*, 91, 93–114.

Rogers, R.W. (1983) Cognitive and physiological processes in fear appeals and attitude change: a revised theory of protection motivation. In J.T. Cacioppo and R.E. Petty (eds) *Social Psychophysiology: A Source Book*. New York: Guilford Press, 153–76.

Rosenstock, I.M. (1966) Why people use health services, *Millbank Memorial Fund Quarterly*, 44, 94–124.

Rosenstock, I.M. (1974) Historical origins of the health belief model, *Health Education Monographs*, 2, 1–8.

Rosenstock, I.M., Strecher, V.J. and Becker, M.H. (1988) Social learning theory and the health belief model, *Health Education Quarterly*, 15, 175–83.

Rotter, J.B. (1954) *Social Learning and Clinical Psychology*. Englewood Cliffs, NJ: Prentice-Hall.

Rotter, R.B. (1966) Generalized expectancies for internal and external control of reinforcement, *Psychological Monographs: General and Applied*, 80 (**whole no. 609**), 1–28.

Royal College of Physicians (1992) *Smoking and the Young*. Sudbury, UK: Lavenham Press.

Rutter, D.R. (1989) Models of belief-behaviour relationships in health, *Health Psychology Update*, **November**, 8–10.

Rutter, D.R. and Quine, L. (eds) (2002) *Changing Health Behaviour*. Buckingham: Open University Press.

Rutter, D.R., Quine, L. and Chesham, D.J. (1993) *Social Psychological Approaches to Health*. London: Harvester-Wheatsheaf.

Saltzer, E.B. (1982) The weight loss of control (WLOC) scale: a specific measure for obesity research, *Journal of Personality Assessment*, 46, 620–8.

Schneider, D.J. (1991) Social cognition, *Annual Review of Psychology*, 42, 527–61.

Schwarzer, R. (1992) Self-efficacy in the adoption and maintenance of health behaviors: theoretical approaches and a new model. In R. Schwarzer (ed.) *Self-efficacy: Thought Control of Action*. London: Hemisphere, 217–43.

Schwarzer, R. and Fuchs, R. (1995) Self-efficacy and health behaviours. In M. Conner and P. Norman (eds) *Predicting Health Behaviour: Research and Practice with Social Cognition Models*. Buckingham: Open University Press, 163–96.

Seydel, E., Taal, E. and Wiegman, O. (1990) Risk-appraisal, outcome and self-efficacy expectancies: cognitive factors in preventive behavior related to cancer, *Psychology and Health*, 4, 99–109.

Sheeran, P. (2002) Intention-behavior relations: a conceptual and empirical review. In W. Strobe and M. Hewstone (eds) *European Review of Social Psychology*, Vol. 12. Chichester: Wiley, 1–30.

Steptoe, A. and Wardle, J. (2001) Locus of control and health behaviour revisited: a multivariate analysis of young adults from 18 countries, *British Journal of Health Psychology*, 92, 659–72.

Steptoe, A., Wardle, J., Vinck, J., Tuomisto, M., Holte, A. and Wichstrom, L. (1994) Personality and attitudinal correlates of healthy and unhealthy lifestyles in young adults, *Psychology and Health*, 9, 331–43.

Sutton, S. (2002) Using social cognition models to develop health behaviour interventions: problems and assumptions. In D. Rutter and L. Quine (eds) *Changing Health Behaviour*. Buckingham: Open University Press, 193–208.

Taylor, S. (1991) *Health Psychology*. New York: McGraw-Hill.

Taylor, S., Lichtman, R.R. and Wood, J.V. (1984) Attributions, beliefs about control and adjustment to breast cancer, *Journal of Personality and Social Psychology*, **46**, 489–502.

Tennen, H., Affleck, G., Allen, D.A., McGrade, B.J. and Ratzan, S. (1984) Causal attributions and coping with insulin-dependent diabetes, *Basic and Applied Social Psychology*, **5**, 131–42.

Trafimow, D. and Fishbein, M. (1995) Do people really distinguish between behavioural and normative beliefs?, *British Journal of Social Psychology*, **34**, 257–66.

Trafimow, D., Sheeran, P., Conner, M. and Finlay, K.A. (2002) Evidence that perceived behavioral control is a multidimensional construct: perceived control and perceived difficulty, *British Journal of Social Psychology*, **41**, 101–21.

Turk, D.C. and Salovey, P. (1986) Clinical information processing: bias inoculation. In R.E. Ingham (ed.) *Information Processing Approaches to Clinical Psychology*. New York: Academic Press, 305–23.

Van der Pligt, J. (1994) Risk appraisal and health behaviour. In D.R. Rutter and L. Quine (eds) *Social Psychology and Health: European Perspectives*. Aldershot: Avebury Press, 131–52.

Van der Pligt, J., de Vries, N.K., Manstead, A.S.R. and Van Harreveld, F. (2000) The importance of being selective: weighting the role of attribute importance in attitudinal judgment, *Advances in Experimental Social Psychology*, **32**, 135–200.

Van der Velde, W. and Van der Pligt, J. (1991) AIDS-related behavior: coping, protection motivation, and previous behavior, *Journal of Behavioral Medicine*, **14**, 429–51.

Wallston, K.A., Wallston, B.S. and Devellis, R. (1978) Development of multidimensional health locus of control (MHLC) scales, *Health Education Monographs*, **6**, 160–70.

Wallston, K.E. (1992) Hocus-pocus, the focus isn't strictly locus: Rotter's social learning theory modified for health, *Cognitive Therapy and Research*, **16**, 183–99.

Wardle, J. and Steptoe, A. (1991) The European health and behaviour survey: rationale, methods and initial results from the United Kingdom, *Social Science and Medicine*, **33**, 925–36.

Weinstein, W.D. (1988) The precaution adoption process, *Health Psychology*, **7**, 355–86.

Weinstein, W.D. (1993) Testing four competing theories of health-protective behavior, *Health Psychology*, **12**, 324–33.

Weinstein, W.D. (2000) Perceived probability, perceived severity, and health-protective behavior, *Health Psychology*, **19**, 65–74.

Weinstein, N.D. and Sandman, P.M. (1992) The precaution adoption process model. In K. Glanz, B.K. Rimer and F.M. Lewis (eds) *Health Behavior and Health Education: Theory, Research, and Practice*, 3rd edition. San Francisco, CA: Jossey-Bass, 121–43.

Weinstein, N.D., Rothman, A.J. and Sutton, S.R. (1998) Stage theories of health behavior: conceptual and methodological issues, *Health Psychology*, **17**, 290–9.

Weiss, G.L. and Larson, D.L. (1990) Health value, health locus of control, and the prediction of health protective behaviors, *Social Behavior and Personality*, **18**, 121–36.

Whitehead, M. (1988) The health divide. In *Inequalities in Health: The Black Report and the Health Divide*. London: Penguin, 217–356.

Winett, R.A. (1985) Ecobehavioral assessment in health life-styles: concepts and methods. In P. Karoly (ed.) *Measurement Strategies in Health Psychology*. Chichester: Wiley, 147–81.

Witenberg, S.H., Blanchard, E.B., Suls, J., Tennen, H., McCoy, G. and McGoldrick, M.D. (1983) Perceptions of control and causality as predictors of compliance with hemodialysis, *Basic and Applied Social Psychology*, **1**, 319–36.

Wurtele, S.K., Britcher, J.C. and Saslawsky, D.A. (1985) Relationships between locus of control, health value and preventive health behaviours among women, *Journal of Research in Personality*, **19**, 271–8.

| 2 | CHARLES ABRAHAM AND |
| | PASCHAL SHEERAN |

THE HEALTH BELIEF MODEL

1 General background

In the 1950s US public health researchers began developing psychological models designed to enhance the effectiveness of health education pro-grammes (Hochbaum 1958; Rosenstock 1966). Demographic variables such as socioeconomic status, gender, ethnicity and age were known to be associated with preventive health behaviours and use of health services (Rosenstock 1974). Such antecedents could not, however, be modified through health education. Moreover, even when services were publicly financed, the effects of socioeconomic status were not eliminated. Effective health education was needed to target potentially modifiable individual characteristics which predicted preventive behaviour and health service usage and which, ideally, reflected differences in socialization histories, indexed by demographic variables.

Beliefs provided a link between socialization and behaviour. Beliefs are enduring individual characteristics which shape behaviour and can be acquired through primary socialization. Beliefs are also modifiable and can differentiate between individuals from the same background. If persuasive methods can be used to change behaviour-related beliefs and these inter-ventions also result in behaviour change this provides a theoretical and practical basis for evidence-based health education.

The relationship between health beliefs and behaviours was con-ceptualized primarily in terms of Lewin's (1951) idea of valence, that is, making a behaviour more or less attractive. This resulted in an expectancy-value model in which events believed to be more or less likely were seen to be positively or negatively evaluated by the individual. In particular, the likelihood of experiencing a health problem, the severity of the con-sequences of that problem and the perceived benefits of a health behaviour, in combination with its potential costs, were seen as key beliefs that shaped health behaviour. Early research found that these health beliefs were correlated with health behaviours and so could be used to differentiate between those who did and did not undertake such behaviours. The model was initially applied to preventive behaviours but later successfully extended to identify the correlates of health service usage and adherence to medical advice (Becker *et al.* 1977b).

Rosenstock (1974) attributed the first health belief model (HBM) research to Hochbaum's (1958) studies of the uptake of tuberculosis X-ray screening. Hochbaum found that perceived susceptibility to tuberculosis and the belief that people with the disease could be asymptomatic (making screening beneficial) distinguished between those who had and had not attended for chest X-rays. Similarly, a prospective study by Kegeles (1963) showed that perceived susceptibility to the worst imaginable dental problems and awareness that visits to the dentist might prevent these problems were useful predictors of the frequency of dental visits over the next three years. Haefner and Kirscht (1970) took this research one step further and demonstrated that a health education intervention designed to increase participants' perceived susceptibility, perceived severity and anticipated benefits resulted in a greater number of check-up visits to the doctor compared to controls over the following eight months. Thus, by the early 1970s a series of studies suggested that these key health beliefs provided a useful framework for understanding individual differences in health behaviour and for designing behaviour change interventions.

The HBM had the advantage of specifying a discrete set of common sense cognitions that appeared to mediate the effects of demographic variables and were amenable to educational intervention. This model could be applied to a range of health behaviours and provided a basis for shaping public health behaviour and training health care professionals to work from their patients' subjective perceptions of illness and treatment. Consensus regarding the utility of the HBM was important for public health research and, simultaneously, placed social cognition modelling at the centre of health service research programmes.

The HBM was consolidated when Becker *et al.* (1977b) published a consensus statement from the Carnegie Grant Subcommittee on Modification of Patient Behaviour for Health Maintenance and Disease Control. This paper considered a range of alternative approaches to understanding the social psychological determinants of health and illness behaviour and endorsed the HBM framework. The components of the model were defined and further research on the relationships between individual beliefs and health behaviours was called for.

2 Description of the model

The HBM focused on two aspects of individuals' representations of health and health behaviour: threat perception and behavioural evaluation. Threat perception was construed as two key beliefs, perceived susceptibility to illness or health problems and anticipated severity of the consequences of illnesses. Behavioural evaluation also consisted of two distinct sets of beliefs, those concerning the benefits or efficacy of a recommended health behaviour and those concerning the costs of, or barriers to, enacting the behaviour. In addition, the model proposed that cues to action can activate health behaviour when appropriate beliefs are held. These 'cues' included a diverse range of triggers including individual perceptions of symptoms, social influence and health education campaigns. Finally, an individual's general health motivation, or 'readiness to be concerned about health matters', was included in later versions of the model (e.g. Becker *et al.* 1977b). There were therefore six distinct constructs specified by the HBM.

As Figure 2.1 indicates, there were no clear guidelines on how to operationalize the links between perceived susceptibility, severity and overall threat perception. Similarly, although it was suggested that perceived benefits were 'weighted against' perceived barriers (Becker *et al.* 1977b), no formula for creating an overall behavioural evaluation measure was developed. Consequently, the model has usually been operationalized as a series of up to six separate independent variables which potentially account for variance in health behaviours. Even the definition of these six constructs was left open to debate. Rosenstock (1974) and Becker and Maiman (1975) illustrate how various researchers used somewhat different operationalizations of these constructs and, in a meta-analysis of predictive applications of the HBM, Harrison *et al.* (1992) concluded that this lack of operational homogeneity weakens the HBM's status as a coherent psychological model of the prerequisites of health behaviour. Nevertheless, a series of studies have shown that these various operationalizations allowed identification of beliefs correlated with health behaviours (e.g. Janz and Becker 1984).

3 Summary of research

3.1 Overview of HBM applications and research strategies

The HBM has been applied to the prediction of an impressively broad range of health behaviours among a wide range of populations. Table 2.1 illustrates the range of behaviours which have been examined. Three broad areas can be identified: (a) preventive health behaviours, which include health-promoting (e.g. diet, exercise) and health-risk (e.g. smoking) behaviours as well as vaccination and contraceptive practices; (b) sick role behaviours, particularly adherence to recommended medical regimens; and (c) clinic use, which includes physician visits for a variety of reasons.

Early HBM studies focused on prediction of preventive health behaviours. One of the first reviews of research (Becker *et al.* 1977a) examined 20 studies, 13 of which were investigations of preventive actions. These 13 studies examined seven distinct behaviours (X-ray screening for TB, polio and influenza vaccination, use of safety gloves, pap test, preventive dental visits and screening for Tay–Sachs trait). In contrast, six of the remaining

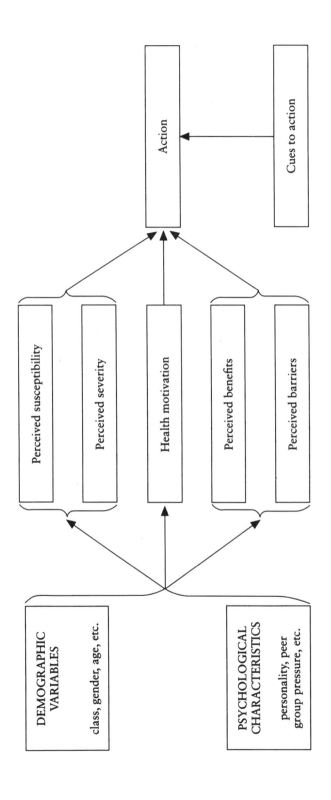

Figure 2.1   The health belief model

Table 2.1   Illustrative applications of the HBM

Behaviour	Researchers
Preventive behaviours	
Screening	
• genetic	Becker *et al.* (1975), Tay–Sachs trait; Hoogewerf *et al.* (1990) Faecal occult blood
• health	King (1984) Hypertension; Orbell *et al.* (1995) Cervical cancer; Hay *et al.* (2003) Colorectal cancer; Rawl *et al.* (2001) Colorectal cancer
	Aiken *et al.* (1994a, 1994b) mammography; Simon and Das (1984) STI test; Dorr *et al.* (1999) HIV test.
Risk behaviours	
• smoking	Gianetti *et al.* (1985), Mullen *et al.* (1987), Penderson *et al.* (1982), Stacy and Lloyd (1990)
	Li *et al.* (2003) exposure to environmental tobacco smoke
• alcohol	Beck (1981), Gottlieb and Baker (1986), Portnoy (1980)
• eating meat	Weitkunat *et al.* (2003)
Influenza vaccination	Oliver and Berger (1979), Cummings *et al.* (1979), Larson *et al.* (1982), Rundall and Wheeler (1979)
Breast self-examination	Calnan (1985), Champion (1984), Owens *et al.* (1987), Ronis and Harel (1989), Umeh and Rogan-Gibson (2001), Norman and Brain (in press)
Contraceptive use (including condom use)	Eisen *et al.* (1985), Hester and Macrina (1985), Lowe and Radius (1987)
	Drayton *et al.* (2002), Abraham *et al.* (1992; 1996), Lollis *et al.* (1997), Adih and Alexander (1999), Volk, and Koopman (2001), Winfield and Whaley (2002)
Diet and exercise	Aho (1979a), Langlie (1977)
	Silver Wallace (2002) in relation to osteoporosis prevention
Dental behaviours	
• dental visits	Chen and Land (1986), Kegeles (1963)
• brushing/flossing	Chen and Tatsuoka (1984)
Others	Ogionwo (1973) cholera prevention; Quine *et al.* (1998) safety helmet use
	Ali (2002) coronary heart disease prevention
Sick role/adherence behaviours	
Anti-hypertensive regimens	Hershey *et al.* (1980), Kirscht and Rosenstock (1977), Nelson *et al.* (1978), Taylor (1979)
Diabetic regimens	Bradley *et al.* (1987), Brownlee-Duffeck *et al.* (1987), Harris and Lynn (1985), Wdowik *et al.* (2001)
Renal disease regimen	Cummings *et al.* (1982), Hartman and Becker (1978), Heinzelmann (1962)
Psychiatric regimens	Kelly *et al.* (1987), Perkins (1999), Smith *et al.* (1999)
Parental adherence to children's regimens	Becker *et al.* (1977b) obesity; Gordis *et al.* (1969) rheumatic fever; Becker *et al.* (1972), Charney *et al.* (1967) Otitis medea; Becker *et al.* (1978) asthma

Table 2.1 cont'd

Others	Reid and Christensen (1998) regimen for urinary tract infection Abraham *et al.* (1999) malaria prophylaxis regimens
Clinic use Physician visits	
• preventive	Berkanovich *et al.* (1981), Leavitt (1979), Kirscht *et al.* (1976), Norman and Conner (1993)
• parent and child	Becker *et al.* (1972, 1977a), Kirscht *et al.* (1978)
• psychiatric	Connelly *et al.* (1982), Connelly (1984), Pan and Tantam (1989), Rees (1986)

seven studies of sick role behaviours concerned adherence to penicillin prescriptions. When Janz and Becker reviewed the HBM literature in 1984, smoking, alcohol use, dieting, exercise and attendance at blood pressure screening had been added to the list of preventive behaviours examined from an HBM perspective. Studies of sick role behaviours also increased to include adherence to regimens for hypertension, insulin-dependent and non-insulin-dependent diabetes, end-stage renal disease, obesity and asthma. Studies often examined a range of outcomes relevant to a particular regimen. For example, Cummings *et al.*'s (1982) study of end-stage renal disease patients included measures of serum phosphorus and potassium levels, fluid intake, weight gain and patients' self-reports of diet and medication. Subsequent research has extended the range of behaviours examined to include contraceptive use, including condom use, and personal dental behaviours such as teeth brushing and flossing as well as screening for faecal occult blood, colorectal cancer and sexually transmitted diseases.

Most HBM studies have employed cross-sectional designs, although Janz and Becker's (1984) review found that 40 per cent of identified HBM studies (n = 18) were prospective. Prospective studies are important because simultaneous measurement of health beliefs and (especially self-reported) behaviour may be subject to memory and social desirability biases and do not permit causal inferences (Field 2000). Most studies also have used self-report measures of behaviour but some have used physiological measures (e.g. Bradley *et al.* 1987), behavioural observations (e.g. Alagna and Reddy 1984; Dorr *et al.* 1999; Hay *et al.* 2003) or medical records (e.g. Orbell *et al.* 1995; Drayton *et al.* 2002) as outcome measures. While the majority of measures of health beliefs employ self-completion questionnaires, structured face-to-face (e.g. Cummings *et al.* 1982; Volk and Koopman 2001) and telephone (e.g. Grady *et al.* 1983) interviews have also been employed. Use of random sampling techniques is commonplace and specific representation of low-income and minority groups is also evident (e.g. Becker *et al.* 1974; Mullen *et al.* 1987; Ronis and Harel 1989; Winfield and Whaley 2002).

Findings from research studies employing the HBM are reviewed below. We first examine evidence for the predictive utility of the model's four major constructs: susceptibility, severity, benefits and barriers. Second, findings relating to cues to action and health motivation, which have received less empirical attention, are considered. Third, the issue of combining health beliefs and the potential importance of interactions among beliefs is examined. Finally, we discuss the extent to which health beliefs have been successful in mediating the effects of social structural variables and past behaviour.

3.2   Utility of perceived susceptibility, severity, benefit and barrier constructs

Two quantitative reviews of research using the HBM with adults have been published (Janz and Becker 1984; Harrison *et al.* 1992).[1] These reviews adopted different strategies in quantifying findings from research studies. Janz and Becker's (1984) review employed a vote count procedure (see Cooper 1986: 36). A significance ratio was calculated 'wherein the number of positive and statistically significant findings for an HBM dimension are divided by the total number of studies which reported significance levels for that dimension'. Janz and Becker's significance ratios shows the percentage of times each HBM construct was statistically significant in the predicted direction across 46 studies. Across all studies, the significance ratios are very supportive of HBM predictions. Susceptibility was significant in 81 per cent of studies (30/37), severity in 65 per cent (24/37), benefits in 78 per cent (29/37) and barriers in 89 per cent (25/28). When prospective studies only (n = 18) were examined, findings appeared to confirm a predictive role for these health beliefs. The ratios were 82, 65, 81 and 100 per cent for susceptibility, severity, benefits and barriers based on 17, 17, 16 and 11 studies, respectively. Results show that barriers are the most reliable predictor of behaviour, followed by susceptibility and benefits, and finally severity.

Figure 2.2 presents significance ratios separately for preventive, sick role and clinic utilization behaviours based in each case on the number of studies examined by Janz and Becker.[2] Across 24 studies of preventive behaviours, barriers were significant predictors in 93 per cent of hypotheses, susceptibility in 86 per cent, benefits in 74 per cent and severity in 50 per cent. Barriers were also the most frequent predictor in 19 studies of sick role behaviours (92 per cent), with severity second (88 per cent) followed by benefits (80 per cent) and susceptibility (77 per cent). There were only three clinic use studies examined in the review. Benefits were significant in all studies, susceptibility was significant in two out of three and severity was significant in one out of three. Barriers were significant in one of the two studies of clinic use which examined this component. It is interesting to note that while severity has only a moderate effect upon preventive behaviour or clinic utilization, it is the second most powerful predictor of sick role behaviour. Janz and Becker suggest that these differences might be due to respondents' difficulty in conceptualizing this component when they are asymptomatic or when the effects of the health threat are unfamiliar or only occur in the long term.

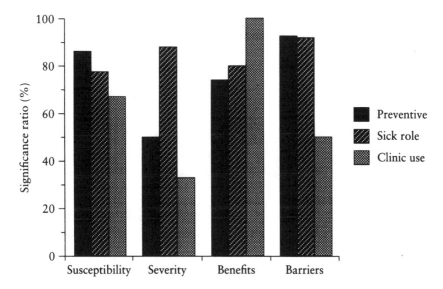

Figure 2.2 Significance ratios for HBM constructs for preventive, sick-role and clinic use behaviours (after Janz and Becker 1984)

Janz and Becker's findings appear to provide strong support for the HBM across a range of behaviours but limitations of the vote count procedure suggest caution in interpreting these results. The significance ratios only reveal how often HBM components were significantly associated with behaviour, not how large the effects of HBM measures were on outcomes (e.g. behaviour). Moreover, significance ratios give equal weighting to findings from studies with large and small numbers of participants and do not differentiate between bivariate relationships between an HBM construct and behaviour and multivariate associations. In addition, Janz and Becker's analysis did not properly control for multiple behavioural outcomes.

Harrison *et al.*'s (1992) meta-analytic review of the HBM addressed these methodological issues. Harrison and colleagues originally identified 234 published empirical tests of the HBM. Of these, only 16 studies (i.e. 6.8 per cent) measured all four major components and included reliability checks. This clearly demonstrates the extent to which operationalizations of the HBM have failed to measure all constructs or provide psychometric tests of measures (see Conner 1993). The meta-analysis involved converting associations between HBM constructs and behaviour measures, in each study, into a common effect size, namely Pearson's r. A weighted average of these effect sizes was then computed for each component (see Rosenthal 1984). Figure 2.3 shows that, across all studies, the average correlations between HBM components and behaviour were 0.15, 0.08, 0.13 and 0.21 for susceptibility, severity, benefits and barriers, respectively. While these correlations are all statistically significant, they are small with individual constructs accounting for between just one-half and 4 per cent of the variance in behaviour, across studies. Unlike Janz and Becker (1984), Harrison *et al.* found that HBM components had different associations in cross-sectional versus longitudinal designs. Both benefits and barriers had significantly larger effect sizes in prospective than in retrospective research, whereas in the case of severity, the effect size was significantly larger in retrospective studies.

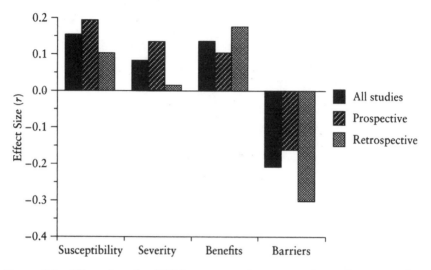

Figure 2.3   Effect sizes for HBM constructs for prospective and retrospective studies (after Harrison *et al.* 1992)

Overall, the results of quantitative reviews of the susceptibility, severity, benefits and barriers constructs suggest that these variables are very often found to be significant predictors of health-related behaviours but that their effects are small. A number of caveats are important here. First, the effects of individual health beliefs should be combined and the combined effect may be greater than the sum of individual effects. Second, Harrison *et al.* (1992) adopted very strict criteria for inclusion in their review and the effect sizes they obtained are based on findings from only 3515 respondents. Finally, Harrison *et al.* point out that their effect sizes also show considerable heterogeneity, which suggests that design or measurement differences across studies or different conceptualizations of the constructs influenced the results. We can conclude that, while tests of the predictive utility of these HBM constructs are supportive, poor operationalizations of the model and failure to check both the reliability and the validity of constructs is a significant drawback in many studies applying the HBM.

3.3 Utility of cues to action and health motivation constructs

Cues to action and health motivation have been relatively neglected in empirical tests of the HBM. Neither Janz and Becker (1984) nor Harrison *et al.* (1992) include these components in their reviews because of the paucity of studies examining these variables. One reason for researchers' failure to operationalize these components may be the lack of clear construct definitions. Cues to action can include a wide range of experiences and so have been operationalized differently by different researchers. For example, Grady *et al.* (1983) found significant associations between the numbers of family members with breast and other cancers and participation in a breast self-examination teaching programme. These authors did not, however, refer to these measures as 'cues to action', while an almost identical variable in Keesling and Friedman's (1987) study of skin cancer prevention was conceptualized in this way.

Physicians' advice or recommendations have been found to be successful cues to action in the contexts of smoking cessation (Weinberger *et al.* 1981; Stacy and Lloyd 1990) and flu vaccination (Cummings *et al.* 1979). Postcard reminders have also been successful (e.g. Larson *et al.* 1982; Norman and Conner 1993), though the effect of other media cues to action is less clear. While Ogionwo (1973) found that a radio, film and poster campaign was successful in attempts to prevent cholera, Bardsley and Beckman (1988) reported a negative effect of an advert for alcoholism treatment. Mullen *et al.* (1987) found no effect for memory of a mass media campaign upon smoking and Li *et al.* (2003) found that reported exposure to antismoking campaigns on radio, TV and billboards was not associated with young people's exposure to tobacco smoke. Knowing someone who is HIV positive or has AIDS has not been predictive of behavioural change among gay men (e.g. McCuskar *et al.* 1989a; Wolcott *et al.* 1990), and Winfield and Whaley (2002) found that a multi-item scale, including assessment of knowledge of others with HIV/AIDS, previous discussion of HIV/AIDS and exposure to HIV/AIDS campaigns, was not significantly correlated with condom use among African American college students. Similarly, Umeh and Rogan-Gibson (2001) found that a multi-item cues-to-action scale including social pressure, recommendations from health care professionals, family experiences and physical symptoms was not associated with reported breast self-examination. However, Aho (1979b) found that knowing someone who had experienced negative side effects from influenza vaccination was negatively related to inoculation behaviour. Perhaps unsurprisingly, measures of 'internal' cues to action, namely the presence or intensity of symptoms, have been generally predictive of behaviour (King 1984; Harris and Lynn 1985; Kelly *et al.* 1987).

Measurements of health motivation have generally comprised just a single item, usually expressing general 'concern' about health, though a small number of researchers have developed psychometric scales (e.g. Maiman *et al.* 1977; Champion 1984; Umeh and Rogan-Gibson 2001). Bivariate relationships between health motivation and health behaviour are generally small but statistically significant (e.g. Ogionwo 1973; Berkanovich *et al.* 1981; Champion 1984; Casey *et al.* 1985; Ali 2002), with some non-significant exceptions (e.g. Harris and Guten 1979; Rayant and Sheiham 1980; Umeh and Rogan-Gibson 2001). Findings from multivariate analyses are mixed, with some studies finding positive relationships (e.g. Portnoy 1980; Thompson *et al.* 1986; Ali 2002) and others finding no association (e.g. King 1982; Wagner and Curran 1984).

Few studies have examined direct versus indirect effects of health motivation. One which did (Chen and Land 1986) found that health motivation was negatively related to perceived susceptibility and positively related to severity but did not directly affect behaviour.

3.4 Combining HBM components

Failures to operationalize the HBM in its entirety may be partly due to the early suggestion that susceptibility and severity could be combined under a single construct, that is 'threat', and similarly, that benefits and barriers should be subtracted from one another rather than treated as separate constructs (Becker and Maiman 1975). Some researchers have used a threat index rather than measure susceptibility and severity separately (e.g. Kirscht *et al.* 1976). This appears to violate the expectancy-value structure of the HBM and so can be seen as an inferior, and perhaps incorrect, operationalization of the model (see Feather 1982).

While most HBM studies measure benefits and barriers, some researchers have also combined benefits and barriers in a single index (e.g. Gianetti *et al.* 1985; Oliver and Berger 1979). This practice raises theoretical and empirical issues. At a theoretical level, Weinstein (1988) suggests that there is a qualitative difference between benefits and barriers, at least in hazard situations, which means that they should be treated as distinct constructs. For example, while barriers relating to taking exercise or giving up salt are certain and concrete (e.g. time and effort, loss of pleasure), the benefits in terms of avoiding hypertension are more hypothetical. At an empirical level, the benefits construct may comprise distinct components, namely the efficacy of the behaviour in achieving an outcome (response efficacy) as well as possible psychosocial benefits such as social approval. Similarly, the barriers construct may comprise both physical limitations on performing a behaviour (e.g. expense) and psychological costs associated with its performance (e.g. distress). It seems unlikely that a single index could adequately represent these different outcome expectancies. An empirical approach to resolving this issue is to employ factor and reliability analyses to assess whether, and which, benefits and barriers can be legitimately combined, from a psychometric perspective (e.g. Abraham *et al.* 1992).

A separate issue concerns whether susceptibility and severity scores should combine additively or multiplicatively as the HBM's expectancy value structure would suggest. This issue has been investigated experimentally from a protection motivation theory perspective by Rogers and Mewborn (1976). These researchers found no support for the predicted susceptibility by severity interaction (see also Weinstein 1982; Maddux and Rogers 1983; Rogers 1983; Ronis and Harel 1989). In a rare HBM study addressing this question, Lewis (1994) noted that the severity manipulation check in Rogers and Mewborn's study was not successful so their data did not represent a useful test of the interaction hypothesis. Lewis's data found no support for the interaction hypothesis using parametric and non-parametric statistical tests on retrospective data. Although, in a prospective study, employing a small sample, the susceptibility × severity interaction contributed a significant proportion of unique variance (sr^2 = 0.12, p < 0.05). Lewis suggests that the equation

threat = susceptibility + (susceptibility × severity)

may better represent the effects of the severity component, at least for some health behaviours, than a simple additive model. Kruglanski and Klar (1985) and Weinstein (1988) concur, suggesting that severity must reach a certain magnitude to figure in health decisions, but once that magnitude has been reached decisions are based solely on perceived susceptibility. The relatively poor findings for the severity component in quantitative reviews appear to support these interpretations, though further research on this issue is required.

3.5 Utility of HBM components in mediating the impact of past experience or social structural position

In a useful review of literature on the impact of past experience of a behaviour upon its future performance, Sutton (1994) points out that almost all health behaviours are capable of being repeated. Janz and Becker (1984: 44) acknowledge that 'some behaviours (e.g. cigarette smoking; tooth-brushing) have a substantial habitual component obviating any ongoing psychosocial decision-making process', but do not address the question of whether health beliefs might have a role in breaking unhealthy habits. While the issue of whether cognitions mediate the effects of past experience has been a central concern of researchers using the theory of reasoned action (see Bentler and Speckart 1979), few HBM studies measure past behaviour.

Some researchers using HBM have explicitly addressed this mediation hypothesis. In a prospective study, Cummings *et al.* (1979) found both direct and indirect effects for 'past experience with flu shots' upon subsequent inoculation behaviour. Perceived efficacy of vaccination (a benefit) and the behavioural intention construct of the theory of reasoned action (Fishbein and Ajzen 1975) were both partial mediators of the effects of experience. Similarly, Norman and Brain (2005) found that perceived susceptibility and barriers both partially mediated the effects of past behaviour on subsequent breast self-examination. Two studies by Otten and van der Pligt (1992) tested whether perceived susceptibility mediated the relationship between past and future preventive health behaviours. While past behaviour was predictive of susceptibility assessments and a proxy measure of future behaviour (behavioural expectation; Warshaw and Davis 1985), susceptibility was negatively associated with expectation and did not mediate the effects of past behaviour. While Otten and van der

Pligt's (1992) studies underline the need for further longitudinal research on this issue.

Another important, and neglected, issue concerns the ability of HBM components to mediate the effects of social structural position upon health behaviour. Cummings *et al.* (1979) found that socioeconomic status (SES) was not related to health beliefs, though both SES and beliefs were significantly related to inoculation behaviour in bivariate analyses. Orbell *et al.* (1995), on the other hand, found that perceived susceptibility and barriers entirely mediated the effects of social class upon uptake of cervical screening. Direct effects were, however, obtained for both marital status and sexual experience. Salloway *et al.* (1978) obtained both direct and indirect effects for occupational status, sex and income and an indirect effect of education upon appointment-keeping at an inner-city hypertension clinic (see also Chen and Land 1990).

Salloway *et al.* (1978) are critical of Rosenstock's (1974) contention that the HBM may be more applicable to middle-class samples because of their orientation toward the future, deliberate planning and deferment of immediate gratification. Salloway *et al.* (1978: 113) point out that working-class people 'are subject to real structural barriers and constrained by real differences in social network structure which are not present in middle-class populations'. Further research is needed to determine the impact of SES upon health beliefs and their relationship to behaviour and to discriminate between the effects of cognitions and the effects of factors such as financial constraints, culture of poverty/network effects, and health system/provider barriers upon the likelihood of health behaviours (Rundall and Wheeler 1979).

4 Developments

Recognizing limitations of the HBM, Rosenstock (1974) suggested that a more comprehensive model of cognitive antecedents could reveal how health beliefs are related to other psychological stages in decision making and action. King (1982) demonstrated how this might be achieved by 'extending' the HBM in a study of screening for hypertension. She included measures of individuals' causal understanding of high blood pressure derived from 'attribution theory' (Kelley 1967), which she theorized as determinants of health beliefs that, in turn, prompted intention formation (Fishbein and Ajzen 1975), a more immediate cognitive antecedent of action. Using a prospective design, King found that eight measures, including intention, could correctly classify 82 per cent of respondents as either attenders or non-attenders. She also reported that four measures, perceived severity, two measures of perceived benefits and the extent to which respondents identified one or many causes of high blood pressure, accounted for 18 per cent of the variance in behavioural intention, which was the best single predictor of attendance. This study is noteworthy because it combined constructs from a number of theories (attribution theory, the HBM and the theory of reasoned action) and created a new model that simultaneously explored the cognitive foundations of health beliefs and sketched a mechanism by which they might generate action. King's research is a good example of how pathways between cognition measures may be empirically examined to provide evidence relating to psychological processes rather than static belief strengths and valences. Unfortunately, studies of this kind are rare in HBM research (but see Quine *et al.*, 1998; Abraham *et al.*, 1999a). This failure to extend the model has distanced it from theoretical advances in social cognition research and later attempts to situate health beliefs in more comprehensive models of the cognitive antecedents of action have tended to abandon the HBM structure in favour of new conceptual frameworks (e.g. protection motivation theory; Prentice-Dunn and Rogers, 1986).

By 1980 work on 'locus of control' by Rotter (1966) and Wallston and Wallston (1982) and, more importantly, 'perceived self-efficacy' by Bandura (1977) had established perceived control as an important determinant of health behaviour. King (1982) included a measure of perceived control derived from attribution theory, which was found to predict attendance. Later, Janz and Becker (1984) also recognized the importance of perceived control but speculated that it might be thought of as a component of perceived barriers rather than an additional theoretical construct. Consequently, the HBM remained unmodified whereas Ajzen added perceived behavioural control to the theory of reasoned action to relaunch it as the theory of planned behaviour (TPB; Ajzen and Madden 1986; Ajzen 1998). Two years later, Rosenstock *et al.* (1988) acknowledged that Janz and Becker (1984) underestimated the importance of self-efficacy and proposed that it be added to the HBM. Subsequent studies have tested the predictive utility of an extended HBM, including self-efficacy, and generally confirmed that self-efficacy is a useful additional predictor (e.g. Silver Wallace 2002; Wallace 2002; Hay *et al.* 2003; Norman and Brain 2005). Self-efficacy may not always enhance the predictive utility of the model, however. When floor or ceiling effects are observed, as when participants are uniformly confident that they can take action, self-efficacy may not provide additional discrimination (e.g. Weitkunat *et al.* 2003).

Unfortunately, unlike King (1982), Rosenstock *et al.* (1988) offered no new theoretical formulation specifying interactions between beliefs and self-efficacy. They suggested that self-efficacy could be added to the other HBM constructs without elaboration of the model's theoretical structure. This may have been short-sighted because subsequent research indicated that key HBM constructs have indirect effects on behaviour as a result of their effect on perceived control and intention which may, therefore, be regarded as more proximal determinants of action (Schwarzer 1992; Abraham *et al.* 1999a).

A number of researchers have included HBM-specified health beliefs in more comprehensive models of the cognitive antecedents of action. For example, Schwarzer's (1992) 'health action process approach' combines constructs from the HBM with those from other social cognitive models.

Susceptibility and severity beliefs are construed as antecedents of outcome expectancies and intention, and intention and self-efficacy are identified as more proximal antecedents of action. Abraham *et al.* (1999a) found that including health beliefs (concerning perceived susceptibility and perceived side effects) in a TPB model helped identify key cognitive antecedents of the intention to adhere to malaria prophylaxis after returning from a malarious region. Like King, Abraham *et al.* found that specific health beliefs enhanced the prediction of intention and that intention was the strongest predictor of adherence. Intention mediated the effects of most cognitions on behaviour although, among a sample taking a drug known to have serious side effects, perceived side effects added to the variance explained in adherence, after controlling for the effects of intention. Jones *et al.* (2001) found that an HBM-derived measure of perceived threat contributed to the prediction of intention to use sunscreen in a model that also included measures of knowledge, norms, importance of short-term negative consequences and self-efficacy. Such research suggests that health beliefs may be more usefully construed as cognitive antecedents of self-efficacy and intention, rather than direct antecedents of action. However, in certain circumstances, particularly salient beliefs about a procedure or medication (e.g. beliefs about perceived side effects) may enhance the prediction of behaviour, controlling for the effects of intention and self-efficacy.

Correspondence between social cognition models has been recognized for some time. For example, Kirscht (1983: 287) noted that HBM constructs could be 'mapped onto' the theory of reasoned action. Prompted by efforts to promote HIV-preventive behaviours, leading theorists held a workshop in 1991 to 'identify a finite set of variables to be considered in any behavioral analysis' (Fishbein *et al.* 2001: 3). Theorists included Fishbein (TPB; e.g. Fishbein and Ajzen 1975), Bandura (social cognitive theory and self-efficacy; e.g. Bandura 1977) and Becker (HBM; e.g. Becker *et al.* 1977a, 1977b). They identified eight core variables important to explaining behaviour and promoting behaviour change. Three variables were regarded as necessary and sufficient prerequisites, namely a strong intention, the necessary skills and the absence of environmental constraints that prevent the specified actions. In addition, five further antecedents were identified as determinants of intention strength: self-efficacy, the belief that advantages (e.g. benefits) outweigh disadvantages (e.g. costs), the perception of greater social (normative) pressure to perform the behaviour than not to perform the behaviour, the belief that the action is consistent with the person's self-image and anticipation of a more positive than negative emotional reaction to undertaking the specified action/s. This framework maps the main constructs from the HBM onto the more general attitude and normative constructs included in the theory of reasoned action. Beliefs about the seriousness of a health threat, personal susceptibility to the threat, efficacy of medication, side effects of medication are all construed as perceived advantages and disadvantages of action which are, in turn, determinants of strength of intention. This produces a logical and parsimonious framework which incorporates the two-stage model of decision making and action inherent in the theory of reasoned action (Fishbein and Ajzen 1975), that is, intention predicts behaviour and is predicted by a series of other cognitive antecedents. This amalgamation of predictive models is a helpful development for researchers wishing to apply social cognition models. However, researchers should continue to explore and measure health beliefs because research has shown that such beliefs can explain additional variance in intention beyond that engendered by general measures of attitude (e.g. semantic differential measures, Fishbein *et al.* 2001: 11). Overall, however, with some exceptions, it may be prudent to regard HBM-specified beliefs as antecedents of intention, rather than predictors of behaviour.

5 Operationalization of the model

Below we outline the steps involved in developing an HBM questionnaire. We briefly review available instruments and analyse a study by Champion (1984) which developed health belief scales to investigate the frequency of breast self-examination. Determination of reliability and validity of scales is addressed in some depth. Finally, we identify some conceptual difficulties with HBM components and briefly address problems of response bias.

5.1 Developing an HBM questionnaire

Formulating hypotheses or research questions clearly so that they translate into relationships between variables, defining an appropriate sample, gaining access to that sample and deciding the mode of data collection (e.g. pencil and paper test or telephone interview) are generally prerequisites of instrument development. There are two ways to determine the content of the items of the questionnaire. The first is to conduct a literature search for previous HBM studies in the area and determine whether previous instruments are published or available from authors. Scales should be checked to determine whether internal reliability is satisfactory and whether the scale has face validity (respondents believe that the scale measures what it says it does). A scale obtained in this way might be used in its entirety but may require modification if it is to be used with a different sample.

HBM scales from the Standardized Compliance Questionnaire (Sackett *et al.*, 1974) have been modified for use in a variety of settings (e.g. Cerkoney and Hart 1980; Bollin and Hart 1982; Connelly 1984) but this instrument may be difficult to obtain and other scales have also been employed. For example, Calnan (1984) and Hallal (1982) employed measures derived from Stillman's (1977) research on breast cancer. Fincham and Wertheimer (1985) used items derived from Leavitt (1979) in their study of uptake of prescriptions while Hoogewerf *et al.* (1990) examined compliance with genetic screening using items from Halper *et al.* (1980). There are also published HBM scales in the areas of compliance with hypertension regimens (Abraham and Williams 1991), children's obesity regimens (Maiman *et al.* 1977), breast self-examination (Champion 1984), and other behaviours.

If no appropriate, previously developed HBM measures are available, researchers must develop their own (see DeVellis 1991, for a general guide to scale development). A useful example of this process is provided by Champion's (1984) study of breast self-examination The first step involves generating items which purport to measure HBM components (the item pool). Again, previous HBM studies can be used as a guide. It is good practice, however, for researchers to conduct semi-structured interviews with 20 or 30 potential respondents in order to determine respondents' perceptions of the health threat and beliefs about the behaviour in an open-ended manner. This process will ensure that questionnaire items are salient to the population of interest and will provide guidance on how well medical terminology and other terms will be understood by respondents. Identification of sample-relevant benefits, barriers and cues to action is likely to provide better behavioural predictors than researcher-imposed conceptualizations. Relevant experts can also be used to develop and select items.

Champion initially developed 20 to 24 items for each HBM component (excluding cues to action) but then retained only those items which at least six out of eight judges (faculty and doctoral students knowledgeable about the HBM) agreed represented the constructs in question. Random presentation of items to judges allowed assessment of the content (or face) validity of each scale, that is, the extent to which the items accurately and adequately reflected the content of HBM constructs.

The next step in developing the instrument is the pilot study. While a small number of studies in the literature report pilots of the instruments employed in the main study (e.g. Eisen *et al.* 1985; Orbell *et al.* 1995), these, unfortunately, are exceptions rather than the rule and this lack of piloting may help to explain some of the difficulties with previous research using the HBM. Champion's pilot questionnaires included the items judged to have good content validity (10 to 12 items for each construct) and employed a five-point Likert scale for responses ('strongly agree' scored 5 and 'strongly disagree' scored 1). The questionnaires were posted to a convenience sample of women along with a prepaid return envelope. Three hundred and one women participated.

Reliability and validity analyses constitute the final step in determining scale items. When a scale has high reliability, random measurement error is low and the items can be viewed as indices of one underlying construct. Scale reliability can be assessed using Cronbach's alpha coefficient (Cortina 1993) or the Spearman–Brown formula (Rust and Golombok 1990). Error over time can be determined by correlating scores on the same scale at separate time points, for example, two weeks apart. Champion determined alpha coefficients for each HBM component, dropping items which reduced the reliability of the scale. While coefficients for three constructs exceeded the generally accepted level of 0.70 (susceptibility = 0.78, severity = 0.78 and barriers = 0.76), the reliabilities for benefits and health motivation were weaker, that is, 0.62 and 0.61, respectively. Two weeks after the original questionnaires were distributed these revised scales were sent to a sub-sample who had agreed to take part in a further study. Correlations were computed between scores on the scales at these two time-points. These test–retest correlations were satisfactory (> 0.70) for four out of the five components (susceptibility = 0.86, severity = 0.76, benefits = 0.47, barriers = 0.76 and health motivation = 0.81).

The construct validity of the scales (the extent to which scales measure what they are designed to measure) was next determined by factor analysing all of the item scores. This statistical procedure sorts individual items into groupings or factors on the basis of correlations between items. Factor analysis showed that, with one exception, items all loaded on the factors (HBM constructs) they were originally assigned to, demonstrating satisfactory construct validity. Criterion validity was also determined by demonstrating that the HBM measures were significantly related to previous practice of breast self-examination. Table 2.2 presents the items used to measure the susceptibility, severity, benefits and barriers constructs, following the reliability and validity checks.

Table 2.2 Items representing susceptibility, severity, benefits and barriers components in a study of breast self-examination (Champion 1984)

HBM constructs, items and reliability

Susceptibility
1 My chances of getting breast cancer are great.
2 My physical health makes it more likely that I will get breast cancer.
3 I feel that my chances of getting breast cancer in the future are good.
4 There is a good possibility that I will get breast cancer.
5 I worry a lot about getting breast cancer.
6 Within the next year I will get breast cancer.

Cronbach's alpha = 0.78

Severity
1 The thought of breast cancer scares me.
2 When I think about breast cancer I feel nauseous.
3 If I had breast cancer my career would be endangered.
4 When I think about breast cancer my heart beats faster.
5 Breast cancer would endanger my marriage (or a significant relationship).
6 Breast cancer is a hopeless disease.
7 My feelings about myself would change if I got breast cancer.
8 I am afraid to even think about breast cancer.
9 My financial security would be endangered if I got breast cancer.
10 Problems I would experience from breast cancer would last a long time.
11 If I got breast cancer, it would be more serious than other diseases.
12 If I had breast cancer, my whole life would change.

Cronbach's alpha = 0.70

Benefits
1 Doing self-breast exams prevents future problems for me.
2 I have a lot to gain by doing self-breast exams.
3 Self-breast exams can help me find lumps in my breast.

Table 2.2   cont'd

---

4   If I do monthly breast exams I may find a lump before it is discovered by regular health exams.
5   I would not be so anxious about breast cancer if I did monthly exams.

Cronbach's alpha = 0.61

Barriers
1   It is embarrassing for me to do monthly breast exams.
2   In order for me to do monthly breast exams I have to give up quite a bit.
3   Self-breast exams can be painful.
4   Self-breast exams are time-consuming.
5   My family would make fun of me if I did self-breast exams.
6   The practice of self-breast exams interferes with my activities.
7   Doing self-breast exams would require starting a new habit, which is difficult.
8   I am afraid I would not be able to do self-breast exams.

Cronbach's alpha = 0.76

While there were some difficulties with Champion's (1984) analyses,[3] this paper provides an example of good practice in the design of a study applying the HBM. Champion rightly contrasts her own study with previous research, pointing out that the validity and reliability of HBM measures has rarely been tested, that multiple-item measures are not routinely employed, that operational definitions vary across studies and that nominal-level operationalizations have limited statistical explorations of the relationships between measures.

5.2 Problems of operationalization: conceptual difficulties with HBM components

Champion's (1984) analysis of methodological problems in HBM research and the heterogeneity of effect sizes obtained by Harrison *et al.* (1992) highlight difficulties with the conceptual definition of HBM constructs. A variety of theorists have drawn attention to problematic assumptions inherent in the HBM, for example the assumption that HBM constructs are unidimensional and that relationships between HBM constructs and behaviour are fixed and linear. In this section we briefly review theoretical issues relevant to the conceptualization of each of the HBM constructs.

Susceptibility
Becker and Maiman (1975: 20) acknowledge the wide variety of operationalizations of susceptibility:

> Hochbaum's questions apparently emphasized the concept of perceived *possibility* of contracting the disease; Kegeles' questions were directed at the *probability* of becoming ill; Heinzelmann requested estimates of likelihood of *recurrence*, while Elling *et al.* asked for similar *re-susceptibility* estimates from the mother concerning her child; and Rosenstock introduced 'self-reference' versus 'reference to

men (women) your age' (as well as 'fixed-alternative' versus 'open-ended' items). [Italics in the original]

Tversky and Kahneman (1981) showed that even quite small changes in the wording of risk choices have significant and predictable effects upon responses. Thus, considerable care needs to be taken in the phrasing of items measuring perceived susceptibility, and multi-item measures are essential.

People may employ cognitive heuristics in their susceptibility judgements. Slovic *et al.* (1977) pointed out that, in general, people seem to overestimate the frequency of rare causes of death and underestimate common causes of death. In particular, events that are dramatic or personally relevant, and therefore easy to imagine or recall, tend to be overestimated. There is also a tendency for people to underestimate the extent to which they are personally vulnerable to health and life-threatening problems. Weinstein (1980) has termed this phenomenon 'unrealistic optimism'. This sense of unique invulnerability has been demonstrated in the context of both relative risk comparisons of self to others (e.g. Weinstein 1984) and subjective versus objective risk appraisals (Gerrard and Warner 1991). Cognitive factors, including perceptions of control, egocentric bias, personal experience and stereotypical beliefs, have been posited as explanations for this tendency, as well as motivational factors, including self-esteem maintenance and defensive coping (see Van der Pligt *et al.* 1993). The impact of these cognitive and motivational processes on risk estimation may help to explain the small effect sizes obtained for associations between perceived susceptibility and health-protective behaviours (Harrison *et al.* 1992).

Weinstein (1988) has also drawn attention to other difficulties with the HBM conceptualization of susceptibility. He suggests that beliefs about susceptibility should be characterized in terms of three stages. The first stage involves the awareness that the health threat exists. The second stage involves determining how dangerous the threat is and how many people are likely to be affected. This is inevitably an ambiguous question and many people will display unrealistic optimism at this stage. Only in the final stage, when the threat has been personalized, will personal susceptibility be acknowledged. This processual account of risk perception implies that susceptibility levels are likely to change over time as populations are influenced by health education and that, consequently, the point at which susceptibility is measured may determine the strength of its association with subsequent health behaviour.

The interpretation of correlations between perceived susceptibility and health behaviour may also be problematic in cross-sectional studies because both positive and negative associations between risk and behaviour are easily interpreted. For example, suppose someone believes (s)he is at risk of HIV infection and therefore decides that (s)he will use a condom during sex. In this case, high susceptibility leads to safer behaviour and so the correlation is positive. The same person, having adopted consistent condom use, however, may now estimate her risk of infection as low. In this case, protective behaviour leads to lowered susceptibility resulting in a negative correlation. Cross-sectional data does not allow determination of the causal relationships between beliefs and behaviour and vice versa. In a review of this issue, Weinstein and Nicolich (1993: 244) concluded that 'the correlation between perceived personal risk and simultaneous preventive behaviors should not be used to assess the effects of perceptions on behavior. It is an indicator of risk perception accuracy.' Gerrard *et al.* (1996) supported this conclusion by examining four prospective studies that measured perceived susceptibility to HIV infection and subsequent safer sexual behaviour. They found no evidence that perceived susceptibility predicts behaviour when the effects of past behaviour were controlled. By contrast, they found a small but significant average weighted association ($r_+ = -0.11$) between past risk behaviour and perceived HIV susceptibility across 26 cross-sectional studies. Gerrard *et al.* point out that sexual behaviour is social and complex and that the impact of perceived susceptibility may be reduced for these reasons. Nonetheless, these findings underline the need for longitudinal studies and analyses that control for the effects of past behaviour in modelling the impact of perceived susceptibility (and other cognitions) on future behaviour. Such findings also suggest that, when evaluating the impact of belief-changing interventions, it is important to assess cognitions immediately after risk information has been received, that is before participants have had an opportunity to change their behaviour.

Finally, individual differences may moderate the relationship between past risk behaviour and perceived susceptibility. For example, Gerrard *et al.* found that this relationship was strongest among older respondents, women (versus men), gay (vs straight) men, and college (vs clinic) samples. Smith *et al.* (1997) found that self-esteem can moderate the effect of past behaviour on perceived susceptibility and Gladis *et al.* (1992) found that, while for most participants previous risk behaviour was positively related to perceived susceptibility, this relationship was reversed among pupils classed as 'repressors'. Myers (2000) further highlighted the importance of this personality trait in studies of health beliefs and cognitions. There is also evidence that personality differences moderate the relationship between perceived risk and subsequent behaviour. For example, Hampson *et al.* (2000) found that perceived risk was associated with a reduction in cigarettes smoked indoors but only for those high in conscientiousness.

Severity

Severity has been conceptualized as a multidimensional construct involving both the medical severity of a disease (pain, complications, etc.) and its psychosocial severity (e.g. the extent to which illness might interfere with valued social roles). Unfortunately, as Haefner (1974: 96) noted: 'examining the literature, one becomes aware of the variation in the selection of particular dimensions of seriousness to be studied'. For example, in a study of osteoporosis prevention, Smith and Rogers (1991) used essays to manipulate three severity dimensions: visibility of disablement (high versus low), time of onset (near versus distant future) and rate of onset (gradual versus sudden). These researchers obtained a significant main effect for visibility and a significant interaction between visibility and time of onset on post-test intention measures. The more visibly disabling descriptions of the effects of osteoporosis were, the stronger were intentions to take preventive action. In addition, low visibility consequences in the distant future were associated with weaker intentions than high visibility consequences with either time of onset. These findings underline the importance of pilot work in identifying salient dimensions of severity including beliefs about visibility and how quickly consequences are likely to occur.

Ronis and Harel (1989) combined elements of the HBM and subjective expected utility (SEU) theory in a study of breast examination behaviours. Since breast examination leads to early detection and treatment, these researchers divided the severity component into severity following action (severity of breast cancer if treated promptly) and severity following inaction (severity of breast cancer if treated late). They found support for this distinction using confirmatory factor analysis. Path analysis showed that severity dimensions did not directly affect behaviour. Rather, the benefits constructs entirely mediated the effects of severity. This study offered an interesting reconceptualization of the threat component of the HBM. Instead of directly influencing behaviour, threat appraisal is thought to contribute to the subjective utility of taking action versus not taking action. This is reflected in Schwarzer's (1992) health action process approach in which perceived threat is construed as a determinant of outcome expectancies and intention. Further research comparing direct effects (Janz and Becker 1984), interactions (e.g. Lewis 1994) and mediational (Ronis and Harel 1989) models of severity would be informative.

Benefits, barriers, cues to action and health motivation

The remaining HBM constructs have also raised problems of multi-dimensionality in operationalizations of the model. As we have noted, the benefits construct comprises both medical and psychosocial benefits of engaging in health-promoting behaviours. Similarly, the barriers component comprises practical barriers to performing the behaviour (e.g. time, expense, availability, transport, waiting time) as well as psychological costs associated with performing the behaviour (pain, embarrassment, threat to well-being or lifestyle and livelihood). Later HBM formulations (Rosenstock *et al.* 1988) included psychological barriers to performing the behaviour. While self-efficacy has received considerable attention (Bandura 1986, 1997), other specific psychological barriers might include poor understanding of complex recommendations (e.g. by a learning disabled person with diabetes) or a lack of social skills (e.g. to negotiate condom use successfully).

As we have seen, the cues to action construct can encompass a variety of influences upon behaviour, ranging from awareness and memory of mass media campaigns, through leaflets and reminder letters, to perceived descriptive and injunctive normative influence exerted by health care professionals and significant others. Thus the coherence of this construct has been questioned by a number of researchers. For example, Weinstein

(1988) argued that the construct does not fit easily alongside the rational expectancy-value structure of the model's major constructs. Mattson (1999) suggested that 'cues to action' could include all persuasive experiences including interpersonal communication, exposure to mass media and internal responses to threat. Conceptualized in this way, cues to action are causally prior to beliefs and the effect of cues on beliefs depends on the content of the persuasive communications (e.g. fear appeals versus self-efficacy enhancing communication). Schwarzer (1992) suggested that actual and perceived cues should be distinguished and that cues to action might be more appropriately construed as antecedents of intention formation and action (once other beliefs were established). Arguably, operationalizations of cues to action could ask respondents about the presence or absence of cues and also ask them to indicate the extent to which cues were available and influenced their decisions (see Bagozzi 1986). Such measures may more closely represent the original conception of 'cues'. The challenge facing researchers is to define this construct so that it can be translated into clearly defined measures that have both theoretical and psychometric coherence or, alternatively, to divide the construct into a series of clearly defined behavioural prompts.

Multi-item measures of health motivation have included a variety of items. For example, Chen and Land's (1986) measure included items relating to control over health and perceived health status while Umeh and Rogan-Gibson (2001) included measures of past performance of a range of health behaviours. This underlines problems with the discriminant validity of the health motivation construct. If health motivation is to be used as a distinct measure, further research is needed to clarify the relationship between this construct and related constructs, including past behaviour, health locus of control (Wallston and Wallston 1982), health value (Kristiansen 1985) and intention, as specified in the theories of reasoned action and planned behaviour (Fishbein and Ajzen 1975).

5.3 Problems of operationalization: response bias

A final problem concerns identifying and controlling for the effects of social desirability bias in HBM studies. Respondents may be aware of the purposes of interviews and questionnaires and so may be motivated to exaggerate both the desirability of their beliefs and behaviours and the consistency between the two. Unfortunately, this issue has received little attention. Prospective studies and objective outcome measures help to reduce bias and individual difference measures of social desirability may also identify participants most likely to shape their responses to present a socially desirable picture of themselves. Sheeran and Orbell (1995) have found that responses to HBM measures may also be subject to bias when questionnaire items are not randomized and can easily be 'read' by respondents. One approach to controlling for this type of bias would be to ask respondents to answer questions referring to both their actual and ideal beliefs.

6 Application of the model: identifying cognitive antecedents of HIV-preventive behaviour

The spread of human immunodeficiency virus (HIV) prompted research into modifiable determinants of HIV-preventive behaviours such as condom use and restriction of sexual partners. Work began with homosexual men but was extended to sexually active adolescents. The HBM had been employed to explore contraceptive behaviour (e.g. Herold 1983; Hester and Macrina 1985) and was explored as a potentially useful theoretical framework for HIV-preventive education. For example, in an early cross-sectional study of the determinants of HIV risk behaviour among homosexual men, Emmons et al. (1986) found that perceived susceptibility was significantly but weakly associated with reported efforts to reduce numbers of sexual partners and strongly but negatively associated with avoidance of anonymous partners. However, in a follow-up study of the same cohort, Joseph et al. (1987) found that health beliefs had little impact on reported behaviour over six months, although perceived susceptibility remained negatively associated with avoidance of anonymous partners. This suggested, surprisingly, that increased susceptibility could render certain groups less likely to take preventive action. The only cognitive variable which was consistently related to future HIV-preventive behaviour was descriptive norm (Cialdini et al. 1991), that is perceptions that peers were changing their behaviour.

A cross-sectional study of homosexual men by McCuskar et al. (1989b) found that health belief measures were not significantly related to condom use but that perceived susceptibility and severity were associated with reported efforts to change, suggesting that these HBM constructs may affect behaviour indirectly through more proximal cognitions, such as intention. A 12-month longitudinal follow-up (McCuskar et al. 1989a) found that past behaviour was the most powerful predictor of subsequent behaviour measures and this was confirmed in other studies. For example, Aspinwall et al. (1991) found that previous numbers of partners accounted for 51 per cent of the variance in reported partner number six months later, with health beliefs accounting for 5 per cent of the variance and health belief interactions, HIV status, partner HIV status and age adding a further 10 per cent. Only past behaviour and perceived barriers to change were significantly associated with subsequent safer sexual behaviour, accounting for 12 per cent of the variance. Collectively, these studies indicate that, among homosexual men, HIV risk behaviour is self-perpetuating, that increased levels of perceived susceptibility could prompt denial in those already aware of their HIV risk and that other measures, including descriptive norms and self-efficacy are more important predictors than HBM-specified variables.

6.1 Utility of the model in identifying the cognitive determinants of HIV-preventive sexual behaviour among young heterosexuals

HIV spread also prompted research into cognitive predictors of adolescent heterosexual sexual behaviour (Boyer and Kegeles 1991). An early cross-sectional survey found that adolescents who believed that condoms were effective in preventing HIV transmission and who felt susceptible to HIV infection were significantly more likely to report always using condoms during intercourse (Hingson *et al.* 1990). However, HBM-specified beliefs accounted for less than 15 per cent of the variance explained. Rosenthal *et al.* (1992) were critical of the measures employed by Hingson *et al.* and reported a cross-sectional study showing that HBM measures were not associated with young men's HIV risk behaviour or young women's behaviour with regular partners. Perceived susceptibility, however, accounted for 13 per cent of the variance in young women's reported HIV risk behaviour with casual partners.

Abraham *et al.* (1996) employed an HBM framework to model the psychological antecedents of adolescent condom use on the east coast of Scotland using a longitudinal design (see also Abraham *et al.* 1992). This study attempted to assess the degree to which health beliefs would predict consistency of condom use over the subsequent year.

6.2 Respondents and procedure

School lists of pupils below the minimum school leaving age were used to select random quota samples of teenagers from two cohorts (16- and 18-year-olds). A postal questionnaire containing HBM-based items was constructed after piloting and a response rate of 64 per cent yielded 690 completed questionnaires. Respondents were sent a second questionnaire one year later, including items concerning their sexual behaviour and condom use over the previous year. A 52 per cent response rate resulted in a longitudinal sample of 258. Of these, 122 reported new sexual partners over the study year and were retained for analysis. These respondents were of particular interest because they had been in a situation in which condom use should have been important, given available HIV-preventive health education campaigns. This sample consisted of 81 women (66 per cent) and 41 men (34 per cent).

6.3 Measures

As well as HBM measures, the initial questionnaire included an intention item because previous work had suggested that the effects of health beliefs may be partially or wholly mediated by intentions (e.g. Cummings *et al.* 1979; King 1982). A measure of perceived condom-use norms was also included because supportive risk-reduction norms had been found to be associated with preventive behaviours among homosexual men (Joseph *et al.* 1987). Intention to use condoms was operationalized using a five-point

Likert item: 'In future I intend to use a condom if I have sex with someone new' (*strongly agree* to *strongly disagree*) and perceived condom-use norm was measured by two seven-point items (Cronbach's alpha = 0.75): 'How many heterosexual men/women of your age would agree with the statement "I will use a condom if I have sex with someone new"?'

Eight HBM measures were included. Perceived susceptibility was measured using four items (alpha = 0.76): 'How likely do you think it is that you will get the AIDS virus in the next five years?' (seven response options from *extremely unlikely* to *extremely likely*); and three items concerning HIV spread, 'Thinking of heterosexual people in Scotland of your age, how many do you think will have been infected by the AIDS virus in (one year/five years/ten years) time?' (seven response options, *none* through *about half* to *all*). Perceived severity was measured using two seven-point items (alpha = 0.63): 'How many people who get the AIDS virus develop AIDS?' and 'How many people who get AIDS actually die of it?' (*none* to *all*).

Eight 5-point Likert items were used to measure perceived benefits of and barriers to condom use. Principal components analysis with varimax rotation yielded three factors for the time 1 sample (Abraham *et al.* 1992). However, one of the resulting measures fell below acceptable reliability for respondents with new partners at time 2 and the construct was operationalized as two single-item measures; perceived condom offensiveness ('I would be offended if someone who wanted to have sex with me suggested protecting themselves against the AIDS virus') and perceived condom casualness ('People would think I wanted casual sex if I carried condoms'). Three items were employed to measure perceived condom effectiveness (alpha = 0.76): 'Using a condom is effective in preventing a man from passing the AIDS virus to a woman', 'Using a condom is effective in preventing a woman from passing the AIDS virus to a man' and 'Using condoms is a good way to avoid unwanted pregnancy'. A measure of perceived condom attractiveness also consisted of three items (alpha = 0.55): 'Most people find condoms awkward to use', 'Condoms would not spoil the pleasure of having sex' and 'A person thinking of having sex with me would probably be pleased if I suggested using a condom'.

Cues to action were measured by asking whether respondents remembered eight specified United Kingdom AIDS-education campaigns (score range 0–8). Finally, a single Likert item ('Health is less important than enjoyment') was used to measure relative health value.

In addition, three measures of previous sexual behaviour were included: lifetime partners, prior condom use and intercourse frequency. Respondents were asked to record the number of people they had ever had sexual intercourse with, whether or not they had ever used a condom during sex (*yes/no*) and how often they had had sexual intercourse in the previous year (*never, once, more than once*). Finally, three demographic measures were included: gender, age and socioeconomic status. Socioeconomic status was indexed using the Registrar General's classification of father's occupation.

The follow-up questionnaire included four items assessing respondents' consistency of condom use ('How often do you use condoms during sex?'; five response options, *never/almost never* through *sometimes* to *almost always/always*) and three consecutive items asking how often in the past year they had: 'had sexual intercourse', 'used a condom during intercourse' and 'not used a condom during intercourse' (five response options, *never, once, most months, most weeks* and *most days*). A ratio score was calculated by dividing the reported frequency of condom use during intercourse in the previous year by the reported frequency of intercourse over the year. This was significantly correlated with responses to the other two items (rs = 0.61, 0.71) and the three response distributions formed a reliable measure (alpha = 0.83).

6.4 Results

Table 2.3 shows means and standard deviations for study variables and zero order correlations (Pearson's r) with time 2 condom use consistency. Intention and perceived condom attractiveness are positively correlated with consistency of use, as would be predicted by the theory of reasoned action. Relative health value is also positively correlated with consistency of use but perceived severity and susceptibility, the costs and barriers measures (apart from condom use attractiveness) and campaign memory are not. This provides little support for the health belief model.

Age was positively correlated with the sexual experience variables (lifetime partners, r = 0.27, p < 0.01; frequency of intercourse, r = 0.31, p < 0.001; prior condom use, r = 0.22, p < 0.01), indicating a common life-experience component. Men reported more lifetime partners, greater frequency of intercourse and were more likely to report prior condom use (rs = 0.37, p < 0.001; 0.19, p < 0.05; 0.18, p > 0.05, respectively). The strongest correlates of condom consistency at follow-up were age, class, lifetime partners and intercourse frequency, with high scores being negatively associated with subsequent consistency of condom use. Men were also more likely to report consistent condom use.

A four-step hierarchical multiple regression analysis was conducted to assess the extent to which the time 1 variables were able to predict reported condom use consistency.[4] In order to assess what predictive power HBM measures and the perceived norm measure would add to the effect of intention, intention was entered first, followed by the other cognitive variables in step 2. Previous behaviour measures were entered in step 3 followed by demographic variables in step 4. As can be seen from Table 2.4, the regression equation failed to reach significance until the previous behaviour measures were entered in step 3.

6.5 Discussion

These results suggest that the HBM measures are not useful predictors of condom use over the subsequent year among adolescents who have new

Table 2.3 Means, standard deviations, and intercorrelations for Abraham *et al.* (1996) study variables (n = 122)

Measure	Correlation with time 2 condom consistency	Range	Mean	Standard deviation
Intention	0.17*	1–5	4.12	0.86
Susceptibility	−0.09	1–5	2.96	0.75
Severity	0.00	1–5	4.19	1.22
Condom offensiveness	0.03	1–5	2.06	0.99
Condom casualness	−0.09	1–5	2.89	1.04
Condom attractiveness	0.18*	1–5	3.24	0.56
Condom effectiveness	0.01	1–5	4.11	0.61
Campaign memory	0.07	1–8	5.8	1.37
Relative health value	0.17*	1–5	1.76	0.71
Condom use norm	0.08	1–7	4.30	1.35
Lifetime partners	−0.27**	0–15	1.80	2.88
Intercourse frequency	−0.23**	1–3	1.99	0.92
SES	−0.27**	1–5	3.28	0.95
Age	−0.26**	16–18	16.85	0.97
Gender	0.17*	–	–	–

Note: * $p < 0.05$ ** $p < 0.01$

sexual partners. This calls into question the utility of the HBM as an adequate theoretical model of the cognitive antecedents of adolescent condom use. It does not, however, rule out the possibility that health beliefs specified by the HBM are prerequisite to adolescent condom use. In a well-informed population, beliefs prerequisite to condom use may be so widely accepted that they no longer distinguish effectively between people who do and do not use condoms. In this study, for example, perceived severity and perceived condom effectiveness were uniformly high and were therefore unlikely to discriminate between degrees of condom use consistency. In such populations, additional cognition measures, over and above those specified by the HBM, may be required to distinguish potential users and non-users (see e.g. Abraham *et al.* 1999b).

The failure of intention to significantly predict condom use consistency is more complex. Intention also failed to predict behaviour in a prospective study of the cognitive antecedents of adolescent condom use conducted by Breakwell *et al.* (1994). Nonetheless, this finding is less convincing because the intention measure employed here was only a single item and because the observed intention–behaviour relationship is likely to have been weakened by a failure to measure the two variables at the same level of specificity. The intention item referred to new partners while the behaviour items referred to condom use in general. Across heterosexual populations more generally, intentions have been found to be reliable predictors of condom use. For example, in a meta-analytic study, Sheeran *et al.* (1999) found an average

Table 2.4 Predictors of consistent condom use among adolescents with new partners in the previous year

Step	Independent variable	Beta[a]	p	Model F	Model p
1	Intention	0.15	0.13	3.20	0.08
2	Susceptibility	0.00	0.97	1.26	0.26
	Severity	0.02	0.78		
	Condom offensiveness	−0.05	0.54		
	Condom casualness	−0.08	0.38		
	Condom attractiveness	0.10	0.27		
	Condom effectiveness	−0.08	0.40		
	Campaign memory	0.01	0.94		
	Relative health value	0.05	0.55		
	Condom use norms	−0.09	0.40		
3	Lifetime partners	−0.22	0.05	1.98[b]	0.03
	Intercourse frequency	−0.27	0.06		
	Previous condom use	0.19	0.07		
4	Age	−0.21	0.02	2.94[c]	0.001
	Gender	0.31	0.00		
	Socioeconomic status	−0.13	0.13		

Notes:
[a] Beta values in final regression equation
[b] $R^2 = 0.19$, adj. $R^2 = 0.10$
[c] $R^2 = 0.31$, adj. $R^2 = 0.24$

weighted correlation of $r_+ = 0.46$ across 21 longitudinal analyses. It is also interesting to note, however, that, in the present study, zero order correlations show that the intention and behaviour measures were significantly correlated for men ($r = 0.33$, $p < 0.05$) but not for women ($r = 0.15$, ns). Similar gender effects on adolescents' HIV-preventive intentions were reported by Petosa and Kirby (1991) and these findings are consistent with the results of qualitative studies suggesting that young women may be disempowered in sexual negotiation so that their good intentions are not translated into action (Holland *et al.* 1990). Sheeran *et al.* (1999) did not find that the intention–behaviour relationship was moderated by gender, but it is possible that this moderation effect will only be observed in younger adolescent samples. Large-scale longitudinal studies of younger adolescents are required to clarify this point.

The effects of past behaviour confirm previous findings that condom use may be self-perpetuating (see Abraham and Sheeran 1993) and that those reporting greatest previous sexual activity are least likely to report consistent condom use. Unfortunately, this suggests that those most at risk from HIV may be the least likely to take precautions. Women and older teenagers also reported less consistent condom use. The effects of age may be mediated by higher numbers of sexual partners. However, the age effect mirrors Schaalma *et al.*'s (1993) observation that older Dutch teenagers had more negative perceptions of condoms, and so underlines the importance of condom promotion interventions with this group.

Overall, this study strongly suggested that cognitions other than those specified by the HBM are required to model potentially modifiable cognitive prerequisites of consistent condom use. This conclusion was supported by Sheeran *et al.* (1999) who found that perceived severity, perceived susceptibility, perceived barriers to condom use and perceived attractiveness of condom use had lower weighted average correlations with condom use (r_+ s = 0.02, 0.06, −0.13 and 0.14, respectively) than measures of subjective norm, descriptive norm, and attitude towards condom use (r_+ s = 0.26, 0.37 and 0.32, respectively).

6.6 Implications of HBM-based studies of HIV-preventive behaviour

Research in this area has highlighted the complexity of HIV-preventive behaviour and the limitations of the HBM. HIV is not highly infectious and the consequences of infection are serious but delayed. Early publicity established a consensus regarding severity but limited transmission routes and delayed effects do not encourage acknowledgement of personal susceptibility. Such ceiling and floor effects may limit the extent to which these measures can distinguish between those who do and those who do not take precautions (Abraham *et al.* 1992). Moreover, increasing perceptions of threat among individuals who already acknowledge personal susceptibility may prompt maladaptive coping in the form of denial and thereby increase the likelihood of risk behaviour (see also Van der Pligt *et al.* 1993).

It has been suggested that the theory of reasoned action may offer a better account of HIV-preventive behaviour than the HBM (Montgomery *et al.* 1989; Brown *et al.* 1991; Sheeran *et al.* 1999), both because it acknowledges the importance of others' approval in the subjective norm construct and because intention formation provides a mechanism through which beliefs might influence behaviour. Studies employing measures derived from the theory of reasoned action offer support for this suggestion, showing that social norms are important determinants of HIV-preventive behaviour and that the effect of health beliefs can be accounted for by intentions (Joseph *et al.* 1987; Fisher *et al.* 1992). These findings support Fishbein *et al.*'s (2001) suggestion that health beliefs are best considered in the context of a more general model including theory of reasoned action constructs.

The social nature of sexual behaviour goes beyond an awareness of others' approval. Sexual behaviour is fundamentally interactive and has high emotional and arousal content. Consequently, perceptions of what peers are doing and of potential partners' attitudes are useful additional predictors (Sheeran *et al.* 1999). Social skills prerequisite to interpersonal negotiation may be more important predictors of safer sexual behaviour than the beliefs specified by the HBM (Abraham and Sheeran 1993, 1994). Self-efficacy, a cognitive component of skill (Bandura 1992, 1997), is also important (Rosenthal *et al.* 1991; Schaalma *et al.* 1993; Sheeran *et al.* 1999), and representations of anticipated affective states such as anticipated regret may also guide HIV-preventive behaviour (Richard and Van der Pligt 1991; Richard *et al.* 1995).

Studies have revealed different psychological antecedents of HIV-preventive behaviour among different groups, e.g. HIV-seropositive homosexual men versus other homosexual men, teenage men versus women, groups of different ages, those in monogamous versus non-monogamous relationships (Aspinwall *et al.* 1991; Richard and Van der Pligt 1991; Abraham *et al.* 1992; Schaalma *et al.* 1993). If relationships between health beliefs and behaviour vary across groups with very different sexual histories, campaigns that target specific beliefs could have different effects among specified sub-groups. Consequently, different groups may require different interventions. For example, Sheeran *et al.* (1999) found that believing that one's partner had a positive attitude towards condom use and communicating with a partner about condom use were more strongly associated with condom use among women than men, highlighting the importance of positive discussion of condom use for women.

Finally, the term HIV-preventive 'behaviour' tends to obscure the complexity of safer sex practice. Condom use, for example, involves a series of behaviours including getting condoms, carrying them, negotiating their use and handling and using them correctly (Abraham *et al.* 1999b). Thus, researchers need to identify the psychological prerequisites of a series of behaviours among a range of different groups. Moreover, these behaviours must be maintained over time, rather than performed on one or two occasions (Montgomery *et al.* 1989). The beliefs specified by the HBM may be too distant from the cognitive processes involved in the regulation of such practices to provide an optimal model of modifiable psychological antecedents. Focusing on the particular cognitive antecedents of well-specified behaviours may provide the best guide for health educators in this, and other, health domains.

7 Intervention studies

We have examined the utility of the HBM as a model of cognitive predictors of health-related behaviour. Accurate prediction is an indicator of veridical explanation. As Sutton (1998: 1317) observed, 'models that do not enable us to predict behaviour are unlikely to be useful as explanatory models'. Useful explanatory models are those that identify antecedents of behaviour, especially modifiable antecedents which create opportunities for psychologists and health educators to intervene to change behaviour. Thus, to the extent that the beliefs specified by the HBM are predictive of health behaviours and are amenable to change (within a specified population) the model provides a blueprint for health promotion targets. The model was initially developed to guide public health and health promotion initiatives and it has inspired researchers interested in behaviour change interventions for decades (e.g. Haefner and Kirscht 1970). We have noted limitations in the predictive utility of the HBM. These findings suggest concomitant limitations in the effectiveness of behaviour-change interventions that target HBM-specified beliefs. Nonetheless, HBM constructs are correlated with a range of health-related behaviours and changing these beliefs may prompt behaviour change (whether or not this involves simultaneous changes in cognitions not specified by the HBM – e.g. intentions).

Below, we consider behaviour change intervention evaluations that explicitly refer to the HBM and target HBM-specified beliefs. Hardeman *et al.*'s (2002) systematic review of interventions applying the TPB highlights the challenges inherent in reviewing intervention evaluations selected on the basis of their application of particular theoretical models. Intervention evaluations may apply a source theory to a greater or lesser extent, use different study designs, target different behaviours and employ different (sometime superficially described) multi-component interventions with different populations. We conducted a review using various electronic databases. This review suggests that the literature on HBM-based behaviour-change interventions is similar in size to the equivalent TPB literature. Hardeman *et al.* found 13 studies that had applied the TPB to behaviour change interventions. Table 2.5 lists 17 HBM-based, behaviour-change intervention evaluations that illustrate the diversity of this literature. We did not retain intervention evaluations that used knowledge and health beliefs as outcome measures (e.g. Booth *et al.* 1999; Out and Lafreniere 2001; Aoun *et al.* 2002), those primarily based on other theoretical frameworks (e.g. fear arousal interventions, or those based on protection motivation theory or the theory of planned behaviour) or evaluations that only draw upon the HBM to interpret results.

There is evidence of selectivity in the choice of health behaviours targeted for intervention; some behaviours have been targeted several times (e.g. mammogram screening) whereas other behaviours have not been targeted. Some were derived directly from the HBM (e.g. Carmel *et al.* 1996; Toro Alfonso *et al.* 2002) whereas others drew upon HBM and other social cognition models in order to target a broader range of cognitions (e.g. Strecher *et al.* 1994; Lu 2001). Some interventions took the form of educational presentations to groups in classes or workshops (e.g. Ford *et al.* 1996; Abood *et al.* 2003) and/or involved the distribution of leaflets or booklets (e.g. Carmel *et al.* 1996; Hawe *et al.* 1998). Others were delivered at an individual level (referred to variously as 'educational' or 'counselling' interventions) and often involved assessment of the recipient's current beliefs before new information and persuasive arguments were presented (e.g. Cummings *et al.* 1981; Jones *et al.* 1988a, 1988b; Hegel 1992; Champion 1994). Such interventions are tailored to the individual's cognitions. Computer-generated, individually tailored letters have also been used (Strecher *et al.* 1994). All of these interventions relied on information provision and verbal persuasion as means to change HBM-specified beliefs.

Table 2.5 Evaluations of behaviour change interventions based on the HBM

Behaviour	Target group	Researchers	Intervention (✓ = Effective)
Preventive behaviours			
Smoking cessation	Adult patients	Strecher et al. (1994)	Tailored letters ✓
	Women with cardiac risk	Schmitz et al. (1999)	Individual educational programme
Breast self-examination	Female adolescents	Ludwick and Garczkowski (2001)	Teaching with video role model ✓
	Tiwanese beauticians	Lu (2001)	Instruction, practice and follow-up ✓
Mammogram screening	Elderly minority women	Fox et al. (2001)	Postal advice on cost ✓
	Women (40–48 years)	Champion (1994)	Home interview ✓
	Women (35+ years)	Champion (1995)	Home interview ✓
	Women (50–85 years)	Champion et al. (2003)	Various (5 interventions) ✓
Safer sexual practices	Men who have sex with men	Toro-Alfonso et al. (2002)	Workshop ✓
Condom use	Low-cost sex workers	Ford et al. (1996)	Outreach group educational programmes ✓
Teenage contraception	Adolescents	Eisen et al. (1992)	HBM-based sex education
Healthy diet	University employees	Abood et al. (2003)	Eight-week worksite intervention ✓
Sun exposure protection	Elderly kibbutz members	Carmel et al. (1996)	Multi-component intervention ✓
Measles vaccination	Parents (pre-vaccination)	Hawe et al. (1998)	Modified postal reminder card ✓
Adherence behaviours			
Time in treatment	Alcohol clinic patients	Rees (1986)	Weekly group meeting
Fluid restrictions	Male hemodialysis patients	Hegel et al. (1992)	HBM-based counselling
Keeping appointments	ER patients (11 problems)	Jones et al. (1988b)	HBM-promoting interviews ✓

Thirteen of the 17 evaluations in Table 2.5 (i.e. 76 per cent) found evidence of behaviour change following HBM-based interventions. This is encouraging but, because these evaluations were not selected on the basis of methodological rigour, conclusions regarding effectiveness should be examined on a study-by-study basis. For example, some evaluations did not include a control group (e.g. Carmel *et al.* 1996) and weaknesses inherent in before-and-after designs mean that observed changes in such evaluations cannot be confidently assigned to the intervention. Other evaluations employed randomized controlled trials (RCTs) and some investigated moderator effects (see Baron and Kenny 1986). For example, Strecher *et al.* (1994) found that their computer-tailored letters were effective for moderate but not heavy smokers in two studies using random assignment to an intervention or control group. Some evaluations also report intervention effects on hypothesized cognitive mediators (e.g. changes in targeted health beliefs). We will highlight methodological and theoretical issues emerging from this literature by considering five of these 17 intervention evaluations in greater detail.

Ludwick and Gaczkowski (2001) used a pre- post-test design without a control group to evaluate an HBM-based intervention to increase breast self-examination (BSE) among 93 14 to 18-year-old US teenagers. The intervention was a school-based, multi-stage teaching session delivered by an undergraduate nursing student. Fibrocystic changes and risks of contracting breast cancer were explained to classes in order to increase knowledge, perceived susceptibility and severity. Cards which could be placed in showers were distributed as cues to action. Classes also watched a video which explained breast anatomy, showed teenagers performing BSE and demonstrated mammography. In addition, classes watched a demonstration of BSE on a breast model and practised BSE on breast models under supervision. The intervention was evaluated by questionnaire one month after the teaching session. Self-reported BSE increased significantly. For example, the proportion who had never performed BSE fell from 64 per cent to 32 per cent. HBM components were measured using multi-item scales but the authors do not report pre- post-test comparisons of HBM measures. It is, therefore, unclear whether the observed self-report behaviour change could be explained by changes in the target HBM cognitions. Although the increase in reported BSE initiation is substantial, this evaluation is weak because no control group was included and the follow-up was short-term. Thus, for example, the results do not clarify whether the completion of BSE-related questionnaires on its own might have prompted increased BSE (without the class) or what proportion of these teenagers were still performing BSE at three months or a year post-intervention.

Lu (2001) assessed the effectiveness of a work-site intervention designed to promote BSE among women who scored highly on a measure of perceived barriers to BSE. High scoring women were allocated by place of work to a control group (n = 40) or intervention group (n = 30). The educational programme was based on the HBM, the theory of reasoned action and Bandura's (1977) social cognitive theory. A brief description indicates that the intervention included BSE instructions and practice using breast models as well as discussion of individual barriers to BSE performance. In addition, participants received a monthly reminder telephone call. The intervention was evaluated using self-report questionnaires three months later. HBM constructs were measured using multi-item scales derived from Champion's work (see e.g. Table 2.2). Significant differences between the intervention and control group were found for reported BSE, BSE accuracy, perceived susceptibility, perceived benefits and barriers, perceived competency, perceived normative influence, and intention, but not for perceived seriousness at three-month follow-up. However, these analyses did not control for pre-intervention scores (e.g. using ANCOVA) and no mediation analysis is reported. Consequently, it is unclear whether differences between the intervention and control groups on HBM-specified beliefs accounted for differences in reported BSE. Multiple regression analyses indicated that perceived competency and normative influence were significant predictors of BSE frequency (with perceived competency accounting for 13 per cent of the variance in BSE frequency) but that HBM-specified beliefs did not add to the variance explained in BSE. This implies that HBM-specified beliefs may not be the most important cognitive targets for BSE-promoting interventions.

The intervention evaluations reported by Lu (2001) and Ludwick and Gaczkowski (2001) suggest that educational programmes, including BSE instruction, practice with breast models and follow-up reminders, are likely to promote BSE (see also Champion 1995). However, more sophisticated intervention evaluation designs, such as randomized controlled trials (RCTs), with longer term follow-up, are required before conclusions can be reached about evidence-based practice for health educators in this field. Although these interventions were, at least partially, inspired by the HBM, it is unclear whether their apparent effectiveness depends on promotion of HBM-specified beliefs. It is possible, for example, that enhanced self-efficacy, rather than changes in HBM-specified beliefs, is crucial to the effectiveness of such BSE educational programmes.

Champion (1994) reported a more robust evaluation of an intervention designed to promote mammography attendance in women over 35 years. An RCT was used to compare four conditions: a no-intervention control group, an information-giving intervention, an individual counselling intervention designed to change HBM-specified beliefs and a combined intervention designed both to provide information and change health beliefs. Self-reported adherence to mammography attendance guidelines was assessed for 301 women one year later. Controlling for pre-intervention compliance, the results indicated that only the combination intervention had a significantly greater post-intervention adherence rate than the control group, with this group being almost four times more likely to adhere. Thus, this evaluation establishes that both information provision and belief-change interventions are required to maximize mammography adherence (see also Champion and Huster 1995; Mandelblatt and Yabroff 1999). The belief-change interventions resulted in greater perceived seriousness, greater benefits and reduced barriers but did not increase perceived susceptibility. However, no mediation analysis was reported and, since knowledge and perceived control were also enhanced, the findings do not demonstrate conclusively that HBM-specified belief changes were critical to intervention effectiveness.

Jones *et al.* (1988b) report an RCT of an intervention designed to persuade patients using hospital emergency services to make and keep follow-up appointments with their own doctor. The sample comprised 842 patients with 11 presenting problems (chest pain, hypertension, asthma, otitis media, diabetes, urinary tract infection, headache, urethritis [men], vaginitis [women], low back pain, and rash) which did not require hospitalization. An intervention for individual patients was developed. This involved assessment of patients' HBM-specified beliefs and delivery of protocol-based, condition-specific educational messages to target beliefs that were not accepted by recipients. The intervention was designed to increase the patients' perceived susceptibility to illness complications, perceived seriousness of the complications, and benefits of a follow-up referral appointment in terms of avoiding further complications. It was delivered by a research nurse during required nursing care. Four intervention conditions were tested:

1 a routine care, control group;
2 an individual, nurse-delivered hospital intervention;
3 the hospital intervention combined with a follow-up telephone call; and
4 a follow-up telephone call without the hospital intervention.

Only 33 per cent of the control group patients scheduled a follow-up appointment whereas 76 per cent of the hospital intervention group, 85 per cent of the telephone intervention group and 85 per cent of the combined intervention did so. Twenty four per cent of the control group kept a follow-up appointment compared to 59 per cent in the hospital intervention group, 59 per cent in the telephone intervention group and 68 per cent in the combination group. Thus, the combination intervention worked most effectively. Jones *et al.* did not conduct a cost-effectiveness analysis but noted that the telephone intervention alone might be the most effective practical intervention when costs such as staff training and staff time are taken into account.

Jones *et al.* (1988b) found that presenting problem had a moderating effect on the intervention impact, that is there were no significant differences between conditions in relation to keeping a follow-up appointment for four of the 11 illness groups (i.e. diabetes, headache, urethritis and vaginitis). The results of this study were also reported separately for asthmatic patients (Jones *et al.* 1987a), hypertensive patients (Jones *et al.* 1987b), low back pain patients (Jones *et al.* 1988a), urinary tract patients (Jones *et al.* 1991a) and chronic versus acute patients (Jones *et al.* 1991b). Mediation analysis was conducted. The researchers found that among those patients who had scheduled a follow-up appointment, the interventions did not have an effect on keeping an appointment. This suggests that the interventions were effective because they prompted appointment scheduling. Availability of child care and being older than 30 years also made keeping a scheduled appointment more likely. These mediation and moderation analyses help clarify how the intervention/s work and for whom. However, the researchers did not report analyses testing whether differences in pre- and post-intervention HBM-specified beliefs could account for the effect of the intervention on scheduling follow-up appointments.

In a study of dialysis patients, Hegel *et al.* (1992) compared an individual HBM-based educational intervention with a behavioural intervention based on operant conditioning (involving reinforcements such as lottery tickets, videotapes and access to a private television) and a combined HBM and reinforcement programme. Weight gain between dialysis sessions was used as an index of adherence to recommended fluid intake restrictions and three studies with very small samples (ns = 4, 3 and 1) were conducted. Results indicated that none of the interventions led to changes in perceived susceptibility, seriousness, benefits, or concern. Patients who received reinforcement but not patients who received the HBM intervention perceived fewer barriers to adherence. The HBM intervention led to short-term adherence gains compared to standard treatment but these gains were not maintained. The reinforcement intervention led to increased adherence that was maintained over time and reinforcement combined with HBM did not improve adherence relative to the reinforcement-only condition. These findings suggest that techniques based on operant conditioning may be more successful than individual HBM educational interventions in changing cognitions (perceived barriers) and behaviour (weight gain) among patients needing to follow a restricted diet. Replication with larger samples is required before drawing conclusions or making recommendations regarding evidence-based practice but these findings highlight the importance of comparing intervention techniques and exploring the mechanisms (e.g. cognition change) underlying intervention-generated behaviour change.

These illustrative evaluation studies demonstrate that the HBM has inspired behaviour change interventions across a range of health behaviours. A number of these interventions have been shown to be effective and so could have implications for the behaviour of health care professionals and health educators. However, these studies also highlight six key shortcomings in studies evaluating HBM-inspired interventions. First, some evaluation designs are limited due to the lack of appropriate control groups, lack of randomization to condition, samples that do not support generalization or short-term follow-up. Second, the variety of behaviours targeted and the multidimensionality of HBM constructs means that the nature of persuasive messages may differ across behaviours and thereby undermine the validity of cross-behaviour comparisons. For example, one intervention may attempt to reduce perceived barriers by informing patients of available financial support (e.g. Fox *et al.* 2001) whereas another attempts to reduce barriers by enhancing communication about risk and precautions in sexual relationships (e.g. Toro-Alfonso *et al.* 2002). The target HBM construct is the same (perceived barriers) but the content of the intervention is quite different. Third, the HBM, like other social cognition models, specifies targets for cognition change but does not describe processes responsible for belief change. It is possible to combine models like the HBM with cognition change theories such as the elaboration likelihood model (Petty and Cacioppo 1986; see Quine *et al.* 2001 for an empirical example) or cognitive dissonance theory (Festinger 1957; see Stone *et al.* 1994 for an empirical example) in order to design interventions with theory-based targets and theory-based intervention techniques. However, this approach is not typical of HBM-based interventions. Consequently, the selection of intervention techniques (as opposed to cognition targets) is often not, or not explicitly, theory-based. Fourth, interventions usually comprise a variety of techniques, making it unclear which particular technique (or combinations of techniques) are crucial to effectiveness. For example, in considering the BSE-promoting interventions by Ludwick and Gaczkowski (2001) and Lu (2001), we might ask whether practice examination of breast models is crucial to effectiveness or whether reminders are necessary to ensure maintenance. In order to identify specific behaviour-change techniques, evaluations need to examine the effects of particular intervention techniques both on their own and in combination (Michie and Abraham 2004). Fifth, in order to establish whether an intervention generates behaviour change because it alters target beliefs, it is necessary both to measure cognitions and behaviour pre- and post-intervention and to conduct mediation analysis (Baron and Kenny 1986). However, mediation analysis is rarely reported in HBM-inspired intervention evaluations. Consequently, even when HBM-inspired interventions are effective in changing behaviour, it is unclear whether such effects are due to changes in HBM-specified beliefs. Sixth, once an effective technique is identified it is important to explore moderating effects such as patient type and mode of delivery to establish for whom (and how) the intervention is most likely to be effective. In summary, although the HBM has inspired the development of effective behaviour change interventions, the lack of programmatic experimental work means that we are unable to identify a series of belief-changing techniques that are likely to prove useful in intervention design generally. Moreover, we are unable to say whether effective HBM-inspired interventions work because they change HBM-specified beliefs.

8 Future directions

The HBM has provided a useful theoretical framework for investigators of the cognitive determinants of a wide range of behaviours for more than thirty years. The model's common sense constructs are easy for non-psychologists to assimilate and can be readily and inexpensively operationalized in self-report questionnaires. The HBM has focused researchers' and health care professionals' attention on modifiable psychological prerequisites of behaviour and provided a basis for practical interventions across a range of behaviours. Research to date has, however, predominantly employed cross-sectional correlational designs and further prospective experimental studies are required to clarify the causal direction of belief–behaviour relationships. The proposed mediation of socioeconomic influences on health behaviour by health beliefs also remains unclear. Research identifying which beliefs or cognitions mediate the effects of socioeconomic status in relation to particular health behaviours (e.g. Orbell *et al.* 1995) would be especially valuable.

Despite the impressive record of HBM-inspired research, numerous limitations have been identified which detract from the contribution this model can make to future modelling of the cognitive determinants of behaviour. The common-sense, expectancy-value framework of the HBM simplifies health-related representational processes, and qualitative distinctions between beliefs encompassed by each construct may be important to understanding why an individual does or does not undertake a specified behaviour. Such broadly defined theoretical components mean that different operationalizations may not be strictly comparable. Further elaboration of HBM constructs, as seen in Weinstein's (1988) precaution adoption process (PAP), may therefore be necessary. The model also excludes cognitions that have been shown to be powerful predictors of behaviour. In contrast to the theory of reasoned action, it fails to address the importance of intention formation or the influence that others' approval may have upon our behaviour. It portrays individuals as asocial, economic decision makers and consequently fails to account for behaviour under social and affective control. This is evident in applications to sexual behaviour, where, despite initial optimism, it has failed to distinguish between 'safer' and 'unsafe' behaviour patterns. The model is also limited because it does not articulate hierarchical or temporal relationships between cognitions. Despite King's (1982, 1984) innovative extension, the model has not distinguished between proximal and distal antecedents of behaviour. More recent models, such as the theory of planned behaviour (Ajzen and Madden 1986) and protection motivation theory (Prentice-Dunn and Rogers 1986) propose direct and indirect cognitive influences on behaviour. This facilitates a more powerful analysis of data and a clearer indication of how interventions might exert their effects. For example, if a certain level of perceived severity must be reached before perceived susceptibility becomes dominant in guiding behaviour, this would explain why severity generally has weak associations with behaviour and suggest that this variable should be regarded as a more distal cognitive antecedent (Schwarzer 1992). Intentions and perceived self-efficacy may mediate the effects of health beliefs on behaviour (Cummings *et al.* 1979; Warwick *et al.* 1993), confirming Rosenstock's (1974: 371) suggestion that HBM constructs could be seen as 'the setting for ... subsequent responses at other stages in the decision process' leading to action. More recent research has focused upon specifying cognitions which distinguish between people who intend and subsequently undertake behaviours and people with equivalent intentions who do not act (Abraham *et al.* 1999b; Gollwitzer 1999; Sheeran 2002; Sheeran and Abraham 2003). Health beliefs may, therefore, be seen as increasingly distant from action facilitation and self-regulation processes. Nonetheless, even if other models specify stronger predictors of behaviour, in certain instances, beliefs about susceptibility, benefits of treatment or barriers to performing health behaviours may be influential in sustaining action or inaction. Consequently, it is important to explore such beliefs when designing predictive models (e.g. Abraham *et al.* 1999a).

Systematic examination of evaluations of HBM-inspired interventions could clarify patterns of effectiveness across this literature. However, given the heterogeneity of evaluation designs, intervention techniques, target behaviours and populations it seems likely that reviews focusing on interventions designed to change particular behaviours for particular populations will be most informative (e.g. Kelley *et al.* 2001). For example, in a review of 63 interventions designed to increase mammography use, Yabroff and Mandelblatt (1999) found that four theory-based interventions drawing upon the HBM (see Aiken *et al.* 1994; Champion 1994) increased mammography utilization, on average, by 23 per cent compared to usual care. This is an impressive finding. The review also indicated that theory-based cognitive interventions that did not involve interpersonal interaction (e.g. those distributing letters or videos) were not effective. Meta-analyses of this kind can identify types of intervention and modes of intervention delivery that are effective in changing specified health behaviours. This information could then be used to design experimental studies that isolate particular techniques and combinations of techniques and measure potential mediators, including pre- and post-intervention beliefs. Such findings would permit identification of techniques that are effective in changing particular behaviours and allow these techniques to be tested against one another (see e.g. Hegel *et al.* 1992). Such research could also illuminate change mechanisms by identifying psychological mediators.

Understanding underlying psychological changes that account for behaviour change would facilitate the transfer of behaviour-change techniques across behavioural domains and a catalogue of effective techniques would provide a foundation for a psychologically based technology of behaviour change. Without this work, intervention design will continue to be theory-inspired rather than evidence-based and health promoters will continue to reinvent theory-based intervention methods rather than reapplying those that have been found to be successful in relation to particular behaviours or groups of behaviours (Michie and Abraham 2004). Much remains to be done to determine the role of HBM constructs in interventions that successfully transform health-related behaviour.

Notes

1 There is also a substantial literature using children as participants which is not considered here (see Gochman and Parcel 1982 for review).

2 The number of hypotheses examined for each HBM component varies across behaviour types. The relevant numbers for vulnerability, severity, benefits and

barriers in the case of preventive behaviours are 21, 18, 19 and 14 respectively. In the case of sick role behaviours the number of hypotheses are 13, 16, 15 and 12 respectively.

3 Champion's (1984) paper refers to the regression of breast self-examination practice upon HBM components as evidence for construct validity. We would argue that such data are indicative of criterion validity. There is also some difficulty with interpretation of the factor analysis in that a three-factor solution for the perceived severity component was not pursued. An item relating to having 'relatives and friends with breast cancer' (p. 83) was not interpreted as a cue to action, a component of the HBM which was ignored in Champion's analysis. Finally, further item development on the benefits component should properly have been conducted in order to improve its poor reliability.

4 Abraham *et al.* (1996) reported a more detailed analysis of these data using a sequence of hierarchical multiple regressions to map out a path analysis of associations between study variables.

5 Jones *et al.* (1988a: 1177) refer to these analyses as identifying 'mediating variables' but the results indicate moderating effects (Baron and Kenny 1986). Although, as we note, these authors also undertake mediation analyses.

References

Abood, D.A., Black, D.R. and Feral, D. (2003) Smoking cessation in women with cardiac risk: a comparative study of two theoretically based therapies, *Journal of Nutrition Education and Behavior*, **35**, 260–67.

Abraham, C., Clift, S. and Grabowski, P. (1999a) Cognitive predictors of adherence to malaria prophylaxis regimens on return from a malarious region: a prospective study, *Social Science and Medicine*, **48**, 1641–54.

Abraham, C. and Sheeran, P. (1993) In search of a psychology of safer-sex promotion; beyond beliefs and texts, *Health Education Research: Theory and Practice*, **8**, 245–54.

Abraham, C. and Sheeran, P. (1994) Modelling and modifying young heterosexuals' HIV-preventive behaviour: a review of theories, findings and educational implications, *Patient Education and Counselling*, **23**, 173–86.

Abraham, C. and Sheeran, P. (2003) Implications of goal theories for the theories of reasoned action and planned behaviour, *Current Psychology*, **22**, 264–80.

Abraham, C., Sheeran, P., Abrams, D. and Spears, R. (1996) Health beliefs and teenage condom use: a prospective study, *Psychology and Health*, **11**, 641–55.

Abraham, C., Sheeran, P., Norman, P., Conner, M., de Vries, N. and Otten, W. (1999b) When good intentions are not enough: modeling post-intention cognitive correlates of condom use, *Journal of Applied Social Psychology*, **29**, 2591–612.

Abraham, C., Sheeran, P., Spears, R. and Abrams, D. (1992) Health beliefs and the promotion of HIV-preventive intentions amongst teenagers: a Scottish perspective, *Health Psychology*, **11**, 363–70.

Abraham, I.L. and Williams, B.M. (1991) Hypertensive elders perception and management of their disease: health beliefs or health decisions?, *Journal of Applied Gerontology*, **10**, 444–54.

Adih, W.H. and Alexander, C.S. (1999) Determinants of condom use to prevent HIV infection among youth in Ghana, *Journal of Adolescent Health*, **24**, 63–72.

Aho, W.R. (1979a) Smoking, dieting and exercise: age differences in attitudes and behaviour relevant to selected health belief model variables, *Rhode Island Medical Journal*, **62**, 95–102.

Aho, W.R. (1979b) Participation of senior citizens in the Swine Flu inoculation programme: an analysis of health belief model variables in preventive health behaviour, *Journal of Gerontology*, **34**, 201–8.

Aiken, L. S., West, S. G., Woodward, C. K. and Reno, R. R. (1994a) Health beliefs and compliance with mammography-screening: recommendations in asymptomatic women, *Health Psychology*, **13**, 122–9.

Aiken, L. S., West, S. G., Woodward, C. K., Reno, R. R. and Reynolds, K. D. (1994b) Increasing screening mammography in asymptomatic women: evaluation of a second generation theory-based program, *Health Psychology*, **13**, 526–38.

Ajzen, I. (1998) Models of human social behaviour and their application to health psychology, *Psychology and Health*, **13**, 735–9.

Ajzen, I. and Madden, T.J. (1986) Prediction of goal-directed behaviour: attitudes, intentions and perceived behavioral control, *Journal of Experimental Social Psychology*, **22**, 453–74.

Alagna, S.W. and Reddy D.M. (1987) Predictors of proficient technique and successful lesion detention in breast self-examination, *Health Psychology*, **3**, 113–27.

Ali, N.S. (2002) Prediction of coronary heart disease preventive behaviors in women: a test of the Health Belief Model, *Women and Health*, **35**, 83–96.

Aoun, S., Donovan, R.J., Johnson, L. and Egger, G. (2002) Preventive care in the context of men's health, *Journal of Health Psychology*, **7**, 243–52.

Aspinwall, L.G., Kemeny, M.E., Taylor, S.E., Schneider, S.G. and Dudley, J.P. (1991) Psychosocial predictors of gay men's AIDS risk-reduction behaviour, *Health Psychology*, **10**, 432–44.

Bagozzi, R.P. (1986) Attitude formation under the theory of reasoned action and a purposeful behaviour reformulation, *British Journal of Social Psychology*, **25**, 95–107.

Bandura, A. (1977) Self-efficacy: towards a unifying theory of behavioural change, *Psychological Review*, **84**, 191–215.

Bandura, A. (1986) *Social Foundations of Thought and Action*. Englewood-Cliffs, NJ: Erlbaum.

Bandura, A. (1992) Exercise of personal agency through the self-efficacy mechanism. In R. Schwarzer (ed.) *Self-efficacy: Thought Control of Action*. Washington, DC: Hemisphere, 3–38.

Bandura, A. (1997) *Self-Efficacy: The Exercise of Control*. New York: Freeman.

Bardsley, P.E. and Beckman, L.J. (1988) The health belief model and entry into alcoholism treatment, *International Journal of the Addictions*, **23**, 19–28.

Baron, R. and Kenny D.A. (1986) The moderator-mediator variable distinction in social psychological research: conceptual, strategic, and statistical considerations, *Journal of Personality and Social Psychology*, **51**, 1173–82.

Beck, K.H. (1981) Driving while under the influence of alcohol: relationship to attitudes and beliefs in a college sample, *American Journal of Drug and Alcohol Abuse*, **8**, 377–88.

Becker, M.H., Drachman, R.H. and Kirscht, P. (1972) Predicting mothers' compliance with pediatric medical regimens, *Journal of Pediatrics*, **81**, 843.

Becker, M.H., Drachman, R.H. and Kirscht, P. (1974) A new approach to explaining sick-role behaviour in low income populations, *American Journal of Public Health*, **64**, 205–16.

Becker, M.H., Haefner D.P., Kasl, S.V., Kirscht, J.P., Maiman, L.A. and

Rosenstock, I.M. (1977a) Selected psychosocial models and correlates of individual health-related behaviors, *Medical Care*, 15, 27–46.

Becker, M.H., Haefner D.P. and Maiman L.A. (1977b) The health belief model in the prediction of dietary compliance: a field experiment, *Journal of Health and Social Behaviour*, 18, 348–66.

Becker, M.H., Kaback, M.M., Rosenstock, I.R. and Ruth, M. (1975) Some influences of public participation in a genetic screening program, *Journal of Community Health*, 1, 3–14.

Becker, M.H. and Maiman, L.A. (1975) Sociobehavioural determinants of compliance with health and medical care recommendations, *Medical Care*, 13, 10–24.

Becker, M.H., Radius, S.M. and Rosenstock, I.M. (1978) Compliance with a medical regimen for asthma: a test of the health belief model, *Public Health Reports*, 93, 268–77.

Bentler, P.M. and Speckart, G. (1979) Models of attitude-behaviour relations, *Psychological Review*, 86, 452–64.

Berkanovich, E., Telesky, C. and Reeder, S. (1981) Structural and social psychological factors on the decision to seek medical care for symptoms, *Medical Care*, 19, 693–709.

Bollin N.W. and Hart, L.K. (1982) The relationship of health belief motivations, health focus of control and health valuing to dietary compliance of haemodialysis patients, *American Association of Nephrology Nurses and Technicians Journal*, 9, 41–7.

Booth, R.E., Zhang, Y. and Kwiatkowski, C.F. (1999) The challenge of changing drug and sex risk behaviors of runaway and homeless adolescents, *Child Abuse and Neglect*, 23, 1295–306.

Boyer, C.B. and Kegeles, S.M. (1991) AIDS risk and prevention among adolescents, *Social Science and Medicine*, 33, 11–23.

Bradley, C., Gamsu, D.S. and Moses S.L. (1987) The use of diabetes-specific perceived control and health belief measures to predict treatment choice and efficacy in a feasibility study of continuous subcutaneous insulin infusion pumps, *Psychology and Health*, 1, 133–46.

Breakwell, G.M., Millward, L.J. and Fife-Schaw, C. (1994) Commitment to 'safer' sex as a predictor of condom use among 16–20 year olds, *Journal of Applied Social Psychology*, 24, 189–217.

Brown, L.K., DiClemente, R.J. and Reynolds, L.A. (1991) HIV prevention for adolescents: the utility of the health belief model, *AIDS Education and Prevention*, 3, 50–9.

Brownlee-Duffeck, M., Peterson, L. and Simonds, J.F. (1987) The role of health beliefs in the regimen adherence and metabolic control of adolescents and adults with diabetes mellitus, *Journal of Consulting and Clinical Psychology*, 55, 139–44.

Calnan, M. (1984) The health belief model and participation in programmes for the early detection of breast cancer: a comparative analysis, *Social Science and Medicine*, 19, 823–30.

Calnan, M. (1985) An evaluation of the effectiveness of a class teaching breast self-examination, *British Journal of Medical Psychology*, 53, 317–29.

Carmel, S., Shani, E. and Rosenberg, L. (1996) Skin cancer protective behaviors among the elderly: explaining their response to a health education program using the health belief model, *Educational Gerontology*, 22, 651–68.

Casey, R., Rosen, B., Glowasky, A. and Ludwig, S. (1985) An intervention to improve follow-up of patients with otitis media, *Clinical Pediatrics*, 24, 149–52.

Cerkoney, K.A. and Hart, K.L. (1980) The relationship between the health belief model and compliance of persons with diabetic regimens, *Diabetes Care*, 3, 594–8.

Champion, V. and Huster, G. (1995) Effect of interventions on stage of mammography adoption, *Journal of Behavioral Medicine*, 18, 169–87.

Champion, V., Maraj, M., Hui, S., Perkins, A. J., Tierney, W., Menon, U. and Skinner, C. S. (2003) Comparison of tailored interventions to increase mammography screening in nonadherent older women, *Preventive Medicine*, 36, 150–8.

Champion, V.L. (1984) Instrument development for health belief model constructs, *Advances in Nursing Science*, 6, 73–85.

Champion, V. L. (1994) Strategies to increase mammography utilization, *Medical Care*, 32, 118–29.

Champion, V.L. (1995) Results of a nurse-delivered intervention on proficiency and nodule detection with BSE, *Oncology Nursing Forum*, 22, 819–24.

Charney, E., Bynum, R. and Eldridge, D. (1967) How well do patients take oral penicillin? A collaborative study in private practice, *Journal of Pediatrics*, 40, 188.

Chen, M. and Land, K.C. (1986) Testing the Health Belief Model: Lisrel analysis of alternative models of causal relationships between health beliefs and preventive dental behaviour, *Social Psychology Quarterly*, 49, 45–60.

Chen, M. and Land, K.C. (1990) Socioeconomic status (SES) and the health belief model: LISREL analysis of unidimensional versus multidimensional formulations, *Journal of Social Behaviour and Personality*, 5, 263–84.

Chen, M. and Tatsuoka, M. (1984) The relationship between American women's preventive dental behaviour and dental health beliefs, *Social Science and Medicine*, 19, 971–8.

Cialdini, R.B., Kallgren, C.A. and Reno, R.R. (1991) A focus theory of normative conduct: a theoretical refinement and reevaluation of the role of norms in human behavior, *Advances in Experimental Social Psychology*, 24, 201–34.

Connelly, C.E. (1984) Compliance with outpatient lithium therapy, *Perspectives in Psychiatric Care*, 22, 44–50.

Connelly, C.E., Davenport, Y.B. and Nurnberger, J.I. (1982) Adherence to treatment regimen in a lithium carbonate clinic, *Archives of General Psychiatry*, 39, 585–8.

Conner, M. (1993) Pros and cons of social cognition models in health behaviour, *Health Psychology Update*, 14, 24–30.

Cooper, H.M. (1986) *Integrating Research: A Guide for Literature Reviews*. London: Sage Publications.

Cortina, J.M. (1993) What is coefficient alpha? An examination of theory and applications, *Journal of Applied Psychology*, 78, 98–104.

Cummings, K.M., Becker, M.H. and Kirscht, J.P. (1982) Psychosocial factors affecting adherence to medical regimens in a group of haemodialysis patients, *Medical Care*, 20, 567–79.

Cummings, K.M., Becker, M.H., Kirscht, J.P. and Levin, N.W. (1981) Intervention strategies to promote compliance with medical regimens by ambulatory haemodialysis patients, *Journal of Behavioral Medicine*, 4, 111–27.

Cummings, K.M., Jette, A.M. and Brock, B.M. (1979) Psychological determinants of immunization behaviour in a swine influenza campaign, *Medical Care*, 17, 639–49.

DeVellis, R. F. (1991) *Scale Development: Theory and Applications*. Newbury Park, CA: Sage Publications.

Dorr, N., Krueckeberg, S., Strathman, A. and Wood, M.D. (1999) Psychosocial correlates of voluntary HIV antibody testing in college students, *AIDS Education and Prevention*, **11**, 14–27.

Drayton, V.L.C., Montgomery, S.B., Modeste, N.N. and Frye-Anderson, B.A. (2002) The Health Belief Model as a predictor of repeat pregnancies among Jamaican teenage mothers, *International Quarterly of Community Health Education*, **21**, 67–81.

Eisen, M., Selman, G.L. and McAlister, A.L. (1985) A health belief model to adolescents' fertility control: some pilot program findings, *Health Education Quarterly*, **12**, 185–210.

Eisen M., Zellman, G. L. and McAlister A. L. (1992) A health belief model-social learning theory approach to adolescents' fertility control: findings from a controlled field trial, *Health Education Quarterly*, **19**, 249–62.

Emmons, C., Joseph, J., Kessler, R.C., Wortman, C.B., Montgomery, S.B. and Ostrow, D. (1986) Psychosocial predictors of reported behaviour change in heterosexual men at risk for AIDS, *Health Education Quarterly*, **13**, 331–45.

Erblich, J., Bovbjerg, D.H. and Valdimarsdottir, H.B. (2000) Psychological distress, health beliefs, and frequency of breast self-examination, *Journal of Behavioral Medicine*, **23**, 277–92.

Feather, N.T. (1982) *Expectations and Actions: Expectancy-value Models in Psychology*. Hillsdale, NJ: Erlbaum.

Festinger, L. (1957) *A Theory of Cognitive Dissonance*. Stanford, CA: Stanford University Press.

Field, A. (2000) *Discovering Statistics: Using SPSS for Windows*. London: Sage Publications.

Fincham, J.E. and Wertheimer, A.L. (1985) Using the health belief model to predict initial drug therapy defaulting, *Journal of Psychology*, **118**, 101–5.

Fishbein, M. and Ajzen, I. (1975) *Belief, Attitude, Intention and Behavior: An Introduction to Theory and Research*. Reading, MA: Addison-Wesley.

Fishbein. M., Triandis, H. C., Kanfer, F. H., Becker M., Middlestadt, S. E. and Eichler, A. (2001) Factors influencing behaviour and behaviour change. In A. Baum, T. A. Revenson and J. E. Singer (eds) *Handbook of Health Psychology*. Mahwah, NJ: Lawrence Erlbaum Associates, 3–17.

Fisher, J.D., Misovich, S.J. and Fisher, W.A. (1992) Impact of perceived social norms on adolescents' AIDS-risk behaviour and prevention. In R.J. DiClemente (ed.) *Adolescents and AIDS: A Generation in Jeopardy*. Newbury Park, CA: Sage Publications, 17–136.

Ford, K., Wirawan, D.N., Fajans, P., Meliawan, P., MacDonald, K. and Thorpe, L. (1996) Behavioural interventions for reduction of sexually transmitted disease/HIV transmission among female commercial sex workers and clients in Bali, Indonesia, *AIDS*, **10**, 213–22.

Fox, S. A., Stein, J. A., Sockloskie, R. J. and Ory, M. G. (2001) Targeted mailed materials and the Medicare beneficiary: increasing mammogram screening among the elderly, *American Journal of Public Health*, **91**, 55–61.

Gerrard, M., Gibbons, F. X. and Bushman, B. J. (1996) Relation between perceived vulnerability to HIV and precautionary sexual behaviour, *Psychological Bulletin*, **119**, 390–409.

Gerrard, M. and Warner, T.D. (1991) Antecedents of pregnancy among women marines, *Journal of the Washington Academy of Sciences*, **80**, 1015.

Gianetti, V.J., Reynolds, J. and Rihen, T. (1985) Factors which differentiate smokers from ex-smokers among cardiovascular patients: a discriminant analysis, *Social Science and Medicine*, **20**, 241–5.

Gladis, M. M., Michela, J. L., Walter, H. J. and Vaughan, R. D. (1992) High school students' perceptions of AIDS risk: realistic appraisal or motivated denial?, *Health Psychology*, 11, 307–16.

Gochman, D.S. and Parcel, G.S. (eds) (1982) Children's health beliefs and health behaviours, *Health Education Quarterly*, 9, 104–270.

Gollwitzer, P. M. (1999) Implementation intentions: Strong effects of simple plans. *American Psychologist*, 54, 493–503.

Gordis, L., Markowitz, M. and Lilienfeld, A.M. (1969) Why patients don't follow medical advice: a study of children on long-term antistreptococcal prophylaxis, *Journal of Pediatrics*, 75, 957–68.

Gottleib, N.H. and Baker, J.A. (1986) The relative influence of health beliefs, parental and peer behaviours and exercise program participation on smoking, alcohol use and physical activity, *Social Science and Medicine*, 22, 915–27.

Grady, K.E., Kegeles, S.S., Lund, A.K., Wolk, C.H. and Farber, N.J. (1983) Who volunteers for a breast self-examination program? Evaluating the bases for self-selection, *Health Education Quarterly*, 10, 79–94.

Haefner, D.P. (1974) The health belief model and preventive dental behavior. In M.H. Becker (ed.) *The Health Belief Model and Personal Health Behavior.* Thorofare, NJ: Slack, 93–105.

Haefner, D.P. and Kirscht, J.P. (1970) Motivational and behavioural effects of modifying health beliefs, *Public Health Reports*, 85, 478–84.

Hallal, J.C. (1982) The relationship of health beliefs, health locus of control, and self-concept to the practice of breast self-examination in adult women, *Journal of Nursing Research*, 31, 127–42.

Halper, M., Winawer, S. and Body, R. (1980) Issues of patient compliance. In S. Winawer, D. Schottenfeld and P. Sherlock (eds) *Colorectal Cancer: Prevention, Epidemiology and Screening.* New York: Raven Press, 299–310.

Hampson, S. E., Andrews, J. A., Barckley, M., Lichenstein, E. and Lee, M. E. (2000) Conscientiousness, perceived risk and risk reduction behaviors: a preliminary study, *Health Psychology*, 19, 496–500.

Hardeman, W., Johnston, M., Johnston, D. W., Bonetti, D., Wareham, N. and Kinmonth, A. L. (2002) Application of the theory of planned behaviour in behaviour change interventions: a systematic review, *Psychology and Health*, 17, 123–58.

Harris, D.M. and Guten, S. (1979) Health protective behaviour: an exploratory study, *Journal of Health and Social Behaviour*, 20, 17–29.

Harris, R. and Lynn, M.W. (1985) Health beliefs, compliance and control of diabetes mellitus, *Southern Medical Journal*, 2, 162–6.

Harrison, J.A., Mullen, P.D. and Green, L.W. (1992) A meta-analysis of studies of the health belief model with adults, *Health Education Research*, 7, 107–16.

Hartman, P.E. and Becker, M.H. (1978) Non-compliance with prescribed regimen among chronic haemodialysis patients, *Journal of Dialysis and Transplantation*, 7, 978–86.

Hawe, P., McKenzie, N. and Scurry, R. (1998) Randomised controlled trial of the use of a modified postal reminder card in the uptake of measles vaccination, *Archives of Disease in Childhood*, 79, 136–40.

Hay, J.L., Ford, J.S., Klein, D., Primavera, L.H., Buckley, T.R. Stein, T.R. *et al.* (2003) Adherence to colorectal cancer screening in mammography-adherent older women, *Journal of Behavioral Medicine*, 26, 553–76.

Hegel, M.T., Ayllon, T., Thiel, G. and Oulton, B. (1992) Improving adherence to fluid restrictions in makle hemodialysis patients: a comparison of cognitive and behavioural approaches, *Health Psychology*, 11, 324–30.

Heinzelmann, F. (1962) Factors in prophylaxis behaviour in treating rheumatoid fever: an exploratory study, *Journal of Health and Human Behaviour*, 3, 73.

Herold, E.S. (1983) The health belief model: can it help us to understand contraceptive use among adolescents?, *Journal of School Health*, 53, 19–21.

Hershey, J.C., Morton, B.G., Davis, J.R. and Reichgolt, M.J. (1980) Patient compliance with antihypertensive medication, *American Journal of Public Health*, 70, 1081–9.

Hester, N.R. and Macrina, D.M. (1985) The health belief model and the contraceptive behaviour of college women: implications for health education, *Journal of American College Health*, 33, 245–52.

Hingson, R.W., Strunin, L., Berlin, B.M. and Heeren, T. (1990) Beliefs about AIDS, use of alcohol and drugs, and unprotected sex among Massachusett's adolescents, *American Journal of Public Health*, 80, 372–7.

Hochbaum, G.M. (1958) *Public Participation in Medical Screening Programs: A Socio-Psychological Study*. Public Health Service Publication No. 572. Washington, DC: United States Government Printing Office.

Holland, J., Ramazanoglu, C., Scott, S., Sharpe, S. and Thomson, R. (1990) Sex, gender and power: young women's sexuality in the shadow of AIDS, *Sociology of Health and Illness*, 12, 336–50.

Hoogewerf, P.E., Hislop, T.G., Morrison, B.J., Burns, S.D. and Sitzo, R. (1990) Health belief and compliance with screening for faecal occult blood, *Social Science and Medicine*, 30, 721–6.

Janz, N. and Becker, M.H. (1984) The health belief model: a decade later, *Health Education Quarterly*, 11, 1–47.

Jones, F., Abraham, C., Harris, P., Schulz, J. and Chrispin C. (2001) From knowledge to action regulation: modeling the cognitive prerequisites of sunscreen use in Australian and UK samples, *Psychology and Health*, 16, 191–206.

Jones, P. K., Jones, S. L. and Katz, J. (1987a) Improving compliance for asthmatic patients visiting the emergency department using a health belief model intervention, *Journal of Asthma*, 24, 199–206.

Jones, P. K., Jones, S. L. and Katz, J. (1987b) Improving follow-up among hypertensive patients using a health belief model intervention, *Archives of Internal Medicine*, 147, 1557–60.

Jones, S. L., Jones, P. K. and Katz, J. (1988a) Compliance for low-back pain patients in the emergency department: a randomized trail, *Spine*, 13, 553–6.

Jones, S. L., Jones, P. K. and Katz, J. (1988b) Health belief model intervention to increase compliance with emergency department patients, *Medical Care*, 26, 1172–84.

Jones, S.L., Jones, P.K. and Katz, J. (1991a) A randomized trial to improve compliance in urinary tract patients in the emergency department, *Annals of Emergency Medicine*, 19, 16–20.

Jones, S.L., Jones, P.K. and Katz, J. (1991b) Compliance in acute and chronic patients receiving a health belief model intervention in the emergency department, *Social Science and Medicine*, 32, 1183–9.

Joseph, J., Montgomery, S.B., Emmons, C., Kessler, R.C., Ostrow, D., Wortman, C.B. *et al.* (1987) Magnitude and determinations of behavioural risk reduction: longitudinal analysis of a cohort at risk for AIDS, *Psychology and Health*, 1, 73–96.

Keesling, B. and Friedman, H.S. (1987) Psychological factors in sunbathing and sunscreen use, *Health Psychology*, 6, 477–93.

Kegeles, S.S. (1963) Why people seek dental care: a test of a conceptual framework, *Journal of Health and Human Behaviour*, 4, 166.

Kelley, H.H. (1967) Attribution theory in social psychology. In D. Levine (ed.) *Nebraska Symposium on Motivation*. Lincoln: University of Nebraska Press, 192–241.

Kelley, K., Bond, R. and Abraham, C. (2001) Effective approaches to persuading pregnant women to quit smoking: a meta-analysis of intervention evaluation studies, *British Journal of Health Psychology*, 6, 207–28.

Kelly, G. R., Mamon, J. A. and Scott, J. E. (1987) Utility of the health belief model in examining medication compliance among psychiatric outpatients, *Social Science and Medicine*, 25, 1205–11.

King, J.B. (1982) The impact of patients' perceptions of high blood pressure on attendance at screening: an extension of the health belief model, *Social Science and Medicine*, 16, 1079–91.

King, J.B. (1984) Illness attributions and the health belief model, *Health Education Quarterly*, 10, 287–312.

Kirscht, J.P. (1983) Preventive health behaviour: a review of research and issues, *Health Psychology*, 2, 277–301.

Kirscht, J.P., Becker M.H. and Eveland, P. (1976) Psychological and social factors as predictors of medical behaviour, *Journal of Medical Care*, 14, 422–31.

Kirscht, J.P., Becker, M.H., Haefner, D.P. and Maiman, L.A. (1978) Effects of threatening communications and mothers' health beliefs on weight change in obese children, *Journal of Behavioural Medicine*, 1, 147–57.

Kirscht, J.P. and Rosenstock, I.M. (1977) Patient adherence of antihypertensive medical regimens, *Journal of Community Health*, 3, 115–24.

Kristiansen, C.M. (1985) Value correlates of preventive health behaviour, *Journal of Personality and Social Psychology*, 49, 748–58.

Kruglanski, A.W. and Klar, Y. (1985) Knowing what to do: on the epistemology of actions. In J. Kuhl and J. Beckmann (eds) *Action Control: From Cognition to Behaviour*. Berlin: Springer-Verlag, 41–60.

Langlie, J.K. (1977) Social networks, health beliefs and preventive health behaviour, *Journal of Health and Social Behaviour*, 18, 244–60.

Larson, E.B., Bergman, J. and Heidrich, F. (1982) Do postcard reminders improve influenza vaccination compliance?, *Journal of Medical Care*, 20, 639–48.

Leavitt, F. (1979) The health belief model and utilization of ambulatory care services, *Social Science and Medicine*, 13, 105–12.

Lewin, R.W. (1951) *Field Theory in Social Science*. New York: Harper.

Lewis, K.S. (1994) An examination of the health belief model when applied to diabetes mellitus, unpublished Doctoral dissertation, University of Sheffield.

Li, C., Unger, J. B., Schuster, D., Rohrbach, L. A., Howard-Pitney, B. and Norman, G. (2003) Youths' exposure to environmental tobacco smoke (ETS) associations with health beliefs and social pressure, *Addictive Behaviors*, 28, 39–53.

Lollis, C.M., Johnson, E.H. and Antoni, M.H. (1997) The efficacy of the health belief model for predicting condom usage and risky sexual practices in university students, *AIDS Education and Prevention*, 9, 551–63.

Lowe, C.S. and Radius, S.M. (1987) Young adults' contraceptive practices: an investigation of influences, *Adolescence*, 22, 291–304.

Lu, Z J. (2001) Effectiveness of breast self-examination nursing interventions for Taiwanese community target groups, *Journal of Advanced Nursing*, 34, 163–70.

Ludwick R. and Gaczkowski T. (2001) Breast self-exams by teenagers: outcome of a teaching program, *Cancer Nursing*, 24, 315–19.

McCuskar, J., Stoddard, A.M., Zapka, J.G., Zorn, M. and Mayer, K.H. (1989a) Predictors of AIDS-preventive behaviour among homosexually active men: a longitudinal analysis, *AIDS*, 3, 443–8.

McCuskar, J., Zapka, J.G., Stoddard, A.M. and Mayer, K.H. (1989b) Responses to the AIDS epidemic among homosexually active men: factors associated with preventive behaviour, *Patient Education and Counselling*, 13, 15–30.

Maddux, J.E. and Rodgers, R.W. (1983) Protection motivation and self-efficacy: a revised theory of fear appeals and attitude change, *Journal of Experimental Social Psychology*, 19, 469–79.

Maiman, L.A., Becker, M.H., Kirscht, J.P., Haefner, D.P. and Drachman, R.H. (1977) Scales for measuring health belief model dimensions: a test of predictive value, internal consistency and relationships among beliefs, *Health Education Quarterly*, 4, 215–31.

Mandelblatt, J. S and Yabroff, K. R. (1999) Effectiveness of interventions designed to increase mammography use: a meta-analysis of provider-targeted strategies, *Cancer Epidemiology Biomarkers and Prevention*, 8, 759–67.

Mattson, M. (1999) Towards a reconceptualization of communication cues to action in the health belief model: HIV test counselling, *Communication Monographs*, 66, 240–65.

Michie, S. and Abraham, C. (2004) Interventions to change health behaviours: evidence-based or evidence inspired?, *Psychology and Health*, 19, 29–49.

Montgomery, S.B., Joseph, J.G., Becker, M.H., Ostrow, D.G., Kessler, R.C. and Kirscht, J.P. (1989) The health belief model in understanding compliance with preventive recommendations for AIDS: how useful?, *AIDS Education and Prevention*, 1, 303–23.

Mullen, P.D., Hersey, J.C. and Iversen, D.C. (1987) Health behaviour compared, *Social Science and Medicine*, 24, 973–81.

Myers, L. B. (2000) Identifying repressors: a methodological issue for health psychology, *Psychology and Health*, 15, 205–14.

Nelson, E.C., Stason, W.B. and Neutra, R.R. (1978) Impact of patients' perceptions on compliance with treatment for hypertension, *Journal of Medical Care*, 16, 893–906.

Norman, P. and Brain, K. (2005) An application of the extended health belief model to the prediction of breast self-examination among women with a family history of breast cancer, *British Journal of Health Psychology*, 10, 1–16.

Norman, P. and Conner, M. (1993) The role of social cognition models in predicting attendance at health checks, *Psychology and Health*, 8, 447–62.

Ogionwo, W. (1973) Socio-psychological factors in health behaviour: an experimental study of methods and attitude change, *International Journal of Health Education*, 16 (supplement), 1–14.

Oliver, R.L. and Berger, P.K. (1979) A path analysis of preventive care decision models, *Journal of Consumer Research*, 6, 113–22.

Orbell, S., Crombie, I. and Johnston, G. (1995) Social cognition and social structure in the prediction of cervical screening uptake, *British Journal of Health Psychology*, 1, 35–50.

Otten, W. and van der Pligt, J. (1992) Risk and behaviour: the mediating role of risk appraisal, *Acta Psychologia*, 80, 325–46.

Out, J. W. and Lafreniere, K. (2001) Baby think it over: using role play to prevent teen pregnancy, *Adolescence*, 36, 571–82.

Owens, R.G., Daly, J., Heron, K. and Lemster, S.J. (1987) Psychological and social characteristics of attenders for breast screening, *Psychology and Health*, 1, 303–13.

Pan, P. and Tantam, D. (1989) Clinical characteristics, health beliefs and compliance with maintenance treatment: a comparison between regular and irregular attenders at a depot clinic, *Acta Psychiatrica Scandinavica*, 79, 564–70.

Penderson, L.L., Wanklin, J.M. and Baskerville, J.C. (1982) Multivariate statistical models for predicting change in smoking behaviour following physician advice to stop smoking, *Journal of Preventive Medicine*, 11, 536–49.

Perkins, D.O. (2002) Predictors of noncompliance in patients with schizophrenia, *Journal of Clinical Psychiatry*, 63, 1121–8.

Petosa, R. and Kirby, J. (1991) Using the health belief model to predict safer sex intentions among adolescents, *Health Education Quarterly*, 18, 463–76.

Petty R.E. and Cacioppo, J.T. (1986) The elaboration likelihood model of persuasion. In L. Berkowitz (ed.) *Advances in Experimental Social Psychology*, Vol. 19. New York: Academic Press, 123–205.

Portnoy, B. (1980) Effects of a controlled usage alcohol education program based on the health belief model, *Journal of Drug Education*, 10, 181.

Prentice-Dunn, S. and Rogers, R.W. (1986) Protection motivation theory and preventive health; beyond the health belief model, *Health Education Research: Theory and Practice*, 3, 153–161.

Quine, L., Rutter, D. R. and Arnold, L. (1998) Predicting and understanding safety helmet use among schoolboy cyclists: a comparison of the theory of planned behaviour and the health belief model, *Psychology and Health*, 13, 251–69.

Quine, L., Rutter, D.R. and Arnold, L. (2001) Persuading school-age cyclists to use safety helmets: effectiveness of an intervention based on the theory of planned behaviour, *British Journal of Health Psychology*, 6, 327–45.

Rawl, S., Champion, V., Menon, U., Loehrer, P.J., Vance, G.H. and Skinner, C.S. (2001) Validation of scales to measure benefits of and barriers to colorectal cancer screening, *Journal of Psychosocial Oncology*, 19, 47–63.

Rayant, G. A. and Sheiham, A. (1980) An analysis of factors affecting compliance with tooth-cleaning recommendations, *Journal of Clinical Periodontology*, 7, 289–99.

Rees, D.W. (1986) Changing patients' health beliefs to improve compliance with alcohol treatment: a controlled trial, *Journal of Studies on Alcoholism*, 47, 436.

Reid, L.D. and Christensen, D.B. (1988) A psychosocial perspective in the explanation of patients' drug-taking behaviour, *Social Science and Medicine*, 27, 277–85.

Richard, R. and Van der Pligt, J. (1991) Factors affecting condom use among adolescents, *Journal of Community and Applied Social Psychology*, 1, 105–16.

Richard, R., Van der Pligt, J. and De Vries, N. (1995) Anticipated affective reactions and prevention of AIDS, *British Journal of Social Psychology*, 34, 9–21.

Rogers, R.W. (1983) Cognitive and physiological processes in fear appeals and attitude change: a revised theory of protection motivation. In J. Cacioppo and R. Petty (eds) *Social Psychophysiology*. New York: Guilford, 153–76.

Rogers, R.W. and Mewborn, C.R. (1976) Fear appeals and attitude change: effects of a threat's noxiousness, probability of occurrence and the efficacy of coping responses, *Journal of Personality and Social Psychology*, 34, 54–61.

Ronis, D.L. and Harel, Y. (1989) Health beliefs and breast examination behaviours: analysis of linear structural relations, *Journal of Psychology and Health*, 3, 259–85.

Rosenstock, I.M. (1966) Why people use health services, *Milbank Memorial Fund Quarterly*, 44, 94–124.

Rosenstock, I.M. (1974) Historical origins of the health belief model, *Health Education Monographs*, 2, 1–8.

Rosenstock, I.M., Strecher, V.J. and Becker, M.H. (1988) Social learning theory and the health belief model, *Health Education Quarterly*, 15, 175–83.

Rosenthal, D., Hall, C. and Moore, S.M. (1992) AIDS, adolescents and sexual risk taking: a test of the health belief model, *Australian Psychologist*, 27, 166–71.

Rosenthal, D., Moore, S. and Flynn, I. (1991) Adolescent self-efficacy, self-esteem, and sexual risk taking, *Journal of Community and Applied Social Psychology*, 1, 77–88.

Rosenthal, R. (1984) *Meta-analysis Procedures for Social Research*. Beverly Hills, CA: Sage Publications.

Rotter, J.B. (1966) Generalized expectancies for internal versus external control of reinforcement, *Psychological Monographs*, 80, whole no. 609, 1–28.

Rundall, T.G. and Wheeler, J.R. (1979) The effect of income on use of preventive care: an evaluation of alternative explanations, *Journal of Health and Social Behaviour*, 20, 397–406.

Rust, J. and Golombok, S. (1990) *Modern Psychometrics*. London: Routledge.

Sackett, D.L., Becker, M.H. and MacPherson, A.S. (1974) *The Standardized Compliance Questionnaire*. Hamilton, Ontario: McMaster University.

Salloway, J.C., Pletcher, W.R. and Collins, J.J. (1978) Sociological and social psychological models of compliance with prescribed regimen: in search of a synthesis, *Sociological Symposium*, 23, 100–21.

Schaalma, H., Kok, G. and Peters, L. (1993) Determinants of consistent condom use by adolescents: the impact of experience of sexual intercourse, *Health Education Research: Theory and Practice*, 8, 255–69.

Schmitz, J.M., Spiga, R., Rhoades, H.M., Fuentes, F. and Grabowski, J. (1999) Nutrition education worksite intervention for university staff: application of the health belief model, *Nicotine and Tobacco Research*, 1, 87–94.

Schwarzer, R. (1992) Self-efficacy in the adoption and maintenance of health behaviours: theoretical approaches and a new model. In R. Schwarzer (ed.) *Self-efficacy: Thought Control of Action*. Washington, DC: Hemisphere, 217–42.

Sheeran, P. (2002) Intentions-behavior relations: a conceptual and empirical review. In W. Stroebe and M. Hewstone (eds) *European Review of Social Psychology*, 12, 1–36.

Sheeran, P. and Abraham, C. (2003) The importance of temporal stability of intention relative to other moderators of the intention–behavior relation, *Personality and Social Psychology Bulletin*, 29, 205–15.

Sheeran, P., Abraham, C. and Orbell, S. (1999) Psychosocial correlates of condom use: A meta-analysis, *Psychological Bulletin*, 125, 90–132.

Sheeran, P. and Orbell, S. (1995) How confidently can we infer health beliefs from questionnaire responses?, *Psychology and Health*, 11, 273–90.

Silver Wallace, L. (2002) Osteoporosis prevention in college women: application of the expanded health belief model, *American Journal of Health Behavior*, 26, 163–72.

Simon, K.J. and Das, A. (1984) An application of the health belief model toward educational diagnosis for VD education, *Health Education Quarterly*, 11, 403–18.

Slovic, P., Fischoff, B. and Lichtenstein, S. (1977) Behavioral decision theory, *Annual Review of Psychology*, 28, 1–39.

Smith, G.E., Gerrard, M. and Gibbons, F.X. (1997) Self-esteem and the relation between risk behaviour and perceptions of vulnerability to unplanned pregnancy in college women, *Health Psychology*, 16, 137–46.

Smith, J.A., Hughes, I.C.T. and Budd, R.J. (1999) Non-compliance with antipsychotic medication: users' views on advantages and disadvantages, *Journal of Mental Health*, 8, 287–96.

Smith Klohn, L. and Rogers, R.W. (1991) Dimensions of severity of health threat: the persuasive effects of visibility, time of onset and rate of onset on young women's intentions to prevent osteoporosis, *Health Psychology*, 10, 323–9.

Stacy, R.D. and Lloyd, B.H. (1990) An investigation of beliefs about smoking among diabetes patients: information for improving cessation efforts, *Journal of Patient Education and Counselling*, 15, 181–9.

Stillman, M. (1977) Women's health beliefs about breast cancer and breast self-examination, *Nursing Research*, 26, 121–7.

Stone, J., Aronson, E., Crain, A. L., Winslow, M. P. and Fried, C. B. (1994) Inducing hypocrisy as a means of encouraging young adults to use condoms, *Personality and Social Psychology Bulletin*, 20, 116–28.

Strecher, V. J., Kreuter, M., DenBoer, D. J., Kobrin, S., Hospers, H. J. and Skinner, C. S. (1994) The effects of computer-tailored smoking cessation messages in Family Practice settings, *Journal of Family Practice*, 39, 262–70.

Sutton, S.R. (1994) The past predicts the future: interpreting behaviour-behaviour relationships in social-psychological models of health behaviours. In D.R. Rutter and L. Quine (eds) *Social Psychology and Health: European Perspectives*. Aldershot: Avebury Press, 71–88.

Sutton, S. (1998) Predicting and explaining intentions and behavior: how well are we doing?, *Journal of Applied Social Psychology*, 15, 1317–38.

Taylor, D.W. (1979) A test of the health belief model in hypertension. In R.B. Haynes, D.W. Taylor and K.L. Sackett (eds) *Compliance in Health Care*. Baltimore, MD: Johns Hopkins University Press, 103–9.

Thompson, R.S., Michnich, M.E., Gray, J., Friedlander, L. and Gilson, B. (1986) Maximizing compliance with hemoccult screening for colon cancer in clinical practice, *Medical Care*, 24, 904–14.

Toro-Alfonso, J., Varas-Dias, N. and Andujar-Bello, I. (2002) Evaluation of an HIV/AIDS prevention intervention targeting latino gay men and men who have sex with men in Puerto Rico, *AIDS Education and Prevention*, 14, 445–56.

Tversky, A. and Kahneman, D. (1981) The framing of decisions and the psychology of choice, *Science*, 211, 453–8.

Umeh, K. and Rogan-Gibson, J. (2001) Perceptions of threat, benefits, and barriers in breast self-examination amongst young asymptomatic women, *British Journal of Health Psychology*, 6, 361–72.

Van der Pligt, J., Otten, W., Richard, R. and Van der Velde, F. (1993) Perceived risk of AIDS: unrealistic optimism and self-protective action. In J.B. Prio and G.D. Reeder (eds) *The Social Psychology of HIV Infection*. Hillsdale, NJ: Erlbaum, 39–58.

Volk, J.E. and Koopman, C. (2001) Factors associated with condom use in Kenya: a test of the health belief model, *AIDS Education and Prevention*, 13, 495–508.

Wagner, P.J. and Curran, P. (1984) Health beliefs and physician identified 'worried well', *Health Psychology*, 3, 459–74.

Wallace, L. S. (2002) Osteoporosis prevention in college women: application of the expanded health belief model, *American Journal of Health Behaviour*, 26, 163–72.

Wallston, K.A. and Wallston, B.S. (1982) Who is responsible for your health? The construct of health locus of control. In G.S. Sanders and J. Suls (eds) *The Social Psychology of Health and Illness*. Hillsdale, NJ: Erlbaum, 65–95.

Warshaw, P.R. and Davis, F.D. (1985) Disentangling behavioral intention and behavioral expectation, *Journal of Experimental Social Psychology*, 21, 213–28.

Warwick, P., Terry, D. and Gallois, C. (1993) Extending the theory of reasoned action: the role of health beliefs. In D.J. Terry, C. Gallois and M. McCamish (eds) *The Theory of Reasoned Action: Its Application to AIDS-Preventive Behaviour.* Oxford: Pergamon Press, 117–34.

Wdowik, M.J., Kendall, P.A., Harris, M.A. and Auld, G. (2001) Expanded health belief model predicts diabetes self-management in college students, *Journal of Nutrition Education.* 33, 17–23.

Weinberger, M., Green, J.Y. and Mandin, J.J. (1981) Health beliefs and smoking behaviour, *American Journal of Public Health*, 71, 1253–5.

Weinstein, N.D. (1980) Unrealistic optimism about future life events, *Journal of Personality and Social Psychology*, 39, 806–20.

Weinstein, N.D. (1982) Unrealistic optimism about susceptibility to health problems, *Journal of Behavioural Medicine*, 5, 441–60.

Weinstein, N.D. (1984) Why it won't happen to me: perceptions of risk factors and illness susceptibility, *Health Psychology*, 3, 431–57.

Weinstein, N.D. (1988) The precaution adoption process, *Health Psychology*, 7, 355–86.

Weinstein, N.D. and Nicolich, M. (1993) Correct and incorrect interpretations of correlations between risk perceptions and risk behaviours, *Health Psychology*, 12, 235–45.

Weitkunat, R., Pottgiesser, C., Meyer, N., Crispin, A., Fischer, R., Schotten, K., Kerr, J. and Ueberla, K. (2003) Perceived risk of bovine spongiform encephalopathy and dietary behaviour, *Journal of Health Psychology*, 8, 373–81.

Werch, C.E. (1990) Behavioural self-control strategies for deliberately limiting drinking among college students, *Journal of Addictive Behaviours*, 15, 119–28.

Winfield, E.B. and Whaley, A.L. (2002) A comprehensive test of the health belief model in the prediction of condom use among African American college students, *Journal of Black Psychology*, 28, 330–46.

Wolcott, D.L., Sullivan, G. and Klein, D. (1990) Longitudinal change in HIV transmission risk behaviours by gay male physicians, *Journal of Psychosomatics*, 31, 159–67.

Yabroff, K. R. and Mandelblatt, J. S. (1999) Interventions targeted towards patients to increase mammography use, *Cancer Epidemiology Biomarkers and Prevention*, 8, 749–57.

PAUL NORMAN, HENK BOER
AND ERWIN R. SEYDEL

PROTECTION MOTIVATION THEORY

1 General background

Protection motivation theory (PMT) was developed by Rogers (1975) as a framework for understanding the impact of fear appeals. A revision of PMT (Rogers 1983) extended the theory to provide a more general account of the impact of persuasive communications, with an emphasis on the cognitive processes that mediate behaviour change. Subsequent research on PMT has typically taken two forms: first, PMT has been used as a framework to develop and evaluate persuasive communications; and second, PMT has been used as a social cognition model to predict health behaviour.

The origins of PMT lie in early work on the persuasive impact of fear appeals that focused on the conditions under which fear appeals may influence attitudes and behaviour. A central question of this work was whether fear appeals could, in themselves, influence attitudes and behaviour, or whether their effects were more indirect. The Yale Programme of Research on Communication and Attitude Change (Hovland *et al.* 1953) provided a systematic study of the ways in which, and the conditions under which, fear appeals may be effective in changing attitudes and behaviour. The research was based on the fear-drive model which proposed that fear acts as a driving force that motivates trial and error behaviour. If a communication evokes fear, then the recipient will be motivated to reduce this unpleasant emotional state. If the communication also contains behavioural advice, following this advice is one way to reduce the threat. If following the behavioural advice leads to a reduction of fear, then the behavioural response will be reinforced and the probability of performing the behaviour in the future is enhanced. However, if following the behavioural advice does not lead to a reduction of fear, or if the communication does not contain behavioural advice, alternative maladaptive coping responses, such as avoidance or denial, may be used as means for reducing the level of aroused fear.

The fear-drive model proposed a non-monotonic relationship between fear arousal and the probability of following recommended behavioural advice (i.e. acceptance). In particular, Janis (1967) argued that as well as motivating the recipient to find ways to reduce the danger (i.e. facilitation), fear may also lead to a more critical evaluation of the recommended advice (i.e. interference). As fear increases (from zero level), facilitation is assumed to increase at a faster rate than interference. However, above a certain (optimal) level, the interfering effects of fear are assumed to increase faster than the facilitating effects. As a result, an inverted U-shaped relationship is predicted between fear arousal and acceptance of a recommended action. However, in a review of early studies (between 1953 and 1980) on the effectiveness of fear appeals, Sutton (1982) found little evidence for the hypothesized inverted U-shaped relationship. Instead, strong evidence was found for a positive linear relationship between fear arousal and acceptance. In addition, Sutton (1982) reported that the perceived effectiveness of the recommended action had an independent effect on acceptance.

PMT was developed by Rogers (1975) to provide conceptual clarity to work on fear appeals. In particular, Rogers (1975) sought to identify the key variables in fear appeals as well as their cognitive mediational effects. PMT was based on the work of Hovland *et al.* (1953) who proposed that there are three main stimulus variables in a fear appeal: (a) the magnitude of noxiousness or severity of an event, (b) the probability of the event occurrence if no protective behaviour is adopted or existing behaviour modified, and (c) the efficacy of a recommended coping response to reduce or eliminate the noxious event. Rogers (1975) included these variables in the original formulation of PMT and further proposed that each stimulus variable initiates a corresponding cognitive mediational process. Thus the magnitude of noxiousness of an event initiates perceptions of severity, the probability that the event will occur initiates perceptions of vulnerability, and the availability of an effective coping response initiates perceptions of response efficacy. In other words, the impact of the stimulus variables in a fear appeal is mediated by perceived severity, vulnerability and response efficacy. These perceptions, in turn, influence protection motivation (i.e. intention to follow the behavioural advice). Protection motivation is seen to be the proximal determinant of protective behaviour as it 'arouses, sustains, and directs activity' (Rogers 1975: 94).

Rogers (1983) subsequently revised PMT to provide a more general theory of persuasive communication and underlying cognitive mediating processes. In particular, the revised version of PMT includes a broader range of factors that initiate cognitive processes. In addition to persuasive communications, other stimulus variables or sources of information were included such as observational learning, past experience and personality. PMT was also expanded to incorporate additional cognitive mediating processes, including perceptions of the rewards of maladaptive responses, self-efficacy and response costs, that were organized into two independent cognitive mediating processes focusing on threat appraisal and coping appraisal.

PMT therefore has similarities with Leventhal's (1970) parallel response model which distinguishes between two independent control processes that are initiated by a fear appeal. The first, fear control, focuses on attempts to reduce the emotional threat (e.g. avoidance) while the second, danger control, focuses on attempts to reduce the threatened danger (e.g. following behavioural advice). The parallel response model is important in that it proposes that protection motivation results from danger control processes (i.e. cognitive responses) rather than from fear control processes (i.e. emotional responses). A similar distinction is made by Lazarus (1991) between primary appraisal processes that focus on the nature of the threat, and secondary appraisal processes that focus on the coping responses available to the individual.

2 Description of the model

PMT outlines the cognitive responses resulting from fear appeals (see Figure 3.1). Rogers (1983) proposed that various environmental (e.g. fear appeals) and intrapersonal (e.g. personality) sources of information can initiate two independent appraisal processes: threat appraisal and coping appraisal.

Threat appraisal focuses on the source of the threat and factors that increase or decrease the probability of maladaptive responses (e.g. avoidance, denial, wishful thinking). Individuals' perceptions of the *severity* of, and their *vulnerability* to, the threat are seen to inhibit maladaptive responses. In relation to smoking, for example, smokers may consider the seriousness of lung cancer and their chances of developing the disease in the future. Fear is an additional, intervening variable, between perceptions of severity and vulnerability and the level of appraised threat. Thus, greater levels of fear will be aroused if an individual perceives him or herself to be vulnerable to a serious health threat and this will increase an individual's motivation to engage in protective behaviour. While perceptions of severity and vulnerability serve to inhibit maladaptive responses, there may be a number of *intrinsic* (e.g. pleasure) and *extrinsic* (e.g. social approval) *rewards* that increase the likelihood of maladaptive responses. For example, smokers may believe that smoking helps to regulate weight or that it facilitates interaction in social settings.

Coping appraisal focuses on the coping responses available to the individual to deal with the threat and factors that increase or decrease the probability of an adaptive response, such as following behavioural advice. Both the belief that the recommended behaviour will be effective in reducing the threat (i.e. *response efficacy*) and the belief that one is capable of performing the recommended behaviour (i.e. *self-efficacy*) increase the probability of an adaptive response. For example, smokers may consider the extent to which quitting smoking would reduce their chances of developing lung cancer in the future and whether they are capable of doing so. While perceptions of response efficacy and self-efficacy serve to increase

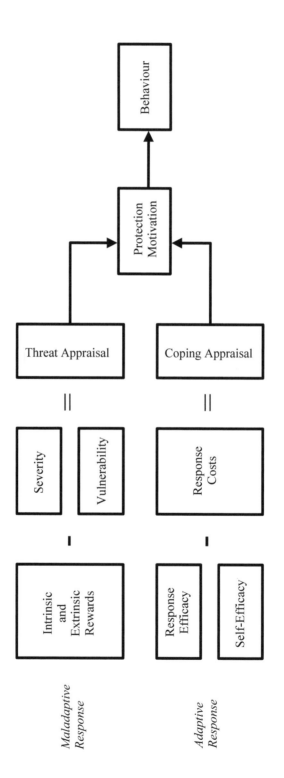

Figure 3.1 A schematic representation of the cognitive mediating processes of protection motivation theory

the probability of an adaptive response, there may be a number of *response costs* or barriers (e.g. availability of resources) that inhibit performance of the adaptive behaviour. For example, smokers may believe that quitting smoking may lead to increased craving.

Protection motivation (i.e. intention to perform a recommended behaviour) results from the two appraisal processes and is a positive function of perceptions of severity, vulnerability, response efficacy and self-efficacy, and a negative function of perceptions of the rewards associated with maladaptive responses and the response costs of the adaptive behaviour. For protection motivation to be elicited, perceptions of severity and vulnerability should outweigh the rewards associated with maladaptive responses. In addition, perceptions of response efficacy and self-efficacy should outweigh the response costs of the adaptive behaviour. However, most applications of PMT simply consider the additive effects of these variables on protection motivation. Protection motivation, which is typically equated with behavioural intention, is seen to direct and sustain protective behaviour. Protection motivation therefore operates as a mediating variable between the threat and coping appraisal processes and protective behaviour.

In the original version of PMT, perceived severity, vulnerability and response efficacy were hypothesized to combine in a multiplicative fashion to elicit protection motivation. This multiplicative function was proposed as it was assumed that protection motivation would not be elicited if the value of any of these three components was zero. Despite the intuitive appeal of such a combinational rule, empirical support for this multiplicative function has been lacking and, in the revised version of PMT, Rogers (1983) proposed a simpler additive model. Most applications of PMT only consider the main effects of perceptions of severity, vulnerability, response efficacy, self-efficacy and response costs. The rewards associated with maladaptive responses are rarely considered as 'the conceptual distinction between the reward value of a risk behaviour and cost of a preventative measure may not be clear' (Abraham *et al.* 1994: 271). For example, the reward of 'increased sexual pleasure' associated with unprotected sex could be rephrased as a response cost associated with condom use (i.e. 'reduced sexual pleasure'). The following review of research on PMT therefore examines the predictive utility of the five main components of the model (i.e. perceptions of severity, vulnerability, response efficacy, self-efficacy, response costs).

3 Summary of research

PMT provides a framework for understanding the effects of fear appeals and the social cognitive variables underlying health protective behaviour. Tests of PMT have typically taken two forms. First, the main components of PMT are manipulated in persuasive communications and their effects on protection motivation and behaviour evaluated. Second, PMT is used as a social cognition model to predict health behaviour. Research on PMT has been subjected to a number of narrative reviews (Boer and Seydel 1995; Rogers and Prentice-Dunn 1997; Conner and Norman 1998) as well as two meta-analyses (Floyd *et al.* 2000; Milne *et al.* 2000) which are described below.

3.1 Meta-analyses

Floyd *et al.* (2000) conducted a meta-analysis of 65 studies. Studies were included in the meta-analysis provided they measured at least one PMT component and included intention and/or behaviour as a dependent variable. Sixteen of the studies measured only one PMT component, whereas 49 contained multiple PMT components. In addition, 27 of the studies only measured intention, 22 only measured behaviour, and 16 measured both intention and behaviour. The results of the meta-analysis are presented in Table 3.1, combined across the different dependent variables. Floyd *et al.* (2000) reported d_+ (sample weighted standardized mean differences) as an estimate of the effect size for each component. Cohen (1992) suggests that d_+ values of 0.20, 0.50 and 0.80 represent small, medium and large effect sizes, respectively.

Table 3.1   Summary of meta-analyses of protection motivation theory

	Floyd *et al.* (2000)[a]	Milne *et al.* (2000)[b]		
	Intention and behaviour	Intention	Concurrent behaviour	Future behaviour
Severity	0.39***	0.10***	0.10***	0.07
Vulnerability	0.41***	0.16***	0.13***	0.12**
Response efficacy	0.54***	0.29***	0.17***	0.09
Self-efficacy	0.88***	0.33***	0.36***	0.22***
Response costs	−0.52***	−0.34***	−0.32***	−0.25***
Protection motivation	−	−	0.82***	0.40***

Note: [a] Reported coefficients are d_+ = sample weighted standardized mean differences. [b] Reported coefficients are r_+ = sample weighted average correlations. ** $p < 0.01$. *** $p < 0.001$.

As can be seen from Table 3.1, significant effects were found for all PMT components. The effect sizes for the threat appraisal variables (i.e. perceived severity and vulnerability) were in the small to medium range. In contrast, the effect sizes for the coping appraisal variables (i.e. perceived response efficacy, self-efficacy and response costs) were in the medium to large range. Self-efficacy was found to have the largest effect size. More detailed analyses were conducted to examine the performance of PMT for different kinds of behaviours. For example, a distinction was made between initiation behaviours (i.e. beginning an adaptive behaviour such as breast self-examination) and cessation behaviours (i.e. stopping a maladaptive behaviour such as smoking). The threat appraisal variables were found to have similar effect sizes for each type of behaviour, whereas the coping appraisal variables were found to have larger effect sizes for cessation behaviours than for initiation behaviours. Floyd *et al.* (2000) also examined the performance of PMT in relation to the prediction of intention versus behaviour. Both the threat and coping appraisal variables were found to have larger effect sizes when intention was the dependent variable compared to when behaviour was the dependent variable. Overall, the results of the Floyd *et al.* (2000) meta-analysis suggest that coping appraisal variables, and especially self-efficacy, provide the strongest predictions of protection motivation (i.e. intention) and behaviour.

This pattern of results was, to a large extent, replicated in a more detailed meta-analysis of PMT studies conducted by Milne *et al.* (2000). Milne *et al.* (2000) employed stricter inclusion criteria so that only empirical applications of PMT to health-related intentions, concurrent behaviour or future behaviour were included in the meta-analysis. Only 12 studies, with 13 independent samples, were deemed suitable for inclusion in the meta-analysis. Most of these studies were concerned with the prediction of intention, while a minority of studies focused on the prediction of concurrent or future behaviour. The results of this meta-analysis are also presented in Table 3.1. Milne *et al.* (2000) reported r_+ (sample weighted average correlations) as an estimate of the effect size for each component of PMT in relation to intention, concurrent behaviour and future behaviour. Cohen (1992) suggests that r_+ values of 0.10, 0.30 and 0.50 represent small, medium and large effect sizes, respectively.

Considering first the prediction of intention, significant effects were found for all PMT components. Small effect sizes were found for the threat appraisal variables (i.e. perceived severity and vulnerability), whereas the effect sizes for the coping appraisal variables (i.e. perceived response efficacy, self-efficacy and response costs) were in the medium to large range. Response costs had the largest effect size, followed by self-efficacy. Milne *et al.* (2000) also reported fail-safe N (FSN) values that indicate the number of null findings that would be required to make a calculated effect non-significant. Interestingly, with the exception of self-efficacy, all the FSN values fell well short of Rosenthal's (1991) tolerance level (of 5k + 10), suggesting the calculated effects are not robust and that they could be easily reduced to non-significance by unretrieved or future null results. A similar pattern of results was found for the prediction of concurrent behaviour. Again, all effects were significant with small effect sizes for the threat appraisal variables and small to medium effect sizes for the coping appraisal variables. Self-efficacy was found to have the largest effect size and was the only variable close to Rosenthal's (1991) tolerance level. In addition, Milne *et al.* (2000) calculated the effect size for the correlation between protection motivation and concurrent behaviour which was found to be large and robust. Finally, a small number of studies examined the relationship between PMT and future behaviour. Only perceived vulnerability, self-efficacy, response costs and protection motivation were found to have significant effects, although these were somewhat attenuated in comparison to the effect sizes calculated for the prediction of intention and concurrent behaviour. In addition, only the correlation between protection motivation and future behaviour approached robustness, as indicated by the FSN value. However, the fact that the FSN values fell short of Rosenthal's (1991) tolerance level is most likely a consequence of the modest number of prospective PMT studies.

Overall, the results of the meta-analyses conducted by Floyd *et al.* (2000) and Milne *et al.* (2000) indicate that the coping appraisal variables provide stronger predictions of protection motivation and behaviour than do threat appraisal variables. The threat appraisal variables (i.e. perceived severity and vulnerability) are typically found to have small effects sizes, whereas the coping appraisal variables (i.e. perceived response efficacy, self-efficacy and response costs) are typically found to have medium effects sizes. In addition, protection motivation is typically found to be a strong predictor of concurrent and, to a lesser extent, future behaviour. It is notable that all of the PMT variables provide stronger predictions of intention and concurrent behaviour than of future behaviour. Moreover, many of the relationships, while significant, appear not to be robust, indicating the need for further replication.

The meta-analyses reported by Floyd *et al.* (2000) and Milne *et al.* (2000) were based on the results of studies employing a wide range of methodologies. In particular, they included both experimental studies, in which the PMT components were manipulated and their effects evaluated, and correlational studies in which PMT was used as a social cognition model to predict health behaviour. As a result, it is difficult to tease out the predictive power of PMT as a social cognition model of health behaviour versus its utility as a framework for developing and evaluating interventions. The following narrative review of PMT studies therefore focuses solely on its use as a social cognition model to predict a range of health-related behaviours (see Table 3.2). Experimental studies that have sought to test PMT by manipulating its components are considered in Section 7.

3.2 Health behaviour

PMT has been used to predict a range of health-promoting (e.g. exercise and diet) and health-compromising (e.g. smoking and alcohol consumption) behaviours. In relation to exercise and dietary behaviour, only a small number of studies have employed PMT, and these have tended to use cross-sectional designs. For example, Plotnikoff and Higginbottom (1998) applied PMT to the prediction of exercise and dietary intentions and behaviour among a group of patients who had recently experienced a myocardial infarction or angina. In a path analysis, self-efficacy was the only PMT variable to emerge as a significant predictor of exercise intentions (although fear also had a weak effect on intention). Intention, in turn, was the only significant predictor of exercise behaviour. Similarly, self-efficacy

Table 3.2 Illustrative applications of protection motivation theory

Behaviour	Authors
Exercise and diet	Plotnikoff and Higginbottom (1995, 1998, 2002)
Smoking	Greening (1997)
Binge drinking	Ben-Ahron *et al.* (1995); Murgraff *et al.* (1999)
Sexual behaviours	Abraham *et al.* (1994); Aspinwall *et al.* (1991); Bengel *et al.* (1996); Eppright *et al.* (1994); Greening *et al.* (2001); Sheeran and Orbell (1996); Van der Velde and Van der Pligt (1991)
Screening behaviours	Boer and Seydel (1995); Hodgkins and Orbell (1998); Orbell and Sheeran (1998); Seydel *et al.* (1990)
Treatment adherence	Bennett *et al.* (1998); Flynn *et al.* (1995); Norman *et al.* (2003); Palardy *et al.* (1998); Rudman *et al.* (1999); Taylor and May (1996)

was the only significant predictor of intentions to follow a low-fat diet. Intention was predictive of engaging in a low-fat diet, along with perceived vulnerability and fear. Plotnikoff and Higginbottom (1995, 2002) have also conducted PMT studies on exercise and dietary behaviour with randomly selected community samples drawn from areas of Australia with high incidence rates of cardiovascular disease. Considering exercise, Plotnikoff and Higginbottom (2002) found self-efficacy to be the strongest predictor of exercise intentions, although weak effects were also found for perceived severity and perceived vulnerability (negative relationship). Intention was again predictive of exercise behaviour, along with self-efficacy and perceived vulnerability (negative relationship). In relation to dietary behaviour, Plotnikoff and Higginbottom (1995) found that self-efficacy and response efficacy were strong predictors of intentions to follow a low-fat diet. Intention, in turn, was predictive of dietary behaviour along with self-efficacy. However, it should be noted that the above studies were cross-sectional in design and used stage-based measures of behaviour that may be confounded with intention (see Sutton, Chapter 6 in this volume).

There have been relatively few tests of PMT in relation to the prediction of health-compromising behaviours. For example, Murgraff *et al.* (1999) used PMT to examine students' binge drinking behaviour over a two-week period. Perceived severity and self-efficacy were predictive of intentions to drink within safe limits. The PMT variables were unable to predict drinking behaviour at two-week follow-up, although it should be noted that Murgraff *et al.* (1999) also included a measure of past behaviour in their regression analyses which may have masked the influence of the PMT variables. In support of this interpretation, a number of baseline PMT measures (i.e. perceived vulnerability, rewards, self-efficacy and intention) had significant correlations with drinking behaviour at two-week follow-up. In an earlier cross-sectional study, Ben-Ahron *et al.* (1995) examined the ability of PMT to discriminate between students classified as binge and non-binge drinkers. This study is noteworthy in that it also contained measures of the intrinsic and extrinsic rewards associated with binge drinking. All of the PMT constructs, with the exception of response efficacy (of drinking within safe daily limits), were found to discriminate between binge and non-binge drinkers, although a negative relationship was found for perceived severity. Considering smoking behaviour, Greening (1997) reported that PMT was predictive of concurrent smoking behaviour in a sample of adolescents. Smokers were more likely to downplay the health risks associated with smoking (i.e. perceived severity) and the response efficacy of not smoking, although they were also more likely to acknowledge greater personal vulnerability to smoking-related diseases.

3.3 Sexual behaviours

PMT has also been applied to the prediction of AIDS-risk reducing intentions and behaviour, although there have been few prospective applications of the model. Aspinwall *et al.* (1991) examined the predictive utility of PMT in relation to a number of AIDS-risk reducing behaviours in a sample of gay men. Self-efficacy and perceived vulnerability were predictive of reductions in the number of sexual partners over a six-month follow-up period. Self-efficacy was also predictive of reductions in the number of anonymous sexual partners, and response costs (i.e. barriers to change) were predictive of unprotected anal receptive intercourse over the same time period. Greening *et al.* (2001) examined the predictive utility of PMT over a one-year period in a sample of sexually active rural African American female adolescents. PMT was found to be predictive of condom use at one-year follow-up, although only self-efficacy emerged as a significant predictor after controlling for baseline condom use. Moreover, contrary to predictions, low levels of self-efficacy were predictive of condom use. A closer inspection of the study, however, reveals a lack of correspondence between the measurement of self-efficacy, which focused on preventing a pregnancy and using contraceptives, and the dependent variable (i.e. condom use). In addition, the sample size (n = 61) meant that the cases-to-independent variables ratio was low for a regression analysis. Finally, the study did not report the simple bivariate correlation between self-efficacy and condom use. As a result, the negative relationship between self-efficacy and condom use found in the regression analysis may have been the result of a suppressor effect, given the strong effect observed for past behaviour.

Other studies have examined the ability of PMT to predict AIDS-risk reducing behaviour using cross-sectional designs. Bengel *et al.* (1996) found that self-efficacy was related to more frequent condom use and fewer sexual partners among a sample of male and female heterosexuals. However, perceived vulnerability was related to more frequent condom use, as well as a higher number of sexual partners. Similar results have been reported by Eppright *et al.* (1994), who found that perceptions of vulnerability were related to the performance of what they termed adaptive (i.e. being abstinent, avoiding sharing bodily fluids, using condoms) and maladaptive (i.e. reducing partners, being careful about selecting infection-free partners) behaviours. The coping appraisal variables they considered (i.e. self-efficacy and response-efficacy) were non-significant predictors, although it should be noted that there was a lack of correspondence between these measures and the dependent variables.

Other PMT studies have focused solely on the prediction of AIDS-risk related intentions. For example, Van der Velde and Van der Pligt (1991) examined the predictors of AIDS-risk related intentions among hetero-sexual men and women and homosexual men with multiple partners. Considering the results for the heterosexual sample, perceived vulnerability, response efficacy and self-efficacy were all found to have direct positive effects on condom use intentions. In addition, perceived severity had an indirect effect on condom use intentions through a measure of fear. Similar results were found among the homosexual sample with perceived severity, response efficacy and self-efficacy having positive direct effects on safe sex intentions. However, a negative relationship was found between perceived vulnerability and safe sex intentions. Abraham *et al.* (1994) found that self-efficacy and response costs were predictive of condom use intentions among a sample of male and female adolescents. Similar findings have been reported by Sheeran and Orbell (1996) in a sample undergraduate students. However, Abraham *et al.* (1994) also found a negative relationship between perceived vulnerability and intentions to limit the number of sexual partners.

Taken together, the above results suggest that PMT is a useful framework for understanding AIDS-risk reduction intentions and behaviour. Self-effi-cacy consistently emerges as the most important predictor, with response efficacy, response costs and perceived severity also emerging as significant predictors in some studies. However, a conflicting pattern of results has been found for the vulnerability component, such that in some studies perceived vulnerability has a positive relationship with AIDS-risk reduction intentions and behaviour, whereas in other studies the relationship is negative. Similar conclusions have been reached by Farin (1994) in a meta-analysis of PMT and HIV-protective behaviour. Self-efficacy and response efficacy emerged as the best predictors of HIV-protective behaviour, although they could only explain 2.2 per cent and 1.8 per cent of the variance in such behaviour. Perceived severity was a weaker predictor, and a conflicting pattern of results was found for perceived vulnerability.

3.4 Cancer-related preventive behaviour

A number of studies have applied PMT to the prediction of cancer-related preventive behaviour, and many of these studies have employed prospective designs. For example, Orbell and Sheeran (1998) reported a prospective study in which PMT measures were used to predict uptake of cervical cancer screening among a sample of never-screened women. Perceived vulnerability, response efficacy (obtaining peace of mind), response costs (perceived potential negative emotional reactions to the test procedure) and self-efficacy were predictive of screening intentions. Intention was, in turn, predictive of actual uptake of screening at one year follow-up, along with perceived vulnerability and response efficacy (belief that any abnormalities would be curable). Boer and Seydel (1996) also used a prospective design to examine the predictors of attendance at breast cancer screening by mammography. Response efficacy and self-efficacy were predictive of screening intentions. However, the PMT measures were unable to predict attendance at screening at two-year follow-up. Hodgkins and Orbell (1998) examined the predictive utility of PMT in relation to breast self-examination (BSE) in a sample of young women (17- to 40-year-olds) over a one-month period. In a path analysis, only self-efficacy was related to BSE intentions. Intention was, in turn, found to be predictive of BSE performance at one-month follow-up. Finally, Seydel *et al.* (1990) examined PMT in relation to a number of cancer-related preventive behaviours in a cross-sectional study. Response efficacy and self-efficacy were found to be predictive of intentions to attend cervical cancer screening and to perform BSE. In addition, perceived severity was also predictive of BSE intentions. Considering the prediction of concurrent behaviour, response efficacy and self-efficacy were predictive of BSE performance, while perceived vulnerability, perceived severity and self-efficacy were predictive of recent uptake of cervical cancer screening.

Overall, the above results suggest that PMT is a useful framework for predicting cancer-related preventive behaviour. Self-efficacy and response efficacy consistently emerge as key predictors, although there is evidence to suggest that threat appraisals (i.e. perceived severity and perceived vulnerability) are also important for the prediction of cancer-related preventive behaviour. One of the strengths of PMT work in this area is the number of prospective studies.

3.5 Medical adherence behaviour

A number of studies have applied PMT to the issue of adherence to medical regimens. For example, Bennett *et al.* (1998) found that the perceived chronicity and perceived severity of asthma were significant predictors of self-reported adherence to corticosteroid medication among a general practice sample of asthma patients. Palardy *et al.* (1998) employed PMT to examine the predictors of self-report adherence to self-care activities among a sample of adolescents with insulin-dependent diabetes mellitus. Perceived severity and response costs emerged as significant predictors of self-report adherence, over and above the influence of the quality of the child–parent relationship and disease severity. Rudman *et al.* (1999) examined renal transplant patients' adherence to a self-monitoring regimen and found that perceived threat, self-efficacy and response costs were predictive of self-monitoring intentions and that self-efficacy and perceived threat were predictive of concurrent adherence behaviour. In a prospective study, Taylor and May (1996) applied PMT to the prediction of compliance to a physiotherapist's treatment recommendations (e.g. application of compression, hot/cold therapy, stretching and strengthening exercises) in a sports injury clinic. Patients completed a PMT questionnaire at the end of their initial appointment and treatment compliance was assessed at the second appointment (3–10 days later). Bivariate analyses revealed that the four main components of PMT were each able to predict compliance, although in a regression analysis only perceived severity and self-efficacy emerged as significant predictors. Unfortunately, the study did not assess intention.

A couple of studies have used PMT as a framework to predict actions taken by one individual (e.g. a parent) to protect another person's health (e.g. their child). For example, Flynn *et al.* (1995) examined parental adherence to physical therapy recommendations for children with muscular dystrophy. Self-efficacy and response efficacy were found to be predictive of adherence intentions, whereas self-efficacy was the sole predictor of adherence. Norman *et al.* (2003) used a prospective design to examined parents' adherence to eye patching recommendations for children with amblyopia. Perceived vulnerability, response efficacy and self-efficacy were predictive of adherence intentions, whereas perceived vulnerability and response costs were predictive of adherence behaviour at two-month follow-up. Interestingly, intention was unrelated to adherence behaviour at follow-up.

Overall, the above studies suggest that PMT can be usefully employed to predict adherence to medical regimens. Both threat appraisal (i.e. perceived severity and perceived vulnerability) and coping appraisal (i.e. response costs and self-efficacy) variables have been found to be predictive of adherence intentions and behaviour, although it is interesting to note that response efficacy has only emerged as a significant predictor of adherence intentions. Despite some encouraging results, work in this area has suffered from two major shortcomings. First, self-report, rather than objective, measures have typically been used to assess adherence behaviour. Second, most PMT studies of adherence behaviour have been cross-sectional in design.

4 Developments

Four main areas for the future development of PMT as a social cognition model of health behaviour are outlined below. First, the role of emotion, and particularly fear, in the model is considered. Second, the ability of PMT variables to predict maladaptive coping responses and the extent to which such responses may impede protection motivation is examined. Third, the sufficiency of the model is assessed through a consideration of the impact of past behaviour on health-protective intentions and behaviour. Fourth, problems associated with interpreting correlations with perceived vulnerability are highlighted.

4.1 Role of emotion

Tanner *et al.* (1991) have questioned the extent to which PMT recognizes the importance of emotional responses to fear appeals. In particular, they argue that Rogers (1975) views fear as an insignificant by-product of the threat appraisal process that has no impact on ongoing appraisal and coping processes. However, Tanner *et al.* (1991) argue that fear arousal may increase an individual's motivation to act in a health protective manner. For example, Plotnikoff and Higginbottom (1995) found that a measure of fear arousal (i.e. '… how frightened you feel when you think about the possibility of having a heart attack') had a significant, though weak, effect on intention to follow a low-fat diet among an 'at risk' community sample. Similarly, Van der Velde and Van der Pligt (1991) found that fear had a direct effect on condom use intentions among a sample of multiple-partner heterosexuals. In contrast, other studies have found non-significant relationships between fear and BSE (Hodgkins and Orbell 1998) and condom use (Abraham *et al.* 1994) intentions. In their meta-analysis, Milne *et al.* (2000) reported significant average correlations between fear and intention ($r_+ = 0.20$) and concurrent behaviour ($r_+ = 0.26$), and a non-significant average correlation between fear and future behaviour ($r_+ = -0.04$). The effect sizes were significant but in the small to medium range, and associated fail-safe N values were well short of recommended tolerance levels indicating the effects not to be robust.

Tanner *et al.* (1991) also argued that an emotional response, such as fear, may act as a source of feedback to heighten the processing of threat and coping information. Thus, Lazarus and Folkman (1984: 227) state that 'when information is appraised for our well-being, it becomes … "hot information" …' and may increase attention to, and comprehension of, information related to the threat. Consistent with this position, Tanner *et al.* (1991) found that students exposed to a high-threat essay that contained coping response information acquired more knowledge than those exposed to a low-threat essay that contained coping response information. Tanner *et al.* (1991) therefore argue that the appraisal processes outlined in PMT should be viewed as sequential or ordered, such that coping appraisal processes are only activated when threat appraisal results in fear.

4.2 Maladaptive coping responses

In addition to assessing the ability of PMT to predict health-protective intentions and behaviour (i.e. adaptive coping responses) it is also possible to apply the model to the prediction of maladaptive coping responses. Thus, when individuals perceive a threat to their well-being in the absence of an effective coping response, they may engage in activities that reduce the fear associated with the threat without dealing with the threat itself. Such strategies may be termed maladaptive coping responses (Rippetoe and Rogers 1987) and include strategies such as denial and avoidance. Thus, high levels of perceived vulnerability and severity and low levels of response efficacy and self-efficacy would be expected to be related to the adoption of maladaptive coping responses. A number of studies have examined the (concurrent) relationships between PMT variables and maladaptive coping responses.

Ben-Ahron *et al.* (1995) considered a number of maladaptive coping responses in relation to binge drinking. These included avoidance (e.g. not thinking about the adverse consequences of binge drinking), wishful thinking (e.g. hoping that medical breakthroughs will nullify the need for behaviour change), fatalism (e.g. believing that the adverse consequences are due to fate rather than personal action) and religious faith (e.g. trusting that God will provide protection). A number of significant relationships between PMT variables and maladaptive coping responses were identified using path analysis. Thus, avoidance was predicted by perceived severity and self-efficacy (negative relationship), while the use of religious faith as a coping strategy was predicted by response efficacy and self-efficacy (negative relationships). Abraham *et al.* (1994) examined a range of maladaptive coping responses in response to the threat of HIV/AIDS among a sample of adolescents. Path analysis revealed negative relationships between response efficacy and wishful thinking, and between self-efficacy and both wishful thinking and denial. In addition, response costs associated with condom use were found to be predictive of denial, fatalism and irrational fear. Similarly, Hodgkins and Orbell (1998) found that the response costs associated with BSE were predictive of the use of avoidance as a coping strategy.

The above studies indicate that PMT can be usefully employed to predict maladaptive, as well as adaptive, coping responses. Future research may therefore seek to confirm these initial findings. In addition, Tanner *et al.* (1991) have argued that engaging in maladaptive coping responses may impede protection motivation and the adoption of actions to deal with the threat. Thus, Ben-Ahron *et al.* (1995) found that avoidance and religious faith were significant (negative) predictors of intentions to drink within safe limits. Similarly, both denial (Abraham *et al.* 1994) and defensive avoidance (Van der Velde and Van der Pligt 1991) have been found to be significant (negative) predictors of condom use intentions. Finally, Hodgkins and Orbell (1998) reported that avoidance had a negative correlation with BSE at one-month follow-up, although this effect became non-significant in a subsequent regression analysis controlling for PMT variables.

4.3 Sufficiency of PMT

Few PMT studies have examined the impact of past behaviour on health-protective intentions and behaviour. This is despite the fact that work on other social cognition models, such as the theory of planned behaviour (Ajzen 1988), has indicated that past behaviour is a strong predictor of future behaviour (Conner and Armitage 1998). Ouellette and Wood (1998) argue that strong past behaviour–future behaviour relations can be explained in two ways. First, past behaviour may affect future behaviour indirectly through its influence on intention (i.e. a conscious response). Past behaviour should shape individuals' beliefs about the behaviour which in turn influence their intentions and subsequent behaviour. Thus, the effects of past behaviour should be mediated by PMT variables in line with Rogers' (1983) view of prior experience (i.e. past behaviour) as an intrapersonal source of information that may initiate the cognitive appraisal processes outlined in PMT. Second, past behaviour may affect future behaviour directly through the automatic repetition of established routines (i.e. an habitual response). As Triandis (1977) argues, repeated performance of a behaviour may result in the behaviour coming under the influence of automatic processes that typify habitual processes (Eagly and Chaiken 1993).

Past behaviour is typically found to have a direct effect on future behaviour that is not fully mediated by social cognitive variables (see Ouellette and Wood 1998), consistent with the view that the impact of past behaviour on future behaviour reflects the involvement of habitual processes. However, Ajzen (1991) argues that when past behaviour is found to have a direct effect on future behaviour this simply indicates that a model is not sufficient. Assuming that the determinants of a behaviour are stable over time, then the correlation between past behaviour and future can be taken as an indication of the ceiling of a model's predictive validity. If a model is sufficient (i.e. it contains all the important determinants of behaviour), then the addition of past behaviour should not explain additional variance.

PMT studies that have assessed past behaviour typically find that it has a strong and unmediated impact on future behaviour. For example, Hodgkins and Orbell (1998) found that past BSE performance was the sole predictor of BSE at one-month follow-up. Moreover, when past behaviour was entered into the regression equation, the previously significant beta weights for intention and response efficacy became non-significant. Similar results have been reported by Murgraff *et al.* (1999) in relation to students' binge-drinking behaviour. In a regression analysis, past drinking behaviour emerged as the sole predictor of binge drinking at two-week follow-up. Finally, Norman *et al.* (2003) found that past behaviour was the strongest predictor of parents' adherence to eye patching recommendations for children with amblyopia at two-month follow-up. However, the response costs associated with patching also emerged as a significant predictor in the regression analysis indicating that the effect of past behaviour was partially mediated by PMT. Past behaviour has also been found to have a direct effect on intention in a number of PMT studies focusing on AIDS risk-reduction behaviour (Van der Velde and Van der Pligt 1991; Abraham *et al.* 1994) and BSE (Hodgkins and Orbell 1998). The above results suggest that PMT is not a sufficient model of health behaviour and that it would benefit from the inclusion of further variables, particularly in relation to the prediction of behaviour (see Sheeran *et al.*, Chapter 7 in this volume; Sutton, Chapter 6 in this volume).

4.4 Perceived vulnerability

Meta-analyses of PMT studies have found perceived vulnerability to be a relatively weak predictor of intention, concurrent behaviour and future behaviour (Floyd *et al.* 2000; Milne *et al.* 2000). Moreover, the narrative review of PMT studies presented above reveals a mixed pattern of results.

According to PMT, perceived vulnerability should be positively related to health-protective intentions and behaviour. However, a number of studies have reported significant negative correlations between perceived vulnerability and intentions to exercise (Plotnikoff and Higginbottom 2002), drink within safe limits (Ben-Ahron *et al.* 1995), use condoms (Van der Velde and Van der Pligt 1991), limit the number of sexual partners (Abraham *et al.* 1994) and participate in cancer screening programmes (Seydel *et al.* 1990). Similar negative correlations have also been reported with concurrent behaviour in relation to binge drinking (Ben-Ahron *et al.* 1995), eating a low-fat diet (Plotnikoff and Higginbottom 1998) and participating in cervical cancer screening (Seydel *et al.* 1990). In contrast, when significant, perceived vulnerability is typically found to have a positive relationship with future protective behaviour (e.g. Aspinwall *et al.* 1991; Orbell and Sheeran 1998; Norman *et al.* 2003).

When perceived vulnerability has been found to have a negative relationship with health-protective intentions and concurrent measures of behaviour, this has usually been explained by referring to 'defensive avoidance' styles of coping (e.g. Seydel *et al.* 1990). Thus, individuals who feel particularly vulnerable to a health threat may experience high levels of anxiety and thereby engage in various maladaptive coping responses to deal with the anxiety associated with threat (e.g. denial, avoidance). However, as reviewed above, few studies have examined the relationships between PMT constructs and maladaptive coping strategies and, as a result, little evidence exists to support this interpretation of the negative correlations between perceived vulnerability and health-protective intentions and behaviour.

An alternative explanation for the negative findings has been put forward by Weinstein and Nicolich (1993) who suggest that the results of many cross-sectional studies may have been misinterpreted. In particular they argue that, to the extent to which people use their current behaviour to make vulnerability judgements, a negative correlation is to be expected between perceived vulnerability and concurrent protective behaviour. Thus, for example, individuals who engage in high levels of exercise may infer that they are unlikely to develop cardiovascular disease in the future. However, Milne *et al.*'s (2000) meta-analysis provides evidence against such a position given that a significant, but weak, positive correlation was found between perceived vulnerability and concurrent behaviour. In line with PMT, those currently engaging in a health-protective behaviour may be doing so because they believe themselves to be at risk. Unfortunately, it is difficult to tease apart these two rival positions as it is possible that some individuals may base their risk judgements on their current behaviour whereas others may or may not engage in a behaviour on the basis of their risk perceptions. Clearly, if these opposing two processes are operating in different subsamples then any correlation between perceived vulnerability and concurrent protective behaviour, positive or negative, is likely to be attenuated.

Weinstein and Nicolich (1993) put forward similar arguments when considering the relationship between perceived vulnerability and intention.

According to PMT, individuals who feel vulnerable to a health threat should be more likely to intend to engage in a protective behaviour (i.e. a positive correlation), although it is also possible to argue that individuals who intend to engage in a health-protective behaviour may feel less vulnerable to a health threat (i.e. a positive correlation). However, as before, it is difficult to disentangle whether perceptions of vulnerability drive health-protective intentions or whether these intentions are used to infer perceptions of vulnerability. The significant positive correlation found between perceived vulnerability and intention in the Milne *et al.* (2000) meta-analysis would suggest that perceptions of vulnerability determine health-protective intentions, in line with PMT. However, given the relatively small size of the correlation it is possible that perceptions of vulnerability only determine health-protective intentions in some situations and/or among some individuals.

When considering the prediction of future behaviour, Weinstein and Nicolich (1993) only argue for the possibility of a positive relationship between perceived vulnerability and protective behaviour, as has been found in relation to reductions in the number of sexual partners (Aspinwall *et al.* 1991), the uptake of cervical cancer screening (Orbell and Sheeran 1998) and treatment adherence (Norman *et al.* 2003). In addition, Milne *et al.* (2000) reported a small, but significant, positive correlation between perceived vulnerability and future behaviour in their meta-analysis. These results are encouraging in that they suggest that perceptions of vulnerability may determine future protective behaviour. However, both Aspinwall *et al.* (1991) and Norman *et al.* (2003) reported that the significant effect of perceived vulnerability on future behaviour disappeared when past behaviour was included in the regression equation. This suggests that the 'apparent link between perceived risk and longitudinal changes in behavior is actually explained by the covariability of a sense of risk and behavior at [time] 1' (Joseph *et al.* 1987: 242).

Finally, Van der Velde and Hooykaas (1996) have advocated the use of conditional measures of perceived vulnerability when testing relationships between perceived vulnerability and health-protective intentions and behaviour. In PMT studies, perceived vulnerability is typically measured by asking respondents to estimate the chances that an event will occur in the future (e.g. 'How likely is it that you will become infected with the AIDS virus in the next two years?'). Such questions provide unconditional measures of perceived vulnerability as respondents can take into account an unspecified range of factors when providing their estimates. In contrast, conditional measures of perceived vulnerability ask respondents to estimate the chances that an event will occur in the future if preventive action is, or is not, taken (e.g. 'How likely is it that you will become infected with the AIDS virus in the next two years, if you don't use condoms?'). Van der Velde and Hooykaas (1996) argue that conditional measures of perceived vulnerability more closely resemble the perceived vulnerability construct as developed in PMT, as respondents estimate their vulnerability if no preventive action is taken. Conditional measures may also help to disentangle the nature of the relationship between perceived vulnerability and health-protective intentions and behaviour in cross-sectional studies. For example, Van der Velde and Hooykaas (1996) reported that a conditional measure of perceived vulnerability (for not using condoms) had a significant positive correlation with condom use intentions among STD clinic attendees (with private partners only and with prostitution partners) in line with PMT predictions. In contrast, an unconditional measure of perceived vulnerability was found to have a significant negative correlation with condom use intentions among attendees with prostitution partners and a non-significant, positive, correlation among attendees with private partners only.

5 Operationalization of the model

In this section the various steps required to develop measures of the main PMT constructs are outlined. These steps broadly mirror the recommendations made by DeVellis (1991) for the development of reliable and valid scales. Most of the PMT studies reviewed in this chapter report few details on the development of PMT measures, although there are a number of exceptions that are highlighted below.

The first stage in the development of a PMT questionnaire is to determine the content of the items to be used in the questionnaire and this can be achieved in one of two ways. First, it is possible to conduct a literature review of previous PMT studies on the health behaviour of interest to identify whether there are any previous, published or unpublished, instruments that could be used. The second, and in many ways preferred, alternative is to develop the questionnaire items specifically for the planned study. The first step in this process is to generate an item pool to cover the PMT constructs. This is ideally achieved by conducting semi-structured interviews with a sample drawn from the target population (e.g. 20 to 30 members) to determine the salient beliefs about the health threat and health behaviour under consideration.

Only a small number of PMT studies have followed such an approach when developing PMT measures. Norman *et al.* (2003) conducted pilot interviews with 20 parents of children who had been prescribed an eye patch for the treatment of amblyopia in their study on treatment adherence. The semi-structured interviews were based around PMT and consisted of initial open-ended questions followed by further prompts and probes in order to generate ideas for the wording and content of the item pool. Example questions are given in Table 3.3 (from Searle *et al.* 2000). Plotnikoff and Higginbottom (1995, 1998, 2002) conducted pilot interviews to generate item pools in their studies on exercise and dietary behaviour in response to the threat of cardiovascular disease. In addition, they also conducted focus group discussions in order to supplement information from the interviews. Rather than conduct interviews, an alternative approach is to conduct an elicitation study. Hodgkins and Orbell (1998) administered a short questionnaire to a sample of 40 women to ascertain salient cognitions about breast cancer and performing BSE. The questionnaire consisted of a series of questions reflecting the main components of PMT. For example, in relation to perceptions of severity, the women were asked, 'In what way would you consider contracting breast cancer would affect your life?'. The most frequently mentioned (i.e. modal) beliefs for each of the model's constructs were included in the PMT questionnaire used in the main study. A similar approach was also followed by Orbell and Sheeran (1998) in their study on cervical cancer screening. Having generated an item pool, the items can be reviewed to ensure that each of the PMT constructs is adequately covered and that the items appear to reflect the specific PMT constructs under consideration (i.e. have face/content validity). One way of achieving this is to give the items to experts to judge.

Table 3.3   Example interview questions from Searle *et al.* (2000)

Severity
In your opinion, what are the potential consequences of your child's visual impairment?

Vulnerability
What are your thoughts about how your child's visual impairment will change over time?

Response efficacy
What are the benefits/advantages of wearing a patch?

Self-efficacy
As a parent, to what extent do you feel that you can carry out the treatment requirements?

Response costs
What are the things/factors that hinder or prevent your child from wearing the patch?

Rewards of maladaptive response
Are there any benefits/advantages of not wearing a patch?

The next stage in the development of a PMT questionnaire is to administer the questionnaire items to a development, or pilot, sample. A pilot stage allows an opportunity to check respondents' comprehension of the items and to detect any potential difficulties that are likely to occur when respondents complete the questionnaire in the main study. In addition, a number of reliability and validity checks can be conducted at this stage. For example, the individual items can be assessed to ensure that they produce a good range of scores and are not excessively skewed. These items can then be combined to form scales to measure each of the model's constructs. The internal reliability of the scales is typically assessed using Cronbach's (1951) coefficient alpha. It is also possible to assess the test–retest reliability of the scales by administering the questionnaire to the same sample (or a sub-sample) at a second time point, usually one or two weeks later. Initial analyses can also be conducted to examine how the scales relate to each other and to other variables (e.g. age, gender, risk status, etc.) in order assess their construct validity. Finally, factor analyses can be conducted to ensure that the items load onto factors in line with the structure of PMT, thereby providing evidence for the factorial validity of the scales (Comrey 1988). Researchers typically employ exploratory factor analysis to investigate the factor structure (i.e. latent constructs) underlying the questionnaire items, although a more appropriate procedure is to conduct confirmatory factor analysis.

There are only a few PMT studies that have included a pilot study when developing PMT measures. Plotnikoff and Higginbottom (2002) reported that they conducted a pilot test of their questionnaire with 95 people from the target population. In addition, 46 respondents were interviewed to establish that respondents were able to comprehend the questionnaire instructions and response formats. A similar procedure was followed in earlier studies by Plotnikoff and Higginbottom (1995, 1998). Taylor and May (1996) conducted a pilot study with 267 patients with a wide range of sports injuries. Respondents completed a PMT questionnaire which was factor analysed to ensure that items loaded onto factors in line with the four main PMT constructs. Reliable scales were subsequently constructed to measure each of these constructs. Murgraff *et al.* (1999) followed a similar approach when developing a PMT questionnaire in relation to binge drinking among students. One hundred and ninety-six students completed a pilot questionnaire which was analysed in three stages. First, the means and standard deviations of individual items were calculated to ensure that each had an adequate spread of responses. Second, scales to measure each of the PMT constructs were constructed and the item–total correlations were examined in order to delete items that reduced a scale's internal reliability. Third, the remaining items were subjected to a principal components analysis and, in the main, were found to load onto factors in line with the structure of PMT.

Some PMT studies that do not include a pilot study will conduct a factor analysis of the questionnaire items used in the main study. For example, Norman *et al.* (2003) reported that all PMT items were factor analysed in order to aid the development of reliable measures of the main constructs. Plotnikoff and Higginbottom (1995) factor analysed the vulnerability, response efficacy, self-efficacy and protection-motivation items, while Plotnikoff and Higginbottom (1998, 2002) factor analysed only the response efficacy, self-efficacy and protection-motivation items. Other studies have reported factor analyses of items measuring specific constructs. For example, Abraham *et al.* (1994) conducted separate factor analyses on items measuring perceptions of vulnerability and response costs. The vulnerability items were found to load onto two factors, reflecting perceptions of vulnerability to the AIDS virus at a personal and at a group level. Items measuring response costs associated with condom use were also found to load onto two factors focusing on pleasure loss and reputation concerns. Sheeran and Orbell (1996) factor analysed items measuring the response costs of using condoms and the rewards of not using condoms, but found that they were unidimensional. Finally, Orbell and Sheeran (1998) conducted a factor analysis of items assessing various expectancies associated with cervical cancer screening and identified three factors focusing on response efficacy, response costs and the possibility of finding abnormal cells and/or another health problem.

The above studies indicate that when PMT items are subjected to a factor analysis, they tend to load onto factors in line with the structure of PMT (e.g. Taylor and May 1996; Murgraff *et al.* 1999; Norman *et al.* 2003). However, few studies have reported such analyses. Instead, items measuring specific PMT constructs are sometimes factor analysed to determine whether or not they are unidimensional in nature (e.g. Abraham *et al.* 1994; Sheeran and Orbell 1996; Orbell and Sheeran 1998). In addition, when conducted, the factor analyses are typically exploratory in nature. Given the problems associated with exploratory factor analysis and the fact that researchers are able to specify, *a priori*, which items should load onto which factors, there is a strong case for the routine use of confirmatory factor analysis. It is clear that there is a need for future studies to report such factor analyses of PMT items to demonstrate that they load onto factors in line with the structure of PMT. At present, most studies only report the internal reliability (i.e. alpha coefficients) of scales used to measure PMT variables.

A range of items have been used to measure each of the PMT constructs in applications of the model. Considering perceived severity, many studies have measured this construct with single items (e.g. Orbell and Sheeran 1998; Plotnikoff and Higginbottom 1998). When multi-item scales are used these are often found to have poor internal reliability (e.g. Abraham *et al.* 1994; Boer and Seydel 1995; Taylor and May 1996), although there are some notable exceptions (e.g. Sheeran and Orbell 1996; Norman *et al.* 2003). The perceived severity items will typically focus on the physical severity of the health threat (e.g. 'How serious a health problem is a heart attack?'; Plotnikoff and Higginbottom 2002). However, other aspects of the seriousness of the health threat have been considered including the potential impact on psychological well-being (e.g. 'Even if I was infected by HIV, I would still lead a happy life'; Sheeran and Orbell 1996) and involvement in normal activities (e.g. 'I see this injury as a serious threat to my sport/exercise involvement'; Taylor and May 1996).

Perceived vulnerability has, in the main, been assessed using multi-item scales with good levels of internal reliability. The perceived vulnerability items tend to focus on the individual's chances of experiencing the health threat at some point in the future (e.g. 'My chances of developing breast cancer in the future are ... very low/very high'; Hodgkins and Orbell 1998). Some studies ask respondents to consider their vulnerability on the basis of their current and past behaviour (e.g. 'Considering my present and past behaviour my chances of getting health problems from binge drinking are very high'; Murgraff *et al.* 1999). Such a wording is consistent with Weinstein and Nicolich's (1993) argument that people may use their current behaviour to inform vulnerability judgements. An alternative approach is to ask respondents to provide vulnerability ratings if a recommended behaviour is not performed (e.g. 'If left untreated, what are the chances that your child's visual impairment will affect his/her reading ability?'; Norman *et al.* 2003). As Van der Velde and Hooykaas (1996) have argued, such a conditional measure of perceived vulnerability may provide a more accurate assessment of the perceived vulnerability construct as outlined in PMT. Finally, some perceived vulnerability items appear to be confounded with fear or worry (e.g. 'How worried are you about the possibility of catching AIDS?'; Eppright *et al.* 1994).

Many PMT studies have used reliable multi-item measures to assess response efficacy, although a number of studies have employed single item measures (e.g. Eppright *et al.* 1994; Greening 1997; Murgraff *et al.* 1999). Response efficacy items typically focus on the effectiveness of the behaviour to reduce the health threat (e.g. 'Regular exercise will reduce my chances of having a heart attack'; Plotnikoff and Higginbottom 2002). However, it is also possible to focus on other positive outcomes of performing the behaviour, especially in relation to psychological well-being (e.g. 'The test will give me peace of mind'; Orbell and Sheeran 1998). Often, the perceived effectiveness of a behaviour is rated in general terms (e.g. 'Using a condom is effective in preventing a man passing the AIDS virus to a woman'; Abraham *et al.* 1994), rather than in relation to the individual performing the behaviour (e.g. 'The rehabilitation programme designed for me will ensure my complete recovery from this injury'; Taylor and May 1996).

Self-efficacy is typically assessed with multi-item scales with good levels of internal reliability in PMT studies. The self-efficacy items tend to focus on individuals' overall levels of confidence or perceived ability to perform the behaviour (e.g. 'I am capable of starting and continuing drinking at safe levels'; Murgraff *et al.* 1999), or on their perceptions of the ease or difficulty of performing the behaviour (e.g. 'I would find it easy to suggest using a condom to a new partner'; Abraham *et al.* 1994). Some studies ask respondents to rate their confidence that they can perform a behaviour when faced with specific obstacles (e.g. 'Choose mainly low-fat foods when you feel too lazy to prepare a meal'; Plotnikoff and Higginbottom 1998). Alternatively, respondents may be asked to indicate the extent to which specific obstacles may prevent them from performing the behaviour (e.g. Boer and Seydel 1995; Orbell and Sheeran 1998).

Response costs have been measured in fewer PMT studies, although they tend to be assessed with reliable multi-item scales. The items typically focus on various negative aspects of performing the behaviour (e.g. 'The test will make me feel anxious'; Orbell and Sheeran 1998). The rewards associated with maladaptive responses are rarely assessed. As Abraham *et al.* (1994) argue, any reward associated with not performing the recommended behaviour (e.g. 'Sex would be more exciting without a condom') can be rephrased as a response cost of performing the recommended behaviour (i.e. 'Sex would be *less* exciting *with* a condom'). In support of such a position, Sheeran and Orbell (1996) found only one factor underlying items measuring various response costs of using condoms and rewards of not using condoms. Nonetheless, Murgraff *et al.* (1999) were able to construct a rewards scale in relation to binge drinking (e.g. 'I sometimes drink beyond safe daily limits as a relaxation strategy').

Finally, protection motivation is typically equated with intention to perform a behaviour in PMT studies. Studies have therefore employed a mixture of single-item and reliable multi-item measures that ask respondents to indicate whether they intend to, plan to, are likely to, or are willing to engage in a behaviour (e.g. 'Do you plan to follow a low-fat diet for at least the next six months?'; Plotnikoff and Higginbottom 1998). Often respondents are asked to indicate their intention to perform a behaviour either at some point in the future (e.g. 'In the future I will use dental floss regularly'; Sheeran and Orbell 1996) or without a time frame (e.g. 'I intend to drink within safe limits as a regular habit'; Murgraff *et al.* 1999). In only a few PMT studies are respondents asked to indicate their intention to perform a behaviour within a specified timeframe (e.g. 'I intend to carry out BSE in the next month'; Hodgkins and Orbell 1998).

In summary, many PMT studies have employed multi-item scales, with adequate levels of internal reliability, to measure the model's constructs. However, there are a number of general comments that can be made on the way in which the PMT constructs have been operationalized. First, few studies report having conducted an elicitation, or pilot, study in order to identify the salient beliefs about the health threat and health behaviour under consideration in the target population. Second, factor analyses of PMT items demonstrating that they load onto factors in line with the structure of PMT are rarely reported. Future studies should therefore ensure that these two activities are conducted in order to ensure the construction of reliable multi-item measures. This, in turn, is likely to increase the statistical power of subsequent analyses (Lipsey 1990). Third, the measurement of the perceived vulnerability construct would be improved by the use of conditional vulnerability measures that ask respondents to indicate their vulnerability if a recommended behaviour is not followed (c.f. Van der Velde and Hooykaas 1996). Fourth, many items that have been used to measure the coping appraisal variables and protection motivation have failed to specify an appropriate time frame. As a result, measures of cognitions and future behaviour may have a low level of correspondence which is likely to attenuate the size of subsequent correlations (Fishbein and Ajzen 1975). Finally, PMT has considerable overlap with other social cognition models of health behaviour reviewed in this book. For example, measures of perceived severity and vulnerability are also included in the health belief model, while intention is a key variable in the theory of planned behaviour and self-efficacy is the cornerstone of social cognitive theory. Recommendations for the measurement of these variables are therefore also outlined in other chapters (Abraham and Sheeran, Chapter 2 in this volume; Conner and Sparks, Chapter 5 in this volume; Luszczynska and Schwarzer, Chapter 4 in this volume).

6 Application of the model

In this section an application of PMT to the prediction of exercise intentions and behaviour is described. Regular exercise has been linked to a range of physical and mental health benefits. For example, the physical health benefits include reduced risk for coronary heart disease (Powell *et al.* 1987), stroke (Paffenbarger and Hyde 1984) and hypertension (Siscovick *et al.* 1985) as well as increased metabolism of carbohydrates (Lennon *et al.* 1983) and fats (Rosenthal *et al.* 1983). Considering the mental health benefits, regular exercise has been linked to reduced levels of anxiety (Singer 1992), reduced life stress (Brown 1991), positive mood states (Folkins and Sime 1981) and enhanced satisfaction with physical shape (King *et al.* 1989). Given the various health benefits, regular exercise has been advocated as a key component of a healthy lifestyle (DoH 1992). However, a significant proportion of the UK population continue to lead a sedentary lifestyle. For example, the 1986 General Household Survey indicated that only one in three men and one in five women participated in any sport or recreational activity (OPCS, 1989). As a result, there is a clear need for research on the proximal, social cognitive, determinants of exercise behaviour. PMT may provide an appropriate framework for identifying these determinants.

To date, there have been few applications of PMT to the prediction of exercise behaviour (see Section 3 above). Plotnikoff and Higginbottom (1998) applied PMT to predict the exercise intentions and behaviour of a sample of cardiac patients. Self-efficacy was found to be the strongest predictor of exercise intentions (along with a weak effect for fear). Intention, in turn, was the only significant predictor of exercise behaviour. Plotnikoff and Higginbottom (2002) conducted a similar study with a sample of people drawn from 'at-risk' communities in Australia. Self-efficacy was again found to be the strongest predictor of exercise intentions, with weak effects also reported for perceived severity and perceived vulnerability (negative relationship). Intention was a significant predictor of exercise behaviour along with self-efficacy and perceived vulnerability (negative relationship). However, the above studies have two important methodological limitations; first, they employed cross-sectional designs and, second, exercise behaviour was measured using a stage-based measure that may be confounded with intention.

The present study reports an application of PMT to the prediction of exercise intentions and behaviour over a one-week period among a sample of undergraduates. The data are drawn from a previous study reporting the impact of a PMT-based health education intervention (Milne *et al.* 2002). Only data from those participants in the control arm of the study are presented below.

6.1 Respondents and procedure

The present sample comprises 76 undergraduate students at a UK university. The age range of the sample was 18–28 years (M = 19.92,

SD = 1.76) and included 19 males and 57 females. Respondents completed a PMT questionnaire at time 1 and were followed up one week later when they reported on their exercise behaviour over the past week.

6.2 Measures

All PMT items were measured on seven-point Likert response scales, consisting of belief statements followed by appropriate response categories. Scales to measure each of the PMT constructs were constructed by averaging across items. The following PMT constructs were assessed.

Threat appraisal measures
Perceived severity was assessed using six items focusing on the physical and psychological severity of experiencing developing coronary heart disease (e.g. 'If I were to develop CHD I would suffer a lot of pain'; alpha = 0.62). *Perceived vulnerability* to coronary heart disease was measured with two items (e.g. 'I am unlikely to develop CHD in the future'; alpha = 0.76). Four items were used to measure *fear* (e.g. 'The thought of developing CHD makes me feel very frightened–not at all frightened'; alpha = 0.93).

Coping appraisal measures
Response efficacy was assessed using two items focusing on the effectiveness of regular exercise to reduce the risk of developing coronary heart disease. However, it was not possible to combine these two items into a reliable scale. As a result, a single item measure of response efficacy was used which was chosen on the basis of stronger correlations with exercise intentions and behaviour (i.e. 'If I were to engage in at least one 20-minute session of vigorous exercise a week I would lessen my chance of developing CHD'). *Self-efficacy* was measured with four items (e.g. 'I feel confident in my ability to partake in at least one 20-minute session of vigorous exercise during the next week'; alpha = 0.83). Two items were used to measure *response costs* (e.g. 'Taking at least one 20-minute session of vigorous exercise during the next week would cause me too many problems'; alpha = 0.74).

Exercise intentions and behaviour
Protection motivation, as assessed by *intention* to exercise over the next week, was measured using two items (e.g. 'I intend to partake in at least one 20-minute session of vigorous exercise during the next week'; alpha = 0.83). *Time 1 exercise* behaviour was measured using a single item that asked respondents to indicate how many times they had engaged in vigorous exercise over the previous week. The same item was used to measure *time 2 exercise* behaviour at one-week follow-up.

6.3 Results

The means, standard deviations and intercorrelations between the main study variables are presented in Table 3.4. All PMT variables were found to

Table 3.4 Means, standard deviations and intercorrelations between the main study variables

	1	2	3	4	5	6	7	8	9
1 Severity		0.39***	0.44***	0.34**	0.26*	-0.22	0.25*	0.36**	0.15
2 Vulnerability			0.36**	0.38***	0.00	-0.17	0.29*	0.14	0.02
3 Fear				0.44**	0.28*	-0.35**	0.41***	0.18	0.16
4 Response efficacy					0.23*	-0.30**	0.40***	0.09	0.21
5 Self-efficacy						-0.77***	0.62***	0.55***	0.55***
6 Response costs							-0.63***	-0.43***	-0.51***
7 Intention								0.54***	0.56***
8 Time 1 Exercise									0.58***
9 Time 2 Exercise									
Mean	4.91	3.79	4.38	5.05	4.94	2.68	4.59	1.18	0.95
SD	0.97	1.09	1.49	1.38	1.61	1.31	2.01	1.94	1.74

Note: *p < 0.05, **p < 0.01, ***p < 0.001. N = 76.

have significant correlations with exercise intentions, in line with expectations. It is noteworthy that the coping appraisal variables tended to have stronger correlations with intention than did the threat appraisal variables. Intention, in turn, was found to have the strongest correlation with exercise behaviour at time 2. In addition, two of the coping appraisal variables, self-efficacy and response costs, were also found to have significant correlations with time 2 exercise behaviour. Finally, past exercise behaviour had strong correlations with both exercise intentions and time 2 exercise behaviour.

A hierarchical regression analysis was performed to assess the ability of PMT to predict exercise intentions (see Table 3.5). The PMT variables were entered at the first step and were able to explain 53 per cent of the variance in exercise intentions, $R^2 = 0.53$, $F(6,69) = 13.08$, $p < 0.001$. Only self-efficacy emerged as a significant independent predictor. When past behaviour was entered at the second step it was found to produce a significant increment in the amount of variance explained, R^2 change $= 0.06$, F change $(1,69) = 9.67$, $p < 0.01$. The effect of self-efficacy was reduced to non-significance and past behaviour was the sole significant predictor in the final regression model which explained 59 per cent of the variance in exercise intentions, $R^2 = 0.59$, $F(7,68) = 14.00$, $p < 0.001$.

A similar hierarchical regression analysis was performed to assess the ability of PMT to predict exercise behaviour at one-week follow-up (see Table 3.6). Intention (i.e. protection motivation) was entered at the first step and was able to explain 31 per cent of the variance in time 2 exercise behaviour, $R^2 = 0.31$, $F(1,74) = 32.93$, $p < 0.001$. The addition of the PMT variables failed to produce a significant increment in the amount of variance explained, R^2 change $= 0.09$, F change $(6,68) = 1.72$, ns. At this stage, the variables in the model were able to explain 40 per cent of the variance in exercise behaviour, $R^2 = 0.40$, $F(7,68) = 6.45$, $p < 0.001$, with intention emerging as the only significant independent predictor. Entering past behaviour at the final step produced a significant increment in the amount of variance explained, R^2 change $= 0.08$, F change $(1,67) = 10.49$, $p < 0.01$. Past behaviour was the only significant predictor in the final regression model which explained 48 per cent of the variance in exercise behaviour, $R^2 = 0.48$, $F(8,67) = 7.73$, $p < 0.001$.

6.4 Discussion

PMT was found to be highly predictive of both exercise intentions and behaviour. Considering the prediction of exercise intentions, the PMT variables explained 53 per cent of the variance with self-efficacy emerging as the sole significant predictor. The PMT variables were also able to explain 40 per cent of the variance in exercise behaviour at one-week follow-up. It is interesting to note that intention was the sole predictor of time 2 exercise suggesting, in line with the theoretical structure of PMT, that intention acts as mediator variable between the threat and coping appraisal variables and protective behaviour. The present results are consistent with previous cross-sectional PMT-exercise applications that have found self-efficacy to be the

Table 3.5 Regression analysis predicting exercise intentions

Step	Variable	Beta	Beta
1	Severity	−0.07	−0.15
	Vulnerability	0.18	0.15
	Fear	0.12	0.14
	Response efficacy	0.14	0.18
	Self-efficacy	0.39**	0.23
	Response costs	−0.23	−0.23
2	Time 1 exercise		0.31**
R²		0.53***	0.59***
R² change			0.06**

Note: **p < 0.01, *** p < 0.001. N = 76.

Table 3.6 Regression analysis predicting time 2 exercise behaviour

Step	Variable	Beta	Beta	Beta
1	Intention	0.55***	0.38**	0.22
2	Severity		0.05	−0.06
	Vulnerability		−0.12	−0.13
	Fear		−0.10	−0.06
	Response efficacy		−0.04	−0.12
	Self-efficacy		0.22	0.08
	Response costs		−0.13	−0.16
3	Time 1 exercise			0.39**
R²		0.31***	0.40***	0.48***
R² change			0.09	0.08**

Note: **p < 0.01, ***p < 0.001. N = 76.

strongest predictor of exercise intentions which, in turn, have been found to be the strongest predictor of exercise behaviour (Plotnikoff and Higginbottom, 1998, 2002). The present results are also broadly in line with meta-analyses of PMT (Floyd *et al.* 2000; Milne *et al.* 2002) that have reported that coping appraisal variables tend to have stronger correlations with intentions and behaviour than do threat appraisal variables.

The addition of past behaviour produced significant increments in the amounts of variance explained in both exercise intentions and behaviour. In both cases the effects of PMT variables were reduced to non-significance and past behaviour emerged as the sole predictor. Similar results have been found in other applications of PMT to BSE (Hodgkins and Orbell 1998), binge drinking (Murgraff *et al.* 1999), condom use (Abraham *et al.* 1994) and treatment adherence (Norman *et al.* 2003). Such findings question the sufficiency of PMT as a model of health behaviour (Ajzen 1991) and highlight the need to consider additional predictors of health-protective intentions and behaviour. However, it is also possible that a strong relationship between past and future behaviour, especially for repeated behaviours such as exercise, may reflect the operation of habitual responses (Ouellette and Wood 1998).

There are a number of study limitations which mean that the present results should be interpreted with some caution. First, the sample size was relatively small. This is likely to have reduced the statistical power of the regression analyses given the number of independent predictors (see Cohen 1992). It is notable that perceived vulnerability and response costs were marginally significant (i.e. $p < 0.10$) in the regression analysis predicting exercise intentions. Second, it was not possible to construct a reliable measure of response efficacy which may have attenuated the predictive power of this construct in the regression analyses. Third, the study only examined exercise behaviour over a brief time interval (i.e. one week). The ability of PMT to predict exercise behaviour over longer time periods remains to be demonstrated. Fourth, it is possible to question the generalizability of the present results given the nature of the sample (i.e. undergraduate students). Finally, exercise behaviour was assessed using a single-item, self-report measure of the number of times participants engaged in vigorous exercise over the previous week. While such a measure ensured a high level of correspondence with the PMT measures, it would also be useful to employ more reliable/valid measures of physical activity such as the Stanford 7-Day Recall Questionnaire (Sallis *et al.* 1985) in future studies.

Despite these criticisms, the present results are of practical importance. In particular, they suggest that attempts to increase exercise behaviour should first focus on enhancing feelings of self-efficacy. As discussed later in this chapter, Bandura (1986) has outlined various sources of self-efficacy that could be targeted in an intervention. Enhancing self-efficacy is likely to lead to stronger intentions which, in the present study, were found to be predictive of exercise behaviour. Encouragingly, there are a number of PMT-based intervention studies that have reported significant effects for self-efficacy manipulations on exercise intentions (e.g. Stanley and Maddux 1986; Wurtele and Maddux 1987; Fruin *et al.* 1992). However, similar effects have not been reported in relation to exercise behaviour (e.g. Wurtele and Maddux 1987; Milne *et al.* 2002). Taken together, these results suggest that while enhancing self-efficacy may lead to increased motivation to exercise, other volitional strategies such as the formation of implementation intentions (Gollwitzer 1999; Sheeran *et al.*, Chapter 7 in this volume) may be required to translate strong intentions into action. For example, Milne *et al.* (2002) reported a PMT-based intervention that was found to have a significant impact on exercise intentions. However, the intervention was found to have little effect on exercise behaviour at one-week follow-up with 35 per cent of participants in the intervention group having exercised versus 38 per cent in the control group. It was only when the PMT intervention was combined with a volitional intervention, instructing participants to form an implementation intention specifying when and where they would exercise during the next week, that a significant impact on behaviour was observed, with 91 per cent having exercised at one-week follow-up. Moreover, it appears that this effect was not due solely to the volitional intervention. In another study on testicular self-examination (TSE), Milne and Sheeran (2002) reported that an implementation intention intervention alone had little impact on behaviour (21 per cent performance at one-month follow-up) compared to a PMT intervention (28 per cent) or a control condition (18 per cent). However, combining the PMT and implementation intention interventions had a dramatic impact on TSE performance (62 per cent).

7 Intervention studies

PMT has been tested extensively in experimental settings. PMT developed out of early work on fear appeals that sought to identify the conditions under which persuasive communications may produce attitude and behaviour change (Rogers 1975, 1983). PMT identifies the key variables that need to be targeted to change health behaviour and numerous studies have attempted to manipulate PMT constructs to produce such change. As Milne *et al.* (2000) note, it is possible to distinguish between two types of PMT intervention studies: (a) 'health education' interventions that are broadly based on PMT and (b) experimental manipulations of specific PMT variables.

7.1 Designing PMT interventions

In health education interventions, the intervention group receives information about a health threat and recommended action whereas the control group receives information on an unrelated topic or receives no information. The health education intervention typically provides general factual information on the health threat and an appropriate coping response, based on PMT constructs. For example, in an intervention to encourage participation in mammography screening (Boer and Seydel 1995), women in the intervention group were sent a PMT-based leaflet entitled *Breast Examination* that described the relative high vulnerability of older women to breast cancer and the high response efficacy of mammography screening. Feelings of self-efficacy towards participating in the screening programme were encouraged by explaining that mammography is a straightforward procedure with little discomfort. Three days after receiving the leaflet the women received a PMT questionnaire. Women in the control group received no information, simply receiving the PMT questionnaire.

Other studies have directly manipulated specific PMT variables. In these studies participants typically read a persuasive communication in which specific PMT variables have been independently manipulated prior to their measurement in a PMT questionnaire. Most of these studies seek to manipulate specific PMT variables through the presentation of information designed to produce high versus low levels of the targeted construct. For example, participants in one condition may receive information designed to increase perceptions of vulnerability whereas participants in the other condition may receive information designed to decrease perceived vulnerability. A good example of such a study is provided by Fruin *et al.* (1992). Participants were presented with material about exercise in which a number of PMT variables (i.e. response efficacy, response costs, self-efficacy) were independently manipulated resulting in a $2 \times 2 \times 2$ between-subjects factorial design with two levels (high vs low) for each factor. After reading the information, participants completed a PMT questionnaire. Other studies seek to manipulate specific PMT variables in order to encourage only health protective behaviour (i.e. present vs absent). For example, Wurtele and Maddux (1987) presented essays to sedentary female undergraduates that recommended beginning a regular exercise programme. The essays were designed so that perceptions of vulnerability, severity, response efficacy and self-efficacy were independently manipulated, such that the specific manipulation was either present or absent (rather than presenting high versus low versions for each variable). After reading the essays, participants completed a PMT questionnaire.

Specific PMT constructs have been manipulated in a variety of ways in intervention studies. Considering threat appraisal variables, Stainback and Rogers (1983) manipulated the perceived severity of excessive drinking by arguing that it may cause either severe injury (i.e. high severity) or minor irritation (i.e. low severity) to internal organs. In a study designed to increase dietary intake of calcium among female students, Wurtele (1988) manipulated perceptions of vulnerability to osteoporosis. The high vulnerability essay 'presented recent findings on the incidence of bone loss in young women along with several reasons why young women may be at risk for osteoporosis' (p. 630). The essay concluded by stating that there was a high probability that the reader would develop some form of osteoporosis. In contrast, the low vulnerability essay argued that 'osteoporosis is primarily a disease of older women and presented several reasons why young women are at low risk for this condition' (p. 630). The essay concluded by stating that the reader's risk for developing osteoporosis was low.

Many studies have combined the perceived severity and vulnerability components so that the potential threat of an illness or disease is manipulated. For example, Rippetoe and Rogers (1987) manipulated the perceived threat of breast cancer by presenting women with either a high- or low-threat essay. The high-threat essay described 'breast cancer in graphic detail, contained vivid descriptions of radical chemotherapy side effects and a radical mastectomy and emphasized college-age women's vulnerability to breast cancer because of stress and diets with increased fat' (p. 599). In contrast, the low-threat essay described 'breast cancer as a less severe disease with few physical or emotional consequences. It also emphasized the rarity of the disease among college-age women and college-age women's decreased vulnerability to the illness' (p. 599).

Considering coping appraisal variables, response efficacy has been manipulated in essays that argue that there is an effective method to prevent or treat a disease or that there is no such method. For example, Fruin *et al.* (1992) presented high school students with essays on cardiovascular disease and exercise. The high response efficacy essay emphasized the effectiveness of regular exercise in reducing their risk of developing cardiovascular disease. In contrast, the low response efficacy essay stated that 'Many people do not believe that regular exercise is effective in preventing cardiovascular disease' (p. 60). To manipulate self-efficacy it is necessary to argue that the individual either has or lacks the ability to perform the recommended coping response. Rippetoe and Rogers (1987) therefore provided information that emphasized a woman's ability to perform breast self-examination and to incorporate it into her health routine, in the high self-efficacy essay. In contrast, the low self-efficacy essay highlighted the difficulty of performing a good breast self-examination and accurately detecting a lump. Finally, only one study has attempted to manipulate response costs directly (Fruin *et al.* 1992). In the high response costs essay the possible negative side effects of engaging in regular exercise were highlighted, whereas the low response costs essay stated that any negative side effects are 'quite minor and easily overcome' (p. 60).

7.2 Meta-analysis of PMT intervention studies

Milne *et al.* (2000) assessed the impact of PMT interventions through a meta-analysis of cognition changes following experimental manipulations of specific PMT variables (see Table 3.7). Milne *et al.* (2000) reported r_+ (sample weighted average correlations) as an estimate of the relevant effect sizes rather than d_+ (sample weighted standardized mean differences) that is a more common measure of effect size in experimental studies. Their meta-analysis consisted of eight studies that included specific manipulations of PMT constructs and considered the effects of the manipulations on corresponding PMT cognitions. As shown in Table 3.7, manipulations of the threat appraisal variables led to significant changes in corresponding perceptions of severity and vulnerability. The effect sizes are large according to Cohen's (1992) guidelines. The effect sizes for manipulations of response efficacy and self-efficacy, though smaller, were significant and in the medium to large range. Only manipulations of response costs were unable to produce a significant effect, although it should be noted that only one study (Fruin *et al.* 1992) attempted directly to manipulate perceptions of response costs. Furthermore, for all the significant effect sizes with the exception of self-efficacy, the *fail-safe* N values fell well above recommended tolerance levels, indicating the effects to be robust. It is noteworthy that the experimental manipulations tend to be more successful at changing threat than coping appraisal cognitions.

There were too few PMT-based health education intervention studies to be able to conduct a meaningful meta-analysis. Milne *et al.* (2000) therefore conducted a vote count of the percentage of times the interventions

Table 3.7   Summary of the Milne *et al.* (2002) meta-analysis of cognition changes following experimental manipulations of protection-motivation theory variables

	r_+
Severity	0.66***
Vulnerability	0.63***
Response efficacy	0.42***
Self-efficacy	0.32***
Response costs	0.09

Note: r_+ = sample weighted average correlations.
***p < 0.001.

produced significant changes in PMT cognitions. The health education interventions were unable to produce significant changes in perceptions of severity and vulnerability (0 per cent significance ratios), although there was some evidence of an impact of such interventions on response efficacy (50 per cent significance ratio) and self-efficacy (100 per cent significance ratio). These findings can be contrasted with a similar vote count conducted for experimental manipulations of specific PMT variables which revealed 100 per cent significance ratios for manipulations of the four main PMT constructs. However, it is clear that there are too few studies at this stage to make any reliable conclusions on the effectiveness of PMT-based health education interventions to change threat and coping appraisal cognitions.

It is important to highlight that the analyses conducted by Milne *et al.* (2000) only considered the impact of PMT interventions on changes in threat and coping appraisals. Of more importance is the impact of such interventions on protection motivation (i.e. intention) and behaviour. In the following narrative review of PMT intervention studies the impact of manipulating specific PMT variables, as well as health education inter-ventions, on a range of health-protective intentions and behaviours is considered (see Table 3.8).

7.3 Narrative review of PMT intervention studies

Considering the impact of manipulating specific PMT variables, the largest number of studies have focused on exercise. For example, Courneya and Hellsten (2001) presented students with essays that manipulated each of the four main PMT constructs. Only the perceived severity manipulation was found to have a significant effect on exercise intentions. However, most other studies have reported significant effects for self-efficacy manipulations on exercise intentions (Stanley and Maddux 1986; Wurtele and Maddux 1987; Fruin *et al.* 1992), and significant effects have also been reported for perceived vulnerability (Wurtele and Maddux 1987) and response efficacy (Stanley and Maddux 1986) manipulations. A number of experimental studies have also focused on safe sex intentions in response to the threat of

Table 3.8 Examples of intervention studies based on protection motivation theory

Behaviour	*Authors*
Exercise	Courneya and Hellsten (2001); Fruin *et al.* (1992); Milne *et al.* (2002)[a][b]; Stanley and Maddux (1986); Wurtle and Maddux (1987)[b]
Smoking	Maddux and Rogers (1983)
Alcohol-related	Stainback and Rogers (1983)
Sexual behaviours	Kyes (1995); Tanner *et al.* (1989, 1991); Yzer *et al.* (1998)
Breast self-examination	Rippetoe and Rogers (1987)
Testicular self-examination	Milne and Sheeran (2002)[a][b]; Steffen (1990)[a]
Mammography	Boer and Seydel (1996)[a]
Dental behaviours	Beck and Lund (1981)[b]

Note: All the above studies report experimental manipulations of specific PMT constructs with the exception of those marked with [a] which are 'health education' interventions. All studies examined the impact of the manipulations/interventions on intentions. Only those marked with [b] also examined the impact on behaviour.

sexually transmitted diseases (STDs) or AIDS. For example, Yzer *et al.* (1998) presented female undergraduate students with newspaper articles that manipulated perceptions of vulnerability to AIDS and self-efficacy to engage in safe sex practice, although only the self-efficacy manipulation was found to have a significant effect on safe sex intentions. Tanner *et al.* (1989) also found a self-efficacy manipulation to have a significant effect on condom use intentions. In contrast, manipulating other PMT constructs has been found to have little effect on safe sex intentions (e.g. Kyes 1995).

Only a small number of experimental studies have focused on other health behaviours. For example, Maddux and Rogers (1983) manipulated the four main PMT constructs and found that response efficacy and self-efficacy had significant effects on intentions to quit smoking among a sample of student smokers. Rippetoe and Rogers (1987) manipulated threat of breast cancer as well as response efficacy and self-efficacy in relation to performing BSE. All three manipulations were found to impact on BSE intentions. In relation to the threat of osteoporosis, Wurtele (1988) found that a perceived vulnerability manipulation had significant effects on women's intentions (to take calcium supplements, to increase dietary intake of calcium and to pick up a free calcium supplement) and their behaviour (in terms of their dietary intake of calcium and picking up a free calcium supplement) assessed at two-week follow-up. The response efficacy manipulation was only found to have a significant effect on intentions to take calcium supplements. Beck and Lund (1981) manipulated beliefs about the severity of, and patients' vulnerability to, periodontal disease. Only the severity manipulation was found to have an effect on intentions to use disclosing tablets and, at four-week follow-up, dental flossing behaviour. Finally, Stainback and Rogers (1983) presented high- versus low-threat information to high school students which was found to influence intentions to remain abstinent and not to drink and drive.

There have been relatively few PMT-based health education interventions reported in the literature. Steffen (1990) evaluated a leaflet on testicular self-examination (TSE) among a sample of male undergraduates. The leaflet, that focused on the prevalence and symptoms of testicular cancer as well as the efficacy of TSE and how to perform it, was found to increase intentions to perform TSE, compared to the control group. Similar results have been reported by Milne and Sheeran (2002) who found that a PMT-based leaflet had a significant effect on intentions to perform TSE, although this effect did not translate into increased performance of TSE at one-month and one-year follow-up. Boer and Seydel (1995) found that a PMT-based leaflet to encourage participation in mammography screening for breast cancer among a community sample of older women increased screening intentions. Unfortunately, it was not possible to assess the impact of the leaflet on the uptake of mammography screening as attendance was extremely high in both the intervention and control groups. Finally, Milne *et al.* (2002) assessed the impact of a PMT-based health education intervention on exercise intentions and behaviour. The intervention was found to have a significant effect on intention that remained over a two-week follow-up period. However, the intervention had no effect on exercise behaviour.

7.4 Summary and discussion

Although experimental tests of PMT have taken two forms, the majority of studies have assessed the effect of independently manipulating specific PMT variables rather than evaluating the impact of PMT-based health education interventions. These studies have shown that manipulations of specific PMT variables have been successful in producing changes in corresponding cognitions (Milne *et al.* 2000). Interestingly, larger effect sizes are typically found for manipulations of perceived severity and perceived vulnerability than for manipulations of response efficacy and self-efficacy, thereby indicating that attempts to change threat appraisals have been more successful than those to change coping appraisals. However, when the effects of manipulating specific PMT variables on health-related intentions are considered, manipulations of self-efficacy are typically more effective than manipulations of other PMT constructs. In terms of motivating people to engage in health behaviour, these results suggest that interventions should attempt to change perceptions of self-efficacy, even though such perceptions are difficult to change. Bandura (1991) has outlined four main sources of self-efficacy that could be targeted in interventions. First, feelings of self-efficacy can be enhanced through personal mastery experience. For example, a behaviour may be split into a series of sub-goals so that mastery of each is achieved in turn. Second, self-efficacy may be enhanced through observing others successfully perform the behaviour (i.e. vicarious experience). Third, standard persuasive techniques can be employed to enhance self-efficacy, as has been attempted in most PMT intervention studies. Fourth, an individual's physiological state may be used as a source of information, such that an individual may infer that high levels of anxiety or arousal indicate that he/she is not capable of performing a recommended action. This may be particularly pertinent when processing high-threat information. As a result, relaxation techniques may be usefully employed to help maintain feelings of self-efficacy.

PMT intervention studies typically assess cognitions immediately after participants have read a persuasive communication, thereby only assessing the immediate impact of PMT interventions. As a result, if the effects of interventions diminish over time, these studies are likely to overestimate their impact. Follow-up assessments of PMT variables are rarely conducted to assess the longer term impact of interventions. To date, only two studies have sought to manipulate and measure PMT variables at a separate time points. Boer and Seydel (1995) sent a PMT-based leaflet to women in the intervention group to encourage attendance at mammography screening. Women in the control group received no leaflet. Three days later all women were sent a PMT questionnaire. Women in the intervention group were found to have stronger perceptions of response efficacy and self-efficacy and stronger intentions to attend screening. Milne *et al.* (2002) developed a PMT-based intervention to increase exercise. PMT variables were assessed immediately after the intervention and again at one- and two-week follow-up. The intervention was found to have significant effects on all PMT variables assessed immediately afterwards and at both follow-up points. Such findings are encouraging as they suggest that cognition changes following PMT interventions may be relatively stable over time. However, it is clear that further work is required to assess the longer term impact of PMT interventions. Moreover, few studies have assessed the impact of PMT interventions on subsequent behaviour. Some encouraging results have been reported in the literature (e.g. Beck and Lund 1981; Wurtele 1988), although other studies have failed to report significant effects (e.g. Wurtele and Maddux 1987; Milne and Sheeran 2002; Milne *et al.* 2002). Such findings are disappointing as they suggest that PMT interventions may have a limited impact on behaviour, despite evidence that points to their utility in changing health-protective cognitions and intentions.

Few studies have tested whether the effects of PMT interventions are mediated by PMT variables. Some studies have reported correlations between manipulated PMT variables and intention (e.g. Stanley and Maddux 1986; Courneya and Hellsten 2001), but have failed to report full mediational analyses (cf. Baron and Kenny 1986). A notable exception is the Rippetoe and Rogers (1987) study that assessed the impact of manipulating threat, response efficacy and self-efficacy on BSE intentions. The manipulations were found to have significant effects on corresponding cognitions and BSE intentions, although path analysis provided support for a mediational model as no direct effects were found for the PMT manipulations on BSE intentions; instead, the effects were mediated by corresponding PMT variables. For example, the effect of the self-efficacy manipulation was fully mediated by the self-efficacy measure which was a significant predictor of intention. Such findings are encouraging in that they suggest that PMT interventions influence health-protective intentions through changing PMT variables, thereby providing strong support for the model.

In addition to assessing the impact of PMT interventions on health-protective intentions and behaviour (i.e. adaptive coping responses), it is also possible to assess their impact on maladaptive coping responses. Thus, according to PMT, individuals may engage in various strategies in order to reduce the fear associated with the threat without dealing with the threat itself. Such responses can be termed maladaptive coping responses (Rippetoe and Rogers 1987). Only a few studies have examined the impact of PMT manipulations on maladaptive coping responses (e.g. Rippetoe and Rogers 1987; Fruin *et al.* 1992; Yzer *et al.* 1998). The most thorough investigation has been conducted by Rippetoe and Rogers (1987) who examined the impact of threat, response efficacy and self-efficacy manipulations in relation to breast cancer and BSE. Both adaptive (i.e. BSE intentions, rational problem solving) and maladaptive (i.e. avoidance, wishful thinking, religious faith, fatalism, hopelessness) coping responses were assessed. The threat manipulation increased the likelihood of both adaptive and maladaptive coping responses, consistent with the idea that threat appraisal is a necessary, but not sufficient, condition for protection motivation. In contrast, the coping appraisal manipulations were found to have significant effects on specific coping responses. For example, women who read the high self-efficacy essay were more likely to engage in adaptive responses (i.e. BSE intentions, rational problem solving), whereas those who read the low self-efficacy essay were more likely to feel hopeless. Using path analysis, Rippetoe and Rogers (1987) also found that the manipulated PMT variables were able to mediate the impact of the PMT manipulations on maladaptive coping responses. For example, the effect of the self-efficacy manipulation on hopelessness was mediated by changes in self-efficacy.

Finally, Milne *et al.* (2002) have highlighted various practical and ethical considerations that should be considered when developing PMT-based intervention studies. First, Milne *et al.* (2002) note that while there is good evidence that experimental manipulations of specific PMT variables are able to change corresponding cognitions and intentions, applying such manipulations to real-world health education intervention programmes may be difficult. It is not generally ethical to manipulate specific variables in a high versus low level in health education settings as doing so would involve providing some individuals with false information (e.g. incorrectly providing information to some individuals that they are at low or high risk of developing a serious disease). One possible solution to this problem is either to provide or not to provide information on the specific PMT variables (i.e. present vs absent), as has been done in some experimental PMT studies (e.g. Yzer *et al.* 1998). Second, Milne *et al.* (2002) note that most experimental PMT studies do not have a control group who receive no information (see Ripptoe and Rogers 1987 for an exception). As a result, it is difficult to assess the impact of the different interventions relative to not receiving an intervention. Milne *et al.* (2002) therefore suggest that when applying PMT to real-world health education intervention programmes it may be more appropriate to test the impact of a PMT health education intervention (relative to a control group) in which all PMT components are addressed in a single intervention. However, the disadvantage of such an approach is that it is not possible to assess the relative impact of different components of the intervention. Such interventions are therefore likely to provide only limited information for the future theoretical development of PMT.

8 Future directions

PMT includes many of the key social cognitive determinants of health behaviour reviewed in this book. It shares a number of similarities with the health belief model (Rosenstock 1974; Abraham and Sheeran, Chapter 2 in this volume). For example, the health belief model includes perceived vulnerability and severity as well as the perceived benefits of, and barriers to, performing a health-protective action which are analogous to the response efficacy and response costs constructs of PMT. However, PMT also includes self-efficacy and protection motivation (i.e. intention) which have been found to be among the most powerful predictors of health behaviour and are included in the theory of planned behaviour (Ajzen 1988; Conner and Sparks, Chapter 5 in this volume). In addition, PMT posits that protection motivation acts as a mediating variable between the threat and coping appraisal variables and health behaviour, again in line with the theory of planned behaviour. Given that PMT includes a range of threat and coping appraisal variables that have been found to be important in other models, it is not surprising that PMT has been found to be a useful model for predicting health-protective intentions and behaviour, with meta-analyses reporting significant effects for all PMT variables (Floyd *et al.* 2000; Milne *et al.* 2000). However, it is worth noting that many of the significant relationships identified in the meta-analyses appear not to be robust and would therefore benefit from further replication. In addition, there are a number of issues that need to be addressed in future research.

There is a clear need for more prospective tests of PMT. This would assist the future theoretical development of PMT in three important ways. First, the use of prospective designs would provide an opportunity to examine the proposed mediating role of protection motivation (i.e. intention) in more detail. According to PMT, the threat and coping appraisal variables should act through (i.e. be mediated by) intention. Meta-analyses (Floyd *et al.* 2000; Milne *et al.* 2000) indicate that the threat and coping appraisal variables provide only weak predictions of future behaviour, whereas intention has been found to be a consistent, and moderately strong, predictor of future behaviour. This pattern of results is consistent with a mediational hypothesis, although it needs to be formally tested in prospective studies in which intention is entered into a regression equation after the threat and coping appraisal variables when predicting future behaviour (cf. Baron and Kenny 1986). Second, the use of prospective designs would provide a more appropriate test of the relationship between perceived vulnerability and health-protective behaviour. As Weinstein and Nicolich (1993) argue, in cross-sectional studies it is unclear whether a positive or negative correlation should be expected between perceived vulnerability and health-protective behaviour. Prospective designs, coupled with the use of conditional measures of perceived vulnerability (Van der Velde and Hooykaas 1996), are required to disentangle the relationship between perceived vulnerability and health-protective behaviour. Third, the use of prospective designs would allow an opportunity to assess the sufficiency of the model in more detail. Measures of past behaviour should be included which, if PMT is a sufficient model of health-protective intentions and behaviour, should not add to the variance explained by the model's constructs (cf. Ajzen 1991).

Future tests of PMT should also focus on maladaptive coping responses. Thus, in the absence of an effective coping response, individuals may engage in activities to reduce the fear associated with a health threat without dealing with the threat itself (Rippetoe and Rogers 1987). A few studies have reported significant correlations between PMT constructs and various maladaptive coping responses, such as avoidance, denial and wishful thinking (e.g. Abraham *et al.* 1994; Ben-Ahron *et al.* 1995; Hodgkins and Orbell 1998). Engaging in maladaptive coping responses may also interfere with protection motivation, as has been noted in some studies (e.g. Van der Velde and Van der Pligt 1991; Abraham *et al.* 1994; Ben-Ahron *et al.* 1995). However, these initial findings require replication.

One of the strengths of PMT is that it has been subjected to numerous experimental tests. The majority of these studies have sought to assess the impact of manipulating specific PMT variables. Milne *et al.*'s (2000) meta-analysis of cognition changes following experimental manipulations of specific PMT variables found large effect sizes for the threat appraisal variables and medium to large effect sizes for the coping appraisal variables. It is interesting to note that Milne *et al.*'s (2000) meta-analysis indicates that self-efficacy manipulations have the weakest impact on corresponding cognitions, whereas the narrative review of experimental studies presented earlier in this chapter suggests that self-efficacy manipulations have the most consistent impact on health-protective intentions. Future work may therefore consider additional ways of manipulating self-efficacy (cf. Bandura 1991), especially given that self-efficacy is the strongest PMT predictor of health-protective intentions.

Despite some encouraging results, there are a number of issues that future experimental tests of PMT need to address. Most experimental tests measure cognitions and intentions immediately after respondents have been exposed to an experimental manipulation. As such, these studies only assess the immediate impact of manipulating PMT variables (for exceptions, see Boer and Seydel 1995; Milne *et al.* 2002). Future experimental studies should therefore assess the longer term impact of manipulating PMT variables. In addition, few studies have assessed the impact of PMT manipulations on subsequent behaviour (for exceptions see Beck and Lund 1981; Wurtele and Maddux 1987; Wurtele 1988; Milne *et al.* 2002) and this issue also needs more attention in future work. In addition, when experimental manipulations of PMT variables have been found to impact on health-protective intentions and behaviour, few studies have tested whether their effects are mediated by PMT variables (see Rippetoe and Rogers 1987). Thus, there is a clear need for mediational analyses to assess the extent to which PMT manipulations have their impact through changing corresponding PMT variables. Finally, experimental studies should also examine the impact of manipulating specific PMT variables on maladaptive coping responses.

In conclusion, PMT has received strong support from correlational studies that have used PMT as a social cognition model to predict health behaviour and, to a lesser extent, from experimental studies that have manipulated specific PMT variables. Moreover, given its sound theoretical foundation and its overlap with other social cognition models, PMT is likely to continue to be an important model of health behaviour. In addition, as outlined above, there are various issues that require attention in future studies and these are likely to stimulate further research on PMT.

References

Abraham, C.S., Sheeran, P., Abrams, D. and Spears, R. (1994) Exploring teenagers' adaptive and maladaptive thinking in relation to the threat of HIV infection, *Psychology and Health*, 9, 253–72.

Ajzen, I. (1988) *Attitudes, Personality and Behavior*. Milton Keynes: Open University Press.

Ajzen, I. (1991) The theory of planned behavior, *Organizational Behavior and Human Decision Processes*, 50, 179–211.

Aspinwall, L.G., Kemeny, M.E., Taylor, S.E., Schneider, S.G. and Dudley, J.P. (1991) Psychosocial predictors of gay men's AIDS risk-reduction behavior, *Health Psychology*, 10, 432–44.

Bandura, A. (1986) *Social Foundations of Thought and Action: A Cognitive Social Theory*. Englewood Cliffs, NJ: Prentice-Hall.

Bandura, A. (1991) Self-efficacy mechanism in physiological activation and health-promoting behavior. In J. Madden (ed.) *Neurobiology of Learning, Emotion and Affect*. New York: Raven Press, 229–70.

Baron, R.M. and Kenny, D.A. (1986) The moderator–mediator distinction in social psychological research: conceptual, strategic, and statistical considerations, *Journal of Personality and Social Psychology*, 51, 1173–82.

Beck, K.H. and Lund, A.K. (1981) The effects of threat seriousness and personal efficacy upon intentions and behavior, *Journal of Applied Social Psychology*, 11, 401–15.

Ben-Ahron, V., White, D. and Phillips, K. (1995) Encouraging drinking at safe limits on single occasions: the potential contribution of protection motivation theory, *Alcohol and Alcoholism*, 30, 633–9.

Bengel, J., Belz-Merk, M. and Farin, E. (1996) The role of risk perception and efficacy cognitions in the prediction of HIV-related preventive behavior and condom use, *Psychology and Health*, 11, 505–25.

Bennett, P., Rowe, A. and Katz, D. (1998) Reported adherence with preventive asthma medication: a test of protection motivation theory, *Psychology, Health and Medicine*, 3, 347–54.

Boer, I. and Seydel, E.R. (1995) Protection motivation theory. In M. Conner and P. Norman (eds) *Predicting Health Behaviour*. Buckingham: Open University Press, 95–120.

Brown, J.D. (1991) Staying fit and staying well: physical fitness as a moderator of life stress, *Journal of Personality and Social Psychology*, 60, 555–61.

Cohen, J. (1992) A power primer, *Psychological Bulletin*, 112, 155–9.

Comrey, A.L. (1988) Factor analytic methods of scale development in personality and clinical psychology, *Journal of Consulting and Clinical Psychology*, 56, 754–61.

Conner, M. and Armitage, C. (1998) Extending the theory of planned behavior: a review and avenues for further research, *Journal of Applied Social Psychology*, 28, 1429–64.

Conner, M. and Norman, P. (1998) Health behaviour. In M. Johnston and D. Johnston (eds) *Health Psychology, Comprehensive Clinical Psychology*, Vol. 8. Oxford: Pergamon, 1–37.

Courneya, K.S. and Hellsten, L.A.M. (2001) Cancer prevention as a source of exercise motivation: an experimental test using protection motivation theory, *Psychology, Health and Medicine*, 6, 59–64.

Cronbach, L.J. (1951) Coefficient alpha and the internal structure of tests, *Psychometrika*, 16, 297–334.

DeVellis, R.F. (1991) *Scale Development: Theory and Applications*. Newbury Park, CA: Sage Publications.

DoH (Department of Health) (1992) *The Health of the Nation*. London: HMSO.

Eagly, A.H. and Chaiken, S. (1993) *The Psychology of Attitudes*. Fort Worth, TX: Harcourt Brace Jovanovich.

Eppright, D.R., Tanner, J.F. Jr and Hunt, J.B. (1994) Knowledge and the ordered protection motivation model: tools for preventing AIDS, *Journal of Business Research*, 30, 13–24.

Farin, E. (1994) Eine Metaanalyse Empirischer Studien zum Prädiktiven Wert Kognitiver Variablen der HIV-Bezogenen Risikowahrnehmung und-Verabeitung für das HIV-Risikoverhalten. Dissertation, Universität Freiburg.

Fishbein, M. and Ajzen, I. (1975) *Belief, Attitude, Intention, and Behavior*. New York: Wiley.

Floyd, D.L., Prentice-Dunn, S. and Rogers, R.W. (2000) A meta-analysis of protection motivation theory, *Journal of Applied Social Psychology*, 30, 407–29.

Flynn, M.F., Lyman, R.D. and Prentice–Dunn, S. (1995) Protection motivation theory and adherence to medical treatment regimens for muscular dystrophy, *Journal of Social and Clinical Psychology*, 14, 61–75.

Folkins, C.H. and Sime, W.E. (1981) Physical fitness training and mental health, *American Psychologist*, 36, 373–89.

Fruin, D.J., Pratt, C. and Owen, N. (1992) Protection motivation theory and adolescents' perceptions of exercise, *Journal of Applied Social Psychology*, 22, 55–69.

Gollwitzer, P.M. (1999) Implementation intentions: strong effects of simple plans, *American Psychologist*, 54, 493–503.

Greening, L. (1997) Adolescents' cognitive appraisals of cigarette smoking: an application of the protection motivation theory, *Journal of Applied Social Psychology*, 27, 1972–85.

Greening, L., Stoppelbein, L. and Jackson, M. (2001) Health education programs to prevent teen pregnancy, *Journal of Adolescent Health*, 28, 257–8.

Hodgkins, S. and Orbell, S. (1998) Can protection motivation theory predict behaviour? A longitudinal study exploring the role of previous behaviour, *Psychology and Health*, 13, 237–50.

Hovland, C., Janis, I.L. and Kelley, H. (1953) *Communication and Persuasion*. New Haven CT: Yale University Press.

Janis, I.L. (1967) Effects of fear arousal on attitude change: recent developments in theory and experimental research. In L.Berkowitz (ed.) *Advances in Experimental Social Psychology*, Vol. 3. New York: Academic Press, 166–224.

Joseph, J.G., Montgomery, S.B., Emmons, C.A., Kirscht, J.P., Kessler, R.C., Ostrow, D.G. *et al.* (1987) Perceived risk of AIDS: assessing the behavioral and psychosocial consequences in a cohort of gay men, *Journal of Applied Social Psychology*, 17, 231–50.

King, A.C., Taylor, C.B., Haskell, W.L. and DeBusk, R.F. (1989) Influence of regular aerobic exercise on psychological health: a randomized, controlled trial of healthy middle-aged adults, *Health Psychology*, 8, 305–24.

Kyes, K.B. (1995) Using fear to encourage safer sex: an application of protection motivation theory, *Journal of Psychology and Human Sexuality*, 7, 21–37.

Lazarus, R.S. (1991) Progress on a cognitive–motivational–relational theory of emotion, *American Psychologist*, 46, 819–34.

Lazarus, R.S. and Folkman, S. (1984) *Stress, Appraisal, and Coping*. New York: Springer.

Lennon, D., Stratman, F.W., Shrago, E., Nagle, F.J., Hanson, P.G., Maddon, M. and Spennetta, T. (1983) Total cholesterol and DHL cholesterol changes during acute, moderate intensity exercise in men and women, *Metabolism*, 32, 244–9.

Leventhal, H. (1970) Findings and theory in the study of fear communications. In L.Berkowitz (ed.) *Advances in Experimental Social Psychology*, Vol. 5. New York: Academic Press, 119–86.

Lipsey, M.W. (1990) *Design Sensitivity: Statistical Power for Experimental Research*. Beverly Hills, CA: Sage Publications.

Maddux, J.E. and Rogers, R.W. (1983) Protection motivation and self-efficacy: a revised theory of fear appeals and attitude change, *Journal of Experimental Social Psychology*, 19, 469–79.

Milne, S., Orbell, S. and Sheeran, P. (2002) Combining motivational and volitional interventions to promote exercise participation: protection motivation theory and implementation intentions, *British Journal of Health Psychology*, 7, 163–84.

Milne, S. and Sheeran, P. (2002) Combining motivational and volitional interventions to prevent testicular cancer. Paper presented to the 13th General Meeting of the European Association of Experimental Social Psychology, San Sebastian, Spain, June.

Milne, S., Sheeran, P. and Orbell, S. (2000) Prediction and intervention in health-related behavior: a meta-analytic review of protection motivation theory, *Journal of Applied Social Psychology*, 30, 106–43.

Murgraff, V., White, D. and Phillips, K. (1999) An application of protection motivation theory to riskier single-occasion drinking, *Psychology and Health*, 14, 339–50.

Norman, P., Searle, A., Harrad, R. and Vedhara, K. (2003) Predicting adherence to eye patching in children with amblyopia: an application of protection motivation theory, *British Journal of Health Psychology*, 8, 67–82.

OPCS (Office of Population Censuses and Surveys) (1989) *General Household Survey*. London: HMSO.

Orbell, S. and Sheeran, P. (1998) 'Inclined abstainers': a problem for predicting health-related behaviour, *British Journal of Social Psychology*, 37, 151–65.

Ouellette, J. and Wood, W. (1998) Habit and intention in everyday life: the multiple processes by which past behavior predicts future behavior, *Psychological Bulletin*, 124, 54–74.

Paffenbarger, R.S. and Hyde, R.T. (1984) Exercise in the prevention of coronary heart disease, *Preventive Medicine*, 13, 3–22.

Palardy, N., Greening, L., Ott, J., Holderby, A. and Atchison, J. (1998) Adolescents' health attitudes and adherence to treatment for insulin-dependent diabetes mellitus, *Developmental and Behavioral Pediatrics*, 19, 31–7.

Plotnikoff, R.C. and Higginbottom, N. (1995) Predicting low-fat diet intentions and behaviors for the prevention of coronary heart disease: an application of protection motivation theory among an Australian population, *Psychology and Health*, 10, 397–408.

Plotnikoff, R.C. and Higginbottom, N. (1998) Protection motivation theory and the prediction of exercise and low-fat diet behaviors among Australian cardiac patients, *Psychology and Health*, 13, 411–29.

Plotnikoff, R.C. and Higginbottom, N. (2002) Protection motivation theory and exercise behaviour change for the prevention of coronary heart disease in a high-risk, Australian representative community sample of adults, *Psychology, Health and Medicine*, 7, 87–98.

Powell, K.E., Thompson, P.D., Caspersen, C.J. and Kendrick, J.S. (1987) Physical activity and the incidence of coronary heart disease, *Annual Review of Public Health*, 8, 253–87.

Rippetoe, P.A. and Rogers, R.W. (1987) Effects of components of protection motivation theory on adaptive and maladpative coping with a health threat, *Journal of Personality and Social Psychology*, 52, 596–604.

Rogers, R.W. (1975) A protection motivation theory of fear appeals and attitude change, *Journal of Psychology* 91, 93–114.

Rogers, R.W. (1983) Cognitive and physiological processes in fear appeals and attitude change: a revised theory of protection motivation. In J.T. Cacioppo and R.E. Petty (eds) *Social Psychophysiology: A Source Book*. New York: Guilford Press, 153–76.

Rogers, R.W. and Prentice-Dunn, S. (1997) Protection motivation theory. In D.S. Gochman (ed.) *Handbook of Behavior Research, Vol. 1: Personal and Social Determinants*. New York: Plenum, 113–32.

Rosenstock, I.M. (1974) Historical origins of the health belief model, *Health Education Monographs*, 2, 1–8.

Rosenthal, M., Haskell, W.L., Solomon, R., Widstrom, A. and Reavan, G.M. (1983) Demonstration of a relationship between level of physical training and insulin stimulated glucose utilization in normal humans, *Diabetes*, 32, 408–11.

Rosenthal, R. (1991) *Meta-analytic procedures for social research* (2nd edition). Newbury Park, CA: Sage Publications.

Rudman, L.A., Gonzales, M.H. and Borgida, E. (1999) Mishandling the gift of life: noncompliance in renal transplant patients, *Journal of Social and Applied Psychology*, 29, 834–51.

Sallis, J.F., Haskell, W.L., Wood, P.D., Fortmann, S.P., Rogers, T., Blair, S.N. and Paffenbarger, R.S. (1985) Physical activity assessment in the five-city project, *American Journal of Epidemiology*, 121, 91–106.

Searle, A., Vedhara, K., Norman, P., Frost, A. and Harrad, R. (2000) Compliance with eye patching in children and its psychosocial effects: a qualitative application of protection motivation theory, *Psychology, Health and Medicine*, 5, 43–54.

Seydel, E., Taal, E. and Wiegman, O. (1990) Risk-appraisal, outcome and self-efficacy expectancies: cognitive factors in preventive behaviour related to cancer, *Psychology and Health*, 4, 99–109.

Sheeran, P. and Orbell, S. (1996) How confidently can we infer health beliefs from questionnaire responses?, *Psychology and Health*, 11, 273–90.

Singer, R.N. (1992) Physical activity and psychological benefits: a position statement, *The Sport Psychologist*, 6, 199–203.

Siscovick, D.S., LaPorte, R.E., and Newman, J.M. (1985) The disease specific benefits and risks of physical activity and exercise, *Public Health Reports*, 100, 180–8.

Stainback, R.D. and Rogers, R.W. (1983) Identifying effective components of alcohol abuse prevention programs: effects of fear appeals, message style and source expertise, *International Journal of Addictions*, 18, 393–405.

Stanley, M.A. and Maddux, J.E. (1986) Cognitive processes in health enhancement: investigation of a combined protection motivation and self-efficacy model, *Basic and Applied Social Psychology*, 7, 101–13.

Steffen, V.J. (1990) Men's motivation to perform testicle self-exam: effects of prior knowledge and an education brochure, *Journal of Applied Social Psychology*, 20, 681–702.

Sutton, S. (1982) Fear-arousing communications: a critical examination of theory and research. In J.R. Eiser (ed.) *Social Psychology and Behavioural Medicine*. London: Wiley, 303–37.

Tanner, J.F. Jr, Day, E. and Crask, M.R. (1989) Protection motivation theory: an extension of fear appeals theory in communication, *Journal of Business Research*, 19, 267–76.

Tanner, J.F. Jr, Hunt, J.B. and Eppright, D.R. (1991) The protection motivation model: a normative model of fear appeals, *Journal of Marketing*, 55, 36–45.

Taylor, A.H. and May, S. (1996) Threat and coping appraisal as determinants of compliance with sports injury rehabilitation. An application of protection motivation theory, *Journal of Sports Sciences*, 14, 471–82.

Tozuka, T., Hayakawa, M. and Fukuda, H. (2001) Determinants of preventive intentions for endocrine disrupters: an application of the protection motivation theory, *Japanese Journal of Experimental Social Psychology*, 41, 26–36.

Triandis, H.C. (1977) *Interpersonal Behavior*. Monterey, CA: Brooks-Cole.

Van der Velde, F.W. and Van der Pligt, J. (1991) AIDS-related behavior: coping, protection motivation, and previous behavior, *Journal of Behavioral Medicine*, 14, 429–51.

Van der Velde, F.W. and Hooykaas, C. (1996) Conditional versus unconditional risk estimates in models of AIDS-related risk behaviour, *Psychology and Health*, 12, 87–100.

Van der Velde, F.W. and Van der Pligt, J. (1991) AIDS-related behavior: coping, protection motivation, and previous behavior, *Journal of Behavioral Medicine*, 14, 429–51.

Weinstein, N.D. and Nicolich, M. (1993) Correct and incorrect interpretations of correlations between risk perceptions and risk behaviors, *Health Psychology*, 12, 235–45.

Wurtele, S.K. (1988) Increasing women's calcium intake: the role of health beliefs, intentions and health value, *Journal of Applied Social Psychology*, 18, 627–39.

Wurtele, S.K. and Maddux, J.E. (1987) Relative contributions of protection motivation components in predicting exercise intentions and behavior, *Health Psychology*, 6, 453–66.

Yzer, M.C., Fisher, J.D., Bakker, A.B., Siero, F.W. and Misovich, S.J. (1998) The effects of information about AIDS risk and self-efficacy on women's intention to engage in AIDS-preventive behavior, *Journal of Applied Social Psychology*, 28, 1837–52.

4 | ALEKSANDRA LUSZCZYNSKA
AND RALF SCHWARZER

SOCIAL COGNITIVE THEORY

1 General background

The present chapter examines the role that Social Cognitive Theory (SCT) plays in the adoption, initiation, and maintenance of health behaviours. It describes the key constructs of social cognitive theory (Bandura 1977, 1992, 2000a, 2000b), such as perceived self-efficacy and outcome expectancies, and it also refers to other constructs, such as goals and socio-structural impediments and facilitators.

Historically, SCT dates back to the 1970s when a paradigm shift took place from a focus on behaviour to a focus on cognitions. Bandura's first book in 1959 was on *Adolescent Aggression* which was followed in 1973 by *Aggression: A Social Learning Analysis*, still based on behavioural analysis and examining role models. After having found out how people learn by observation, Bandura extended this idea to abstract modelling of rule-governed behaviour and to disinhibition through vicarious experience. Then, in 1977, he published his *Social Learning Theory* that markedly altered the direction that psychology was to take in subsequent decades. The landmark article on self-efficacy was also published at this time (Bandura 1977). The discipline became aware of the prominent role of social modelling in human motivation, thought and action. Until that time, researchers had focused on learning through the consequences of one's behaviour. Bandura demonstrated that the tedious and hazardous process of trial and error learning can be shortcut through social modelling of knowledge and competencies. Social modelling is not simply response mimicry; rather individuals generate new behaviour patterns in a similar way by going beyond what they have seen or heard. In addition to cultivating new competencies, social modelling affects motivation by instilling behavioural outcome expectations. In his 1986 book, *Social Foundations of*

Thought and Action: A Social Cognitive Theory, Bandura fully developed his Social Cognitive Theory of human functioning. In this model of triadic reciprocal causation, people are actors as well as products of their environment. This work has been crowned by the 1997 book *Self-Efficacy: The Exercise of Control* (Bandura 1997).

According to SCT, behavioural change is made possible by a personal sense of control. If people believe that they can take action to solve a problem instrumentally, they become more inclined to do so and feel more committed to the decision. Perceived self-efficacy pertains to personal action control or agency. People who believe that they can cause events may lead more active and self-determined lives. This 'can do' cognition mirrors a sense of control over one's environment. It reflects the belief of being able to master challenging demands by means of adaptive action. Self-efficacy makes a difference in how people feel, think and act (Bandura 1977, 1997). A low sense of self-efficacy is associated with depression, anxiety and helplessness. It has been found that a strong sense of personal efficacy is related to better social integration. In terms of thinking, a strong sense of competence facilitates cognitive processes and performance in a variety of settings, including quality of decision making, goal setting and academic achievement (Maddux 1995; Bandura 1997, 2001; Bandura *et al.* 2002).

Outcome expectancies, the other key construct in social cognitive theory, are beliefs about the consequences of one's action. Physical, social and self-evaluative outcome expectancies have been distinguished. One's behaviour may provoke bodily changes, responses from others, or feelings about oneself. Together with self-efficacy they influence goal setting and goal pursuit.

Social cognitive theory has been applied to such diverse areas as school achievement, emotional disorders, mental and physical health, career choice, and sociopolitical change. Social cognitive theory has become a fundamental resource in clinical, educational, social, developmental, health and personality psychology.

2 Description of the model

According to social cognitive theory (SCT), human motivation and action are extensively regulated by forethought. This anticipatory control mechanism involves expectations that might refer to outcomes of undertaking a specific action. The theory outlines a number of crucial factors that influence behaviour. The first factor is perceived self-efficacy, which is concerned with people's beliefs in their capabilities to perform a specific action required to attain a desired outcome. Outcome expectancies are the other core construct of SCT which are concerned with people's beliefs about the possible consequences of their actions. Besides these two cognitions, SCT also includes goals and perceived impediments and opportunity structures. These constructs are displayed in Figure 4.1, which illustrates their interplay throughout the behaviour change process.

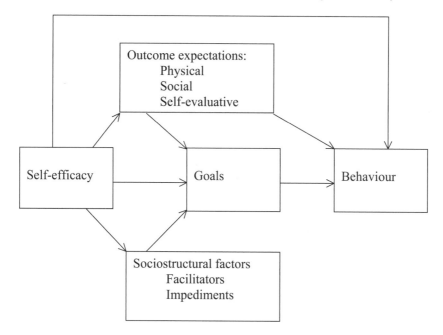

Figure 4.1 An illustration of social cognitive theory (see Bandura 2000b)

2.1 Self-efficacy and outcome expectancies as core SCT constructs

Perceived self-efficacy is concerned with individuals' beliefs in their capability to exercise control over challenging demands and their own functioning. In a unifying theory of behaviour change, Bandura hypothesized that expectations of self-efficacy are self-regulatory cognitions that determine whether instrumental actions will be initiated, how much effort will be expended, and how long it will be sustained in the face of obstacles and failures. Self-efficacy has an influence on preparing for action because self-related cognitions are a major ingredient in the motivation process. Self-efficacy levels can enhance or impede motivation. Persons with low self-efficacy harbour pessimistic thoughts about their likely accomplishments and personal development. Self-efficacy is directly related to behaviour. Perceived self-efficacy represents the confidence that one can employ the skills necessary to resist temptation, cope with stress, and mobilize one's resources required to meet the situational demands. Self-efficacy beliefs affect the amount of effort to change risk behaviour and the persistence to continue striving in the face of barriers and setbacks that may undermine motivation. Self-efficacy is based on different sources (Bandura 1997). First, self-efficacy beliefs can be enhanced through personal accomplishment or mastery, as far as success is attributed internally and can be repeated. A second source is vicarious experience. When a 'model person', that is similar to the individual, successfully masters a difficult situation, social comparison processes can enhance self-efficacy beliefs.

Third, self-efficacy beliefs can also be enhanced through verbal persuasion by others (e.g. a health educator reassures a patient that she will certainly perform cancer screening properly due to her competence). The last source of influence is emotional arousal, that is, the person may experience no apprehension in a threatening situation and, as a result, may feel capable of mastering the situation. These four informational sources vary in strength and importance in the order presented here, with personal mastery being the strongest source of self-efficacy.

Self-efficacy can also influence behaviour change through the emotions that might arise while pursuing the goal. Optimistic self-beliefs about one's own competence create positive affective states instead of negative ones, such as anxiety. Negative emotions may generate cognitive confusion that leads to worse solutions while facing problems (see Maddux and Lewis 1995).

Further, optimistic self-beliefs about one's ability to execute an action successfully can also influence other cognitions, motivational and affective processes, and selection processes. According to SCT, self-efficacy influences the appraisal of stressful stimuli (threat, harm or challenge). In this way it may affect subsequent emotional states of an individual.

Self-efficacy is not the same as unrealistic optimism, since it is based on experience and does not lead to unreasonable risk taking. Instead, it leads to venturesome behaviour that is within reach of one's capabilities. Compared to similar constructs such as self-esteem, self-concept, sense of control, and so on, the essential distinction between those and self-efficacy lies in three aspects: (a) self-efficacy implies an internal attribution (a person is the cause of the action), (b) it is prospective, referring to future behaviours, and (c) it is an operative construct, which means that this cognition is proximal to the critical behaviour. Self-efficacy can be better understood by contrasting it to a different construct, namely *outcome expectancies*, that also plays a central role in Bandura's (1997) theory.

While perceived self-efficacy refers to personal action control or agency, outcome expectancies pertain to the perception of possible consequences of one's action. Outcome expectancies can be organized along three dimensions: (a) area of consequences, (b) positive or negative consequences, and (c) short-term or long-term consequences. Areas of consequences can be split into three. *Physical outcome expectations*, such as expectations of discomfort or disease symptoms, refer to the anticipation of what will be experienced after behaviour change takes place. These include both the short- and long-term effects of behaviour change. For example, immediately after quitting smoking, an ex-smoker might observe a reduction of coughing (positive consequence) and a higher level of muscle tension (negative consequence). In the long run, an ex-smoker might expect lower susceptibility to respiratory infections (positive consequence) but an increased susceptibility to weight gain (negative consequence). *Social outcome expectancies* refer to anticipated social responses after behaviour change. Smokers might expect disapproval from friends who continue to smoke, or, positively, they might expect their family to congratulate them on quitting smoking. In the long run, ex-smokers might expect that they will increase their chances to find and maintain an attractive partner or a better job. *Self-evaluative outcome expectations* refer to the anticipation of experiences, such as being ashamed, being proud of oneself, or satisfied, due to internal standards. This three-factor structure of outcome expectancies has been empirically supported (see Dijkstra *et al.* 1997).

Expectancies about outcomes of personal actions and self-efficacy beliefs include the option to cope instrumentally with health threats by taking preventive action. These action beliefs and personal resource beliefs reflect a functional optimism. Empirically, the distinction between them may be difficult to confirm because they often operate in tandem. In making judgements about health-related goals, people often unite personal agency with appropriate means. Perceived self-efficacy may include outcome expectancies because individuals believe that they can produce the responses necessary for desired outcomes. It might also be argued that outcome expectancies, or judgements about what will happen if an individual performs a certain action, assume that the person might be able to perform the action leading to these results. On the other hand, outcome expectancies and self-efficacy beliefs may diverge in certain situations. For example, many smokers may believe that quitting would lead to positive health outcomes but, at the same time, do not feel confident in their ability to quit.

Both outcome expectancies and self-efficacy beliefs play influential roles in adopting new health behaviours, eliminating detrimental habits, and maintaining what has been achieved. These constructs are seen as direct predictors of behaviours. They also operate through indirect pathways, affecting goal setting and the perception of sociostructural factors.

2.2 Goals, sociostructural factors, and their relations to self-efficacy and outcome expectancies

In adopting a desired behaviour, individuals first form a *goal* and then attempt to execute the action. Goals serve as self-incentives and guides to health behaviours. According to SCT, a distinction can be made between distal goals and proximal goals. The latter regulate the amount of invested effort and guide action. Intentions, as defined in other social cognitive theories, are more similar to proximal goals than to distal goals (Bandura 1997). Terms such as 'I intend to' or 'I aim to' reflect goals. All major theories agree upon the suggestion that goals or intentions should be as specific as possible in order to facilitate subsequent action (Fishbein and Ajzen 1975; Bandura 1997; Gollwitzer 1999), although the preferred terms differ between these theories. There is a continuum from distal to proximal goals, as well as a continuum from goal intentions to implementation intentions. In any case, goals (or intentions) are seen as direct and sometimes sufficient predictors of behaviour.

Outcome expectancies encourage the decision to change one's behaviour. People weigh the pros and cons of a certain behaviour which means that they harbour positive and negative outcome expectancies. Depending on this decisional balance they may develop an intention to act or an intention not to act (DiClemente *et al.* 1985).

People would not set goals for themselves if they thought that the pursuit of such goals would have more disadvantages than advantages. Thus, outcome expectancies are seen as important determinants in the initial formation of intentions, but are less important in the later phases of action control. Self-efficacy, on the other hand, seems to be crucial, especially after the formation of an intention to adopt a health behaviour when the task is to translate the intention into action and to self-regulate the goal pursuit process. According to SCT, forming a goal is a necessary but not sufficient condition; it is a precondition but does not ensure that an individual will actually pursue the goal (Bandura 2000b).

Self-efficacy beliefs affect behaviours indirectly through their impact on goals. Self-efficacy, among other factors, influences which challenges people decide to meet and how high they set their goals. Persons with high self-efficacy in a specific domain select more challenging and ambitious goals. Optimistic self-beliefs about one's capability to exert control over one's actions influence how people respond to discrepancies between their personal goals and their performance. Compared to those with low optimistic self-beliefs, self-efficacious individuals invest more effort when the discrepancies are larger (see DeVellis and DeVellis 2000). High self-efficacy not only improves goal setting, but leads to more persistence in pursuing the goal. Self-efficacy also promotes the effective use of cognitive resources, diagnosing and searching for solutions when obstacles arise (Maddux and Lewis 1995).

Goal setting also depends on perceived sociostructural factors. Sociostructural factors refer to the impediments (barriers) or opportunities that reside in living conditions, health systems, political, economic or environmental systems (Bandura 1997). Optimistic self-beliefs about one's efficacy also control how people perceive opportunities and impediments. Self-efficacy influences whether individuals pay attention to opportunities or barriers in their life circumstances. Self-efficacious individuals who, for example, intend to exercise might focus on cues in their environment, such as hiking paths and cycling routes. Those who are less confident about their physical competence might focus instead on the lack of a gym in their neighbourhood. People with strong self-efficacy recognize that they are able to overcome obstacles, and focus on opportunities. They believe that they are able to exercise control, even if the environment provides constraints rather than opportunities (see Bandura 1997, 2000b). Perceived self-efficacy has become the core construct within social cognitive theory. If people are seen as self-organizing, proactive, self-reflecting, and self-regulating creatures, being actors as well as products of their environment, then they must be driven by self-beliefs that allow them to make judgements and to exert control wherever necessary.

3 Summary of research

In the following section, relationships between constructs from SCT and specific health behaviours are reviewed. A number of studies on the adoption of health practices have measured self-efficacy, outcome expectancies, goals and impediments to assess their impact on the initiation and performance of health-related practices. As people proceed from considering precautions in a general way toward shaping a behavioural intention, contemplating detailed action plans, and actually performing a health behaviour on a regular basis, they crystallize expectations about the outcomes of their actions and beliefs in their capabilities to initiate change. Perceived self-efficacy and outcome expectancies, therefore, are seen to be related to the adoption of health-promoting behaviours in a variety of settings. Most of the research that claims to test SCT assesses only these two constructs.

There is a growing number of studies merging SCT with other approaches, such as the transtheoretical model (TTM) or the theory of planned behaviour (TPB). For example, researchers have looked at the determinants of sun-protective practices of pre-school staff towards their students (James *et al.* 2002). Self-efficacy regarding the ability to apply sunscreen lotion and to protect students from sun exposure, positive outcome expectancies about sun protection, and impediments to sunscreen use were assessed along with perceived norms for sun avoidance and sunscreen use. Self-efficacy turned out to exert the strongest direct effect on protective behaviour, that is, applying and reapplying sunscreen, and to be the only significant predictor of sun avoidance behaviour (using long-sleeved shirts, hats, setting up shaded areas). Self-efficacy also predicted outcome expectancies and impediments related to sunscreen use, in line with the assumptions of SCT. Perceived norms and impediments to use sunscreen predicted sunscreen behaviours, but they were not significantly associated with sun avoidance behaviour.

Similarly, a study on vigorous physical activity among schoolgirls provided strong support for SCT, modest support for the theory of planned behaviour, and only weak support for the theory of reasoned action (Motl *et al.* 2002). First, by means of confirmatory factor analysis, self-efficacy and behavioural control emerged as separate constructs, although their intercorrelation was high (0.67). Second, self-efficacy was the stronger predictor of moderate and vigorous physical activity, whereas behavioural control predicted only vigorous activity.

Table 4.1 provides details of a number of studies that have tested SCT components as predictors of health behaviours. All these studies examine the role of self-efficacy, since SCT emphasizes self-efficacy as the main and the most proximal predictor and antecedent of human behaviour. Some authors seem to believe that SCT is equivalent to self-efficacy theory, provoking repeated statements by Bandura (1997) that SCT is not a 'one-factor theory'. There are hundreds of studies that include perceived self-efficacy, but in the present context, we focus on some typical studies that shed light on the particular function that self-efficacy may have in predicting health behaviour change, mainly in combination with other SCT constructs. The following section describes the results of such studies in more detail.

Table 4.1 Illustrative applications of social cognitive theory

Behaviours	SCT Predictors	Authors and dates of publications
Adherence to medication and rehabilitation	Self-efficacy	Taylor et al. (1985), Toshima et al. (1992), Clark and Dodge (1999), Catz et al. (2000), Bosse et al. (2002), Molassiotis et al. 2002, Stewart et al. (2003)
	Self-efficacy, outcome expectancies	Murphy et al. (2002), Williams and Bond (2002)
Sexual risk behaviours	Self-efficacy	Trobst et al. (2002)
	Self-efficacy, goals	Kok et al. (1992)
	Self-efficacy, outcome expectancies	Dilorio et al. (1997); Dilorio et al. (2000a), Dilorio et al. (2000b), Semple et al. (2000), Dilorio et al. (2001)
Physical exercise	Self-efficacy	Ewart (1992), Holman and Lorig (1992), Strauss et al. (2001)
	Self-efficacy, goals	Rodgers et al. (2002)
	Self-efficacy, outcome expectancies	Rovniak et al. (2002)
	Self-efficacy, outcome expectancies, perceived impediments	Dishman et al. (1992)
	Self-efficacy, perceived impediments	Booth et al. (2000)
	Self-efficacy, outcome expectancies, goals	Dzewaltowski (1989)
Nutrition and weight control	Self-efficacy	Senecal et al. (2000), Savoca and Miller (2001), Dearden et al. (2002), Pinto et al. (2002b)
	Self-efficacy, outcome expectancies	Conn (1997), Anderson et al. (2000), Resnicow et al. (2000)
	Self-efficacy, goals	Schnoll and Zimmerman (2001)
	Self-efficacy, perceived impediments	Van Duyn et al. (2001)

Table 4.1   cont'd

Detection behaviours	Self-efficacy	Alagna and Reddy (1987), Chalmers and Luker (1996)
	Self-efficacy, outcome expectancies	Champion (1990), Umeh and Rogan-Gibson (2001), Cormier *et al.* (2002), Kremers *et al.* (2000), Schnoll *et al.* (2002)
	Self-efficacy, outcome expectancies, goals	Seydel *et al.* (1990)
Addictive behaviours	Self-efficacy	Dijkstra and De Vries (2000), Shiffman *et al.* 2000, Christiansen *et al.* (2002), Gwaltney *et al.* (2002)
	Self-efficacy, outcome expectancies	Dijkstra *et al.* (1999), Cohen and Fromme (2002)

3.1 Adherence to medication and rehabilitation

Adherence to medication requirements or suggested treatment is related to self-regulatory beliefs. New treatments for HIV can improve immune status and decrease mortality, but nearly one-third of patients miss medication doses every five days (see Catz *et al.* 2000). This poor compliance may result partly from patients' experience of adverse side effects, but it may also be due to a lack of self-regulatory skills. Studies on adherence in highly active antiretroviral therapy (HAART) provide consistent findings on the predictors of medication adherence. Non-compliance is known to be related to the complexity and to the adverse side effects of treatment. Considering psychosocial factors, it is also related to lack of social support and lack of self-efficacy (Catz *et al.* 2000). For example, Molassiotis *et al.* (2002) have found that adherence to antiretroviral medication in patients with HIV was strongly related to self-efficacy (that is, optimistic self-beliefs about the ability to follow the medication regimen). These optimistic self-beliefs, together with anxiety and nausea, explained 30 per cent of variance of adherence to the recommended treatment. The relation between social support and medication adherence was weaker than the relation between self-efficacy and medication adherence. Low self-efficacy, together with low outcome expectancies regarding the benefits following the treatment regimen, have also been found to be related to low medication adherence in HIV symptomatic women or women with AIDS (Murphy *et al.* 2002).

Self-efficacy has been also found to be related to adherence to recommended treatments for different chronic health problems. Among older patients with cardiac disease, adherence to a complex treatment has also been found to depend on self-efficacy. Taking medicine as prescribed, getting adequate exercise, managing stress, and following a recommended diet were explained by self-efficacy beliefs measured four and 12 months earlier (see Clark and Dodge 1999). Optimistic self-beliefs have also been shown to mediate the relation between emotional distress and adherence to medical regimen and glycemic control in patients with diabetes (Stewart *et al.* 2003). Another study on compliance with a diabetic regimen showed that self-efficacy was associated with patients' compliance with blood glucose testing, diet, and exercise (Williams and Bond 2002). Patients with the highest rates of glucose testing were found to have high self-efficacy and high outcome expectancies. Those with high outcome expectancies, but low self-efficacy, did not have blood tests performed as often as recommended. Additionally, perceived family support was associated with diabetic self-care. However, when the effects of self-efficacy were controlled, social support no longer predicted compliance. These results are perfectly in line with SCT, which emphasizes the role of self-efficacy as the main self-regulatory factor in health behaviour change.

Recovery from disease or adaptation after surgery are influenced by self-regulatory beliefs, such as self-efficacy. Recovery of cardiovascular function in post-coronary patients is similarly enhanced by beliefs in one's physical and cardiac efficacy (Taylor *et al.* 1985). Cognitive-behavioural treatment of patients with rheumatoid arthritis has been found to enhance their efficacy beliefs, reduce pain and joint inflammation, and improve psychosocial functioning (O'Leary *et al.* 1988). Moreover, patients' confidence in their ability to resume life activities after severe injury followed by an amputation of a limb was among the most powerful psychosocial predictors of post-surgical adaptation. A study on patients after amputation or reconstruction of a leg showed that their recovery and adaptation two years after surgery was predicted not only by socioeconomic status, but also by self-efficacy (Bosse *et al.* 2002). Patients with chronic obstructive pulmonary disease tend to avoid physical exertion due to discomfort, but rehabilitation programmes insist on adherence to an exercise regimen. Compliance with such regimens was found to improve after these patients received a treatment that increased their confidence in their own capabilities (see Toshima *et al.* 1992).

3.2 Sexual risk behaviours

Perceived self-efficacy has been studied to explain unprotected sexual behaviour, such as not using contraceptives to avoid unwanted pregnancies. Teenage women with a high rate of intercourse have been found to use contraceptives more effectively if they believed they could exercise control over their sexual activities (Levinson 1982; Wang *et al.* 2003). Most of the studies referring to risky sexual behaviours have examined social cognitive predictors of condom use. Optimistic beliefs in one's capability to negotiate safer sex practices has emerged as the most important predictor of protective behaviours (Basen-Engquist 1992; Kasen *et al.* 1992; Wulfert and Wan 1993).

The social cognitive predictors of condom use have been studied in various populations. Support for SCT has been provided in a study of sexually active college students (Dilorio *et al.* 2000b). Self-efficacy was found to be directly related to condom use, but optimistic self-beliefs were also indirectly related to condom use, through the effect of self-efficacy on outcome expectancies. In line with Bandura's (1997) theory, self-efficacy predicted emotional state (anxiety), but this state was unrelated to health protective behaviour. Amongst sexually active adolescents, those who expressed confidence in their ability to put on a condom and in being able to refuse intercourse with a sexual partner were more likely to use condoms consistently. In addition, holding favourable outcome expectancies, associated with condom use, predicted more protective behaviours (Dilorio *et al.* 2001).

Condom use amongst HIV-positive gay and bisexual men can be explained by constructs from SCT. Men with anonymous sexual partners have been found to have the lowest scores on self-efficacy and outcome expectancies regarding condom use, negotiation with their partners and disclosure (see Semple *et al.* 2000). Unprotected anal intercourse was predicted by low outcome expectancies for safer sex negotiation. It was related to low self-efficacy for condom use and for negotiation. Results confirming the beneficial role of self-efficacy and outcome expectancies have been also obtained in other high-risk groups, such as patients with sexually transmitted diseases (see Dilorio *et al.* 1997).

Kok *et al.* (1992) reported a study on drug addicts' use of condoms and clean needles. Intentions and behaviours were predicted by attitudes, social norms and self-efficacy beliefs. Perceived self-efficacy correlated with the intention to use clean needles ($r = 0.35$), clean needle use ($r = 0.46$), the intention to use condoms ($r = 0.74$), and condom use ($r = 0.67$). Self-efficacy has also been found to discriminate high- and low-risk groups that differ in shared needle usage and sexual contacts with drug addicts (Trobst *et al.* 2002).

Both outcome expectancies and self-efficacy might refer to the same area of skills necessary to achieve a specific goal. For example, regarding safe sexual behaviour, they might refer to communication skills. Self-efficacy includes the confidence in one's ability to communicate about safe sex practices, whereas expectancies may pertain to outcomes of safer sex communication. Both factors should be directly related to actual safe sex communication and practice (see Dilorio *et al.* 2000a). In a sample of students, communication self-efficacy was directly and indirectly (via expectancies about outcomes of communication) related to the frequency of talking about safe sex practices with a partner. Both social cognitive variables predicted actual condom use. These associations were stronger than the relation between safe sex communication and safe sex practice itself.

3.3 Physical exercise

Regular physical exercise depends on the optimistic self-belief of being able to perform the behaviour appropriately. Perceived self-efficacy has been found to be a major instigating force in forming intentions to exercise and in maintaining the practice for an extended time period (Shaw *et al.* 1992; McAuley 1993; Rodgers *et al.* 2002; Rovniak *et al.* 2002).

Studies using objective measures of physical activity, such as a motion detector monitoring physical activity over a certain time period, have shown that self-efficacy is related to a high level of physical activity among 10- to 16-year-old adolescents (Strauss *et al.* 2001). The prediction of self-reported levels of physical activity might differ from the prediction of electromechanically measured activity. In a sample of young adults, outcome expectancies, perceived barriers and physical self-efficacy explained approximately 26 per cent of the variance of physical activity, measured by means of self-report (Dishman *et al.* 1992). However, an objective index of physical activity (a motion sensor worn by participants for a week) was unrelated to self-efficacy, but was related to outcome expectancies and perceived barriers. Endurance in physical performance has been found to be dependent on experimentally created efficacy beliefs in a series of experiments on competitive efficacy by Weinberg *et al.* (1979, 1980).

Participation in regular physical activity has been identified as the key health behaviour in preventing chronic disease. In a self-management programme, rheumatoid arthritis patients were successfully motivated to engage in regular physical exercise by enhancing their perceived self-efficacy (Holman and Lorig 1992). In applying self-efficacy theory to recovery from heart disease, patients who suffered a myocardial infarction were prescribed a moderate exercise regimen (Ewart 1992). Self-efficacy beliefs predicted both under-exercise and over-exertion during programmed exercise. In an intervention with older adults, an increase in beliefs about the ability to overcome barriers led to increased adherence to physical activity up to 12 months (Brassington *et al.* 2002). In a random sample of persons over 60 years old, physical activity was found to be related to perceived environmental barriers (such as access to local facilities and finding footpaths for safe walking) and self-efficacy (see Booth *et al.* 2000). The results were in line with Bandura's (2000a) suggestion that self-efficacy is related to sociostructural factors that are relevant for health behaviours, such as perceived environmental facilitators and impediments, and with the assumption that these sociostructural factors are directly related to health behaviours (see Figure 4.1).

There are a few studies that have compared the predictive power of constructs derived from different theories. Dzewaltowski (1989) compared the predictive utility of the theory of reasoned action and SCT in the field of exercise motivation. The exercise behaviour of 328 students was recorded for seven weeks and then related to prior measures of different cognitive factors. Behavioural intention was measured by asking the individuals about the likelihood that they would perform exercise behaviour. Attitude toward physical exercise, perceived behavioural control and beliefs about the subjective norms concerning exercise were assessed. The theory of reasoned action fitted the data, as indicated by a path analysis. Exercise behaviour correlated with intention (r = 0.22), attitude (r = 0.18) and behavioural control beliefs (r = 0.13). In addition, three social-cognitive variables were assessed: (a) strength of self-efficacy to participate in an exercise programme when faced with impediments, (b) 13 expected outcomes multiplied by the evaluation of those outcomes, and, finally, (c) self-satisfaction or dissatisfaction with level of activities and multiple outcomes of exercise. Exercise behaviour was correlated with perceived self-efficacy (r = 0.34), outcome expectancies (r = 0.15) and dissatisfaction (r = 0.23), as well as with the interactions of these factors. Individuals with higher scores on the three social cognitive constructs at the onset of the programme exercised more days per week. Those who were confident that they could adhere to the strenuous exercise programme, who were dissatisfied with their present level of physical activity, and who expected positive outcomes also exercised more. Theory of reasoned action variables did not account for any unique variance in exercise behaviour after controlling for the social cognitive factors. These findings indicate that SCT provides powerful explanatory constructs. Other studies using constructs from different theories also show that the effects of self-efficacy on physical activity are stronger than those of other psychosocial determinants (see Rovniak *et al.* 2002).

3.4 Nutrition and weight control

Aspects of diet and weight control can also be governed by self-efficacy beliefs (Glynn and Ruderman 1986; Bagozzi and Warshaw 1990; Hofstetter *et al.* 1990; Shannon *et al.* 1990; Senecal *et al.* 2000). In the context of weight control, it has been found that self-efficacy operates best in concert with general lifestyle changes, including physical exercise and provision of social support. In relation to diet, nationally representative surveys of US adults on daily food intake has shown that self-efficacy is among the factors most consistently and strongly associated with higher consumption of fruit and vegetables (see Van Duyn *et al.* 2001).

According to SCT, self-efficacy is connected to outcome expectancies and goal setting. Self-efficacy has been shown to be a significant predictor of physical, social and self-evaluative outcome expectancies regarding healthy nutrition (Anderson *et al.* 2000). A study using an objective measure of nutrition behaviour, namely grocery receipts, demonstrated that the effect of self-efficacy on fat, fibre, fruit and vegetable intake was mediated by physical outcome expectations. Nutrition goal setting was linked to higher dietary fibre self-efficacy and actual fibre intake. Compared to students who did not set a nutrition goal, goal setters scored 15 per cent higher in optimistic self-beliefs on dietary fibre intake and reported a 91 per cent higher consumption of fibre (see Schnoll and Zimmerman 2001). In a similar study, self-efficacy to eat more fruit and vegetables as well as outcome expectancies in terms of fruit and vegetable intake predicted a 24-hour recall of actual fruit and vegetables intake (Resnicow *et al.* 2000). Additionally, these fruit- and vegetable-specific predictors were inversely related to an unhealthy diet, that is, high-fat cooking.

Studies aimed at predicting nutrition in vulnerable populations or patients with chronic or terminal diseases usually provide support for SCT. The nutrition of women 65 years or older has been found to be related to current self-efficacy, but not to outcome expectancies (Conn 1997). Besides knowledge about proper nutrition, dietary self-efficacy and perceived spousal support were associated with dietary behaviours amongst Type 2 diabetes patients (Savoca and Miller 2001). Diabetes-related self-efficacy was found to be strongly related to maintenance of diabetes self-care (diet, exercise and glucose testing; see Bond 2002). The most powerful effects were observed when strong optimistic self-beliefs were combined with strong beliefs about outcomes (Bond 2002). Nutrition and exercise self-efficacy were also connected to the maintenance of diet and physical activity in breast cancer patients (Pinto *et al.* 2002b).

Self-efficacy has also been found to be a significant determinant of caregiver behaviour. Self-efficacious caregivers supplied their 6- to 18-month old children with healthy foods and washed their children's hands more often (see Dearden *et al.* 2002). Improving medical students' knowledge as well as their nutrition self-efficacy might translate into better professional practice in future physicians. When consulting cardiovascular patients, medical students with higher nutrition self-efficacy addressed the topic of preventive nutrition more frequently (see Carson *et al.* 2002).

3.5 Detective behaviours

The role of SCT has also been analysed in the context of symptom detection behaviours. Various studies have employed breast self-examination (BSE) as an example of a detective health behaviour. Persons with high confidence in their capability to perform BSE are more likely to engage in regular self-examination (Alagna and Reddy 1987; Chalmers and Luker 1996). Positive and negative outcome expectancies also influence intentions; perceived benefits and barriers of engaging in BSE have been found to predict intentions as well as concurrent BSE behaviour (Champion 1990; Umeh and Rogan-Gibson 2001). Some studies have provided evidence that both outcome expectancies and perceived self-efficacy are the best joint predictors of the intention to engage in regular breast cancer detection behaviours (Meyerowitz and Chaiken 1987; Seydel *et al.* 1990).

Research involving high-risk populations also provides support for SCT. A study on first-degree relatives of prostate cancer patients supports the role of self-efficacy for screening behaviours. Physician recommendation, knowledge and risk estimation were only poor predictors, whereas self-efficacy beliefs and positive outcome expectancies were more closely linked to prostate cancer screening (Cormier *et al.* 2002). In another study on 50- to 60-year-old patients, participation in endoscopic colorectal cancer screening was examined. Self-efficacy, followed by the individuals' beliefs about the outcome of participation, discriminated between those who participated in the screening and those who did not (Kremers *et al.* 2000).

Cancer screening might be a first step on the way to change everyday health behaviours. However, people who enrol in a single cancer screening (e.g. lung cancer) do not necessarily have high self-efficacy regarding behaviours related to this cancer (e.g. regular screening, quitting smoking). Women who smoked heavily were asked to participate in lung cancer screening that involved sputum cytology, chest X-ray, bronchoscopy and spiral computer tomography (Schnoll *et al.* 2002). Almost two-thirds of those who participated in screening were classified as having low self-efficacy regarding smoking cessation. A minority of the women (25 per cent) reported high levels of negative outcome expectancies of quitting smoking, although most of them (76 per cent) reported high positive outcome expectancies of quitting. Finally, only very few women actually quit smoking after consultation with an oncologist. The results are in line with SCT, which emphasizes the role of self-efficacy in the process of behaviour change. Despite relatively high expectations about quitting smoking, the participants were unable to change their smoking habits. Persons who undergo cancer screening and are probably aware of the high risk of the disease might still be unable to change their risk behaviours, because they possess low optimistic-self beliefs.

3.6 Addictive behaviours

Optimistic self-beliefs also influence the process of changing addictive behaviours. Confidence to overcome barriers can predict attempts to quit smoking (Dijkstra and DeVries 2000). Nicotine abstinence of self-quitters depends on various demographic, physiological, cognitive and social factors, but only a few factors are common predictors of maintaining abstinence. These are physiological factors, such as lower nicotine dependence, longer duration of previous abstinence and, as a cognitive factor, high perceived self-efficacy (see Ockene *et al.* 2000).

Finally, poor self-efficacy is associated with lapses. Coping successfully with high-risk situations as they occur during the maintenance period is dependent on self-efficacy. Confidence in one's ability to abstain from smoking might refer to particular environmental or affective contexts, such as feelings of irritation or sadness, socializing with smokers, or being in a bar or a restaurant. Gwaltney *et al.* (2002) found that lapse episodes within a four-week abstinence period were predicted by abstinence self-efficacy. Abstinence self-efficacy differentiated between the temptation episodes in which the former smoker was able to resist smoking and situations that ended up with lapses. In a study on lapses and relapses of smokers who attempted to quit, self-efficacy was measured daily in order to analyse whether changes in optimistic self-beliefs precede lapses during 25 days after quitting smoking (Shiffman *et al.* 2000). On days when both groups were abstinent, persons who never lapsed during the monitoring period reported higher daily self-efficacy than those who lapsed. Daily average self-efficacy over the lapse-to-relapse interval was lower among persons who relapsed than daily average post-lapse self-efficacy among those who did not. Self-efficacy after the lapse significantly predicted subsequent behaviour.

Various researchers have verified relationships between perceived self-efficacy and relapse occurrence or time to relapse, with correlations ranging from −0.34 to −0.69 (see Colletti *et al.* 1985; DiClemente *et al.* 1985; Wilson *et al.* 1990). Kok *et al.* (1992) conducted several studies on the influence of perceived self-efficacy on non-smoking intentions and behaviours. Cross-sectionally, perceived self-efficacy was correlated r = 0.66 with intention, and r = 0.71 with reported behaviour (see also DeVries *et al.* 1988). These relationships were replicated longitudinally, although with less impressive coefficients (DeVries *et al.* 1989). In a longitudinal study on substance use amongst young adults, Cohen and Fromme (2002) showed that self-efficacy, along with positive and negative outcome expectancies, predicted alcohol, marijuana and other drug use, all measured at the same wave of data collection. Self-efficacy was also related to both positive and negative outcome expectancies. However, the SCT constructs did not predict behaviour measured one year later: the only significant determinant of substance use frequency was past behaviour measured one year earlier.

Hierarchies of tempting situations correspond to hierarchies of self-efficacy: the more a critical situation induces craving, the greater the perceived efficacy needed to prevent relapse (Velicer *et al.* 1990). Efficacy beliefs to resist temptation to smoke have been shown to predict reduction in the number of cigarettes smoked (r = −0.62), the amount of tobacco per smoke (r = −0.43), and the nicotine content (r = −0.30) (Godding and Glasgow 1985). Laboratory studies have revealed that efficacy beliefs about resisting smoking along with the affective response in a stressful social situation are associated with smoking urges (Niaura *et al.* 2002).

The role of outcome expectancies for smoking behaviour (intention to quit smoking and quitting smoking) have been further studied by Dijkstra *et al.* (1999). The authors emphasized the role of self-evaluative outcome expectations, that is, being ashamed, current feelings of regret, being satisfied in the case of quitting, and regretting smoking if illness due to smoking would occur. The stronger the self-evaluative outcome expectations, the greater the chances to quit smoking. The short-term health and social outcome expectancies seemed to be more important than expectancies about long-term health outcomes. Positive outcome expectations were better predictors of quitting smoking than negative ones (see Dijkstra *et al.* 1999). The role of positive and negative outcome expectancies might differ. Positive outcome expectancies for the consumption of cigarettes, alcohol or marijuana in early adolescence have been found to predict substance use one year later (Ellickson and Hays 1992). The minor role of negative outcome expectancies for behaviour change has been shown in cross-sectional studies on alcohol consumption. Heavily drinking students who drank alone expected more negative drinking consequences than those who drank heavily in a social context or who did not drink heavily. Those who were most likely to develop alcohol dependence had the highest negative outcome expectancies. Again, the crucial role of self-efficacy was confirmed: heavy drinkers had lower self-efficacy than those who drank less or who drank only in social situations (Christiansen *et al.* 2002).

4 Developments

Over the years, the notion of self-efficacy has become so appealing to health psychologists that it has been incorporated into most health behaviour theories. Becker and Rosenstock (1987) integrated it into their health belief model, mainly by reinterpreting what used to be 'barriers' to action. Ajzen (1991) has extended the theory of reasoned action to the theory of planned behaviour by adding a predictor labelled 'perceived behavioural control', which is seen to be synonymous with self-efficacy. In contrast, his long-time co-author Fishbein (2001) has simply incorporated self-efficacy (in the same sense as Bandura) into his own revision of their theory of reasoned action. In the context of US nationwide attempts to prevent HIV infections by promoting condom use, the leading health behaviour theorists, including Bandura and Fishbein, were asked to come up with an integrated framework to guide research on this topic (Fishbein *et al.* 1992). This workshop may have served as a stimulating factor for the inclusion of self-efficacy as an additional construct in some of the other theories.

Earlier, Maddux and Rogers (1983) had already included self-efficacy as a major determinant in their protection motivation theory. The theory most similar to SCT is the health action process approach (HAPA), but with an elaboration of the goal pursuit phase (see Schwarzer 1992; Renner and Schwarzer 2003). HAPA includes self-efficacy, outcome expectancies and intentions but has been designed to acknowledge in particular the fact that post-intentional processes are the most proximal predictors of actual behaviours. Thus, planning and initiative as well as maintenance and recovery from lapses are addressed in addition to the other predictors.

These models and theories are described in more detail in other chapters of this book. Thus, 'self-efficacy models' are no longer really distinct from other approaches because the key construct that was originally developed within Bandura's social cognitive theory has subsequently proved to be an essential component in all major models.

4.1 Phase-specific self-efficacy

Due to its popularity and unquestionable effects on human behaviour, researchers have proposed some further theoretical developments of the self-efficacy construct. Bandura (1997) suggested that self-efficacy should always refer to the particular task or specific behaviour that is being predicted. Other researchers suggest that optimistic self-beliefs might also be conceptualized as being more general, or that they should be tailored to particular stages of behaviour change.

Behaviour change can be described as a competent self-regulation process in which individuals monitor their responses to taxing situations, observe similar others facing similar demands, appraise their coping resources, create optimistic self-beliefs, plan a course of action, perform the critical action, and evaluate its outcome. Endorsing a process approach to behaviour change, Marlatt *et al.* (1995) proposed five categories of self-efficacy for corresponding stages of motivation and prevention. They differentiated kinds of self-efficacy that are crucial for primary and secondary prevention, namely resistance self-efficacy and harm-reduction self-efficacy. Moreover, action self-efficacy, coping self-efficacy and recovery self-efficacy are seen as making a difference in treatment adherence and relapse prevention. These five categories are explained in more detail below.

Resistance self-efficacy refers to the confidence in one's ability to avoid any substance use in the first place, which pertains to primary prevention. This implies resisting peer pressure to smoke, drink or take drugs. It has been found repeatedly that the combination of peer pressure and low self-efficacy predicts the onset of smoking and substance use in adolescents (Conrad *et al.* 1992). Ellickson and Hays (1991) studied the determinants of future substance use in 1138 8th- and 9th-graders in ten junior high schools. As potential predictors of onset, they analysed pro-drug social influence, resistance self-efficacy and perception of drug-use prevalence. Social influence or exposure to drug users combined with low self-efficacy for drug resistance predicted experimentation with drugs nine months later. Resistance self-efficacy was no longer predictive in the sub-sample of students who were already involved with drugs. In a study on smoking onset, Stacy *et al.* (1992) examined pro-smoking social influence and resistance self-efficacy in a sample of 1245 Californian high-school students. Perceived self-efficacy moderated the effect of peer pressure. As expected, many adolescents succumbed to pro-smoking influence, but those high in resistance self-efficacy were less vulnerable to interpersonal pressure to smoke.

Harm-reduction self-efficacy refers to one's confidence in being able to reduce the risk behaviour after having become involved with tobacco or drugs, which pertains to secondary prevention. Once a risk behaviour has commenced, the notion of resistance loses its significance. It is then of more importance to control further damage and to strengthen the belief that one is capable of minimizing the risk. This is particularly useful since most adolescents at least experiment with cigarettes and alcohol, which can be regarded as a normal stage in puberty when youngsters face developmental tasks, including self-regulation in tempting situations. Substance use can be seen as being normative rather than deviant and might reflect a healthy exploratory behaviour and a constructive learning process (Newcomb and Bentler 1988). The conflict here is between solving normative developmental tasks, on the one hand, and initiating a risk behaviour that might accumulate and habitualize to a detrimental lifestyle pattern, on the other. Thus, the question is, how can a drug be curiously explored without becoming a gateway drug? The answer lies in the notion of harm-reduction self-efficacy. The individual must acquire not only the competence and skills, but also the optimistic belief in control of the impending risk. The aim of secondary prevention is to let adolescents experiment while at the same time empowering them to minimize and eliminate substance use later on. In one study, college students participated in one of three treatments: (a) an alcohol information class dealing with the negative consequences of alcohol, (b) a moderation-oriented cognitive-behavioural skills-training class, and (c) an assessment-only control group (Baer *et al.* 1992; Baer 1993). The second treatment group was trained to enhance their harm-reduction self-efficacy, and this resulted in a decrease in alcohol consumption.

The above two types of self-efficacy are related to prevention. The process requires self-regulatory skills that enable an individual to deal with barriers specific for initiation, maintenance and recovery. The distinction proposed by Marlatt *et al.* (1995) has been further developed to specify self-efficacy beliefs that are typical for a particular phase of behaviour change (see Schwarzer and Renner 2000; Luszczynska and Schwarzer 2003; Renner and Schwarzer 2003). The next sections provide further details on this topic.

People initiate behaviour change when a critical situation arises. This requires that they firmly believe that they are capable of performing the action. *Pre-action self-efficacy* (Luszczynska and Schwarzer 2003) is an optimistic belief where an individual develops an intention to change. Individuals high in pre-action self-efficacy imagine success, anticipate potential outcomes of diverse strategies, and are more likely to initiate a new behaviour. People low in pre-action self-efficacy imagine failure, harbour self-doubts, and tend to procrastinate instead of giving the action a try. Pre-action self-efficacy refers to the first phase of the process, in which an individual does not yet act, but develops a motivation to do so. Action self-efficacy (Marlatt *et al.* 1995) is a similar construct, but it refers to what happens after a decision to change has been made. It addresses the confidence to attain one's desired abstinence goal. When intentions to quit are translated into preparatory acts, the individual needs optimistic self-beliefs to make detailed plans about how to refrain from the substance and to initiate instrumental actions. This applies to unaided cessation as well as to formal treatment settings. Action self-efficacy has been found to predict attempts to quit smoking (Marlatt 1998).

Later, a health-related behaviour needs to be maintained. Coping self-efficacy or *maintenance self-efficacy* (Luszczynska and Schwarzer 2003) describe optimistic beliefs about one's capability to deal with barriers that arise during the maintenance period. A new health behaviour might turn out to be much more difficult to adhere to than expected, but a self-efficacious person responds confidently with better strategies, more effort and prolonged persistence to overcome such hurdles. This kind of self-efficacy refers to mobilizing resources to continue successful adoption. Coping self-efficacy, a similar construct, relates to anticipatory coping with relapse crises. After one has made a successful attempt to quit, long-term maintenance is called for. At this stage, quitters are confronted with high-risk situations, such as experiencing negative affect or temptations in positive social situations. Lapses are likely to occur unless the quitter can mobilize alternative coping strategies. Relapse prevention training aims at making use of a variety of situation-tailored coping strategies, which in turn enhances coping self-efficacy (Curry 1993; Gruder *et al.* 1993; Marlatt 1998). While coping self-efficacy refers to a particular orientation to risk situations and lapse prevention, maintenance self-efficacy refers to beliefs about the ability to promote further success by strengthening one's own skills or searching for new resources.

Recovery self-efficacy (Marlatt *et al.* 1995; Luszczynska and Schwarzer 2003) is closely related to coping self-efficacy, although both tap different aspects within the maintenance stage (similar to the distinction between resistance and harm-reduction self-efficacy in the prevention stage). If a lapse occurs, individuals can fall prey to the 'abstinence violation effect', that is, they attribute their lapse to internal, stable and global causes, dramatize the event, and interpret it as a full-blown relapse (Marlatt and Gordon 1985). High self-efficacious individuals, however, avoid this effect by attributing the lapse to a high-risk situation and by finding ways to control the damage and to restore hope. Recovery self-efficacy pertains to one's conviction to get back on track after being derailed. The person trusts his/her competence to regain control after a setback or failure.

4.2 General self-efficacy

In another theoretical approach, self-efficacy has been conceptualized as a general optimistic belief that refers to a global confidence in one's coping ability across a wide range of demanding or novel situations (Sherer *et al.* 1982; Schwarzer and Jerusalem 1995). General self-efficacy reflects a broad and stable sense of personal competence to deal effectively with a variety of stressful situations (Scholz *et al.* 2002), and it might refer to a number of different domains of functioning in which people judge how efficacious they feel. This approach is not in opposition to Bandura's (1997) position that perceived self-efficacy should mainly be conceptualized in a situation-specific manner. It might be more compatible to analyse specific intentions or specific behaviours in the context of self-efficacy specific for a particular task. However, general self-efficacy allows for the possibility of explaining a broader pattern of coping with life and readjusting after stressful life events in the long run (Luszczynska *et al.* in press).

The highest level of generality is given when broad optimistic self-beliefs are examined, for instance when individuals under stress have to readapt to novel life circumstances over an extended period of time. In a study with cardiac surgery patients, Schröder *et al.* (1998) found that patients with high general self-efficacy scores recovered better one week after surgery and experienced better quality of life half a year later than their counterparts with low general self-efficacy.

4.3 Environmental factors and predictors of cognitions

Besides self-efficacy and outcome expectancies, other more peripheral constructs of SCT have caught the attention of researchers. The theory includes a general hypothesis of reciprocity between the individual's cognitions, environment, and behaviour. Sociostructural factors, such as economic and educational conditions and socioeconomic status, affect behaviours through their impact on people's cognitions (Bandura *et al.* 2002). Most of the studies on health behaviours target the relations between cognitions and behaviour. Recent years have seen renewed interest in environmental factors (see Baranowski *et al.* 1999; Sallis *et al.* 2000; Dzewaltowski *et al.* 2002). According to SCT, environmental variables might influence psychosocial processes and subsequent behaviours. It has been suggested that there are four environmental factors that might affect health behaviours and cognitions: (a) feelings of connection between people in the environment, (b) feelings of autonomy in the environment that support taking control over one's own actions, (c) skill-building opportunities in the environment, and (d) healthy norms that refer to group norms in the environment, suggesting that a healthy behaviour is a normative one (see Dzewaltowski *et al.* 2002a, 2002b). These characteristics of the environment might be developed by influencing the behaviours and cognitions of leaders, educators or caregivers. The behaviours of educators or caregivers might, in turn, influence the cognitions and behaviours of their students or patients.

5 Operationalization of the model

5.1 Operationalization of SCT constructs: guidelines for questionnaire design

Sometimes, researchers misunderstand theoretical constructs and, as a consequence, develop psychometric scales that lack construct validity or content validity. To assure a complete understanding of constructs, it is mandatory to provide algorithms for test construction or at least operational definitions, i.e. test item examples. In the area of sociocultural impediments and facilitators, this remains a difficult task since a very broad range of possible factors might be of interest in studies based on SCT, including social support, social integration, ethnic group membership, education, knowledge, intelligence, affluence or poverty, etc.

The definition of goals is easier since this is the same as the one for intentions. Typically, one-item seven-point scales are used that have the structure 'I intend to do X within the next week (day, month, etc.)'. In line with other theories, the level of specificity is adjustable. One could say 'I intend to eat five portions of vegetable per day, starting tomorrow', or one could say 'I intend to eat a healthy diet in the near future'. Both are intentions or goals, varying in level of specificity. Bandura (1997) mentions a continuum from proximal to distant goals. It is up to the researcher and the context of the study to select the most appropriate level. In any case, it is preferred to focus on behaviour instead of outcomes. Instead of 'to lose weight', one would choose 'to eat fewer calories'.

There are some good rules of thumb to assess outcome expectancies and perceived self-efficacy. To simplify test construction, one can keep in mind that outcome expectancies are best worded with if/then statements, and self-efficacy items as confidence statements. The semantic structure of outcome expectancies is: 'If . . . (a behaviour), then . . . (consequences)'. An example of a positive outcome expectancy is 'If I reduce my dietary fat intake, I will become slim'. An example of a negative one is 'If I reduce my dietary fat intake, I cannot enjoy my favourite desserts any longer'.

For self-efficacy, the corresponding wording could be: 'I am confident that I can . . . (perform an action), even if . . . (a barrier)'. An example of a self-efficacy item is: 'I am confident that I can skip desserts even if my family continues to eat them in my presence'. This rule need not be applied rigidly, but might serve as a heuristic.

It is suggested to assess a variety of (a) barriers that might arise if an individual tries to change a behaviour, and (b) outcome expectancies, both positive and negative. Individuals face various social, personal, and environmental obstacles or barriers. For example, people have many reasons why they should quit smoking or why they find it better to continue. Therefore, questionnaire items should refer to multiple possible barriers and outcomes that are specific for a health behaviour. It is also suggested not to present different constructs neatly separated in the questionnaire, but rather to scramble them so that respondents are not able to find out about the constructs.

Following these general rules, researchers usually develop their own measures of SCT constructs that pertain to their particular research context. Table 4.2 displays examples of the operationalization of the main SCT constructs. For brevity, we refer to one behaviour only, namely condom use.

5.2 Measures of behaviour-specific self-efficacy

All components of SCT are usually measured in a behaviour-specific way. As self-efficacy is the most often employed construct of the SCT, self-efficacy scales that are more or less adequate have been published for all kinds of health behaviours. Various psychometric instruments have been developed to assess self-efficacy for physical activities (see Barling and Abel 1983; Motl *et al.* 2002; Rodgers *et al.* 2002). The scales are usually adjusted to the age and development of the respondents. For example, children are asked whether they would be physically active during their free time even if they could watch TV or play video games instead (see Motl *et al.* 2002). Physical exercise self-efficacy scales for patients coping with chronic disease have been designed by Holman and Lorig (1992) and Toshima *et al.* (1992). A scale to measure nutrition self-efficacy has been developed by Schwarzer and Renner (2000). The scale refers to barriers that arise while developing the motivation to initiate health behaviour change (e.g. 'How certain are you that you could overcome the following barriers?' 'I can manage to stick

Table 4.2 Social cognitive theory components: examples of questionnaire items

Variable	*Question example*	*Response scale*
Self-efficacy: behaviour specific	I can use condoms even if I would have to negotiate it with my partner	Completely false to Exactly true 1–2–3–4
Phase-specific self-efficacy: pre-action	I can use condoms even if I have to develop a precise plan how to negotiate it with my partner	
Phase-specific self-efficacy: maintenance	I can use condoms even if I have to negotiate with my partner	
Phase-specific self-efficacy: recovery	I can return to using condoms even if I failed a few times to use them as planned	
Outcome expectancies: physical	If I use condoms I would avoid health problems (such as chlamydia)	Completely false to Exactly true 1–2–3–4
Outcome expectancies: social	If I use condoms my partner might be happy that I take care of him/her	
Outcome expectancies: self-evaluative	If I use condoms I would be proud of myself	
Goals	Starting tomorrow, I intend to use condoms during sexual intercourse	Completely false to Exactly true 1–2–3–4
Sociostructural factors: impediments	In my country, high-quality condoms are expensive	Completely false to Exactly true 1–2–3–4
Sociostructural factors: facilitators	In my town, one can easily buy condoms in public restrooms, drugstores, or chemists	

to healthful food, even if I have to rethink my entire way of nutrition'). The items also refer to the barriers that are specific for the maintenance period (e.g. 'I can manage to stick to healthful food, even if I do not receive a great deal of support from others when making my first attempts').

There are two basic methods to design a risk-behaviour self-efficacy scale. One is to confront the individual with a list or hierarchy of tempting situations and to assess situation-specific self-efficacy in line with these demands. The second approach aims at the restricted use of substances, asking participants whether in general they feel competent to control the behaviour in question (irrespective of specific risk situations). In the domain of smoking, for example, the first method has been chosen by Colletti *et al.* (1985) and Velicer *et al.* (1990). Dijkstra and DeVries (2000) elaborated a smoking self-efficacy scale that reflects different barriers that might arise during adoption, maintenance and recovery after lapses. For example, barriers pertaining to emotional states (e.g. being stressed), social situations (e.g. seeing someone enjoying a smoke), or lack of skills (e.g. telling smokers to quit smoking during a party) might occur during the maintenance period. In research on drinking, this method has been preferred by Annis (1982), Annis and Davis (1988), and DiClemente *et al.* (1985). The second approach was chosen by Godding and Glasgow (1985), Shiffman *et al.* (2000), and Gwaltney *et al.* (2002) to assess smoking self-efficacy.

Compliance with a medical recommendation might refer to more than one health behaviour. Patients with diabetes or those having suffered a myocardial infarction are usually asked to comply with medication or to have blood glucose tests, but also to increase their physical activity and to change their diet. Therefore, self-efficacy scales that assess the ability to perform such behaviours in each regimen area have been developed (see Williams and Bond 2002).

6 Application of the model

SCT can be validated by analysing the relations between measured SCT constructs and a selected behaviour. The predictive power of SCT can also be tested by means of experimental manipulation of its components and assessing the effects of this manipulation on behaviour. The National Institute of Mental Health (NIMH) Multisite HIV Prevention Trial Group (1998, 2001; O'Leary *et al.* 2000) employed both approaches to validate the theory, and their work forms the basis of the example application described here. To explore the role of self-efficacy, outcome expectancies and goal setting on behaviour, researchers from the NIMH developed an intervention based on SCT aimed at reducing sexual risk behaviours. The study was primarily designed to test whether a manipulation aimed at increasing self-efficacy and positive outcome expectancies would affect behaviour change.

6.1 Participants and procedure

The participants of the NIMH Multisite HIV Prevention Trial (2001) were randomly assigned to one of two conditions. Controls received a one-hour education session on HIV. The second group received an intervention based on SCT. All were interviewed four times: prior to the intervention, and 3, 6 and 12 months after the intervention. The treatment consisted of seven 90- to 120-minute small group sessions. The SCT intervention dealt with outcome expectancies, condom use and non-use, and goal setting, with feedback. Modelling and mastery experience of condom use by means of individual practice were provided. Skills aimed at condom use and condom negotiation were explicitly developed. At all waves of measurement, data about sexual behaviours, drug use, STD (sexually transmitted diseases) symptoms and HIV testing were collected.

Participants were recruited in 37 clinics at seven cities across the USA. A group consisted of at-risk men and women who had reported unprotected sexual intercourse during 90 days prior to the study and who met at least one of the HIV risk criteria, such as having had STD, having had sex with one or more new sexual partners, etc. All the measurement waves elicited information about sexual behaviour, drug use, STD symptoms and HIV testing. Self-efficacy and outcome expectancies (as detailed in section 5.3) were measured three months after the intervention. The participants were randomly selected to one of two conditions. Controls received one hour of education on HIV. The second group received seven 90- to 120-minute small group treatment sessions. The intervention, based on SCT, aimed at increase of knowledge, outcome expectancies, and self-efficacy regarding condom use.

6.2 Measures

The NIMH Multisite HIV Prevention Trial Group (2001) developed a safe-sex self-efficacy scale tapping the barriers to be overcome, such as having a conversation with the partner about safe sex practices, dealing with partner resistance, and leaving the situation. The respondents were asked whether they were confident that they could (a) refuse to have sex or leave the situation if the partner wouldn't allow the use of a condom or have safe sex, (b) convince the partner that the respondent and the partner should use a condom or have safe sex, even if s/he says 'I hate those things', (c) convince the partner that the two of them should use a condom or have safe sex, even if both prefer doing it with the feel of bare skin. The responses were made on an 11-point scale anchored at *not at all confident* to *completely confident*. Outcome expectancies were measured regarding three areas mentioned by Bandura (1997, 2000b). Physical outcome expectancies were referred to by lack of physical pleasure associated with condom use (e.g. 'Condoms ruin the mood'). Social outcome expectancies referred to partner's potential reactions (e.g. 'My sex partner would get mad if I said we had to use condoms'). Self-evaluative outcome expectancies dealt with feelings about the self as the result of condom use (e.g. 'I would feel more responsible if we used a condom').

In the study, condom use and safe sex behaviour measurement elicited information about sexual behaviour, drug use, STD symptoms and HIV testing (NIMH Multisite HIV Prevention Trial Group, 1998, 2001; O'Leary *et al.* 2000). Behaviours were measured by means of self-reported consistent condom use during 90 days before data collection. Other measures included STD reinfection rate (compared with post-intervention record) as obtained from clinical records, point prevalence of chlamydia and gonorrhea (assessment with DNA amplification of urine specimens [ligase chain reaction; LCR]), and self-reports of STD symptoms during the 90 days before data collection.

6.3 Results

A significant increase in consistent condom use or sexual abstinence was found in the intervention groups, compared to controls. Forty-two per cent of intervention participants (versus 27 per cent of controls) acted in a consistently safe way at three months, 44 per cent (versus 33 per cent of controls) at six months, and 43 per cent (versus 34 per cent of controls) at 12-month follow-up.

Compared to the control group, self-efficacy, physical, social, and self-evaluative outcome expectancies were significantly higher in the experimental group at the three-month follow-up (see NIMH Multisite HIV Prevention Trial Group 2001). The SCT variables entered as a group produced significant increases in the variance accounted for across three behavioural measures. Self-efficacy and outcome expectancies, measured at baseline, predicted 10, 11 and 12 per cent of variance of consistent condom use, number of unprotected sexual acts and use of condom at last sexual act, respectively. Self-efficacy and outcome expectancies measured at three-month follow-up explained 36, 23 and 23 per cent of variance of respective measures of condom use (O'Leary *et al.* 2000).

The treatment based on SCT had an impact on the rates of reported STD symptoms (see NIMH Multisite HIV Prevention Trial Group 1998). In the control group conditions, 36.6 per cent of the participants reported symptoms of STD one year after the intervention. Among the participants in the intervention group, only 27.7 per cent reported STD symptoms one year after the intervention. In addition, both groups were compared on the basis of the content clinical charts. Of the control group men, 6.6 per cent were treated for gonorrhea in the follow-up year, compared to 3.6 per cent of the intervention condition men.

The intervention was significantly related to an increase in self-reported condom use (the NIMH Multisite HIV Prevention Trial Group, 2001). Results of urine specimens analysed at the one-year follow-up did not bring hard evidence for SCT: differences between controls and intervention group were not significant (NIMH Multisite HIV Prevention Trial Group 1998). However, some tendencies were observed. Compared to controls, fewer persons from the intervention group had gonorrhea (0.9 per cent versus 1.5 per cent). The evidence for chlamydia indicated little difference between the intervention group and controls (2.9 per cent versus 2.8 per cent). When men and women patients from STD clinics and patients recruited at the health service organizations (mostly primary care clinics) were analysed separately, a different result for chlamydia emerged. STD clinic patients who participated in the intervention were infected with chlamydia slightly more often (3.6 per cent of men and 2.1 per cent of women) than controls (1.8 per cent of men and 1.9 per cent of women). Regarding health service organization patients (only women recruited), the results were the opposite, that is, participants of the intervention group had less chlamydia (4.3 per cent versus 2.6 per cent).

To test the mediation hypothesis, logistic regression (repeated-measures models) with consistent condom use or abstinence as the outcome was conducted. The mediators (outcome expectancies and self-efficacy) were included in one equation; the other equation was calculated without the mediators. Group assignment turned out to be a significant predictor of a behaviour measured at follow-ups. Persons who participated in the intervention reported significantly more frequent consistent condom use (odds ratio = 1.68) compared to the control group participants. Intervention effects were significantly reduced when each social cognitive variable was entered into regression. Each variable contributed to the mediation effect. Reduction of intervention regression coefficients from 0.52 to between 0.48 (for self-efficacy) and 0.44 was found. This means that the effectiveness of the programme was due partly to changes in participants' outcome expectancies and self-efficacy.

6.4 Discussion

The results based on the self-report data lend support to SCT. Self-reported safe sex behaviour was changed by means of an intervention using SCT as the theoretical background. Compared to the control group, the effect of intervention might be considered to be small. However, the control group also received an intervention which aimed at imparting knowledge about safe sexual behaviours. This might account for the relatively small between-groups difference. The authors of the study emphasized that the effects of social cognitive variables were small, which might result from the sample size and its diversity.

Self-efficacy contributed to the mediation effect to a lesser degree than any of three measured indexes of outcome expectancies. This result is in line with some theoretical approaches to the role of optimistic self-beliefs. For persons who are still initiating the process of behaviour change, outcome expectancies might be more important for initiating the behaviour. For those who are already maintaining a new behaviour and are fighting with obstacles, self-efficacy is the most important cognition on the way to developing a new habit (see Schwarzer 2001). In the group studied, most of the participants were initiating, rather than maintaining, a new behaviour, namely regular condom use. Between one-half and one-quarter adopted the behaviour after the intervention. Therefore, stronger effects of outcome expectancies were to be expected. Analyses performed in the sub-group of participants who successfully adopted regular condom use could result in a different pattern of findings. While outcome expectancies help to form an intention and initiate a new behaviour, their effect decreases as individuals adopt the behaviour. Self-efficacy, then, continues to play a major role during the attempts to maintain a newly adopted behaviour. The incessant struggle to adhere to the intended level of health-promoting action requires, in particular, self-efficacy whereas the decisional balance of pros and cons remains relatively constant when being maintained.

The portion of results that were based on objective data did not provide support for SCT. In most cases, the results were in line with theory, although no statistically significant differences were found. Prevalence of diseases, estimated by means of LCR urine analysis, showed less gonorrhea in men and women from all kinds of clinics, and less chlamydia in health service organization patients. More frequent evidence of chlamydia in the intervention group than among controls might result from the fact that the participants of the control group, recruited in STD clinics, were treated for sexually transmitted diseases more often than persons who received the intervention. Such a result was found in the charts of patients in STD clinics. Therefore, control group patients could already have been cured from some forms of STD at one-year follow-up, although, in general, they could be infected more often.

7 Using social cognitive theory (SCT) to develop interventions

The constructs included in SCT belong to those most often analysed or measured in order to test the effectiveness of interventions aimed at health behaviour change. For example, in 265 nutrition interventions published in the 1980s and 1990s, outcome expectancies or self-efficacy were used in about 90 per cent of the studies (see Contento et al. 2002). Contento et al. (2002) conclude from their review that changes in preferences or different attitudes seem to be of less importance than changes in self-efficacy or outcome expectancies. Changes in SCT constructs (i.e. self-efficacy and outcome expectancies) and behavioural skills are more likely to produce changes in nutrition behaviour. The examples of intervention studies that report experimental manipulations of specific SCT constructs are displayed in Table 4.3.

Interventions might include strategies designed to increase participants' sense of mastery and ability to handle difficult situations that might arise during initiation or maintenance of a health-promoting behaviour. Another kind of treatment based on SCT might be education about a behaviour and benefits of its adoption. Programmes based on SCT might lead to change in targeted theoretical outcomes, such as self-efficacy, outcome expectancies or health behaviour change.

SCT has been employed to develop interventions to change multiple health behaviours. In this section, the effectiveness of such interventions is discussed. We compare the effectiveness of interventions that use mastery experience and vicarious experience to enhance SCT components. Finally, the short- and long-term effects of these interventions are addressed.

Table 4.3 Examples of intervention studies that report experimental manipulations of specific SCT constructs

Behaviours	Authors and dates of publications
Adherence to medication and rehabilitation	O'Leary *et al.* (1988)
Sexual risk behaviours	Lawrence *et al.* (1997), The National Institute of Mental Health Multisite HIV Prevention Trial Group (1998, 2001)
Physical exercise	Parent and Fortin (2000), Bock *et al.* (2001), Brassington *et al.* (2002), Dishman *et al.* (2004)
Nutrition and weight control	Carson *et al.* (2002), Wilson *et al.* (2002), Baranowski *et al.* (2003)
Detective behaviours	Meyerowitz and Chaiken (1987), Luszczynska (2004)
Addictive behaviours	Dijkstra *et al.* (1998), Dijkstra and De Vries (2001), Winkleby *et al.* (2001)

7.1 Mastery and vicarious experience interventions enhancing SCT components

There are two main sources of perceived self-efficacy (see Bandura 1997). Personal mastery experience, such as practising a behaviour, is most effective for self-efficacy enhancement because it provides observable evidence for goal attainment. Vicarious experience, such as observing a model person who is able to perform a difficult behaviour, can also enhance self-efficacy. Including one of these two components in the treatment might differentiate between successful and unsuccessful interventions. Exercise interventions that do not incorporate mastery experience might increase outcome expectancies, without changing self-efficacy or behaviour (see Hallam and Petrosa 1998). In such treatments, individuals have no chance to deal with the barriers during the intervention and to overcome them. Later, if they are faced with the barriers while attempting to perform the behaviour, they might fail and re-evaluate their ability to overcome these barriers as being low.

Vicarious and mastery experience might be obtained by means of computerized interventions. For example, treatment of children might include multimedia games aimed at behaviour change. Based on SCT, the education activities in the game might be designed to increase preferences for healthy behaviour, for example healthy food consumption (see Baranowski *et al.* 2003). Using multiple exposures, this approach has been found to increase mastery in asking for healthy foods at home and when eating out. It also increased skills for preparing healthy food by means of virtual recipes and virtual food preparation. A study on increased fruit and vegetable consumption showed that, compared to controls, pre-adolescents participating in such an intervention increased their consumption significantly (see Baranowski *et al.* 2003).

Health behaviour change might by obtained by vicarious experience only, in which a person models a desirable health behaviour. A study on patients after coronary artery bypass graft surgery showed that an intervention in which former patients exemplify the physically active lives they lead after the surgery can affect post-operative exercise (see Parent and Fortin 2000). Patients who received the intervention developed stronger self-efficacy than controls five days after surgery, and they reported more walking and stair climbing and a higher level of general activity. Four weeks after surgery, patients who participated in vicarious experience intervention reported a more active lifestyle.

Not all interventions lead to a linear increase of perceived self-efficacy. McAuley and co-workers (1999) studied the physical activity of older adults participating in a 12-month exercise course (aerobic or stretching and toning groups). The results revealed a curvilinear pattern of growth of self-efficacy during the first six months of training and a decrease over the next six months. However, frequency of participation in exercise appeared to be a significant predictor of overall growth in self-efficacy. This result supports the assumption of SCT that mastery experience builds up optimistic self-beliefs.

SCT identifies five components that might lead to the adoption of a health behaviour, especially risk reduction behaviour (Bandura 1997). These are provision of information, mastery of self-protective skills and self-efficacy for implementation of these skills, social competence and social support for the adoption of protective actions. Following these suggestions, Lawrence and colleagues (1997) developed an intervention that included HIV/AIDS education, teaching and rehearsing skills targeting social competence (negotiations with a partner, refusal), mastery of self-protective skills (condom application and increasing sterility of intravenous drug application), technical competence, generating a supportive climate amongst participants, and normalizing self-protective behaviours. The intervention targeted a high-risk population of incarcerated women, of whom approximately one-third were drug users, and almost one-half were treated for sexually transmitted diseases. Most respondents reported a high number of lifetime sex partners. Incarcerated women had opportunities to meet their partners in private and to have sexual intercourse during their imprisonment. Compared to baseline, after the intervention the women reported higher self-efficacy and frequency of communication with their partners about condom use. They also exhibited more knowledge about AIDS. The participants also improved in skills of condom application. These changes were sustained throughout the six-month follow-up.

7.2 Short- and long-term effects of SCT-based interventions

Interventions designed to increase compliance with healthy nutrition, physical activity or cancer screening are not always successful in changing the long-term maintenance of a behaviour. Using SCT and the transtheoretical model, Pinto and colleagues (2002a) developed a fully automated counselling system, available by phone, aimed at promoting physical activity in sedentary adults. The intervention, available for six months, resulted in behaviour change during the availability of the counselling. People who received automatic information promoting moderate intensity of physical activity met more recommendations regarding activity than controls. They also reported significantly higher daily kilocalorie expenditure than controls, who received automatic information on nutrition. However, the results were not maintained six months after the first measurement. In a similar study, telephone-based exercise counselling was provided to sedentary older adults (Brassington *et al.* 2002). After 12 months of intervention, adherence to suggested physical activity increased. The increments in self-efficacy and fitness outcome expectancies were related to a more active lifestyle. The authors, however, did not provide information about whether the change was maintained a few months after the end of the treatment.

Individually tailored interventions based on SCT might affect behaviour more strongly and lead to better maintenance than non-tailored interventions. To increase physical activity, a typical treatment based on SCT would aim at improving self-efficacy and discussing benefits and barriers to activity. In one study, self-help guidebooks, mailed three times to the participants, were tailored by targeting the deficiencies found in previous assessment responses in the participants' use of self-efficacy (see Bock *et al.* 2001). The respondents showed increased self-efficacy after the treatment and at six-month follow-up. Those who maintained physical activity at follow-up had higher self-efficacy beliefs at post-test and follow-up. Individuals who achieved the recommended levels of physical activity by the end of the intervention were more likely to maintain their physical activity level half a year later.

Not all interventions designed in line with SCT lead to changes in the target health behaviours. Social cognitive constructs of sense of community, self-efficacy, outcome expectancies, incentive value, policy control and leadership competence guided a programme for students from low-income neighbourhoods. The intervention aimed at a reduction of alcohol and drug use. No decrease of alcohol consumption or use of tobacco and other psychoactive substances was observed after completion of the programme (Winkleby *et al.* 2001). The post-treatment measurement, however, revealed increased levels of the social cognitive constructs. The lack of behaviour change might result from a lack of adjustment of the intervention to culture and developmental level. Other studies have demonstrated that culturally and developmentally tailored interventions based on SCT might bring short-term changes in behaviour. The changes might be not maintained, however. For example, HIV-risk-reduction treatment based on SCT, tailored for African – American pre-adolescents and young adolescents, affected the use of condoms six months after the intervention. However, the rate of condom use decreased at 12-month follow-up, and the differences became non-significant (see Stanton *et al.* 1996).

SCT might be combined successfully with other theoretical approaches. The theoretical background of the intervention should depend on the targeted population and the behaviour itself. For example, if the target group is more likely to suffer from cognitive deficits, an intervention might be based on learning theory. In one study, older adults with Type-2 diabetes took part in a treatment aimed at nutrition improvement, based on learning theory, principles of information processing and SCT. After the intervention, the measures of fasting, plasma glucose, total cholesterol and glycated hemoglobine changed significantly in the treatment group, compared to matched controls (see Miller *et al.* 2002). Some studies have shown that a treatment based on SCT might be as effective as an intervention that combines the social cognitive approach with an intervention aimed at increasing motivation. These two kinds of interventions (SCT combined and SCT) affected self-efficacy levels as well as fruit and vegetable intake among adolescents, whereas a mere education-based intervention did not change their nutrition (see Wilson *et al.* 2002).

8 Future directions

Theoretical approaches to health behaviours need to elaborate further on the process of behaviour change. This process might refer to developing an intention to change, that requires specific self-regulatory skills, and to maintaining that change. The construct of perceived self-efficacy has been the most powerful single resource factor in predicting the process of behaviour change. However, self-efficacy is not the 'magic bullet' to solve all problems that can arise in the prediction and changing of health behaviour. Amongst another powerful predictors, peer pressure and social norms usually have high predictive value, although some studies have found a negligible effect of perceived norms on nutrition behaviour and dieting (Field *et al.* 2001). Another strong determinant of behaviour, namely social support, also has a high potential as a resource factor. On the other hand, social influence might be confounded with self-efficacy. The degree to which peer pressure makes a difference also depends on the individual's resistance self-efficacy. The degree to which social support operates also rests on one's self-efficacy to build, maintain and mobilize social networks (Jessor 1998; Wills *et al.* 2000).

An open question remains regarding the optimal degree of specificity of the self-efficacy construct. According to Bandura (1997), perceived self-efficacy should always be as situation-specific as possible. This specificity issue can even be further subdivided into a formal and a substantial facet. In a formal or temporal sense, Marlatt *et al.* (1995) conceptualized five kinds of self-efficacy that reflect different stages. In a substantial sense, one has to tailor the questions to the situation, for example smoking cessation or condom use. Although there is nothing wrong with more and more specificity, there still exist domain-specific and also highly general measures that have considerable predictive value (Schwarzer and Jerusalem 1995). High specificity of self-efficacy enables the prediction of only a narrow range of behaviours, such as high-fibre food consumption (see Schnoll and Zimmerman 2001). A general measure of self-efficacy gives the opportunity to assess self-efficacy in a parsimonious way, if the study deals with the adoption of a general lifestyle, general stress adaptation, or overall compliance with a range of recommended healthy practices.

The author of SCT defines self-efficacy as 'beliefs in one's capabilities to organize and execute the courses of action' (Bandura 1997: 3). Therefore, self-efficacy not only refers to beliefs about an individual's ability to execute a specific behaviour (e.g. 'I can eat healthy food'), but also to an individual's ability to regulate the behaviour change process (e.g. 'I can eat healthy food despite lack of support from my spouse'). Due to the continuous influence that self-efficacy has at different stages or phases throughout this process, its measurement might be adjusted to the particular point in time when self-regulation is at stake, for example at the moment of initiation of healthy nutrition, or at the moment of maintenance, or at the moment of recovery after a lapse. An adjustment of the self-efficacy concept to various phases in the health behaviour change process might help to explain how and why individuals successfully adopt healthy lifestyles (see Marlatt et al. 1995; Luszczynska and Schwarzer 2003). Developing phase-specific self-efficacy skills by means of intervention could, for example, help to get those on their way who are still undecided about what to do. For them, enhancement of pre-action self-efficacy could be helpful. Therefore, future interventions based on SCT should be tailored to the specific phase of the health behaviour change process.

Perceived self-efficacy has to be optimistic to generate motivational power and should be somewhat overly optimistic. It should not exceed a certain limit where unrealistic optimism would lead to disappointment or harm. Many interventions have focused on risk communication to lower defensive optimism. The idea is to allow people to understand how much they really are at risk, which should affect their behaviour (see Ruiter et al. 2001). Perception of risk or threat is usually seen as a facilitator for deciding to change a behaviour (see Weinstein 2003), but mostly in the early stages of behaviour change, that is, when the motivation to change is developed. Therefore, treatments might combine different approaches, increasing both risk perception and self-efficacy, but they should be tailored to the advancement of the participants in the change process. If intention formation (developing the motivation) is the aim of an intervention, then the treatment should aim at risk perception, outcome expectancies and self-efficacy. If instead maintenance is to be analysed or promoted, self-efficacy is crucial for goal pursuit, whereas risk perception and outcome expectancies lose their influence.

Health self-regulation encompasses a broad range of cognitions and behaviours. Further studies could benefit from work in other fields, in particular from relapse prevention theory (Marlatt et al. 1995) and self-regulation theories (Karoly 1993; Carver and Scheier 1998). Self-regulatory constructs other than self-efficacy might help to explain further post-intentional processes of health behaviour change. Theories of volition emphasize that self-regulation refers to an individual's ability to focus the attention on the task at hand and to keep a favourable emotional balance (see Carver and Scheier 1998). Self-competencies that refer to regulation of attentional and emotional components of goal-directed behaviour might play a crucial role across all phases of health behaviour change. In different stages of goal pursuit, people need to pay attention and stay with the task at hand. They need to concentrate even when an interference to attend to another task emerges. Moreover, controlling interfering emotions such as boredom, anger, distress, exhaustion, anxiety or reluctance requires a number of cognitive skills (Karoly 1993). Self-regulation of attention and emotion might be seen as a stable personal disposition, an individual's characteristic that enables habitual control over recurrent actions, as well as in the process of behaviour change (see Karoly 1993; Luszczynska *et al.* 2004).

To test the validity of SCT versus other theories of health behaviour change, experimental studies are required. So far, most of the studies that aim at examining determinants from different theories are mainly correla- tional and cross-sectional. A minority includes experimental manipulations and examines the maintenance of behaviour change by means of follow-up assessment (see Section 7). Future research that tests the application of the theories should include the manipulation of constructs from SCT in one studied group, and manipulation of the constructs from a different theory (such as TPB) in the other group. For example, at the stage of intention development, one group could be treated by improving positive attitudes and subjective norms (TPB) whereas the other group could be treated by improving self-efficacy and outcome expectancies (SCT). At the stage of goal pursuit, on the other hand, one group could be treated by improving perceived behavioural control (TPB) whereas the other could be treated by enhancing self-efficacy (SCT) or a combination of self-efficacy, action planning and relapse prevention (HAPA). It is unlikely that one will ever find an acid test to compare all models with each other since they are partly incompatible, as are, for example, stage models versus continuum models (see Sutton, Chapter 6 in this volume). Researchers tend to prefer eclectic approaches such as selecting attractive elements from one model and implanting them into another one which can be seen as a means of theory evolution.

Further studies are needed to identify the essential mechanisms that operate in the process of behaviour change. Different perspectives lead to an emphasis on different variables and mechanisms. A psychological per- spective would underscore social influence and the social context of self- regulation. A lifespan developmental perspective would accentuate perso- nal history and life events, as well as gains and losses. The present health psychological view pertains to short time periods that are typically involved in coping with addictive behaviours and in thorny cessation attempts. Regardless of the perspective, self-regulatory cognitions, such as self- efficacy, are decisive factors for health self-regulation.

References

Ajzen, I. (1991) The theory of planned behavior, *Organizational Behavior and Human Decision Processes*, 50, 179–211.

Alagna, S.W. and Reddy, D.M. (1987) Predictors of proficient technique and successful lesion detection in breast self-examination, *Health Psychology*, 3, 113–27.

Anderson, E.S., Winett, R.A. and Wojcik, J.R. (2000) Social-cognitive determinants of nutrition behavior among supermarket food shoppers: a structural equation analysis, *Health Psychology*, 19, 479–86.

Annis, H.M. (1982) *Inventory of Drinking Situations*. Ontario, Canada: Addiction Research Foundation.

Annis, H.M. and Davis, C.S. (1988) Assessment of expectancies. In D.M. Donovan and G.A. Marlatt (eds) *Assessment of Addictive Behaviors*. New York: Guilford, 84–111.

Baer, J.S. (1993) Etiology and secondary prevention of alcohol problems with young adults. In J.S. Baer, G.A. Marlatt and R. J. McMahon (eds) *Addictive Behaviors Across the Lifespan: Prevention, Treatment, and Policy Issues*. Newbury Park, CA: Sage Publications, 111–37.

Baer, J.S., Marlatt, G.A., Kivlahan, D.R., Fromme, K., Larimer, M.E. and Williams, E. (1992) An experimental test of three methods of alcohol risk reduction with young adults, *Journal of Consulting and Clinical Psychology*, 60, 974–9.

Bagozzi, R.P. and Warshaw, P.R. (1990) Trying to consume, *Journal of Consumer Research*, 17, 127–40.

Bandura, A. (1977) Self-efficacy: toward a unifying theory of behavioral change, *Psychological Review*, 84, 191–215.

Bandura, A. (1986) *Social Foundations of Thought and Action: A Social Cognitive Theory*. Englewood Cliffs, NJ: Prentice-Hall.

Bandura, A. (1992) Self-efficacy mechanism in psychobiologic functioning. In R. Schwarzer (ed.) *Self-efficacy: Thought Control of Action*. Washington, DC: Hemisphere, 355–94.

Bandura, A. (1997) *Self-efficacy: The Exercise of Control*. New York: Freeman.

Bandura, A. (2000a) Exercise of human agency through collective efficacy, *Current Directions of Psychological Science*, 9, 75–8.

Bandura, A. (2000b) Cultivate self-efficacy for personal and organizational effectiveness. In E.A. Locke (ed.) *The Blackwell Handbook of Principles of Organizational Behavior*. Oxford: Blackwell, 120–36.

Bandura, A. (2001) Social cognitive theory: an agentic perspective, *Annual Review of Psychology*, 52, 1–26.

Bandura, A., Barbaranelli, C., Caprana, C.V. and Pastorelli, C. (2002) Self-efficacy beliefs as shapers of children's aspirations and career trajectories, *Child Development*, 72, 178–206.

Baranowski, T., Baranowski, J., Cullen, K.W., Marsh, T., Islam, N., Zakerei, I. *et al.* (2003) Squire's Quest: dietary outcome evaluation of a multimedia game, *American Journal of Preventive Medicine*, 24, 52–61.

Baranowski, T., Weber Cullen, K. and Baranowsky, J. (1999) Psychosocial correlates of dietary intake: advancing dietary interventions, *Annual Review of Nutrition*, 19, 17–40.

Barling, J. and Abel, M. (1983) Self-efficacy and tennis performance, *Cognitive Therapy and Research*, 7, 265–72.

Basen-Engquist, K. (1992) Psychosocial predictors of 'safer-sex' behaviors in young adults, *Aids Education and Prevention*, 4, 120–34.

Becker, M.H. and Rosenstock, I.M. (1987) Comparing social learning theory and the health belief model. In W.B. Ward (ed.) *Advances in Health Education and Promotion*, Vol. 2. Greenwich, CT: JAI, 245–9.

Bock, B.C., Marcus, B.H., Pinto, B.M. and Forsyth, L.H. (2001) Maintenance of physical activity following an individualized motivationally tailored intervention, *Annals of Behavioral Medicine*, 23, 79–87.

Bond, M.J. (2002) The roles of self-efficacy, outcome expectancies and social support in the self-care behaviors of diabetics, *Psychology, Health and Medicine*, 7, 127–41.

Booth, M.L., Owen, N., Bauman, A., Clavisi, O. and Leslie, E. (2000) Social-cognitive and perceived environmental influences associated with physical activity in older Australians, *Preventive Medicine*, 31, 15–22.

Bosse, M.J., McKenzie, E.J., Kellam, J.F., Burgess, A.R., Webb, L.X., Swiontkowski, M.F. *et al.* (2002) An analysis of outcomes of reconstruction or amputation after leg-threatening injuries, *New England Journal of Medicine*, 347, 1924–31.

Brassington, G.S., Atienza, A.A., Perczek, R.E., DiLorenzo, T.M. and King, A.C. (2002) Intervention-related cognitive versus social mediators of exercise adherence in the elderly, *American Journal of Preventive Medicine*, 23, 80–6.

Carson, J.A.S., Gilham, M.B., Kirk, L.M., Reddy, S.T. and Battles, J.B. (2002) Enhancing self-efficacy and patient care with cardiovascular nutrition education, *American Journal of Preventive Medicine*, 23, 296–302.

Carver, C.S. and Scheier, M.F. (1998) *On the Self-regulation of Behavior*. New York: Cambridge University Press.

Catz, S.L., Kelly, J.A., Bogart, L.M., Benotsch, E.G. and McAuliffe, T.L. (2000) Patterns, correlates, and barriers to medication adherence among persons prescribed new treatments for HIV disease, *Health Psychology*, 19, 124–33.

Chalmers, K.I. and Luker, K.A. (1996) Breast self-care practices in women with primary relatives with breast cancer, *Journal of Advanced Nursing*, 23, 1212–20.

Champion, V.L. (1990) Breast self examination in women 35 and older: a prospective study, *Journal of Behavioral Medicine*, 13, 523–30.

Christiansen, M., Vik, P.W. and Jarchow, A. (2002) College student heavy drinking in social contexts versus alone, *Addictive Behaviors*, 27: 393–404.

Clark, M.M. and Dodge, J.A. (1999) Exploring self-efficacy as a predictor of disease management, *Health Education and Behaviour*, 26, 72–89.

Cohen, E.S. and Fromme, K. (2002) Differential determinants of young adult substance use and high risk sexual behavior, *Journal of Applied Social Psychology*, 32, 1124–50.

Colletti, G., Supnick, J.A. and Payne, T.J. (1985) The smoking self-efficacy questionnaire (SSEQ): preliminary scale development and validation, *Behavioral Assessment*, 7, 249–60.

Conn, V.S. (1997) Older women: social cognitive correlates of health behaviour, *Women and Health*, 26, 71–85.

Conrad, K.M., Flay, B.R. and Hill, D. (1992) Why children start smoking cigarettes: predictors of onset, *British Journal of Addiction*, 87, 1711–24.

Contento, I.R., Randell, J.S. and Basch, C.E. (2002) Review and analysis of education measures used in nutrition education intervention research, *Journal of Nutrition Education and Behavior*, 34, 2–25.

Cormier, L., Kwan, L., Reid, K. and Litwin, M. (2002) Knowledge and beliefs among brothers and sons of men with prostate cancer, *Urology*, 59, 895–900.

Curry, S.J. (1993) Self-help interventions for smoking cessation, *Journal of Consulting and Clinical Psychology*, **61**, 790–803.

Dearden, K.A., Quan Ie, N., Do, M., Marsh, D.R., Schroeder, D.G., Pachon, H. *et al.* (2002) What influences healthy behavior? Learning from caregivers of young children in Viet Nam, *Food and Nutrition Bulletin*, **23**, 119–29.

DeVellis, B.M. and DeVellis, R.F. (2000) Self efficacy and health. In A. Baum, T.A. Revenson and J.E. Singer (eds) *Handbook of Health Psychology*. Mahwah, NJ: Erlbaum, 235–47.

DeVries, H., Dijkstra, M. and Kok, G.J. (1989) Self-efficacy as a determinant of the onset of smoking and interventions to prevent smoking in adolescents. Paper presented to the First European Congress of Psychology, Amsterdam, July.

DeVries, H., Dijkstra, M. and Kuhlman, P. (1988) Self-efficacy: the third factor besides attitude and subjective norm as a predictor of behavioural intentions, *Health Education Research*, **3**, 273–82.

DiClemente, C.C., Prochaska, J.O. and Gibertini, M. (1985) Self-efficacy and the stages of self-change of smoking, *Cognitive Therapy and Research*, **9**, 181–200.

Dijkstra, A., Bakker, M. and DeVries, H. (1997) Subtypes within a precontemplating sample of smokers: a preliminary extension of the stages of change, *Addictive Behaviors*, **22**, 327–37.

Dijkstra, A. and DeVries, H. (2000) Self-efficacy expectations with regard to different tasks in smoking cessations, *Psychology and Health*, **15**, 501–11.

Dijkstra, A. and DeVries, H. (2001) Do self-help interventions in health education lead to cognitive changes, and do cognitive changes lead to behavioural change?, *British Journal of Health Psychology*, **6**, 121–34.

Dijkstra, A., DeVries, H., Kok, G. and Roijackers, J. (1999) Self-evaluation and motivation to change: social cognitive constructs in smoking cessation, *Psychology and Health*, **14**, 747–59.

Dijkstra, A., DeVries, H. and Roijackers, J. (1998) Computerized tailored feedback to change cognitive determinants of smoking: a Dutch field experiment, *Health Education Research*, **13**, 197–206.

Dilorio, C., Dudley, W.N., Kelly, M., Soet, J.E., Mbwara, J. and Sharpe Potter, J. (2001) Social cognitive correlates of sexual experience and condom use among 13- through 15-year-old adolescents, *Journal of Adolescent Health*, **29**, 208–16.

Dilorio, C., Dudley, W.N., Lehr, S. and Soet, J.E. (2000a) Correlates of safer sex communication among college students, *Journal of Advanced Nursing*, **32**, 658–65.

Dilorio, C., Dudley, W.N., Soet, J., Watkins, J. and Maibach, E. (2000b) A social cognitive model for condom use among college students, *Nursing Research*, **49**, 208–14.

Dilorio, C., Maibach, E., O'Leary, A., Sanderson, C.A. and Celentano, D. (1997) Measurement of condom use self efficacy and outcome expectancies in a geographically diverse group of STD patents, *AIDS Education and Prevention*, **9**, 1–13.

Dishman, R.K., Darracott, C.R. and Lambert, L.T. (1992) Failure to generalize determinants of self-reported physical activity to a motion sensor, *Medicine and Science in Sports and Exercise*, **24**, 904–10.

Dishman, R.K., Motl, R.W., Saunders, R., Felton, G., Ward, D.S., Dowda, M. *et al.* (2004) Self-efficacy partially mediates the effects of a school-based physical-activity intervention among adolescent girls, *Preventive Medicine*, **38**, 628–36.

Dzewaltowski, D.A. (1989) Toward a model of exercise motivation, *Journal of Sport and Exercise Psychology*, **11**, 251–69.

Dzewaltowski, D.A., Estabrooks, P.A., Gyurcsik, N.C. and Johnston, J.A. (2002a) Promotion of physical activity through community development. In J.L. Van Raalte and B.W. Brewer (eds) *Exploring Sport and Exercise Psychology*, 2nd edition. Washington, DC: American Psychological Association, 209–33.

Dzewaltowski, D.A., Estabrooks, P.A. and Johnston, J.A. (2002b) Healthy young places promoting nutrition and physical activity, *Health Education Research*, 17, 541–51.

Ellickson, P.L. and Hays, R.D. (1991) Beliefs about resistance self-efficacy and drug prevalence: do they really affect drug use?, *International Journal of the Addictions*, 25, 1353–78.

Ellickson, P.L. and Hays, R.D. (1992) On becoming involved with drugs: modelling adolescent drug use over time, *Health Psychology*, 11, 377–85.

Ewart, C.K. (1992) The role of physical self-efficacy in recovery from heart attack. In R. Schwarzer (ed) *Self-efficacy: Thought Control of Action*. Washington, DC: Hemisphere, 287–304.

Field, A.E., Camargo, C.A., Taylor, C.B., Berkey, C.S., Roberts, S.B. and Colditz, G.A. (2001) Peer-parent, and media influences on the development of weight concerns and frequent dieting among preadolescent and adolescent girls and boys, *Pediatrics*, 107, 54–60.

Fishbein, M. (2001) Sexually transmitted diseases: psychosocial aspects. In N. J. Smelser and P. B. Baltes (eds) *The international encyclopedia of the social and behavioral sciences*, Vol. 21. Oxford, England: Elsevier, 26–32.

Fishbein, M. and Ajzen, I. (1975) *Belief, Attitude, Intention, and Behavior: An Introduction to Theory and Research*. Reading, MA: Addison-Wesley.

Fishbein, M., Bandura, A., Triandis, H.C., Kanfer, F.H., Becker, M.H. and Middlestadt, S.E. (1992) *Factors Influencing Behavior and Behavior Change: Final Report – Theorist's Workshop*. Rockville, MD: National Institute of Mental Health.

Glynn, S.M. and Ruderman, A.J. (1986) The development and validation of an eating self-efficacy scale, *Cognitive Therapy and Research*, 10, 403–20.

Godding, P.R. and Glasgow, R.E. (1985) Self-efficacy and outcome expectations as predictors of controlled smoking status, *Cognitive Therapy and Research*, 9, 583–90.

Gollwitzer, P.M. (1999) Implementation intentions: strong effects of simple plans, *American Psychologist*, 54, 493–503.

Gruder, C.L., Mermelstein, R.J., Kirkendol, S., Hedeker, D., Wong, S.C., Schreckengost, J. *et al.* (1993) Effects of social support and relapse prevention training as adjuncts to a televised smoking-cessation intervention, *Journal of Consulting and Clinical Psychology*, 61, 113–20.

Gwaltney, C.J., Shiffman, S., Paty, J.A., Liu, K.S., Kassel, J.D., Gnys, M. *et al.* (2002) Using self-efficacy judgements to predict characteristics of lapses to smoking, *Journal of Consulting and Clinical Psychology*, 70, 1140–9.

Hallam, J. and Petrosa, R. (1998) A worksite intervention to enhance social cognitive theory constructs to promote exercise adherence, *American Journal of Health Promotion*, 13, 4–7.

Hofstetter, C.R., Sallis, J.F. and Hovell, M.F. (1990) Some health dimensions of self-efficacy: analysis of theoretical specificity, *Social Science and Medicine*, 31, 1051–6.

Holman, H.R. and Lorig, K. (1992) Perceived self-efficacy in self-management of chronic disease. In R. Schwarzer (ed) *Self-efficacy: Thought Control of Action*. Washington, DC: Hemisphere, 305–23.

James, A.S., Tripp, M.K., Parcel, G.S., Sweeney, A. and Gritz, E.R. (2002) Psychosocial correlates of sun-protective practices of preschool staff toward their students, *Health Education Research*, 17, 305–14.

Jessor, R. (ed) (1998) *New Perspectives on Adolescent Risk Behavior*. New York: Cambridge University Press.

Karoly, P. (1993) Mechanisms of self-regulation: a system view, *Annual Review of Psychology*, 44, 23–52.

Kasen, S., Vaughn, R.D. and Walter, H.J. (1992) Self-efficacy for AIDS preventive behaviors among tenth-grade students, *Health Education Quarterly*, 19, 187–202.

Kok, G., Den Boer, D., DeVries, H., Gerards, F., Hospers, H.J. and Mudde, A.N. (1992) Self-efficacy and attribution theory in health education. In R. Schwarzer (ed) *Self-efficacy: Thought Control of Action*. Washington, DC: Hemisphere, 245–62.

Kremers, S.P., Mesters, I., Pladdet, I.E., van den Borne, B. and Stockbrügger, R.W. (2000) Participation in a sigmoidoscopic colorectal cancer screening program: a pilot study, *Cancer Epidemiology, Biomarkers and Prevention*, 9, 1127–30.

Lawrence, J.S., Eldridge, G.D., Shelby, M.C., Little, C.E., Brasfield, T.L. and O'Bannon, R.E. III (1997) HIV risk reduction for incarcerated women: a comparison of brief interventions based on two theoretical models, *Journal of Consulting and Clinical Psychology*, 65, 504–9.

Levinson, R.A. (1982) Teenage women and contraceptive behavior: focus on self-efficacy in sexual and contraceptive situations. Unpublished PhD thesis, Stanford University, Stanford, California.

Luszczynska, A. (2004) Change in breast self-examination behavior: effects of intervention on enhancing self-efficacy, *International Journal of Behavioral Medicine*, 11, 95–103.

Luszczynska, A. and Schwarzer, R. (2003) Planning and self-efficacy in the adoption and maintenance of breast self-examination: a longitudinal study on self-regulatory cognitions, *Psychology and Health*, 18, 93–108.

Luszczynska, A., Diehl, M., Gutiérrez-Doña, B., Kuusinen, P. and Schwarzer, R. (2004) Measuring one component of dispositional self-regulation: attention control in goal pursuit, *Personality and Individual Differences*, 37, 555–66.

Luszczynska, A., Gutiérrez-Doña B. and Schwarzer R. (in press) General self-efficacy in various domains of human functioning: evidence from five countries, *International Journal of Psychology*.

McAuley, E. (1993) Self-efficacy and the maintenance of exercise participation in older adults, *Journal of Behavioral Medicine*, 16, 103–13.

McAuley, E., Katula, J., Mihalko, S.L., Blissmer, B., Duncan, T.E., Pena, M. *et al.* (1999) Mode of physical activity and self-efficacy in older adults: a latent growth curve analysis, *Journals of Gerontology. Series B, Psychological Sciences and Social Sciences*, 54, 283–92.

Maddux, J.E. (1995) *Self-efficacy, Adaptation, and Adjustment: Theory, Research, and Application*. New York: Plenum.

Maddux, J.E. and Lewis, J. (1995) Self-efficacy and adjustment. Basic principles and issues. In J.E. Maddux (ed.) *Self-efficacy, Adaptation, and Adjustment: Theory, Research, and Application*. New York: Plenum, 37–68.

Maddux, J.E. and Rogers, R.W. (1983) Protection motivation and self-efficacy: a revised theory of fear appeals and attitude change, *Journal of Experimental Social Psychology*, 19, 469–79.

Marlatt, G.A. (1998) *Harm Reduction: Pragmatic Strategies for Managing High-Risk Behaviours.* New York: Guilford Press.

Marlatt, G.A., Baer, J.S. and Quigley, L.A. (1995) Self-efficacy and addictive behavior. In A. Bandura (ed) *Self-efficacy in Changing Societies.* New York: Cambridge University Press, 289–315.

Marlatt, G.A. and Gordon, J.R. (eds) (1985) *Relapse Prevention.* New York: Guilford.

Meyerowitz, B.E. and Chaiken, S. (1987) The effect of message framing on breast self-examination attitudes, intentions, and behavior, *Journal of Personality and Social Psychology,* **52,** 500–10.

Miller, C.K., Edwards, L., Kissling, G. and Sanville, L. (2002) Nutrition education improves metabolic outcomes among older adults with diabetes mellulitis: results from a randomized controlled trial, *Preventive Medicine,* **34,** 252–9.

Molassiotis, A., Nahas-Lopez, V., Chung, W.Y., Lam, S.W., Li, C.K. and Lau, T.F. (2002) Factors associated with adherence to antiretroviral medication in HIV-infected patients, *International Journal of STD and AIDS,* **13,** 301–10.

Motl, R.W., Dishman, R.K., Saundres, R.P., Dowda, M., Felton, G., Ward, D.S. *et al.* (2002) Examining social-cognitive determinants of intention and physical activity among Black and White adolescent girls using structural equation modelling, *Health Psychology,* **21,** 459–67.

Murphy, D.A., Greenwell, L. and Hoffman, D. (2002) Factors associated with antiretroviral adherence among HIV-infected women with children, *Women and Health,* **36,** 97–111.

Newcomb, M.D. and Bentler, P.M. (1988) *Consequence of Adolescent Drug Use: Impact on the Lives of Young Adults.* Beverly Hills, CA: Sage Publications.

Niaura, R., Shadel, W.G., Britt, D.M. and Abrams, D.B. (2002) Response to social stress, urge to smoke, and smoking cessation, *Addictive Behaviors,* **27,** 241–50.

NIMH (National Institute of Mental Health) Multisite HIV Prevention Trial Group (1998) The NIMH Multisite HIV prevention trial: reducing HIV sexual risk behavior, *Science,* **280,** 1889–94.

NIMH Multisite HIV Prevention Trial Group (2001) Social-cognitive theory mediators of behavior change in the National Institute of Mental Health Multisite HIV Prevention Trial, *Health Psychology,* **20,** 369–76.

Ockene, J.K., Emmons, K.M., Mermelstein, R.J., Perkins, K.A., Bonollo, D.S., Voorhees, C.C. *et al.* (2000) Relapse and maintenance issues for smoking cessation, *Health Psychology,* **19,** 17–31.

O'Leary, A., Maibach, E., Ambrose, T.K., Jemmot III, J.B. and Celentano, D.D. (2000) Social cognitive predictors of sexual risk behavior change among STD clinic patients, *AIDS and Behavior,* **4,** 309–16.

O'Leary, A., Shoor, S., Lorig, K. and Holman, H.R. (1988) A cognitive-behavioral treatment for rheumatoid arthritis, *Health Psychology,* **7,** 527–42.

Parent, N. and Fortin, F. (2000) A randomized controlled trial of vicarious experience through peer support for male first-time cardiac surgery patients: impact on anxiety, self-efficacy expectation, and self-reported activity, *Heart and Lung,* **29,** 389–400.

Pinto, B.M., Friedman, R., Marcus, B.H., Kelly, H., Tennstedt, S. and Gillman, M.W. (2002a) Effects of computer-based, telephone-counseling system on physical activity, *American Journal of Preventive Medicine,* **23,** 113–20.

Pinto, B.M., Maruyama N.C., Clark, M.M., Cruess, D.G., Park, E. and Roberts, M. (2002b) Motivation to modify lifestyle risk behaviors in women treated for breast cancer, *Mayo Clinic Proceedings,* **77,** 122–9.

Renner, B. and Schwarzer, R. (2003) Social-cognitive factors predicting health behavior change. In J. Suls and K. Wallston (eds) *Social Psychological Foundations of Health and Illness*. Oxford: Blackwell, 169–96.

Resnicow, K., Wallace, D.S., Jackson, A., Digirolamo, A., Odom, E., Wang, T. *et al.* (2000) Dietary change through African American churches: baseline results and program description of the eat for life trial, *Journal of Cancer Education*, **15**, 156–63.

Rodgers, W.M., Hall, C.R., Blanchard, C.M., McAuley, E. and Munroe, K.J. (2002) Task and scheduling self-efficacy as predictors of exercise behavior, *Psychology and Health*, **27**, 405–16.

Rovniak, L.S., Anderson, E.S., Winett, R. A. and Stephens, R.S. (2002) Social cognitive determinants of physical activity in young adults: a prospective structural equation analysis, *Annals of Behavioral Medicine*, **24**, 149–56.

Ruiter, R.A.C., Abraham, C. and Kok, G. (2001) Scary warnings and rational precautions: a review of the psychology of fear appeals, *Psychology and Health*, **16**, 613–30.

Sallis, J.F., Prochaska, J.J. and Taylor, W.C. (2000) A review of correlates of physical activity and fitness in children and adolescents, *Medicine and Science in Sports and Exercise*, **32**, 963–75.

Savoca, M. and Miller, C. (2001) Food selection and eating patterns: themes found among people with type-2 diabetes mellitus, *Journal of Nutrition Education*, **33**, 224–33.

Schnoll, R.A., Miller, S.M., Unger, M., McAleer, C., Halbherr, T. and Bradley, P. (2002) Characteristics of female smokers attending a lung cancer screening program: a pilot study with implications for program development, *Lung Cancer*, **37**, 257–65.

Schnoll, R. and Zimmerman, B.J. (2001) Self-regulation training enhances dietary self-efficacy and dietary fiber consumption, *Journal of the American Dietetic Association*, **101**, 1006–11.

Scholz, U., Gutiérrez-Doña, B., Sud, S. and Schwarzer, R. (2002) Is general self-efficacy a universal construct? Psychometric findings from 25 countries, *European Journal of Psychological Assessment*, **18**, 242–51.

Schröder, K.E.E., Schwarzer, R. and Konertz, W. (1998) Coping as a mediator in recovery from cardiac surgery, *Psychology and Health*, **13**, 83–97.

Schwarzer, R. (1992) Self-efficacy in the adoption and maintenance of health behaviors: theoretical approaches and a new model. In R. Schwarzer (ed.) *Self-efficacy: Thought Control of Action*. Washington, DC: Hemisphere, 217–42.

Schwarzer, R. (2001) Social-cognitive factors in changing health-related behavior, *Current Directions in Psychological Science*, **10**, 47–51.

Schwarzer, R. and Jerusalem, M. (1995) Generalized self-efficacy scale. In J. Weinman, S. Wright and M. Johnston (eds) *Measures in Health Psychology: A User's Portfolio. Causal and Control Beliefs*. Windsor, UK: NFER-NELSON, 35–7.

Schwarzer, R. and Renner, B. (2000) Social-cognitive predictors of health behavior: action self-efficacy and coping self-efficacy, *Health Psychology*, **19**, 487–95.

Semple, S.J., Patterson, T.L. and Grant, I. (2000) Partner type and sexual risk behavior among HIV positive gay and bisexual men: social cognitive correlates, *AIDS Education and Prevention*, **12**, 340–56.

Senecal, C., Nouven, A. and White, D. (2000) Motivation and dietary self-care in adults with diabetes: are self-efficacy and autonomous self-regulation complementary or competing constructs?, *Health Psychology*, **19**, 452–7.

Seydel, E., Taal, E. and Wiegman, O. (1990) Risk-appraisal, outcome and self-efficacy expectancies: cognitive factors in preventive behavior related to cancer, *Psychology and Health*, **4**, 99–109.

Shannon, B., Bagby, R., Wang, M.Q. and Trenkner, L. (1990) Self-efficacy: a contributor to the explanation of eating behavior, *Health Education Research*, **5**, 395–407.

Shaw, J.M., Dzewaltowski, D.A. and McElroy, M. (1992) Self-efficacy and causal attributions as mediators of perceptions of psychological momentum, *Journal of Sport and Exercise Psychology*, **14**, 134–47.

Sherer, M., Maddux, J.E., Mercandante, B., Prentice-Dunn, S., Jacobs, B. and Rogers, R.W. (1982) The self-efficacy scale: construction and validation, *Psychological Reports*, **51**, 663–71.

Shiffman, S., Balabanis, M.H., Paty, J.A., Engberg, J., Gwaltney, C.J., Liu, K.S. *et al.* (2000) Dynamic effects of self-efficacy on smoking lapse and relapse, *Health Psychology*, **19**, 315–23.

Stacy, A.W., Sussman, S., Dent, C.W., Burton, D. and Flay, B.R. (1992) Moderators of peer social influence in adolescent smoking, *Personality and Social Psychology Bulletin*, **18**, 163–72.

Stanton, B.F., Li, X., Ricardo, I., Galbraith, J., Feigelman, S. and Kaljee, L. (1996) A randomized, controlled trial of an AIDS prevention program for low-income African American youths, *Archives of Pediatrics and Adolescent Medicine*, **150**, 363–72.

Stewart, S.M., Lee, P.W., Waller, D., Hughes C.W., Low, L.C., Kennard, B.D. *et al.* (2003) A follow up study of adherence and glycemic control among Hong Kong youths with diabetes, *Journal of Pediatric Psychology*, **28**, 67–79.

Strauss, R.S., Rodzilsky, D., Burack, G. and Colin, M. (2001) Psychosocial correlates of physical activity in healthy children, *Archives of Pediatrics and Adolescent Medicine*, **155**, 897–902.

Taylor, C.B., Bandura, A., Ewart, C.K., Miller, N.H. and DeBusk, R.F. (1985) Exercise testing to enhance wives' confidence in their husbands' cardiac capability soon after clinically uncomplicated acute myocardial infarction, *American Journal of Cardiology*, **55**, 635–8.

Toshima, M.T., Kaplan, R.M. and Ries, A.L. (1992) Self-efficacy expectancies in chronic obstructive pulmonary disease rehabilitation. In R. Schwarzer (ed.) *Self-efficacy: Thought Control of Action*. Washington, DC: Hemisphere, 325–54.

Trobst, K.L., Herbst, J.H., Masters, H.L. III and Costa, P.T. Jr (2002) Personality pathways to unsafe sex: personality, condom use and HIV risk behaviors, *Journal of Research in Personality*, **36**, 117–33.

Umeh, K. and Rogan-Gibson, J. (2001) Perceptions of threat, benefits, and barriers in breast self-examination amongst asymptomatic women, *British Journal of Health Psychology*, **6**, 361–72.

Van Duyn, M.A., Kristal, A.R., Dodd, K., Campbell, M.K., Subar, A.F., Stables, G. *et al.* (2001) Association of awareness, intrapersonal and interpersonal factors, and stage of dietary change with fruit and vegetable consumption: a national survey, *American Journal of Health Promotion*, **16**, 69–78.

Velicer, W.F., DiClemente, C.C., Rossi, J.S. and Prochaska, J.O. (1990) Relapse situations and self-efficacy: an integrative model, *Addictive Behaviors*, **15**, 271–83.

Wills, T.A., Gibbons, F.X., Gerrard, M. and Brody, G. (2000) Protection and vulnerability processes for early onset of substance use: a test among African-American children, *Health Psychology*, **19**, 253–63.

Wang, R.-H., Wang, H.-H. and Hsu, M.-T. (2003) Factors associated with adolescent pregnancy – a sample of Taiwanese female adolescents, *Public Health Nursing*, **20**, 33–41.

Weinberg, R.S., Gould, D. and Jackson, A. (1979) Expectations and performance: an empirical test of Bandura's self-efficacy theory, *Journal of Sport Psychology*, **1**, 320–31.

Weinberg, R.S., Yukelson, D. and Jackson, A. (1980) Effects of public and private efficacy expectations on competitive performance, *Journal of Sport Psychology*, **2**, 340–9.

Weinstein, N.D. (2003) Exploring the links between risk perceptions and preventive health behavior. In J. Suls and K. Wallston (eds) *Social Psychological Foundations of Health and Illness*. Oxford: Blackwell, 22–53.

Williams, K.E. and Bond, M.J. (2002) The roles of self-efficacy, outcome expectancies and social support in the self-care behaviors of diabetics, *Psychology, Health and Medicine*, **7**, 127–41.

Wilson, D.K., Friend, R., Teasley, N., Green, S., Reaves, I.L. and Sica, D.A. (2002) Motivational versus social cognitive interventions for promoting fruit and vegetable intake and physical activity in African American adolescents, *Annals of Behavioral Medicine*, **24**, 310–19.

Wilson, D.K., Wallston, K.A. and King, J.E. (1990) Effects of contract framing, motivation to quit, and self-efficacy on smoking reduction, *Journal of Applied Social Psychology*, **20**, 531–47.

Winkleby, M.A., Feighery, E.C., Altman, D.A., Kole, S. and Tencati, E. (2001) Engaging ethnically diverse teens in a substance use prevention advocacy program, *American Journal of Health Promotion*, **15**, 433–6.

Wulfert, E. and Wan C.K. (1993) Condom use: a self-efficacy model, *Health Psychology*, **12**, 346–53.

5 MARK CONNER AND
PAUL SPARKS

THEORY OF PLANNED BEHAVIOUR
AND HEALTH BEHAVIOUR

1 General background

The theory of planned behaviour (TPB; Ajzen 1988, 1991) is an extension
of the earlier theory of reasoned action (TRA; Fishbein and Ajzen 1975;
Ajzen and Fishbein 1980), which continues to attract attention in psychology (Sheppard *et al.* 1988; Ajzen 2001). Both models are considered
deliberative processing models that imply that people's attitudes are formed
after careful consideration of available information. The TRA origins are in
Fishbein's work on the psychological processes by which attitudes cause
behaviour (Fishbein 1967a) and in an analysis of the failure to predict
behaviour from individuals' attitudes. The former work used an expectancy-value framework (Peak 1955) to explain the relationship between
beliefs and attitudes, and interposed a new variable, behavioural intention,
between attitudes and behaviour; the latter work generated a powerful
explanation of the conditions under which strong attitude–behaviour
relationships might be expected (the principle of compatibility).

Based on an analysis of previous studies of the relationship between
attitudes and behaviour, Fishbein and Ajzen (1975; Ajzen and Fishbein
1977) developed the principle of compatibility (Ajzen 1988).[1] This principle
holds that each attitude and behaviour has the four elements of action,
target, context and time, and states that correspondence between attitudes
and behaviour will be greatest when both are measured at the same degree
of specificity with respect to each element (see Ajzen and Fishbein 2005 for
a recent discussion). Hence, any behaviour consists of (a) an action (or
behaviour), (b) performed on or toward a target or object, (c) in a particular
context, (d) at a specified time or occasion. For example, a person concerned about oral hygiene (a) brushes (b) her teeth (c) in the bathroom (d)
every morning after breakfast. In the study of health behaviours commonly

it is the repeat performance of a single behaviour (e.g. teeth brushing) or general class of behaviours (e.g. healthy eating) across contexts and times that we wish to predict (Ajzen 1988). Attitudes and behaviour will be most strongly related when both are assessed at the same level of specificity with regard to these four elements. Thus, general attitudes should predict general classes of behaviours and specific attitudes should predict specific behaviours. Considerations of compatibility are particularly important in developing appropriate measures for components of the TRA/TPB.

2 Description of the model

The TRA suggests that the proximal determinant (or cause) of volitional behaviour is one's behavioural intention to engage in that behaviour. Behavioural intention represents a person's motivation in the sense of her or his conscious plan, decision or self-instruction to exert effort to perform the target behaviour. Attitudes towards a specific behaviour impact on performance of the behaviour via intentions. Thus in the TRA the issue of how the unobservable attitude is transformed into observable action is clarified by interposing another psychological event: the formation of an intention between the attitude and the behaviour. However, the theory is less clear about the factors that lead attitudes to be translated into intentions. One possibility is that it is the anticipated opportunity to perform the behaviour that promotes the formation of an intention. The TRA includes a second determinant of intention, subjective norm. This component represents the perceived social pressure from others to perform the target behaviour. The TRA restricts itself to the prediction of volitional behaviours. Those behaviours requiring skills, resources or opportunities that are not freely available are not considered to be within the domain of applicability of the TRA. As a result, they are likely to be poorly predicted by the TRA (Fishbein 1993).

The TPB was developed to broaden the applicability of the TRA beyond purely volitional behaviours by incorporating explicit considerations of perceptions of control over performance of the behaviour as an additional predictor of behaviour (Ajzen 1988, 1991). Consideration of perceptions of control, or perceived behavioural control (PBC), are important because they extend the applicability of the theory beyond easily performed, volitional behaviours to those complex goals and behaviours which are dependent upon performance of a complex series of other behaviours, but which are of considerable importance in terms of health outcomes (e.g. healthy eating). It is this lack of actual control which attenuates the power of intentions to predict behaviour (Ajzen and Fishbein 2005). However, given the myriad of problems defining and measuring actual control (Ajzen and Fishbein 2005), perceptions of control (PBC) have tended to be employed. To the extent that PBC accurately reflects actual control, it should provide good predictions of behaviour. The inclusion of PBC in the TPB provides information about the potential constraints on action as perceived by the actor, and explains why intentions do not always predict behaviour.

The TPB depicts behaviour as a linear regression function of behavioural intention and perceived behavioural control:

$$B = w_1 BI + w_2 PBC \tag{1}$$

where B is behaviour, BI is behavioural intention, PBC is perceived behavioural control, and w_1 and w_2 are regression weights. Contrary to some commentators' misconceptions, the value of these regression weights needs to be empirically determined and will likely vary as a function of both the behaviour and the population being examined.

The link between intention and behaviour reflects the fact that people tend to engage in behaviours they intend to perform. However, the link between PBC and behaviour is more complex. PBC is held to exert both direct and interactive (with behavioural intentions) effects on behaviour. This is based on the following rationale: that however strongly held, the implementation of an intention into action is at least partially determined by personal and environmental barriers, thus, 'The addition of perceived behavioral control should become increasingly useful as volitional control over behavior decreases' (Ajzen 1991: 185). Therefore, in situations where prediction of behaviour from intention is likely to be hindered by the level of actual (i.e. volitional) control, PBC should (a) facilitate the implementation of behavioural intentions into action, and (b) predict behaviour directly (Armitage and Conner 2001). Ajzen (1988) is explicit in stating that it is actual control which is important here, in that people will tend to perform (and exert extra effort to perform) desirable behaviours they have control over, and not perform behaviours they have little or no control over. Hence, measures of actual control would be preferable here. However, because such measures are difficult to obtain, perceptions of control (PBC) are used as proxy measures for actual control. PBC will predict behaviour directly to the extent that the measure matches actual control (Ajzen 1988). The review of Armitage and Conner (2001) indicated the interaction between intentions and PBC to be significant in approximately half of reported tests, while Sheeran *et al.* (2003) showed that where PBC proved to be accurate it provided stronger predictions of behaviour and moderated the intention–behaviour relationship.

2.1 Determinants of intention

In the TRA, attitudes are one predictor of behavioural intention. Attitudes are the overall evaluations of the behaviour by the individual. Fishbein and Ajzen (1975: 6) define an attitude as 'a learned disposition to respond in a consistently favorable or unfavorable manner with respect to a given object'. Applying the principle of compatibility, the relevant attitudes are those towards performance of the behaviour, assessed at a similar level of specificity to that used in the assessment of behaviour. The TRA also specifies subjective norms as the other determinant of intentions. Subjective norms consist of a person's beliefs about whether significant others think he/she should engage in the behaviour. Significant others are individuals or groups whose preferences about a person's behaviour in this domain are important to him or her. Subjective norms are assumed to assess the social pressures individuals feel to perform or not perform a particular behaviour from salient referents. The TPB incorporates a third predictor of intentions, perceived behavioural control, which is the individual's perception of the extent to which performance of the behaviour is easy or difficult. Control is seen as a continuum with easily executed behaviours at one end (e.g. eating a readily available, liked food) and behavioural goals demanding resources, opportunities and specialized skills (e.g. becoming a world-class chess player) at the other end. Hence, behavioural intention is a linear regression function of attitudes, subjective norms and perceived behavioural control:

$$BI = w_3A + w_4SN + w_5PBC \tag{2}$$

where BI is behavioural intention, A is attitude toward the behaviour, SN is subjective norm, PBC is perceived behavioural control, and w_3 to w_5 are empirical weights indicating the relative importance of the determinants of intention. The equation indicates that intentions are a function of one's evaluation of personally engaging in the behaviour, one's perception that significant others think you should or should not perform the behaviour, and perceptions of one's control over performance of the behaviour. Without the PBC component, equation 2 represents the TRA. It is worth noting that, unlike other variables, PBC has links with both the intentions and behaviour components in the TPB. The PBC–intention link represents the fact that, in general, individuals are more disposed (i.e. intend) to engage in positively valued behaviours that are believed to be achievable (cf. Bandura 1986).

The weights in equation 2 are assumed to vary as a function of the behaviour and the population under study. Ajzen (1991) states that 'The relative importance of attitude, subjective norm, and perceived behavioral control in the prediction of intention is expected to vary across behaviors and situations' (p.188). Research indicates that there may be individual differences in the weights placed on the different components, with some individuals tending to base their intentions on attitudes and others on norms across behaviours (Trafimow and Findlay 1996). In addition, in situations where (for example) attitudes are strong, or where normative influences are powerful, PBC may be less predictive of intentions. Indirect evidence for this has been found in studies that have shown that measures of attitude strength (e.g. Sparks *et al.* 1992) and individual differences in sociability (e.g. Trafimow and Findlay 1996) increase the relative predictive power of attitudes and subjective norms, respectively.

2.2 Determinants of attitudes

Just as intentions are held to have determinants, so the attitude, subjective norm and perceived behavioural control components are also held to have determinants. The determinants are sometimes referred to as indirect measures. However, it is worth noting that both the direct and indirect measures of each of the components are considered to be measures of one and the same construct (Ajzen and Fishbein 1980). Attitude is a function of salient behavioural beliefs, which represent perceived consequences or other attributes of the behaviour. Following expectancy-value conceptualizations (Peak 1955), consequences are composed of the multiplicative combination of the perceived likelihood that performance of the behaviour will lead to a particular outcome and the evaluation of that outcome. These expectancy-value products are then summed over the various salient consequences:

$$A = \sum_{i = 1}^{i = p} b_i \cdot e_i \tag{3}$$

where b_i is the behavioural belief that performing the behaviour leads to some consequence i (thus b_i is the subjective probability that the behaviour has the consequence i), e_i is the evaluation of consequence i, and p is the number of salient consequences over which these values are summed. It is not claimed that an individual performs such calculations each time he or she is faced with a decision about performing a behaviour, but rather that the results of such considerations are maintained in memory and retrieved and used when necessary (Eagly and Chaiken 1993). However, it is also possible for the individual to retrieve the relevant individual beliefs and evaluations when necessary. Fishbein (1993) claims equation 3 is not a model of a process but is a computational representation aimed to capture the output of a process that occurs automatically as a function of learning (see Ajzen and Fishbein 2000). This part of the model, the relationship between attitudes and beliefs, is based on Fishbein's (1967a, 1967b) *summative model of attitudes*. It is assumed that a person may possess a large number of beliefs about a particular behaviour, but that at any one time only some of these are likely to be salient. It is the salient beliefs which are assumed to determine a person's attitude. This link between attitudes and behavioural beliefs is generally strong (Van den Putte 1991; Armitage and Conner 2001).

2.3 Determinants of subjective norm

Subjective norm is a function of normative beliefs, which represent perceptions of specific significant others' preferences about whether one should or should not engage in a behaviour. This is quantified in the model as the subjective likelihood that specific salient groups or individuals (referents) think the person should or should not perform the behaviour, multiplied by the person's motivation to comply with that referent's expectation. Motivation to comply is the extent to which the person wishes to comply with the specific wishes of the referent on this issue. These products are then summed across salient referents:

$$SN = \sum_{j=1}^{j=q} nb_j \cdot mc_j \qquad (4)$$

where SN is the subjective norm, nb_j is the normative belief (i.e. a subjective probability) that some referent j thinks one should perform the behaviour, mc_j is the motivation to comply with referent j, and q is the number of salient referents. It should be noted that the distinction between behavioural beliefs and normative beliefs is somewhat arbitrary (Miniard and Cohen 1981) and there is often considerable correlation between the two (O'Keefe 1990). However, there is some merit in maintaining a distinction between the determinants of behaviour that are attributes of the person and those which are attributes of the social environment (see Eagly and Chaiken 1993: 171; Trafimow and Fishbein 1995). The expectancy-value nature of equation 4 has been noted by a number of authors (e.g. Eagly and Chaiken 1993) and is supported by strong correlations between normative beliefs and subjective norms (Van den Putte 1991; Armitage and Conner 2001).

2.4 Determinants of perceived behavioural control

Judgements of perceived behavioural control are influenced by beliefs concerning whether one has access to the necessary resources and opportunities to perform the behaviour successfully, weighted by the perceived power of each factor (Ajzen 1988, 1991). The perception of factors likely to facilitate or inhibit the performance of the behaviour are referred to as control beliefs. These factors include both internal (information, personal deficiencies, skills, abilities, emotions) and external (opportunities, dependence on others, barriers) control factors. People who perceive they have access to the necessary resources and perceive that there are opportunities (or lack of obstacles) to perform the behaviour are likely to perceive a high degree of behavioural control (Ajzen 1991). Ajzen (1991) has suggested that each control factor is weighted by its perceived power to facilitate or inhibit performance of the behaviour. The model quantifies these beliefs by multiplying the frequency or likelihood of occurrence of the factor by the subjective perception of the power of the factor to facilitate or inhibit the performance of the behaviour:

$$PBC = \sum_{k=1}^{k=r} c_k \cdot p_k \qquad (5)$$

where PBC is perceived behavioural control, c_k is the perceived frequency or likelihood of occurrence of factor k, p_k is the perceived facilitating or inhibiting power of the factor k, and r is the number of control factors. The similarity of equation 5 to an expectancy-value computation is again worth noting. Correlations between control beliefs and PBC is supportive of the multiplicative composite (Armitage and Conner 2001).

2.5 Commentary

The causal model the TPB represents is illustrated in Figure 5.1. Behaviour is determined by intention to engage in the behaviour and perceptions of control over performance of the behaviour. Intention is determined by attitude towards the behaviour, subjective norms and perceived behavioural control. Attitude is determined by perceptions of the likelihood of salient outcomes and their evaluation. Subjective norm is determined by normative beliefs and motivation to comply with salient referents. PBC is determined by the perceived presence or absence of requisite resources and opportunities and the perceived power of these factors to facilitate or inhibit performance of the behaviour. Actual control influences the impact of PBC on intention and behaviour. The model is held to be a complete theory of behaviour in that any other influences on behaviour are held to have their impact upon behaviour via influencing components of the TPB. However, it is perhaps more correctly regarded as a theory of the proximal determinants of behaviour.

3 Summary of research

The TRA/TPB has been applied to the prediction of a wide range of different behaviours, including health-relevant behaviours, with varying degrees of success. There are a number of narrative reviews (e.g. Liska 1984; Eagly and Chaiken 1993; Sparks 1994; Manstead and Parker 1995; Jonas and Doll 1996; Ajzen and Fishbein 2005) as well as quantitative reviews of the TRA (Sheppard *et al.* 1988; Van den Putte 1991) and TPB (e.g. Armitage and Conner 2001). Here we summarize meta-analytic reviews of the TPB, discuss key issues raised, and summarize applications to health behaviours.

3.1 Meta-analytic reviews of the TPB

A series of meta-analyses have now been reported for the TPB, including general reviews (e.g. Ajzen 1991; Armitage and Conner 2001; Trafimow *et al.* 2002), those focusing on health behaviours (Godin and Kok 1996), and those focusing on specific behaviours (e.g. exercise: Blue 1995; Hausenblas *et al.* 1997; Hagger *et al.* 2002; condom use: Sheeran and Taylor 1999; Albarracin *et al.* 2001).

In a review of early studies using the TPB, Ajzen (1991) reported the multiple correlation between intentions (BI) and attitude (A), subjective norm (SN) and perceived behavioural control (PBC) to be 0.71 (across 16

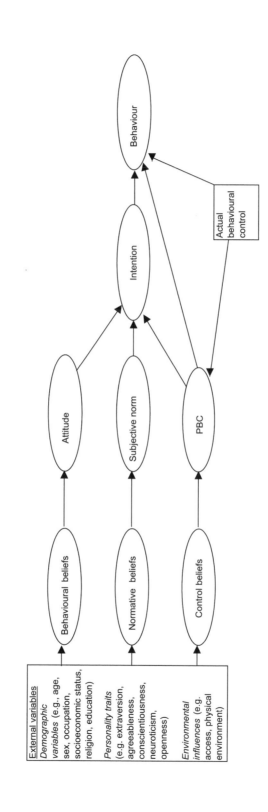

Figure 5.1 The theory of planned behaviour

studies). Similarly, Van den Putte (1991) computed a value of R = 0.64 across 37 studies, but noted a marked variation between behaviours. Trafimow *et al.* (2002), in a review of studies which distinguish between two aspects of PBC (difficulty and control), reported R = 0.66. In the most comprehensive review to date, Armitage and Conner (2001) reported R = 0.63 across 154 studies. Finally, Godin and Kok (1996) in a review of 76 applications of the TPB to health behaviours reported R = 0.64, whilst noting considerable variation between studies. Overall, A, SN and PBC account for between 40 and 50 per cent of the variance in intentions across studies. When considering sample weighted mean correlations (r_+) A and PBC generally emerged as stronger predictors than SN (e.g. in Armitage and Conner 2001, A–BI r_+ = 0.49, SN–BI r_+ = 0.34, PBC–BI r_+ = 0.43).

In relation to the prediction of behaviour (B), Ajzen (1991) reported the mean R = 0.51 between BI, PBC and behaviour, while Van den Putte (1991) computed a value of 0.46. Similar values are reported by the reviews of Trafimow *et al.* (2002) (R = 0.60), Armitage and Conner (2001) (R = 0.52) and Godin and Kok (1996) (R = 0.58). Thus overall, BI and PBC account for between 21 and 36 per cent of the variance in behaviour. Godin and Kok (1996) noted considerable variation in this figure, from 16 per cent for clinical screening behaviours to 41 per cent for addictive behaviours. In the majority of reviews intention accounts for more variance in behaviour than PBC (e.g. Armitage and Conner 2001, BI–B r_+ = 0.47, PBC–B r_+ = 0.37). Despite this power of intentions, the Armitage and Conner (2001) review also indicated that on average PBC predicts a significant 2 per cent additional variance in behaviour after controlling for intentions.

In order to summarize the overall size of relationships among variables in the TRA/TPB we conducted a meta-analysis of meta-analyses of relationships in the TRA/TPB (cp. Sutton 1998). Only meta-analyses which focused on the TRA or TPB and included the sample-weighted mean correlation (r_+) between TRA/TPB components along with total number of participants included in the analyses (n) and the number of hypotheses tested (k) were used. The meta-analysis of Godin and Kok (1996) had to be excluded because n was not reported. The included meta-analyses focus on the TRA (Sheppard *et al.* 1988; Van den Putte 1991), the TPB (Armitage and Conner 2001; Hagger *et al.* 2002; Trafimow *et al.* 2002; McEachan *et al.* 2005), or both the TRA and TPB (Hausenblas *et al.* 1997; Sheeran and Taylor 1999; Albarracin *et al.* 2001). Given that there is some overlap in included studies between these meta-analyses we should be cautious in interpreting the findings. In addition, we should note that the range of behaviours considered extends beyond health behaviours. The findings as summarized in Table 5.1 give some indication of the overall size of relationships among variables in the TRA/TPB. Based on Cohen's (1992) power primer, the relationships between intention and behaviour and between attitude and intention equate to large effect sizes $(r_+ \sim 0.5)$, with the majority of other relationships in the medium $(r_+ \sim 0.3)$ to large $(r_+ \sim 0.5)$ range. Only the subjective norm–behaviour relationship equates to a medium $(r_+ \sim 0.3)$ to small $(r_+ \sim 0.1)$ effect size. Regression analysis of the data in Table 5.1 indicate intention and PBC to explain 25.6 per cent of the variance in behaviour (intention beta = 0.40, p < 0.001; PBC beta = 0.18, p < 0.001), while attitude, subjective norm and PBC explain 33.7 per cent of the variance in intentions (attitude beta = 0.36, p < 0.001; subjective norm beta = 0.15, p < 0.001; PBC beta = 0.25, p < 0.001). Finally, it is worth noting that the correlations between the direct and indirect measures (e.g. attitudes and behavioural beliefs) varied between 0.49 and 0.54, which equates to a large effect size.

Table 5.1 A meta-analysis of meta-analyses of relationships in the TRA/TPB

Relationship	k	n	r_+
BI–B	420	82712	0.48
PBC–B	241	55444	0.35
A–B	126	28495	0.36
SN–B	122	28410	0.16
A–BI	497	111558	0.51
SN–BI	472	109111	0.34
PBC–BI	386	95877	0.43
A–SN	120	30440	0.36
A–PBC	91	26626	0.41
SN–PBC	91	26626	0.26
BB–A	137	29652	0.54
NB–SN	124	25270	0.49
CB–PBC	18	2744	0.52

Note: Included meta-analyses were Sheppard *et al.* 1988; van den Putte, 1991; Hausenblas *et al.* 1997; Sheeran and Taylor 1999; Albarracin *et al.* 2001; Armitage and Conner 2001; Hagger *et al.* 2002; Trafimow *et al.* 2002; McEachan *et al.* 2005. BB = behavioural beliefs; NB = normative beliefs; CB = control beliefs.

3.2 Key issues raised in reviews of the TPB

Applications of the TRA and TPB have tended to rely on self-reports, despite evidence to suggest the vulnerability of such data to self-presentational biases (e.g. Gaes *et al.* 1978). Armitage and Conner (2001) compared the multiple correlations of intention and PBC with objective and self-reported behaviour. The TPB accounted for large, highly significant proportions of the variance in prospective measures of both objective (R^2 = 0.20, k = 19) and self-reported (R^2 = 0.31, k = 44) behaviour. Researchers should be cognizant of the problems of self-report data, and wherever possible take accurate and objective multiple measures of behaviour.

Figure 5.1 recognizes the importance of background factors such as sociodemographic variables within the TPB but assumes they are mediated by TPB variables. However, some studies have found a direct, unmediated effect of background variables on intentions or behaviour. In contrast, the majority of studies have demonstrated that background factors influence intentions and behaviour indirectly by their effects on behavioural, normative or control beliefs (see Ajzen and Fishbein 2005 for a review).

One common criticism of the TRA/TPB has been that it assumes that all behaviour is rational and fails to take account of other non-cognitive or irrational determinants of human behaviour (e.g. Gibbons *et al.* 1998; van der Pligt and de Vries 1998). In this regard, Ajzen and Fishbein (2005) note that typical applications of the TRA/TPB devote little attention to the role of emotion which may be relevant to a range of health behaviours. Such emotions would be considered background variables in the TRA/TPB and might be expected to influence intentions and behaviour via their impact on beliefs and attitudes. However, this criticism highlights potential problems with the way in which typical TRA/TPB studies are conducted. In particular, differences may exist between the contemplation of a behaviour (e.g. when filling in a TPB questionnaire) and its actual performance in a real-life context. It may be that the beliefs activated when completing the questionnaire are different from the ones accessible at the point of performing the behaviour (Ajzen and Sexton 1999), leading to the attitudes, norms, PBC and intentions being poor representations of those which exist in the behavioural situation and thus being poor predictors of action. It may be particularly difficult for individuals to correctly anticipate the strong emotions that drive their behaviour in real life (Ajzen and Fishbein 2005). This would lead to problems with incorporating emotional factors within typical TRA/TPB applications. Nevertheless, it should be noted that there is usually considerable consistency between intentions and behaviours where one might expect considerable differences in emotional state between the context in which the questionnaire is completed and the one in which the behaviour is performed (e.g. condom use; Albarracin *et al.* 2001 report intention–behaviour $r_+ = 0.45$ across 96 data sets).

3.3 Review of applications of the TPB to health behaviours

3.3.1 *Drug use*
A range of licit and illicit drug use has been explored with both the TRA and TPB. These include alcohol use, tobacco smoking and the use of illicit drugs such as cannabis, ecstasy and cocaine. In a recent meta-analysis of prospective applications of the TPB to health behaviours, McEachan *et al.* (2005) located 18 studies examining alcohol use (n = 3), tobacco smoking (n = 7), or illicit drug use (n = 8). Across these studies A, SN and PBC were able to explain a frequency-weighted average of 53 per cent of the variance in intentions with PBC being the strongest predictor ($r_+ = 0.55$), A the second strongest predictor ($r_+ = 0.52$), and SN being the weakest predictor ($r_+ = 0.43$). In relation to behaviour, BI and PBC were able to predict a frequency-weighted average of 39 per cent of the variance in behaviour with BI being a stronger predictor ($r_+ = 0.55$) than PBC ($r_+ = 0.46$). This level of prediction was over an average period of 200 days.

3.3.2 *Sexual behaviours*
A number of sexual behaviours have been examined including condom use in relation to the threat of AIDS, but also other contraceptive behaviours,

casual sex and number of sexual partners. In addition, a range of different population groups have been examined including general populations, heterosexual and homosexual samples and sex workers. There have been several reviews of the application of the TPB to sexual behaviours (Godin and Kok 1996) or condom use (Sheeran and Taylor 1999). Albarracin *et al.* (2001) report the most inclusive review of the application of the TRA and TPB to condom use including a maximum of 96 datasets. Across studies A, SN and PBC explained 50 per cent of the variance in intentions with A (r_+ = 0.58) and PBC (r_+ = 0.45) being stronger predictors than SN (r_+ = 0.39). BI and PBC accounted for an average 30 per cent of the variance in behaviour with the BI–behaviour relationship (r_+ = 0.45) being considerably stronger than the PBC–behaviour relationship (r_+ = 0.25). Indeed, across studies, PBC failed to increase significantly the amount of variance explained in condom use over and above that explained by intentions.

McEachan *et al.* (2005) located 17 prospective studies examining general safer sex behaviours (n = 8), or condom use (n = 9). Across these studies a frequency-weighted average of 49 per cent of the variance in intentions was explained by A, SN and PBC, with A being the strongest predictor (r_+ = 0.43), SN the second strongest predictor (r_+ = 0.38), and PBC being the weakest predictor (r_+ = 0.35). A frequency-weighted average of 28 per cent of the variance in behaviour was explained by BI and PBC, with BI being the stronger predictor (r_+ = 0.39) and PBC the weaker predictor (r_+ = 0.23). These latter predictions were over an average period of 133 days.

3.3.3 Other risk-related behaviours

Both the TRA and TPB have been applied to a number of other risk behaviours such as safe riding of motorbikes, various risk-related driving violations such as exceeding the posted speed limit in cars, and sun protective behaviours. McEachan *et al.* (2005) located six prospective studies examining bike riding safety use (n = 3), car driving behaviours (n = 1), or sun protective behaviours (n = 2). Across these studies A, SN and PBC were able to explain a frequency-weighted average of 54 per cent of the variance in intentions with PBC being the strongest predictor (r_+ = 0.66), SN the second strongest predictor (r_+ = 0.51), and A being the weakest predictor (r_+ = 0.50). In relation to behaviour, BI and PBC were able to predict a frequency-weighted average of 39 per cent of the variance in behaviour with BI being a stronger predictor (r_+ = 0.58) than PBC (r_+ = 0.51). This was over an average period of 98 days.

3.3.4 Physical activity

Participation in a range of physical activity/exercise behaviours including various sports and leisure time activities has been studied using the TRA/TPB in a variety of samples. Reviews of applications of the TPB to physical activity include Godin and Kok (1996) and Hausenblas *et al.* (1997). However, the most comprehensive review to date has been provided by Hagger *et al.* (2002) in a review of 72 independent studies. Across studies, A, SN and PBC explained 45 per cent of the variance in intentions with

A ($r_+ = 0.48$) and PBC ($r_+ = 0.44$) being stronger predictors than SN ($r_+ = 0.25$). It was found that BI and PBC accounted for an average 27 per cent of the variance in behaviour across studies with intention ($r_+ = 0.42$) having slightly more predictive power than PBC ($r_+ = 0.31$). McEachan *et al.* (2005) located 47 studies examining physical activity. Across these studies a frequency-weighted average of 40 per cent of the variance in intentions was explained by A, SN and PBC, with PBC being the strongest predictor ($r_+ = 0.47$), A the second strongest predictor ($r_+ = 0.46$), and SN the weakest predictor ($r_+ = 0.26$). A frequency-weighted average of 33 per cent of the variance in behaviour was explained by BI and PBC, with BI being the stronger predictor ($r_+ = 0.49$) and PBC the weaker predictor ($r_+ = 0.39$). These latter predictions were over an average period of 78 days.

3.3.5 Dietary behaviours
The TPB has been applied to a range of dietary behaviours including reduction in fat intake and healthy eating. McEachan *et al.* (2005) located 19 prospective TPB studies examining healthy eating (n = 8), fruit and vegetable intake (n = 3), reducing fat intake (n = 4), restricting sugar intake (n = 1), taking dietary supplements (n = 2) or eating breakfast foods (n = 1). Across studies a frequency-weighted average of 41 per cent of the variance in BI was explained by A, SN and PBC, with A being the strongest predictor ($r_+ = 0.47$), SN the second strongest predictor ($r_+ = 0.40$), and PBC the weakest predictor ($r_+ = 0.36$). A frequency-weighted average of 16 per cent of the variance in behaviour was explained by BI and PBC, with BI being the stronger predictor ($r_+ = 0.36$) and PBC the weaker predictor ($r_+ = 0.29$). These latter predictions were over an average period of 187 days.

3.3.6 Screening behaviours
Health screening attendance has been investigated using the TPB in a number of studies. McEachan *et al.* (2005) located 12 prospective applications of the TPB to breast or testicular self-examination (n = 5), cervical screening (n = 2), or health screening (n = 5). Across studies a frequency-weighted average of 44 per cent of the variance in BI was explained by A, SN and PBC, with A being the strongest predictor ($r_+ = 0.56$), PBC the second strongest predictor ($r_+ = 0.43$), and SN the weakest predictor ($r_+ = 0.34$). A frequency-weighted average of 16 per cent of the variance in behaviour was explained by BI and PBC, with BI being the stronger predictor ($r_+ = 0.32$) and PBC the weaker predictor ($r_+ = 0.19$). These latter predictions were over an average period of 68 days.

3.3.7 Conclusions from studies applying the TPB to health behaviours
The TPB has been applied to a wide range of health behaviours. In a number of cases the number of studies is considerable (e.g. Hagger *et al.* 2002 identified over 70 applications of the TPB to physical activity; see Table 5.2). In the vast majority of cases these have been successful applications in that the TPB has been able to explain considerable variation in intentions and action across behaviours. In relation to behaviour, this is

despite there being a considerable time gap between the measurement of TPB variables and subsequent behaviour (mean = 127 days across the prospective applications to health behaviours in McEachan *et al.* 2005). However, it is also the case that there is significant variation in the findings between studies. Some of this variation appears to be attributable to difference between behaviours (see Godin and Kok 1996; McEachan *et al.* 2005). For example, McEachan *et al.* (2005) found TPB variables to explain the most variance in BI to use drugs or engage in risk behaviours (53–54 per cent variance) and the least variance in BI to take physical activity and engage in dietary behaviours (40–41 per cent variance). There was also variability in which construct was the best predictor of BI with A being the strongest for sexual, dieting and screening behaviours, and PBC the strongest for drug taking, physical activity and risk behaviours. McEachan *et al.* (2005) also report the TPB variables to explain the most variance in drugs use or engaging in risk behaviours (39 per cent variance) and the least variance in dietary and screening behaviours (16 per cent variance). BI and PBC were generally both strong predictors of engaging in all health behaviours, although in each case intention was the strongest predictor of behaviour. McEachan *et al.* (2005) discuss the implications of such findings for the application of the TPB to differing health behaviours.

Table 5.2 Illustrative applications of the TPB to various health behaviours

Research area	*Example applications*
Smoking	Godin *et al.* (1992) Frequency of smoking
Alcohol use	Johnston and White (2003) Binge drinking
Illicit drug use	McMillan and Conner (2003) Amphetamine use
Condom use	Agnew (1998) In adults
Physical activity	Sparks *et al.* (2004) Attendance at a health club
Dietary behaviours	Armitage and Conner (1999b) Healthy eating
Road use behaviours	Elliott *et al.* (2003) Exceeding posted speed limit
Sun protective behaviours	Terry and Hogg (1996) Sunscreen use
Screening attendance	Norman and Conner (1993) Cervical screening
Breast/testicular self-examination	Steadman *et al.* (2002) Breast self-examination
Adherence to medication	Abraham *et al.* (1999) Anti-malarial medication

4 Developments

Two related areas of development concern the role of additional predictors in the TPB: first, new predictors incorporated through reconceptualizations of each of the major constructs (Bagozzi *et al.* 2001; Ajzen 2002a; Hagger and Chatzisarantis 2005); and second, new predictors that constitute useful additions to the model (Conner and Armitage 1998). These are commented on here.

4.1 Multiple component view of the TPB

4.1.1 Components of intentions

The construct of intention is central to the TRA/TPB. Intentions capture the motivational factors that influence a behaviour, how hard people are willing to try, how much effort they would exert to perform the behaviour (Ajzen 1991: 181) or the self-instructions individuals give themselves to act (Triandis 1977). There has been some variation in how the intention construct has been operationalized in TRA/TPB studies. Warshaw and Davis (1985) made the distinction between measures of behavioural intentions (e.g., 'I intend to perform behaviour x') and self-predictions (e.g., 'How likely is it that you will perform behaviour x?'). Sheppard *et al.*'s (1988) meta-analysis indicated the latter to be more predictive of behaviour. Beyond this, Bagozzi (1992) has suggested that attitudes may first be translated into desires (e.g., 'I want to perform behaviour x') which then develop into intentions to act, which direct action (see Perugini and Bagozzi 2003). The meta-analysis of Armitage and Conner (2001) specifically considered the role of intentions, desires and self-predictions in the context of the TPB. Intentions and self-predictions were stronger predictors of behaviour than desires when PBC was included as a predictor. The meta-analytic data indicated that the most variance in behaviour was explained by employing measures of intentions and PBC (Armitage and Conner 2001). When added to the clearer causal argument that can be made for intentions in determining behaviour this provides strong support for employing a measure of intentions rather than a self-prediction or desire measure. However, given the commonly very high level of correlation between measures of desire, intention and expectation it is perhaps not surprising that the majority of studies reviewed by Armitage and Conner (2001) employed mixed measures of intention (combining measures of intention, self-prediction and/or desire). The extent to which a second-order factor (i.e. motivation) might usefully account for the more differentiated components of intentions, expectations and desires has yet to be examined in the literature.

Ajzen and Fishbein (2005) also argue that willingness to perform a behaviour (e.g. Gibbons *et al.* 1998), personal norm with respect to the behaviour (Parker *et al.* 1995) or identification with the behaviour (i.e. self-identity; e.g. Armitage and Conner 1999a; Conner *et al.* 1999) are each closely related to intention. In each case the high correlation with intentions (i.e. lack of divergent validity) and failure to explain substantial variance in behaviour after taking account of intentions (i.e. lack of predictive validity) is noted. However, given the number of studies that have examined self-identity we return to considering its potential as an additional variable later (section 4.2.3).

4.1.2 Components of attitudes

As noted earlier, reviews of the TRA/TPB often demonstrate attitudes to be the best predictor of intentions. In the TRA/TPB attitudes towards behaviours are measured by semantic differential scales (Osgood *et al.* 1957). However, research on attitudes towards objects has used such measures to distinguish between affective and cognitive measures of attitudes, with the suggestion that the former are more closely related to behaviour (e.g. Breckler and Wiggins 1989; Eagly *et al.* 1994). It is now recognized that similar components of an attitude towards a behaviour can be distinguished in the TRA/TPB. In particular it has been noted that an attitude may contain instrumental (e.g. desirable–undesirable, valuable–worthless) as well as experiential or affective (e.g. pleasant–unpleasant, interesting–boring) aspects (see Ajzen and Driver 1991; Crites *et al.* 1994). However, research with the TPB has been criticized for focusing on the instrumental aspects of attitudes to the detriment of affective aspects (e.g. Bagozzi *et al.* 2001). This is problematic because some research has indicated that intentions may be more closely related to affective than cognitive measures of attitudes. For example, Ajzen and Driver (1992) reported affective measures of attitudes (e.g. pleasant–unpleasant) to be more closely related to intentions than were instrumental (e.g. useful–useless) measures in four out of five behaviours studied (see also Ajzen and Timko 1986; Chan and Fishbein 1993; Manstead and Parker 1995).

Ajzen and Fishbein (2005) have recently indicated that appropriate attitude measures for use in the TPB should contain items representing the instrumental and affective or experiential components of attitudes (see also Fishbein 1993). The two components do tend to be correlated with one another but can be discriminated based on their underlying belief systems (Trafimow and Sheeran 1998), their different functions (Breckler and Wiggins 1989), and empirical differences (Eagly and Chaiken 1993; Bagozzi *et al.* 2001). However, in order to maintain the parsimony of the TPB it has also been suggested that it is useful to distinguish between a higher order construct of attitude and these differentiated components of attitude at a lower order (Ajzen 2002a). This distinction between global and specific components of constructs is common in social psychology (e.g. Vallerand 1997). Thus in relation to instrumental and experiential attitudes, a higher order construct of attitude is invoked to explain the shared variance between these two components. The higher order construct is not measured directly from observed data but is indicated by the first order constructs (i.e. instrumental and experiential attitudes) which are so named because they are derived from the observed data (Bollen 1989). Two forms of such models have been recently proposed. In the first, the higher order constructs are 'caused' by their lower order components (Rhodes and Courneya 2003a). In the second, it is the higher order construct which 'causes' the lower order components (Bagozzi *et al.* 2001; Ajzen 2002a;

Hagger and Chatzisarantis 2005). The latter approach has a number of advantages such as explaining the correlation between lower order components.

This distinction between a higher order construct of attitudes indicated by two lower order constructs (instrumental and affective attitude) has received support in several empirical studies. For example, Bagozzi *et al.* (2001) in relation to the decision to donate bone marrow and Hagger and Chatzisarantis (2005) in relation to both exercise and dieting behaviours demonstrated that first-order measures of instrumental and affective attitudes could be distinguished. They both also showed that the lower order constructs had substantial shared variance which could be explained by a higher order factor representing global attitude. This higher order construct was shown to mediate the effects of the first order constructs on intentions.

In the TRA/TPB attitudes are held to be determined by underlying salient behavioural beliefs (Fishbein 1967a, 1967b). It is assumed that a person may possess a large number of beliefs about a particular behaviour, but that at any one time only some of these are likely to be salient. It is the salient beliefs which are assumed to determine a person's attitude. However, Towriss (1984) noted that while the theory would suggest the use of individually salient beliefs, respondents are normally presented with modal salient beliefs based on pilot work, following the procedures outlined by Ajzen and Fishbein (1980). This procedure has a number of disadvantages. First, procedures (e.g. asking for advantages and disadvantages of the behaviour) for sampling 'behavioural beliefs' about specific behaviours may sample an excessively cognitive subset (i.e. instrumental beliefs) of the influences that actually play on people's attitudes (Wilson *et al.* 1989), and fail to elicit beliefs which are more difficult to articulate (e.g. affective or moral influences; Sparks 1994), yet potentially important influences on attitude formation. A second problem is that the TPB is primarily concerned with individuals' beliefs. The supplying of beliefs by researchers may not adequately capture the beliefs salient to the individual no matter how extensive the pilot work. Several studies have explored the use of individually generated beliefs within the TRA (e.g. Rutter and Bunce 1989; Agnew 1998). For example, in a study on individually generated and modal beliefs about condom use, Agnew (1998) reported that individually generated beliefs were marginally significantly more strongly related to overall attitudes ($r = 0.46$ vs 0.38, $p_{diff} < 0.10$). This does not compare favourably with the moderately strong correlation between modal behavioral beliefs and attitudes more commonly reported (Table 5.1). Thus, while the use of individually generated beliefs is more consistent with the TRA/TPB, it does not appear to reduce measurement error sufficiently to increase levels of prediction of attitudes and so compensate for the additional effort required in data collection.

Another problem related to the use of modal beliefs concerns the relative importance of beliefs. A number of authors have suggested that the prediction of attitudes might be improved by adding a measure of importance or relevance of the attribute to the attitude towards the behaviour, although the evidence is mixed (e.g. Agnew 1998). Nevertheless, information about belief importance could usefully inform the design of interventions to change behaviour in segments of the population stratified by key beliefs (Van der Pligt and de Vries 1998; see Van der Pligt *et al.* 2000 for a discussion; see also Bagozzi and Edwards 1998 for a 'laddering' technique for exploring the underlying belief structure).

4.1.3 Components of norms

A number of researchers have argued that further attention needs to be paid to the concept of normative influences within the TRA/TPB (e.g. Conner and Armitage 1998). For example, both Godin and Kok (1996) and Armitage and Conner (2001) noted that subjective norms were the weakest predictor of intentions in the TPB. Similarly, Sheppard *et al.* (1988) and Van den Putte (1991) noted that subjective norms were weak predictors of intentions across the TRA studies they reviewed. Whilst this could merely reflect the lesser importance of normative factors as determinants of intentions in the behaviours studied, a number of alternative explanations for such weak effects are possible.

The meta-analysis of Armitage and Conner (2001) indicated subjective norm to be the weakest predictor of intentions in the TPB across studies. However, at least partly, this appeared to be attributable to the use of single item measures with lower reliability. Where studies employed reliable multi-item measures subjective norms were significantly stronger predictors of intentions, although still weaker than attitudes or PBC. Another explanation of the weak predictive power of normative measures in the TRA/TPB is the conceptualization of norms used (Cialdini *et al.* 1991). Cialdini *et al.* (1991) call the normative beliefs used in the TRA/TPB injunctive social norms as they concern the social approval of others which motivates action through social reward/punishment, and distinguish them from descriptive social norms which describe perceptions of what others do (see Deutsch and Gerard 1955). The relative predictive power of these normative components is an issue of some debate.

De Vries *et al.* (1995) reported that measures of injunctive and descriptive norms significantly predicted smoking. Recently, Rivis and Sheeran (2003a) have reported a meta-analysis of the role of descriptive norms in the TPB. Across 14 tests with a total n = 5810 they reported $r_+ = 0.46$ for the descriptive norm–intention correlation. In addition, across studies descriptive norms were found to explain a highly significant additional 5 per cent of variance in intentions after taking account of attitudes, subjective norms and PBC.

More recently, Fishbein (1993) and Ajzen and Fishbein (2005) suggested that both subjective norms and descriptive norms be considered indicators of the same underlying concept, social pressure. Similarly to attitudes one might conceive of social pressure as a higher order factor with injunctive and descriptive norms as lower order measures. However, it is unclear whether a formative model with injunctive and descriptive norms producing overall social pressure or a reflective model with social pressure producing injunctive and descriptive norms is more appropriate. The relatively low correlation between the two (Rivis and Sheeran 2003a report r+ = 0.38 for subjective norm and descriptive norm) might be interpreted as supporting the former. The impact of inconsistency between the two components may represent an interesting research focus.

A further distinction in relation to the normative component of the TPB has been made by researchers applying a social identity theory/self-categorization approach (e.g. Terry and Hogg 1996). For example, Terry and Hogg (1996) demonstrated that group norm measures were more predictive of intentions when they employed a measure of group identification (e.g. 'I identify with my friends with regard to smoking') rather than motivation to comply. In two studies, norms only influenced intentions for those who strongly identified with their 'in-group'. Group norms have been operationalized as either what members of the group are perceived to do (e.g. 'Most of my friends smoke'; i.e. descriptive norms) or to think (e.g. 'Most of my friends think smoking is a good thing to do' [see Johnston and White 2003], sometimes referred to as group attitude). Studies using this approach tend to report interactive effects between group norms and group identification rather than main effects (e.g. Terry et al. 1999). However, where the target group is strongly associated with the behaviour (e.g. my smoking friends) then main effects of group identification on intentions have been reported (e.g. Fekadu and Kraft 2001). More research may be required to disentangle further the different normative influences on intentions. We believe that evidence strongly supports the use of measures which tap both injunctive and descriptive norms. Whether additional measures of either group attitude or group identification would increase the predictive power of a second order normative construct requires further research. In particular, for referent groups not defined by the behaviour an interactive model between group attitude (or descriptive norm) and group identification may be appropriate.

There has also been work examining normative beliefs. It should be noted that the distinction between behavioural beliefs and normative beliefs is somewhat arbitrary (Miniard and Cohen 1981), and there is often found to be considerable correlation between the two (O'Keefe 1990; see Table 5.1). Miniard and Cohen (1981) point out that the impact of another person's behaviour can equally be assessed as a behavioural belief (e.g. 'Using a condom would please my partner') or a normative belief (e.g. 'My partner thinks I should use a condom'). However, there is some merit in maintaining a distinction between the determinants of behaviour that are attributes of the person and those which are attributes of the social environment (see Eagly and Chaiken 1993: 171; Trafimow: 1998). Trafimow and Fishbein (1995) present a number of experiments which support the distinction (see Trafimow 1998 for a review).

Other researchers have suggested that rather than the way normative influence is tapped, it is measurement of compliance with this pressure which needs attention. In the TRA/TPB this is tapped by measures of motivation to comply with the perceived pressure from each salient source of social influence. Typically, such items tap the extent to which the individual wants to do what this individual or group wishes them to in general (Fishbein and Ajzen 1975: 306). There has been debate about the most appropriate level of specificity to use in the wording of the motivation to comply item (e.g. O'Keefe 1990). For example, should motivation to comply be in general, specifying a group of behaviours, or be specific to the behaviour in question (the principle of compatibility might suggest this last alternative)? Alternatively, as we noted earlier in relation to social identity theory, a measure of group identification (e.g. 'I identify with my friends with regard to smoking') rather than motivation to comply might be more appropriate. Such an approach would also suggest combining such identification with a different measure of group norm (i.e. descriptive norm or group attitude rather than injunctive norm). Further, Gibbons and Gerrard (1997) draw upon ideas of behavioural prototypes (e.g. the typical smoker) and suggest that positive evaluation and perceived similarity to such prototypes may represent another way in which social influence and comparison processes operate. Rivis and Sheeran (2003b) provide support for this idea in relation to engaging in exercise behaviour. Prototype similarity but not prototype evaluation had an independent effect on both intentions and behaviour in the context of TPB variables, descriptive norms and past behaviour.

4.1.4 Components of PBC

The difference between the TRA and TPB lies in the control component (i.e. PBC) of the TPB. We noted earlier that meta-analytic evidence has generally supported the power of PBC to explain additional variance in intentions and behaviour after controlling for the components of the TRA. The overlap in definition of PBC with Bandura's (1977: 192) definition of self-efficacy, '... the conviction that one can successfully execute the behavior required to produce the outcomes' is striking. Ajzen (1991) argued that the PBC and self-efficacy constructs were synonymous and more recently 'quite similar' (Ajzen 2002a). Congruent with this view of a conceptual overlap between PBC and self-efficacy several researchers (e.g. De Vries *et al.* 1995) have advocated the use of measures of self-efficacy in place of PBC within the TPB. However, this has proved problematic because of differences in the way the two constructs have been operationalized. This latter issue reflects a broader controversy surrounding the nature and measurement of PBC which has a number of threads. A first thread concerns disparities in the definitions and operationalizations used with respect to PBC and the possibility that it represents a multidimensional construct (for reviews see Ajzen 2002a; Trafimow *et al.* 2002). A second thread has questioned the discriminant validity of some operationalizations of PBC as distinct from other components of the TPB.

Early definitions of the PBC construct were intended to encompass perceptions of factors that were both internal (e.g. knowledge, skills, willpower) and external (e.g. time availability, cooperation of others) to the individual. For example, Ajzen and Madden (1986) defined PBC as '... the person's belief as to how easy or difficult performance of the behavior is likely to be' (p. 457). However, the items used to tap PBC included both perceptions of difficulty and perceptions of control over the behaviour (see Sparks *et al.* 1997). In the majority of early applications of the TPB studies tended to employ 'mixed' measures of PBC that included both components. However, more recently opinion appears to have coalesced around the idea of PBC being a multidimensional construct consisting of two separate but related components (Ajzen 2002a; Trafimow *et al.* 2002). In particular, Ajzen (2002a) argues that PBC can be considered as a second-order construct that consists of two components which he labels perceived self-efficacy and perceived controllability. Trafimow *et al.* (2002) label these terms perceived difficulty and perceived control and provide experimental and meta-analytic support for distinguishing the two. However, there seems to be little evidence that these two components show any simple mapping onto control factors internal versus external to the individual (Ajzen 2002a).

The *self-efficacy* component of PBC '. . . deals with the ease or difficulty of performing a behavior, with people's confidence that they can perform it if they want to do so' (Ajzen 2002c). Ajzen (2002a) has suggested that this component of PBC can be tapped by two types of items: first, the perceived difficulty of the behaviour, e.g. 'For me to quit smoking would be . . .' (very difficult–very easy); second, the perceived confidence the individual has that he/she can perform the behaviour, e.g. 'I am confident that I could quit smoking' (definitely false–definitely true). It is clear that perceived confidence items most closely resemble the 'can-do cognitions' involved in assessing self-efficacy (Bandura 1986). Ajzen (2002c) suggests that the *perceived control* component of PBC, 'involves people's beliefs that they have control over the behavior, that performance or non-performance of the behavior is up to them'. Again, two types of items can be distinguished: first, perceived control over performance of the behaviour, e.g. 'How much control do you believe you have over quitting smoking?' (no control–complete control); second, perceptions of control analogous to the locus of control concept, e.g. 'It is mostly up to me whether I quit smoking' (strongly disagree–strongly agree).

Kraft *et al.* (2005) note that in the majority of TPB studies PBC has been assessed by a mixture of these four different types of items. This might explain why low internal reliabilities have been reported for such measures of PBC (see Notani 1998). Ajzen (2002a) has suggested that formative research could allow the selection of a set of items which adequately tap PBC and show good internal reliability. This might avoid the complexity of employing a second-order PBC factor based on separate measures of perceived self-efficacy and perceived controllability.

A second thread to research with the PBC construct has focused on discriminant validity. Fishbein and colleagues (Chan and Fishbein 1993; Fishbein 1997; Leach *et al.* 2001) note two problems with employing perceived difficulty items to tap PBC: first, there is no necessary association between an individual's perceptions of how difficult a behaviour is held to be and how much they perceive control over performing it; second, easy–difficult items overlap conceptually and empirically with semantic-differential items designed to tap affective attitudes. The argument is that an individual is likely to hold a positive affective attitude toward an easy to perform behaviour and a negative affective attitude toward a difficult to perform behaviour. Leach *et al.* (2001) showed that perceived difficulty items appeared to tap both attitudes and self-efficacy in relation to condom use. Kraft *et al.* (2005) also provided evidence for an empirical overlap between perceived difficulty items and affective attitude for physical activity and recycling behaviours.

This review of existing research suggests at least three possibilities in relation to measuring PBC within the TPB. First, Ajzen (2002a) has suggested that the use of formative research within a behavioural domain can result in the appropriate selection of items with a unidimensional structure. Such items might reflect perceived difficulty, perceived confidence, and/or perceived control as appropriate. Second, measures can explicitly tap the two components of PBC identified by Ajzen (2002a): perceived self-efficacy and perceived controllability. Ajzen and Fishbein (2005) argue that items concerned with the ease or difficulty of performing a behaviour, or confidence in one's ability to perform it, tend to load on the former, whereas items that address control over the behaviour, or the extent to which its performance is up to the actor, load on the second factor. Research could then either explore the relative predictive power of these two components (see Trafimow *et al.* 2002) or, as Ajzen (2002a) suggested, explore the power of a second-order factor of PBC based on these two components (e.g. see Hagger and Chatzisarantis, 2005). Third, measures of PBC could be selected which explicitly avoid perceived difficulty items because of concerns about overlap with affective attitudes. Such measures might be selected to be unidimensional (i.e. PBC) or bidimensional (i.e. perceived self-efficacy and perceived controllability). Armitage and Conner (1999a, 1999b) provided evidence to support a distinction between self-efficacy and 'perceived control over behaviour', utilizing measures that do not rely on perceived ease or difficulty.

Future research will need to explore further these different possibilities and their implications. Evidence from previous meta-analyses is mixed. For example, while Armitage and Conner (2001) report evidence that measures of self-efficacy compared to measures of controllability were better predictors of intentions ($r_+ = 0.44$ vs 0.23) and behaviour ($r_+ = 0.35$ vs 0.18), self-efficacy was no better than unidimensional measures of PBC for intentions ($r_+ = 0.44$ vs 0.44) or behaviour ($r_+ = 0.35$ vs 0.40). Similarly, Trafimow *et al.* (2002) showed perceived difficulty compared to perceived control to have stronger correlations with both intentions ($r_+ = 0.53$ vs 0.27) and behaviour ($r_+ = 0.48$ vs 0.27). Thus it seems clear that measures tapping perceived self-efficacy tend to be more predictive than measures which tap perceived controllability. In contrast, Rhodes and Courneya (2003b) argue for a focus on controllability because it shows better discriminant validity with intention than does self-efficacy. However, neither approach addresses the suggestion of Ajzen (2002a) that either a reliable unidimensional measure of PBC or a second-order measure of PBC based on perceived self-efficacy and perceived controllability would be at least as strong predictors of intentions and behaviour.

Another issue in relation to the PBC component of the TPB is the assessment of underlying control beliefs. There has been some variation in how such beliefs have been tapped (Manstead and Parker 1995). Ajzen (1991) suggests that control beliefs 'assess the presence or absence of requisite resources and opportunities' (p.196). These beliefs are assumed to be based upon various forms of previous experience with the behaviour. These factors might be elicited in a pilot study by the question 'What factors might prevent or help you perform behavior x?'. However, there has been some variation in how modal control beliefs have been operationalized. Ajzen and Madden (1986) assessed PBC to be based upon the sum of frequency of occurrence of various facilitators and inhibitors. Others (e.g. Godin and Gionet 1991) have employed a formulation closer to that used to assess self-efficacy to gauge the extent to which a particular barrier will make performance of the behaviour more difficult, e.g. 'How likely is being drunk to inhibit your use of a condom?' (likely–unlikely). Ajzen (1991) suggests a formulation closer to that employed to assess the other beliefs in the TPB. Control beliefs are tapped by items assessing the frequency with which a facilitator or inhibitor of the behaviour occurs, e.g. 'I can climb in an area that has good weather' (likely–unlikely) weighted by its perceived power to facilitate or inhibit performance of the behaviour, e.g. 'Good weather makes mountain climbing …' (easier–more difficult) with both items scored as bipolar items. This format has been employed by several authors (e.g. Ajzen and Driver 1991; Parker *et al.* 1995). Further research might usefully assess the relationship of underlying beliefs to overall perceptions of control and whether different sets of control beliefs underlie the different dimensions of PBC. For example, Armitage and Conner (1999a) provided evidence to suggest that control beliefs were antecedents of self-efficacy, but correlated only weakly with perceived control.

4.2 Additional predictors

The sufficiency of the TRA/TPB has received considerable attention (Eagly and Chaiken 1993: 168–93, see Conner and Armitage 1998) with a number of additional constructs to be added being suggested. Ajzen (1991) suggested the openness of the TPB to such developments, 'The theory of planned behavior is, in principle, open to the inclusion of additional predictors if it can be shown that they capture a significant proportion of variance in intention or behavior after the theory's current variables have been taken into account' (p.199). In this section we consider four additional constructs: anticipated affective reactions, moral norms, self-identity and past behaviour. In each case theoretical (Fishbein 1993) and empirical (Ajzen 1991) justifications for their inclusion in the TPB are considered. Although a range of other constructs (e.g. personality dimensions; Conner and Abraham 2001) have been addressed sporadically in the literature there is as yet insufficient published research to evaluate their contribution. As the TRA/TPB 'has the great virtue of parsimony' (Charng *et al.* 1988: 303) we would argue that the evidence needs to be strong to justify serious consideration being given to additional variables.

4.2.1 Anticipated regret

As noted earlier, the traditional method for eliciting behavioural beliefs may fail to elicit affective outcomes associated with performance of the behaviour (see Manstead and Parker 1995; Van der Pligt and de Vries 1998). Such anticipated affective reactions to the performance or non-performance of a behaviour may be important determinants of attitudes and intentions (Triandis 1977; Van der Pligt and de Vries 1998), especially in situations where the consequences of the behaviour are unpleasant or negatively affectively laden. Emotional outcomes are commonly factored into decision making (Van der Pligt *et al.* 1998). Anticipated regret is a negative, cognitive-based emotion that is experienced when we realize or imagine that the present situation could have been better had we acted differently. This concept of anticipated regret has been considered in a number of TPB studies.

Factor analytic studies (Richard *et al.* 1996; Sheeran and Orbell 1999) have demonstrated that regret is distinct from the other components of the TPB (attitude, subjective norm and PBC). Studies have shown anticipated regret to add to the prediction of intentions over and above the components of the TPB for a range of behaviours including eating junk foods, using soft drugs and alcohol use (Richard *et al.* 1996). In a recent meta-analysis of TPB studies using regret, Sandberg and Conner (2005) found the correlation between regret and intentions to be $r_+ = 0.47$ (n = 11098 participants, k = 24 studies). More importantly, regret explained an additional 7.0 per cent of the variance in intentions after taking account of attitude, subjective norm and PBC (p<0.0001). For regret to be further considered as an additional predictor of intentions we need research demonstrating independent effects for anticipated regret when controlling for both instrumental and experiential attitudes.

4.2.2 Moral norms

Cialdini *et al.* (1991) distinguished between injunctive, descriptive and moral norms. We have commented on how the first two might usefully be considered components of a social norm construct. The latter are the individual's perception of the moral correctness or incorrectness of performing a behavior (Ajzen 1991) and take account of '... personal feelings of ... responsibility to perform, or refuse to perform, a certain behavior' (Ajzen 1991: 199). Moral norms might be expected to have an important influence on the performance of those behaviours with a moral or ethical dimension (e.g. Beck and Ajzen 1991). Ajzen (1991) suggested that moral norms work in parallel with attitudes, subjective norms and PBC, and directly influence intentions. For example, Beck and Ajzen (1991) included a measure of moral norm in their analysis of dishonest actions, and found it significantly increased the amount of variance accounted for in intention (by 3–6 per cent), and made a significant contribution to the prediction of each intention. Manstead (2000) provides a useful review of research with the moral norm construct. Conner and Armitage (1998) reported the correlation between moral norms and intentions to be $r_+ = 0.50$ across 11 TPB studies. Moral norm added (on average) 4 per cent to the prediction of intention, a change which was significant. These findings imply that moral norm would be a useful addition to the TPB, at least for those behaviours where moral considerations are likely to be important.

4.2.3 Self-identity

Self-identity may be defined as the salient part of an actor's self which relates to a particular behaviour. It reflects the extent to which an actor sees him or herself fulfilling the criteria for any societal role, for example, 'someone who is concerned with green issues' (Sparks and Shepherd 1992: 392). Several authors have addressed the extent to which self-identity might be a useful addition to the TRA/TPB (e.g. Sparks and Shepherd 1992). Conner and Armitage (1998) reported that across six TPB studies self-identity had a correlation of $r_+ = 0.27$ with intentions and only explained an additional 1 per cent of variance in intentions after taking account of other TPB variables. They interpreted this as not providing support for the role of self-identity as a useful addition to the TPB. Ajzen and Fishbein (2005) come to a similar conclusion but suggest self-identity might be best considered as an alternative measure of intentions. This view would not be supported by the meta-analysis of Conner and Armitage (1998) where the self-identity–intention correlation was modest. Despite these negative conclusions about self-identity, given the results of authors such as Sparks and Shepherd (1992), it is reasonable to assume that there are certain behaviours where self-identity will provide additional predictions of intentions. Further research is needed to identify the characteristics of behaviours or the conditions (e.g. for predicting maintenance of a behaviour) under which self-identity becomes a useful addition to the TPB.

4.2.4 Past behaviour

The influence of past behaviour on future behaviour is an issue that has attracted considerable attention (see Eagly and Chaiken 1993: 178–82 for a review). It is argued that many behaviours are determined by one's previous behaviour rather than cognitions such as described in the TRA/TPB (Sutton 1994). The argument is based on the results of a number of studies showing past behaviour to be the best predictor of future behaviour (e.g. Mullen *et al.* 1987). Conner and Armitage (1998) provide an empirical review of the impact of past behaviour within the TPB. They reported relatively large past behaviour–future behaviour, past behaviour–intention, past behaviour–attitude, and past behaviour–PBC correlations. Ajzen (1991) regards the role of past behaviour as a test of sufficiency of the TPB and that its effects should be mediated by PBC: repetition of behaviour should lead to enhanced perceptions of control. On this basis, one might predict that past behaviour should be most strongly correlated with PBC, although this was not supported in the review of Conner and Armitage (1998). What is of particular interest is the contribution of past behaviour to the predictions of intentions and behaviour once the TPB variables are taken into account. Ajzen (1991) reports that across three studies, the amount of variance added to the prediction of behavior by past behaviour (mean 2.1 per cent) was so small as to reflect common method variance due to use of similar response formats for the two measures. Conner *et al.* (1999) manipulated the degree of similarity in response formats for the two measures of behaviour but found this to explain only a modest amount of variance. Conner and Armitage (1998) found that after taking account of attitude, subjective norms and PBC, past behaviour, on average, explained a further 7.2 per cent of the variance in intentions (across 12 studies). Similarly, past behaviour explained a mean 13.0 per cent of variance in behaviour after taking account of intentions and PBC (across seven studies) (see also Ouellette and Wood 1998). Despite these strong effects of past behaviour within the TPB we should be cautious in giving past behaviour the same status as other predictors in the TPB. It is clear that past behaviour cannot be used to explain future performance of an action (i.e. individuals do not perform a behaviour *because* they have performed it in the past), although habit may be one way of conceptualizing this effect (Sutton 1994).

Ajzen (2002b) provides a stimulating review of the effects of past on later behaviour. He notes that the residual impact of past behaviour on later behaviour after taking account of intentions noted in a number of studies is influenced by several factors. In particular, weaker effects are observed when measures of intention and behaviour are matched on the principle of compatibility. Also, strong, well-formed intentions appear to be associated with an attenuation of the effect of past behaviour. In addition, where expectations are realistic and specific plans for implementation of intentions have been developed, little impact of past behaviour on later behaviour is observed after controlling for intentions (Ajzen 2002b). Finally, experience of the behaviour may lead to a change in intentions and a reverting to a previous pattern of behaviour (Ajzen and Fishbein 2005).

5 Operationalization of the model

This section describes the formulation of measures of each of the model components. Extensive details of applying the TRA can be found in Ajzen and Fishbein (1980), while Ajzen (1991) provides an outline of the TPB and Ajzen (2002c) supplies a clear step-by-step guide to producing a TPB-based questionnaire. For those wishing to construct a TPB questionnaire, we recommend that the current section is read in conjunction with the Ajzen (2002c) text, so that similarities and differences within question formulation can be identified and considered. While the examples provided in Ajzen (2002c) give a clear demonstration of how to construct a questionnaire assessing walking 'on a treadmill for at least 30 minutes each day in the forthcoming month', the examples provided here relate to a series of different behaviours around a common theme, or behavioural category (viz. exercising). Thus, Ajzen (2002c) provides a comprehensive example of measures for one particular behaviour, so that the reader can see how to construct a questionnaire (concerning a specified behaviour) that complies with the *principle of compatibility* requirement. The present text, on the other hand, provides some examples of measures from published research so that the reader can see (a) examples of measures applied to somewhat different behaviours within a common theme, and (b) the variation between research studies in the level of specificity and in adherence to the target, action, context, time (TACT) principle.

5.1 Behaviour

> Selecting and assessing a behavioral criterion is often the most difficult part of any behavioral study.
>
> (Fishbein 1997: 81)

In considering the development of appropriate measures of each of the components of the TPB, it is common to begin with developing a clear conceptualization of the behaviour or behavioural categories we wish to predict. The principle of compatibility indicates that measures of behaviours and components of the TPB need to be formulated at the same level of specificity with regard to action, target, context and time. Hence, we need to make an unambiguous decision about the level at which we wish to predict behaviour with regard to these four elements. Specification of the action, target, context and time frame for the behaviour will greatly assist the specification of the TPB measures. For example, we may wish to predict running (action) a marathon (target) in Berlin (context) in September next year (time frame), or walking (action) for an hour (target) in the countryside (context) later today (time frame).[2] In the latter example, the TPB measures would be taken on one day and the measure of behaviour would need to be taken at a later stage (e.g. the next day). Obviously, aggregation of behaviours across time frames, contexts, targets and actions is possible. The minimum specification would require an action and time frame to be stated. Such clear specification allows easy application of the principle of compatibility with respect to the TPB measures. Assessment of such a behaviour might involve simple self-reports of whether the behaviour was performed in the specified context over the appropriate time period (in this example the behaviour is assessed on the following day):

I walked for an hour in the countryside yesterday.

Definitely did not 1 2 3 4 5 6 7 Definitely did[3]

An alternative item might simply require the participant to mark whether the behaviour was or was not performed:

I did/did not walk for an hour in the countryside yesterday.

(delete as appropriate)

Ideally, of course, one could take more objective behaviour measures. Sparks *et al.* (2004), for example, made use of computer records of attendance at a health club; but more often than not it is either difficult or impossible to obtain appropriate objective behaviour measures (even in this case, the measure was not one of actual exercise behaviour!). The reliability of self-report measures may be expected to vary as a function of the behaviour and context in question, with some (perhaps more 'sensitive' in one way or other) behaviours raising the suspicion that self-reports may be less than accurate (Ajzen and Fishbein 2005).

5.2 Behavioural intention

Behavioural intention measures tend to use a number of standard wordings that incorporate the same level of specificity with respect to action, target, context and time frame as used in the behaviour measure. For example:

I intend to exercise at X health club at least four times each week during the next two weeks. *Definitely do* 1 2 3 4 5 6 7 *Definitely do not*

I will make an effort to exercise at X health club at least four times each week during the next two weeks. *Definitely false* 1 2 3 4 5 6 7 *Definitely true*

I will try to exercise at X health club at least four times each week during the next two weeks. *Definitely will not* 1 2 3 4 5 6 7 *Definitely will*

Adapted from Sparks *et al.* (2004)

From a psychometric point of view multiple-item measures are more appropriate than single-item measures because of increased reliability.

5.3 Attitudes

Attitudes are a person's evaluation of the target behaviour and are typically measured by using items such as:

My taking regular physical activity over the next 6 months would be:

Harmful	1 2 3 4 5 6 7	Beneficial
Unpleasant	1 2 3 4 5 6 7	Pleasant
Unenjoyable	1 2 3 4 5 6 7	Enjoyable
Bad	1 2 3 4 5 6 7	Good
Foolish	1 2 3 4 5 6 7	Wise

Adapted from Norman *et al.* (2000)

Here participants evaluate the behaviour described at the appropriate level of specificity on a series of semantic differentials (taken from the evaluative dimension of Osgood *et al.* 1957). Typically 4–6 such differentials are used and these tend to show high internal reliability (alpha > 0.9). While at one stage it was suggested that researchers need only ensure that such items were evaluative and formed a single factor, several dimensions have been identified in a number of studies (Ajzen and Driver 1992). More recently, Ajzen (2002c) has suggested that steps be taken to ensure that both instrumental (e.g. worthless–valuable; harmful–beneficial; unimportant–important) and experiential (e.g. unpleasant–pleasant; unenjoyable–

enjoyable; unsatisfying–satisfying) items should be included within attitude measures. Measurement of instrumental and experiential components of attitudes allows the analysis of the lower and higher order components of attitudes noted earlier (section 4.1.2).

Alternatively, attitudes may be assessed by simply asking the respondent more direct questions about their attitudes (see Ajzen and Fishbein 1980: 55). For example:

> My attitude towards my exercising at X health club is ...
> *Extremely unfavourable* 1 2 3 4 5 6 7 *Extremely favourable*
> *Extremely negative*   1 2 3 4 5 6 7 *Extremely positive*
> Adapted from Sparks *et al.* (2004)

This latter 'more purely evaluative' method has been recommended by Zanna and Rempel (1988) for measuring attitudes since it allows research participants to express their general evaluation of the behaviour without the researcher prejudging what the basis (e.g. cognitive or affective) of that attitude might be.

5.4 Subjective norm

In early descriptions of the subjective norm construct it was alternatively described as a 'person's ... perception that most people who are important to him think he should or should not perform the behavior in question' (Ajzen and Fishbein 1980: 57) and a 'person's perception of the social pressures put on him to perform or not perform the behavior in question' (p.6). There is a difference in these two definitions (consider the example of voting for a particular political party in a secret ballot!) but the construct has traditionally been operationalized as the person's subjective judgement concerning whether significant others would want him or her to perform the behaviour or not, using items such as:

> Most people who are important to me think I:
> Should   1 2 3 4 5 6 7   Should not
> take regular physical activity over the next 6 months.
> Adapted from Norman *et al.* (2000)

There are a number of well-known problems with the use of single items (see Armitage and Conner 2001) and additional items have been suggested to make a multi-item scale, although there is little reliability data on such measures. ·

> People who are important to me would:
> Approve 1 2 3 4 5 6 7 Disapprove
> of my taking regular physical activity over the next 6 months.

> People who are important to me want me to take regular physical activity over the next 6 months.
> Likely 1 2 3 4 5 6 7 Unlikely
> Adapted from Norman *et al.* (2000)

More recently, it has been suggested that measures of subjective norm should include both injunctive normative influences (such as those given above which reflect what significant others think the person should do) and descriptive normative influences (such as the items given below which reflect what significant others are perceived to do with respect to the behaviour in question):

> Most of my friends exercise regularly.
>> Strongly disagree   1 2 3 4 5 6 7   Strongly agree
>
> Most of my family members exercise regularly.
>> Strongly disagree   1 2 3 4 5 6 7   Strongly agree
>>> Adapted from Rhodes and Courneya (2003a)

Measurement of injunctive and descriptive norm components of subjective norms would allow the analysis of the lower and higher order components of norms noted earlier (section 4.1.3).

5.5 Perceived behavioural control

PBC represents the overall control the individual perceives him or herself to have over performance of the behaviour. Typical items used to measure PBC would be the following:

> How much control do you have over whether you exercise for at least 20 minutes, three times per week for the next fortnight?
>> No control   1 2 3 4 5 6 7   Complete control
>
> I feel in complete control of whether I exercise for at least 20 minutes, three times per week for the next fortnight.
>> Completely false   1 2 3 4 5 6 7   Completely true
>
> For me to exercise for at least 20 minutes, three times per week for the next fortnight will be
> ...   Very easy   1 2 3 4 5 6 7   Very difficult
>
> I am confident that I can exercise for at least 20 minutes, three times per week for the next fortnight.   Strongly disagree   1 2 3 4 5 6 7   Strongly agree
>> Adapted from Terry and O'Leary (1995)

The internal reliability of PBC items has frequently been found to be low (e.g. Ajzen 2002a; Sparks 1994), such that separate assessment of controllability (e.g. the first two items above) and self-efficacy (e.g. the second two items above) is now recommended (Ajzen 2002a). Measurement of controllability and self-efficacy components would allow the analysis of the lower and higher order components of PBC noted earlier (section 4.1.4). The problem of the adequate measurement of PBC has received a good deal of attention in recent years (e.g. Ajzen 2002a). For example, if we consider the sorts of item that are currently used to assess the construct, part of the problem with inter-item reliability may be due to differences in the way lay people conceptualize the notion of 'control' and the notion of 'difficulty' (Chan and Fishbein 1993; Sparks *et al.* 1997). People may consider the performance of a behaviour to be 'under their control' yet at the same time consider it to be difficult to carry out. Mixing unipolar and bipolar scales among PBC items may contribute to this problem, which may also be exacerbated by question order context effects when items are either randomly or systematically ordered in questionnaires (e.g. Budd 1987).

5.6 Behavioural beliefs

In the TRA/TPB the relevant behavioural beliefs are those salient to the individual. However, most applications of these models employ modal salient beliefs derived from pilot studies with a representative sample of individuals drawn from the population of interest (see Rutter and Bunce 1989 for an exception). The pilot studies typically consist of semi-structured interviews or questionnaire studies in which participants are asked to list the characteristics, qualities and attributes of the object or behaviour (Ajzen and Fishbein 1980: 64–71). For example, participants are asked 'What do you see as the advantages and disadvantages of [behaviour]?' The most frequently mentioned (modal) beliefs are then used in the final questionnaire, with commonly between six and 12 beliefs being employed.

Examples of belief strength and outcome evaluation items are given below. Belief strength assesses the subjective probability that a particular outcome will be a consequence of performing the behaviour. Such items commonly use response formats such as 'unlikely–likely', 'improbable–probable', or 'false–true' which are scored in a bipolar fashion (e.g. -3 to $+3$, on a seven-point scale) or unipolar fashion (e.g. 1 to 7, on a seven-point scale) (see Ajzen 2002c for a discussion). Outcome evaluations assess the overall evaluation of that outcome and are generally treated as bipolar (-3 negative evaluation to $+3$ positive evaluation) and responded to on 'bad–good' response formats (Ajzen and Fishbein 1980). Belief strength and outcome evaluation are then multiplicatively combined and summed (equation 3) to give an indirect measure of attitude. The problem with such calculations with interval level data has been noted by a number of authors (e.g. French and Hankins 2003), although no completely satisfactory solution has been found. Ajzen (2002c) has recommended the use of optimal rescaling techniques in order to avoid this problem, but this practice is currently not common in published research and has attracted criticism (French and Hankins 2003).

Belief strength
My taking regular physical activity would make me feel healthier.
                         Unlikely   1 2 3 4 5 6   7   Likely
My taking regular physical activity would make me lose weight.
                         Unlikely   1 2 3 4 5 6   7   Likely

Outcome evaluation
Feeling healthier would be...   Bad   1 2 3 4 5 6 7   Good
Losing weight would be...   Bad   1 2 3 4 5 6 7   Good
                                        Adapted from Norman *et al.* (2000)

5.7 Normative beliefs

As with behavioural beliefs, most studies employ modal rather than individually salient referent groups as the basis of normative items and derive these from pilot studies with a representative sample of individuals from the population of interest (see Steadman *et al.* 2002 for an exception). Ajzen and Fishbein (1980) suggest that we ask about the groups or individuals who would approve or disapprove of you performing the behaviour or who come to mind when thinking about the target behaviour (pp.74–75). For example, participants might be asked, 'Are there any groups or individuals who come to mind when thinking about behaviour x?' The most frequently mentioned (modal) referents are then incorporated in the final questionnaire. Typically two to six referent groups are included. Below we give examples of normative belief and motivation to comply items. Normative beliefs are the person's perceptions of whether specific referents would want him or her to perform the behaviour under consideration. These items are typically responded to on a 'should not–should' or 'unlikely–likely' response format and scored in a bipolar fashion, i.e. −3 strong negative pressure to perform to +3 strong positive pressure to perform. Motivation to comply is operationalized as the person's willingness to comply with the expectations of the specific referents. Such items are typically responded to on 'not at all–strongly' or 'unlikely–likely' response formats and treated as unipolar scales, i.e. +1 low motivation to comply, +7 strong motivation to comply. This scoring procedure is used because people are considered unlikely to be motivated to do the opposite of what they perceive significant others want them to do. The relevant normative beliefs and motivations to comply are then multiplicatively combined and summed (equation 4) to give an indirect measure of normative pressure.

> *Normative belief strength*
> My friends think I should take regular physical activity.
> > Unlikely 1 2 3 4 5 6 7 Likely
> Health experts think I should take regular physical activity.
> > Unlikely 1 2 3 4 5 6 7 Likely
>
> *Motivation to comply*
> With regard to physical activity, I want to do what my friends think I should.
> > Strongly disagree 1 2 3 4 5 6 7 Strongly agree
> With regard to physical activity, I want to do what health experts think I should.
> > Strongly disagree 1 2 3 4 5 6 7 Strongly agree
> > > Adapted from Norman *et al.* (2000)

5.8 Control beliefs

For control beliefs, the few studies which have reported these items have also used modal control beliefs derived from pilot studies with samples representative of the target population, although presumably salient control factors are the most appropriate measures. Ajzen and Driver (1992) suggest that individuals are asked to list the factors and conditions that make it easy or difficult to perform the target behaviour and the most frequently mentioned (modal) items are used in the final questionnaire. For example, participants might be asked 'What factors might prevent you or help you eat fruit as part of your midday meal?' However, perhaps because of their infrequent use to date, there has been some variation in how control beliefs have been operationalized. Below we give examples of both control belief and power items. Control beliefs assess the presence or absence of facilitating or inhibiting factors and are commonly scored on 'never–frequently', 'false–true', 'unavailable–available', or 'unlikely–likely' response formats. Ajzen (1991) suggests that control is best treated as a bipolar scale (−3 inhibits to +3 facilitates), although a unipolar scoring appears more appropriate for certain response formats (e.g. +1 'never' to +7 'frequently'). Perceived power items assess the power of the item to facilitate or inhibit performance of the behaviour. Power items are also problematic: response formats include 'less likely–more likely', 'more difficult–easier', and 'not important–very important'. Ajzen (1991) reports mixed evidence concerning whether these should be scored as unipolar or bipolar, although the wording of the response format may suggest the most appropriate scoring to use. The relevant items are then multiplicatively combined and summed (equation 5) to give an indirect measure of perceived behavioural control. This offers a promising avenue for exploration, offering an opportunity to identify those factors that underpin people's perceptions of control. However, precisely how these control beliefs combine to influence PBC requires more attention since this research is currently at a preliminary stage.

Control beliefs
I have free time...   Never   1 2 3 4 5 6 7   Frequently
I am near sports facilities...   Never   1 2 3 4 5 6 7   Frequently

Power
Having free time makes taking regular physical activity ...
                    Less likely   1 2 3 4 5 6 7   More likely
Being near sports facilities makes taking regular physical activity ...
                    Less likely   1 2 3 4 5 6 7   More likely

Adapted from Norman *et al.* (2000)

6 Application of the model: food choice

There have been a number of applications of the TPB to food choice (see Sparks 1994; Conner and Armitage 2002 for reviews). In this section we discuss the application of the TPB to healthy food choices through the example of Conner *et al.*'s (2002) study of attitudes towards healthy eating over a six-year period.[4] In this study healthy eating was described as a diet low in fat and high in fruit and vegetables and fibre. Study of the predictors of the performance of healthy eating over such a prolonged period is important because it is only over these prolonged periods that associated health benefits are likely to accrue.

6.1 Respondents and procedure

This was a questionnaire study in which participants were selected from a number of general practices in the UK. A total of 248 participants completed the initial questionnaire (59 males; 189 females; mean age 47.4

years). Of these 144 also completed a second questionnaire six years later. Attrition analyses comparing TPB variables at time 1 for respondents who completed both or only the first questionnaire revealed no significant multivariate difference: $F(7,240) = 1.21$, ns, indicating that those who remained in the sample were not biased compared to those who did not remain in the sample.

6.2 Measures

The questionnaire included the following measures to assess central components of the TPB. *Intention* to eat a healthy diet was assessed as the mean of five items, each measured on seven-point bipolar scales, e.g. 'I intend to eat a healthy diet in the future' (definitely do not–definitely do; all scored -3 to $+3$). Cronbach's alpha was 0.95. Test–retest reliability over a six-month time period was acceptable ($r = 0.48$, $p < 0.01$). *Attitude* was assessed as the mean of six semantic differential scales, e.g. 'My eating a healthy diet would be/is ...' (bad–good, harmful–beneficial, unpleasant–pleasant, unenjoyable–enjoyable, foolish–wise, unnecessary–necessary), all scored -3 to $+3$; alpha = 0.83; test-retest $r = 0.51$, $p < 0.01$). *Subjective norm* was assessed by a single item, e.g. 'People who are important to me think I should eat a healthy diet' (unlikely–likely), scored -3 to $+3$). Reliability was acceptable (test–retest $r = 0.38$, $p < 0.01$). *Perceived behavioural control* (PBC) was assessed as the mean of six, seven-point unipolar ($+1$ to $+7$) items, e.g. 'For me to eat a healthy diet in the future is ...' (difficult–easy) 'I am confident that if I ate a healthy diet I could keep to it' (strongly disagree–strongly agree); alpha = 0.74; test–retest $r = 0.53$, $p < 0.01$.

Behavioural beliefs[5] were assessed by seven items (derived from pilot interviews): 'Eating a healthier diet would make me physically fitter; Eating a healthier diet would make me healthier; By eating a healthier diet I would lose weight; Eating a healthier diet would help me live longer; Eating a healthier diet would make feel good about myself; Eating a healthier diet would take time (e.g. choosing healthier foods, preparing healthier foods, etc.); A healthier diet would be expensive'. The response scales were marked 'unlikely' and 'likely' at their end points and were scored from -3 to $+3$. The 'outcomes' identified in the behavioural belief questions were evaluated on a response scale labelled from bad to good (scored -3 to $+3$) in response to questions of the form: 'Being physically fitter would be ...' (bad–good). Each behavioural belief was multiplied by the corresponding outcome evaluation and these products summed.[6]

Normative beliefs were assessed in relation to four referents (derived from pilot interviews): friends, health experts, family and workmates. The normative belief questions were of the same format: 'My friends think I should eat a healthier diet' (unlikely–likely), scored -3 to $+3$. Corresponding to each normative belief was a motivation to comply question, assessed by statements worded in the form: 'With regard to eating, I want to do what friends think I should' (strongly disagree–strongly agree), scored 1 to 7. Each normative belief was multiplied by the corresponding motivation to comply and these products summed.

Control beliefs were assessed with 11 items (derived from pilot interviews): 'Lack of support from people with whom I share food; The limited choice of healthier food when eating out; Obscure and difficult to understand advice about healthier eating; Stressful situations; Having free time on my hands; Being anxious/upset; Seeing others eat unhealthy foods; Feeling depressed; The poor taste of a healthier diet; Being in a hurry at meal times; Lack of easy access to places selling healthier foods (e.g. large supermarkets)'. The power items were of the same format: 'Lack of support from whom I share food makes my eating a healthier diet . . .' (unlikely-likely), scored −3 to +3. Control belief items corresponded to each of the above power items (e.g. 'People with whom I eat food support me in eating a healthier diet' (never–frequently), scored 1 to 7. Each power item was multiplied by the corresponding control belief and these products summed.

Behaviour was assessed at the second time point by using a 33-item food frequency questionnaire (FFQ). The items of food were commonly consumed food categories that were arranged in terms of food groups. These were: dairy products; meats and fish; bread and cereals; fruit and vegetables; desserts and snacks. Each food was rated on the frequency it was eaten, on a scale with six categories: two or more times a day; every day; three to five times a week; one to two times a week; one to three times a month; and rarely/never. This measure was a slightly adapted version of the FFQ developed and validated by Cade and Margetts (1988). Using this measure, standard portion size data and nutritional data measures of *percentage fat intake* (i.e. percentage of calories derived from all fat in the diet; M = 34.9, SD = 6.45), *fibre intake* (i.e. grams of fibre consumed per day; M = 9.65, SD = 3.40), and *fruit/vegetable intake* (i.e. portions of fruit and vegetables consumed per day; M = 4.23, SD = 0.96) were computed. To compute an overall measure of healthy eating behaviour, each of the three measures was standardized and a sum computed (after multiplying the percentage calories from fat measure by −1), such that higher scores indicate more healthy eating.

6.3 Results

For the analysis, the correlations amongst the TPB components were first calculated (Table 5.3). All variables except normative beliefs and control beliefs were significantly correlated with intentions, while all variables except subjective norms and normative beliefs were significantly correlated with behaviour. The strongest predictor of intentions was PBC while the strongest predictor of behaviour was intentions. Multiple regressions of behavioural intentions onto attitudes, subjective norms and perceived behavioural control were computed. The final beta coefficients showed that all three variables exerted an independent predictive effect on behavioural intentions with PBC being the strongest predictor (Table 5.4). The multiple correlation (R) between the three predictors and behavioural intention was 0.63, indicating that 40 per cent of the variance in intention scores could be

Table 5.3 Means, standard deviations and intercorrelations for study variables

Variables	1	2	3	4	5	6	7	8	Mean	SD
1 Healthy eating behavior	1.00	0.37**	0.16	−0.09	0.37**	0.20*	0.09	0.20*	0.10	2.24
2 Intentions		1.00	0.35**	0.24**	0.57**	0.43**	0.22	0.15	1.89	1.22
3 Attitude			1.00	0.07	0.36**	0.19**	0.10	0.10	2.03	0.96
4 Subjective norm				1.00	−0.01	0.42**	0.60**	0.03	1.51	1.66
5 PBC					1.00	0.14*	0.06	0.35	5.14	1.16
6 Behavioural beliefs						1.00	0.37**	0.37	4.76	2.64
7 Normative beliefs							1.00	0.43	6.06	6.04
8 Control beliefs								1.00	−1.59	4.93

Note: * p < 0.05, ** p < 0.01. For correlations with behaviour *n* = 144, for other correlations *n* = 248

Table 5.4   Hierarchical regressions of intentions onto TPB variables (n = 248)

Predictors	Unstandardized Beta	Standard Error of Beta	Beta
Attitude	0.132	0.048	0.147**
Subjective norm	0.115	0.024	0.237**
PBC	0.530	0.055	0.515**

Note: ** $p < 0.001$. R^2 = 0.400, $p < 0.001$.

Table 5.5   Hierarchical regressions of behaviour onto TPB variables (n = 144)

Predictors	Unstandardized Beta	Standard Error of Beta	Beta
Intentions	0.400	0.150	0.247**
PBC	0.370	0.142	0.241**

Note: ** $p < 0.001$. R^2 = 0.180, $p < 0.001$.

'explained' by these predictors ($F(3,244)$ = 54.1, $p < 0.001$). Table 5.5 reports the results of the regression of behaviour onto TPB variables. Intention and PBC were entered and explained 18 per cent of the variance in behaviour with both being significant ($F(2,141)$ = 14.2, $p < 0.001$).

A final analysis attempted to identify those beliefs which might form an appropriate focus for intervention. This was achieved by identifying those beliefs most strongly associated with variations in their direct predictor, e.g. which behavioural beliefs were most strongly associated with variations in attitude. A median split was conducted on attitude, subjective norm and PBC in order to create groups with high versus low levels on these constructs. A t-test was then used to identify which beliefs had different means for these two groups. For attitudes only three beliefs showed significant differences ($p < 0.05$): Eating a healthier diet would make me physically fitter; Eating a healthier diet would make me healthier; A healthier diet would be expensive. For subjective norms all four beliefs showed significant differences ($p < 0.001$), but the largest differences were for: My friends think I should eat a healthier diet; My family think I should eat a healthier diet. For PBC eight beliefs showed significant differences ($p < 0.05$), but the largest differences were for: Seeing others eat unhealthy foods; The poor taste of a healthier diet; Being in a hurry at meal times.

6.4 Summary of study findings and implications

The above study demonstrates the application of the TPB to understanding healthy eating. Intentions were well predicted by each of the other components of the model, with PBC being the strongest predictor. In addition, both intentions and PBC were significant predictors of behaviour, with both having similar predictive power. The amounts of explained variance in both intentions and behaviour are similar to the average values for dietary behaviour reported in meta-analyses (41 per cent and 16 per cent respectively in McEachan *et al.* 2005). In this context, the variance explained in behaviour is impressive given the six-year time period over which predictions were made. Nevertheless, the overall amount of variance explained in behaviour is modest, perhaps because intentions changed during the six-year period between the assessment of the TPB variables and the final measure of behaviour. In this regard it is interesting to note that Conner *et al.* (2002) showed that intentions were significantly stronger predictors of healthy eating behaviour six years later among those whose intentions remained stable over the initial six months.

The study identifies attitude, subjective norms and PBC as strong predictors of intentions, and intentions and PBC as strong direct predictors of behaviour. There are practical implications that can be drawn from these findings. Interventions to promote health outcomes through changing various aspects of healthy eating should target attitudes, subjective norms and PBC in order to increase healthy eating intentions and behaviour. Fishbein and Ajzen (1975) suggest that persuasive communications targeting beliefs about the salient outcomes of a behaviour are the best way to change attitudes. For example, analysis of the behavioural beliefs assessed in this study indicated that the three beliefs which most strongly (p < 0.001) differentiated those with positive and negative attitudes to healthy eating were: Eating a healthier diet would make me physically fitter; Eating a healthier diet would make me healthier; A healthier diet would be expensive. These might form useful targets for interventions designed to change attitudes toward healthy eating. Analysis of normative beliefs indicated that the two beliefs which most strongly (p < 0.001) differentiated those with positive and negative subjective norms to healthy eating were: My friends think I should eat a healthier diet; My family think I should eat a healthier diet. These might form useful targets for interventions designed to change subjective norms toward healthy eating. Bandura (1986) outlines four ways in which self-efficacy, or in this case PBC, can be directly enhanced; through personal mastery experience by the setting and achieving of sub-goals (e.g. eating or avoiding particular foods), through observing others' success, through standard persuasive techniques, and through the use of relaxation techniques (e.g. to control feelings of arousal or anxiety). The TPB would suggest a further way of changing PBC, through changing the control beliefs underlying PBC. For example, analysis of the control beliefs assessed in this study indicated that the three beliefs which most strongly (p < 0.001) differentiated those with high and low PBC toward healthy eating were: Seeing others eat unhealthy foods; The poor taste of a healthier diet; Being in a hurry at meal times. These might form useful targets for interventions designed to change attitudes toward healthy eating.

7 Behavioural interventions

The title of Ajzen and Fishbein's (1980) seminal work on the theory of reasoned action made reference to the theory's role in 'understanding' and 'predicting' behaviour. Because of its popularity in applied research, it is not surprising that the issue of the theory's possible additional role in behavioural interventions has been raised. In fact, Eagly (1992) has been quite explicit in stating that 'interest in attitude theory is widespread and quite intense because of the desire of many groups to change attitudes and behaviors' (p. 705).

On the one hand, the claim that changing a person's beliefs will lead to changes in other model components (including behaviour) has led to a growing interest in the model for intervention work. On the other hand, Ajzen and Fishbein's (2005) suggestion that the validity of central proposals of the theory can be tested by intervention work focuses attention on the benefits of intervention work to the assessment of the theory itself. For example, Ajzen and Fishbein (2005) suggest that successful modification of TRA/TPB predictors should lead to a change in intentions and/or behaviour; if it does not, Ajzen and Fishbein (2005) concede that this would indicate a falsification of the theory. This latter suggestion would seem to us to be unwarranted unless one could be certain that one is measuring and monitoring changes in *all* the influences on intentions and behaviours.

Ajzen and Fishbein (1980) suggested a number of ways in which the TRA can be used to change behavioural intentions and behaviour. Their approach focuses on the targeting of underlying beliefs. Ajzen and Fishbein (1980) argue that changing these underlying beliefs should bring about long-lasting change in (for example) attitudes, intentions and behaviour. Generally speaking, there are two stages involved in using the TPB to develop an intervention. First, it is important to determine which variables should be targeted: clearly, it would be counter-productive to target variables that did not account for variance in behavioural intention or behaviour. Second, the message content must be identified. This is done by either identifying new salient beliefs that the recipient is not aware of, or more commonly by targeting and changing existing salient beliefs (see Sutton 2002b for a more detailed consideration of this issue).

Table 5.6 summarizes a number of TPB intervention studies. As an example of research which has used the TPB[7] as a basis for intervention designed to influence people's motives to engage in health-related behaviours, we consider the work of Brubaker and Fowler (1990) on testicular self-examination.

Table 5.6 Illustrative applications of intervention studies using the TPB to various health behaviours

Research area	Example applications
Smoking	Godin *et al.* (1992) Frequency of smoking
Road safety	Parker *et al.* (1996) Restricting driving speed
Exercise	Courneya and McAuley (1995) Exercise programme
Diet	Beale and Manstead (1991) Infants' sugar intake
Miscellaneous	Brubaker and Fowler (1990) Testicular self-examination

Brubaker and Fowler (1990) were concerned about the recent increase in the incidence of testicular cancer in the USA and the lack of knowledge young men had about carrying out testicular self-examination (TSE) in order to detect the disease. They consequently designed a study in which they attempted 'to evaluate the effect of a persuasive message based on the theory of reasoned action on the performance of TSE' (p.1413). Male undergraduate students (*n* = 114) were randomly assigned to one of three conditions:

1 in the *theory-based message* group, participants heard a message based on the TRA;
2 in the *informational message* group, participants heard a message containing more general information about, for example, the incidence of testicular cancer and how it can be treated;
3 in the *no-message* group, participants received no message at all.

The information that participants received was presented in the form of an audio-taped dialogue lasting for about 10 minutes between, ostensibly, a doctor and some students (these roles were taken, in fact, by actors). For the *theory-based message* group, the dialogue consisted of the actors 'challenging misconceptions' about TSE that had been identified in previous research in the form of beliefs that had differentiated between males who performed TSE and males who did not. Brubaker and Fowler mention the examples of 'TSE is difficult to perform; TSE can lead to early detection of cancer; TSE does not take a lot of time to perform' as beliefs that were addressed in this way.

A subsequent questionnaire, focused on performing TSE during the next month, assessed, for example, intentions, attitudes, subjective norm, self-efficacy, behavioural beliefs, normative beliefs, outcome evaluations and motivation to comply. In follow-up telephone calls one week and four weeks later, participants were asked for a self-report of their TSE behaviour since the experimental procedure. The results clearly showed differences between participants who received messages and those who did not (e.g. the former reported more TSE, greater intentions and more positive attitudes). However, there was no evidence of differences between the *theory-based message* group and the *informational message* group on the key dependent variables. Despite the lack of clear findings, it is important to note that this study sought to modify the structure of people's beliefs about the behaviour in question. This is in line with how Ajzen and Fishbein would propose the TRA and TPB should be used in interventions aimed at influencing people's behavioural motives. However, we would reiterate our earlier comment that the method by which this is effected is an issue beyond the remit of the TPB/TRA. Researchers may select ineffective methods, or may influence model components that they did not intend to influence, or may discover effective strategies which they had not expected to work. The range of methods open to them is very broad (Fishbein and Ajzen 2004), and the effectiveness of different methods may be expected to be highly context-dependent. And, of course, while some attitudes and behaviours may be amenable to change, others may be more entrenched and intransigent.

Hardeman *et al.* (2002) recently reviewed studies using the TPB to promote behaviour change (see examples in Table 5.6). A total of 24 intervention studies were identified, although the TPB was used to develop the intervention in only half the studies. In the other half of the studies the TPB was only used in relation to assessing the effects of the intervention. Where the results were reported, the interventions were effective in changing intentions in approximately half the studies and behaviour in approximately two-thirds, although the effect sizes tended to be small. However, two main problems with interpreting these findings are apparent. First, many studies did not conduct an initial TPB study to identify appropriate targets for intervention. Second, many studies did not test the effectiveness of interventions in changing targeted cognitions before examining impacts on intentions and behaviour. Hardeman *et al.* (2002) indicate that many interventions they examined appeared to be poorly designed, that 'interventions were seldom explicitly developed to target specific components of the model' (p. 149) and that this area should focus more on whether any observed effects are mediated by changes in TPB components.

What then should we make of the role of the TPB in behavioural change interventions? While the issue of persuasion and attitude change has a long, and perhaps chequered, history within social psychology, a set of sure-fire techniques for manipulating or influencing people's attitudes and behaviour is not available to us. Moreover, theories of attitude change and theories (such as the TPB) addressing the relationship between attitudes and behaviour are quite distinct areas of research (Eagly 1992). So, at one level, the role of the TPB needs to be considered in the context of other theoretical issues that need to be dealt with in implementing intervention work: 'The theory of planned behavior can provide general guideline [sic] ... but it does not tell us what kind of intervention will be most effective' (Ajzen 2004: 2; see also Fishbein and Ajzen 2004). Thus, for example, the popularity of the Elaboration Likelihood Model (Petty and Cacioppo 1986) as a model of persuasion could be used to supplement the TPB in intervention work (Quine *et al.* 2001). However, the matter of how to construct strong arguments in order to bring about central route persuasion and (presumably) changes in belief structure is but one issue that requires research attention.

Evidence which indicates that a change in people's beliefs can bring about changes in attitudes, intentions and/or behaviour (Ajzen and Fishbein 2005) lends some support to the basic causal sequence at the heart of the TPB. However, even here, one needs to be open to the possible role of demand characteristics or other biasing factors. Objective behaviour measures are often difficult to obtain and the reliability of self-report measures merits critical scrutiny, as we have indicated above. What the TPB does offer is a theory of volitional behaviour which posits an explicit causal relationship between people's beliefs and their subsequent actions. It is thus apparent that changes in those beliefs will lead to behavioural changes, all other things being held equal. Moreover, Ajzen and Fishbein (1980) suggest that if one is interested in attitude change one might 'try to influence some of the beliefs that are salient in a subject population or try to introduce novel, previously nonsalient, beliefs' (p.224). There also seems to have been little research addressing this latter issue directly, although implications for this possibility are to be found in the literature (e.g. Millar and Millar 1990). Clearly further research is required on this issue.

Important in this context is not only that the role of the TPB in intervention work should not be overstated but also that a realistic assessment of the contribution of the theory to intervention work is required. In the Hardeman *et al.* (2002) review, the authors note that researchers 'seem to see the theory as more useful in identifying cognitive targets for change than in offering suggestions on how these cognitions might be changed' (p.149). We feel this to be the most appropriate approach given the current formulation of the TPB. While from an applied perspective behaviour change may be seen as the most important criterion for judging the effectiveness of an intervention, from a theory development perspective other criteria may be relevant. In relation to theory development the key issue is the light that intervention studies can throw on supposed causal relationships in the TPB. For such an aim, experimental designs which allow a focused manipulation of one construct and observation of the effects on other constructs are required (see Sutton 2002a). Thus, for example, we require interventions that can be shown to change PBC (without directly changing A and SN) and to observe the effects on BI and behaviour. This might be difficult to achieve in many applied settings. However, in our view, the development and testing of such focused interventions are important tasks for the further development of the TPB.

8 Future directions

8.1 Compatibility

Although the TPB might be expected to provide some predictive power when the demands of 'compatibility' are complied with, we should consider the suggestion made by Ajzen (1988) that individuals' actions on specific occasions are not essentially what psychologists are interested in: rather, what is of interest are 'regularities in behavior, consistent patterns of action, response tendencies' (p.46). The 'aggregation' of behaviour was discussed earlier. In a related way, it is not altogether clear that we would want to dispense with attitudes towards the target when considering attitudes towards particular actions. For example, attitudes towards purchasing foods produced by certain technologies may well be affected by more general attitudes towards these technologies as well as by attitudes towards specific purchase behaviours, especially if attitudes towards purchase focus on the outcomes of purchase (rather than, for example, on the processes by which the foods were produced).

Recent work on temporal construals (e.g. Trope and Libermann 2000) would also suggest that people's representations of a given behaviour may be expected to vary partly as a function of the temporal distance from behavioural enactment: for example, at greater temporal distance, a behaviour is likely to be represented in more abstract terms than it is at less temporal distance. Such variations in construals might be expected to be intimately connected to belief salience.

On a related theme, Lord *et al.* (1984) have suggested that attitudes towards targets will only correspond with actual behaviours if the attitude target matches the person's representation of the attitude target. So, for example, if people's representation of a low-fat diet or of a production technology does not match their actual subsequent first-hand experience with those 'targets', then poor attitude–behaviour relationships might be expected.

8.2 Moderator variables

A significant body of work in recent years has examined the role of moderator variables within the TPB (i.e. variables that influence the magnitude of relationships between TPB constructs). The value of this work for applied researchers lies in identifying the conditions which maximize the relationships between TPB variables. From a theoretical perspective such moderators help elucidate the range of conditions under which the theory works. A range of moderator variables have been examined in relation to the TPB. These can be broadly split into additional variables and properties of components of the TPB. The former include anticipated regret, moral norms and past behaviour. The latter include accessibility, direct experience, involvement, certainty, ambivalence, affective-cognitive consistency and temporal stability (see Cooke and Sheeran 2004 for a review of 44 such studies).

For example, anticipated regret has been posited as a moderator of intention–behaviour relationships on the basis that high levels of regret may bind people to their intentions and so strengthen their intentions because failing to act would be associated with aversive affect (Sheeran and Orbell 1999). Several studies have demonstrated this effect in relation to exercising (Sheeran and Abraham, 2003) and smoking initiation (Conner *et al.* 2005, Study 2). Abraham and Sheeran (2003, Study 1) also reported a similar moderating effect of anticipated regret on exercise intention–behaviour relationships. Impressively, a second study by these authors manipulated regret and demonstrated similar moderation effects.

The predominant basis on which intentions are formed has also been examined as a moderator of intention–behaviour relationships in a number of studies. For example, Sheeran *et al.* (1999) showed that intentions more aligned with attitudes than subjective norms were significantly stronger predictors of behaviour. It was argued that this was because attitudinally aligned intentions were more intrinsically motivated (Ryan *et al.* 1996). More recently, Godin *et al.* (2005) demonstrated across a number of studies that intentions that were most closely aligned with moral norms were significantly stronger predictors of behaviour. It was argued that such intentions were more consistent with an individual's core self-identity. The final additional variable moderator that has been examined is past behaviour. Norman *et al.* (2000) found PBC to be a significantly stronger predictor of exercise behaviour for those who had exercised frequently in the past. This was interpreted as being attributable to PBC being more accurate for those who had more experience of exercise (i.e. had exercised more frequently in the past).

In relation to properties of components of the TPB the focus has been on attitudes and intentions. In the Cooke and Sheeran (2004) meta-analytic review accessibility, direct experience, certainty, ambivalence and affective-cognitive consistency all significantly moderated attitude–behaviour relationship, while ambivalence, certainty and involvement all moderated the attitude–intention relationship. All these properties plus certainty also significantly moderated the intention–behaviour relationship. In each case greater accessibility, greater involvement, more direct experience, more certainty, less ambivalence and greater affective-cognitive consistency were associated with significantly stronger relationships.

Temporal stability appears to be a particularly important moderator of relationships with behaviour. In the Cooke and Sheeran (2004) review it emerged as the strongest moderator. As Ajzen (1996) has argued '... to obtain accurate prediction of behavior, intentions ... must remain reasonably stable over time until the behavior is performed' (p.389). Intentions measured prior to performance of a behaviour may change as a result of new information or unforeseen obstacles resulting in a reduced predictive power. The moderating role of temporal stability has been addressed in several recent studies of health behaviours. Conner *et al.* (2002) found a significant intention stability moderation effect in relation to healthy eating over a period of six years, such that intentions were stronger predictors of behaviour when intentions were stable. Similar results have been reported in relation to smoking initiation (Conner *et al.* 2005), attending health screening and eating a low fat diet (Conner *et al.* 2000). Sheeran and Abraham (2003) found intention stability both to moderate the intention–behaviour relationship for exercising and, more importantly, to mediate the impacts of various other moderators of the intention–behaviour relationship (e.g. anticipated regret, certainty, etc.). This suggests that a number of these other moderators may have their effect on intention–behaviour relationships through changing the temporal stability of intentions. Nevertheless, the stability of intentions is an emergent property of an individual's intention and subsequent research may well show it to be dependent on other more directly modifiable aspects of intentions (e.g. prioritizing one particular intention/goal over other competing intentions/goals).

8.5 Conclusion

A rather critical stance towards the TPB has been taken here since we believe that this is the best foundation on which to make progress (see also discussion by Sarver 1983; Liska 1984; Eagly and Chaiken 1993). Its contribution may be seen as both significant and limited for health behaviours: significant because at one level of analysis it increases our understanding of many health-related behaviours; limited because it deals with perceptions of control and not with actual control issues themselves (but see Figure 5.1). In the broad social environment there will be a number of influences on people's health and on their behaviour: any of these that do not impinge on people's perceptions of control will not be accessible to analysis via the TPB. Health behaviours need to be understood not only in terms of people's beliefs, values, perceived social pressure and perceived control but also in terms of the individual's behavioural history and the broader social pressures that may be operating. While the TPB is concerned with proximal psychological influences on behaviour, we have to recognize the broader social structure within which these influences develop.

Notes

1 This was originally called the principle of correspondence (Fishbein and Ajzen 1975; Ajzen and Fishbein 1977).
2 As Ajzen (2002c) notes, 'Defining the TACT elements is somewhat arbitrary' (p.2).
3 The response options may be structured in various ways: for example, as numbers to circle, boxes to tick, or as lines to put crosses or ticks on.
4 Note that only the data from time points 1 and 3 of the Conner *et al.* (2002) study are reported here.
5 Data on behavioural, normative and control beliefs was not reported in the Conner *et al.* (2002) paper.
6 Internal reliability measures are not reported for belief-based measures as we believe it is most appropriate to consider individual beliefs as formative rather than reflective indicators of the construct (see Conner *et al.* 2001).
7 The Brubaker and Fowler (1990) study is, in fact, a study of an extended TRA incorporating a measure of self-efficacy.

References

Abraham, C., Clift, S. and Grabowski, P. (1999) Cognitive predictors of adherence to malaria prophylaxis regimens on return from a malarious region: a prospective study, *Social Science and Medicine*, 48, 1641–54.

Abraham, C. and Sheeran, P. (2003) Evidence that anticipated regret strengthens intentions, enhances intention stability, and improves intention–behaviour consistency, *British Journal of Health Psychology*, 9, 269–78.

Agnew, C. (1998) Modal versus individually-derived behavioural and normative beliefs about condom use: comparing measurement alternatives of the cognitive underpinnings of the theories of reasoned action and planned behaviour, *Psychology and Health*, 13, 271–87.

Ajzen, I. (1988) *Attitudes, Personality and Behavior*. Milton Keynes: Open University Press.

Ajzen, I. (1991) The theory of planned behavior, *Organizational Behavior and Human Decision Processes*, 50, 179–211.

Ajzen, I. (1996) The directive influence of attitudes on behavior. In P. Gollwitzer and J.A. Bargh (eds) *Psychology of Action*. New York: Guilford, 385–403.

Ajzen, I. (2001) Nature and operation of attitudes, *Annual Review of Psychology*, **52**, 27–58.

Ajzen, I. (2002a) Perceived behavioural control, self-efficacy, locus of control, and the theory of planned behaviour, *Journal of Applied Social Psychology*, **32**, 1–20.

Ajzen, I. (2002b) Residual effects of past on later behavior: habituation and reasoned action perspectives, *Personality and Social Psychology Review*, **6**, 107–22.

Ajzen, I. (2002c) Constructing a TpB questionnaire: conceptual and methodological considerations, from www.people.umass.edu/aizen/pdf/tpb.measurement.pdf, accessed 12 July 2004.

Ajzen, I. (2004) Behavioral interventions based on the theory of planned behavior, from http://www.people.umass.edu/aizen/pdf/tpb.intervention.pdf, accessed 12 July 2004.

Ajzen, I. and Driver, B.L. (1992) Application of the theory of planned behavior to leisure choice, *Journal of Leisure Research*, 24, 207–224.

Ajzen, I. and Fishbein, M. (1977) Attitude–behavior relations: a theoretical analysis and review of empirical research, *Psychological Bulletin*, **84**, 888–918.

Ajzen, I. and Fishbein, M. (1980) *Understanding Attitudes and Predicting Social Behavior*. Englewood-Cliff, NJ: Prentice-Hall.

Ajzen, I. and Fishbein, M. (2000) Attitudes and the attitude–behavior relation: reasoned and automatic processes, *European Review of Social Psychology*, **11**, 1–33.

Ajzen, I. and Fishbein, M. (2005) The influence of attitudes on behavior. In D. Albarracin, B.T. Johnson and M.P. Zanna (eds) *Handbook of Attitudes and Attitude Change: Basic Principles*. Mahwah, NJ: Erlbaum, in press.

Ajzen, I. and Madden, T.J. (1986) Prediction of goal directed behavior: attitudes, intentions and perceived behavioral control, *Journal of Experimental Social Psychology*, **22**, 453–74.

Ajzen, I. and Sexton, J. (1999) Depth of processing, belief congruence, and attitude–behavior correspondence. In S. Chaiken and Y. Trope (eds) *Dual-process Theories in Social Psychology*. New York: Guilford, 117–38.

Ajzen, A. and Timko, C. (1986) Correspondence between health attitudes and behavior, *Journal of Basic and Applied Social Psychology*, 7, 259–76.

Albarracin, D., Johnson, B. T., Fishbein, M. and Muellerleile, P. A. (2001) Theories of reasoned action and planned behavior as models of condom use: a meta-analysis, *Psychological Bulletin*, **127**, 142–61.

Armitage, C. J. and Conner, M. (1999a) The theory of planned behaviour: assessment of predictive validity and 'perceived control', *British Journal of Social Psychology*, **38**, 35–54.

Armitage, C. J. and Conner, M. (1999b) Distinguishing perceptions of control from self-efficacy: predicting consumption of a low fat diet using the theory of planned behavior, *Journal of Applied Social Psychology*, **29**, 72–90.

Armitage, C. J. and Conner, M. (2001) Efficacy of the theory of planned behaviour: a meta-analytic review, *British Journal of Social Psychology*, **40**, 471–99.

Bagozzi, R.P. (1992) The self-regulation of attitudes, intentions and behaviour, *Social Psychology Quarterly*, **55**, 178–204.

Bagozzi, R.P. and Edwards, E.A. (1998) Goal setting and goal pursuit in the regulation of body weight, *Psychology and Health*, **13**, 593–621.

Bagozzi, R. P., Lee, K.-H. and Van Loo, M.F. (2001) Decisions to donate bone marrow: the role of attitudes and subjective norms across cultures, *Psychology and Health*, **16**, 29–56.

Bandura, A. (1977) Self-efficacy: toward a unifying theory of behavioural change, *Psychological Review*, **84**, 191–215.

Bandura, A. (1986) *Social Foundations of Thought and Action: A Cognitive Social Theory*. Englewood Cliffs, NJ: Prentice-Hall.

Beale, D.A. and Manstead, A.S.R. (1991) Predicting mothers' intentions to limit frequency of infants' sugar intake: testing the theory of planned behavior, *Journal of Applied Social Psychology*, **21**, 409–31.

Beck, L. and Ajzen, I. (1991) Predicting dishonest actions using the Theory of Planned Behavior, *Journal of Research in Personality*, **25**, 285–301.

Blue, C. L. (1995) The predictive capacity of the theory of reasoned action and the theory of planned behavior in exercise research: an integrated literature review, *Research in Nursing and Health*, **18**, 105–21.

Bollen, K.A. (1989) *Structural Equations with Latent Variables*. New York: Wiley.

Breckler, S. J. and Wiggins, E. C. (1989) Affect versus evaluation in the structure of attitudes, *Journal of Experimental Social Psychology*, **25**, 253–71.

Brubaker, R.G. and Fowler, C. (1990) Encouraging college males to perform testicular self-examination: evaluation of a persuasive message based on the revised theory of reasoned action, *Journal of Applied Social Psychology*, **17**, 1411–22.

Budd, R.J. (1987) Response bias and the theory of reasoned action, *Social Cognition*, **5**, 95–107.

Cade, J.E. and Margetts, B.M. (1988) Nutrient sources in the English diet: quantitative data from three English towns, *International Journal of Epidemiology*, **17**, 844–8.

Chan, D.K. and Fishbein, M. (1993) Determinants of college women's intentions to tell their partners to use condoms, *Journal of Applied Social Psychology*, **23**, 1455–70.

Charng, H.-W., Piliavin, J. A. and Callero, P. L. (1988) Role identity and reasoned action in the prediction of repeated behavior, *Social Psychology Quarterly*, **51**, 303–17.

Cialdini, R.B., Kallgren, C.A. and Reno, R.R. (1991) A focus theory of normative conduct: a theoretical refinement and re-evaluation of the role of norms in human behaviour, *Advances in Experimental Social Psychology*, **24**, 201–34.

Cohen, J. (1992) A power primer, *Psychological Bulletin*, **112**, 155–9.

Conner, M. and Abraham, C. (2001) Conscientiousness and the theory of planned behavior: towards a more complete model of the antecedents of intentions and behavior, *Personality and Social Psychology Bulletin*, **27**, 1547–61.

Conner, M. and Armitage, C.J. (1998) Extending the theory of planned behavior: a review and avenues for further research, *Journal of Applied Social Psychology*, **28**, 1430–64.

Conner, M. and Armitage, C.J. (2002) *The Social Psychology of Food*. Buckingham: OU Press.

Conner, M., Kirk, S.F.L., Cade, J.E. and Barrett, J.H. (2001) Why do women use dietary supplements? The use of the theory of planned behaviour to explore beliefs about their use, *Social Science and Medicine*, **52**, 621–33.

Conner, M., Norman, P. and Bell, R. (2002) The Theory of Planned Behavior and healthy eating, *Health Psychology*, **21**, 194–201.

Conner, M., Sandberg, T., McMillan, B. and Higgins, A.(2005) Role of anticipated regret, intentions and intention stability in adolescent smoking initiation, *British Journal of Health Psychology*, in press.

Conner, M., Sheeran, P., Norman, P. and Armitage, C.J. (2000) Temporal stability as a moderator of relationships in the theory of planned behaviour, *British Journal of Social Psychology*, **39**, 469–93.

Conner, M., Warren, R., Close, S. and Sparks, P. (1999) Alcohol consumption and the theory of planned behavior: an examination of the cognitive mediation of past behavior, *Journal of Applied Social Psychology*, **29**, 1675–703.

Cooke, R. and Sheeran, P. (2004) Moderation of cognition–intention and cognition–behaviour relations: a meta-analysis of properties of variables from the theory of planned behaviour, *British Journal of Social Psychology*, **43**, 159–86.

Courneya, K.S. and McCauley, E. (1995) Cognitive mediators of the social influence–exercise adherence relationship: a test of the theory of planned behavior, *Journal of Behavioral Medicine*, **18**, 499–515.

Crites, S.L., Fabrigar, L.R. and Petty, R.E. (1994) Measuring the affective and cognitive properties of attitudes: conceptual and methodological issues, *Personality and Social Psychology Bulletin*, **20**, 619–34.

Deutsch, M. and Gerard, H. B. (1955) A study of normative and informational social influences upon human judgment, *Journal of Abnormal and Social Psychology*, **51**, 629–36.

De Vries, H., Backbier, E., Kok, G. and Dijkstra, M. (1995) The impact of social influences in the context of attitude, self-efficacy, intention and previous behaviour as predictors of smoking onset, *Journal of Applied Social Psychology*, **25**, 237–57.

Eagly, A.H. (1992) Uneven progress: social psychology and the study of attitudes, *Journal of Personality and Social Psychology*, **63**, 693–710.

Eagly, A.H. and Chaiken, S. (1993) *The Psychology of Attitudes*. Fort Worth, TX: Harcourt Brace Jovanovich.

Eagly, A. H., Mladinic, A. and Otto, S. (1994) Cognitive and affective bases of attitudes towards social groups and social policies, *Journal of Experimental Social Psychology*, **30**, 113–37.

Elliott, M. A., Armitage, C. J. and Baughan, C. J. (2003) Drivers' compliance with speed limits: an application of the theory of planned behavior, *Journal of Applied Psychology*, **88**, 964–72.

Fekadu, Z. and Kraft, P. (2001) Expanding the theory of planned behaviour: the role of social norms and group identification, *Journal of Health Psychology*, **7**, 33–43.

Fishbein, M. (1967a) Attitude and the prediction of behavior. In M. Fishbein (ed.) *Readings in Attitude Theory and Measurement*. New York: Wiley, 477–92.

Fishbein, M. (1967b) A behavior theory approach to the relations between beliefs about an object and the attitude toward the object. In M. Fishbein (ed.) *Readings in Attitude Theory and Measurement*. New York: Wiley, 389–400.

Fishbein, M. (1993) Introduction. In D.J. Terry, C. Gallois and M. McCamish (eds) *The Theory of Reasoned Action: Its Application to AIDS-preventive Behaviour*. Oxford: Pergamon, xv–xxv.

Fishbein, M. (1997) Predicting, understanding, and changing socially relevant behaviors: lessons learned. In C. McGarty and S.A. Haslam (eds) *The Message of Social Psychology*. Oxford: Blackwell, 77–91.

Fishbein, M. and Ajzen, I. (1975) *Belief, Attitude, Intention, and Behavior*. New York: Wiley.

Fishbein, M. and Ajzen, I. (2004) Theory-based behavior change interventions: comments on Hobbis and Sutton (2004), *Journal of Health Psychology*, **10**: 27–31.

French, D. P. and Hankins, M. (2003) The expectancy-value muddle in the theory of planned behaviour – and some proposed solutions, *British Journal of Health Psychology*, 8, 37–55.

Gaes, G. G., Kalle, R. J. and Tedeschi, J. I. (1978) Impression management in the forced compliance situation: two studies using the bogus pipeline, *Journal of Experimental Social Psychology*, 9, 491–501.

Gibbons, F. X. and Gerrard, M. (1997) Health images and their effects on health behavior. In B. P. Buunk and F. X. Gibbons (eds) *Health, Coping, and Social Comparisons*. Hillsdale, NJ: Erlbaum, 63–94.

Gibbons, F. X., Gerrard, M., Ouellette, J. and Burzette, R. (1998) Cognitive antecedents to adolescent health risk: discriminating between behavioural intention and behavioural willingness, *Psychology and Health*, 13, 319–39.

Godin, G., Conner, M. and Sheeran, P. (2005) Bridging the intention–behavior 'gap': the role of moral norm, *British Journal of Social Psychology*, in press.

Godin, G. and Gionet, N. J. (1991) Determinants of an intention to exercise of an electric power commission's employees, *Ergonomics*, 34, 1221–230.

Godin, G. and Kok, G. (1996) The theory of planned behavior: a review of its applications to health-related behaviors, *American Journal of Health Promotion*, 11, 87–98.

Godin, G., Valois, P., Lepage, L. and Desharnais, R. (1992) Predictors of smoking behaviour – an application of Ajzen's theory of planned behaviour, *British Journal of Addiction*, 87, 1335–43.

Hagger, M. and Chatzisarantis, N.L.D. (2005) First- and higher-order models of attitudes, normative influences, and perceived behavioural control in the theory of planned behaviour, *British Journal of Social Psychology*, in press.

Hagger, M., Chatzisarantis, N. and Biddle, S. (2002) A meta-analytic review of the theories of reasoned action and planned behavior in physical activity: predictive validity and the contribution of additional variables, *Journal of Sport and Exercise Psychology*, 24, 3–32.

Hardeman, W., Johnston, M., Johnston, D., Bonetti, D, Wareham, N.J. and Kinmonth, A.L. (2002) Application of the theory of planned behaviour in behaviour change interventions: a systematic review, *Psychology and Health*, 17, 123–58.

Hausenblas, H. A., Carron, A. V. and Mack, D. E. (1997) Application of the theories of reasoned action and planned behavior to exercise behavior: a meta-analysis, *Journal of Sport and Exercise Psychology*, 19, 36–51.

Johnston, K.L. and White, K.M. (2003) Binge-drinking: a test of the role of group norms in the theory of planned behaviour, *Psychology and Health*, 18, 63–77.

Jonas, K. and Doll, J. (1996) A critical evaluation of the Theory of Reasoned Action and the Theory of Planned Behavior, *Zeischrift fur Sozialpsychologie*, 18–31.

Kraft, P., Rise, J., Sutton, S. and Roysamb, E. (2005) Perceived difficulty in the theory of planned behaviour: perceived behavioural control or affective attitude?, *British Journal of Social Psychology*, in press.

Leach, M., Hennesy, M. and Fishbein, M. (2001) Perception of easy–difficult: attitude or self-efficacy?, *Journal of Applied Social Psychology*, 31, 1–20.

Liska, A.E. (1984) A critical examination of the causal structure of the Fishbein/Ajzen attitude-behavior model, *Social Psychology Quarterly*, 47, 61–74.

Lord, C.G., Lepper, M.R. and Mackie, D. (1984) Attitude prototypes as determinants of attitude–behavior consistency, *Journal of Personality and Social Psychology*, 46, 1254–66.

McEachan, R., Conner, M. and Lawton, R. (2005) A meta-analysis of theory of planned behaviour studies: the impact of behaviour type. Submitted for publication.

McMillan, B. and Conner, M. (2003) Applying an extended version of the theory of planned behavior to illicit drug use among students, *Journal of Applied Social Psychology*, **33**, 1662–83.

Manstead, A. S. R. (2000) The role of moral norm in the attitude–behavior relation. In D. J. Terry and M. A. Hogg (eds) *Attitudes, Behavior, and Social Context*. Mahwah, NJ: Lawrence Erlbaum Associates, 11–30.

Manstead, A. S. R. and Parker, D. (1995) Evaluating and extending the Theory of Planned Behaviour. In W. Stroebe and M. Hewstone (eds) *European Review of Social Psychology*, **6**, 69–95.

Millar, M.G. and Millar, K.U. (1990) Attitude change as a function of attitude type and argument type, *Journal of Personality and Social Psychology*, **59**, 217–28.

Miniard, P.W. and Cohen, J.B. (1981) An examination of the Fishbein–Ajzen behavioural–intentions model's concepts and measures, *Journal of Experimental Social Psychology*, **17**, 309–39.

Mullen, P. D., Hersey, J. C. and Iverson, D. C. (1987) Health behavior models compared, *Social Science and Medicine*, **24**, 973–83.

Norman, P. and Conner, M.T. (1993) The role of social cognition models in predicting attendance at health checks, *Psychology and Health*, **8**, 447–62.

Norman, P., Conner, M. and Bell, R. (2000) The theory of planned behaviour and exercise: evidence for the moderating role of past behaviour, *British Journal of Health Psychology*, **5**, 249–61.

Notani, A.S. (1998) Moderators of perceived behavioural control's predictiveness in the theory of planned behaviour: a meta-analysis, *Journal of Consumer Psychology*, **3**, 207–22.

O'Keefe, D. (1990) *Persuasion*. London: Sage Publications.

Osgood, C.E., Suci, G.J. and Tannenbaum, P.H. (1957) *The Measurement of Meaning*. Urbana, IL: University of Illinois Press.

Ouellette, J.A. and Wood, W. (1998) Habit and intention in everyday life: the multiple processes by which past behavior predicts future behavior, *Psychological Bulletin*, **124**, 54–74.

Parker, D., Manstead, A.S.R. and Stradling, S.G. (1995) Extending the TPB: the role of personal norm, *British Journal of Social Psychology*, **34**, 127–37.

Parker, D., Stradling, S.G. and Manstead, A.S.R. (1996) Modifying beliefs and attitudes to exceeding the speed limit: an intervention study based on the theory of planned behavior, *Journal of Applied Social Psychology*, **26**, 1–19.

Peak, H. (1955) Attitude and motivation. In M.R. Jones (ed.) *Nebraska symposium on motivation*, Vol. 3. Lincoln, NE: University of Nebraska Press, 149–88.

Perugini, M. and Bagozzi, R.P. (2003) The distinction between desires and intentions, *European Journal of Social Psychology*, **33**, 1–15.

Petty, R.E. and Cacioppo, J.T. (1986) *Communication and Persuasion: Central and Peripheral Routes of Attitude Change*. New York: Springer Verlag.

Quine, L., Rutter, D. R. and Arnold, L. (2001) Persuading school-age cyclists to use safety helmets: effectiveness of an intervention based on the Theory of Planned Behaviour, *British Journal of Health Psychology*, **6**, 327–45.

Rhodes, R. E. and Courneya, K. S. (2003a) Investigating multiple components of attitude, subjective norm, and perceived control: an examination of the theory of planned behaviour in the exercise domain, *British Journal of Social Psychology*, **42**, 129–46.

Rhodes, R. E. and Courneya, K. S. (2003b) Self-efficacy, controllability and intention in the theory of planned behavior: measurement redundancy or causal dependence, *Psychology and Health*, 18, 79–91.

Richard, R., Van der Pligt, J. and de Vries, N. (1996) Anticipated affect and behavioral choice, *Basic and Applied Social Psychology*, 18, 111–29.

Rivis, A. and Sheeran, P. (2003a) Descriptive norms as an additional predictor in the theory of planned behaviour: a meta-analysis, *Current Psychology*, 22, 218–33.

Rivis, A. and Sheeran, P. (2003b) Social influences and the theory of planned behaviour: evidence for a direct relationship between prototypes and young people's exercise behaviour, *Psychology and Health*, 18, 567–83.

Rutter, D.R. and Bunce, D.J. (1989) The theory of reasoned action of Fishbein and Ajzen: a test of Towriss's amended procedure for measuring beliefs, *British Journal of Social Psychology*, 28, 39–46.

Ryan, R., Sheldon, K. M., Kasser, T. and Deci, E. L. (1996) All goals are not created equal: an organismic perspective on the nature of goals and their regulation. In P. M. Gollwitzer and J. A. Bargh (eds) *The Psychology of Action*. London: Guildford Press, 7–26.

Sandberg, T. and Conner, M. (2005) A meta-analysis of the role of regret in the theory of planned behaviour. Submitted for publication.

Sarver, V.T. Jr (1983) Ajzen and Fishbein's 'theory of reasoned action': a critical assessment, *Journal for the Theory of Social Behaviour*, 13, 155–63.

Sheeran, P. and Abraham, C. (2003) Mediator of moderators: temporal stability of intention and the intention–behavior relationship, *Personality and Social Psychology Bulletin*, 29, 205–15.

Sheeran, P., Norman, P. and Orbell, S. (1999) Evidence that intentions based on attitudes better predict behaviour than intentions based on subjective norms, *European Journal of Social Psychology*, 29, 403–06.

Sheeran, P. and Orbell, S. (1999) Augmenting the theory of planned behavior: roles for anticipated regret and descriptive norms, *Journal of Applied Social Psychology*, 29, 2107–42.

Sheeran, P. and Taylor, S. (1999) Predicting intentions to use condoms: a meta-analysis and comparison of the theories of reasoned action and planned behavior, *Journal of Applied Social Psychology*, 29, 1624–75.

Sheeran, P., Trafimow, D. and Armitage, C. J. (2003) Predicting behaviour from perceived behavioural control: tests of the accuracy assumption of the theory of planned behaviour, *British Journal of Social Psychology*, 42, 393–410.

Sheppard, B.H., Hartwick, J. and Warshaw, P.R. (1988) The theory of reasoned action: a meta-analysis of past research with recommendations for modifications and future research, *Journal of Consumer Research*, 15, 325–339.

Sparks, P. (1994) Attitudes towards food: applying, assessing and extending the 'theory of planned behaviour'. In D.R. Rutter and L. Quine (eds) *Social Psychology and Health: European Perspectives*. Aldershot: Avebury Press, 25–46.

Sparks, P., Guthrie, C.A. and Shepherd, R. (1997) The dimensional structure of the perceived behavioral control construct, *Journal of Applied Social Psychology*, 27, 418–38.

Sparks, P., Harris, P.R. and Lockwood, N. (2004) Predictors and predictive effects of ambivalence, *British Journal of Social Psychology*, 43, 371–83.

Sparks, P., Hedderley, P. and Shepherd, R. (1992) An investigation into the relationship between perceived control, attitude variability and the consumption of two common foods, *European Journal of Social Psychology*, 22, 55–71.

Sparks, P. and Shepherd, R. (1992) Self-identity and the theory of planned behavior

– assessing the role of identification with green consumerism, *Social Psychology Quarterly*, **55**, 388–99.

Steadman, L., Rutter, D. R. and Field, S. (2002) Individually elicited versus modal normative beliefs in predicting attendance at breast screening: examining the role of belief salience in the Theory of Planned Behaviour, *British Journal of Health Psychology*, **7**, 317–30.

Sutton, S. (1994) The past predicts the future: interpreting behaviour–behaviour relationships in social psychological models of health behaviour. In D. R. Rutter and L. Quine (eds) *Social Psychology and Health: European Perspectives*. Aldershot: Avebury, 71–88.

Sutton, S. (1998) Explaining and predicting intentions and behavior: how well are we doing?, *Journal of Applied Social Psychology*, **28**, 1318–39.

Sutton, S. (2002a) Testing attitude–behaviour theories using non-experimental data: an examination of some hidden assumptions, *European Review of Social Psychology*, **13**, 293–323.

Sutton, S. (2002b) Using social cognition models to develop health behaviour interventions: problems and assumptions. In D. Rutter and L. Quine (eds) *Changing Health Behaviour*. Buckingham: OU Press, 193–208.

Terry, D.J. and Hogg, M. A. (1996) Group norms and the attitude–behavior relationship: a role for group identification, *Personality and Social Psychology Bulletin*, **22**, 776–93.

Terry, D.J., Hogg, M. and White, K.M. (1999) The theory of planned behaviour: self-identity, social identity and group norm, *British Journal of Social Psychology*, **28**, 225–44.

Terry, D.J. and O'Leary, J.E. (1995) The theory of planned behaviour: the effects of perceived behavioural control and self-efficacy, *British Journal of Social Psychology*, **34**, 199–220.

Towriss, J. G. (1984) A new approach to the use of expectancy value models, *Journal of the Market Research Society*, **26**, 63–75.

Trafimow, D. (1998) Attitudinal and normative processes in health behavior, *Psychology and Health*, **13**, 307–17.

Trafimow, D. and Findlay, K. (1996) The importance of subjective norms for a minority of people, *Personality and Social Psychology Bulletin*, **22**, 820–8.

Trafimow, D. and Fishbein, M. (1995) Do people really distinguish between behavioral and normative beliefs?, *British Journal of Social Psychology*, **34**, 257–66.

Trafimow, D. and Sheeran, P. (1998) Some tests of the distinction between cognitive and affective beliefs, *Journal of Experimental Social Psychology*, **34**, 378–97.

Trafimow, D., Sheeran, P., Conner, M. and Findlay, K.A. (2002) Evidence that perceived behavioral control is a multidimensional construct: perceived control and perceived difficulty, *British Journal of Social Psychology*, **41**, 101–21.

Triandis, H. C. (1977) *Interpersonal Behavior*. Monterey, CA: Brooks/Cole.

Trope, Y. and Libermann, N. (2000) Temporal construal and time-dependent changes in preference, *Journal of Personality and Social Psychology*, **79**, 876–89.

Vallerand, R.J. (1997) Towards a hierarchical model of intrinsic and extrinsic motivation. In M.P. Zanna (ed.) *Advances in Experimental Social Psychology*. New York: Academic Press, 271–359.

Van den Putte, B. (1991) *On the theory of reasoned action*. Unpublished doctoral dissertation, University of Amsterdam, the Netherlands.

Van der Pligt, J. and de Vries, N. K. (1998) Belief importance in expectancy-value models of attitudes, *Journal of Applied Social Psychology*, **28**, 1339–54.

Van der Pligt, J., de Vries, N.K., Manstead, A.S.R. and van Harreveld, F. (2000) The importance of being selective: weighing the role of attribute importance in attitudinal judgment, *Advances in Experimental Social Psychology*, **32**, 135–200.

Van der Pligt, J., Zeelenberg, M., van Dijk, W.W., de Vries, N.K. and Richard, R. (1998) Affect, attitudes and decisions: let's be more specific. In W. Stroebe and M. Hewstone (eds) *European Review of Social Psychology*. Chichester: Wiley, 33–66.

Warshaw, P. R. and Davis, F. D. (1985) Disentangling behavioral intentions and behavioral expectations, *Journal of Experimental Social Psychology*, **21**, 213–28.

Wilson, T.D., Dunn, D.S., Kraft, D. and Lisle, D.J. (1989) Introspection, attitude change, and attitude–behaviour consistency: the disruptive effects of explaining why we feel the way we do. In L. Berkowitz (ed.) *Advances in Experimental Social Psychology*. New York: Academic Press, 287–343.

Zanna, M.P. and Rempel, J.K. (1988) Attitudes: a new look at an old concept. In D.Bar-Tal and A.W.Kruglanski (eds) *The Social Psychology of Knowledge*. Cambridge: University Press, 315–34.

STEPHEN SUTTON

STAGE THEORIES OF HEALTH BEHAVIOUR

1 General background

That a whole chapter is dedicated to stage theories in this edition of the book is indicative of the enormous amount of interest and research activity that such theories have generated in recent years. This chapter discusses three stage theories: the transtheoretical model (TTM; Prochaska and DiClemente 1983; Prochaska *et al.* 1992, 2002; Prochaska and Velicer 1997), the precaution adoption process model (PAPM; Weinstein and Sandman 1992, 2002a, 2002b), and the health action process approach (HAPA; Schwarzer 1992, 1999, 2001, 2004; Schwarzer and Fuchs 1995a, 1995b), although we argue that the last is not a genuine stage theory but a continuum theory like the theory of planned behaviour (TPB; Ajzen 1991, 2002; Conner and Sparks, Chapter 5 in this volume). Other stage theories that should be mentioned, but are not discussed in this chapter, are the health behaviour goal model (Gebhardt 1997; Maes and Gebhardt 2000), the Rubicon model, or model of action phases (Heckhausen 1991; Gollwitzer 1996), a four-stage model that forms the theoretical background to the work on implementation intentions (see Sheeran *et al.*, Chapter 7 in this volume), the AIDS risk reduction model (Catania *et al.* 1990), and theories of delay in seeking health care (Safer *et al.* 1979; Andersen *et al.* 1995).

We start by presenting a hypothetical three-stage theory to explain the assumptions of stage theories and how they differ from continuum theories, and we then discuss the TTM, the PAPM and the HAPA in turn. The decision to discuss three theories necessitated some modifications to the recommended chapter format. In particular, because the PAPM and the HAPA are relatively new and have limited evidence bases compared with the TTM, sections on *developments* and *application of the model* are not included for these two theories.

1.1 A hypothetical three-stage theory

Figure 6.1 shows a hypothetical three-stage theory, in which the stages are assumed to be discrete. According to the theory, a person can move from Stage I to Stage III only via Stage II. The lower case letters a–e are causal factors that are hypothesized to influence the stage transitions. Increases in factors a–c are assumed to increase the likelihood that the person will move from Stage I to Stage II; similarly, increases in factors c–e are held to increase the likelihood that a person in Stage II will move to Stage III. Thus, variables a–e are the independent variables and the transitions from one stage to the next are the dependent variables. In the simplest case, the latter can be treated as dichotomous: a person either stays in the same stage or moves to the next.

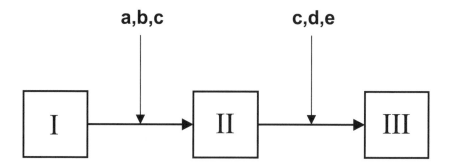

Figure 6.1   Hypothetical three-stage model

A key assumption of stage theories is that different factors are important at different stages. In this example, the set of factors that influence the transition from Stage I to Stage II, {a, b, c}, differs from the set of factors that influence the transition from Stage II to Stage III, {c, d, e}. Note that factor c influences both transitions. This is allowable, even if c has the same effect size for each of the two transitions, because the causal factors still differ as a set.

A more fully specified version of the theory would also specify the causal relationships among the explanatory factors that influence each transition. For example, for the first transition, one might specify that factors a, b and c each have direct effects on the probability of stage movement but that a also has an indirect effect via b. This amounts to specifying a separate causal model for each transition.

This is a very simple stage theory. In principle, a stage theory could include only two stages, but in this case there would be only one forward stage transition, so the assumption that different factors influence different transitions would not apply.

A stage theory may be made more complex by incorporating additional stages and additional explanatory variables, and by allowing backward transitions and transitions to non-adjacent stages. However, even the simple three-stage theory outlined above has a more complex structure than most of the theories discussed in this book. A corollary of this more complex structure is that stage theories are also more difficult to test than other kinds of theories. More specifically, stage theories should be contrasted with *continuum* theories. A classic example of a continuum theory is the theory of reasoned action (TRA; Ajzen and Fishbein 1980; Conner and Sparks, Chapter 5 in this volume). According to the TRA, the likelihood of performing the target behaviour is a linear function of the strength of intention to do so, which is treated as a continuous variable. A person may move to action from any point on the intention continuum, though their probability of doing so is assumed to be higher the further along the continuum they are. Two *pseudostages*, I and II, could be created by arbitrarily dividing the intention continuum into two segments. People in these two pseudostages would be expected to differ on variables that are assumed to influence intention strength (i.e. attitude and/or subjective norm). However, this would not be a genuine stage theory for the following reasons:

1   the 'stages' have been arbitrarily created by dividing a continuum;
2   there is no assumption that people in Pseudostage I (low intention) have to move into Pseudostage II (high intention) before they can move to action;
3   everyone in the target population is assumed to have an intention with respect to performing the target behaviour; similarly, everyone is assumed to have an attitude and a subjective norm with respect to the target behaviour;
4   the factors that influence movement along the continuum (i.e. attitude and/or subjective norm), and that therefore increase the likelihood of action, are assumed to be the same at every point on the continuum and to have the same effect sizes at every point on the continuum; and
5   the same intervention (i.e. one designed to increase attitude and/or subjective norm) would be used regardless of the recipient's position on the continuum.

2 The transtheoretical model (TTM)

2.1 Description of the model

The TTM is the dominant stage model in health psychology and health promotion. It was developed in the 1980s by a group of researchers at the University of Rhode Island (hereafter referred to as the Rhode Island group). The model derived partly from an analysis of systems of psychotherapy but some of the first empirical applications were to smoking cessation (e.g. DiClemente and Prochaska 1982; Prochaska and DiClemente 1983), and smoking remains the most popular application of the model. Although it is often referred to simply as the stages of change model, the TTM includes several different constructs: the *stages of change*, the *pros and cons of changing* (together known as *decisional balance*), *confidence and temptation*, and the *processes of change* (Table 6.1). The TTM was an

Table 6.1   The TTM constructs, adapted from Prochaska *et al.* (2002)

Construct	Description
Stages of change	
Precontemplation	Has no intention to take action within the next six months
Contemplation	Intends to take action within the next six months
Preparation	Intends to take action within the next 30 days and has taken some behavioural steps in this direction
Action	Has changed overt behaviour for less than six months
Maintenance	Has changed overt behaviour for more than six months
Decisional balance	
Pros	The benefits of changing
Cons	The costs of changing
Self-efficacy	
Confidence	Confidence that one can engage in the healthy behaviour across different challenging situations
Temptation	Temptation to engage in the unhealthy behaviour across different challenging situations
Processes of change	
Experiential processes	
Consciousness raising	Finding and learning new facts, ideas, and tips that support the healthy behaviour change
Dramatic relief	Experiencing the negative emotions (fear, anxiety, worry) that go along with unhealthy behavioural risks
Self-reevaluation	Realizing that the behaviour change is an important part of one's identity as a person
Environmental reevaluation	Realizing the negative impact of the unhealthy behaviour or the positive impact of the healthy behaviour on one's proximal social and physical environment
Self-liberation	Making a firm commitment to change
Behavioural processes	
Helping relationships	Seeking and using social support for the healthy behaviour change
Counterconditioning	Substituting healthier alternative behaviours and cognitions for the unhealthy behaviour
Reinforcement management	Increasing the rewards for the positive behaviour change and decreasing the rewards of the unhealthy behaviour
Stimulus control	Removing reminders or cues to engage in the unhealthy behaviour and adding cues and reminders to engage in the healthy behaviour
Social liberation	Realizing that the social norms are changing in the direction of supporting the healthy behaviour change

attempt to integrate these different constructs drawn from different theories of behaviour change and systems of psychotherapy into a single coherent model; hence the name transtheoretical.

The stages of change provide the basic organizing principle. The most widely used version of the model specifies five stages: pre-contemplation, contemplation, preparation, action and maintenance. The first three stages are pre-action stages and the last two stages are post-action stages (although preparation is sometimes defined partly in terms of behaviour change). People are assumed to move through the stages in order, but they may relapse from action or maintenance to an earlier stage. People may cycle through the stages several times before achieving long-term behaviour change.

The pros and cons are the perceived advantages and disadvantages of changing one's behaviour. They were originally derived from Janis and Mann's (1977) model of decision making, though similar constructs occur in most theories of health behaviour. Note that applications to smoking cessation usually assess the pros and cons of smoking which are assumed to be equivalent to the cons and pros of changing (quitting) respectively.

Confidence is similar to Bandura's (1986) construct of self-efficacy (see Luszczynska and Schwarzer, Chapter 4 in this volume). It refers to the confidence that one can carry out the recommended behaviour across a range of potentially difficult situations. The related construct of temptation refers to the temptation to engage in the unhealthy behaviour across a range of difficult situations.

Finally, the processes of change are the covert and overt activities that people engage in to progress through the stages. The Rhode Island group has identified 10 such processes that appear to be common to a number of different behaviours: five experiential (or cognitive-affective) processes and five behavioural processes (Table 6.1).

In stage theories, the transitions between adjacent stages are the dependent variables, and the other constructs are variables that are assumed to influence these transitions – the independent variables. The processes of change, the pros and cons of changing, and confidence and temptation are all independent variables in this sense. Descriptions of the TTM to date have not specified the causal relationships among these variables. It is not clear, for example, whether the processes of change influence pros, cons, confidence and temptation, which in turn influence stage transitions; whether these variables have independent effects on stage transitions; or whether some other causal model is assumed to hold. It would be helpful if the Rhode Island group specified causal models for each of the four forward stage transitions.

The TTM has been applied to a wide range of different health behaviours (Table 6.2). Because the stronger research designs have been used mainly in applications of the model to smoking cessation and to adoption and maintenance of physical exercise, the remainder of this section focuses on these behaviours.

Table 6.2   Illustrative applications of the TTM

Behaviour	Authors
Smoking	DiClemente *et al.* (1991); Prochaska *et al.* (1993)[a]; Kraft *et al.* (1999); Borland *et al.* (2000); Aveyard *et al.* (2003)[a]
Drinking	Budd and Rollnick (1996); Migneault *et al.* (1999)
Drug use	Isenhart (1994); Belding *et al.* (1996)
Exercise	Marcus and Simkin (1993); Courneya *et al.* (2001); Blissmer and McAuley (2002)[a]
Healthy eating	Domel *et al.* (1996); Steptoe *et al.* (1996)
Condom use	Evers *et al.* (1998); Brown-Peterside *et al.* (2000)[a]
Mammography screening	Rakowski *et al.* (1992); Clark *et al.* (2002)[a]
Sun protection	Rossi *et al.* (1994)[a]; Weinstock *et al.* (2002)[a]

[a] Intervention studies.

2.2 Summary of research

This section is organized by the four research designs that can be used to test predictions from stage theories (Weinstein *et al.* 1998c). These are: cross-sectional studies comparing people in different stages; examination of stage sequences; longitudinal prediction of stage transitions; and experimental studies of matched and mismatched interventions.

2.2.1 Cross-sectional studies
A very large number of studies of the TTM have used cross-sectional designs in which participants are classified into stages and compared on theoretically relevant variables (i.e. processes of change, pros and cons, confidence and temptation). Stage theories predict *discontinuity patterns* (Weinstein *et al.* 1998c; Kraft *et al.* 1999; Sutton 2000b). In our three-stage example, variable b would be predicted to increase between Stage I and Stage II but to show no difference between Stage II and Stage III, whereas variable d would be predicted to show no difference between Stage I and Stage II but to increase between Stage II and Stage III (Figure 6.2). This section focuses on two important meta-analyses of cross-sectional studies on the TTM (Rosen 2000; Marshall and Biddle 2001).

Rosen (2000) identified 34 studies, most of which were unpublished dissertations, that reported cross-sectional data on use of change processes by stage and included the action stage (because this is the stage in which behavioural processes are predicted to peak and cognitive-affective processes are predicted to decline). Although Rosen did not formally test for linearity and departure from linearity, he noted that

> For most health problems, use of behavioral processes increased fairly linearly from precontemplation through action … [and] was typically constant or increased slightly between action and maintenance. Only

for smoking did use of behavioral processes decline substantially between action and maintenance ... Behavioral processes peaked during action or maintenance in 85% of all studies.

(Rosen 2000: 596–7)

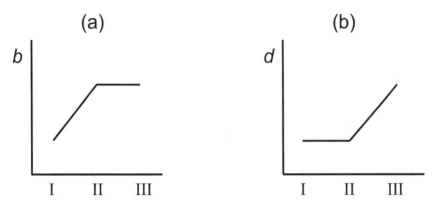

Figure 6.2   Two discontinuity patterns in a cross-sectional comparison of people in three different stages

For smoking in particular, this is clear evidence of a discontinuity at the action stage. However, the decline in use of behavioural processes between action and maintenance is not informative about factors that facilitate this transition because it is implausible that *less* frequent use of behavioural processes would increase the likelihood of the transition. A more plausible explanation is that people in the maintenance stage need to use behavioural processes less frequently, that is, that the change in use is a consequence of the transition.

Rosen (2000) found that in less than half (41 per cent) of studies did experiential processes peak in contemplation or preparation, as predicted by the TTM. This proportion varied by behaviour. Use of experiential processes peaked in contemplation or preparation in four out of five studies of smoking. By contrast, use of these processes increased fairly linearly with stage of exercise adoption, peaking during action or maintenance in 11 out of 12 studies. For other health behaviours, experiential processes were not consistently associated with any particular stage.

Rosen (2000) also noted that the steepest increase in use of all change processes typically occurred between the pre-contemplation and contemplation stages of change, particularly in the case of cognitive-affective processes. This could be interpreted as evidence for a discontinuity at the contemplation stage, though Rosen (p.603) highlights the difficulty of interpreting this change in process use: 'Does this indicate that engagement in these processes motivates precontemplators to change their intentions? Or only that people who are already considering change are more likely to use cognitive-affective and behavioral processes of change?'

Rosen (2000) also reported some interesting findings for use of specific processes. For example, consciousness raising was used most in the contemplation or preparation stages in 80 per cent of studies on smoking and psychotherapy but was used most in the action or maintenance stages in 88 per cent of studies on substance abuse, exercise and diet change; and reinforcement management was used most in the action or maintenance stage in nearly all studies of exercise, smoking and psychotherapy but was used most during contemplation or preparation in two-thirds of the studies on substance abuse and diet change.

The mainly linear patterns found by Rosen (2000), particularly for behavioural processes, do not provide strong support for a stage model. If differences between process use between adjacent stages are interpreted as causal effects of process use on stage transition, Rosen's findings suggest that interventions should encourage the use of behavioural processes *throughout the process of change* from pre-contemplation through action. As noted, the findings for experiential processes were more variable.

One problem with Rosen's (2000) analysis is that he combined studies that used different staging methods. Given the differences between the different methods, it would be preferable to combine only studies of a particular behaviour that used the same staging method.

Table 6.3 Mean sample-weighted corrected effect sizes (d₊) for differences between adjacent stages from the meta-analysis by Marshall and Biddle (2001)

Variable	k	PC vs C	C vs PR	PR vs A	A vs M
Self-efficacy	15–19	0.59*	0.36*	0.60*	0.72*
Pros	11–13	0.97*	0.01	0.24*	0.23*
Cons	11–13	−0.46*	−0.28*	−0.37*	−0.24*
Behavioural processes	5				
Counter-conditioning		0.74*	0.62*	0.62*	0.37*
Helping relationships		0.55*	0.10	0.44*	−0.05
Reinforcement management		0.97*	0.34	0.58*	0.03
Self-liberation		1.18*	0.41*	0.72*	0.04
Stimulus control		0.83*	0.15	0.49*	0.14
Experiential processes	5				
Consciousness raising		0.93*	0.10	0.47*	0.04
Dramatic relief		0.65*	−0.18	0.27*	−0.07
Environmental re-evaluation		0.74*	−0.01	0.36*	−0.13
Social liberation		0.63*	0.19	0.32*	0.07
Self-re-evaluation		0.98*	0.01	0.57*	−0.15*

Note: k = number of independent samples; PC = precontemplation; C = contemplation; PR = preparation; A = action; M = maintenance.
* p < 0.05

Marshall and Biddle (2001) conducted a meta-analysis of applications of the TTM to physical activity and exercise. Unlike Rosen (2000), they excluded dissertations but they did include published conference abstracts.

Effect sizes for comparisons of adjacent stages are shown in Table 6.3. All the effect sizes for self-efficacy were positive and significant; the effect size differed for different comparisons, though this was not tested formally. The effect sizes for the pros of changing were all positive and significant except for contemplation to preparation. The cons of changing showed significant decreases across successive stages. Effect sizes for the processes of change were based on fewer studies (k = 5) than for the other variables. For each of the behavioural processes, the largest effect was for the transition from pre-contemplation to contemplation and the smallest effect was for the transition from action to maintenance; the difference between action and maintenance was non-significant for four out of five processes. For the experiential processes, the largest effect again occurred between pre-contemplation and contemplation. Differences between action and maintenance were non-significant for four processes and significantly negative (i.e. showed a decrease) for the fifth (self-re-evaluation).

Do these results support a stage model? For pros and experiential processes, there is clear evidence for a discontinuity pattern. There is a steep increase between pre-contemplation and contemplation, little or no increase between contemplation and preparation, and an increase between preparation and action. For both behavioural and experiential processes, there is further evidence of discontinuity in that preparation to action is associated with an increase whereas action to maintenance is not.

Marshall and Biddle (2001) interpret their findings as mainly supportive of the TTM predictions. However, our interpretation of the findings in terms of discontinuity patterns leads to somewhat different conclusions. If we assume that a difference in process use between two adjacent stages reflects a causal effect of process use on the likelihood of making the transition, then Marshall and Biddle's findings suggest, for example, that pre-contemplators who use behavioural processes relatively frequently (compared with others in that stage) are more likely to move to the contemplation stage but that people in the action stage who use behavioural processes relatively frequently (compared with others in that stage) are *not* more likely to move to the maintenance stage (with the possible exception of counter-conditioning). It seems unlikely that the TTM would make these predictions. Similarly, the findings suggest that contemplators who make more frequent use of experiential processes are not more likely than others in the same stage to move to the preparation stage.

This highlights an important difference in the way in which the Rhode Island group interprets cross-sectional data on stage differences and the interpretation suggested by Weinstein *et al.* (1998c) and Sutton (2000b). Consider Figure 6.3, which shows a hypothetical pattern of means across stages; assume that this represents the findings for behavioural processes. The Rhode Island group would interpret the relatively frequent use of behavioural processes among people in the action and maintenance stages as indicating that use of these processes is particularly important at these stages and therefore needs to be encouraged. The alternative interpretation focuses on the *differences* between adjacent stages rather than the absolute

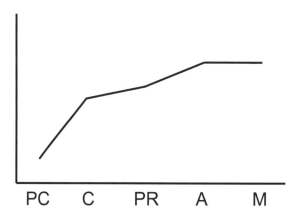

PC   C   PR   A   M

Figure 6.3 Hypothetical pattern of means across the five TTM stages. [PC = pre-contemplation; C = contemplation; PR = preparation; A = action; M = maintenance.]

levels. The steepest increase occurs between pre-contemplation and contemplation, suggesting that relatively frequent use of behavioural processes among those in the pre-contemplation stage may increase the likelihood that they move to the contemplation stage. Similarly, the lack of a difference in behavioural process use between action and maintenance could be interpreted as suggesting that relatively frequent use of behavioural processes is not beneficial in moving people to the maintenance stage. Of course, this alternative interpretation assumes a specific causal model in which behavioural process use is treated as a potential cause but not a consequence of the stage transition. Clearly, these two interpretations may have very different implications for intervention. The interpretation advocated here is consistent with the way that cross-sectional data on other theories of health behaviour are usually interpreted: the analysis focuses on the association between differences between individuals on one variable and differences between individuals on a second variable.

Following the practice of the Rhode Island group, many cross-sectional studies of the TTM report the results in terms of T-scores. T-scores are standardized scores with a mean of 50 and a standard deviation of 10. This practice creates a problem when an investigator wishes to compare absolute levels of a variable across studies or to combine them in a meta-analysis. Consider two studies that use the same staging algorithm. Even if the means and standard deviations for each stage on a theoretically relevant variable such as the pros of changing based on the raw (unstandardized) scores are *identical* in the two studies, the mean T-scores and standard deviations will differ if the distributions of individuals across stages differ between the two studies. Similarly, consider two studies, again using the same staging algorithm, but one reports data on all five stages and the other reports data on only the first four stages (there is no one in the maintenance stage in the second study). Even if the means and standard deviations based on raw scores for the first four stages on a variable such as the pros of changing are identical in the two studies, the mean T-scores and standard deviations will in general differ between the studies. Primary studies of the TTM should therefore always report stage means and standard deviations based on the raw scores as well as, or instead of, means and standard deviations based on T-scores. Meta-analyses that combine data across studies in the way that Rosen (2000) did should use the means based on the raw scores. The technique used by Marshall and Biddle (2001), namely to compute standardized effect sizes for each pair of adjacent stages, is not affected by this problem.[1]

2.2.2 *Examination of stage sequences*

Longitudinal data can be used to examine sequences of transitions through the stages. Several studies have reported the full set of transition probabilities for the five-stage version of the TTM: Carbonari *et al.* (1999) for smoking cessation; Cardinal and Sachs (1995), Peterson and Aldana (1999), Plotnikoff *et al.* (2001) and Cardinal *et al.* (2002) for exercise/ physical activity; and Evers *et al.* (1998) for condom use. Some of these studies used latent transition analysis (LTA[2]; Collins and Wugalter 1992) to test particular models; the others used a less formal approach. Most of these studies claimed support for the TTM, though it is not clear exactly what predictions the TTM would make.

It should be emphasized that stage models predict discontinuities in the transition probabilities. A pattern in which the transition probabilities for a given stage declined steadily with increasing distance in both directions would be consistent with a pseudostage model (Weinstein *et al.* 1998c). It should also be noted that the analysis of transition probabilities assumes that stage is measured not only validly but also reliably; in other words, that observed changes in stage reflect true changes and not simply random measurement error.

In most of the transition matrices reported in the studies listed above, initial pre-action stage of change predicted being in action or maintenance at follow-up: those in the preparation stage at baseline were more likely to be in action or maintenance at follow-up than those in contemplation, and those in contemplation were more likely to be in action or maintenance than those in pre-contemplation. This is what the Rhode Island group calls a *stage effect* (e.g. Prochaska *et al.* 2004). It is a highly consistent finding in the literature on the TTM. However, on their own, stage effects do not provide strong evidence for a stage model because pseudostage models may yield similar effects. For example, continuous measures of intention predict future behaviour, and if such an intention measure is categorized into, say, three categories, one would expect to find a (pseudo)stage effect. Nevertheless, stage effects mean that stage measures may be of practical value; for example, in measuring progress towards smoking cessation. However, they may not be the best measures for this purpose (Farkas *et al.* 1996; Pierce *et al.* 1998; Abrams *et al.* 2000; Sutton 2000a).

2.2.3 Longitudinal prediction of stage transitions

As well as examining stage sequences, longitudinal data can be used to test whether different theoretically relevant variables predict stage transitions among people in different baseline stages. The assumption is that such predictors represent causal factors that influence stage movement. Analyses of longitudinal data should be stratified by stage and should compare people who move to the next stage in the sequence with those who remain in a given stage with respect to baseline characteristics.

No prospective studies in the domain of exercise/physical activity have used the TTM variables to predict stage transitions. By contrast, there have been a number of such studies in the domain of smoking cessation. Two of these (DiClemente *et al.* 1985; Prochaska *et al.* 1985) used an old staging algorithm and an early version of the TTM. They were reviewed by Sutton (2000a). Nine more recent studies were reviewed by Sutton (2005): De Vries and Mudde (1998); Hansen (1999); Herzog *et al.* (1999); Velicer *et al.* (1999); Dijkstra and De Vries (2001); Segan *et al.* (2002, 2004a, 2004b); Dijkstra *et al.* (2003).[3] The findings are briefly summarized here. The study by Segan *et al.* (2004a) is discussed in detail in Section 2.5.

These nine studies found some evidence that different predictors are associated with different stage transitions. For example, Segan *et al.* (2004b) found that the pros and cons of smoking did not predict movement out of the pre-contemplation or contemplation stages. (In fact, none of the TTM measures predicted movement out of the pre-contemplation stage.) Pros and cons seemed to be important only for movement out of the preparation stage, for which lower pros of smoking and *lower* cons of smoking predicted forward movement.

However, there were few consistent findings across the nine studies, providing little support for the TTM. Most of the studies used relatively long follow-up periods (at least six months). Future studies should use shorter follow-up periods to minimize the likelihood of missing stage transitions (with the proviso that at least six months is required to detect the transition from action to maintenance).

2.2.4 Experimental studies

The strongest evidence for a stage theory would be to show consistently in randomized experimental studies that stage-matched interventions are more effective than stage-mismatched interventions in moving people to the next stage in the sequence. In our three-stage example, an intervention that was designed to increase variables a and b would be predicted to be more effective in moving people in Stage I to Stage II than an intervention designed to increase variables d and e; conversely, the second intervention should be more effective than the first for people in Stage II. Such evidence would be strengthened by showing that the interventions do indeed influence the target variables and by mediation analyses yielding results consistent with the hypothesis that this was the mechanism through which the interventions had their effects on stage movement.

Only three studies to date have compared matched and mismatched interventions within the framework of the TTM or closely related models (Dijkstra *et al.* 1998a; Quinlan and McCaul 2000; Blissmer and McAuley 2002). The first and second of these, which were on smoking cessation, are considered first.

Dijkstra *et al.* (1998a) compared the effectiveness of individually tailored letters designed either to increase the pros of quitting and reduce the cons of quitting (outcome information) or to enhance self-efficacy, or both. Smokers were categorized into four stages of change: preparers (planning to quit within the next month); contemplators (planning to quit within the next six months); pre-contemplators (planning to quit within the next year or in the next five years); and immotives (planning to quit sometime in the future but not in the next five years, to smoke indefinitely but cut down, or to smoke indefinitely without cutting down). The sample size for the main analyses was 1100.

On the basis of two earlier cross-sectional studies (De Vries and Backbier 1994; Dijkstra *et al.* 1996), it was hypothesized that immotives would benefit most from outcome information only, preparers from self-efficacy enhancing information only, and the other two groups from both types of information. Thus, counter-intuitively, pre-contemplators and contemplators were predicted to benefit from the same kind of information. A close examination of the cross-sectional studies reveals only partial empirical support for these hypotheses (Sutton 2000a). In the event, the Dijkstra *et al.* (1998a) study showed only weak evidence for a beneficial effect of stage-matched information. With respect to the likelihood of making a forward stage transition, assessed at 10-week follow-up, there were no significant differences between the three types of information among smokers in any of the four stages. However, preparers who received the self-efficacy-enhancing information only were significantly more likely to have quit smoking for seven days at follow-up than preparers in the outcome information only condition. Combining immotives and pre-contemplators, the percentage of smokers who made a forward stage transition did not differ significantly between those who received stage-matched and stage-mismatched information. Among contemplators and preparers combined, the percentage who made a forward stage transition and the percentage who quit for seven days were higher among those who received the stage-matched information than among those who received the stage-mismatched information, but these comparisons were only marginally significant ($p < 0.10$). It is not clear why the researchers combined the stages in this way (immotives and pre-contemplators; contemplators and preparers), given the hypothesis of the study.

Quinlan and McCaul (2000) compared a stage-matched intervention, a stage-mismatched intervention, and an assessment-only condition in a sample of 92 college-age smokers in the pre-contemplation stage. The stage-matched intervention consisted of activities designed to encourage smokers to think more about quitting smoking. The stage-mismatched intervention consisted of action-oriented information and activities intended for smokers who are ready to quit smoking. At one month, 30 participants had progressed to contemplation, one participant had progressed to preparation, and five participants had progressed to action. Contrary to the hypothesis, a greater percentage of participants in the stage-mismatched condition (54 per cent) progressed than in the stage-matched (30 per cent) or assessment-only (35 per cent) conditions; however, this difference was not significant. Significantly more smokers in the stage-mismatched condition tried to quit smoking than in the stage-matched condition.

Quinlan and McCaul (2000) suggest that a mismatched intervention may have different effects depending on whether it is matched to a later stage in the sequence (as in their own study) or to an earlier stage. For example, although it may not be detrimental for smokers in the pre-contemplation stage to receive an intervention designed for those in the preparation stage, it may be counterproductive to give preparers an intervention designed for pre-contemplators. The Dijkstra *et al.* (1998a) study provided very weak support for this hypothesis. Nevertheless, it may be worth testing in future studies.

In the most recent study, Blissmer and McAuley (2002) studied physical activity. 288 university staff were randomly assigned to four conditions, including: (a) stage-matched materials (personalized, stage-appropriate covering letter plus stage-matched manuals) delivered via campus mail on a monthly basis; and (b) stage-mismatched materials delivered in the same way. After 16 weeks, 40.4 per cent of the matched group had progressed one or more stages compared with 31.8 per cent of the mismatched group. This difference was in the predicted direction. The authors did not report a significance test, but secondary analysis showed that it did not approach significance at the 0.05 level: $\chi^2(2) = 0.91$, $p = 0.634$. A limitation of the study, which the authors acknowledge, is that 57 per cent of participants were in the action or maintenance stage at baseline, and the short follow-up period would have prevented those who had recently entered the action stage from progressing to maintenance.

Considered together, these three experimental studies of matched and mismatched interventions found little or no evidence for the stage model predictions. Intervention studies that have compared TTM-based stage-matched interventions with generic, non-matched interventions or no-intervention control conditions are considered in Section 2.6.

2.3 Developments

This section outlines several variants of the TTM. First, a group of researchers in the Netherlands has developed a version of the TTM and applied it in a number of studies of smoking cessation (e.g. Dijkstra *et al.* 1996, 1997, 1998a, 2003; De Vries and Mudde 1998). The stage definitions in the Dutch version of the model differ from the most widely used TTM definitions in that the pre-action stages are defined purely in terms of intention: preparation is defined as planning to quit in the next month and contemplation as planning to quit in the next six months but not in the next month. In some studies, the group has subdivided the pre-contemplation stage. For example, Dijkstra *et al.* (1998b) defined *immotives* as smokers who are not planning to quit in the next five years or who may be planning never to quit and pre-contemplators as smokers who are planning to quit in the next five years but not in the next six months. Dijkstra and De Vries (2001) relabelled the latter group *postponers*. However, this distinction was not made in a recent study of stage transitions (Dijkstra *et al.* 2003).

In the Dutch version of the TTM, the main factors hypothesized to influence stage transitions are self-efficacy and positive and negative outcome expectancies (the pros and cons of quitting), drawn from Bandura's (1986) social cognitive theory (see Luszczynska and Schwarzer, Chapter 4 in this volume). These correspond respectively to confidence and the cons and pros of smoking in the TTM, although the latter are operationalized differently in the Dutch version. Processes of change are not emphasized in the Dutch version. In some studies, the set of independent variables has been expanded to include social influence, based on the attitude–social influence–efficacy (ASE) model (De Vries and Mudde 1998; De Vries *et al.* 1998). Research on the Dutch version of the TTM has included cross-sectional comparisons of people in different stages (e.g. Dijkstra *et al.* 1996), longitudinal studies of predictors of stage transitions (e.g. Dijkstra *et al.* 2003), an experimental match–mismatch study (Dijkstra *et al.* 1998a, discussed in Section 2.2), and evaluations of individually tailored interventions (e.g. Dijkstra *et al.* 1998b).

In a similar development, several studies in the domains of healthy eating and physical exercise have used variables from the TPB (Ajzen 1991, 2002; Conner and Sparks, Chapter 5 in this volume) in conjunction with the stages of change from the TTM (e.g. Courneya 1995; Courneya *et al.* 1998, 2001; Armitage and Arden 2002; Armitage *et al.* 2003, 2004). For example, in a longitudinal study, Courneya *et al.* (2001) used the TPB variables as predictors of stage transitions in the exercise domain, although they compared stage progression, regression and staying in the same stage rather than stage-to-stage transitions. There was some evidence for differential prediction. Subjective norm, for example, only predicted progression from the pre-contemplation stage. However, a single-item measure of intention emerged as a strong and consistent predictor across stages. Courneya and colleagues suggest that the stages of change for exercise should incorporate what they call intention *choice* (i.e. what the person intends to do) in the post-action stages as well as the pre-action stages and that intention *strength* should be included in the model as an independent predictor of stage transitions.

In an earlier study, Courneya *et al.* (1998) treated stage of change, coded as a continuous variable, as a potential mediator of the intention–behaviour relationship. Their model specified that intention influences stage which in turn influences behaviour. The theoretical basis for these proposed relationships seems dubious, first because it does not respect the stage theory assumptions and second because stage of change is defined in terms of behaviour and so cannot be a cause of behaviour.

None of these studies included the TTM independent variables, so it was not possible to show that the TPB variables were more strongly associated with stage or were better predictors of stage transitions than the TTM variables or whether they contributed additional predictive power. There are some similarities between the two sets of variables. For example, behavioural beliefs in the TPB are similar in some respects to the pros and cons in the TTM. However, they differ from pros and cons in that they are based theoretically on the expectancy-value principle and they distinguish between expectancy (belief strength) and value (outcome evaluation).

2.4 Operationalization of the model

2.4.1 Stages of change

Two main methods have been used to measure stages of change: multi-dimensional questionnaires and staging algorithms. In multidimensional questionnaires such as the University of Rhode Island Change Assessment (URICA; McConnaughy *et al.* 1983, 1989), each stage is measured by a set of questionnaire items, and scores are derived for each individual representing their position on each dimension. This approach has a number of problems, the most serious of which is that it allows people to score highly on more than one 'stage' (and many people do), which is inconsistent with the assumption of discrete stages (Sutton 2001). By contrast, a staging algorithm uses a small number of questionnaire items to allocate participants to stages in such a way that no individual can be in more than one stage. This approach has a number of advantages over multidimensional questionnaires: it is much simpler and the stages are clearly defined and mutually exclusive. Perhaps not surprisingly, the few studies that have compared the two approaches have found low concordance between them (e.g. Belding *et al.* 1996; Sfikaki 2001). The staging algorithm approach has been used in the vast majority of studies that have applied the TTM to smoking and exercise.

Table 6.4 shows a staging algorithm for smoking that has been used in a large number of studies since it was first introduced by DiClemente *et al.* (1991). Pre-contemplation, contemplation and preparation are defined in terms of current behaviour, intentions and past behaviour (whether or not the person has made a 24-hour quit attempt in the past year), whereas action and maintenance are defined purely in terms of behaviour; ex-smokers' intentions are not taken into account.

Critics have pointed out a number of serious problems with this algorithm, some of which stem from the way that contemplation and preparation are defined (Pierce *et al.* 1996; Sutton 2000a; Etter and Sutton 2002; Borland *et al.* 2003). For example, according to this algorithm, a smoker cannot be in the preparation stage unless he or she has made a recent quit attempt. Thus, a smoker can never be 'prepared' for his or her first quit attempt (Sutton 1996b).

Farkas *et al.* (1996) tabulated some of the different definitions used in the studies of smoking by the Rhode Island group between 1983 and 1991. They note that the different classifications have never been compared

Table 6.4 TTM measures for adult smoking, from http://www.uri.edu/research/cprc/measures.htm

---

Stages of change

Are you currently a smoker?
- Yes, I currently smoke
- No, I quit within the last 6 months (ACTION STAGE)
- No, I quit more than 6 months ago (MAINTENANCE STAGE)
- No, I have never smoked (NON-SMOKER)

(For smokers only) In the last year, how many times have you quit smoking for at least 24 hours?

(For smokers only) Are you seriously thinking of quitting smoking?
- Yes, within the next 30 days (PREPARATION STAGE if they have one 24-hour quit attempt in the past year – refer to previous question ... if no quit attempt then CONTEMPLATION STAGE)
- Yes, within the next 6 months (CONTEMPLATION STAGE)
- No, not thinking of quitting (PRE-CONTEMPLATION STAGE)

Processes of change (short form)

The following experiences can affect the smoking habit of some people. Think of any similar experiences you may be currently having or have had in the last month. Then rate the FREQUENCY of this event on the following five-point scale.

1 = Never, 2 = Seldom, 3 = Occasionally, 4 = Often, 5 = Repeatedly

1	When I am tempted to smoke I think about something else.	☐
2	I tell myself I can quit if I want to.	☐
3	I notice that non smokers are asserting their rights.	☐
4	I recall information people have given me on the benefits of quitting smoking.	☐
5	I can expect to be rewarded by others if I don't smoke.	☐
6	I stop to think that smoking is polluting the environment.	☐
7	Warnings about the health hazards of smoking move me emotionally.	☐
8	I get upset when I think about my smoking.	☐
9	I remove things from my home or place of work that remind me of smoking.	☐
10	I have someone who listens when I need to talk about my smoking.	☐
11	I think about information from articles and ads about how to stop smoking.	☐
12	I consider the view that smoking can be harmful to the environment.	☐
13	I tell myself that if I try hard enough I can keep from smoking.	☐
14	I find society changing in ways that makes it easier for non-smokers.	☐
15	My need for cigarettes makes me feel disappointed in myself.	☐
16	I have someone I can count on when I'm having problems with smoking.	☐
17	I do something else instead of smoking when I need to relax.	☐

18   I react emotionally to warnings about smoking cigarettes.   ☐
19   I keep things around my home or place of work that remind me
     not to smoke.   ☐
20   I am rewarded by others if I don't smoke.   ☐

Scoring:
Experiential processes
    Consciousness raising   4, 11
    Environmental re-evaluation   6, 12
    Self-re-evaluation   8, 15
    Social liberation   3, 14
    Dramatic relief   7, 18
Behavioral processes
    Helping relationships   10, 16
    Self-liberation   2, 13
    Counterconditioning   1, 17
    Reinforcement management   5, 20
    Stimulus control   9, 19

Self-efficacy/temptation (short form)
Listed below are situations that lead some people to smoke. We would like to know
HOW TEMPTED you may be to smoke in each situation. Please answer the
following questions using the following five-point scale.

1 = Not at all tempted, 2 = Not very tempted, 3 = Moderately tempted, 4 = Very
tempted, 5 = Extremely tempted

1   With friends at a party.   ☐
2   When I first get up in the morning.   ☐
3   When I am very anxious and stressed.   ☐
4   Over coffee while talking and relaxing.   ☐
5   When I feel I need a lift.   ☐
6   When I am very angry about something or someone.   ☐
7   With my spouse or close friend who is smoking.   ☐
8   When I realize that I haven't smoked for a while.   ☐
9   When things are not going my way and I am frustrated.   ☐

Scoring:
Positive affect/social situation   1, 4, 7
Negative affect situations   3, 6, 9
Habitual/craving situations   2, 5, 8

Decisional balance (short form)
The following statements represent different opinions about smoking. Please rate
HOW IMPORTANT each statement is to your decision to smoke according to the
following five-point scale.

Table 6.4 *cont'd*

1 = Not important, 2 = Slightly important, 3 = Moderately important, 4 = Very important, 5 = Extremely important

1　Smoking cigarettes relieves tension.　☐
2　I'm embarrassed to have to smoke.　☐
3　Smoking helps me concentrate and do better work.　☐
4　My cigarette smoking bothers other people.　☐
5　I am relaxed and therefore more pleasant when smoking.　☐
6　People think I'm foolish for ignoring the warnings about cigarette　☐
　　smoking.

Scoring:
PROS   1, 3, 5
CONS   2, 4, 6

Note: It states on the website that 'All measures are copyright Cancer Prevention Research Center, 1991. Dr James O. Prochaska, Director of the CPRC, is pleased to extend his permission for you to use the Transtheoretical Model-based measures available on this website for research purposes only, provided that the appropriate citation is referenced.'

empirically. This lack of standardization makes it difficult to compare results from different studies and to accumulate the research findings into a coherent body of knowledge. Using data from a large sample of smokers from the California Tobacco Survey, Farkas *et al.* compared the DiClemente *et al.* (1991) staging algorithm with an earlier algorithm used by the Rhode Island group that classified smokers into pre-contemplation, contemplation and relapse stages. The two algorithms produced markedly different stage distributions. For example, the earlier algorithm classified almost half the sample in the most advanced stage (relapse) whereas the revised scheme placed only 16 per cent in the most advanced stage (preparation). The two algorithms would lead to very different conclusions concerning the proportion of smokers for whom action-oriented programmes are appropriate. Farkas and colleagues also showed that the earlier stage measure provided better prediction of cessation and quit attempts assessed at 1 to 2-year follow-up than the revised algorithm and that both schemes allocated smokers with very different probabilities of quitting to the same stage (see also Pierce *et al.* 1996).

A variety of different staging algorithms have been used in the domain of exercise/physical activity. Marshall and Biddle (2001) recommend the one proposed by Marcus and Simkin (1993; see also Reed *et al.* 1997), which is shown in Table 6.5. Although this scheme does not suffer from the logical problems of the DiClemente *et al.* (1991) smoking algorithm, it seems somewhat implausible to treat irregular exercise (preparation) as a discrete stage between contemplation and action, implying that people move from no exercise to irregular exercise to regular exercise and that irregular exercise is qualitatively different from regular exercise.

A problem with most staging algorithms is that the time periods are

Table 6.5   Staging algorithm for exercise, from Marcus and Simkin (1993)

Items

1   I currently do not exercise
2   I intend to exercise in the next 6 months
3   I currently exercise *regularly*
4   I have exercised *regularly* for the past 6 months

Scoring

Pre-contemplation: Item 1 = true and Item 2 = false.
Contemplation: Item 1 = true and Item 2 = true.
Preparation: Item 1 = false and Item 3 = false.
Action: Item 3 = true and Item 4 = false.
Maintenance: Item 3 = true and Item 4 = true.

---

arbitrary. For instance, action and maintenance are usually distinguished by whether or not the duration of behaviour change exceeds six months. Changing the time periods would lead to different stage distributions. The use of arbitrary time periods casts doubt on the assumption that the stages are qualitatively distinct, that is, that they are true stages rather than pseudostages (Sutton 1996a; Bandura 1997, 1998).

The staging algorithms listed on the Rhode Island group's website show inconsistencies across different health behaviours. For example, in the algorithm for adoption of mammography (Rakowski *et al.* 1992), action and maintenance are defined partly in terms of intentions (planning to have a mammogram in the coming year). Like the DiClemente *et al.* (1991) algorithm, this algorithm has logical flaws. For instance, it is possible for a woman to move directly from contemplation to maintenance simply by forming an intention, without passing through the action stage and without changing her behaviour.

2.4.2 TTM independent variables

Table 6.4 shows the measures of the other TTM variables for adult smoking as listed on the Rhode Island group's website. These are all the short-form measures; the long forms are also listed on the website.

Descriptions of the development of the long forms of the measures can be found in Velicer *et al.* (1985) for decisional balance, DiClemente (1981), DiClemente *et al.* (1985) and Velicer *et al.* (1990) for confidence and temptation, and Prochaska *et al.* (1988) for the processes of change. Fava *et al.* (1995) outline the development of the short forms of these measures, except for confidence. In its studies of smoking cessation, the Rhode Island group has favoured the temptation measure over the confidence measure, because the scores tend to be highly (negatively) correlated and the temptation measure 'is more easily responded to by subjects in some of the stages' (Velicer *et al.* 1990: 273). However, the assumption that the two measures are interchangeable has been challenged by Segan *et al.* (2004a).

Compared with the long forms, the short-form measures are more suitable for use in studies that use telephone interviewing and in intervention studies involving repeated assessment. Using the short forms, all the constructs in the TTM can be measured with a total of 35 items. However, it is likely that the reliability of the short-form measures is lower than that of the long forms, and content validity may also be compromised because a construct may not be adequately represented by two or three items. For example, the short-form decisional balance scale does not include items about the health consequences of smoking, the financial costs, or the belief that smoking helps keep weight down.

In the measures of the TTM independent variables, scale scores are created by computing the sum or the mean of the item scores. The short-form processes of change measure consists of 10 two-item scales assessing recent frequency of use; aggregate scores can also be created for the experiential and behavioural processes respectively. Borland *et al.* (2000) improved the wording of several of the items and also discussed some remaining problems. The short-form temptation measure has three subscales: positive affect or social situations; negative affect situations; and habitual/craving situations. An aggregate temptation score can also be computed. Finally, the short-form decisional balance measure comprises two subscales representing the pros and cons of smoking, respectively. The usual practice is to standardize these separately and then compare them (see Section 2.2).

The Rhode Island group's website lists measures of the TTM independent variables for exercise and some other health-related behaviours, though the full set of measures is not given for all the behaviours listed. Note that, for many behaviours, the confidence measure may be more appropriate than the temptation measure.

2.5 Application of the model: smoking relapse

2.5.1 Introduction

The study by Segan *et al.* (2004a) on predictors of relapse to smoking cessation was selected as the example application of the TTM. In their rationale for the study, the authors point out that most quit attempts end in failure and that a better understanding of the factors involved in relapse is needed to improve success rates. They also note that most studies that have applied the TTM to smoking have focused on current smokers and that surprisingly little attention has been paid to the post-cessation stages. The key questions addressed by this study are: do the post-cessation stages help us understand the process of staying abstinent, and can TTM measures predict relapse?

From the perspective of the TTM, relapse is a transition from the action or maintenance stage to one of the pre-action stages (pre-contemplation, contemplation or preparation). The model predicts that use of four of the five behavioural change processes (helping relationships, counter-conditioning, reinforcement management and stimulus control) influences progression from action to maintenance (Prochaska *et al.* 1992), the implication being that, having quit, the smoker needs to use these processes frequently in order to stay abstinent for six months and thus move into the maintenance stage.

2.5.2 Method

Participants were 325 cigarette smokers who called the Quitline telephone counselling and information service in Victoria, Australia, and were quit at either the three-month follow-up and/or the six-month follow-up. The mean age was 39 years (range 17 to 78) and 55 per cent were women; mean cigarette consumption at baseline was 21 cigarettes a day.

Participants were recruited into the study after their reason for calling the Quitline had been dealt with. Of the callers asked to participate in the study, 77 per cent did so. They completed a telephone interview (time 1) and were posted the same questionnaire at three months (time 2) and six months (time 3), and a shorter version at 12 months (time 4). Response rates to the follow-ups were 76 per cent, 74 per cent and 68 per cent respectively.

The sample was part of a larger study that had several intervention groups. Segan *et al.* (2004a) argue that the interventions should not be regarded as an interfering factor because they are presumed to have their effect by influencing the TTM independent variables, not by producing change in fundamentally different ways.

The predictor variables consisted of the short-form measures of the processes of change, the pros and cons of smoking, and temptation to smoke (see Section 2.4).[4] Two of the experiential change processes, dramatic relief and social liberation, were not measured. Minor modifications were made to the wording of some of the change process items (see Borland *et al.* 2000). At follow-up, smoking status was assessed by the question 'Are you currently a cigarette smoker?' (Yes/No), and length of abstinence by the question 'How long ago did you quit?', answered in days, weeks or months.

In the analysis, Segan *et al.* (2004a) compared ex-smokers who had quit for less than one month and ex-smokers who had quit for more than one month. Although the TTM does not make this distinction, the authors present both theoretical and empirical reasons for using this time point. For example, relapse rates are likely to differ significantly between these groups.

In terms of the TTM stages, those who were quit at time 2 were in the action stage; those who were still abstinent at time 3 were either still in the action stage or had moved to maintenance. Ex-smokers who had quit for less than one month at time 3 were in the action stage; those who were still off smoking at time 4 had moved to the maintenance stage. Ex-smokers who had quit for more than one month at time 3 were in action or maintenance; those who were still abstinent at time 4 had moved to the maintenance stage.

Predictors of relapse were examined by conducting a series of logistic regression analyses (one for each predictor measure), controlling in each case for intervention condition and length of abstinence.

2.5.3 Results

Relapse between time 2 and time 3 Thirty per cent of the 247 participants who were quit at time 2 relapsed by time 3. Relapse at time 3 was predicted by higher aggregate temptations (p = 0.001), higher positive/social temptations (p < 0.001), higher habit/addictive temptations (p = 0.03), higher negative/affective temptations (p = 0.004), higher aggregate behavioural change processes (p = 0.01), higher reinforcement management (p = 0.02) and higher helping relationships (p = 0.03). There were significant interactions for the aggregate behavioural processes and reinforcement management (p = 0.03 and 0.02 respectively). For those who had quit for less than one month higher levels of behavioural process use and reinforcement management predicted relapse, whereas for those who had quit for more than one month the levels of these variables were similar for both relapsers and quitters.

Relapse between time 3 and time 4 Thirty-five per cent of the 204 participants who were quit at time 3 relapsed by time 4. Relapse was predicted by higher aggregate temptations (p = 0.005), higher positive/social temptations (p = 0.001) and higher habit/addictive temptations (p = 0.007).

2.5.4 Discussion

The authors note a number of potential limitations of the study. First, there may be predictors of relapse that are specific to very recent ex-smokers in the acute withdrawal phase (i.e. quit for less than a week), but it was not possible to examine this because of the relatively small sample size in this group. Second, the sample consisted of smokers who had sought help by phoning a quitline; it is possible that the predictors of relapse would be different in smokers who try to quit without help. Third, the short-form measures may not adequately assess the TTM constructs (see Section 2.4).

Use of behavioural processes predicted relapse between time 2 and time 3 (though not between time 3 and time 4). However, the findings were contrary to the TTM predictions, with *more frequent* use of behavioural processes predicting relapse between time 2 and time 3. The authors suggest that higher use of behavioural processes may indicate greater difficulties with staying quit and hence greater likelihood of relapse. The only TTM variables that predicted relapse in both time periods were higher levels of temptations to smoke, a finding that is consistent with Marlatt and Gordon's (1985) relapse prevention model.

There was some evidence that predictors of relapse differed between those who had quit for less than one month and those who had quit for more than one month. Based on these findings and other evidence, Segan *et al.* (2004a) suggest that by dividing ex-smokers into those who have quit for less than six months (actors) and those who have quit for more than six months (maintainers), the TTM provides an overly simplistic account of the post-cessation phase.

This research group has recently developed a new model that specifies seven 'perspectives' (stages) in the process of smoking cessation, including four post-cessation stages (Borland 2000; Borland *et al.* 2004; Segan *et al.* 2004a). Based on a detailed and insightful analysis of the task of quitting smoking, the model is a promising alternative to the TTM and is potentially applicable to other health behaviours.

2.6 Intervention studies

The TTM implies that interventions should be matched to the participant's stage by targeting the variables that are assumed to influence the transition from that stage to the next. Such interventions should be more effective than generic interventions in which all participants are treated the same irrespective of their stage of change. TTM-based interventions have been developed for a range of different target behaviours, including condom use (Brown-Peterside *et al.* 2000) and sun protective behaviours (Weinstock *et al.* 2002), as well as smoking cessation (Prochaska *et al.* 1993). Some TTM-based interventions not only match materials to the participant's stage but also individually tailor the information on the basis of the other TTM variables.

A number of studies have compared TTM-based stage-matched interventions with generic, non-matched interventions or no-intervention control conditions. Four reviews have summarized the evidence on effectiveness. Riemsma *et al.* (2003) identified 23 randomized controlled trials of TTM-based interventions for smoking cessation and concluded that 'limited evidence exists for the effectiveness of stage based interventions in changing smoking behaviour' (p.1175). Using more lenient selection criteria, Spencer *et al.* (2002) identified 22 intervention studies on smoking and reached a more positive conclusion. Bridle *et al.* (in press) found 37 randomized controlled trials of TTM-based interventions targeting seven health-related behaviours (including 13 studies on smoking cessation and seven on physical activity). They concluded that 'Overall ... there was limited evidence for the effectiveness of stage-based interventions as a basis for behavior change or for facilitating stage progression ...'. Finally, Van Sluijs *et al.* (2004) identified 29 trials of TTM-based lifestyle interventions in primary care (including 14 studies on smoking cessation and 13 on physical activity) and came to a similar conclusion.

All these reviews included studies that were not proper applications of the TTM. For an intervention to be labelled as TTM-based, it should (a) stratify participants by stage and (b) target the theory's independent variables (pros and cons, confidence and temptation, processes of change), focusing on different variables at different stages. Many of the studies included in the reviews did not meet this requirement. For example, the Newcastle exercise project involved an intervention based on motivational interviewing and apparently did not stratify participants by stage of change or target the TTM's independent variables (Harland *et al.* 1999).

Not surprisingly, the interventions that come closest to a strict application of the TTM are those developed by the Rhode Island group. The group's studies of TTM-based smoking cessation interventions have yielded mainly positive findings (e.g. Prochaska *et al.* 1993, 2001a, 2001b;

Pallonen *et al.* 1998). By contrast, adaptations of these interventions evaluated by other research groups in the UK and Australia have yielded mainly negative results (Aveyard *et al.* 1999, 2001, 2003; Borland *et al.* 2003; Lawrence *et al.* 2003).

None of these studies speaks directly to the validity or otherwise of the TTM. There have been no process analyses published to date demonstrating that TTM-based interventions do indeed influence the variables they target in particular stages and that forward stage movement can be explained by these variables.

2.7 Future directions

The TTM has been very influential and has popularized the idea that behaviour change involves movement through a series of discrete stages. It has also stimulated the development of innovative interventions. However, the model cannot be recommended in its present form. Fundamental problems with the definition and measurement of the stages need to be resolved. Although a cursory glance at the huge literature on the TTM gives the impression of a large body of mainly positive findings, a closer examination reveals that there is remarkably little supportive evidence. It would be helpful if the Rhode Island group presented a fuller specification of the model that (a) stated which variables influence which stage transitions and (b) specified the causal relationships among the pros and cons, confidence and temptation, and processes of change. Predictions from the model should be tested using strong research designs: longitudinal studies of stage transitions with short time intervals and experimental studies of matched and mismatched interventions (Weinstein *et al.* 1998c). Studies of stage-matched interventions should examine whether the interventions influence the variables targeted in particular stages and whether forward stage transitions can be explained by these variables.

It would also be helpful if the Rhode Island group addressed the detailed critiques of the TTM by, among others, Sutton (1996a, 2000a, 2001), Carey *et al.* (1999), Joseph *et al.* (1999), Rosen (2000) and Littell and Girvin (2002), and responded to Weinstein *et al.*'s (1998c) exposition of the conceptual and methodological issues surrounding stage theories.

3 The precaution adoption process model (PAPM)

3.1 Description of the model

The PAPM was originally developed to describe the process by which people come to adopt the precaution of testing their homes for radon (a naturally occurring carcinogenic gas). The model was first described by Weinstein (1988) but was subsequently revised. This section focuses on the revised version, which was first presented by Weinstein and Sandman (1992). The theory specifies seven discrete stages in the process

of precaution adoption (Figure 6.4). In Stage 1, people are unaware of the
health issue. People in Stage 2 are aware of the issue but they have never
thought about adopting the precaution; they are not personally engaged
by the issue. People who reach Stage 3 are undecided about whether or
not to adopt the precaution. If they decide against adopting the precaution, they move into Stage 4. If they decide in favour, they move into Stage
5. Having reached Stage 5, people who act on their decision move to
Stage 6. Finally, for some behaviours, a seventh stage (maintenance) may
be appropriate.

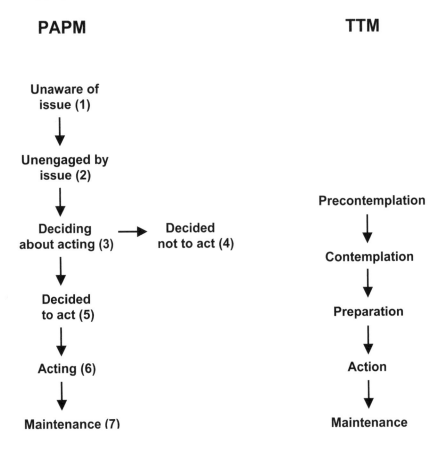

Figure 6.4 The PAPM compared with the TTM, from Weinstein and Sandman
(2002a). [Only the acting/action and maintenance stages can be regarded as
equivalent across the two models.]

The PAPM differs from the TTM in a number of ways (Figure 6.4). It has
more stages: seven instead of five. Unlike the TTM, there is a stage (decided
not to act) that is a side-path from the main sequence (although a person
who reaches this stage may of course return to Stage 3 at some point and

continue moving towards action). The decided to act stage is similar to the preparation stage in the TTM (at least when preparation is defined purely in terms of intentions or plans and not in terms of past behaviour). At first glance, deciding about acting appears to be similar to contemplation in the TTM. However, being undecided about doing something may not be the same as seriously thinking about doing something in the next six months. Weinstein and Sandman (1992) suggest that the contemplation stage may include both individuals who are undecided about action and those who have already decided to act. Note that, unlike the TTM, none of the pre-action stages in the PAPM refers to specific time periods, which means that they are less arbitrary and perhaps more likely to represent genuine stages. Finally, the PAPM in effect splits the TTM pre-contemplation stage into three stages (1, 2 and 4), which seem to represent important distinctions; in particular, it seems important to distinguish between (a) having never thought about adopting a precaution and (b) having thought about it and decided not to act.

Table 6.6 Stage transitions allowable under the PAPM

	1	2	3	4	5	6
1	✓	✓				
2		✓	✓			
3			✓	✓	✓	
4			✓	✓		
5			✓		✓	✓
6						✓

Table 6.6 shows a transition matrix for the six-stage version of the PAPM (without the maintenance stage). Allowable transitions are indicated by ticks. The diagonal consists entirely of ticks, meaning that a person can stay in any of the stages indefinitely. For example, one person may remain blissfully unaware of the health threat while another person may be constantly trying to decide what to do. Transitions above the diagonal represent forward movements. The ticks in this part of the matrix indicate the transitions illustrated in Figure 6.4, for example moving from being unaware about the issue to being aware but unengaged. Transitions in the upper diagonal that do not have a tick represent forward skips. Such skips may sometimes occur. For example, a person may make a decision to do something on the spur of the moment without having thought about it. Thus, they may move directly from Stage 2 to Stage 5, skipping Stage 3. It is possible to interpret this example in terms of the person moving rapidly through the intervening stage rather than skipping it completely. Conceptually, it is neater to proscribe skips and to assume that change follows the sequence postulated in Figure 6.4. In practice, it is difficult or impossible to distinguish between the two interpretations.

Transitions below the diagonal represent backward movements. Weinstein and Sandman (2002a: 71) state that 'Movement backwards towards an earlier stage can ... occur, without necessarily going through all the intermediate stages, though obviously it is not possible to go from later stages to Stages 1 or 2.'

Table 6.7 shows the factors that are likely to influence key transitions in the PAPM. Weinstein and Sandman (2002b) emphasize the importance of media messages in shifting people from Stage 1 to Stage 2. They also state that the factors that influence stage transitions may differ for different

Table 6.7 Issues likely to determine progress between stages, from Weinstein and Sandman (2002b)

Stage transition	Important issues
Stage 1 to Stage 2	Media messages about the hazard and precaution
Stage 2 to Stage 3	Communications from significant others
	Personal experience with hazard
Stage 3 to Stage 4 or Stage 5	Beliefs about hazard likelihood and severity
	Beliefs about personal susceptibility
	Beliefs about precaution effectiveness and difficulty
	Behaviours and recommendations of others
	Perceived social norms
	Fear and worry
Stage 5 to Stage 6	Time, effort and resources needed to act
	Detailed 'how-to' information
	Reminders and other cues to action
	Assistance in carrying out action

behaviours. Although the factors listed in Table 6.7 seem plausible, and there is a lot of indirect supporting evidence, there is as yet little direct evidence from the few studies of the PAPM that have been conducted to date.

3.2 Summary of research

To date, the PAPM has been applied to only a limited number of behaviours (Table 6.8). This review focuses on the longitudinal studies and an important experimental match–mismatch study; all these studies were applications to radon testing. An intervention study on osteoporosis prevention (Blalock *et al.* 2002), which did not involve a comparison of matched and mismatched interventions, is discussed in Section 3.4. First, however, we discuss the Clemow *et al.* (2000) cross-sectional study on mammography screening because it raises an important issue about the role of past behaviour.

Clemow *et al.* (2000) applied the PAPM in a large sample (n = 2507) of women aged 50–80 in Massachusetts whom they describe as

Table 6.8 Applications of the PAPM

Behaviour	Authors
Home radon testing	Weinstein and Sandman (1992); Weinstein *et al.* (1998a)[a]
Hepatitis B vaccine acceptance	Hammer (1998)
Osteoporosis prevention	Blalock *et al.* (1996, 2002[a])
Mammography screening	Clemow *et al.* (2000)

[a] Intervention studies.

'underutilizers' of mammography, that is women who had never had a mammogram or who had not had one in the 24 months prior to the survey or who had had a mammogram in the previous 24 months but had not had one in the 24 months prior to the last mammogram. The staging algorithm they used differed from the recommended one (see Section 3.3). Participants were first classified into three groups with respect to their intention to have a mammogram in the next year or two: (a) definitely planning (Stage 5); (b) thinking about (Stage 3); and (c) not planning. (No respondent stated that they had never heard of a mammogram.) A second question was used to divide the not planning group into three stages: (a) never seriously considered getting a mammogram (Stage 2); (b) considered getting a mammogram, but decided against it (Stage 4); and (c) have thought about it but still undecided (Stage 3b). Clemow *et al.* do not report a full comparison of adjacent stages, but their data show some evidence for discontinuity patterns. For example, compared with women in Stage 2, those in Stage 3 were significantly more likely to say that they worried 'a little' or 'a lot' about breast cancer. However, the two groups also differed with respect to the percentage that had had a prior mammogram (53.8 per cent in Stage 3 vs 11.6 per cent in Stage 2). This is a potentially important confounding factor. Ideally, such stage comparisons should control for past behaviour, for example by dividing the sample into those who had and those who had not had a previous mammogram. Such an analysis could also address the question of whether past behaviour is a moderator of stage transitions: the factors that influence a particular transition may differ depending on whether or not participants have prior experience of the behaviour.

Weinstein and Sandman (1992) briefly report results from three prospective studies of home radon testing that examined movement from the pre-action stages to the action stage (ordering a test). The staging algorithm used in these studies defined Stage 4 as 'test not needed', which may not be quite the same as 'decided not to test' in the recommended algorithm (see Section 3.3). The findings, which are summarized in Table 6.9, show that the percentage who subsequently ordered a test was much higher among those in the plan-to-test stage than among those in the other pre-action stages; differences between these other pre-action stages were relatively small. (Weinstein and Sandman note that the higher rate of testing by undecided participants in Study II may be a consequence of the rather aggressive intervention that occurred after their stage of testing had been assessed.) Although not tested formally, this is evidence not simply for what the Rhode Island group calls a *stage effect* (Prochaska *et al.* 2004) but for the predicted discontinuity pattern. No studies of the PAPM have examined other stage transitions over time or have investigated predictors of stage transitions in longitudinal studies.

Table 6.9   Stages of testing adoption and subsequent test orders (per cent ordering a test), from Weinstein and Sandman (1992)

Prior stage	Study I n = 263	Study II 647	Study III 453
Never thought about it	—[a]	2.0	5.3
Not needed	3.6	4.2	4.8
Undecided	3.3	12.9	3.5
Plan to test	26.2	23.6	28.2

[a] 'Never thought about it' was not given as a response option in this study.

Weinstein *et al.* (1998a) reported an experimental study of the PAPM that compared matched and mismatched interventions. Participants (residents of Columbus, Ohio) first viewed a general informational video in their homes and were then staged by asking 'What are your thoughts about testing your home for radon?' in a telephone interview. The statements used for classifying people into Stages 2–5 were very similar to those in the recommended algorithm (see Section 3.3). The statement for the action stage was 'I have already completed a test, have a test in progress, or have purchased a test.' Stage 1 people, who had never heard about radon testing, had already been screened out of the study. Those people who were in either the *undecided* or the *decided to test* stage were randomly assigned to one of four experimental conditions and were sent the appropriate intervention materials and a questionnaire. A follow-up telephone interview was conducted nine to ten weeks after participants returned the questionnaire to find out whether they had purchased a radon test kit and, if not, to ascertain their final stage. (Weinstein *et al.* (1998a) note that buying a test kit is not equivalent to testing, but that they chose to use test kit purchase as the main outcome to avoid lengthening the follow-up period.)

The four experimental conditions were:

1   *High likelihood*. Participants in this condition received a five-minute video designed to convince them that they had a moderate to high chance of finding high radon levels in their homes. The covering letter mentioned that test kits could be ordered from the American Lung Association (ALA) but did not include an order form.

2 *Low effort.* The five-minute video sent to participants in this condition described how to select a kit type (including a specific recommendation), find and purchase a kit, and conduct a test. The procedure was described as simple and inexpensive. They were also sent a form to order test kits from the ALA.

3 *Combination.* Participants in this condition received a 10-minute video that simply combined the high-likelihood and low-effort videos and the same letter and order form as people in the low-effort condition.

4 *Control.* Participants in the control condition received a letter stating that their assistance in viewing a second video was not needed.

Manipulation checks showed that the high-likelihood intervention increased perceived radon risk and the low-effort intervention increased perceived ease of testing, as intended. The outcome results are shown in Table 6.10. The main outcome was the percentage of people who progressed *one or more* stages towards testing. This criterion (rather than forward movement of only a single stage) was chosen because people in the undecided stage who moved to the decided to test stage may have already possessed the information or skills required to progress further to the action stage. As predicted, both the stage by high-likelihood treatment interaction and the stage by low-effort treatment interaction were significant. The high-likelihood treatment was much more effective among undecided participants than among decided-to-act participants, and the low-effort treatment was more effective among the decided-to-act participants than among the undecided participants. This is clear evidence for the greater effectiveness of stage-matched over stage-mismatched interventions.

Table 6.10 Percentage of participants who progressed one or more stages toward testing, from Weinstein *et al.* (1998a)

	Condition			
Pre-intervention stage	*Control*	*High-likelihood*	*Low-effort*	*Combination*
Undecided	18.8 (138)	41.7 (144)	36.4 (130)	54.5 (139)
Decided-to-test	8.0 (339)	10.4 (338)	32.5 (329)	35.8 (345)

Note: The group size in each cell is shown in parentheses.

There was no evidence that the stage-mismatched interventions were counter-productive: they were still more effective than the control condition. The combination treatment was the most effective but, as Weinstein *et al.* (1998a) point out, it was approximately twice as long as each of its two components and therefore more expensive. However, it is possible that the high-likelihood video with an accompanying letter that included instructions on how to buy a test kit and an order form would be as effective as the combination treatment.

Table 6.11   PAPM stage classification algorithm, from Weinstein and Sandman (2002b)

1 Have you ever heard about {home radon testing}?	
No	Stage 1
Yes [go to 2]	
2 Have you {tested your own house for radon}?	
Yes	Stage 6
No [go to 3]	
3 Which of the following best describes your thoughts about {testing your home}?	
I've never thought about {testing}	Stage 2
I'm undecided about {testing}	Stage 3
I've decided I don't want to {test}	Stage 4
I've decided I do want to {test}	Stage 5

Note: The words in curly brackets could be replaced with other precautions to develop a staging algorithm for these precautions.

The Weinstein *et al.* (1998a) study is an exemplary study that provides a model for how stage theories can be tested experimentally.

3.3 Operationalization of the model

Table 6.11, from Weinstein and Sandman (2002b), gives a stage classification algorithm that would be suitable for any behaviour for which a maintenance stage is not applicable. These include behaviours that, if they are performed at all, are usually performed only once, for example having a predictive genetic test for inherited breast/ovarian cancer. Of course, virtually any behaviour can be repeated: a person may test their home for radon, then move house and test their new home for radon. If a significant proportion of people in the sample have adopted the precaution before, then it may be necessary to take past behaviour into account in the analysis and to reword the staging algorithm. Consider, for example, applying the model to participation in mammography screening. If the investigator is interested only in *first-time* attendance for screening, he or she could either select a sample of women who have recently reached the lower age limit for screening and use the algorithm in Table 6.11 to stage them or select a sample of women who have never been screened and follow them over time until some of them have their first screen, using the algorithm to stage the sample on a number of occasions. Women who have had one mammogram could be allocated to stages with respect to having another mammogram. This would require modifications to the algorithm. Stage 1 would not be applicable for these women. And the statement used to classify women in Stage 2 could be reworded to something like 'I haven't thought about whether to have another mammogram'. (An alternative approach would be to classify women who have had repeated mammograms in accordance with the recommended schedule as being in the maintenance stage. However, it would be difficult to know how to classify women who have had more than one mammogram but whose pattern of attendance does not conform to the recommend schedule.)

The PAPM can also be applied to deliberate changes in ongoing behaviours such as the frequency of taking exercise or the amount of salt consumed per day. In this case, it is necessary to define a criterion level of behaviour, for example doing at least 30 minutes of moderate physical activity every day. Here it would be appropriate to specify a maintenance stage, possibly defined in terms of duration as in the TTM, for example having maintained at least 30 minutes of moderate physical activity a day for at least six months. However, as noted earlier, such time periods are arbitrary and do not have face validity as marking a transition between discrete stages.

3.4 Intervention studies

Apart from the Weinstein *et al.* (1998a) study, only one PAPM-based intervention study has been published to date. Blalock *et al.* (2002) described the effects of an osteoporosis prevention programme in which they compared a tailored education intervention, based partly on the PAPM, with a non-tailored intervention among women aged between 40 and 56 in North Carolina. Women in the tailored education group (n = 273) were sent two individually tailored packets and participated in a brief telephone counselling session. The packets contained separate cards for calcium and exercise. The messages were partly tailored on precaution adoption stage of change. If the participant was in the *action* stage (defined as being above the recommended criterion for the behaviour at baseline), the card included a message reinforcing that behaviour. If the participant was in the *engaged* stage (not obtaining an adequate amount of calcium/exercise at baseline but thinking about or trying to increase their level), the card included a tailored message reinforcing her interest in change. If she was in the *unengaged* stage (not obtaining an adequate amount of calcium/exercise at baseline and not thinking about trying to increase their level), the card included a message encouraging her to think about trying to get more calcium/exercise. Thus, rather than targeting factors assumed to influence stage transitions, the tailored interventions tried to encourage forward movement (or staying in the action stage) in a simple, direct way.

The telephone counselling session took place about three weeks after the woman had received the first tailored packet. If a woman was above the criterion level, the session simply reinforced her current behaviour. If a woman was below the criterion but wanted to change, she was guided through a structured protocol that included goal setting, behavioural contracting, identifying potential barriers to change, and relapse prevention strategies. The second tailored packet was sent to participants immediately after the counselling session. This listed the behavioural goals that had been set, included a copy of the behavioural contract(s), and provided tips on overcoming the barriers that had been identified.

Women in the non-tailored education group (n = 274) received two packets of information with similar content to those received by the tailored education group but with no individual tailoring. In addition, women in this group did not receive telephone counselling.

Among women in the unengaged and engaged stages at baseline, calcium intake increased significantly between baseline and three-month follow-up, and these increases were maintained at the six- and twelve-month follow-ups. Among women in the engaged stage, the tailored group showed greater increases than the non-tailored group at each follow-up. Among women in the action stage at baseline, for whom further increases in calcium intake were not appropriate, the non-tailored group showed an increase but the tailored group did not. There were no significant differences between the intervention conditions for exercise. Thus, this study yielded limited evidence for the greater effectiveness of the tailored intervention. This was a well-conducted study, but the tailored intervention was based loosely on a simplified version of the PAPM, and the study does not provide direct evidence bearing on the validity of the model.

3.5 Future directions

Although only a handful of studies using the PAPM have been conducted to date, it is a promising approach. The stages (particularly for the six-stage version, without the maintenance stage) have greater face validity than the TTM stages and make important distinctions that are not made by the TTM. Given the problems with the TTM, researchers and practitioners who are thinking of using the TTM should seriously consider the PAPM as an alternative.

Key tasks for future research are to specify the variables that are important for each of the stage transitions and to test whether they predict and influence these transitions. The factors listed in Table 6.7 provide a useful starting point, though they will need to be precisely operationalized in empirical studies. As noted in Section 3.1, Weinstein and Sandman (2002b) suggest that the factors that influence particular stage transitions may differ for different behaviours (in contrast to the TTM, which holds that stage transitions for many different behaviours are influenced by variables from the same limited set); however, they do not make any specific predictions about this. The model should be applied to a wider range of behaviours, including those that are relevant for novel threats where many people will fall into the early stages as well as those that are relevant for more established threats. It would be helpful if future studies of the PAPM used staging algorithms that were as similar as possible to the recommended version (Table 6.11) and sufficiently large sample sizes to avoid the need to collapse stages.

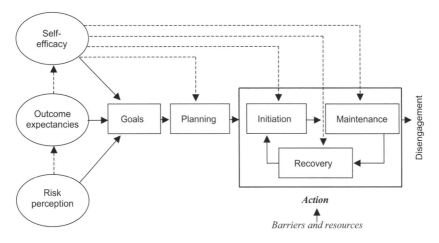

Figure 6.5   The HAPA, adapted from Schwarzer (2004)

4 The health action process approach (HAPA)

4.1 Description of the model

The third theory to be discussed in this chapter is the HAPA. A number of different versions of the theory have been published and different names have been used for the same constructs. The description of the theory presented here is based on the most recent publications including Ralf Schwarzer's website (Schwarzer 2004), from which Figure 6.5 is taken.

The HAPA postulates at least two distinct phases or stages: a *motivation* (or pre-intentional) phase and a *volition* phase (also called a self-regulatory or action phase). The latter is further subdivided into a planning phase, an initiation phase and a maintenance phase. In the motivation phase, three variables are held to influence intention (or goals) directly: risk perception (sometimes referred to as risk awareness or threat), and outcome expectancies and self-efficacy from Bandura's (1986) social cognitive theory (see Luszczynska and Schwarzer, Chapter 4 in this volume). The model suggests a causal order among these three predictors: '. . . threat is specified as a distal antecedent that helps to stimulate outcome expectancies which further stimulate self-efficacy' (Schwarzer 2004). Taken literally, the arrows would be interpreted as follows: people who, for whatever reason, have higher risk perceptions will, *as a consequence*, develop more favourable outcome expectancies; and those who develop more favourable outcome expectancies will, *as a consequence*, have a higher level of self-efficacy. Or, to put it differently, an increase in risk perceptions leads to an increase in outcome expectancies, which in turn leads to an increase in self-efficacy.

The volition phase is represented by the right-hand part of Figure 6.5. Descriptions of this phase of the HAPA focus on the cognitions involved in initiating and controlling the action. For example, the formation of detailed action plans is seen as essential to translate intentions into action

(Gollwitzer 1999; Sheeran *et al.*, Chapter 7 in this volume). Self-efficacy is regarded as having a key role in all phases. This leads to the notion of *phase-specific* self-efficacy. *Maintenance self-efficacy*, for example, refers to optimistic beliefs about one's ability to deal with barriers that arise during the maintenance period.

Although the motivation phase of the HAPA is well specified as a causal model, the volition phase is a framework (or 'heuristic', to use Schwarzer's

Table 6.12   Applications of the HAPA

Behaviour	Authors
Single-occasion drinking	Murgraff *et al.* (2003)
Smoking	Schwarzer and Fuchs (1995a)
Exercise	Schwarzer and Fuchs (1995a); Lippke *et al.* (2004a, 2004b,[a] in press); Ziegelmann, *et al.* (2004a),[a] Sniehotta *et al.* (in press-a,[a] in press-b)
Healthy eating	Schwarzer and Fuchs (1995a, 1995b); Schwarzer and Renner (2000); Renner and Schwarzer (in press)
Resisting dieting	Garcia and Mann (2003)
Condom use	Schwarzer and Fuchs (1995a)
Cancer screening	Schwarzer and Fuchs (1995a)
Breast self-examination	Garcia and Mann (2003); Luszczynska and Schwarzer (2003); Luszczynska (2004)[a]
Testicular self-examination	Barling and Lehmann (1999)

[a] Intervention studies.

(2001) term) that needs further specification before the theory can be fully operationalized and tested. Empirical applications of the model have only recently started to try to represent the volition phase by including measures of planning and phase-specific self-efficacy as well as behaviour (e.g. Sniehotta *et al.* in press-b).

4.2 Summary of research

Applications of the HAPA are listed in Table 6.12. Several cross-sectional studies of the HAPA have investigated predictors of intentions (Schwarzer and Fuchs 1995a; Garcia and Mann 2003) or current or recent behaviour (Barling and Lehmann 1999; Renner and Schwarzer in press). Other HAPA studies have used longitudinal designs to examine the predictors of behaviour as well as intentions (Schwarzer and Fuchs 1995b; Schwarzer and Renner 2000; Luszczynska and Schwarzer 2003; Murgraff *et al.* 2003; Lippke *et al.* 2004a, in press; Sniehotta *et al.* in press-b). The target behaviours in these studies included exercise, healthy eating, single-occasion drinking and breast self-examination. In some cases, the studies

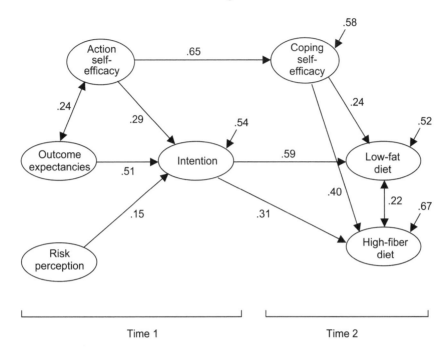

Figure 6.6 Path model predicting healthy eating among Berlin residents, from Renner and Schwarzer (2003). [See Schwarzer and Renner (2000) for the full set of parameter estimates.]

involved interventions; intervention studies are considered in Section 4.4. This section briefly describes three of the longitudinal studies to illustrate how the HAPA has been tested in practice.

Schwarzer and Renner (2000) reported an application of the theory to healthy eating in 524 residents of Berlin who completed a questionnaire on two occasions six months apart. Risk perception (perceived risk of heart disease, high blood pressure and a stroke), outcome expectancies, action self-efficacy and intention were measured at time 1; coping self-efficacy, low-fat dietary intake and high-fibre dietary intake were measured at time 2. The results for the model fitted on the full sample are shown in Figure 6.6 (from Renner and Schwarzer 2003). Intention was predicted by risk perception, outcome expectancies and action self-efficacy, with 46 per cent of the variance explained. Coping self-efficacy was strongly predicted by action self-efficacy. The two behaviour variables were predicted by intention and coping self-efficacy; the model explained 48 per cent of the variance in low-fat dietary intake and 33 per cent of the variance in high-fibre dietary intake.

Luszczynska and Schwarzer (2003) applied the model to breast self-examination (BSE) in a sample of 418 students in Poland who completed questionnaires on two occasions 12–15 weeks apart. (Although not mentioned in the paper, this study involved an intervention designed to increase BSE; see Luszczynska 2004.) Risk perception, outcome expectancies, pre-action self-efficacy and intention were measured at wave 1; planning, maintenance self-efficacy, recovery self-efficacy and BSE behaviour were measured at wave 2. Pre-action self-efficacy and outcome expectancies

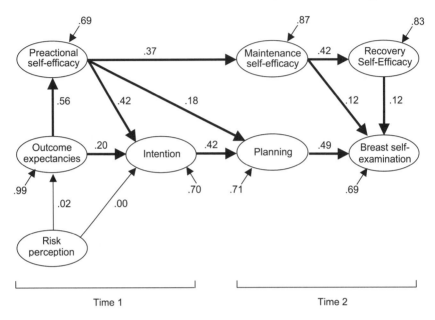

Figure 6.7 Path model predicting breast self-examination among students in Poland, from Luszczynska and Schwarzer (2003). [The arrows in bold indicate paths significant at $p < .05$.]

but not risk perception were significant predictors of intention (Figure 6.7). Intention and pre-action self-efficacy were significant predictors of planning. Planning, maintenance self-efficacy and recovery self-efficacy were significant predictors of BSE behaviour. The model explained 30 per cent of the variance in intention, 29 per cent of the variance in planning; and 31 per cent of the variance in BSE behaviour.

Sniehotta *et al.* (in press-b) reported a three-wave longitudinal study of 307 heart disease patients in rehabilitation. They estimated three versions of the HAPA, the most complete of which included the following variables: risk perception, outcome expectancies and task self-efficacy measured at time 1; coping self-efficacy, planning and action control (or 'self-regulation', as the authors also refer to it) assessed at time 2; and behaviour (exercise) assessed at time 3, four months after discharge. Task self-efficacy and outcome expectancies were significant predictors of intention; task self-efficacy significantly predicted coping self-efficacy; intention and coping self-efficacy significantly predicted planning; coping self-efficacy, intention

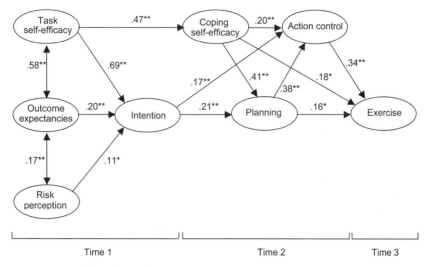

Figure 6.8   Path model predicting exercise in heart disease patients, from Sniehotta *et al.* (in press-b). [*p < .05; **p < .01.]

and planning significantly predicted action control; and coping self-efficacy, planning and action control significantly predicted exercise (Figure 6.8). Thus, the findings were consistent with a model in which planning and action control mediate the effects of intention on behaviour; planning and action control partly mediate the effect of coping self-efficacy on behaviour; and action control partly mediates the effect of planning on behaviour.

As these three examples show, different versions of the HAPA have been examined in different studies. The way that some of the constructs have been operationalized has also varied across studies (see Section 4.3). This lack of standardization makes it difficult to compare findings from different studies.

4.3 Operationalization of the model

Recommendations for operationalizing risk perception, outcome expectancies and self-efficacy were given by Schwarzer and Fuchs (1995b). Detailed recommendations for operationalizing the constructs in the second half of the model have not been published to date. In practice, the measures used have varied between studies.

With regard to *risk perception*, some studies (e.g. Schwarzer and Renner 2000; Lippke *et al.* 2004a) used comparative measures in which participants were asked to estimate their risk compared with other people of the same age and sex. On the other hand, Sniehotta *et al.* (in press-b) used an absolute measure; the sample item they give is: 'If I keep my lifestyle the way it was prior to the acute treatment ... I will suffer from coronary health problems' (four-point scale from *not at all true* to *exactly true*). In their study of healthy eating, Schwarzer and Fuchs (1995b) combined a comparative measure with an absolute measure. Note that the items used by Sniehotta *et al.* (in press-b) were conditional on a specified behaviour (not changing my lifestyle) whereas those used in the other HAPA studies were unconditional. Weinstein *et al.* (1998b) recommend the use of conditional measures to try to avoid the problem of respondents taking account of possible future changes in their behaviour when estimating their risk.

For *outcome expectancies*, most of the HAPA studies have used the 'if–then' format recommended by Schwarzer and Fuchs (1995b). For example, one of the items used by Schwarzer and Renner (2000) was 'If I stick to a low-fat diet then I will need to spend more time preparing the meals.' Some studies (e.g. Schwarzer and Fuchs 1995b; Lippke *et al.* in press) measured both positive and negative outcome expectancies and treated them as separate predictors. Other studies (e.g. Luszczynska and Schwarzer 2003) have assessed only positive outcome expectancies.

For *self-efficacy*, Schwarzer and Fuchs (1995b) recommend a series of statements in the format 'I am confident that I can perform *behaviour X*, even if *barrier Y*', where each statement refers to a different potential barrier. Several of the HAPA studies have used this format, though the measures used by Schwarzer and Fuchs (1995b) and Lippke *et al.* (2004a) did not refer to specific barriers; nor did the measure of task self-efficacy used by Sniehotta *et al.* (in press-b). The notion of phase-specific self-efficacy implies that both the behaviour and the barriers may differ between different phases. See Luszczynska and Sutton (2005) for suggestions for wording phase-specific items.

In the HAPA studies, *intentions* have been assessed by asking respondents to rate statements in the format 'I intend to *perform behaviour X*.' The following item from Lippke *et al.* (2004a) is typical: 'I intend to exercise for 20 minutes or longer on at least two days per week on a regular basis' (four-point scale from *not at all true* to *absolutely true*).

The few studies that included measures of *action planning* (also called action plans) used similar measures. For example, the measure used by Sniehotta *et al.* (in press-b) consisted of four items: 'I have made a detailed plan regarding (a) when to do my physical exercise, (b) where to exercise, (c) how to do my physical exercise, and (d) how often to do my physical exercise.' Responses were given on six-point scales ranging from *not at all true* to *exactly true*. Although several of the intervention studies refer to *coping planning* (see Section 4.4), no measures of this construct have been published to date.

Action control has been measured in only one study to date (Sniehotta *et al.* in press-b).[5] The construct was measured by six items representing 'the different action control of comparative self-monitoring, awareness of standards, and self-regulatory effort': 'During the last four weeks, I have ... (a) constantly monitored myself whether I exercise frequently enough; (b) watched carefully that I trained for at least 30 minutes with the recommended strain per unit; (c) had my exercise intention often on my mind; (d) always been aware of my prescribed training program; (e) really tried to exercise regularly; (f) tried my best to act in accordance to my standards.'

It is worth noting that, of the HAPA studies conducted to date, only Murgraff *et al.* (2003) rigorously applied the *principle of compatibility*, widely used in studies of the TRA and the TPB, which implies that, in order to maximize predictive power, the definition of the target behaviour should occur with essentially the same wording in all of the questions.

4.4 Intervention studies

Three recent studies based on the HAPA have examined the effect of brief interventions designed to encourage the formation of detailed plans with respect to future physical activity in samples of orthopaedic and heart disease patients.

Sniehotta *et al.* (in press-a) evaluated the effectiveness of action planning and combined action and coping planning in 211 heart disease patients who had just completed a cardiac rehabilitation programme. Participants in the action planning group were asked to form up to three action plans about when, where and how they would exercise or engage in extra everyday physical activities after discharge. Participants in the combined planning group were additionally asked to form up to three coping plans about strategies to overcome anticipated barriers. The interventions were administered by trained consultants in a one-to-one setting and lasted up to 30 minutes. Participants wrote down their plans on a planning sheet, which was handed in at the end of the session. Compared with a no-intervention control condition, there was a significant effect for combined planning but not for action planning alone on self-reported physical activity two months after discharge.

Lippke *et al.* (2004b) tested a similar, though briefer, intervention combining action and coping planning in 560 orthopaedic patients. Compared with a no-intervention control condition, the planning intervention had no effect on intentions but led to a significant increase in action planning (assessed immediately) and also significantly increased the percentage of participants who reported exercising at the recommended level six weeks after discharge (though not at two weeks after discharge). When the sample was divided by baseline stage ('non-intenders', 'intenders' and 'actors'), the intervention was found to have a significant effect on outcome only in the intenders at six-week follow-up. The authors argue that the planning intervention was 'matched' for the intenders but not for those in the other two stages. However, they did not test the stage by intervention interaction. It also seems likely that some participants would have changed stage between baseline and the end of the rehabilitation period when the intervention was administered.

The planning intervention in this study actually consisted of two different experimental conditions: interviewer-assisted and self-administered. In a comparison of these two conditions, Ziegelmann *et al.* (2004) found that the interviewer-assisted intervention led to more detailed action plans and to a significantly higher duration of physical activity two weeks after discharge but not at six weeks.

Finally, in a study on breast self-examination (BSE), Luszczynska (2004) evaluated the effectiveness of a single-session intervention designed to enhance pre-action and maintenance self-efficacy and positive outcome expectancies in a sample of 417 students in Poland. The intervention consisted of several components, including a film showing a woman performing BSE, practice with a silicone model of a breast, and a leaflet. Relative to the no-intervention control condition, the intervention significantly increased pre-action self-efficacy and outcome expectancies but not maintenance self-efficacy and led to a significant increase in frequency of BSE 12–15 weeks later.

4.5 Future directions

In considering possible avenues for future research, it is important to appreciate that the HAPA *as tested to date* is not a stage theory in the way that the TTM and PAPM are stage theories. Take the Schwarzer and Renner (2000) study, for example, which was discussed in Section 4.2. Like the other longitudinal studies of the HAPA, this study treated the different waves as if they corresponded to different phases in the process of behaviour change. Thus, action self-efficacy, which 'makes a difference in the pre-actional phase' (p.488), was measured at time 1, whereas coping self-efficacy, which 'describes optimistic beliefs about one's capability to deal with barriers that arise during the maintenance period' (p.488), was measured at time 2. However, it makes little sense to treat the two waves as corresponding to different phases because (a) the behaviours studied were ongoing, (b) continuous measures of intention and behaviour were used, and (c) it seems likely that there were people in different phases at each wave. Applications of the HAPA have predicted intention as a continuous measure in samples that include people who are already performing the behaviour, and have predicted future behaviour as a continuous measure in samples that include people who are already performing the behaviour as well as people who are not and people with low intentions to perform it as well as people with high intentions to perform it.

In fact, as is clear from a glance at Figures 6.6, 6.7 and 6.8, the HAPA as tested to date is the same type of theory as the TPB. Indeed, it could be regarded as a possible alternative to the TPB, and future studies should directly compare the two theories. (See Garcia and Mann (2003) for a cross-sectional comparison of the HAPA, the TPB and several other models in the prediction of intentions.) Although they are similar in structure, a key difference between the two theories is that recent versions of the HAPA have specified planning as a mediator of the intention–behaviour relationship. Note that identifying such mediating variables helps to explain the intention–behaviour relationship, in the sense of specifying the causal mechanism, but it does not reduce the intention–behaviour gap.

Planning could also *moderate* the effect of intention on behaviour: people who form action plans may be more likely to translate their goal intentions into action. Of the HAPA studies to date, only Murgraff *et al.* (2003) tested this hypothesis; they found no evidence for interactions between intentions and any of the HAPA variables on behaviour, although some of their measures differed from those used by Schwarzer's group. However, Jones *et al.* (2001), in a study of sunscreen use that was partly influenced by the HAPA, found evidence for both mediating and moderating effects of prior planning (see also Abraham *et al.* 1999). A moderating influence of planning is consistent with the theory underlying implementation intentions (Gollwitzer 1999; Sheeran *et al.*, Chapter 7 in this volume).

In order to turn the HAPA into a genuine stage theory, the stages would need to be defined and a staging algorithm developed. To date, only one HAPA study has included a stage classification (Lippke *et al.* 2004b, in press). Stage was assessed only at baseline, so it was not possible to examine stage transitions. Discussions of the HAPA imply that it may be useful to specify at least *three* stages:

1 a pre-intentional stage, in which the person has not formed an intention with respect to the target behaviour;
2 a post-intentional, pre-actional (or planning) stage, in which the person has formed an intention to perform the target behaviour; and
3 a post-actional stage, in which the person has initiated the behaviour.

Having defined the stages, the model should specify the factors that influence the stage transitions. For example, risk perceptions, outcome expectancies and (pre-action) self-efficacy could be specified as the factors that influence the transition from the pre-intentional stage to the post-intentional, pre-action stage. Further stages could be specified. For example, Schwarzer's statement, repeated in a number of his publications, that risk perceptions only 'set the stage' for later processes could be interpreted as implying that the pre-intention stage should be divided into a stage in which the person is not aware of the health threat (or is aware of it but does not feel vulnerable) and a stage in which the person is aware of the threat (or feels at risk). Such a respecified HAPA would resemble the PAPM, and studies designed to test the theory would look rather different from the studies reviewed in Section 4.2.

5 Concluding remarks

Stage theories are appealing because they seem to capture some of the complexities of the process of health behaviour change. However, the more complex structure of stage theories means that they are more difficult to test and to apply in practice than continuum theories like the TPB. Wherever possible, future studies should use strong research designs to test predictions from stage theories. It is remarkable that only four experimental studies of matched and mismatched interventions have been published to date. A prerequisite for such studies is that a stage theory is completely specified so that not only are the stages clearly defined but the independent variables, and the causal relationships among them, are also clearly specified. To date, research on stage theories has been dominated by the TTM. However, partly in response to the problems that have been identified with this model, alternative stage theories are beginning to attract attention and hold promise for future research and practice.

Notes

1 The use of T-scores creates another problem. Cross-sectional studies show that the pros of changing tend to increase across stages whereas the cons of changing tend to decrease. The Rhode Island group thinks that the crossover of the pros and cons has psychological significance. For example, referring to the contemplation stage, Prochaska and Velicer (1997: 39) state: 'This balance between the costs and benefits of changing can produce profound ambivalence that can keep people stuck in this stage for long periods of time.' However, if the pros are increasing and the cons are decreasing, the use of T-scores *guarantees* that the lines will cross over. This will be the case even if the lines based on the raw scores do not cross over. Thus, the crossover is artifactual. The exact position of the crossover point depends on a number of factors, including the set of stages over which the data are standardized and the sample sizes in each stage.

2 LTA extends previous approaches to analysing discrete latent variables (latent class theory and Markov techniques) to models that include both static and dynamic latent variables such as stage membership. In the simplest case where there is only a single indicator of stage membership, no latent class (discrete grouping variable such as experimental versus control condition), and only two time points, LTA provides estimates of two types of parameters: the proportion of the population in each stage at each occasion of measurement; and the probabilities of being in each of the stages at time 2 conditional on stage membership at time 1 (i.e. the transition probabilities). LTA can be used to ascertain how well a particular theoretical model fits the data. Goodness-of-fit statistics can be used to compare competing models. LTA requires specialist software; a Windows version of the program can be downloaded from http://methcenter.psu.edu. See Martin *et al.* (1996) for an application to the TTM.

3 The study by Perz *et al.* (1996) is not included in this list because the analyses were either not properly prospective or failed to stratify by stage; see Hansen (1999) and Segan *et al.* (2004c) for detailed critiques of this study.

4 Several non-TTM measures were also included but are not reported here.

5 Murgraff *et al.* (2003) used a combined measure of action planning and action control.

Acknowledgements

The author wishes to thank Neil Weinstein, Alexander Rothman, Ron Borland and Pål Kraft for stimulating discussions about stage theories, and Ralf Schwarzer and Catherine Segan for kindly providing copies of their in-press and submitted papers.

References

Abraham, C., Sheeran, P., Norman, P., Conner, M., De Vries, N. and Otten W. (1999) When good intentions are not enough: modeling postdecisional cognitive correlates of condom use, *Journal of Applied Social Psychology*, 29, 2591–612.

Abrams, D. B., Herzog, T. A., Emmons, K. M. and Linnan, L. (2000) Stages of change versus addiction: a replication and extension, *Nicotine and Tobacco Research*, 2, 223–9.

Ajzen, I. (1991) The theory of planned behavior, *Organizational Behavior and Human Decision Processes*, 50, 179–211.

Ajzen, I. (2002) *The Theory of Planned Behavior*. Retrieved 1 September 2004, from http://www.people.umass.edu/aizen

Ajzen, I. and Fishbein, M. (1980) *Understanding Attitudes and Predicting Social Behavior*. Englewood Cliffs, NJ: Prentice-Hall.

Andersen, B. L., Cacioppo, J. T. and Roberts, D. C. (1995) Delay in seeking a cancer diagnosis: delay stages and psychophysiological comparison processes, *British Journal of Social Psychology*, 34, 33–52.

Armitage, C. J. and Arden, M. A. (2002) Exploring discontinuity patterns in the transtheoretical model: an application of the theory of planned behaviour, *British Journal of Health Psychology*, 7, 89–103.

Armitage, C. J., Povey, R. and Arden, M. A. (2003) Evidence for discontinuity patterns across the stages of change: a role for attitudinal ambivalence, *Psychology and Health*, 18, 373–86.

Armitage, C. J., Sheeran, P., Conner, M. and Arden, M. A. (2004) Stages of change or changes of stage? Predicting transitions in transtheoretical model stages in relation to healthy food choice, *Journal of Consulting and Clinical Psychology*, 72, 491–9.

Aveyard, P., Cheng, K. K., Almond, J., Sherratt, E., Lancashire, R., Lawrence, T. *et al.* (1999) Cluster randomized controlled trial of expert system based on the transtheoretical ('stages of change') model for smoking prevention and cessation in schools, *British Medical Journal*, 319, 948–53.

Aveyard, P., Griffin, C., Lawrence, T. and Cheng, K. K. (2003) A controlled trial of an expert system and self-help manual intervention based on the stages of change versus standard self-help materials in smoking cessation, *Addiction*, 98, 345–54.

Aveyard, P., Sherratt, E., Almond, J., Lawrence, T., Lancashire, R., Griffin, C. *et al.* (2001) The change-in-stage and updated smoking status results from a cluster-randomized trial of smoking prevention and cessation using the transtheoretical model among British adolescents, *Preventive Medicine*, 33, 313–24.

Bandura, A. (1986) *Social Foundations of Thought and Action: A Social Cognitive Theory*. New York: Prentice-Hall.

Bandura, A. (1997) The anatomy of stages, *American Journal of Health Promotion*, 12, 8–10.

Bandura, A. (1998) Health promotion from the perspective of social cognitive theory, *Psychology and Health*, 13, 623–49.

Barling, N. R. and Lehmann, M. (1999) Young men's awareness, attitudes and practice of testicular self-examination: a Health Action Process Approach, *Psychology, Health and Medicine*, 4, 255–63.

Belding, M. A., Iguchi, M. Y. and Lamb, R. J. (1996) Stages of change in methadone maintenance: assessing the convergent validity of two measures, *Psychology of Addictive Behaviors*, 10, 157–66.

Blalock, S. J., DeVellis, B. M., Patterson, C. C., Campbell, M. K., Orenstein, D. R. and Dooley, M. A. (2002) Effects of an osteoporosis prevention program incorporating tailored education materials, *American Journal of Health Promotion*, 16, 146–56.

Blalock, S. J., DeVellis, R. F., Giorgino, K. B., DeVellis, B. M., Gold, D. T., Dooley, M. A. *et al.* (1996) Osteoporosis prevention in premenopausal women: using a stage model approach to examine the predictors of behavior, *Health Psychology*, 15, 84–93.

Blissmer, B. and McAuley, E. (2002) Testing the requirements of stages of physical activity among adults: the comparative effectiveness of stage-matched, mismatched, standard care, and control interventions, *Annals of Behavioral Medicine*, 24, 181–9.

Borland, R. (2000). The Steps to Stop Program: underlying theory and structure of the advice provided. Unpublished manuscript.

Borland, R., Balmford, J. and Hunt, D. (2004) The effectiveness of personally tailored computer-generated advice letters for smoking cessation, *Addiction*, 99, 369–77.

Borland, R., Balmford, J., Segan, C., Livingston, P. and Owen, N. (2003) The effectiveness of personalized smoking cessation strategies for callers to a Quitline service, *Addiction*, 98, 837–46.

Borland, R., Segan, C. and Velicer, W. (2000) Testing the transtheoretical model for smoking change: Victorian data, *Australian Journal of Psychology*, 52, 83–8.

Bridle, C., Riemsma, R. P., Pattenden, J., Sowden, A. J., Mather, L., Watt, I. S. *et al.* (in press) Systematic review of the effectiveness of health interventions based on the transtheoretical model, *Psychology and Health*.

Brown-Peterside, P., Redding, C. A. and Leigh, R. (2000) Acceptability of a stage-matched expert system intervention to increase condom use among women at high risk of HIV infection in New York City, *AIDS Education and Prevention*, 12, 171–81.

Budd, R. J. and Rollnick, S. (1996) The structure of the Readiness to Change Questionnaire: a test of Prochaska and DiClemente's transtheoretical model, *British Journal of Health Psychology*, 1, 365–76.

Carbonari, J. P., DiClemente, C. C. and Sewell, K. B. (1999) Stage transitions and the transtheoretical 'stages of change' model of smoking cessation, *Swiss Journal of Psychology*, 58, 134–44.

Cardinal, B. J., Jacques, K. M. and Levy, S. S. (2002) Evaluation of a university course aimed at promoting exercise behavior, *Journal of Sports Medicine and Physical Fitness*, 42, 113–19.

Cardinal, B. J. and Sachs, M. L. (1995) Prospective analysis of stage-of-exercise movement following mail-delivered, self-instructional exercise packets, *American Journal of Health Promotion*, 9, 430–2.

Carey, K. B., Purnine, D. M., Maisto, S. A. and Carey, M. P. (1999) Assessing readiness to change substance abuse: a critical review of instruments, *Clinical Psychology Science and Practice*, 6, 245–66.

Catania, J. A., Kegeles, S. M. and Coates, T. J. (1990) Towards an understanding of risk behavior: an AIDS risk reduction model (ARRM), *Health Education Quarterly*, 17, 53–72.

Clark, M. A., Rakowski W., Ehrich, B., Rimer, B. K., Velicer, W. F., Dube, C. E. *et al.* (2002) The effect of stage-matched and tailored intervention on repeat mammography, *American Journal of Preventive Medicine*, 22, 1–7.

Clemow, L., Costanza, M. E., Haddad, W. P., Luckmann, R., White, M. J. and Klaus D. (2000) Underutilizers of mammography screening today: characteristics of women planning, undecided about, and not planning a mammogram, *Annals of Behavioral Medicine*, **22**, 80–8.

Collins, L. M. and Wugalter, S. E. (1992) Latent class models for stage-sequential dynamic latent variables, *Multivariate Behavioral Research*, **27**, 131–57.

Courneya, K. S. (1995) Understanding readiness for regular physical activity in older individuals: an application of the theory of planned behavior, *Health Psychology*, **14**, 80–7.

Courneya, K. S., Nigg, C. R. and Estabrooks, P. A. (1998) Relationships among the theory of planned behavior, stages of change, and exercise behavior in older persons over a three year period, *Psychology and Health*, **13**, 355–67.

Courneya, K. S., Plotnikoff, R. C., Hotz, S. B. and Birkett, N. J. (2001) Predicting exercise stage transitions over two consecutive 6-month periods: a test of the theory of planned behaviour in a population-based sample, *British Journal of Health Psychology*, **6**, 135–50.

De Vries, H. and Backbier, E. (1994) Self-efficacy as an important determinant of quitting among pregnant women who smoke: the Ø-pattern, *Preventive Medicine*, **23**, 166–74.

De Vries, H. and Mudde, A. N. (1998) Predicting stage transitions for smoking cessation applying the attitude–social influence–efficacy model, *Psychology and Health*, **13**, 369–85.

De Vries, H., Mudde, A. N., Dijkstra, A. and Willemsen, M. C. (1998) Differential beliefs, perceived social influences, and self-efficacy expectations among smokers in various motivational phases, *Preventive Medicine*, **27**, 681–9.

DiClemente, C. C. (1981) Self-efficacy and smoking cessation maintenance: a preliminary report, *Cognitive Therapy and Research*, **5**, 175–87.

DiClemente, C. C. and Prochaska, J. O. (1982) Self-change and therapy change of smoking behavior: a comparison of processes of change in cessation and maintenance, *Addictive Behaviors*, **7**, 133–42.

DiClemente, C. C., Prochaska, J. O., Fairhurst, S. K., Velicer, W. F., Velasquez, M. M. and Rossi, J. S. (1991) The process of smoking cessation: an analysis of precontemplation, contemplation, and preparation stages of change, *Journal of Consulting and Clinical Psychology*, **59**, 295–304.

DiClemente, C. C., Prochaska, J. O. and Gibertini, M. (1985) Self-efficacy and the stages of self-change of smoking, *Cognitive Therapy and Research*, **9**, 181–200.

Dijkstra, A., Bakker, M. and De Vries, H. (1997) Subtypes within a sample of precontemplating smokers: a preliminary extension of the stages of change, *Addictive Behaviors*, **22**, 327–37.

Dijkstra, A. and De Vries, H. (2001) Do self-help interventions in health education lead to cognitive changes, and do cognitive changes lead to behavioural change?, *British Journal of Health Psychology*, **6**, 121–34.

Dijkstra, A., De Vries, H. and Bakker, M. (1996) Pros and cons of quitting, self-efficacy, and the stages of change in smoking cessation, *Journal of Consulting and Clinical Psychology*, **64**, 758–63.

Dijkstra, A., De Vries, H., Roijackers, J. and van Breukelen, G. (1998a) Tailored interventions to communicate stage-matched information to smokers in different motivational stages, *Journal of Consulting and Clinical Psychology*, **66**, 549–57.

Dijkstra, A., De Vries, H., Roijackers, J. and van Breukelen, G. (1998b) Tailoring information to enhance quitting in smokers with low motivation to quit: three basic efficacy questions, *Health Psychology*, **17**, 513–19.

Dijkstra, A., Tromp, D. and Conijn, B. (2003) Stage-specific psychological determinants of stage transition, *British Journal of Health Psychology*, **8**, 423–37.

Domel, S. B., Baranowski, T., Davis, H. C., Thompson, W. O., Leonard, S. B. and Baranowski, J. (1996) A measure of stages of change in fruit and vegetable consumption among fourth- and fifth-grade school children: reliability and validity, *Journal of the American College of Nutrition*, **15**, 56–64.

Etter, J-F. and Sutton, S. (2002) Assessing 'stage of change' in current and former smokers, *Addiction*, **97**, 1171–82.

Evers, K. E., Harlow, L. L., Redding, C. A. and LaForge, R. G. (1998) Longitudinal changes in stages of change for condom use in women, *American Journal of Health Promotion*, **13**, 19–25.

Farkas, A. J., Pierce, J. P., Gilpin, E. A., Zhu, S-H., Rosbrook, B., Berry, C. *et al.* (1996) Is stage-of-change a useful measure of the likelihood of smoking cessation?, *Annals of Behavioral Medicine*, **18**, 79–86

Farkas, A. J., Pierce, J. P., Zhu, S-H., Rosbrook, B., Gilpin, E. A., Berry, C. *et al.* (1996) Addiction versus stages of change models in predicting smoking cessation, *Addiction*, **91**, 1271–80.

Fava, J. L., Velicer, W. F. and Prochaska, J. O. (1995) Applying the transtheoretical model to a representative sample of smokers, *Addictive Behaviors*, **20**, 189–203.

Garcia, K. and Mann, T. (2003) From 'I wish' to 'I will': social-cognitive predictors of behavioral intentions, *Journal of Health Psychology*, **8**, 347–60.

Gebhardt, W. A. (1997) Health behaviour goal model: towards a theoretical framework for health behaviour change. Unpublished doctoral dissertation, Leiden University.

Gollwitzer, P. M. (1996) The volitional benefits of planning. In P. M. Gollwitzer and J. A. Bargh (eds) *The Psychology of Action: Linking Cognition and Motivation to Behavior*. New York: Guilford, 287–312.

Gollwitzer, P. M. (1999) Implementation intentions: strong effects of simple plans, *American Psychologist*, **54**, 493–503.

Hammer, G. P. (1998) Factors associated with hepatitis B vaccine acceptance among nursing home workers, *Dissertation Abstracts International*, **59**(1-B): 0182.

Hansen, J. (1999) The stages and processes of change for smoking cessation: testing the transtheoretical model, *Dissertation Abstracts International*, **59**(9-B): 5083.

Harland, J., White, M., Drinkwater, C., Cinn, D., Farr, L. and Howel, D. (1999) The Newcastle exercise project: a randomised controlled trial of methods to promote physical activity in primary care, *British Medical Journal*, **319**, 828–32.

Heckhausen, H. (1991) *Motivation and Action*. New York: Springer-Verlag.

Herzog, T. A., Abrams, D. B., Emmons, K. M., Linnan, L. and Shadel, W. G. (1999) Do processes of change predict smoking stage movements? A prospective analysis of the transtheoretical model, *Health Psychology*, **18**, 369–75.

Isenhart, C. E. (1994) Motivational subtypes in an inpatient sample of substance abusers, *Addictive Behaviors*, **19**, 463–75.

Janis, I. L. and Mann, L. (1977) *Decision Making: A Psychological Analysis of Conflict, Choice and Commitment*. New York: Free Press.

Jones, F., Abraham, C., Harris, P., Schulz, J. and Chrispin, C. (2001) From knowledge to action regulation: modeling the cognitive prerequisites of sun screen use in Australian and UK samples, *Psychology and Health*, **16**, 191–206.

Joseph, J., Breslin, C. and Skinner, H. (1999) Critical perspectives on the transtheoretical model and stages of change. In J. A. Tucker, D. M. Donovan and G.

A. Marlatt (eds) *Changing Addictive Behavior: Bridging Clinical and Public Health Strategies*. New York: Guilford, 160–90.

Kraft, P., Sutton, S. R. and Reynolds, H. M. (1999) The transtheoretical model of behaviour change: are the stages qualitatively different?, *Psychology and Health*, **14**, 433–50.

Lawrence, T., Aveyard, P., Evans, O. and Cheng, K. K. (2003) A cluster randomised controlled trial of smoking cessation in pregnant women comparing interventions based on the transtheoretical (stages of change) model to standard care, *Tobacco Control*, **12**, 168–77.

Lippke, S., Ziegelmann, J. and Schwarzer, R. (2004a) Behavioral intentions and action plans promote physical exercise: a longitudinal study with orthopedic rehabilitation patients, *Journal of Sport and Exercise Psychology*, 26, 470–83.

Lippke, S., Ziegelmann, J. and Schwarzer, R. (2004b) Initiation and maintenance of physical exercise: stage-specific effects of a planning intervention, *Research in Sports Medicine*, 12, 221–40.

Lippke, S., Ziegelmann, J. and Schwarzer, R. (in press) Stage-specific adoption and maintenance of physical activity: testing a three stage model, *Psychology of Sport and Exercise*.

Littell, J. H. and Girvin, H. (2002) Stages of change: a critique, *Behavior Modification*, **26**, 223–73.

Luszczynska, A. (2004) Change of breast self-examination: the effects of intervention on enhancing self-efficacy, *International Journal of Behavioral Medicine*, 11, 95–103.

Luszczynska, A. and Schwarzer, R. (2003) Planning and self-efficacy in the adoption and maintenance of breast self-examination: a longitudinal study on self-regulatory cognitions, *Psychology and Health*, 18, 93–108.

Luszczynska, A. and Sutton, S. (2005) Attitudes and expectations. In J. Kerr, R. Weitkunat and M. Moretti (eds) *ABC of Behavior Change*. Edinburgh: Elsevier, 71–84.

McConnaughy, E. A., DiClemente, C. C., Prochaska, J. O. and Velicer, W. F. (1989) Stages of change in psychotherapy: a follow-up report, *Psychotherapy*, 4, 494–503.

McConnaughy, E. A., Prochaska, J. O. and Velicer, W. F. (1983) Stages of change in psychotherapy: measurement and sample profiles, *Psychotherapy: Theory, Research and Practice*, 20, 368–75.

Maes, S. and Gebhardt, W. (2000) Self-regulation and health behavior: the health behavior goal model. In M. Boekaerts, P. R. Pintrich and M. Zeidner (eds) *Handbook of Self-regulation: Theory, Research and Applications*. San Diego, CA: Academic Press, 343–68.

Marcus, B. H. and Simkin, L. R. (1993) The stages of exercise behavior, *Journal of Sports Medicine and Physical Fitness*, 33, 83–8.

Marlatt, G. A. and Gordon, J. R. (eds) (1985) *Relapse Prevention: Maintenance Strategies in the Treatment of Addictive Behaviors*. New York: Guilford.

Marshall, S. J. and Biddle, S. J. H. (2001) The transtheoretical model of behavior change: a meta-analysis of applications to physical activity and exercise, *Annals of Behavioral Medicine*, **23**, 229–46.

Martin, R. A., Velicer, W. F. and Fava, J. L. (1996) Latent transition analysis to the stages of change for smoking cessation, *Addictive Behaviors*, **21**, 67–80.

Migneault, J. P., Velicer, W. F., Prochaska, J. O. and Stevenson, J. F. (1999) Decisional balance for immoderate drinking in college students, *Substance Use and Misuse*, 34, 1325–46.

Murgraff, V., McDermott, M. R. and Walsh, J. (2003) Self-efficacy and behavioral enactment: the application of Schwarzer's Health Action Process Approach to the prediction of low-risk, single-occasion drinking, *Journal of Applied Social Psychology*, 33, 339–61.

Pallonen, U. E., Velicer, W. F., Prochaska, J. O., Rossi, J. S., Bellis, J. M., Tsoh, J. Y. *et al.* (1998) Computer-based smoking cessation interventions in adolescents: description, feasibility, and six-month follow-up findings, *Substance Use and Misuse*, 33, 935–65.

Perz, C. A., DiClemente, C. C. and Carbonari, J. P. (1996) Doing the right thing at the right time? The interaction of stages and processes of change in successful smoking cessation, *Health Psychology*, 15, 462–8.

Peterson, T. R. and Aldana, S. G. (1999) Improving exercise behavior: an application of the stages of change model in a worksite setting, *American Journal of Health Promotion*, 13, 229–32.

Pierce, J. P., Farkas, A. J. and Gilpin, E. A. (1998) Beyond stages of change: the quitting continuum measures progress towards successful smoking cessation, *Addiction*, 93, 277–86.

Pierce, J. P., Farkas, A., Zhu, S-H., Berry, C. and Kaplan, R. M. (1996) Should the stage of change model be challenged?, *Addiction*, 91, 1290–2.

Plotnikoff, R. C., Hotz, S. B., Birkett, N. J. and Courneya, K. S. (2001) Exercise and the transtheoretical model: a longitudinal test of a population sample, *Preventive Medicine*, 33, 441–52.

Prochaska, J. O. and DiClemente, C. C. (1983) Stages and processes of self-change of smoking: toward an integrative model of change, *Journal of Consulting and Clinical Psychology*, 51, 390–5.

Prochaska, J. O., DiClemente, C. C. and Norcross, J. C. (1992) In search of how people change: applications to addictive behaviors, *American Psychologist*, 47, 1102–14.

Prochaska, J. O., DiClemente, C. C., Velicer, W. F., Ginpil, S. and Norcross, J. C. (1985) Predicting change in smoking status for self-changers, *Addictive Behaviors*, 10, 395–406.

Prochaska, J. O., DiClemente, C. C., Velicer, W. F. and Rossi, J. S. (1993) Standardized, individualized, interactive, and personalized self-help programs for smoking cessation, *Health Psychology*, 12, 399–405.

Prochaska, J. O., Redding, C. A. and Evers, K. E. (2002) The transtheoretical model and stages of change. In K. Glanz, B. K. Rimer and F. M. Lewis (eds) *Health Behavior and Health Education: Theory, Research, and Practice* (3rd edition). San Francisco: Jossey-Bass, 99–120.

Prochaska, J. O. and Velicer, W. F. (1997) The transtheoretical model of health behavior change, *American Journal of Health Promotion*, 12, 38–48.

Prochaska, J. O., Velicer, W. F., DiClemente, C. C. and Fava, J. L. (1988) Measuring the processes of change: applications to the cessation of smoking, *Journal of Consulting and Clinical Psychology*, 56, 520–8.

Prochaska, J. O., Velicer, W. F., Fava, J. L., Rossi, J. S. and Tsoh, J. Y. (2001a). Evaluating a population-based recruitment approach and a stage-based expert system intervention for smoking cessation, *Addictive Behaviors*, 26, 583–602.

Prochaska, J. O., Velicer, W. F., Fava, J. L., Ruggiero, L., Laforge, R. G., Rossi, J. S. *et al.* (2001b) Counselor and stimulus control enhancements of a stage-matched expert system intervention for smokers in a managed care setting, *Preventive Medicine*, 32, 23–32.

Prochaska, J. O., Velicer, W. F., Prochaska, J. M. and Johnson J. L. (2004) Size, consistency, and stability of stage effects for smoking cessation, *Addictive Behaviors*, **29**, 207–13.

Quinlan, K. B. and McCaul, K. D. (2000) Matched and mismatched interventions with young adult smokers: testing a stage theory, *Health Psychology*, **19**, 165–71.

Rakowski, W., Dube, C. E., Marcus, B. H., Prochaska, J. O., Velicer, W. F. and Abrams, D. B. (1992) Assessing elements of women's decisions about mammography, *Health Psychology*, **11**, 111–18.

Reed, G. R., Velicer, W. F., Prochaska, J. O., Rossi, J. S. and Marcus, B. H. (1997) What makes a good staging algorithm: examples from regular exercise, *American Journal of Health Promotion*, **12**, 57–66.

Renner, B. and Schwarzer, R. (2003) Social-cognitive factors in health behavior change. In J. Suls and K. A. Wallston (eds) *Social Psychological Foundations of Health and Illness*. Oxford: Blackwell, 169–96.

Renner, B. and Schwarzer, R. (in press) The motivation to eat a healthy diet: how intenders and nonintenders differ in terms of risk perception, outcome expectancies, self-efficacy, and nutrition behavior, *Polish Psychological Bulletin*.

Riemsma, R. P., Pattenden, J., Bridle, C., Sowden, A. J., Mather, L., Watt, I. S. *et al.* (2003) Systematic review of the effectiveness of stage based interventions to promote smoking cessation, *British Medical Journal*, **326**, 1175–7.

Rosen, C. S. (2000) Is the sequencing of change processes by stage consistent across health problems? A meta-analysis, *Health Psychology*, **19**, 593–604.

Rossi, J. S., Blais, L M. and Weinstock, M. A. (1994) The Rhode Island Sun Smart Project: skin cancer prevention reaches the beaches, *American Journal of Public Heath*, **84**, 672–4.

Safer, M. A., Tharps, Q., Jackson, T. and Leventhal, H. (1979) Determinants of three stages of delay in seeking care at a medical clinic, *Medical Care*, **17**, 11–29.

Schwarzer, R. (1992) Self-efficacy in the adoption and maintenance of health behaviors: theoretical approaches and a new model. In R. Schwarzer (ed.) *Self-efficacy: Thought Control of Action*. Washington, DC: Hemisphere, 217–43.

Schwarzer, R. (1999) Self-regulatory processes in the adoption and maintenance of health behaviors: the role of optimism, goals, and threats, *Journal of Health Psychology*, **4**, 115–27.

Schwarzer, R. (2001) Social-cognitive factors in changing health-related behavior, *Current Directions in Psychological Science*, **10**, 47–51.

Schwarzer, R. (2004) *Modeling Health Behavior Change: The Health Action Process Approach (HAPA)*. Retrieved 10 June 2004, from http://userpage.fu-berlin.de/hapa.htm

Schwarzer, R. and Fuchs, R. (1995a) Changing risk behaviors and adopting health behaviors: the role of self-efficacy beliefs. In A. Bandura (ed.) *Self-efficacy in Changing Societies*. New York: Cambridge University Press, 259–88.

Schwarzer, R. and Fuchs, R. (1995b) Self-efficacy and health behaviours. In M. Conner and P. Norman (eds) *Predicting Health Behaviour: Research and Practice with Social Cognition Models*. Buckingham: Open University Press, 163–96.

Schwarzer, R. and Renner, B. (2000) Social-cognitive predictors of health behavior: action self-efficacy and coping self-efficacy, *Health Psychology*, **19**, 487–95.

Segan, C. J., Borland, R. and Greenwood, K. M. (2002) Do transtheoretical model measures predict the transition from preparation to action in smoking cessation?, *Psychology and Health*, **17**, 417–35.

Segan, C. J., Borland, R. and Greenwood, K. M. (2004a) Can transtheoretical model measures predict relapse from the action stage of change among ex-smokers who quit after calling a quitline? Manuscript submitted for publication.

Segan, C. J., Borland, R. and Greenwood, K. M. (2004b) Do transtheoretical model measures predict forward stage transitions among smokers calling a quitline? Manuscript submitted for publication.

Segan, C. J., Borland, R. and Greenwood, K. M. (2004c) What is the right thing at the right time? Interactions between stages and processes of change among smokers who make a quit attempt, *Health Psychology*, **23**, 86–93.

Sfikaki, M. (2001) Comparison of methods for assessing stage of change among heroin addicts in treatment: evaluation of a Greek sample. Unpublished Master's thesis, University of London.

Sniehotta, F. F., Scholz, U. and Schwarzer, R. (in press-a) Action plans and coping plans for physical exercise: a longitudinal intervention study in cardiac rehabilitation, *British Journal of Health Psychology*.

Sniehotta, F. F., Scholz, U. and Schwarzer, R. (in press-b) Bridging the intention–behaviour gap: planning, self-efficacy, and action control in the adoption and maintenance of physical exercise, *Psychology and Health*.

Spencer, L., Pagell, F., Hallion, M. E. and Adams, T. B. (2002) Applying the transtheoretical model to tobacco cessation and prevention: a review of the literature, *American Journal of Health Promotion*, **17**, 7–71.

Steptoe, A., Wijetunge, S., Doherty, S. and Wardle, J. (1996) Stages of change for dietary fat reduction: associations with food intake, decisional balance and motives for food choice, *Health Education Journal*, **55**, 108–22.

Sutton, S. (2000a) A critical review of the transtheoretical model applied to smoking cessation. In P. Norman, C. Abraham and M. Conner (eds) *Understanding and Changing Health Behaviour: From Health Beliefs to Self-regulation*. Reading, England: Harwood Academic Press, 207–25.

Sutton, S. (2000b) Interpreting cross-sectional data on stages of change, *Psychology and Health*, **15**, 163–71.

Sutton, S. (2001) Back to the drawing board? A review of applications of the transtheoretical model to substance use, *Addiction*, **96**, 175–186.

Sutton, S. (2005) Do the transtheoretical model variables predict stage transitions? A review of the longitudinal studies. Manuscript in preparation.

Sutton, S. R. (1996a) Can 'stages of change' provide guidance in the treatment of addictions? A critical examination of Prochaska and DiClemente's model. In G. Edwards and C. Dare (eds) *Psychotherapy, Psychological Treatments and the Addictions*. Cambridge: Cambridge University Press, 189–205.

Sutton, S. R. (1996b) Further support for the stages of change model?, *Addiction*, **91**, 1281–92.

Van Sluijs, E. M. F., Van Poppel, M. N. M. and Van Mechelen, W. (2004) Stage-based lifestyle interventions in primary care: are they effective?, *American Journal of Preventive Medicine*, **26**, 330–43.

Velicer, W. F., DiClemente, C. C., Prochaska, J. O. and Brandenburg, N. (1985) Decisional balance measure for assessing and predicting smoking status, *Journal of Personality and Social Psychology*, **48**, 1279–89.

Velicer, W. F., DiClemente, C. C., Rossi, J. R. and Prochaska, J. O. (1990) Relapse situations and self-efficacy: an integrative model, *Addictive Behaviors*, **15**, 271–83.

Velicer, W. F., Norman, G. J., Fava, J. L. and Prochaska, J. O. (1999) Testing 40 predictions from the transtheoretical model, *Addictive Behaviors*, **24**, 455–69.

Weinstein, N. D. (1988) The precaution adoption process, *Health Psychology*, 7, 355–86.

Weinstein, N. D., Lyon, J. E., Sandman, P. M. and Cuite, C. L. (1998a) Experimental evidence for stages of health behavior change: the precaution adoption process model applied to home radon testing, *Health Psychology*, 17, 445–53.

Weinstein, N. D., Rothman, A. J. and Nicolich, M. (1998b) Use of correlational data to examine the effects of risk perceptions on precautionary behavior, *Psychology and Health*, 13, 479–501.

Weinstein, N. D., Rothman, A. J. and Sutton, S. R. (1998c) Stage theories of health behavior: conceptual and methodological issues, *Health Psychology*, 17, 290–9.

Weinstein, N. D. and Sandman, P. M. (1992) A model of the precaution adoption process: evidence from home radon testing, *Health Psychology*, 11, 170–80.

Weinstein, N. D. and Sandman, P. M. (2002a) Reducing the risks of exposure to radon gas: an application of the precaution adoption process model. In D. Rutter and L. Quine (eds) *Changing Health Behaviour: Intervention and Research with Social Cognition Models*. Buckingham, England: Open University Press, 66–86.

Weinstein, N. D. and Sandman, P. M. (2002b) The precaution adoption process model. In K. Glanz, B. K. Rimer and F. M. Lewis (eds) *Health Behavior and Health Education: Theory, Research, and Practice* (3rd edition). San Francisco, CA: Jossey-Bass, 121–43.

Weinstock, M. A., Rossi, J. S., Redding, C. A. and Maddock, J. E. (2002) Randomized controlled community trial of the efficacy of a multicomponent stage-matched intervention to increase sun protection among beachgoers, *Preventive Medicine*, 35, 584–92.

Ziegelmann, J. P., Lippke, S. and Schwarzer, R. (2004) Adoption and maintenance of physical activity across the lifespan: Planning interventions in orthopedic rehabilitation patients. Manuscript submitted for publication.

7	PASCHAL SHEERAN, SARAH MILNE, THOMAS L. WEBB AND PETER M. GOLLWITZER

IMPLEMENTATION INTENTIONS AND HEALTH BEHAVIOUR

1 General background

1.1 The intention–behaviour relation

Several theories that have been used extensively to predict health behaviours construe the person's *intention* to act as the most immediate and important predictor of subsequent action, such as the theory of planned behaviour (TPB; Ajzen 1991; Conner and Sparks, Chapter 5 in this volume) and protection motivation theory (PMT; Rogers 1983; Norman *et al.*, Chapter 3 in this volume). Intentions can be defined as the instructions that people give themselves to perform particular behaviours or to achieve certain goals (Triandis 1980) and are characteristically measured by items of the form 'I intend to do/achieve X.' Intentions are the culmination of the decision-making process; they signal the end of deliberation about a behaviour and capture the standard of performance that one has set oneself, one's commitment to the performance, and the amount of time and effort that will be expended during action (Gollwitzer 1990; Ajzen 1991; Webb and Sheeran 2005). Given the centrality of the concept of intention to models of health behaviour, it is important to ask how well intentions predict behaviour.

Sheeran (2002) approached this question by conducting a meta-analysis of meta-analyses of prospective tests of the intention–behaviour relation. Across 422 studies involving a sample of 82,107 participants, intentions accounted for 28 per cent of the variance in behaviour, on average. $R^2 = 0.28$ constitutes a 'large' effect size according to Cohen's (1992) power primer, which suggests that intentions are 'good' predictors of behaviour. Moreover, 28 per cent of the variance may underestimate the 'true' relation between intention and behaviour because this value was not corrected for measurement artefacts such as lack of reliability or scale correspondence (see Sutton 1998; Sheeran 2002 for reviews).

However, Sheeran's (2002) meta-analysis does not address the question that most health psychologists probably really want answered, namely, to what extent do intentions predict behaviour *change*? An answer to this question can be gleaned from a meta-analysis of 51 studies (n = 8166) that reported intercorrelations among past behaviour, intention and future behaviour (Sutton and Sheeran 2003). Using these correlations as the input matrix for hierarchical regression shows that, not surprisingly, past behaviour is a good predictor of future behaviour (R^2 = 0.26). Importantly, however, intention is associated with a highly significant increment in the variance; an additional 7 per cent of the variance in behaviour was explained after prior performance had been taken into account. Thus, intentions have a reliable association with behaviour change, though the magnitude of this effect size is small-to-medium (cf. Cohen 1992).

Orbell and Sheeran (1998) pointed out that indices of association (such as percentage variance) do not illuminate the *sources* of consistency and discrepancy between intention and behaviour. To gain insight into this issue, Orbell and Sheeran decomposed the intention–behaviour relation into a 2 (intention: to act vs not to act) × 2 (behaviour: acted vs did not act) matrix (see also McBroom and Reid 1992). This decomposition reveals that intention–behaviour consistency is attributable to participants with positive intentions who subsequently act (termed 'inclined actors') and to participants with negative intentions who do not act ('disinclined abstainers'). Discrepancies between intentions and behaviour, on the other hand, can be attributed to participants with positive intentions who do not act ('inclined abstainers') and participants with negative intentions who ultimately perform the behaviour ('disinclined actors'). Orbell and Sheeran (1998) found that inclined abstainers – rather than disinclined actors – are principally responsible for the intention–behaviour 'gap'. This conclusion was confirmed in a review of health behaviours by Sheeran (2002). Across studies of exercise, condom use and cancer screening, the median proportion of participants with positive intentions who did not perform the behaviour was 47 per cent whereas the median proportion of participants with negative intentions who acted was only 7 per cent. These findings indicate that barely more than one-half of people with positive intentions to engage in health behaviours successfully translate those intentions into action.

1.2 Explaining intention–behaviour discrepancies

Why is it so difficult for people to enact their intentions? We suspect that three processes underlie intention–behaviour discrepancies. The first process is *intention viability* which refers to the idea that it is impossible for most decisions to find expression in the absence of particular abilities, resources or opportunities. That is, a behavioural intention can only be realized if the person possesses actual control over the behavioural performance (Ajzen 1991). Sheeran *et al.* (2003) tested this idea by developing a proxy measure of actual control (PMAC) using participants' post-behavioural attempt assessments of control (e.g. 'How difficult was it for you to exercise twice in the last week?'). Validity of the PMAC was established by demonstrations that (a) PMAC scores did not reflect self-serving attributions for failures to enact one's intentions, and (b) a measure of accuracy of perceived behavioural control (PBC) derived from the PMAC moderated the PBC–behaviour relation. More important, and consistent with the viability hypothesis, findings from studies of low-fat diet and exercise both showed that intentions were associated with behaviour only when intentions were viable, i.e. when participants possessed actual control over the behaviour according to the PMAC. However, because intention viability refers to actual – and not to perceived – control, initiatives to promote intention – behaviour consistency by this route are likely to prove resource–intensive (e.g. in terms of provision of appropriate training, facilities and compensation to make people's intention to exercise viable). Thus, economic and policy interventions may be more appropriate for increasing intention viability whereas psychological interventions may be more appropriate in relation to the other processes.

The second process that is relevant to discriminating between disinclined actors and inclined abstainers concerns *intention activation*. The activation level of an intention refers to the extent to which contextual demands alter the salience, direction or intensity of a focal intention relative to other intentions. To see the importance of situational demands on cognitive and motivational resources, consider that for any particular time and context that a researcher chooses to specify in a measure of a health behaviour intention (e.g. 'Do you intend to exercise at the gym twice in the next week?'), research participants are likely to have multiple, and often conflicting, goals pertaining to the same point in time (e.g. 'Every evening this week is going to be spent writing that report for work') and context ('I must ask Ian and Sarah about their trip to Reykjavik when I see them at the gym'). Moreover, accumulated evidence indicates that situational features activate goals and subsequent behavioural pursuit of those goals in a manner that operates outside people's conscious awareness (e.g. Bargh *et al.* 2001; Aarts *et al.* 2004). Relatedly, when particular goals involve short-term affective costs (e.g. foregoing a tempting dessert) or require mobilization of effort (e.g. bringing a change of clothes to work), then people may be especially vulnerable to more enjoyable or pressing alternatives. Thus, the relative activation level of any particular goal intention may be reduced by environmental activation of alternative goal representations.

Diminution of the activation level of a focal intention can have two important consequences – *prospective memory failure* and *goal reprioritization*. Prospective memory failure occurs when people forget to perform the behaviour. Empirical support for this explanation of intention–behaviour discrepancies comes from retrospective reports by inclined abstainers. For example, Orbell *et al.* (1997) found that 70 per cent of participants who intended to perform a breast self-examination but did not do so offered 'forgetting' as their reason for non-performance (see also

Milne *et al.* 2002). Goal reprioritization occurs when an intention fails to attract sufficient activation to permit its realization and is postponed or abandoned (at least temporarily). Consistent with this idea, Milne *et al.* (2002) found that 45 per cent of participants who failed to enact their intention to exercise said that they were 'too busy', while Abraham *et al.* (1999) found that intentions to use a condom were not enacted because the goal of having sex was more important at the time than was the goal of protecting oneself against HIV/AIDS. Similarly, numerous studies attest to the lack of salience of pregnancy prevention *in situ* (reflected in statements such as 'I could not be bothered at the time' or 'We were carried away in the heat of the moment') as explanations of contraceptive non-use (see Sheeran *et al.* 1991 for a review).

The third process that can help to explain the intention–behaviour gap concerns *intention elaboration*. People may fail to engage in, or to elaborate in sufficient detail, an analysis of the particular actions and contextual opportunities that would permit realization of their intention. Most of the behaviours of interest to health psychologists are goals that can be achieved by performing a variety of behaviours (e.g. the goal or outcome 'losing weight' can be achieved by performing exercise behaviours, dietary behaviours or both, cf. Bagozzi and Kimmel 1995) or – equivalently – behavioural categories such as exercising or dieting that may be indexed by a variety of specific actions (Abraham and Sheeran 2004; see Sewacj *et al.* 1980 for an empirical example). Moreover, health behaviours, may involve complex action sequences wherein the failure to initiate relevant preparatory behaviours is likely to undermine goal pursuit. For example, the intention to use a condom might only be realized if the person has (a) bought, stored or carried condoms, (b) suggested using one to a sexual partner, and (c) thought of ways of overcoming a partner's reluctance to use a condom (Abraham *et al.* 1998; Sheeran *et al.* 1999). Understanding that health goals involve hierarchies of single acts undertaken in specific situational contexts clarifies how important it is to identify both the means (action) and the context (internal or external cue) that will permit intention realization – especially in the case of behaviours that involve deadlines or windows of opportunity (e.g. a health check appointment). In the absence of such elaboration, the person is likely to miss opportunities to act, or not know how to act even if an opportunity presents itself.

1.3 Theoretical background to implementation intentions

The strategy of forming implementation intentions has been proposed as an effective tool for handling problems with sub-optimal activation or elaboration of goal intentions (Gollwitzer 1993, 1996, 1999; Gollwitzer and Schaal 1998; Gollwitzer *et al.* 2005). The theoretical background to the implementation intention construct is the model of action phases (MAP; Heckhausen and Gollwitzer 1987; Gollwitzer 1990). The MAP is a framework for understanding goal achievement that is based on the distinction between the motivational issue of goal setting (intention formation) and the volitional issue of goal striving (intention realization). The model assumes that the principles that govern intention formation and intention realisation are qualitatively different. Whereas intention formation is guided by people's beliefs about the desirability and feasibility of particular courses of action, intention realization is guided by conscious and unconscious processes that promote the initiation and effective pursuit of the goal. The distinction between intention formation and intention realization is important because it clarifies the distinctiveness of the concept of implementation intentions. Traditional models such as the TPB and PMT focus on the motivational phase of action. The primary concern of these theories is with the specific types of feasibility and desirability considerations that determine intention formation – little attention is paid to how intentions are translated into action (Oettingen and Gollwitzer 2001; Sheeran 2002). Research on implementation intentions, on the other hand, provides an explicit theoretical analysis of processes that govern the enactment of intentions.

2 Description of the model

2.1 The nature of implementation intentions

Implementation intentions are if–then plans that connect good opportunities to act with cognitive or behavioural activities that will be effective in accomplishing one's goals. Whereas behavioural or goal intentions specify what one wants to do or achieve (i.e. 'I intend to do/achieve X'), implementation intentions specify the behaviour that one will perform in the service of goal achievement and the situational context in which one will enact it (i.e. 'If situation Y occurs, then I will initiate goal-directed behaviour Z!'). Implementation intentions are subordinate to goal intentions because, whereas a goal intention indicates *what* one will do, an implementation intention specifies the *when, where*, and *how* of what one will do.

To form an implementation intention, the person must first identify a response that will lead to goal attainment and, second, anticipate a suitable occasion to initiate that response. For example, the person might specify the behaviour 'go jogging for 20 minutes' and specify a suitable opportunity as 'tomorrow morning before work' in order to enact the goal intention to exercise. Implementation intention formation is the mental act of linking the anticipated critical situation with the effectual goal-directed response. This process involves a conscious act of willing that results in an association in memory between mental representations of the specified opportunities (situations) and the means of attaining goals (cognitive or behavioural responses).

2.2 Operation of implementation intentions

Implementation intentions promote intention realization by instigating psychological processes that enhance both the identification of the critical situation and the execution of the goal-directed response. That is, implementation intentions enable people both to *see* and to *seize* opportunities to achieve their goals.

2.2.1 Identification of the critical situation

Specifying a good opportunity to act in the if-component of an implementation intention means that the critical situation becomes highly accessible. This heightened accessibility enhances information processing related to the specified cue; more particularly, it becomes easy to detect and attend to the critical situation when one encounters it later. Aarts *et al.* (1999) obtained evidence that implementation intentions enhance cue accessibility in an experiment that asked one-half of participants to form an implementation intention about how they would later collect a coupon from a nearby room; the other half of participants (controls) formed an irrelevant implementation intention about how they would spend the coupon. All of the participants then took part in an ostensibly unrelated word recognition task (their task was to indicate as quickly and accurately as possible whether or not letter strings were words or non-words). Among the letter strings presented were words related to the location of room where the coupon should be collected (e.g. 'corridor', 'swing-door'). Analysis of the response latencies indicated that participants who formed if–then plans were much faster at recognizing the words related to the critical situation than were control participants. Implementation intentions increased the accessibility of environmental cues that participants had anticipated in their plans.

Webb and Sheeran (2004a, Experiment 1) used a classic linguistic illusion to test whether the heightened accessibility engendered by implementation intentions could enhance the detection of critical cues – even when detection is extremely difficult. Participants were presented with a short piece of text and simply asked to count the number of instances of the letter 'F'. The illusion resides in the fact that there are six instances of the letter F in the text but most people count only three because they miss the Fs in the word 'of', which occurs three times. Consistent with predictions, almost all control participants who simply familiarized themselves with the letter prior to the task counted only three Fs. Participants who formed an implementation intention (e.g. 'As soon as I see the letter F, I will add one more to my count!'), on the other hand, counted significantly more instances of the letter. Equivalent findings were obtained by Gollwitzer *et al.* (2002b) in a study that examined identification of elements in the embedded figures test (e.g. Witkin *et al.* 1972). Thus, specifying the critical situation in an if–then plan leads to improved detection of that situation even when the setting means that cue identification is highly challenging.

Heightened accessibility should also mean that the specified situational cues attract and focus attention even though the person is occupied by other concerns. Gollwitzer *et al.* (2002b) tested this idea using a dichotic listening task. Participants were instructed to repeat words presented in one ear (the 'shadowing' task) while ignoring words presented in the other ear (the non-attended channel). In addition, participants had to turn off a light that appeared at irregular intervals as quickly as possible (the secondary task). The key experimental manipulation was the type of words that were presented on the non-attended channel. For one-half of the trials, the words presented to participants represented critical situations that they had earlier specified in implementation intentions to promote the achievement of a personal goal intention; the other half of the trials involved neutral words. Findings indicated that the specified cues were highly disruptive to attention to the focal (shadowing and secondary) tasks. That is, participants were much slower to switch off the light, and repeated the words more slowly and less accurately, when words related to their specified cues were presented on the non-attended channel compared to when neutral words were presented. Thus, words related to the critical situation grabbed participants' attention even though participants were supposed to be concentrating on demanding other tasks. These findings speak to the idea that even though we may be wrapped up in our own thoughts, gripped by powerful emotions, or otherwise absorbed in activities that have nothing to do with an underlying goal intention, the critical situation specified in an if–then plan will penetrate current preoccupations and capture our attention.

2.2.2 Execution of the goal-directed response

Specifying that one will perform a particular goal-directed behaviour in the then-component of a plan, at the moment one has specified in the if-component of the plan, involves a strategic abdication of action control. This is because forming an implementation intention delegates control of behaviour from the self to specified situational cues that directly elicit the behaviour (Gollwitzer 1993). Forming an if–then plan means that the person commits himself or herself in advance to acting as soon as certain contextual constraints are satisfied – nothing needs to be done to ensure action initiation except encounter the specified situation. Action proceeds swiftly and effortlessly, and does not require the person's attention. That is, the execution of a behaviour specified in an implementation intention exhibits features of *automatic* processes.

According to Bargh (1992, 1994), three key features of automatic processes are immediacy, efficiency and lack of awareness. Automaticity characterizes highly over-learned activities such as driving a car or typing. For example, drivers respond quickly to changes in the flow of traffic or road conditions. They can hold a conversation with a passenger despite the demands of so doing while they are driving at the same time (supporting the idea that driving is efficient in terms of cognitive resources). Moreover, drivers need devote little attention to the process of driving itself; they need only be aware of other traffic and their conversation partner. So what evidence is there that action control by implementation intentions exhibits these three features of automaticity?

The *immediacy* of implementation intention effects is supported by several studies that employed speed of responding as the dependent variable.

For example, Webb and Sheeran (2004a, Experiment 3) used a reaction time task to compare whether an implementation intention to respond especially quickly to a critical stimulus (the number 3) led to faster responses compared to a goal intention that had the same aim. Findings indicated that participants who formed if–then plans responded faster to the critical stimulus compared to both non-critical stimuli and participants who only formed goal intentions. A field study by Orbell and Sheeran (2000) afforded a similar conclusion. Patients undergoing joint replacement surgery were asked to form implementation intentions about resuming functional activities upon their discharge from hospital. Despite equivalent goal intentions to resume the activities, behavioural follow-up at three months showed that patients who formed implementation intentions initiated 18 out of 32 activities sooner than did patients who had not formed if–then plans. Implementation intention participants were functionally active 2.5 weeks sooner, on average, than were controls. Gollwitzer and Brandstätter (1997, Experiment 3) measured the time interval between specified opportunities and specified behavioural responses in a study where participants had to make counter-arguments to racist remarks. Findings indicated that participants who formed implementation intentions spoke up in closer temporal proximity to the times they had specified than did participants who only formed goal intentions in relation to the specified opportunities. Thus, participants who make if–then plans are likely to immediately seize the opportunities to act that they have identified – action initiation by implementation intentions is swifter than that generated by goal intentions alone.

The *efficiency* of implementation intention effects is supported by studies that manipulated cognitive load either through selection of the sample (e.g. schizophrenic patients, heroin addicts under withdrawal) or by using a dual task paradigm in experiments with college students (Brandstätter *et al.* 2001; Lengfelder and Gollwitzer 2001). For example, Lengfelder and Gollwitzer (2000, Study 2) found that implementation intentions benefited task performance for schizophrenic patients just as much as for matched controls even though schizophrenic participants are likely to have been preoccupied by unwanted thoughts. Similarly, forming an implementation intention to compose a curriculum vitae increased the likelihood of completing the task by the deadline regardless of whether or not addicts were still experiencing symptoms of opiate withdrawal (Brandstätter *et al.* 2001, Study 1). Finally, two experiments manipulated the amount of mental load participants were experiencing by having them perform two tasks at once (Brandstätter *et al.* 2001). Consistent with the idea that implementation intentions do not require much in the way of cognitive resources, the benefits of if–then plans on task performance did not compromise performance on a secondary task (Study 3) and did not show evidence of task interference even when the task was very difficult (Study 4).

Efficiency is usually construed in terms of the cognitive demands that are placed on participants (e.g. Bargh 1992). However, Webb and Sheeran (2003) also wished to examine how effective were implementation intentions in promoting goal achievement when people's overall capacity for self-control (i.e. 'willpower') was diminished. Their experiment drew upon Baumeister and colleagues' research on 'ego-depletion' (e.g. Baumeister *et al.* 1998; see Muraven and Baumeister 2000, for a review). Ego-depletion refers to the temporary depletion of self-regulatory capacity brought about by an initial act of self-control. For example, Baumeister *et al.* (1998, Experiment 1) showed that participants who had to eat radishes instead of tempting chocolate during an initial task persisted for less time on a subsequent unsolvable puzzle task than did participants who did not have to exert self-control during the initial task (participants were allowed to eat the chocolate). Webb and Sheeran (2003, Experiment 2) induced ego-depletion by asking participants to perform a dual balance-and-maths task that required considerable self-control (or not). Participants then either formed or did not form an implementation intention in relation to a subsequent Stroop colour-naming task. Consistent with previous research, ego-depleted participants performed worse on the Stroop task than did non-depleted controls. However, the effect of ego-depletion was eliminated when participants had formed implementation intentions. Participants who formed if–then plans were as fast and accurate in their Stroop performance as were participants who had not been ego-depleted. These findings are consistent with the idea that implementation intentions are 'efficient' in terms of people's willpower. Even when participants' capacity for self-control was substantially diminished, forming an implementation intention still benefited task performance: 'Ego-fatigo'[1] is no barrier to implementation intention effects.

The third feature of automaticity relevant to the operation of implementation intentions concerns *lack of awareness*. Two aspects of this feature have been investigated, one related to the anticipated situation and the other related to the underlying goal intention. Bayer *et al.* (2002) obtained evidence that awareness of the specified cue is not required for implementation intention effects. Study 1 used a retaliation paradigm wherein participants who had been insulted by an experimenter during an initial study were encouraged to form a goal intention to complain to the rude experimenter. In addition, a subset of participants formed implementation intentions ('As soon as I see this person again, I'll tell her what an unfriendly person she is!'). In a second ostensibly unrelated study, participants had to read a series of positive and negative adjectives used to describe people as quickly as possible. However, 100 milliseconds before each adjective, either the face of the unfriendly experimenter or a neutral face was presented subliminally (participants were not consciously aware of the presentation because the face was pattern masked and appeared for only 10 milliseconds). Findings indicated that participants who formed implementation intentions to tell the unfriendly experimenter what they thought of her exhibited slower responses to positive adjectives and faster responses to negative adjectives following subliminal presentation of a picture of the unfriendly experimenter compared to the neutral face. These findings were not obtained among participants who only formed goal intentions or a second control group who had not been insulted. Thus, awareness of the critical cue is not needed for that specified situation directly to elicit cognitive responses that are consistent with the intended action. Moreover, Bayer *et al.*'s (2002) second study went beyond the activation of relevant cognitive responses, and demonstrated that the specified behavioural responses were initiated even though participants were not aware of the critical situation. Participants who formed an implementation intention to respond especially quickly to triangles in a classification task involving geometric figures showed enhanced performance following subliminal presentation of a triangle but not following subliminal presentation of another symbol.

Sheeran *et al.* (2005, Study 2) examined whether participants need be consciously aware of the goal underlying implementation intentions. Participants were given the conscious task goal to solve a series of puzzles as accurately as possible and they formed either an implementation intention to solve the puzzles quickly (relevant implementation intention condition) or they formed an irrelevant implementation intention. In addition, the goal to respond quickly was primed outside participants' awareness (using a word-recognition task that contained words related to being quick such as 'fast' and 'rapid', cf. Bargh *et al.* 2001), or a neutral goal was primed. Debriefing indicated that participants were not aware of the situational activation of the goal to respond quickly; participants did not recognize a theme to the words in the priming task, nor did they believe that the priming task could have affected their performance on the puzzles. However, despite this lack of awareness of the respective goal, implementation intentions effects were contingent upon the presence of that goal. There was a significant interaction effect on how quickly the puzzles were solved such that solution times were fastest when participants had been primed with the goal to respond quickly and had formed the relevant implementation intention to respond quickly. Participants did not have to be consciously aware of the superordinate goal intention for implementation intentions to affect behavioural performance. In sum, these findings indicate that action initiation by implementation intentions is immediate, efficient, and does not require conscious intent. Forming an if–then plan automates the specified goal-directed response.

2.3 Implementation intentions and overcoming volitional problems in goal pursuit

When people have only formed goal intentions, inadequate activation or elaboration of those intentions can generate volitional problems that undermine goal pursuit – and give rise to inclined abstainers rather than inclined actors. However, these problems can be overcome by the enhanced cue accessibility and automaticity of action initiation engendered by implementation intentions. Forming an implementation intention promotes goal achievement because the person is perceptually ready to encounter the situational cues specified in the if-component of the plan, and because these cues evoke the specified *then* response swiftly and without the need for conscious awareness or effort.

2.3.1 Problems of intention elaboration
Forming an implementation intention elaborates a goal intention because if–then plans specify the behaviour that one will perform in the service of the goal and the situational context in which one will perform it. Whereas the person who has only formed a goal intention still has to identify the specific action(s) that will be effective in achieving their goal *and* identify a good opportunity in which to enact it, all of this work is finished when the person has formed an implementation intention: the plan specifies the *when*, *where*, and *how* of goal achievement in advance. This means that good opportunities to initiate a behaviour that leads to goal attainment are recognized swiftly and precisely, rather than missed. Moreover, encountering a good opportunity instigates action in an immediate and effortless fashion instead of generating deliberation about what behaviour one should perform and/or the need to energize oneself to perform it.

2.3.2 Problems of intention activation
Implementation intentions also help to circumvent problems associated with the activation level of the superordinate goal intention. This is because if–then plans delegate control of behaviour to specified situational cues that serve to elicit action directly. People do not have to devote conscious efforts to being watchful for the critical situation or to remembering their goal intention; the specified cues attract and focus attention (e.g. Gollwitzer *et al.* 2002b; Webb and Sheeran 2004a) even when the goal is not available to conscious awareness (Sheeran *et al.* 2005). This contrasts with the predicament of the person who has only formed goal intentions who must maintain the activation level of the intention in the face of multiple and often competing goals (and is vulnerable to prospective memory failure and goal reprioritization). Although recent research indicates that constructs such as anticipated regret (e.g. Abraham and Sheeran 2003) and temporal stability of intention (e.g. Conner *et al.* 2000; Sheeran and Abraham 2003; see Sheeran 2002 and Cooke and Sheeran 2004 for reviews) provide reliable moderation of the intention–behaviour relation, studies to date suggest little that the person could *deliberately* or strategically do to maintain the activation level of his/her intention (over and above cognitive rehearsal of that self-instruction and/or deployment of mnemonic devices such as diaries or knotted handkerchiefs).

Interestingly, however, recent research has explicitly tested whether implementation intentions can be used to help people overcome contextual threats that usually undermine intention activation and obstruct goal achievement. Three particular contextual threats warrant discussion, namely, situational priming of goals that are antithetical to focal goal pursuit, the presence of attractive distractions, and detrimental self-states such as tiredness or boredom. Sheeran and Webb (2003) tested whether forming an implementation intention to respond quickly to a critical target in a lexical decision task could withstand non-conscious activation of the antithetical goal of responding slowly. Findings showed that whereas performance on non-critical targets was significantly affected by the priming procedure (i.e. participants who had been primed with slowness responded more slowly to non-critical targets than did control participants), the prime had no impact on targets specified in participants' implementation intentions. Equivalent findings were obtained by Gollwitzer (1998) in two studies. The first study showed that participants who had only formed goal intentions in relation to a focal task were susceptible to priming of the goal of cooperation (the prime caused participants to spend time away from the task being helpful). However, when participants had formed an implementation intention in relation to task performance, goal priming had no impact on the amount of time spent helping another person. The second study showed that forming an implementation intention to drive both quickly and accurately overcame situational activation of the goal of 'moving fast' on speed and error rate in a driving simulator. Thus, implementation intentions may be used to offset the impact of situations that activate task-inhibiting or alternative goals – the strategic automaticity of if–then plans can overcome the automatic activation of antithetical goals.

Gollwitzer and Schaal (1998) examined whether implementation intentions could overcome the impact of attractive distractions on the time it took to solve boring arithmetic problems. The arithmetic problems were presented on a computer upon which was mounted a video monitor that played award-winning commercials at particular intervals. All of the participants formed goal intentions to deal with the distractions; in addition, subsets of participants formed implementation intentions either to concentrate on the maths task whenever the commercials were playing (task-facilitating plan) or to ignore the commercials when they played (temptation-inhibiting plan). Inspection of the mean time needed to solve each problem revealed that the temptation-inhibiting implementation intention, in particular, was very effective in overcoming the detrimental effects of distraction. Similar findings were obtained in a study by Milne and Sheeran (2003) that examined the impact of tiredness and boredom on task persistence. Participants worked on a very tedious task that involved clicking a computer mouse each time a circle did not illuminate in sequence. Participants worked on this task for 20 minutes under three conditions; no implementation intention (control), a task-facilitating implementation intention ('When I feel bored or tired, then I will get on with my work'), or a temptation-inhibiting implementation intention ('When I feel bored or tired, then I will ignore it'). Persistence was indexed by the time it took participants to miss two sequences in a row. Findings indicated that participants who formed temptation-inhibiting plans persisted for almost the full 20 minutes on average, whereas control and task-facilitating participants both persisted for only 15 minutes.

In sum, there is good evidence that implementation intentions provide an effective strategy for overcoming contextual threats to intention activation that may undermine the realization of one's goal intentions. If–then plans prove useful (a) whether the threat is within, or outside, conscious awareness and (b) whether the threat resides in the environment or is an internal self-state.

3 Summary of research

3.1 Meta-analytic reviews

Because implementation intentions facilitate identification of good opportunities to act, and initiate action automatically when those opportunities are encountered, forming an implementation intention should make it more likely that decisions become a reality compared to only forming a goal intention. The overall impact of implementation intentions on behavioural performance and goal achievement has been tested in three meta-analyses (Koestner *et al.* 2002; Sheeran 2002; Gollwitzer and Sheeran 2003). The effect size estimate used in each case was d_+ which is the sample-weighted difference between means for an implementation intention condition versus a control condition divided by the within-group standard deviations. According to Cohen's (1992) power primer, $d_+ = 0.20$ should be considered a 'small' effect size, $d_+ = 0.50$ is a 'medium' effect size, whereas $d_+ = 0.80$ is a 'large' effect size (these values equate to sample-weighted average correlations of 0.10, 0.30, and 0.50, respectively). Figure 7.1 presents the effect sizes obtained in the three reviews.

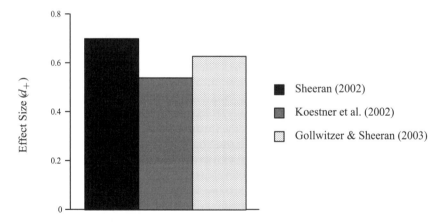

Figure 7.1 Effect sizes in three meta-analyses of the impact of implementation intentions on goal achievement

Sheeran (2002) meta-analysed the first 15 studies of implementation intentions (n = 1611) and obtained an effect size of medium-to-large magnitude, $d_+ = 0.70$. Koestner *et al.* (2002) reviewed 13 studies (n = 826) and obtained $d_+ = 0.54$. However, the most comprehensive review was conducted by Gollwitzer and Sheeran (2003) and involved 85 studies and a total of sample of 8155 participants. This meta-analysis showed that implementation intentions have an effect of medium size on behavioural enactment and goal attainment, $d_+ = 0.63$. Thus, forming an implementation intention makes an important difference to whether or not desired outcomes are obtained compared to the formation of a goal intention on its own.

Several features of Gollwitzer and Sheeran's (2003) analysis serve to underline the efficacy of implementation intentions in promoting goal achievement. First, the review does not suffer from publication bias. Sixty per cent of the studies reviewed were unpublished; moreover, publication status had no impact on the effect size obtained for implementation intentions. Second, 91 per cent of studies involved experimental designs (i.e. random assignment of participants to implementation intention versus control conditions), which increases confidence in the findings. It was also the case that the effect sizes obtained in correlational and experimental studies were equivalent. Third, the composition of the sample did not moderate implementation intention effects. If–then plans were similarly effective in promoting goal achievement among students, members of the general public and people with physical illness. Finally, the efficacy of implementation intentions was not exaggerated by over-reliance on self-report measures of behaviour. In fact, the effect size for implementation intentions increased to $d_+ = 0.72$ in the 52 studies where objective measures of performance were employed. In sum, implementation intentions benefited performance no matter how one looks at the data.

3.2 Narrative review of health behaviours

Relatively little research has used implementation intentions to understand or promote health behaviour change. Only 12 health behaviour studies were published or in press at the time of writing (July 2004). Research to date has examined both health-protective behaviours (exercise, diet, vitamin intake, safety training, and cancer screening) and health-risk behaviours (binge drinking and smoking) and used a variety of samples and measures of behaviour (see Table 7.1). Empirical tests of the benefits of implementation intentions in promoting health behaviours generally have adopted a paradigm wherein all participants complete questionnaire items designed to measure constructs from motivational theories such as the TPB and PMT and are then randomized to conditions where participants complete questions designed to induce implementation intention formation (or they do not complete these questions). Performance of the health behaviour is measured at a later time-point.

3.2.1 Exercise

Three studies examined the impact of implementation intentions on exercise behaviour. Milne *et al.* (2002) randomized n = 248 student participants to three conditions: a no-intervention control group, an intervention based on PMT, and the PMT intervention augmented by implementation intentions. Participants in the implementation intention condition were

Table 7.1   Applications of implementation intentions to health goals

Research area	*Researchers*
Promoting health-protective behaviours	
Exercise	Milne, Orbell, and Sheeran (2002), Prestwich, Lawton, Conner (2003a), Rise, Thompson, and Verplanken (2003)
Diet	Kellar and Abraham (2003), Armitage (2004)
	Verplanken and Faes (1999)
Cancer screening	
Breast self-examination	Orbell, Hodgkins, and Sheeran (1997)
Testicular self-examination	Milne and Sheeran (2002a)
Attendance for breast screening	Steadman, Rutter and Quine (2003)
Attendance for cervical screening	Sheeran and Orbell (2000)
Pill intake	Sheeran and Orbell (1999), Steadman and Quine (2000)
Reducing health-risk behaviours	
Smoking	Higgins and Conner (2003, 2004)
Alcohol consumption	Murgraff, White and Phillips (1996), Webb and Sheeran (2004b)

instructed to complete the following statement: 'During the next week I will partake in at least 20 minutes of vigorous exercise on _____ (day or days) at _____] (time of day) at or in _____ (place)'. Measures of PMT cognitions and behaviour were taken at three time-points over a two-week period. The two PMT groups both showed significant differences in threat appraisal, coping appraisal and goal intention compared to controls following the intervention. However, despite the fact that the PMT intervention-only group exhibited a substantial difference in intention to exercise compared to the control group, there were no differences between the groups in self-reported exercise during the final week of the study. In contrast, participants who had received the PMT intervention and had formed an implementation intention exercised significantly more often compared to both the PMT-only and control groups – even though intention scores among this group were the same as the PMT-only condition. Differences between conditions were much more dramatic when the exercise data were analysed in terms of the percentage of participants who exercised at least once. Whereas only 38 per cent of the control group and 35 per cent of the PMT-only group exercised at least once, fully 91 per cent of participants who formed if–then plans did so.

Prestwich *et al.* (2003a) conducted a similar study but with two important refinements. First, their study involved a full 2 (motivational intervention: decision balance sheet vs control) × 2 (implementation intentions: formed vs not formed) design. Second, Prestwich *et al.* employed an objective measure of fitness (average heart rate while jogging over a fixed distance) as well as two self-reports of exercise behaviour (frequency and duration). The motivational intervention involved completing a decision balance sheet that reflected anticipated gains and losses to self and others that would accrue from increasing exercise by two sessions per week. The implementation intention manipulation asked participants to specify the time, place and type of exercise they would undertake. Findings from the behavioural follow-up taken two weeks post-baseline indicated that participants who had both completed the decision balance sheet and formed an implementation intention exhibited significantly greater change in frequency of exercise, duration of exercise, and fitness level compared to controls (see also Rise *et al.* 2003, for a similar conclusion).

3.2.2 Diet

Verplanken and Faes (1999) conducted the first test of the efficacy of implementation intentions in promoting a healthy diet. Student participants (n = 100) were asked to form implementation intentions to eat healthily on one particular day in the next five days (i.e. plan exactly what they would eat and drink during the specified day). Participants in the control condition did not form this plan. All of the participants were asked to keep a diary for five days in which they recorded everything they ate and drank. As expected, ratings by a dietician (who was blind to the purpose of the study) indicated that participants who formed implementation intentions ate significantly more healthily than did participants who had not planned when and how to eat healthily. Kellar and Abraham (2003) obtained similar findings with respect to students' recommended daily intake of fruit and vegetables over a one-week period.

Armitage (2004) tested the efficacy of implementation intentions in promoting a low-fat diet among a sample of 264 company employees. A well-validated food frequency index was used to assess behaviour over a one-month period (Margetts *et al.* 1989). Participants in the experimental (implementation intention) group received the following instruction at the end of a TPB questionnaire about eating a low-fat diet: 'We want you to plan to eat a low-fat diet during the next month. You are free to choose *how* you will do this, but we want you to formulate your plans in as much detail as possible. Pay particular attention to the situations in which you will implement these plans.' (Blank lines were presented so that participants could write in their plans.) The food frequency measure was used to compute three indices of dietary intake: total fat intake, saturated fat intake, and fat intake as a proportion of total energy intake. Within-participants analyses indicated that participants who formed implementation intentions showed significant reductions in fat intake at follow-up compared to baseline according to all three indices. Participants who had not formed implementation intentions, on the other hand, exhibited no change over the one-month period. Moreover, between-participants analyses indicated that although there were no differences between the groups at baseline, the diet of participants in the experimental group was significantly lower in fat (according to all three indices) than was the diet of control participants. These findings indicate that a simple instruction to form an implementation intention can be effective in promoting a healthy diet among representative samples.

Sheeran and Milne (2002) took a different approach to using implementation intentions to promote healthy eating. Instead of asking participants to plan what healthy foods they would eat, participants were asked to halve their consumption of an unhealthy snack food by planning to consume the foodstuff only on particular occasions. The idea was that participants would probably be unwilling to try to eliminate the foodstuff from their diet and, therefore, an effectual implementation intention would need to respect participants' pre-commitment to indulgence. All of the participants nominated foodstuffs (e.g. burgers, chips, chocolate) and completed a TPB questionnaire concerning their beliefs about halving their consumption of the nominated foodstuff over the following week; in addition, a subset formed implementation intentions. Findings from two studies indicated that forming if–then plans to engage in moderate indulgence significantly reduced self-reported snack food consumption over a one-week period.

3.2.3 *Cancer screening*
The first test of the efficacy of implementation intentions in promoting health-protective behaviour concerned breast self-examination (BSE; Orbell *et al.* 1997). Orbell *et al.* asked one-half of their sample (n = 155) to specify when and where they would perform a BSE in the next month; the other half did not form an if–then plan. Findings indicated that implementation intention participants were significantly more likely to perform an exam than were control participants (rates were 64 per cent and 14 per cent, respectively). This group difference was even greater when data from participants with strong goal intentions were analysed separately (n = 33); here 100 per cent of participants who formed implementation intentions conducted a BSE compared to just 53 per cent of the control participants.

Two studies investigated whether implementation intentions could be used to increase attendance at cancer screening appointments provided by the health service. Sheeran and Orbell (2000) asked half of their sample (n = 114) to form an implementation intention that specified when, where and how they would make an appointment to attend for cervical cancer screening. Screening attendance was determined from medical records three months later. Findings indicated that whereas 68 per cent of the women who did not form an implementation intention attended, this figure rose to 92 per cent among women who formed if–then plans. Steadman *et al.* (2004) examined attendance at breast screening (mammography) clinics (n = 1894). Participants were randomly allocated to one of three conditions: (a) an intervention condition where participants were asked to form implementation intentions designed to overcome three barriers to attendance (i.e. arranging time off work, travelling to the clinic, or changing the appointment), (b) a no-intervention control condition, and (c) a second control condition that did not receive a questionnaire. Medical records indicated that the intervention had no overall impact on attendance rates; rates were approximately 80 per cent in all three groups. However, when findings were analysed separately for participants who had completed the section of the questionnaires designed to induce implementation intentions (i.e. participants who had formed if–then plans), the rate increased from 80 per cent to 92–96 per cent depending on the barrier for which the implementation intention was formed.

3.2.4 Pill intake

Three studies examined regular intake of vitamin pills among college students as a behavioural analogue for medication adherence. Sheeran and Orbell (1999, Study 1) gave participants bottles of vitamin pills and asked them to complete questionnaires based on the TPB about taking vitamins. The implementation intention manipulation asked participants to write down when and where they would take a pill each day. Behaviour was measured by self-report and pill count at 10 days and three weeks postbaseline. Findings indicated that implementation intentions had no discernible impact on the number of missed pills at 10 days – consistent with the idea that motivation can satisfactorily promote behaviour in the short term. However, by three weeks, participants who had formed implementation intentions missed significantly fewer pills than did controls. A second study confirmed the significance of this difference between implementation intention and control groups at three weeks. Moreover, this finding was replicated in an independent study (Steadman and Quine 2000). These results suggest that implementation intentions represent a promising means of helping people with physical illness to take their medication regularly and on time.

3.2.5 Binge drinking

Murgraff *et al.* (1996) used implementation intentions to try to reduce binge drinking among college students. Participants were presented with six possible statements that they could use to refuse a drink (e.g. 'No thanks. I do not want to get drunk. I would rather have just a few tonight') and were asked to choose which one they would use. In addition, participants were asked to 'specify the appropriate time and place in which [their] chosen response would be executed'. Compared to a control group who did not form this plan, the experimental group reported drinking significantly less frequently and showed a significantly greater reduction in drinking frequency over a two-week period. Webb and Sheeran (2004b) obtained equivalent findings in a study that used accessibility of drinking behaviour (assessed by response latencies to the action word *drinking* in a verb verification task) as the dependent variable. Participants formed an implementation intention to distract themselves every time they thought about drinking (or did not). In addition, the goal of socializing was activated by asking participants questions about their social lives or an irrelevant goal was activated. Despite the fact that participants were unaware of the activation of the goal and did not believe goal activation could have influenced their performance on the verb verification task, findings indicated that implementation intentions significantly reduced mental readiness to drink when participants had been primed with the goal to socialize.

3.2.6 Smoking

Two studies have examined the power of implementation intentions to prevent smoking initiation in adolescents. A pilot study by Higgins and Conner (2003) examined smoking initiation over an eight-week period. The experimental group formed an implementation intention about how to refuse an offer of a cigarette while the control group formed an implementation intention in relation to schoolwork. Both groups received a persuasive message against smoking. Results indicated that none of the non-smokers (0 per cent) in the experimental condition (n = 51) went on to try smoking during the eight weeks whereas 6 per cent of non-smokers in the control condition (n = 53), tried smoking in this period. Although these findings are suggestive, the modest sample size precluded statistically significant differences. Higgins and Conner (2004) used a similar design to examine smoking initiation in a larger sample over a period of two years. Adolescents completed questionnaires, read a persuasive message against smoking, and formed an implementation intention to avoid smoking or complete their schoolwork every six months. Findings showed lower levels of self-reported and objectively measured smoking in the relevant implementation intention group across time.

4 Developments

The first question that should be asked about the concept of implementation intentions is: *do* implementation intentions facilitate the translation of intentions into action? Findings from studies in social and health psychology and meta-analyses of those studies would seem to indicate that the answer to this first question is 'yes'. Strategic automatization of goal-directed responses appears to be of considerable benefit in helping people achieve intended performances and outcomes. However, two other questions also should be asked of the concept in order to gain a more complete understanding of how implementation intentions can be used to promote health behaviours, namely, *why* do implementation intentions facilitate translation of intentions into action, and *when* do implementation intentions facilitate translation of intentions into action? Answers to these questions can be gleaned from recent research on mediators and moderators of implementation intention effects, respectively.

4.2 Mediators of implementation intention effects

Two processes are thought to explain the efficacy of forming if–then plans in improving the likelihood of goal attainment compared to only forming a respective goal intention (Gollwitzer, 1993, 1996, 1999; see Section 2). First, implementation intentions promote identification of good opportunities to act. This is supported by demonstrations that implementation intentions increase the accessibility of situational cues (specified in the *if* component of the plan) and that detection of, and attention to, the critical situation is thereby facilitated (Aarts *et al.* 1999; Gollwitzer *et al.* 2002b; Webb and Sheeran 2004a). Second, implementation intentions automate the execution of the goal-directed response (specified in the *then* component of the plan). This is supported by demonstrations that initiation of behaviour in the presence of the critical situation is immediate, efficient, and does not require conscious awareness (Gollwitzer and Brandstätter 1997; Lengfelder and Gollwitzer 2001; Brandstätter *et al.* 2001; Bayer *et al.* 2002; Webb and Sheeran, 2004a, Sheeran *et al.* 2005). The mere formation of a goal intention is not sufficient to produce these effects – the person still has to identify appropriate opportunities and goal-directed behaviours and then mobilize the self to act. Action control in this mode is slow by comparison and requires conscious attention and effort.

Implementation intentions seem to operate in a similar manner to habits and, in fact, the automaticity of implementation intention effects is echoed by demonstrations that habitual behaviour is immediate, efficient, and occurs outside awareness (Aarts and Dijksterhuis 2000a, 2000b; Sheeran *et al.* in press). There are also important parallels between implementation intentions and habits in terms of their underlying mechanism. In both cases, strong associations have developed between particular situational cues and particular goal-directed responses. However, the origins of these strong associations are different. In the case of habits, frequent and consistent performance of a behaviour in a particular context means that strong links develop between the context and the behaviour. In the case of implementation intentions, the same linkage is achieved by getting participants to form this association mentally in an act of will. Hence, the automaticity of implementation intentions is *strategic* and serves the person's current goals whereas the automaticity in habits may be counter-intentional (Gollwitzer and Schaal 1998; Sheeran *et al.* 2005).

Similar to habits, there are two potential mediators of the implementation intention–behaviour relation, namely, the accessibility of the situational cues (opportunities) and the strength of the cue–response associations (opportunity–action links). To demonstrate mediation, the following four conditions need to be satisfied (Baron and Kenny 1986; Kenny *et al.* 1998): first, participants who form implementation intentions should exhibit greater accessibility of situational cues and cue–behaviour associations compared to participants who only form goal intentions. Second, implementation intentions should affect goal achievement. Third, the proposed mediators should be associated with goal achievement. Finally, in a simultaneous regression, the impact of implementation intentions on goal achievement should be attenuated whereas the effect of cue accessibility and cue–behaviour associative strength should remain significant.

The following two studies have tested mediation. Aarts *et al.* (1999) tested whether participants who formed an implementation intention in relation to collecting a coupon later in the experiment showed greater accessibility of situational cues relevant to the location of the room where the coupon should be collected (i.e. faster responses to cues in a lexical decision task). Consistent with predictions, words related to the critical situation (e.g. 'corridor') were more accessible among participants who formed if–then plans (see Section 2.2.1). Importantly, however, Aarts *et al.* also tested whether or not participants collected the coupon. Two aspects of the procedure made collection difficult: (a) collection of the coupon was delayed while participants completed other tasks (such as the lexical decision task) which meant that participants could forget about coupon collection, and (b) participants were instructed to hurry to a location to complete another task in a manner that meant participants had to interrupt pursuit of this goal in order to go to the room where the coupon was located. These procedures seemed to have been effective in obstructing goal achievement. Whereas only 50 per cent of controls who had only formed goal intentions collected a coupon, 80 per cent of participants who formed implementation intentions did so. Thus, implementation intentions affected both cue accessibility (the mediator) and goal achievement. Further analyses indicated that there was a strong relationship between cue accessibility and whether or not participants collected the coupon. Finally, a simultaneous regression of goal achievement on both the mediator and condition indicated that the beta for cue accessibility was significant whereas the effect of forming an implementation intention was reduced to non-significance. In sum, Aarts *et al.*'s (1999) study provides good evidence that the accessibility of situational cues mediates (explains) the impact of implementation intentions on goal achievement.

However, Aarts *et al.*'s experiment did not test the potential mediating role of the strength of cue–response associations. These associations constitute a key parallel between how implementation intentions operate and how habits operate (i.e. situational activation of goal-directed behaviours). Webb and Sheeran (2004c) therefore conducted a replication and refinement of Aarts *et al.* (1999) to provide a simultaneous test of the importance of the accessibility of situational cues and the strength of cue–behaviour links in mediating action control by implementation intentions. The study replicated the key features of the coupon collection paradigm; the main innovation was using a sequential priming procedure in the lexical decision task. This procedure involved the following sequence. Participants were presented with a fixation dot for 1500 milliseconds followed by a priming word for 17 milliseconds. Then a mask was presented immediately to prevent participants from recognizing the priming word. Finally, the target word was presented (participants responded 'yes' or 'no' to whether the target was a word using a button box). The priming words were related to the location of the coupon (e.g. 'corridor', 'right') or were matched neutral words. The target words were the specified behaviour ('collect'), an unrelated behaviour ('confirm'), the location words (cues), and filler words. In this way, it was possible to determine the impact of implementation intentions on both cue accessibility (response latencies to *neutral prime-location cue* targets) and the strength of cue–behaviour links (response latencies to *location prime-specified behaviour* targets) and all other prime-target combinations.

Findings showed, first, that participants who formed implementation intentions were significantly more likely to collect the coupon than were participants who only formed goal intentions (64 per cent versus 39 per cent). Second, participants who formed if–then plans exhibited faster responses both to specified situational cues and to the specified behaviour primed by the respective critical situations in the lexical decision task compared to control participants (there were no differences between the groups on any of the other targets). Third, accessibility of situational cues and the strength of cue–response associations were both strongly associated with coupon collection. Finally, simultaneous regression analyses showed that cue accessibility and cue–behaviour associative strength both reduced the effect of forming implementation intentions on behaviour to non-significance. Thus, both heightened accessibility of the specified opportunity and strong opportunity–action links mediated the impact of if–then plans on coupon collection. These findings support theoretical predictions about the processes underlying action control by implementation intention (Gollwitzer 1993), and provide the best evidence to date that enhanced identification of critical cues and automated execution of behaviour are the mechanisms by which implementation intentions promote goal achievement.

Webb and Sheeran's (2004c) findings also serve to undermine the idea that implementation intention effects can be explained in terms of motivational processes. In fact, there are four lines of evidence that indicate that goal intentions, self-efficacy or other motivational constructs are not responsible for this mode of action control. First, there is no empirical support for the idea that forming if–then plans increases goal intentions or self-efficacy/perceived behavioural control. Several studies measured motivational variables specified by the TPB or PMT both prior to, and after, the formation of an implementation intention – either before the measure of behaviour (Sheeran and Orbell 1999) or at the same time as the measure of behaviour (Orbell *et al.* 1997; Milne *et al.* 2002; Sheeran *et al.* in press). Regardless of when the second measurement of motivation was taken, there were no differences in goal intentions or other motivational constructs either within the implementation intention group or between the implementation intention and control groups. Second, implementation intentions significantly affected the likelihood of goal achievement even when almost all of the participants scored at the top of the scale measuring goal intentions (e.g. Verplanken and Faes 1999; Sheeran and Orbell 2000). Clearly, these findings would be impossible if goal intentions and implementation intentions referred to the same concept. Third, it is well established that the relationship between goal intentions and behaviour is substantially reduced when the time interval between the measurement of intentions and behaviour increases. For example, a meta-analysis by Sheeran and Orbell (1998) found that the correlation between intention and condom use was significantly smaller when the time interval was less than versus greater than one month (rs were 0.33 and 0.44, respectively). However, Sheeran and Silverman (2003) found no difference in the effectiveness of implementation intentions whether or not the specified behaviour was to be performed within or after one month. Indeed, Sheeran and Orbell (1999, Study 1) found that the effectiveness of implementation intentions increased over time while Milne and Sheeran (2002a) showed significant implementation intention effects after one year. Thus, implementation intentions do not follow the temporal trajectory of goal intention effects. Finally, a reanalysis of data from Webb and Sheeran (2003, Experiment 1) indicated that participants who formed implementation intentions exhibited greater task persistence than ego-depleted participants even though both groups had equivalent low scores on the 'Reduced Motivation' subscale of the Multidimensional Fatigue Inventory (MFI-20; Smets *et al.* 1995). In sum, motivation is not the mechanism by which implementation intentions promote goal achievement. Instead, as Webb and Sheeran (2004c) have shown, accessibility of situational cues and the strength of cue–response links are the explanatory processes.

4.2 Moderators of implementation intention effects

Several factors are likely to determine how strongly implementation intentions affect goal achievement. The first key moderator of implementation intentions effects concerns the presence of a self-regulatory problem. If enacting a behaviour is easy and there are few obstacles to performance, then motivational factors (e.g. goal intentions, self-efficacy) should satisfactorily promote action; little additional benefit can be obtained from forming an implementation intention. A good example is Webb and Sheeran's (2003, Experiment 2) analysis of the impact of ego-depletion and implementation intention formation on Stroop performance. Webb and Sheeran found that implementation intentions had a strong effect on task speed and accuracy when participants were ego-depleted. However, when participants were not ego-depleted, implementation intentions did not affect performance – because participants possessed sufficient self-regulatory capacity to perform the task well (see also Lengfelder and Gollwitzer 2001). Similarly, Prestwich *et al.* (2003b, Study 2) found that implementation intentions were least effective in promoting performance among participants who scored high on conscientiousness as a personality trait. Finally, Gollwitzer and Brändstatter (1997, Study 1) used participants' ratings to divide goals into 'easy' versus 'difficult' categories and found that implementation intentions only affected the achievement of difficult goals. These findings all seem to indicate that implementation intention effects are only likely to emerge when the focal behaviour presents a volitional challenge. However, these findings also imply that implementation intentions are most likely to benefit behavioural performance when the task is difficult or when people have difficulty regulating their behaviour.

A second important moderator of action control by implementation intentions is the activation and the strength of the superordinate goal intention. Goal intentions should affect the relationship between if–then plans and goal achievement for three reasons. First, goal intentions are likely to determine the availability, accessibility and elaboration of situational cues and cue–behaviour associations that underlie action control by implementation intentions. Availability will be affected because people who do not intend to perform a health behaviour are unlikely to form an implementation intention that promotes behavioural performance even when they are asked to do so; hence, the relevant opportunity and opportunity–action link will not be present or *available* in memory (cf. Higgins 1996). This availability hypothesis is supported by a reanalysis of Sheeran and Silverman (2003) that showed that 89 per cent of participants who did not intend to go to a health and safety training session failed to formulate an implementation intention despite being instructed to do so. Accessibility of situational cues and cue–behaviour associations is likely to be affected because intention strength should influence how well people encode both the specified situational cue and the link between the cue and response. Depth of encoding of the specified cue and cue–behaviour association should affect the accessibility of these constructs and, thereby, the strength of implementation intention effects. Finally, goal intentions should affect the degree of elaboration of the implementation intention because people with strong goal intentions are likely to give greater time and consideration to ensuring that the specified opportunity is a good one and to ensuring that the response will be effective in achieving the superordinate goal. Consistent with this idea, Sheeran and Armitage (2003) found that the strength of respective goal intentions predicted how well specified were participants' implementation intentions with respect to the *when, where*, and *how* of goal achievement while Rise *et al.* (2003) demonstrated that the degree of specification in the implementation intention predicted the extent to which people performed the target behaviour.

The second reason for believing that action control by implementation intentions depends upon activated and strong goal intentions derives from Aarts and Dijksterhuis's (2000a, 2000b) demonstrations that the cue–response associations that characterize the operation of habits depend upon the activation of a relevant goal. Their studies showed that the automaticity in travel habits was not a mechanistic elicitation of behaviour in the presence of relevant environmental cues. Rather, automaticity of habitual responding was only observed when participants had been primed with the goal to travel (see also Sheeran *et al.* in press). Given the strong parallels between implementation intentions and habits, there are, therefore, good grounds for believing that the situational cues specified in implementation intentions will only elicit goal-directed behaviour as long as the goal that the behaviour serves is activated and strong, i.e. the automaticity in if–then plans should be goal-dependent (cf. Bargh, 1992, 1994).

This brings up the third reason why goal intentions are important. Implementation intention effects could be dysfunctional if this mode of action control did not respect people's goal intentions in a flexible manner. For example, forming an implementation intention to be witty at specified opportunities during a future conversation could prove socially disastrous if one stuck to the plan despite learning that a tragedy has befallen one's companion. Clearly, for implementation intentions to be functional, this form of planning must be able to account for the state (activation, strength) of the respective goal intention.

In fact, empirical findings indicate that strong effects of implementation intentions are contingent upon the presence of strong superordinate goal intentions. For example, Orbell *et al.*'s (1997) study of BSE indicated that implementation intentions were especially effective in promoting performance among participants with positive intentions who formed if–then plans compared to all participants who formed if–then plans (rates were 100 per cent vs 64 per cent, respectively). Sheeran *et al.* (2005) conducted formal moderator analyses and found significant interactions between intention strength and implementation intentions in two studies. Simple slopes analyses for high, medium, and low levels of goal intentions indicated that implementation intentions only affected attendance at workplace health and safety training sessions or the amount of independent study students undertook when participants' goal intentions strongly favoured the behavioural performance. Similarly, Koestner *et al.* (2002) obtained evidence consistent with the idea that implementations effects were especially effective when participants' goal intentions were more self-concordant compared to less self-concordant.

Two studies either activated or deactivated the respective goal intention in order to test the goal-dependency of implementation intentions. An unpublished study by Seehausen, Bayer and Gollwitzer (1994, cited in Gollwitzer 1996) tested participants' memory for situational cues specified in their implementation intentions after a short (15 minutes), or long (48 hours) delay. Findings showed good recall for the specified cues at both follow-ups – consistent with the idea that implementation intentions heighten the accessibility of those cues (Gollwitzer 1993). However, participants who were told that the goal intention would no longer have to be implemented (because other participants had supposedly taken on the task) showed poorer recall after the short delay and virtually no recall after 48 hours. Thus, the effect of implementation intentions on cue accessibility was no longer evident when the goal intention had been abolished by the experimenter. Sheeran *et al.* (in press, Study 2) obtained equivalent findings regarding the importance of goal activation using an objective measure of performance on a puzzle task. Formation of an implementation intention to respond quickly only affected response times when the goal to respond quickly had been activated by a priming procedure. When the conscious task goal to be accurate was active, implementation intentions had no impact on speed of performance. In sum, the state of the respective superordinate goal intention is an important moderator of action control by implementation intentions. Implementation intentions do not involve mechanistic elicitation of action by environmental cues – the superordinate goal must be activated and strong to engender automation of goal-directed responses. If–then plans, therefore, adjust to the goal adaptations that people make in response to changing environmental circumstances. In this way, implementation intentions afford flexible, as well as tenacious, goal pursuit.

A third potential moderator of implementation intention effects is degree of implementation intention formation. Degree of implementation intention formation refers to processes related to formulating one's if–then plans that serve to enhance the accessibility of situational cues and the strength of cue–response links – and should thereby fortify implementation intention effects. Several factors relevant to this idea have been found to moderate the implementation intention–action relation. For example, Gollwitzer *et al.* (2002a) manipulated the strength of participants' commitment to their implementation intention by providing feedback from extensive personality tests that supposedly indicated that participants would benefit from sticking closely to their plans (high commitment) or would benefit from not rigidly adhering to the plan (low commitment). Findings from a cued recall paradigm indicated that the high-commitment group had superior memory for selected opportunities compared to the low-commitment group. Prestwich *et al.* (2003b) examined the efficacy of augmenting implementation intentions with (a) a positive statement about the benefits of planning, (b) cognitive rehearsal of the plan, or (c) the use of environmental cues (a reminder note). Findings indicated that cognitive rehearsal and environmental cues both enhanced the behavioural impact of implementation intentions compared to the positive statement manipulation. Milne and Sheeran (2002b) obtained evidence that rehearsal of the link between the specified cue and the specified response may be crucial. Participants who were instructed to concentrate on the cue–behaviour link when formulating their plan were much more likely to visit a target website than were participants who wrote their implementation intention on a reminder note and put it in a prominent place at home (rates were 87 per cent versus 40 per cent, respectively). Thus, although relatively few studies have tested indicators of degree of implementation intention formation, there is evidence that commitment and cognitive rehearsal both moderate the impact of if–then plans on goal achievement.

5 Operationalization of the model

5.1 Preliminary considerations

The paradigm adopted in most applications of implementation intentions to health goals has involved questionnaire measures of TPB/PMT constructs and past behaviour followed by random assignment to an experimental condition that contains questions designed to induce implementation intention formation or to a control condition that does not contain these questions. Of course, random assignment should ensure that participants in both conditions have equivalent previous experience with, and motivation to achieve, the goal. However, an advantage of taking measures of experience and motivation is that randomization checks can be conducted and any differences on these variables can be controlled in statistical analyses. Relatedly, if the behavioural follow-up involves further direct contact with participants then measures of motivational variables could be taken at the same time as the measure of behaviour. These procedures allow researchers to conduct statistical analyses to ensure that the impact of implementation intentions on goal attainment is not attributable to pre-intervention differences in motivation or past behaviour or to potential differences in motivation accruing from the formation of the if–then plan.

Most health psychology studies have involved passive control conditions, i.e. participants in the no-implementation intention group have not been asked to complete questionnaire items of similar content or duration as participants in the experimental and control group. Strictly speaking, this procedure confounds the impact of the experimental manipulation with potential differences in expectancies and attentional demands between conditions. However, it is worth noting that studies that employed active control conditions wherein participants formed implementation intentions about what to do after they have accomplished their goal (e.g. Aarts *et al.* 1999) or formed plans regarding an irrelevant goal (e.g. Sheeran *et al.* 2005) obtained strong implementation intention effects as well. Never-theless, it seems wise to employ an active control condition whenever possible in order to rule out alternative explanations of differences in behavioural performance or attained outcomes.

Not surprisingly, implementation intentions have greater impact on the achievement of health goals when participants complete the relevant section of the questionnaire designed to induce their formation than when parti-cipants omit that section (e.g. Sheeran *et al.* 2003; Steadman *et al.* 2003). Because implementation intention inductions usually ask participants to specify an appropriate opportunity and goal-directed response in an open-ended format, considerable care must be taken to ensure that participants do not skip relevant items. Answering open-ended questions can be per-ceived as onerous when participants have already completed a long ques-tionnaire and have become used to ticking a box to indicate their response. To alleviate this potential problem, some studies have hinted at the benefits of forming an implementation intention in order to get participants to complete the respective section of the questionnaire (e.g. Orbell *et al.* 1997; Sheeran and Orbell 1999; Milne *et al.* 2002; Milne and Sheeran 2002a). Even though this procedure seemed likely to generate expectancies about the impact of planning, interestingly, none of these studies observed sig-nificant effects on subsequent motivation to perform the behaviour. In sum, careful consideration needs be given to features of the overall questionnaire (e.g. length, order) and to the wording and layout of the implementation intention induction to ensure that participants engage with the process of forming an if–then plan.

5.2 The format of implementation intentions

Implementation intentions have the format 'If situation Y occurs, then I will initiate goal-directed behaviour Z!' The importance of using an if–then format in wording the plan was demonstrated by Oettingen, Hönig, and Gollwitzer (2000, Study 3). All participants were provided with diskettes containing four concentration tasks and were asked to perform these tasks on their computers each Wednesday morning for the next four weeks. Participants in the control condition were asked to indicate what time they would perform the task by responding to the statement 'I will perform as many arithmetic tasks as possible each Wednesday at ____ (self-chosen time before noon)'. Participants in the implementation intention condition, on the other hand, indicated their chosen time by responding to the statement 'If it is Wednesday at ____ (self-chosen time before noon), then I will perform as many arithmetic tasks as possible!' The programme on the diskette recorded the time that participants started to work on the task from the clock on participants' computers.

Despite the apparent similarity between the control and implementation intention instructions, the conditional structure of the implementation intention had a dramatic impact on how closely participants performed the task to their intended time: the mean deviation from the intended start time was five times greater in the control condition (8 hours) compared to the implementation intention condition (1.5 hours). These findings indicate that using the defining if–then format in implementation intention inductions is important to ensure strong implementation intention effects.

5.3 A framework for operationalizing implementation intentions in relation to particular volitional problems

Implementation intention inductions invite people to specify a good opportunity to act in the *if* component of the plan and to specify an effective goal-directed response in the *then* component. The assumption is that people do not require a great deal of knowledge or insight to identify effective goal-directed behaviours or suitable moments to initiate that behaviour (Gollwitzer *et al.* 2005). Indeed, problems are likely to arise if opportunities or actions are imposed on the person forming an implementation intention because (a) imposed responses may be negatively evaluated, (b) imposed opportunities may not be perceived as suitable, and (c) the imposition may be resented such that motivation to pursue the goal is reduced or the person does not devote time or attention to formulating the plan; each of these considerations could diminish the impact of implementation intentions on goal pursuit.

It is useful, nonetheless, to draw together operationalizations of implementation intentions used in previous research to develop a broad framework for specifying what opportunities and goal-directed responses in if–then plans may help to overcome particular problems in translating intentions into action. Because it is difficult to anticipate the varieties of goals and associated self-regulatory problems researchers might wish to examine, this framework is not exhaustive. Rather, the framework tries to bring together the contents (opportunities, responses) in implementation intentions that proved useful in overcoming particular volitional problems in previous research (see Sections 1.3 and 2.3; see also Gollwitzer, 1993, 1996, 1999; Sheeran 2002; Gollwitzer *et al.* 2005).

Figure 7.2 presents a schematization of the framework. Decisions about what opportunities and goal-directed responses might be specified in an implementation intention begin with consideration of whether the dependent variable is a goal (a desired outcome that can be achieved by performing a variety of behaviours) or a behaviour (single action) (see Panel A). If the dependent variable is a goal then an effective goal-directed response must be identified. For example, if the goal is to lose weight then one could specify a particular form of exercise (e.g. jogging) as one goal-directed response and/or controlling one's consumption of high-fat food (e.g. pizza) as another goal-directed response. Specifying an effective goal-directed response in an implementation intention is vital to goal attainment because implementation intentions only promote performance of the goal-directed response; if that response is not effective, then by definition, implementation intentions will not promote achievement of the goal. There are good grounds for supposing that if the person jogs at particular intensity and refrains from eating high-fat foods then weight loss will result (cf. Sewacj *et al.* 1980). However, in many domains pilot studies may be needed to identify what responses that are strongly linked to goal attainment should be specified in the then-component of participants' plans.

The next juncture in the framework is whether the goal-directed response is wanted or unwanted, and consequently, whether the volitional issue involves obtaining a wanted response versus controlling an unwanted response. In the example of weight loss, jogging constitutes a wanted response (one wishes to exhibit this response) whereas eating pizza is an unwanted response (one wishes not to exhibit this response). Figure 7.2 shows that obtaining wanted responses and controlling unwanted responses are not entirely separate issues. However, wanted and unwanted responses also embrace distinctive volitional problems that are considered separately in Panels B and C.

The first volitional problem to do with obtaining a wanted response is getting started. Recall that the formation of a goal intention on its own may mean that the person forgets her intention or misses suitable opportunities to act and, therefore, does not initiate the behaviour. The appropriate implementation intention to overcome this problem is an if–then plan to instigate action, i.e. to specify a suitable opportunity to start to perform the behaviour. For example, in order to instigate jogging, the if–then instigation plan might be 'If it is Wednesday at 5.30 p.m., then I will jog home from work'. Studies by Sheeran and Silverman (2003) and Sheeran and Orbell (2000) both employed this type of plan. The implementation intention induction in the former study asked participants to write down the date, time and location of the health and safety training course they would attend (from a list provided) in order to increase attendance. In the latter study, the implementation intention induction invited participants to write down when (day, date, time), where and how (e.g. by telephone) they would make an appointment to attend for cervical cancer screening. Findings indicated

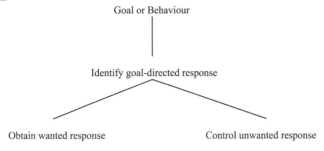

Goal or Behaviour

Identify goal-directed response

Obtain wanted response   Control unwanted response

PANEL B

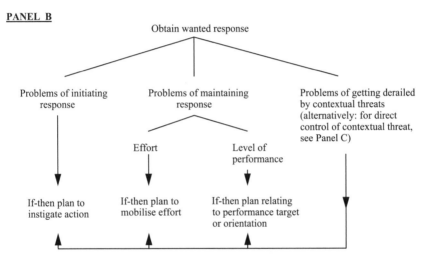

Obtain wanted response

Problems of initiating response

Problems of maintaining response

Problems of getting derailed by contextual threats (alternatively: for direct control of contextual threat, see Panel C)

Effort

Level of performance

If-then plan to instigate action

If-then plan to mobilise effort

If-then plan relating to performance target or orientation

PANEL C

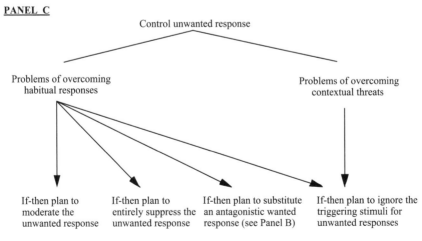

Control unwanted response

Problems of overcoming habitual responses

Problems of overcoming contextual threats

If-then plan to moderate the unwanted response

If-then plan to entirely suppress the unwanted response

If-then plan to substitute an antagonistic wanted response (see Panel B)

If-then plan to ignore the triggering stimuli for unwanted responses

Figure 7.2 A framework for operationalizing implementation intentions in relation to particular volitional problems

that making an appointment was an effective goal-directed response in helping participants attend for cervical cancer screening (all of the women who made an appointment subsequently attended for screening).

A second volitional problem pertaining to wanted responses concerns the tenacity of goal pursuit and difficulties maintaining performance. Response maintenance seems to involve two issues, namely effort and performance orientation. For example, effort must be devoted to jogging, and jogging must be undertaken for particular durations and frequencies for weight loss to accrue. However, people may find it hard to devote requisite effort to the behaviour or orient themselves towards its performance in the manner required to achieve weight loss goals – despite successful initiation of the behaviour. In these instances, the appropriate if–then plans could either mobilize effort (e.g. 'If I feel I am flagging, then I will immediately put more effort into my jogging') or set particular ways of going about performing the behaviour (e.g. 'If I have jogged as far as my home, then I will jog around the block twice more before going inside').

Gollwitzer and Schaal (1998) demonstrated that an if–then plan to mobilize effort ('If a distraction arises, then I will increase my effort at the task at hand') increased performance on boring arithmetic problems. However, this effort mobilization implementation intention only affected task performance when participants had relatively low motivation to solve the problems to begin with; when motivation was high, plans to mobilize effort actually reduced performance – because participants became over-motivated which diminished their ability to solve the problems (see also Milne and Sheeran 2003). Thus, the utility of specifying effort mobilization in the *then* component of an implementation intention depends upon task motivation.

The efficacy of specifying a particular orientation towards a task in one's plan has been demonstrated in several studies. For example, Sheeran *et al.* (2003, Study 3) found that an implementation intention to respond quickly instead of deliberating about one's answer (i.e. 'As soon as I think I have the answer, I will not deliberate but press the corresponding number key as quickly as possible!') increased speed of performance on a puzzle task, without compromising accuracy of responding. Similarly, Endress (2001, cited in Gollwitzer *et al.* 2005) showed that an implementation intention to proceed immediately to generating another use for a household object in a creativity task ('And if I have generated a certain use, then I will immediately turn to generating a further possible use') increased the number of uses generated. Finally, Trötschel and Gollwitzer (2002) demonstrated that supplementing a goal intention to be fair in a cooperation game involving the distribution of a disputed island with an if–then plan about how to respond to specific proposals ('And if I receive a proposal on how to share the island, then I will offer a fair counter proposal!') led to objectively fairer distribution of the island. In sum, specifying the mobilization of effort or task orientations that promote persistence in the *then* component of an implementation intention and specifying appropriate opportunities to deploy these strategies in the *if* component should make it more likely that wanted responses will be pursued tenaciously and maintained over time.

The third volitional problem to do with obtaining wanted responses is ensuring that goal pursuit is not derailed by contextual threats. For example, the goal intention to jog might not be realized because sitting in front of the TV seems more attractive, because there is work that has to be finished, or because one has been invited for a drink with colleagues. That is, jogging may be overwhelmed by personal or environmental influences to do other things. In these instances, successful goal attainment depends upon keeping goal pursuit on track.

Importantly, however, it has been demonstrated that strategically automating the performance of a wanted response can overcome such influences. In other words, the formation of if–then plans to instigate action, mobilize effort or orient oneself towards behavioural performance can overcome contextual threats such as temptations, detrimental self-states and the activation of antithetical goals. Controlling wanted responses in this manner was demonstrated in several of the studies cited above. For example, in Endress's (2001, cited in Gollwitzer *et al.* 2005) study, participants who formed implementation intention to generate uses in the creativity task were not affected by a social loafing manipulation whereas participants who only formed goal intentions were strongly affected by this manipulation. Similarly, participants who formed implementation intentions to behave cooperatively in Trötschel and Gollwitzer's (2002) research were immune to influence by whether the negotiation was loss-framed versus gain-framed, unlike control participants. Finally, studies by Gollwitzer (1998) and Sheeran and Webb (2003) demonstrated that forming an implementation intention with respect to wanted goal-directed responses overcame the impact of primed antagonistic goals that were detrimental to the performance. In sum, strategic automatization of wanted responses can prevent ongoing goal pursuit from being derailed.

The key volitional problem that arises when trying to control an unwanted response such as eating pizza is overcoming habitual responding (see Panel C). A habit involves the automatic activation of a goal and goal-directed response by particular environmental cues and is established through (a) frequent and consistent activation of a particular goal in the presence of those cues, (b) frequent and consistent initiation of a particular action in response to that goal activation, as well as (c) satisfactory reinforcement of both cue–goal and goal–behaviour relations. The problem of overcoming habits is, of course, that habitual responses are reinforced by satisfying experiences – pizza tastes great, improves mood and/or constitutes a treat at the end of the day for many people. In the light of these considerations, the first issue to do with controlling unwanted responses concerns whether people are motivated only to reduce, but not to eliminate, the unwanted response. That is, people may have low motivation to eliminate a behaviour but might be willing to curb its performance. For example, setting up a goal intention never to eat pizza in an empirical study could be unacceptable to participants, whereas the same participants might endorse a goal intention to limit pizza consumption. In such instances, the appropriate if–then plan involves moderating the unwanted response. Thus, the person could attempt to control unwanted pizza consumption by specifying that particular quantities of pizza are consumed only on particular occasions (e.g. 'If it is Saturday evening, then it is OK to eat one small pizza'). Sheeran and Milne (2003) found that participants who specified limiting their consumption of high-fat foodstuffs using this type of implementation intention were successful in reducing intake compared to participants who only formed goal intentions.

Often, of course, people will want to reduce an unwanted response as much as possible and to abolish the response entirely if at all possible. Gollwitzer *et al.* (2005) pointed to the efficacy of specifying three types of if–then plans in facilitating this goal. First, the if–then plan could specify the suppression of the unwanted response (e.g. 'If I feel like ordering pizza at a restaurant, then I will not order it'). Second, the if–then plan could specify the substitution of an antagonistic wanted response (e.g. 'If I feel like ordering pizza at a restaurant, then I will order a salad instead'). Third, the if–then plan could specify an 'ignore' response (e.g. 'If I feel like ordering pizza at a restaurant, then I will ignore that feeling'). Support for utility of specifying suppression and ignore responses in the *then* component of an implementation intention was obtained in studies designed to overcome the automatic activation of stereotypical beliefs (Achtziger 2002; Gollwitzer *et al.* 2002a). For example, the implementation intentions to suppress stereotyping of older people, or prejudice towards homeless people and soccer fans ('And if I see an old person, then I tell myself: Don't stereotype!', 'And if I see a homeless person, then I will tell myself: No prejudice!', and 'And if I see a soccer fan, then I'll not be prejudiced against him!', respectively) were successful in attenuating stereotypical responses – even using priming paradigms where participants typically find it extremely difficult to control their responses (Bargh 1999). Implementation intentions that specified ignoring individuals' group memberships were similarly effective (i.e. 'If I see a homeless person, then I will ignore the fact that she is homeless!' and 'If I see this person, then I will ignore her gender!'). Whether an implementation intention that substitutes unwanted stereotypic responses with wanted egalitarian or fair responses (e.g. 'If I see a soccer fan, then I will judge him on his merits as an individual!', 'If I see a homeless person, then I will treat this person especially fairly!') is also effective in reducing stereotyping – or leads to over-motivation and thereby greater stereotyping – remains to be determined.

The second problem to do with controlling unwanted responses is overcoming contextual threats. Contextual threats can be internal (thoughts or feelings that increase desire for the unwanted response) or external (environments that promote temptation). People can be highly aware of the critical cues that make it difficult to keep sight of one's good intentions (e.g. feelings of agitation or the taste of coffee could be cues for smokers to light up). Moreover, people may be willing to relinquish control over unwanted responses if conducive circumstances make it possible to generate an external attribution for a lapse (Gibbons *et al.* 2003). In these instances, the appropriate if–then plan might be an 'ignore' response to internal ('If I start to think that I deserve pizza because I've had a hard day, then I will ignore that thought!') or external cues ('If there is a smell of baking pizza in the restaurant, then I will ignore it!'). Gollwitzer and Schaal (1998) demonstrated that an implementation intention that specified ignoring attractive distractions enhanced task performance whereas Milne and Sheeran (2003) found that an implementation to ignore detrimental self-states ('As soon as I feel tired or bored, I will ignore that feeling!') promoted task persistence. Similarly, Sheeran *et al.* (2003) found that ignoring feelings of concern about attending clinical psychology appointments ('As soon as I feel concerned about attending my appointment, I will ignore that feeling and tell myself this is perfectly understandable!') was highly effective in promoting attendance. Of course, in all of these studies, the efficacy of specifying ignore responses to deal with contextual threats must be inferred from performance of the focal behaviour, rather than performance of the response *per se*. Further research is required to demonstrate mediation of the implementation intention–goal achievement relation by then-I-will-ignore-it specifications.

6 Application of the model

6.1 Background and design

The present study (Milne and Sheeran 2002a) uses the concept of implementation intentions to try to promote performance of testicular self-examination (TSE) in a longitudinal study among undergraduate men. Testicular cancer is the most common form of cancer among men aged 19–44 years (Imperial Cancer Research Fund 1998). Successful treatment of testicular cancer depends upon confinement of disease to testicular tissue with the consequence that early detection benefits survival rates. For this reason, men are advised to examine their testicles for small hard swellings from puberty onwards. However, evidence shows that very few men perform TSE at the recommended frequency of one month (e.g. Wardle *et al.* 1994), often because of lack of motivation to perform TSE, prospective memory failure, and embarrassment about touching oneself intimately (Steffen and Gruber 1991; Steffen *et al.* 1994).

Because men may not be motivated to perform TSE, and because implementation intentions effects are only obtained when the respective goal intention is strong (Sheeran *et al.* 2005), the study began with a protection motivation theory (PMT) intervention to increase goal intentions to perform TSE before having participants form implementation intentions to promote the realization of their goal. The design adopted was 2 (motivational intervention: PMT vs control) × 2 (implementation intention: formed vs not formed); participants were randomly assigned to one of the four conditions. The motivational intervention was based on PMT because this model has been used successfully to promote goal intentions in previous research (e.g. Milne *et al.* 2002; see Milne *et al.* 2000, and Norman *et al.*, Chapter 3 in this volume, for reviews). The implementation intention manipulation specified the instigation of performance in the *then* component of the plan. This specification should automate performance of TSE and, thereby, alleviate problems with remembering to perform the behaviour and short-term affective costs. Moreover, the if–then plan should facilitate the establishment of TSE performance as part of respondents' routines.

The study had the following hypotheses:

1   the PMT intervention will increase threat and coping appraisal in relation to TSE as well as goal intentions to perform TSE;
2   forming an implementation intention to promote TSE will increase the likelihood of both the performance one month later and the establishment of routine TSE performance over one year; and
3   there will be a significant interaction between the PMT intervention and manipulation of implementation intentions such that the initiation and maintenance of TSE will be greatest when both motivation is enhanced and an if–then plan is formed.

6.2 Method

6.2.1 Participants and procedure

Participants were undergraduate men aged 18 to 42 years at the University of Bath, UK who took part in three waves of data collection over a one-year period. At time 1, a questionnaire containing the motivational and implementation intention manipulations as well as measures of PMT constructs was completed by n = 642 participants. One month later (time 2), n = 432 participants completed a behavioural follow-up by email. At time 3 (one year later), n = 254 participants who still had a university email address were contacted (i.e. participants who had not graduated or were not on placements). Responses were obtained from 173 participants. Representativeness checks showed no significant differences on background or PMT variables, which suggests that the samples at time 2 and time 3 adequately represent the population from which they were drawn.

The time 1 questionnaire contained standard multi-item measures of PMT variables, i.e. measures of goal intentions, perceived vulnerability, perceived severity, fear, response efficacy, self-efficacy, and perceived costs (see Norman *et al.*, Chapter 3 in this volume) as well as measures of background characteristics and past behaviour. Reliabilities proved satisfactory for goal intentions (alpha = 0.72) and other variables (alphas = 0.68 to 0.87) with the exception of perceived severity and response efficacy (single items were analysed). TSE performance at time 2 was measured by one item that asked participants whether or not they had performed a TSE in the previous month (*yes/no*). TSE performance at time 3 was measured by an item that asked whether or not participants had established a routine of performing TSE every month (*yes/no*).

6.2.2 Manipulations

The PMT intervention was presented after the questionnaire measures of background characteristics and past behaviour but before the measures of PMT variables. The intervention comprised a health education leaflet entitled *A Whole New Ball Game* (Imperial Cancer Research Fund 1998) that provided information and persuasive messages about testicular cancer and TSE. Content analysis indicated that the text addressed all of the variables specified by PMT. Control participants did not receive this leaflet.

The implementation intention manipulation was presented as a supplement to the health education leaflet and comprised the following passage:

> Many people find that when they intend to adopt a new health behaviour such as TSE, they then forget to do it or 'never get round to it'. It has been found that when you form a specific plan of exactly how, when and where you will carry out the behaviour you are less likely to forget about it or find you don't get round to doing it. It would be useful for you to make such a plan of when and where you intend to conduct TSE over the next month. Fill in the following statement providing as much contextual information as you can, e.g. on Monday next week, at 8.00 in the morning, in my bathroom, after I have had a shower.

> During the next month I will perform TSE on_____(day) at_____(time) at/in_____(place) add any further contextual information, e.g. after a shower, after breakfast, etc._____

> To ensure you have made a link in your mind between the situation you have outlined above and performing TSE, imagine the situation and tell yourself 'If I find myself *in this situation*, then I will perform TSE.'

6.3 Results

The findings at time 1 were consistent with previous reports of non-performance of TSE (e.g. Wardle *et al.* 1994). Only 8 per cent of the sample reported that they examined their testicles once a month and 62 per cent had never done so. In fact, 45 per cent of participants reported that they had never thought about testicular cancer prior to taking part in the study. Thus, the present study can be construed as an attempt to initiate and maintain a new health behaviour.

Multivariate analysis of variance appropriate to the design supported the first hypothesis. The PMT intervention had a significant positive impact on goal intentions to perform TSE (Ms = 5.41 and 4.96, for PMT and control conditions, respectively), $p < 0.05$. This increase in goal intentions appeared to be due to higher perceived self-efficacy and lower perceived costs among the PMT group compared to the control group (Ms = 5.30 vs 4.85, and 2.04 vs 2.42, respectively), ps < 0.05. The PMT intervention had no significant effects on perceived vulnerability, perceived severity, fear, or response efficacy. Thus, the health education leaflet affected protection motivation (goal intentions) and coping appraisal, but not threat appraisal.

The second hypothesis concerned the impact of implementation intention formation on initiation of TSE performance (measured at one month) and the development of routine TSE performance (measured over one year). Chi-square analyses indicated that if–then plans produced significant and substantive differences in performance at both time-points. Whereas only 22 per cent of control participants initiated TSE performance, 44 per cent of participants who formed implementation intentions did so (see Figure 7.3). Similarly, 15 per cent of the control group reported routine performance of TSE compared to 37 per cent of the planning group. These findings support Hypothesis 2. Forming an implementation intention doubled the rates of initiation and routinization of TSE.

The final hypothesis concerned the potential interaction between the PMT intervention and implementation intention manipulation. As predicted, the interactions turned out to be significant at both one month and one year. Whereas 62 per cent of participants who received both the PMT and implementation intention interventions initiated TSE, only 28 per cent of the PMT-only group, 21 per cent of the plan-only group, and 18 per cent of the combined control group, did so (see Figure 7.4). Importantly, the percentage of participants who received both the PMT and implementation intention interventions that showed routinized TSE performance at one year (64 per cent) was virtually identical to the percentage that initiated performance (62 per cent). These findings contrast with the other conditions where the levels of performance declined (rates were 21 per cent, 11

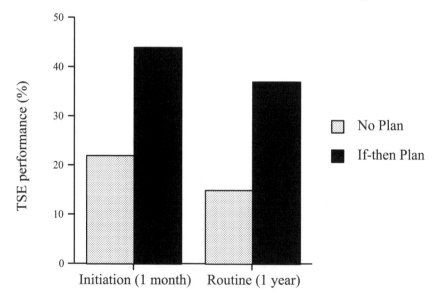

Figure 7.3 Main effects of implementation intention formation on the initiation and maintenance of TSE performance

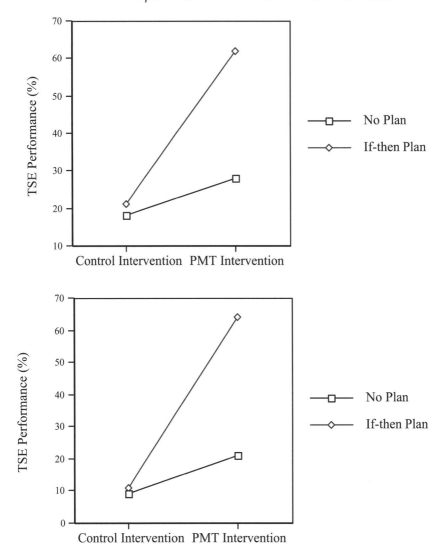

Figure 7.4 Interaction between PMT intervention and implementation intention formation on the initiation and maintenance of TSE performance

Note: Top panel refers to findings at one month and the bottom panel to findings at one year.

per cent, and 9 per cent for the PMT-only, plan-only, and control groups, respectively). Thus, Hypothesis 3 is supported. Initiation and maintenance of TSE was greatest when both motivation was enhanced and an if–then plan was formed.

6.4 Discussion

The contribution of the present research can be summarized as follows. This is the first study to combine a motivational intervention based on PMT with an implementation intention induction in a 2 × 2 between-participants design, and the first study to investigate both the initiation and routinization of a health behaviour that was novel for participants. Moreover, the study employed the longest follow-up period in studies of implementation intentions to date (one year). Findings indicated that the PMT intervention was successful in increasing goal intentions to perform TSE and supported the utility of this model in efforts to enhance people's motivation to achieve health goals (Norman *et al.*, Chapter 3 in this volume). The findings also supported the utility of if–then plans to instigate responses in promoting action initiation. Twice as many participants who formed if–then plans undertook a TSE within one month compared to participants who had not formed plans. The automatization of responding engendered by implementation intentions appears to have helped to overcome prospective memory failure and embarrassment about intimate touching that explained TSE non-performance in previous research (Steffen and Gruber 1994; Steffen *et al.* 1994).

The present findings also provided new evidence that behavioural initiation by implementation intentions can become an established part of people's routines. Whereas only 8 per cent of the no-PMT, no-plan control group had routinized TSE performance at one year, 64 per cent of the combined intervention group were performing TSEs each month. This finding underlines the parallels between action control by if–then plans and action control by habits (Gollwitzer 1999); all that is required for maintenance of the response over time is the presence of the respective situation–goal link. Clearly, delegating control of behaviour to specified situational cues is a powerful means of sustaining health goals, even over relatively long time periods. This temporal trajectory of implementation intention effects contrasts with motivational initiatives to promote health behaviour change where the impact of interventions typically diminishes over time (e.g. McCaul *et al.* 1992).

However, the present findings also speak to the importance of undertaking motivational interventions to enhance goal intentions prior to having participants form implementation intentions when participants have relatively low motivation to achieve the goal to begin with. Findings from both follow-ups showed significant interactions between the PMT and implementation intention interventions such that participants were most likely to initiate and maintain TSE performance in the combined PMT-plus-plan condition compared to each of the other conditions. These findings are consistent with previous demonstrations that strong effects of implementation intentions only emerge when the underlying goal intention is strong (e.g. Sheeran *et al.* 2005). Thus, the concept of implementation intentions should not be construed as a substitute for interventions to promote goal intentions among people with low motivation to achieve health goals. Rather, implementation intention formation is a simple and effective means of overcoming intention–behaviour discrepancies associated with sub-optimal activation or elaboration of goal intentions – when the respective goal intentions strongly favour goal achievement.

7 Future directions

The concept of implementation intentions has a short past and a bright future in health psychology. Accumulated evidence indicates that forming if–then plans makes an important difference to whether or not people realize their goals (Koestner *et al.* 2002; Sheeran 2002; Gollwitzer and Sheeran 2003) – both when goal attainment is contingent upon promoting wanted responses and controlling unwanted responses (Gollwitzer *et al.* 2005; Sheeran 2002). In addition, a good deal of research indicates that implementation intentions promote goal achievement both by facilitating identification of specified opportunities to act and by automating goal-directed responses (Aarts *et al.* 1999; Lengfelder and Gollwitzer 2000; Brandstätter *et al.* 2001; Gollwitzer *et al.* 2002b; Sheeran *et al.* 2003; Webb and Sheeran 2004a, 2004c). Finally, there is evidence that difficulties in behaviour regulation, the state of the respective goal intention, and degree of implementation intention formation all moderate the impact of implementation intention formation on goal achievement. In sum, substantial progress has been made in answering questions about *whether*, *when*, and *why* implementation intentions facilitate the enactment of goal intentions.

Despite this substantial progress, there remains considerable scope for future research in developing new applications, further delineating mediating processes, and identifying additional moderating variables. There have been few applications of the concept of implementation intentions to the promotion of health goals and further rigorous tests of this concept are warranted, especially in relation to controlling unwanted responses (e.g. smoking, excessive alcohol consumption). Most studies to date have also employed undergraduate samples and, consequently, the generalizability of findings need to be determined (cf. Sears 1986). Tailoring the *if* and *then* components of the respective plan and the plan induction, and taking account of social desirability and experimenter biases in measurements of goal intentions constitute important challenges in ensuring that effective goal-directed responses are promoted among clinical samples. Finally, implementation intentions have been deployed virtually exclusively to promote health *actions* in studies to date. However, Milne *et al.* (2003) showed that if–then plans can be used successfully to cope with daily stressors. This finding suggests that using implementation intentions to promote well-being (e.g. quality of life, pain control) among physically ill people constitutes another important avenue for future research.

Only two studies to date formally tested mediators of action control by implementation intentions (Aarts *et al.* 1999; Webb and Sheeran 2004c). Evidence supports the idea that increased accessibility of specified opportunities and strong associations between these opportunities and specified responses are the mechanisms underlying implementation intention effects (Webb and Sheeran 2004c). Further research is required to replicate these findings in other domains and to rule out alternative explanations of implementation intention effects, e.g. in terms of prospective memory. For example, some early studies mistakenly interpreted the impact of implementation intentions in terms of enhanced memory for goal intentions (e.g. Orbell *et al.* 1997; Sheeran and Orbell 1999). However, there appear to be important differences between remembering one's goal intention and action control by implementation intentions. For instance, prospective memory is highly vulnerable to the cognitive demands of ongoing activity (e.g. Marsh *et al.* 2002a; Smith 2003) whereas implementation intention effects are not (e.g. Brandstätter *et al.* 2001). Similarly, in studies of event-based prospective memory, processing of critical cues (i.e. events associated with intentionality) is slower than is the processing of non-critical cues (Marsh *et al.* 2002b) whereas implementation intention studies show superior processing of critical compared to non-critical cues (e.g. Brandstätter *et al.* 2001; Webb and Sheeran 2004a). Further delineation of the distinctiveness of processes associated with prospective memory compared to implementation intentions will be valuable, not only in theoretical terms, but also in terms of understanding how ideas from the literature on prospective memory might best be used to enhance implementation intention effects in applied settings (e.g. Prestwich *et al.* 2003c).

Relatedly, the role of motivational processes in understanding implementation intention effects requires careful explication. It is easy to imagine how a poorly designed implementation intention induction could engender experimenter demand and thereby inadvertently increase participants' subjective norm, or could increase participants' expectations of success and thereby enhance self-efficacy. Although it might seem desirable to increase participants' motivation to perform a behaviour, it is worth remembering that procedures that give rise to over-motivation or draw participants' attention to the operation of their plans could undermine the automaticity in implementation intentions (Gollwitzer and Schaal 1998), and make goal achievement less likely. The analysis presented earlier proposed that goal intentions and self-efficacy are important factors in determining whether or not participants form implementations and how much care and attention participants devote to identifying appropriate opportunities and goal-directed responses and to encoding their if–then plans. These considerations are important because implementation intentions are not a foolproof self-regulatory strategy (Gollwitzer *et al.* 2005). If people's plans are poorly elaborated, such that deliberation about opportunities or goal-directed responses is required *in situ*, if specified opportunities do not arise or prove unsuitable for initiating goal-directed responses, or if the specified responses are impossible to execute or have limited instrumentality in terms of achieving the respective goal, then implementation intention formation will not benefit goal striving. Future research might profitably be directed towards testing the accuracy of this analysis and assessing the role of motivation in determining the strength of implementation intention effects.

There is also considerable scope for further moderator analyses of implementation intention effects. Research into degree of implementation intention formation has so far tested only a small number of factors with a view to enhancing the impact of implementation intentions (e.g. cognitive rehearsal, environmental cues). Future studies could usefully examine the efficacy of different strategies for facilitating the encoding if–then plans (e.g. surprise recall tasks or plan reminders) or for increasing people's commitment to the plan (e.g. inducing anticipated regret about not following one's plan or making one's commitment public). A good deal more research is also required about the role of individual differences in action control by implementation intentions. For example, people who are more conscientious, planful, or high in need for cognition might be more likely to form implementation intentions spontaneously and, therefore, less likely to benefit from plan inductions. Conversely, people who are prone to rumination or procrastination may obtain greater benefit from implementation intention formation. Perhaps the most important issue to do with moderation, however, will be to bring the issues of degree of intention formation and individual differences together to understand how implementation intentions can be used to overcome habits and initiate new behaviour patterns. When particular situation–goal–response links have been satisfactorily reinforced in the past, it is no simple matter trying to suppress or substitute those responses. Future research will need to produce a fine-grained analysis of what kinds of goal-directed responses and opportunities should be specified and what kinds of implementation intention inductions should be deployed for particular samples and particular behaviours in order to enhance the efficacy of implementation intentions in helping people realize their intentions. Undertaking further research on implementation intentions to these ends seems a good plan for health psychologists.

Acknowledgements

We thank Ian Kellar, Andrew Prestwich, Liz Steadman, and Andrea Higgins for providing additional information about their research.

Note

1 We thank Marie Johnston for this wonderful encapsulation of the concept of ego-depletion.

References

Aarts, H. and Dijksterhuis, A. (2000a) Habits as knowledge structures: automaticity in goal-directed behavior, *Journal of Personality and Social Psychology* 78, 53–63.

Aarts, H., and Dijksterhuis, A. (2000b) On the automatic activation of goal-directed behavior: the case of travel habit, *Journal of Environmental Psychology*, 20, 75–82.

Aarts, H., Dijksterhuis, A. and Midden, C. (1999) To plan or not to plan? Goal achievement or interrupting the performance of mundane behaviors, *European Journal of Social Psychology*, 29, 971–9.

Aarts, H., Gollwitzer, P. M. and Hassin, R. (2004) Goal contagion: perceiving is for pursuing, *Journal of Personality and Social Psychology*, 87, 23–37.

Abraham, C. and Sheeran, P. (2003) Anticipated regret and intention–behaviour relations, *British Journal of Social Psychology*, 42, 495–511.

Abraham, C. and Sheeran, P. (2004) Implications of goal theories for the theories of reasoned action and planned behaviour, *Current Psychology*, 22, 218–33.

Abraham, C., Sheeran, P. and Johnson, M. (1998) From health beliefs to self-regulation: theoretical advances in the psychology of action control, *Psychology and Health*, 13, 569–92.

Abraham, C., Sheeran, P., Norman, P., Conner, M., Otten, W. and de Vries, N. (1999) When good intentions are not enough: modelling post-intention cognitive correlates of condom use, *Journal of Applied Social Psychology*, 29, 2591–612.

Achtziger, A. (2002) Sozial-, kognitions- und motivationspsychologische Determinaten des Eindrucksbildungsprozesses unter besonderer Berücksichtigung der Stereotypisier-ung. (Social-cognitive and motivational determinants of evaluating and judging others). Unpublished dissertation, University of Konstanz, Germany.

Ajzen, I. (1991) The theory of planned behavior, *Organizational Behavior and Human Decision Processes*, 50, 179–211.

Armitage, C. J. (2004) Implementation intentions and eating a low-fat diet: a randomized controlled trial, *Health Psychology*, 23, 319–23.

Bagozzi, R. P. and Kimmel, S. K. (1995) A comparison of leading theories for the prediction of goal-directed behaviour, *British Journal of Social Psychology*, 34, 437–61.

Bargh, J. A. (1992) The ecology of automaticity: towards establishing the conditions needed to produce automatic processing effects, *American Journal of Psychology*, 105, 181–99.

Bargh, J. A. (1994) The four horsemen of automaticity: awareness, efficiency, intention, and control in social interaction. In R. S. Wyer Jr. and T. K. Srull (eds) *Handbook of Social Cognition* (2nd edition). Hillsdale, NJ: Erlbaum, 1–40.

Bargh, J. A. (1999) The cognitive monster: the case against the controllability of automatic stereotype effects. In S. Chaiken and Y. Trope (eds), *Dual-process Theories in Social Psychology*. New York: Guilford, 361–82.

Bargh, J. A., Gollwitzer, P. M., Lee-Chai, A., Barndollar, K. and Trötschel, R. (2001) The automated will: nonconscious activation and pursuit of behavioral goals, *Journal of Personality and Social Psychology*, 81, 1014–27.

Baron, R. M. and Kenny, D. A. (1986) The moderator–mediator variable distinction in social psychological research: conceptual, strategic and statistical considerations, *Journal of Personality and Social Psychology*, 51, 1173–82.

Baumeister, R. F., Bratlavsky, E., Muraven, M. and Tice, D. M. (1998) Ego-depletion: is the active self a limited resource?, *Journal of Personality and Social Psychology*, 74, 1252–65.

Bayer, U. C., Moskowitz, G. B. and Gollwitzer, P. M. (2002) Implementation intentions and action initiation without conscious intent. Unpublished manuscript, University of Konstanz, Germany.

Brandstätter, V., Lengfelder, A. and Gollwitzer, P. M. (2001) Implementation intentions and efficient action initiation, *Journal of Personality and Social Psychology*, 81, 946–60.

Cohen, J. (1992) A power primer, *Psychological Bulletin*, 112, 155–9.

Conner, M., Sheeran, P., Norman, P. and Armitage, C.J. (2000) Temporal stability as a moderator of relationships in the theory of planned behaviour, *British Journal of Social Psychology*, 39, 469–93.

Cooke, R. and Sheeran, P. (2004) Moderation of cognition–intention and cognition–behaviour relations: a meta-analysis of properties of variables from the theory of planned behaviour, *British Journal of Social Psychology*, 43, 159–86.

Einstein, G. O. and McDaniel, M. A. (1996) Retrieval processes in prospective memory: theoretical approaches and some new empirical findings. In M. Bradimonte, G. O. Einstein and M. A. McDaniel (eds) *Prospective Memory: Theory and Applications*. Mahwah, NJ: Erlbaum, 115–138.

Gibbons, F. X., Gerrard, M. and Lane, D. J. (2003) A social reaction model of adolescent health risk. In J. Suls and K. A. Wallston (eds) *Social Psychological Foundations of Health and Illness*. Oxford: Blackwell, 107–136.

Gollwitzer, P. M. (1990) Action phases and mindsets. In E. T. Higgins and J. R. M. Sorrentino (eds) *The Handbook of Motivation and Cognition*, Vol. 2. New York: Guilford, 53–92.

Gollwitzer, P. M. (1993) Goal achievement: the role of intentions. In W. Strobe and M. Hewstone (eds) *European Review of Social Psychology*, Vol. 4. Chicester: Wiley, 141–85.

Gollwitzer, P. M. (1996) The volitional benefits of planning. In P. M. Gollwitzer and J. A. Bargh (eds) *The Psychology of Action: Linking Cognition and Motivation to Behavior*. New York: Guilford, 287–312.

Gollwitzer, P. M. (1998) Implicit and explicit processes in goal pursuit. Paper presented at the symposium 'Implicit vs explicit processes' at the Annual Meeting of the Society of Experimental Social Psychology, Atlanta, Georgia.

Gollwitzer, P. M. (1999) Implementation intentions: strong effects of simple plans, *American Psychologist*, 54, 493–503.

Gollwitzer, P. M., Achtziger, A., Schaal, B. and Hammelbeck, J. P. (2002a) Intentional control of stereotypical beliefs and prejudicial feelings. Unpublished manuscript, University of Konstanz.

Gollwitzer, P. M., Bayer, U. C. and McCulluch, K. C. (2005) The control of the unwanted. In R. R. Hassin, J. S. Uleman and J. A. Bargh (eds) *The New Unconscious*. New York: Oxford University Press, 485–515.

Gollwitzer, P. M., Bayer, U. C., Steller, B. and Bargh, J. A. (2002b) Delegating control to the environment: perception, attention, and memory for pre-selected behavioral cues. Unpublished manuscript, University of Konstanz.

Gollwitzer, P. M. and Brandstätter, V. (1997) Implementation intentions and effective goal pursuit, *Journal of Personality and Social Psychology*, 73, 186–99.

Gollwitzer, P. M. and Schaal, B. (1998) Metacognition in action: the importance of implementation intentions, *Personality and Social Psychology Review*, 2, 124–36.

Gollwitzer, P. M. and Sheeran, P. (2003) Bridging the intention-behaviour 'gap' through strategic automatization: meta-analysis of implementation intentions. Manuscript in preparation, New York University.

Heckhausen, H. and Gollwitzer, P. M. (1987) Thought contents and cognitive functioning in motivational versus volitional states of mind, *Motivation and Emotion*, 11, 101–20.

Higgins, A. and Conner, M. (2003) Understanding adolescent smoking: the role of the theory of planned behaviour and implementation intentions, *Psychology, Health and Medicine*, 8, 177–90.

Higgins, A. and Conner, M. (2004) Preventing adolescent smoking using implementation intentions. Manuscript submitted for publication.

Higgins, E. T. (1996) Knowledge activation: accessibility, applicability, and salience. In E. T. Higgins and A. W. Kruglanski (eds) *Social Psychology: Handbook of Basic Principles*. New York: Guilford, 133–68.

Kellar, I. and Abraham, C. (2003) Randomised controlled trial of a research-based intervention promoting fruit and vegetable consumption. Manuscript under review.

Kenny, D. A., Kashy, D. A. and Bolger, N. (1998) Data analysis in social psychology. In D. T. Gilbert, S. T. Fiske and G. Lindzey (eds) *The handbook of Social Psychology*, (4th edition). New York: Oxford University Press, 233–65.

Koestner, R., Lekes, N., Powers, T. A. and Chicoine, E. (2002) Attaining personal goals: self-concordance plus implementation intentions equals success, *Journal of Personality and Social Psychology*, 83, 231–44.

Lengfelder, A. and Gollwitzer, P. M. (2001) Reflective and reflexive action control in patients with frontal brain lesions, *Neuropsychology*, 15, 80–100.

McBroom, W. H. and Reid, F. W. (1992) Towards a reconceptualization of attitude–behavior consistency, *Social Psychology Quarterly*, 55, 205–16.

McCaul, K. D., Glasgow, R. E. and O'Neill, H. K. (1992) The problem of creating habits: establishing health-protective dental behaviors, *Health Psychology*, 11, 101–10.

Margetts, B. M., Cade, J. E. and Osmond, C. (1989) Comparison of a food frequency questionnaire with a diet record, *International Journal of Epidemiology*, 18, 868–73.

Marsh, R. L., Hancock, T. W. and Hicks, J. L. (2002a) The demands of an ongoing activity influence the success of event-based prospective memory, *Psychonomic Bulletin and Review*, 9, 604–10.

Marsh, R. L., Hicks, J. L. and Watson, V. (2002b) The dynamics of intention retrieval and coordination of action in event-based prospective memory. *Journal of Experimental Psychology: Learning, Memory, and Cognition*, 28, 652–659.

Milne, S., Gollwitzer, P. M. and Sheeran, P. (2003) Unpublished raw data, University of Bath.

Milne, S., Orbell, S. and Sheeran, P. (2002) Combining motivational and volitional interventions to promote exercise participation: protection motivation theory and implementation intentions, *British Journal of Health Psychology*, 7, 163–84.

Milne, S. and Sheeran, P. (2002a) Combining motivational and volitional interventions to prevent testicular cancer. Paper presented to the 13th General Meeting of the European Association of Experimental Social Psychology, San Sebastian, June.

Milne, S. and Sheeran, P. (2002b) Making good implementation intentions: comparing associative learning and prospective memory in remembering intentions. Paper presented to the 16th Conference of the European Health Psychology Society, Lisbon, October.

Milne, S. and Sheeran, P. (2003) Unpublished raw data, University of Bath.

Milne, S., Sheeran, P. and Orbell, S. (2000) Prediction and intervention in health-related behaviour: a meta-analytic review of protection motivation theory, *Journal of Applied Social Psychology*, 30, 106–43.

Muraven, M. and Baumeister, R. F. (2000) Self-regulation and depletion of limited resources. Does self-control resemble a muscle?, *Psychological Bulletin*, **126**, 247–59.

Murgraff, V., White, D. and Phillips, K. (1996) Moderating binge drinking: it is possible to change behaviour if you plan it in advance, *Alcohol and Alcoholism*, **6**, 577–82.

Oettingen, G. and Gollwitzer, P.M. (2001) Goal setting and goal striving. In A. Tesser and N. Schwarz (eds) *Intraindividual processes. Volume 1 of the Blackwell Handbook in Social Psychology*. Editors-in-chief: M. Hewstone and M. Brewer. Oxford: Blackwell, 329–47.

Oettingen, G., Hönig, G. and Gollwitzer, P. M. (2000) Effective self-regulation of goal attainment, *International Journal of Educational Research*, **33**, 705–32.

Orbell, S., Hodgkins, S. and Sheeran, P. (1997) Implementation intentions and the theory of planned behavior, *Personality and Social Psychology Bulletin*, **23**, 945–54.

Orbell, S. and Sheeran, P. (1998) 'Inclined abstainers': a problem for predicting health-related behavior, *British Journal of Social Psychology*, **37**, 151–65.

Orbell, S. and Sheeran, P. (2000) Motivational and volitional processes in action initiation: a field study of the role of implementation intentions, *Journal of Applied Social Psychology*, **30**, 780–97.

Prestwich, A., Lawton, R. and Conner, M. (2003a) Use of implementation intentions and the decision balance sheet in promoting exercise behaviour, *Psychology and Health*, **18**, 707–21.

Prestwich, A., Lawton, R. and Conner, M. (2003b) Increasing the impact of implementation intentions: the impact of environmental cues, rehearsal and sufficient plans. Unpublished manuscript, University of Leeds.

Prestwich, A., Lawton, R., Conner, M. and Taylor, S. (2003c) Spontaneous planning: the role of motivation and conscientiousness in the formation of implementation intentions. Unpublished manuscript, University of Leeds.

Rise, J., Thompson, M. and Verplanken, B. (2003) Measuring implementation intentions in the context of the theory of planned behavior, *Scandinavian Journal of Psychology*, **44**, 87–95.

Rogers, R. W. (1983) Cognitive and physiological processes in fear appeals and attitude change: a revised theory of protection motivation. In B. L. Cacioppo and L. L. Petty (eds) *Social Psychophysiology: A Sourcebook*. London: Guildford, 153–76.

Sears, D. O. (1986) College sophomores in the laboratory: influences of a narrow data base on social psychology's view of human nature, *Journal of Personality and Social Psychology*, **51**, 515–30.

Sewacj, D., Ajzen, I. and Fishbein, M. (1980) Predicting and understanding weight loss: intentions, behaviors, and outcomes. In I. Ajzen and M. Fishbein, *Understanding Attitudes and Predicting Social Behavior*. Englewood Cliffs, NJ: Prentice-Hall, 101–12.

Sheeran, P. (2002) Intention–behavior relations: a conceptual and empirical review. In W. Strobe and M. Hewstone (eds) *European Review of Social Psychology*, Vol. 12. Chichester: Wiley, 1–30.

Sheeran, P., Aarts, H., Custers, R., Rivis, A., Webb, T. L. and Cooke, R. (in press) The goal-dependent automaticity of drinking habits, *British Journal of Social Psychology*.

Sheeran, P. and Abraham, C. (2003) Mediator of moderators: temporal stability of intention and the intention–behavior relationship, *Personality and Social Psychology Bulletin*, **29**, 205–15.

Sheeran, P., Abraham, C. and Orbell, S. (1999) Psychosocial correlates of hetero-sexual condom use: a meta-analysis, *Psychological Bulletin*, **125**, 90–132.

Sheeran, P. and Armitage, C. J. (2003). Unpublished raw data, University of Sheffield.

Sheeran, P., Aubrey, R. and Kellett, S. (2003) Unpublished raw data, University of Sheffield.

Sheeran, P. and Milne, S. (2002) Unpublished raw data, University of Sheffield.

Sheeran, P. and Milne, S. (2003) Unpublished raw data, University of Sheffield.

Sheeran, P. and Orbell, S. (1998) Do intentions predict condom use? A meta-ana-lysis and examination of six moderator variables, *British Journal of Social Psychology*, **37**, 231–50.

Sheeran, P. and Orbell, S. (1999) Implementation intentions and repeated behavior: augmenting the predictive validity of the theory of planned behavior, *European Journal of Social Psychology*, **29**, 349–69.

Sheeran, P. and Orbell, S. (2000) Using implementation intentions to increase attendance for cervical cancer screening, *Health Psychology*, **19**, 283–9.

Sheeran, P. and Silverman, M. (2003) Evaluation of three interventions to promote workplace health and safety: evidence for the utility of implementation inten-tions, *Social Science and Medicine*, **56**, 2153–63.

Sheeran, P., Trafimow, D. and Armitage, C. J. (2003) Predicting behaviour from perceived behavioural control: tests of the accuracy assumption of the theory of planned behaviour, *British Journal of Social Psychology*, **42**, 393–410.

Sheeran, P., Webb, T. L. and Gollwitzer, P. M. (2005) The interplay between goal intentions and implementation intentions, *Personality and Social Psychology Bulletin*, **31**, 87–98.

Sheeran, P. and Webb, T. L., (2003) Unpublished raw data, University of Sheffield.

Sheeran, P., White, D. and Phillips, K. (1991) Premarital contraceptive use: a review of the psychological literature, *Journal of Reproductive and Infant Psychology*, **9**, 253–69.

Smets, E. M. A., Garssen, B., Bonke, B. and De Haes, J. C. J. M. (1995) The multi-dimensional fatigue inventory (MFI): psychometric qualities of an instrument to assess fatigue, *Journal of Psychosomatic Research*, **39**, 315.

Smith, R. E. (2003) The cost of remembering to remember in event-based pro-spective memory: investigating the capacity demands of delayed intention per-formance, *Journal of Experimental Psychology: Learning, Memory, and Cognition*, **29**, 347–61.

Steadman, L. and Quine, L. (2000) Are implementation intentions useful for brid-ging the intention–behavior gap in adhering to long-term medication regimens? An attempt to replicate Sheeran and Orbell's (1999) intervention to enhance adherence to daily vitamin C intake. Paper presented to the British Psychological Society Division of Health Psychology Annual Conference, University of Kent at Canterbury, September.

Steadman, L. and Quine, L. (2004). Encouraging young males to perform testicular self-examination: a simple, but effective, implementation intention intervention, *British Journal of Health Psychology*, **9**, 479–87.

Steadman, L., Rutter, D. R. and Quine, L. (2004) An implementation intentions intervention to increase uptake of mammography. Manuscript under review.

Steffen, V. J. and Gruber, V. A. (1991) Direct experience with a cancer self-exam: effects on cognitions and behaviour, *Journal of Social Psychology*, **131**, 165–77.

Steffen, V. J., Sternberg, L., Teegarden, L. A. and Shepherd, K. (1994) Practice and persuasive frame: effects on beliefs, intention and performance of a cancer self-examination, *Journal of Applied Social Psychology*, 24, 897–925.

Sutton, S. (1998) Predicting and explaining intentions and behaviour: how well are we doing?, *Journal of Applied Social Psychology*, 28, 1317–38.

Sutton, S. and Sheeran, P. (2003) Meta-analysis of the theory of planned behaviour and past behaviour. Manuscript in preparation, University of Cambridge.

Triandis, H. C. (1980) Values, attitudes, and interpersonal behaviour. In H. Howe and M. Page (eds) *Nebraska Symposium on Motivation*, Vol. 27. Lincoln, NB: University of Nebraska Press, 195–259.

Trötschel, R. and Gollwitzer, P. M. (2002) Implementation intentions and the control of framing effects in negotiations. Manuscript under review.

Verplanken, B. and Faes, S. (1999) Good intentions, bad habits, and effects of forming implementation intentions on healthy eating, *European Journal of Social Psychology*, 29, 591–604.

Wardle, J., Steptoe, A., Burckhardt, R., Vögele, C., Vila, J., and Zarczynski, I. (1994) Testicular self-examination: attitudes and practices among young men in Europe, *Preventive Medicine*, 23, 206–10.

Webb, T. L. and Sheeran, P. (2003) Can implementation intentions help to overcome ego-depletion?, *Journal of Experimental Social Psychology*, 39, 279–86.

Webb, T. L. and Sheeran, P. (2004a) Identifying good opportunities to act: implementation intentions and cue discrimination, *European Journal of Social Psychology*.

Webb, T. L. and Sheeran, P. (2004b) Unpublished raw data, University of Sheffield.

Webb, T. L. and Sheeran, P. (2004c) Unpublished raw data, University of Sheffield.

Webb, T. L. and Sheeran, P. (2005) Integrating goal theories to understand the achievement of personal goals, *European Journal of Social Psychology*, 35, 69–96.

Witkin, H. A., Lewis, H. B., Hertzman, M., Machover, K., Meissner, P. B. and Wapner, S. (1972) *Personality through Perception: An Experimental and Clinical Study*. Westwood, CT: Greenwood Press.

PREDICTING AND CHANGING HEALTH BEHAVIOUR: FUTURE DIRECTIONS

Introduction

Despite an extensive research base on the application of social cognition models (SCMs) to the prediction of health behaviour, there are a range of issues for future work to address. In this chapter (section 2) we highlight seven issues focusing on (a) the impact of personality traits on health behaviour, (b) the assessment of risk perceptions, (c) the utility of other SCMs, (d) the impact of past behaviour/habit, (e) automatic influences on health behaviour, (f) the predictors of the maintenance of health behaviour, and (g) critiques of the use of SCMs to predict health behaviour. Over recent years there has been a growing interest in the development of interventions based on the main SCMs to change health behaviour (see Rutter and Quine 2002). However, a somewhat mixed pattern of results has been reported in the literature. We therefore also consider (Section 3) general issues relating to the development, evaluation and implementation of theory-based interventions, and highlight some of the reasons why a social cognitive approach to intervention design, to date, has failed to realize its full potential.

2 Predicting health behaviour: future directions

2.1 The impact of personality traits on health behaviour

An extensive literature exists linking personality traits to health outcomes (see Marshall *et al.* 1994); however, relatively little research has focused on the impact of these traits on health behaviour. To date, most research has focused on the influence of the 'big five' personality traits (i.e. neuroticism, extraversion, conscientiousness, openness and agreeableness) on health behaviour (e.g. Siegler *et al.* 1995; Schwartz *et al.* 1999; Conner and Abraham 2001). Personality traits are seen to be distal predictors in the main SCMs that shape beliefs about the behaviour in question which, in turn, determine intention and behaviour. Thus, the impact of personality traits should be mediated by social cognitive variables. For example, Siegler *et al.* (1995) found that the effect of conscientiousness on mammography attendance was mediated by knowledge of breast cancer and the perceived costs of seeking mammography. However, other research has found direct effects for personality traits when predicting health behaviour. For example, extraversion has been shown to explain additional variance in exercise behaviour, over and above that explained by the TPB (e.g. Courneya *et al.* 1999). Similarly, Conner and Abraham (2001) reported that conscientiousness had a direct effect on exercise behaviour, although extraversion and neuroticism only had indirect effects. No effects were found for openness and agreeableness. Research indicates that, in the main, the effects of personality traits on health behaviour are mediated by more proximal social cognitive variables. However, the direct effects found for conscientiousness and extraversion highlight the need for more research on the ways in which these personality traits may impact on health behaviour.

Conscientiousness refers to the ability to control one's behaviour and to complete tasks. Those with high conscientiousness scores are seen to be more organized, careful, dependable, self-disciplined and achievement-oriented than those low in conscientiousness (McCrae and Costa 1987). High conscientiousness scores have also been associated with a greater use of problem-focused, positive reappraisal and support-seeking coping strategies (Watson and Hubbard 1996) and a less frequent use of escape-avoidance and self-blame coping strategies (O'Brien and Delongis 1996). Such characteristics and activities are likely to facilitate the performance of aversive or difficult health behaviours that individuals are motivated to perform. Conscientiousness should therefore moderate the relationship between health beliefs and health behaviour. A few studies have examined the moderating role of conscientiousness with some encouraging results. For example, in a retrospective study, Schwartz *et al.* (1999) found that conscientiousness moderated the relationship between breast cancer-related distress and mammography uptake such that under high levels of distress, those with high conscientiousness scores were more likely to have attended mammography screening than those with low conscientiousness scores. Conscientiousness scores had no differential impact under low levels of distress. Such findings are important as they suggest that high levels of conscientiousness may aid the performance of health-protective behaviours that are associated with high levels of risk or distress.

The moderating role of extraversion on intention–behaviour relations has also been examined in a number of studies on exercise behaviour. Extraverts are seen to have an increased tendency to seek out situations in which opportunities to be active present themselves (Eysenck 1981). Individuals with high extraversion scores may be more likely to encounter opportunities to act on their intentions to exercise, which will therefore increase the strength of intention–behaviour relations. Consistent with this position, extraversion has been found to moderate the relationship between exercise intentions and behaviour (e.g. Rhodes *et al.* 2003). Interestingly, other studies have shown that the direct effect of extraversion on exercise behaviour is primarily due to the activity facet of extraversion, rather than the positive affect or sociability facets (e.g. Rhodes and Courneya 2003). According to McCrae and Costa (1990), the activity facet describes an individual's tendency to be energetic, busy and forceful. With respect to exercise behaviour, it is possible that this facet may also be responsible for the moderating role of extraversion on intention–behaviour relations.

The hypothesis that personality traits may moderate intention–behaviour relations has also been proposed by Kuhl (1985) in his theory of action control. According to Kuhl (1985), for an intention to be translated into action, it must be protected from various alternative, competing action tendencies through the deployment of a number of action control processes (i.e. attention control, encoding control, emotion control, motivation control, environment control, parsimony of information processing). The efficiency of these action control processes is enhanced when individuals are *action oriented*, that is, when individuals simultaneously focus on their present state, their intended future state, the discrepancy between the two states, and different ways to reach their intended future state. Such an orientation is likely to facilitate goal achievement. In contrast, when individuals are *state oriented*, they focus exclusively on their present state or their intended future state and thereby fail to consider ways to reach their intended future state. Such an orientation is likely to inhibit goal achievement. Kuhl (1985) argues that there are individual differences in state versus action orientation. Individuals who are action oriented should therefore be more likely to translate their intentions into action. In other words, state versus action orientation should moderate the intention–behaviour relationship. Unfortunately, evidence for the moderating role of state versus action orientation on the intention–behaviour relationship is mixed. For example, Kendzierski (1990) found significant intention–behaviour correlations among action-oriented, but not state-oriented, participants. However, the differences between the strength of the intention–behaviour correlations obtained for action-oriented and state-oriented participants were not statistically reliable. Norman *et al.* (2003) examined 30 common social and health behaviours over a two-week period. The interaction between intention and state versus action orientation was only significant in one of the 30 moderated regression analyses.

The distinction made by Kruglanski *et al.* (2000) between assessment and locomotion aspects of self-regulation may also be of importance when considering the impact of individual differences on intention–behaviour relations. According to Kruglanski *et al.* (2000), the assessment aspect of self-regulation is concerned with the critical evaluation of choices between different goals and the means to achieve them, whereas the locomotion aspect of self-regulation is concerned with the commitment of psychological resources to ensuring that goal-directed behaviour is initiated and maintained. Kruglanski *et al.* (2000) argue that these aspects of self-regulation are relatively independent and that individual differences exist in assessment and locomotion tendencies. A range of evidence exists to support this position (see Higgins *et al.* 2003). It is clear that both aspects of self-regulation are required for successful goal pursuit inasmuch as it is necessary to both choose an appropriate action (i.e. assessment) and ensure that it is initiated and maintained (i.e. locomotion). However, the locomotion aspect of self-regulation would seem to be of particular importance for the movement from intention to behaviour. Kruglanski *et al.* (2000) have presented evidence that locomotors are more decisive and conscientious, have greater attentional control and higher levels of intrinsic motivation, and place a greater emphasis on expectancy in relation to goal attainment. Such factors are likely to aid the movement from intention to behaviour and, as a result, locomotion scores should moderate the intention–behaviour relationship. In support of this position, Pierro *et al.* (2002) found a significant interaction between exercise intentions and locomotion scores when predicting attendance at a gym, such that the intention–behaviour relationship was stronger among those with high locomotion scores.

In conclusion, Abraham *et al.* (2000) have noted that the literatures on the links between personality and health behaviour and between SCMs and health behaviour have developed in parallel with little cross-referencing. Personality and social cognitive influences may therefore be usefully integrated into a single account of health behaviour (see also Bermudez 1999). In such an account, personality traits are likely to be distal predictors of health behaviour, their impact being mediated by the variables contained in current SCMs. However, given the direct effects of conscientiousness and extraversion on health behaviour reported in some studies it is possible that individual differences may add to the prediction of health behaviour. In addition, personality traits may be important moderators of intention–behaviour relations for certain health behaviours.

2.2 The assessment of risk perceptions

Risk perceptions are central to most SCMs that have been applied to the prediction of health behaviour. For example, models that have been developed specifically to predict health behaviour (i.e. health belief model [HBM], protection motivation theory [PMT]) all contain constructs that explicitly focus on risk perceptions. In addition, other models such as the theory of planned behaviour (TPB) and social cognitive theory (SCT) also focus on perceptions of risk, indirectly, via other constructs. For example, in the TPB, perceptions of risk may be assessed via behavioural beliefs, whereas in the SCT, outcome expectancies may focus on risk perceptions. However, despite the central role afforded to risk perceptions in many SCMs research evidence for a link between risk perceptions and health behaviour is weak. For example, in a meta-analysis of PMT studies, Milne *et al.* (2000) reported that perceived vulnerability had relatively weak correlations with intention (r = 0.16), concurrent behaviour (r = 0.13) and future behaviour (r = 0.12). Moreover, a mixed pattern of results has been reported in the literature. Considering the prediction of health-protective intentions, some studies have reported positive correlations with perceived risk (e.g. Norman *et al.* 1999), whereas other studies have reported negative correlations (e.g. Abraham *et al.* 1994). Similarly, perceived risk has been found to have both positive (e.g. Seydel *et al.* 1990) and negative (e.g. Ben-Ahron *et al.* 1995) correlations with concurrent health-protective behaviour. In contrast, perceived risk typically has a positive relationship with future health-protective behaviour (e.g. Aspinwall *et al.* 1991).

Weinstein and Nicolich (1993) outline a number of reasons for the mixed pattern of results reported in the literature. Considering the relationship between perceived risk and concurrent health behaviour, models such as the HBM and PMT predict a positive correlation between perceived risk and health protective behaviour. For example, individuals who believe they are at risk of HIV infection should be more likely to exhibit consistent condom use. However, Weinstein and Nicolich (1993) argue that people infer vulnerability judgements from their current behaviour and, as a result, negative correlations may be observed between perceived risk and concurrent protective behaviour. For example, individuals who exhibit consistent condom use may infer that they are at low risk of HIV infection. Consistent with this argument, Gerrard *et al.* (1996) reported a small but significant negative average correlation (r = −0.11) between perceived HIV susceptibility and past protective behaviour across 26 cross-sectional studies. Such findings suggest that 'the correlation between perceived personal risk and simultaneous preventive behaviors should not be used to assess the effects of perceptions on behavior. It is an indicator of risk perception accuracy' (Weinstein and Nicolich 1993: 244). However, meta-analyses of the HBM and PMT report significant, but weak, positive correlations between risk perceptions and concurrent protective behaviour (Harrison *et al.* 1992; Milne *et al.* 2000), consistent with the argument that those currently engaging in a health-protective behaviour are doing so because they believe themselves to be at risk. Unfortunately, teasing apart these two rival positions in cross-sectional studies is difficult as some individuals may base their risk judgements on their current behaviour whereas others may or may not engage in a behaviour on the basis of their risk perceptions. The obtained correlation between perceived risk and concurrent behaviour would then be a function of the relatives sizes of these two sub-samples.

Weinstein and Nicolich (1993) put forward similar arguments when considering the relationship between perceived risk and intention. According to PMT, for example, a positive correlation is expected between perceived vulnerability and intention, such that individuals who feel vulnerable to a health threat should be more likely to intend to engage in a protective behaviour. However, it is also possible to argue that individuals who intend to engage in a health protective behaviour may feel less vulnerable to a health threat, thus explaining the negative correlations found in some PMT studies. However, as before, it is difficult to disentangle whether risk perceptions drive intentions to engage in a health-protective behaviour or whether these intentions are used to infer perceptions of risk. The significant positive correlation found between perceived vulnerability and intention in the Milne *et al.* (2000) meta-analysis would suggest that risk perceptions determine health-protective intentions, in line with PMT. However, given the relatively small size of the correlation it is possible that risk perceptions only determine health-protective intentions in some situations and/or among some individuals.

When considering the prediction of future behaviour, Weinstein and Nicolich (1993) only argue for the possibility of a positive relationship between risk perceptions and health behaviour. Thus, perceived risk is seen to be an important determinant of future health behaviour. Perceptions of risk have been found to be predictive of reductions in the number of sexual partners (Aspinwall *et al.* 1991), the uptake of cervical cancer screening (Orbell and Sheeran 1998) and treatment adherence (Norman *et al.* 2003) in various prospective studies. In addition, small but significant positive correlations have been estimated between risk perceptions and future behaviour in meta-analyses of the HBM and PMT (Harrison *et al.* 1992; Milne *et al.* 2000). These results are encouraging as they suggest that perceptions of risk may be predictive of future behaviour. However, Aspinwall *et al.* (1991) reported that the significant effect of perceived vulnerability on future behaviour disappeared when past behaviour was included in the regression equation. Similarly, Gerrard *et al.* (1996) found that perceived susceptibility failed to predict safer sex behaviour in four prospective studies when controlling for the effects of past behaviour. These findings suggest that the 'apparent link between perceived risk and longitudinal changes in behavior is actually explained by the covariability of a sense of risk and behavior at [time] 1' (Joseph *et al.* 1987: 242).

Another possible reason for the weak predictive role of perceived risk may be the way in which risk perceptions are measured. Many studies ask respondents to estimate the chances that an event will occur in the future (e.g. 'How likely is it that you will become infected with the AIDS virus in the next two years?'). As Van der Velde and Hooykaas (1996) note, such questions provide unconditional risk estimates as respondents can take into account an unspecified range of factors, including their current behaviour, when providing a risk estimate. In contrast, conditional risk items ask respondents to estimate the chances that an event will occur in the future if no preventive action is taken (e.g. 'How likely is it that you will become infected with the AIDS virus in the next two years, if you don't use condoms?'). Van der Velde and Hooykaas (1996) argue that conditional risk estimates more closely resemble the perceived vulnerability construct as developed in SCMs such as the HBM and PMT. In support of their position, Van der Velde and Hooykaas (1996) found that an unconditional risk measure had a non-significant relationship with condom use intentions among STD clinic attendees with private partners only and a significant negative correlation among attendees with prostitution partners. In contrast, the expected positive correlation was found among both groups when a conditional perceived risk measure (for not using condoms) was employed. Van der Velde and Hooykaas (1996) therefore recommend the use of conditional measures when assessing the relationships between perceived risk and health-related intentions and behaviour.

The typically weak relationship between perceived risk and health-protective behaviour may also be due to some people underestimating their risk status. In particular, research has shown that most people tend to believe that they are at less risk than their peers. This tendency is referred to as the 'optimistic bias' or 'unrealistic optimism' (Weinstein and Klein 1996) and has been found in relation to a wide range of health problems including diabetes (e.g. Weinstein 1984), high blood pressure (e.g. Weinstein 1987), liver disease, heart disease and strokes (e.g. Harris and Middleton 1994). Weinstein (1983) explains the existence of such optimistic biases by arguing that individuals show selective focus when making comparative risk judgements, for example focusing primarily on their risk-reducing rather than their risk-increasing behaviour. In addition, this selective focus is compounded by egocentrism such that individuals will ignore others' risk-reducing behaviour when making comparative risk judgements. Moreover, there is some evidence that optimistic biases in risk perceptions inhibit the performance of precautionary behaviours (see Helweg-Larsen and Shepperd 2001). The existence of such biases may have important ramifications for attempts to change health behaviour. In particular, such attempts are unlikely to be successful if people do not pay close attention to risk information (Weinstein and Klein 1995), erroneously believing that such information is directed at others who are more at risk than themselves (Weinstein 1988). Unfortunately, research has shown that it can be difficult to eliminate optimistic biases in risk perceptions (Weinstein and Klein 1995).

As the above discussion highlights, there are various reasons for the weak relationship between perceived risk and health behaviour. Risk perceptions are unlikely to have a strong, proximal impact on behaviour, instead being of more importance in the early stages of behaviour. For example, Schwarzer (1992) places perceived risk in the motivation phase of health behaviour in the health action process approach (HAPA), arguing that perceptions of risk may stimulate people to start thinking about the benefits of engaging in a health-protective behaviour and their ability to perform the behaviour which, in turn, determine goal intentions. Similarly, in the precaution adoption process model (PAPM; Weinstein 1988), risk perceptions are held to have their most important effects in the relatively early stages of health behaviour. Moreover, Weinstein (1988) argues that risk perceptions should be characterized in terms of three stages. In the first stage, people are unaware of the health threat. In the second stage, people are aware of the threat but have not accepted that it is personally relevant, i.e. they are unengaged by the health threat. It is only in the third stage that people acknowledge the personal relevance of the health threat and, as a result, start to think about taking health-protective action. Other beliefs about the behaviour (e.g. its effectiveness and difficulty) then come into play and determine whether or not a person decides to act. In later stages, other activities such as the making of plans and the mobilization of relevant resources are required in order to ensure the person initiates and maintains performance of a behaviour. An important implication of the PAPM is that interventions that focus on risk perceptions should encourage movement through the early stages of health behaviour, whereas interventions that focus on the practicalities of performing a behaviour should be more effective in encouraging movement through the later stages of health behaviour. Weinstein *et al.* (1998) have presented experimental evidence in support of this proposition.

2.3 Other social cognition models

The models covered in this book do not represent the full range of SCMs that have been applied to the prediction of health behaviour. Other models, while not attracting as much research attention, nonetheless provide compelling accounts of the proximal determinants of health behaviour. We briefly review work on four such models: (a) the theory of interpersonal behaviour, (b) the theory of trying, (c) self-determination theory, and (d) the prototype/willingness model.

2.3.1 The theory of interpersonal behaviour

According to the theory of interpersonal behaviour (TIB; Triandis 1977, 1980), behaviour is a function of four factors; (a) intentions, (b) habits, (c) facilitating conditions, and (d) physiological arousal. Intentions here are defined as the self-instructions that individuals give themselves to behave in certain ways and are operationalized in a similar manner as in the TPB (Ajzen 1988). Triandis (1980: 204) also affords a predictive role to habits, which are 'situation–behavior sequences that are or have become automatic, so that they occur without self-instruction. The individual is usually not "conscious" of these sequences'. Triandis emphasizes the importance of a close correspondence between the situation, response (i.e. behaviour) and reinforcement in the development of habits, although most applications of the TIB simply assess habit as the frequency of past behaviour. However, even when people have formed strong intentions or have developed strong habits, environmental constraints may be encountered that impede performance of the behaviour. As a result, facilitating conditions (low versus high) are likely to have a strong influence on the likelihood of behaviour. Finally, the likelihood of performance of a behaviour is also dependent on the physiological arousal/state of the individual which may vary from zero (i.e. asleep) to 1.00 (i.e. extremely aroused). In general, increasing levels of physiological arousal are likely to facilitate performance of a behaviour, although under very high levels of arousal behaviour may be impeded. Triandis (1980) proposes that probability of action is a function of intentions plus habits multiplied by physiological arousal and facilitating conditions. Most applications of the model do not assess physiological arousal (or assume it to be optimum) and simply test the additive effects of the remaining three factors (i.e. intention, habit and facilitating conditions) on behaviour.

Intention, in turn, is seen to be a linear function of three factors. First is the consequences component which focuses on the perceived consequences of performing the behaviour weighted by the value attached to these consequences. Second is the affective component which focuses on the affective reactions that the individual associates with performing the behaviour (e.g. joy, displeasure, etc.). Third are social factors which refer to the individual's internalization of his/her reference group's subjective culture as well as specific interpersonal agreements made with other group members. These factors determine the extent to which an individual perceives a behaviour to be appropriate, desirable and morally correct.

The TIB has been successfully applied to a range of health behaviours including exercise (e.g. Godin and Gionet 1991), mammography screening (e.g. Lauver *et al.* 2003), cervical cancer screening (e.g. Seibold and Roper 1979), influenza vaccinations (e.g. Nowalk *et al.* 2004), and HIV-risk related behaviours (e.g. Apostolopoulos *et al.* 2003). For example, Apostolopoulos *et al.* (2003) used the TIB to predict the sexual behaviour of American undergraduates on their spring-break vacation. Variables from the TIB were able to explain 75 per cent of the variance in engaging in casual sex with social influences (i.e. having made a 'pact' to have causal sex), prior experience of casual sex, and facilitating factors (i.e. drinking prior to sexual activity and impulsivity) emerging as significant predictors. The TIB variables also explained 69 per cent of the variance in engaging in unprotected sex with two facilitating factors (i.e. the (un)availability of condoms and impulsivity) emerging as significant predictors.

The TIB has been found to provide strong predictions of health behaviour and, as a result, should provide a sound basis for the development of effective interventions. However, to date, there have been few TIB-based intervention studies. Caron *et al.* (2004) reported an evaluation of the 'Protection Express Program' to encourage safer sexual behaviour among high school students in Canada. The programme draws upon the TIB (and TPB) and a teaching model based on the principles of social cognitive theory (Bandura 1986). Peer educators were used to deliver the intervention to junior high school students. The intervention lasted two to three hours and targeted beliefs identified as predictors of sexual behaviour in a previous study among high school students (Caron *et al.* 1998). The intervention had significant impacts on all TIB and TPB variables at nine-month follow-up although no differences were found between intervention and control schools in postponing sexual intercourse and consistent condom use. The impact of the intervention on the TIB and TPB variables is encouraging and consistent with previous work that has shown that even relatively brief peer-led interventions can impact on psychosocial variables related to condom use (Dunn *et al.* 1998). However, the lack of an impact on behaviour is disappointing but may reflect relatively low levels of sexual activity among this age group.

The TIB has a number of similarities with the TPB, which may explain its strong predictive validity. For example, the cognitive component, social norm component and facilitating/impeding conditions parallel the attitude, subjective norm and perceived behavioural control components of the TPB. In addition, both the TIB and the TPB (a) posit intention to be a key mediating variable between more distal predictor variables and behaviour, (b) state that external variables (e.g. age, gender, personality) should have their influence through the variables contained in the models, (c) emphasize the importance of measuring the predictor variables and behaviour at the same level of specificity in terms of action, target, context and time, and (d) suggest that the relative weights of the predictor variables for both intention and behaviour should vary as a function of the population and behaviour under study.

However, the TIB provides a more inclusive model of health behaviour than the TPB in four ways. First, the TIB explicitly distinguishes between cognitive and affective reactions towards performing a behaviour. It has been suggested that affective reactions are lacking from the TPB and that they may be more important in the prediction of health behaviour (e.g. Van der Pligt and de Vries 1998). Second, the social factors component of the TIB considers a wider range of normative influences than does the subjective norm component of the TPB. Thus, the social factors component refers to perceived appropriateness of performing the behaviour based on group norms, roles and interpersonal agreements. In contrast, subjective norms focus solely on injunctive norms concerning what others would want the individual to do (see Cialdini *et al.* 1991). Third, the TIB also focuses on moral considerations within the social factors component which, again, some researchers have suggested should be added to the TPB (e.g. Manstead 2000). Fourth, and most importantly, the TIB includes habit as a predictor of future behaviour along with intention and facilitating conditions. Triandis (1977) equates habit with the frequency of past behaviour and this, in part, may explain the strong predictive validity of the model reported in many applications, given that past behaviour is often found to be the best predictor of future behaviour (Ouellette and Wood 1998).

A number of additional comments are worth making on the TIB as a model of health behaviour. First, the structure of the TIB suggests that intention should mediate the influence of more distal TIB predictors on behaviour. However, few TIB studies have tested this mediation hypothesis, instead either considering the impact of all the TIB variables on behaviour in a single regression equation (e.g. Apostolopoulos *et al.* 2003) or only examining the predictors of intention (e.g. Gagnon and Godin 2000). Second, many tests of the TIB have been performed in conjunction with other SCMs including the theories of reasoned action (e.g. Boyd and Wandersman 1991) and planned behaviour (e.g. Belanger *et al.* 2002) and the transtheoretical model of change (e.g. Lauver *et al.* 2003). TIB variables are typically found to explain additional variance in intention and behaviour. Third, there is a lack of consistency in the description and operationalization of the model in the literature. Thus, studies may list different constructs as being part of the TIB, employ different labels to describe the same constructs, and operationalize specific TIB variables in different ways. Fourth, the TIB does not explicitly include self-efficacy as a predictor.

Instead, Triandis (1980) argues that perceptions of the ease/difficultly of performing a behaviour are covered by the consequences component. However, this is an important omission given that self-efficacy is widely recognized as being one of the most powerful predictors of health behaviour (see Luszczynska and Schwarzer, Chapter 4 in this volume). Finally, further experimental/intervention work is required both to test the structure of the model and to aid the design of effective health behaviour interventions.

2.3.2 Theory of trying

Bagozzi (1992) developed a 'theory of trying' to describe the influences upon the intention to try and actual trying to achieve a particular goal. These variables are assumed by Bagozzi to replace intention and behaviour in the TPB. Trying is held to be the more relevant variable to predict because behaviour can be successful or unsuccessful without the determining factors being any different. Trying is based on the intention to try, frequency of past trying, and recency of past trying. Intention to try is also based on frequency of past trying along with four other factors: (a) the attitude towards success and expectation of success, (b) the attitude toward failure and expectation of failure, (c) the attitude toward the process and (d) the subjective norm toward trying. Also, particularly in relation to intermediate goal-directed behaviour, intentions to try can be formed towards a range of ways or means of attempting to achieve a goal and individuals must select amongst these means. This distinction is similar to Gollwitzer's (1993) distinction between goal intention (i.e. intention to try to achieve a goal) and behavioural intention (i.e. intention to achieve a goal via a specific means).

Bagozzi (1992) suggests that decisions about the means to achieve a goal are determined by three interrelated processes. First, there are specific self-efficacy considerations. Means which the individual does not perceive themselves as capable of performing are less likely to be adopted, whereas means which the individual perceives to be easily executable are more likely to be performed. Second, instrumental beliefs (or outcome expectancies) will play a role such that only means perceived to be likely to lead to the desired outcome or goal are likely to be adopted. Third, the desirability or affect towards the means will have an impact. More desirable means are more likely to be adopted, while noxious means are likely to be avoided. The outcome of these processes is the choice amongst means and subsequent trying to perform these actions in pursuit of the goal. Presumably successful goal achievement is dependent upon the selection of appropriate means which are indeed efficacious in achieving the goal.

Bagozzi and Edwards (1998) have tested this model in relation to the regulation of body weight. Their model suggests that the three appraisal processes (self-efficacy, instrumental beliefs, affect) act either additively or interactively to determine one's choice of means to an end depending on the perceived difficulty of initiating the behaviour. Where there are few internal or external impediments it is proposed that the three appraisal processes act additively. Thus, the more the action is seen as being within one's capabilities, to lead to the intended outcome, and to be enjoyable or pleasant, the more likely is it to be performed. In contrast, where there are strong internal or external impediments to the action it is proposed that the three processes act interactively. Thus, the behaviour is only likely to be performed if all three appraisal processes are high (i.e. supportive of the behaviour). Bagozzi and Edwards (1998) tested these predictions in relation to young men and women engaging in a range of dieting or exercising behaviours designed to reduce or maintain weight. In line with predictions, they found that for both dieting and exercising behaviours, self-efficacy, outcome expectancy or affect towards the means were sufficient to initiate action (i.e. an additive model). Self-efficacy in particular was an important determinant of each of the dieting and exercising behaviours examined. The formation of intentions, strengthening of commitment, and maintenance of behaviour over time were all increased with high levels of self-efficacy. This effect has also been demonstrated for both dieting (Shannon *et al.* 1992) and exercise (McAuley 1993) behaviours in other studies. However, when exercise behaviours in women were examined separately, a three-way interaction was found between self-efficacy, outcome expectancy and affect. Participation by women in exercise and sporting activities as a means for body weight control occurred only when self-efficacy, outcome expectancy and affect towards means were jointly favourable.

Bagozzi's work with the theory of trying points to the importance of a number of cognitive factors in complex health behaviours such as weight control. A strong motivation or intention to control one's weight is important, but only in terms of providing the motivation to engage in weight control behaviours. In terms of which behaviours are engaged in to control weight, feeling confident that one can perform the behaviour (i.e. self-efficacy) is particularly important. Where the behaviour is difficult, perceiving the behaviour to lead to favoured outcomes (e.g. weight loss) and enjoying the behaviour are also important. These variables could provide important targets for interventions designed to increase weight control efforts.

The importance of the theory of trying lies in its attempt to link goal intentions to the choice of specific courses of action to achieve these goals. The determinants of goal intentions are somewhat similar to models such as the TPB. Bagozzi and Kimmel (1995) report only limited evidence to support the superiority of the theory of trying to the TPB. Thus, where the focus is on a single behaviour the contribution of the theory of trying may be limited. In contrast, where the focus is on a health behaviour goal which can be achieved through different means the theory of trying provides a useful framework for considering the influences on which specific means or behaviours are selected. However, it has been argued that the best predictions may be achieved through examining the predictors of each potential means or behaviour (e.g. using the TPB; see Fishbein 1993). Studies to compare these possibilities are required (see Conner and Norman 1996 for a partial attempt). More generally, further applications of the theory of trying are required before a definitive judgement can be reached about its value in relation to understanding the pursuit of health goals.

2.3.3 Self-determination theory

Self-determination theory (SDT; Deci and Ryan 1985; Ryan and Deci 2000) represents a somewhat different approach to the prediction of health behaviour, focusing on people's psychological needs for competence (Harter 1978), autonomy (Deci 1975), and relatedness (Baumeister and Leary 1995). The main contribution of SDT is the distinction that it makes between different types of motivated behaviour. These are placed along a continuum according to the degree to which the motivation to perform a behaviour is seen to emanate from the self (i.e. is self-determined or autonomous). At one end of the continuum is *amotivation*, a state which reflects a lack of intention to act. Amotivation is seen to be the result from an individual not valuing the target activity, not feeling competent to per-form the activity and not expecting that the activity will lead to a desired outcome. At the other end of the continuum is *intrinsic motivation* which is highly autonomous and represents the prototypical case of self-determination. Behaviour that is regulated by intrinsic motivation is per-formed for its own sake – i.e. for the inherent enjoyment of performing the behaviour.

Between amotivation and intrinsic motivation is *extrinsic motivation* that reflects behaviour that is performed in order to obtain some outcome, other than the inherent satisfaction or enjoyment of performing the behaviour. SDT proposes that behaviours that are extrinsically motivated vary according to their relative autonomy and outlines four regulatory styles that can be used to guide such behaviours. First is *external regulation* where behaviour is performed to satisfy an external demand or reward con-tingency. Second, behaviours that are guided by *introjected regulation* are performed to avoid negative feelings such as guilt or shame. Behaviours guided by these first two regulatory styles are clearly intended, in that individuals will feel competent to perform the behaviours and believe that they will lead to certain outcomes, but they cannot be said to be autono-mous given that the value and regulation of the behaviour have not been internalized and integrated into the self. Third, behaviours guided by *identified regulation* are seen to be more autonomous and self-determined in nature. Such behaviours are experienced by individuals as being important for functioning effectively in the social world. Fourth, and the most autonomous form of extrinsic motivation, is *integrated regulation* which occurs when the value and regulation of the behaviour are fully assimilated to the self. In other words, performance of the behaviour is consistent with the individual's other values and needs. Behaviours guided by these last two regulatory styles share many qualities with those regulated by intrinsic motivation but they are still considered to be the result of extrinsic motivation as they are performed to obtain outcomes other than the inherent enjoyment of performing the behaviour.

In many SDT studies identified, integrated and intrinsic motivation are combined to form an 'autonomous motivation' measure that can be contrasted with more 'controlled' or extrinsic motivation. This distinction between autonomous and controlled motivated behaviour has important implications for the study of intention–behaviour relations. For example, autonomous motivation has been found to be associated with more interest, excitement and confidence which, in turn, is related to enhanced performance, persistence, generalizability and creativity (see Ryan and Deci 2000). In relation to the prediction of health behaviour, more autonomous motivation has been related to greater adherence to medication among people with chronic illnesses (Williams *et al.* 1998b) and, among people with diabetes, to improved glucose control (Williams *et al.* 1998a) and dietary self-care activities (Senécal et al. 2000). In addition, autonomous motivation has also been found to be predictive of weight loss in the obese (Williams *et al.* 1996), smoking cessation (Williams *et al.* 2002), and exercise behaviour (Chatzisarantis *et al.* 1997).

SDT also incorporates a number of sub-theories that seek to outline the factors that may hinder or facilitate different types of motivation, which may form the basis of interventions to encourage more autonomous motivation. Thus cognitive evaluation theory (CET; Deci and Ryan 1985) focuses on the factors that are important in explaining variability in intrinsic motivation. First, intrinsic motivation is likely to be enhanced following feedback that leads to increased feelings of competence (e.g. Deci 1975). However, second, feelings of competence also need to be coupled with a sense of autonomy for intrinsic motivation to be enhanced (e.g. Ryan 1982). Third, introducing extrinsic rewards has been shown to undermine intrinsic motivation (Deci *et al.* 1999). Fourth, situations that are characterized by a sense of security or relatedness may also encourage intrinsic motivation (Ryan and Grolnick 1986). Research on CET has provided strong evidence for the proposed links between intrinsic motivation and the satisfaction of needs for autonomy and competence and, to a lesser extent, for relatedness (see Ryan and Deci 2000). A second sub-theory is organismic integration theory (OIT; Deci and Ryan 1985) which examines the factors that may encourage the internalization and integration of extrinsically motivated and regulated behaviours. First, it is proposed that internalization is more likely to occur when the behaviour is prompted, modelled or valued by important others as this is likely to satisfy the need for relatedness (e.g. Ryan *et al.* 1994). Second, internalization should also be enhanced by engendering feelings of competence (e.g. Vallerand 1997). Third, the experience of autonomy is also likely to lead to greater internalization (e.g. Grolnick and Ryan 1989).

A number of SDT-based intervention studies have been reported in the literature in relation to health behaviour, albeit with mixed results. For example, Williams *et al.* (2002) compared the impact of physicians' use of either autonomy-supportive or controlling interpersonal styles when advising smokers to quit. Unfortunately the counselling style of the physician had no direct effect on cessation rates. However, an indirect effect was observed such that counselling style impacted on the smokers' perceptions of autonomy support which were predictive of autonomous motivation which, in turn, predicted cessation. Similar findings have been reported by Williams *et al.* (2004) in relation to health care activities among patients with diabetes. However, more positive results for SDT-based interventions have been reported in relation to glycemic control (Greenfield *et al.* 1988) and exercise behaviour (Vansteenkiste *et al.* 2004).

To conclude, SDT's importance lies in making the distinction between different types of motivation and highlighting the role of intrinsic motivation in regulating health behaviour. However, more research is needed on a wider range of health behaviours to replicate initial positive findings and on interventions designed to increase autonomous motivation. In addition, more attention needs to be given to the measurement of intrinsic (i.e. autonomous) motivation as a number of inconsistent measures exist in the literature. Finally, further research is required to test whether the effects of autonomous motivation are independent of perceived competence and, to a lesser extent, relatedness.

2.3.4 Prototype/willingness model

SCMs may provide relatively poor predictions of health-impairing, or health-risk, behaviours (see Van den Putte 1991 for a review). It is clear that, good intentions notwithstanding, many young people engage in health-risk behaviours such as unprotected sex (Brooks-Gunn and Furnstenberg 1989). Gibbons and Gerrard (1995, 1997) argue that young people are likely to experience situations in which opportunities to engage in health-risk behaviours present themselves. In such situations, they may be 'willing' to engage in the behaviour given the opportunity to do so. Thus, their behaviour reflects a reaction to the social situation rather than a premeditated intention to engage in a health-risk behaviour. Gibbons and Gerrard (1995, 1997) developed the prototype/willingness model (PWM) to provide an account of such health-risk behaviour among adolescents and young people.

The PWM has three underlying assumptions. The first is that many of the health-risk behaviours performed by young people are neither intentional nor planned. Instead, they are the result of reactions to the risk-conducive situations that many young people are likely to encounter. Second, health-risk behaviours are typically performed with, or in the presence of, others (Nadler and Fisher 1992). In other words, they are *social* events. As a result, social comparison processes are likely to have an important impact on the health-risk behaviour of young people. Third, young people are highly concerned about their social images and, as a result, are likely to be very aware of the social implications of their behaviour (Simmons and Blyth 1987). This may be particularly the case for behaviours that are performed with others in social settings and that are associated with vivid/salient images, for example of the 'typical drinker' or the 'typical smoker' (Gibbons and Gerrard 1997; Blanton *et al.* 2001). Therefore, performing a health-risk behaviour has an important social consequence, i.e. an acceptance of the image associated with the behaviour.

PWM outlines two 'pathways' to health-risk behaviour among adolescents and young adults. The first is a 'reasoned pathway' reflecting the operation of more or less rational decision-making processes as outlined in the major SCMs. In this pathway, health-risk behaviour is based on a consideration of the pros and cons of performing the behaviour. As a result, behavioural intention (or expectation) is seen to be the proximal predictor of health-risk behaviour in this pathway. Gibbons and Gerrard (1995, 1997) use measures of behavioural expectations rather than of behavioural intentions to predict health-risk behaviour (see Sheppard *et al.* 1988), arguing that adolescents may be more likely to acknowledge that they are likely to perform a health-risk behaviour in the future than they are to admit that they intend to do so.

The second pathway to health-risk behaviour is a 'social reaction pathway' which forms the cornerstone of the PWM. This pathway includes four factors that impact on individuals' willingness to engage in health-risk behaviours when they encounter risk-conducive situations. First are *subjective norms* that focus on perceptions of whether important others engage in the behaviour and whether they are likely to approve or disapprove of the individual performing the behaviour. In this way, Gibbons and Gerrard (1995, 1997) highlight the importance of both descriptive and injunctive social norms (Cialdini *et al.* 1991). Second are *attitudes* that are primarily concerned with the perceived likelihood of negative outcomes (e.g. perceived vulnerability). In particular, a willingness to perform a health-risk behaviour in a risk-conducive situation may be associated with a downplaying of the risks associated with the behaviour. *Past behaviour* is the third factor seen to impact on behavioural willingness. Given that many health-risk behaviours attract social approval and are enjoyable, having performed a health-risk behaviour in the past may be associated with more positive subjective norms (Gerrard *et al.* 1996), more positive attitudes (Bentler and Speckart 1979) and a greater willingness to perform the behaviour again in the future (Gibbons *et al.* 1998a). The fourth, and unique, factor in the PWM is the *prototype* associated with the health-risk behaviour, i.e. the image that people have of the type of person who engages in a certain behaviour (e.g. the 'typical ecstasy user'). According to the PWM, prototype favourability (i.e. the extent to which the image is positively evaluated) and prototype similarity (i.e. the perceived similarity between the image and one's self) interact to impact on individuals' willingness to engage in a health-risk behaviour. The four factors identified in the 'social reaction pathway' are seen to have their influence through *behavioural willingness*. Gibbons and Gerrard (1995, 1997) argue that the willingness to engage in a health-risk behaviour in a risk conducive situation provides a better prediction of subsequent behaviour than does behavioural expectation as it reflects the social reactive nature of many of the health-risk behaviours performed by young people.

The PWM has been applied to a variety of health-risk behaviours including smoking (e.g. Blanton *et al.* 1997), unprotected sex (e.g. Thornton *et al.* 2002), alcohol use (e.g. Gerrard *et al.* 2002) and drink-driving (e.g. Gibbons *et al.* 1998b). These studies provide empirical support for various key aspects of the PWM. For example, studies have found behavioural willingness to be predictive of subsequent health-risk behaviour, independent of behavioural expectations (e.g. Gerrard *et al.* 2002). In addition, prototype perceptions have been found to predict both behavioural willingness (e.g. Thornton *et al.* 2002) and health-risk behaviour (e.g. Blanton *et al.* 1997). A good example of a PWM application is provided by the Gibbons *et al.* (1998a) study on unprotected sexual intercourse among college students. Using structural equation modelling, the PWM model was found to explain 66 per cent of the variance in sexual behaviour (i.e. sexual intercourse without using any form of birth control) with past behaviour, behavioural expectation and behavioural willingness having direct, significant effects. In turn, behavioural expectation was predicted by subjective norms, attitudes and past behaviour ($R^2 = 0.55$). These three variables were also predictive of behavioural willingness along with prototype perceptions ($R^2 = 0.40$). It is noteworthy that prototype perceptions only had an effect on behavioural willingness, in line with PWM predictions.

Despite these encouraging findings, there are various issues for future work to address. First, the making of social comparisons is assumed to be a crucial process in the 'social reaction pathway'. However, few studies have tested whether the link between prototype perceptions and health-risk behaviour is stronger among those who engage in social comparisons. For example, Gibbons and Gerrard (1995) found significant interactions between prototype perceptions and social comparisons in relation to reckless driving and ineffective contraception. As expected, stronger prototype–behaviour relations were found among those respondents who reported that they often compared themselves with others in terms of their social behaviour.

Second, the PWM focuses on the images associated with the performance of health-risk behaviours and their impact on behavioural willingness. However, it is also likely that people will have images of the typical person who engages in non-risk behaviour and that these images also impact on behaviour. Gerrard *et al.* (2002) argue that non-risk prototype perceptions are likely to be the result of more extensive deliberations and a desire to avoid being identified with the risk image. As a result, non-risk prototype perceptions may have their impact via the 'reasoned pathway', in contrast to risk-related prototype perceptions that have their impact via the 'social reaction pathway'. In support of this position, Gerrard *et al.* (2002) found that the effect of prototype perceptions of the 'typical drinker' on subsequent behaviour was mediated by behavioural willingness, in line with the PWM. In contrast, prototype perceptions of the 'typical non-drinker' had a direct, unmediated effect on subsequent behaviour. Rivis and Sheeran (2003) have also found that non-risk prototype perceptions, of the 'type of person who exercises at least three times a week', were predictive of exercise intentions and behaviour.

Overall, there is considerable empirical support for the PWM in relation to the prediction of health-risk behaviour among young people. The PWM may add to our ability to predict health behaviour in two main ways. First, the PWM highlights that many health-risk behaviours are not intentional or planned. Instead, people may be reacting to risk-conducive situations in which they are willing to perform the behaviour. As such, the PWM provides an additional account of the 'intention–behaviour gap' (Sheeran 2002) in those situations where people engage in non-intended behaviour. Second, the PWM highlights the importance of prototype perceptions as an additional source of normative influence on health behaviour. As Rivis and Sheeran (2003) have shown, measures of prototype perceptions could usefully be added to current, more 'reasoned', SCMs.

2.4 The role of past behaviour and habit

A major shortcoming of the major SCMs is their inability to account fully for the influence of past behaviour on future behaviour. Past behaviour is often found to have a strong relationship with future behaviour that is not mediated by social cognitive variables. For example, past behaviour has been found to be a strong predictor in TPB applications explaining, on average, an additional 13.0 per cent of the variance in future behaviour (Conner and Armitage 1998). Similar findings have been noted in relation to other SCMs, although tests of the impact of past behaviour on future behaviour are less common than in TPB studies. For example, the HBM has been found to be unable to fully mediate the effects of past behaviour in relation to the uptake of flu immunizations (Cummings *et al.* 1979) and the performance of BSE (Norman and Brain, 2005). Direct effects for past behaviour have also been reported in PMT studies on binge drinking (Murgraff *et al.* 1999), BSE (Hodgkins and Orbell 1998) and treatment adherence (Norman *et al.* 2003), as well as in applications of SCT to alcohol, marijuana and other drug use (Cohen and Fromme 2002). Such findings have led to a call for past behaviour to be included in social cognition models as an additional predictor variable (e.g. Bentler and Speckart 1979). However, Ajzen (1987) has cautioned against such a move, pointing out that past behaviour has no explanatory value – one is unlikely to exercise tomorrow *because* one exercised yesterday. Instead, it is necessary to offer a theoretical account of the ways in which past behaviour may influence future behaviour and this has been provided by Ouellette and Wood (1998) in their review of past behaviour–future behaviour relations. They proposed that past behaviour may have its impact on future behaviour through one of two routes, depending on the frequency of the opportunity to perform the behaviour and the stability of the context in which the behaviour is performed.

First, for behaviours that are performed relatively infrequently in unstable contexts, past behaviour may provide individuals with information that shapes their beliefs about the behaviour which, in turn, determine intention and future behaviour (i.e. a conscious response). For such behaviours, past behaviour affects future behaviour indirectly through its influence on beliefs and intention. Such an account is consistent with the structure of major SCMs. For example, Rogers (1983) sees prior experience (i.e. past behaviour) as an intrapersonal source of information that may initiate the cognitive processes outlined in PMT, while Bandura (1986) contends that personal (mastery) experience is an important source of self-efficacy. Similarly, Ajzen (1991) argues that the impact of past behaviour should be mediated by TPB variables and, in particular, the perceived behavioural control construct.

The second way in which past behaviour may impact on future behaviour is through the formation of a habitual response. Thus, for behaviours that are performed relatively frequently in stable contexts, the impact of past behaviour may reflect the operation of habitual responses which do not require the mediation of intention. For such behaviours, intentions (and other social cognitive variables) may lose their predictive validity and past behaviour will have a direct effect on future behaviour. The idea behind this proposition is that the repeated execution of the same behaviour (i.e. response) in the same context is likely to lead to formation of a habitual response. As a result, the behaviour is performed automatically and efficiently with little effort or conscious awareness in response to relevant stimulus cues. The direct effect of past behaviour on future behaviour can therefore be interpreted in terms of the operation of habits which are 'learned sequences of acts that have become automatic responses to specific cues' (Verplanken and Aarts 1999: 104).

Ouellette and Wood's (1998) analysis of past behaviour–future behaviour relations is important for two main reasons. First, it allows for the direct effect of past behaviour on future behaviour found in many studies to be interpreted in terms of the operation of habits, and second, it delineates the circumstances under which intention and past behaviour are expected to predict behaviour (i.e. frequency of opportunity/stability of context). In particular, for behaviours that are performed relatively infrequently in unstable contexts, intention should be the primary predictor of future behaviour (reflecting the operation of conscious responses), whereas for behaviours that are performed relatively frequently in stable contexts past behaviour is expected to be the primary predictor of future behaviour (reflecting the operation of habitual responses). Ouellette and Wood (1998) conducted a meta-analysis to test these predictions in which behaviours were classified according to whether they had the opportunity to be performed frequently in stable environmental contexts or infrequently in unstable environmental contexts. When the joint effects of past behaviour and intention were assessed in a regression analysis, past behaviour (Beta = 0.45) was found to be a stronger predictor than intention (Beta = 0.27) of frequent/stable behaviours, whereas intention (Beta = 0.62) was a stronger predictor than past behaviour (Beta = 0.12) of infrequent/unstable behaviours. These results are consistent with the idea that infrequent/unstable behaviours are primarily under the control of conscious processes whereas frequent/stable behaviours are primarily under the control of habitual processes. However, certain aspects of both the methodology and the interpretation of the results of Ouellette and Wood's (1998) study have been questioned (Ajzen 2002; Sheeran 2002).

Considering methodological factors, Sheeran (2002) noted that the regression analyses of the joint effects of past behaviour and intention on future behaviour were based on only eight studies of frequent/stable behaviours and six studies of infrequent/unstable behaviours. In addition, given that there was a substantial overlap between the frequency of opportunity of performance and the stability of the context in which the behaviours were performed, the behaviours were classified into frequent/stable versus infrequent/unstable behaviours. As a result of this combination, it is not possible to delineate whether the observed effects are due to the frequency of performance, the stability of the context, or a combination of both.

There are a number of alternative interpretations of the results presented by Ouellette and Wood (1998). In particular, care needs to taken when attributing residual variance to habit, even for frequent/stable behaviours, as the direct effect of past behaviour on future behaviour may simply indicate that a model is not sufficient and that additional, social cognitive, predictors need to be considered. As Ajzen (1991) argues, assuming that the determinants of behaviour remain stable over time, the past behaviour–future behaviour correlation can be taken as an indication of the ceiling of a model's predictive validity. If a model contains all the important proximal determinants of a behaviour (i.e. is sufficient), then the addition of past behaviour in a regression analysis should not explain additional variance in future behaviour. Thus, when a direct effect is found between past behaviour and future behaviour this may simply indicate that the model is not sufficient rather than the operation of habitual responses. In addition, even when past behaviour is found to explain additional variance in future behaviour, part of this effect may be the result of shared method variance inasmuch as measures of past behaviour and future behaviour are likely to be more similar than measures of intention and future behaviour.

Ajzen (2002) has provided a more fundamental critique of Ouellette and Wood's (1998) hypotheses. Ajzen (2002) notes that the habitual account of the direct effect of past behaviour on future behaviour is based on the premise that habitual responses are likely to form when behaviours are performed repeatedly in stable contexts. However, this explanation does not account for the residual impact of past behaviour that is often found for low-frequency behaviours such as attendance at health checks (e.g. Norman and Conner 1996). Furthermore, it is clear that intention is a significant predictor of both infrequent/unstable and frequent/stable behaviours, even in conjunction with past behaviour. Ajzen (2002) argues that for behaviours that are performed frequently, intentions themselves might be automatically activated by situational cues and used to guide behaviour without the necessity of conscious awareness or control. As Heckhausen and Beckmann (1990: 38) propose, 'intents resemble plans about how to act when predetermined cues or conditions occur. Once formed, however, the intents no longer require much conscious control. Instead, they are triggered as automatic or quasi-automatic operations.' In many ways, this conceptualization of well-formed intentions has parallels with the concept of implementation intentions (Gollwitzer 1993), which are seen to mimic habitual responses by linking an intended action to an environmental cue. Finally, Ajzen (2002) notes that inferring the existence of a habit from a strong past behaviour–future behaviour correlation and then using the concept to explain the existence of the strong correlation involves a circular argument. Instead, an independent measure of habit is required in order to be able to use habit as an explanation for the existence of strong past behaviour–future behaviour correlations. Using frequency of past behaviour as a measure of habit strength fails to capture all of the defining features of a habitual response. Habitual behaviours are performed frequently (i.e. have a history of repetition), but they are also performed automatically, efficiently, and with little effort or conscious awareness in response to stable environmental cues. In short, it is necessary to develop measures of habit strength that show discriminant validity with respect to frequency of past behaviour (Ronis *et al.* 1989) when attempting to provide an explanation for the strength of past behaviour–future behaviour relations. A number of measures of habit strength have been reported in the literature.

Alternative self-reported measures of habit strength ask participants to indicate how often they perform a behaviour 'by force of habit' or 'without awareness' (e.g. Kahle and Beatty 1987; Conner and McMillan 1999). Such measures have been found to be predictive of future behaviour, although they have not been shown to moderate intention–future behaviour relations (e.g. Conner and McMillan 1999). In addition, they have two common shortcomings: (a) they ask for simultaneous estimates of behavioural frequency and the extent to which the behaviour is habitual in nature, and (b) they tend to be single-item measures. Verplanken *et al.* (1994) therefore developed a script-based, or response-frequency, measure of habit strength. Participants are presented with a series of habit-related situations and are instructed to respond as quickly as possible with their behavioural choice. The number of times a participant responds with the same behavioural choice over different situations is taken as a measure of habit strength. This measure has been shown to moderate the intention–future behaviour relationship in relation to travel mode choice in line with predictions (Verplanken *et al.* 1998). However, such script-based measures of habit strength have a number of limitations. First, it is possible to question the extent to which habits are akin to behavioural scripts which are knowledge structures that contain 'a standard sequence of events characterizing typical activities' (Abelson 1981: 715). Second, Ajzen (2002) has argued that it may be more appropriate to interpret the response-frequency measure of habit strength as a generalized measure of intention. Third, the measure is restricted to choice behaviours that are executed in different contexts, which goes against the importance that is afforded to the stability of the environmental context in the formation of habits. Fourth, the development of such a measure requires extensive pilot work to identify key situations and, finally, its administration requires a controlled research environment which is not always available when conducting applied research.

Given these criticisms, Verplanken and Orbell (2003) have developed a self-report index of habit strength. The 12-item measure is based on various key features of habitual responses reflecting a history of repetition (e.g. 'X is something I do frequently'), automaticity (e.g. 'X is something I do without having to consciously remember') and the expression of one's identity (cf. Trafimow and Wyer 1993) (e.g. 'X is something that's typically "me"'). The self-report habit index (SRHI) has been found to be a reliable measure that correlates with the response-frequency measure of habit and with frequency of past behaviour. In addition, it has been shown to discriminate successfully between three behaviours differing in average behavioural frequency and between behaviours performed weekly versus daily. Despite the initial promise of this measure, it remains for future work to demonstrate that it can be used to account for strong past behaviour–future behaviour correlations. In particular, the SHRI should be able to mediate the relationship between past behaviour and future behaviour.

2.5 Dual process models

Over the last twenty years, two distinct approaches to understanding the impact of attitudes on behaviour within the field of attitude theory have consolidated: automatic and deliberative (Eagly and Chaiken 1998). These two approaches have been combined in various dual process theories. The most influential of these has been Fazio's (1990) MODE (Motivation and Opportunity as Determinants) model which focuses on automatic and deliberative ways in which attitudes impact on behaviour. The automatic component of this model relies heavily on Fazio's attitudes-to-behaviour model while the deliberative component is more similar to models such as the TPB (Ajzen 1988). Given our focus on deliberative models in this book, this section reviews research on more automatic processes.

Various priming studies have provided evidence for the role of automatic processes in guiding behaviour (e.g. Bargh *et al.* 1996). Bargh (1997: 243) has gone as far as to speculate that behaviour is '99 and 44/100 per cent automatic'. Numerous studies have shown that activating traits, stereotypes or goals outside conscious awareness can automatically elicit behaviour consistent with these constructs. For example, Macrae and Johnson (1998) primed participants with the trait 'helpful' outside their conscious awareness. At the end of the experiment, the experimenter gathered some belongings and asked the participant to follow her to another experiment. She then 'accidentally' dropped her belongings as she approached the door. Participants primed with the 'helpful' trait picked up more items from the floor than did controls (i.e. they behaved in a more 'helpful' way). Bargh *et al.* (1996) has also shown that priming participants with an elderly stereotype leads to them taking longer to walk along a corridor from the experiment room to the nearest lift, compared to non-primed controls. Finally, Bargh and Chartrand (1999) reported that participants primed with an achievement goal were more likely to continue working on a task after being told to stop than non-primed controls.

Such findings are indicative of a direct link between the unconscious activation of goals, traits and/or stereotypes and behaviour. In short, they provide insights into the 'unconscious mechanisms of the mind' (Wegner and Wheatley 1999: 490) that underlie behaviour. However, there are a number of criticisms that can be made of these priming studies (see Sheeran 2002). First, the fact that participants' behaviour can be manipulated through priming traits, stereotypes or goals in the laboratory provides little information on the extent to which priming is responsible for health behaviour outside the laboratory. Second, the behaviours typically considered in priming studies are less involving than those typically studied in applications of SCMs. Third, it remains to be demonstrated that health behaviour is better predicted by priming traits, stereotypes or goals than by more deliberative processes based on the variables outlined in SCMs (e.g. intention). Fourth, it is possible that conscious intentions may mediate the influence of unconscious primes on behaviour. For example, in the Macrae and Johnston (1998) study it is likely that participants primed with 'helpful' traits may have formed an intention to help the experimenter when she dropped her possessions and would have been able to report having such an intention if questioned. Finally, it is important to recognize that unconscious primes on individuals' behaviour can be over-ridden by other active, conscious, goals. For example, in the Macrae and Johnston (1998) study, when participants were told that they running late and had to hurry to the next experiment, the effect of priming 'helpful' traits on helping behaviour disappeared. In other words, the conflicting conscious goal had a more powerful impact on their behaviour. In summary, it remains for future research to determine the extent of the influence of automatic processes (e.g. primes) on health behaviour, particularly vis-à-vis the role of (conscious) goals and intentions.

Work on automatic processes extends beyond priming studies and is not so open to these criticisms. For example, the implicit association test (IAT; Greenwald et al. 1998) has been specifically developed to measure implicit attitudes and used in several studies (see Greenwald and Nosek 2001). The IAT is a computerized method for measuring indirectly the strength of the association between pairs of concepts via a discrimination task. It relies on the assumption that, if two concepts are highly associated (congruent), the discrimination task will be easier, and therefore quicker, when the associated concepts share the same response key than when they require different response keys (see Greenwald et al. 1998, for more details about the procedure). Although the IAT has primarily been used for topics such as prejudice (Dasgupta et al. 2000) and self-esteem (Greenwald and Farnham 2000), a few studies have also investigated the predictive power of the IAT for behaviours such as smoking (Swanson et al. 2001) and consumers' choice of drinking products (Maison et al. 2001). In most of these studies, measures of explicit attitudes have also been assessed. Correlations between explicit and implicit measures tend to be low (on average in the region of

0.20 to 0.30). There is only modest evidence concerning their relative predictive power, with implicit measures showing greater predictive power for some behaviours and explicit measures showing greater predictive power for other behaviours. For example, Stacy *et al.* (2000) reported that implicit attitudes predicted lack of condom use, although the predictive power was modest compared to other studies using explicit attitudes (e.g. Albarracin *et al.* 2001). Indeed not all studies have found implicit measures to show predictive power (e.g. Karpinski and Hilton 2001) and generally the predictive power of explicit attitudes tends to exceed by far the power of implicit attitudes. Although the vast majority of studies have employed the IAT, a range of other implicit measures have been employed including the Extrinsic Affective Simon Task, and Dot Probe Tasks. Fazio and Olson (2003) provide a useful review of these measures.

Wilson *et al.* (2000) recently proposed a model of dual attitudes (MDA). The MDA is interesting because it specifically considers the way in which implicit and explicit attitudes determine behaviour. Wilson *et al.* (2000) distinguish between four main cases where implicit and explicit attitudes conflict (repression, independent systems, motivated overriding, automatic overriding), corresponding to the combination of awareness of the implicit attitude, once activated, and the amount of motivation and cognitive effort needed for the explicit attitude to override the implicit one. According to this framework, implicit attitudes guide behaviour that people do not monitor consciously or that they do not see as an expression of their attitude, whereas explicit attitudes predict controlled behaviours or behaviours that people see as expressive of their attitudes. At present, the empirical evidence supporting these claims comes mainly from research on prejudice and stereotyping (e.g. Fazio *et al.* 1995). Further research with a broader range of behaviours is required. In addition, the theoretical elaboration of Wilson and colleagues is focused only on cases of conflicts between implicit and explicit attitudes. It is not clear what predictions are made when implicit and explicit attitudes are congruent. Perugini (in press) distinguishes between an additive effect (i.e. they explain independent variance in predicting behaviour), a multiplicative effect (i.e. the variance predicted in behaviour is higher when both attitudes are congruent), or a dissociative effect (i.e. the variance in behaviour is predicted by whichever is the more predictive of the two attitudes, with no additional contribution of the other attitude). In relation to smoking, Perugini (in press) reports evidence for a multiplicative effect of implicit and explicit attitudes, while for snacking a dissociative effect was observed. Interactive effects have also been reported for condom use (Marsh *et al.* submitted). In contrast, O'Gorman *et al.* (2004) mainly found evidence for additive effects for sweet consumption. Other research has begun to examine consumption of high-fat foods (Roefs and Janssen 2002) and alcohol (Wiers *et al.* 2002). A more detailed discussion of the interaction between implicit and explicit influences on behaviour can be found in Strack and Deutsch (2004).

Further research on the interaction between implicit and explicit measures of attitudes in determining health behaviour is required to address a number of outstanding questions. First, what is the relative predictive power of explicit and implicit attitudes? Second, for what types of behaviours might we expect one, other or both measures to be important? Third, what conditions promote or inhibit the relative power of implicit and explicit measures to determine behaviour? The answers to these questions are likely to provide us with a fuller understanding of the relative impact of automatic and deliberative influences on health behaviour.

2.6 Maintenance of health behaviour

Research with SCMs has tended to focus on the initiation of health behaviour. This is appropriate for behaviours where health benefits are associated with one-off performance (e.g. immunization). However, other health behaviours (e.g. healthy eating, exercise) provide little or no health benefit unless maintained over prolonged time periods. A greater understanding is required of the factors determining maintenance of health behaviour; it is likely that these will be different from the factors important in the initiation of health behaviour. In addition, although health benefits of maintenance behaviours may be most strongly associated with consistent performance over prolonged time periods, interruptions or lapses may be common for these behaviours (e.g. healthy eating; Conner and Armitage 2002). Hence, an appropriate focus may be on performance over prolonged time periods that minimizes lapses (Shankar *et al.* 2004).

Distinguishing initiation and maintenance is a key component of various stage models (Armitage and Conner 2000) and has been specifically noted in relation to physical activity (Sherwood and Jeffery 2000), weight control (Jeffery *et al.* 1999) and recovery from addictions (Marlatt and Gordon 1985). A complex but key issue is how initiation versus maintenance is defined. Stage models such as the transtheoretical model of change (Prochaska *et al.* 1992) suggest distinguishing the two based on a fixed time period; initiation is the first six months following behaviour change; maintenance is beyond six months. However, this time period is essentially arbitrary and appears to be based on when most relapses occur (Orleans 2000). A more useful, but less easily quantified, distinction between initiation and maintenance might focus on variations in the factors which determine the decision to initiate or maintain the behaviour.

Various theories of the factors important for the maintenance of behaviour have been developed including the relapse prevention model (Marlatt and Gordon 1985) and the transtheoretical model (Prochaska *et al.* 1992). Basic to these theories is the idea that different factors are important in the decision to initiate and maintain a behaviour. This is distinct from other SCMs that assume the same factors underlie initiation and maintenance. The evidence here is mixed. For example, Floyd *et al.* (2000) in their meta-analysis of the PMT reported that response efficacy and self-efficacy had similar effect sizes for both initiation and maintenance behaviours. In relation to the TPB, Sheeran *et al.* (2001) showed the TPB to predict attendance at individual screening appointments, but not repeated attendance. In contrast, Conner *et al.* (2002) reported the TPB to be predictive of long-term healthy eating over a six-year period.

Here we highlight five theories that outline the different factors important in the decision to initiate a behaviour compared to the decision to maintain a behaviour. These theories propose that either different factors or the same factors acting via different processes are important in determining the decision to initiate or maintain a behaviour.

First, Rothman (2000) focuses on the role of outcome expectancies and satisfaction with outcomes in the initiation and maintenance of behaviour. The decision to initiate a behaviour is held to be based on a consideration of the potential benefits afforded by the new pattern of behaviour compared to the current situation (i.e. outcome expectancies). Initiating a new behaviour thus depends on holding favourable expectancies regarding future outcomes. Because the process of behavioural initiation can be conceptualized as the attempt to reduce the discrepancy between a current state and a desired reference state, it is viewed as an approach-based self-regulatory system (Carver and Scheier 1990). In contrast, decisions to maintain a behaviour involve decisions about whether the outcomes associated with the new pattern of behaviour are sufficiently desirable to warrant continued action (King *et al.* 2002). Thus, the decision to maintain a behaviour depends principally on perceived satisfaction with received outcomes. Because the process of behavioural maintenance can be conceptualized as the attempt to maintain the discrepancy between a current state and an undesired reference state, it is viewed as an avoidance-based self-regulatory system (Carver and Scheier 1990). Another implication of this view is that while high expectations may be an important facilitator to initiating a behaviour, these expectations must become more realistic in order that dissatisfaction with the received outcomes does not inhibit maintenance (see also Sears and Stanton 2001). Rothman (2000) suggests that satisfaction will depend upon comparisons of received outcomes with expectations about what rewards a new pattern of behaviour will provide. Thus, interventions which heighten expectations may be useful in initiating behaviour change but be detrimental to the maintenance of a behaviour.

Second, self-efficacy has been found to be a key predictor of initiation and maintenance across a variety of behavioural domains including physical activity (e.g. Dzewaltowski *et al.* 1990), oral health behaviours (e.g. Syrjala *et al.* 2001), cardiac rehabilitation (e.g. Oldridge 1988) and AIDS-preventive behaviours (e.g. Kok *et al.* 1991). It is also a variable that distinguishes action and maintenance stages from earlier stages in the transtheoretical model (e.g. Marcus and Simkin 1994). In addition, in relapse prevention theory (Marlatt and Gordon 1985) the importance of self-efficacy is highlighted in relation to recovering from slips and relapses. Finally, in goal-setting studies, higher self-efficacy is related to sticking to more challenging goals (Locke and Latham 1990). In the HAPA, Schwarzer (1992) argues that successful maintenance is dependent on the implementation of an action plan that includes a set of cognitive and behavioural skills that help people cope with behavioural lapses, and thus prevent complete relapse of the behaviour. Schwarzer (1998) particularly emphasizes coping and recovery self-efficacy as important to maintaining a health behaviour or recovering from a relapse in the behaviour respectively (see Schwarzer and Renner 2000).

Third, social support, though only tangentially included in the major SCMs, may also be important in relation to initiation and maintenance. Some studies have reported that direct measures of social support add to prediction of intentions to engage in health behaviours over and above TPB variables (e.g. healthy eating, Povey *et al.* 1999). In relation to weight loss, for example, social support appears to be an important predictor of initial weight loss attempts and longer term maintenance (Wing *et al.* 1991). In terms of initiation, social support may need to take the form of encouragement from others to try weight loss behaviours, while in terms of maintenance, social support may need to take the form of knowing others with whom to perform the behaviour. Social support has also been found to have small to moderate effects on maintenance of exercise behaviours (Sherwood and Jeffery 2000). Such effects are sometimes direct and at other times mediated by changes in self-efficacy. Social support may be just one important part of a supportive environment that is key to the maintenance of behaviours (Orleans 2000).

Fourth, self-determination theory (SDT; Deci and Ryan 1985) specifies the different motivational determinants that might be relevant to initiation versus maintenance of behaviour. In particular, SDT views successful maintenance as based on the internalization of motivation to act. So while successful initiation of a health behaviour may be possible even where the motivation is external (e.g. a health professional's recommendation), such motivation is not likely to be sufficient to maintain the behaviour. Internalization here refers to the process whereby the individual comes fully to accept the regulation of the behaviour as internally determined. Such internalized motivation has been found to be related to the maintenance of physical activity (Laitakari *et al.* 1996), diabetic dietary self-care (Senécal *et al.* 2000), smoking cessation (Williams *et al.* 2002), and medication adherence (Williams *et al.* 1998b). However, it is unclear whether these impacts of internalized motivation are independent of self-efficacy.

Fifth, the relapse prevention model (RPM; Marlatt and Gordon 1985) provides an account of the factors important to maintenance and relapse from maintenance. RPM focuses on those situations that place an individual at risk from relapse and the coping strategies an individual might use to prevent relapse via increasing self-efficacy. High-risk situations include emotional states and social pressure. Relapse can be tackled by avoiding high-risk situations, increasing self-efficacy and changing the interpretation of minor lapses. The latter is particularly important. Individuals who make internal, stable and global attributions for a lapse are more likely to experience negative emotions, such as guilt, and to relapse. Relapse prevention training has been applied to marijuana dependence (Stephens *et al.* 1994), physical activity (Knapp 1988), weight management (Perri *et al.* 2001), and smoking cessation (Curry and McBride 1994). RPM has usefully focused attention on the importance of successfully managing lapses as a means to increase maintenance of a health behaviour.

The above theories provide useful insights into the factors important to maintenance of health behaviours. A number of conclusions and issues for further research can be drawn. First, the key role of self-efficacy is evident in a number of the above theories. High levels of self-efficacy appear to be important for maintenance and for dealing with temporary lapses. Second, motivation appears as a central construct in a number of the models. For example, in SDT the importance of intrinsic motivation is emphasized, particularly in relation to maintaining health behaviours. Third, the need for integration of these different models of maintenance is apparent. A range of other variables, in addition to motivation and self-efficacy, are outlined in different models including perceived satisfaction with received outcomes, social support and interpretation of lapses. However, it is not clear how these variables might be integrated into a single model. Fourth, there is a need to integrate these maintenance models more formally with the more widely used SCMs that have been found to be successful in predicting the initiation of health behaviour (Shankar *et al.* 2004). An integrated model of the initiation and maintenance of health behaviour would include motivation and self-efficacy as key constructs but also address how social influences impact on initiation and maintenance, consider the role of future and received outcomes, and address lapses in behaviour. Models such as Schwarzer's (1992) HAPA and Bellg's (2003) health behaviour internalization model offer promising directions for future research.

2.7 Critiques of the social cognition approach

The use of SCMs to predict health behaviour has a number of advantages and disadvantages. In this section we briefly outline the main advantages of a social cognition approach before considering in more detail a range of both specific and more general criticisms that have been made of this approach.

The advantages of using SCMs to predict health behaviour are simply rehearsed. First, they provide a clear theoretical background to research, guiding the selection of constructs to measure, procedures for developing reliable and valid measures of these constructs, and a description of the ways in which these constructs combine in order to determine health behaviours. The overlap in key constructs (e.g. intention, self-efficacy, outcome expectancies) between the models can be considered to be convergent evidence that the key social cognitions have been identified (Conner and Norman, Chapter 1 in this volume). Second, to the extent that SCMs identify the variables that are important in determining health behaviour, they should be useful in informing the development of more effective interventions. Third, SCMs provide us with a description of the motivational and volitional processes underlying health behaviours. As a result, they add to our understanding of the proximal determinants of health behaviour.

However, parallel disadvantages can be drawn of a too exclusive focus on SCMs as the only way to understand health behaviour. First, in providing such a clear theoretical framework for predicting health behaviour the use of SCMs may lead us to neglect constructs that are not included in the models but, nonetheless, play an important role in predicting certain behaviours. Thus, the development of SCMs to be widely applicable across a range of behaviours and the drive for parsimony may lead to certain variables that are important for specific behaviours being neglected. As result, the most profitable application of SCMs may involve the use of constructs specified by the SCM under consideration along with additional constructs considered to be important for the particular health behaviour under investigation. Second, while SCMs may identify the key beliefs to target in interventions, they do not always specify the best means to change such cognitions. Moreover, an over-exclusive focus on SCMs may lead to the neglect of other potentially effective interventions, such as increased taxation or legal restrictions, because it is not readily apparent that such interventions would change the cognitions specified in the SCMs.

Critiques of specific SCMs have been discussed in other chapters of this book (e.g. Conner and Sparks, Chapter 5 in this volume, discuss various critiques of the theories of reasoned action and planned behaviour raised by authors such as Sarver 1983; Liska 1984; Eagly and Chaiken 1993). More general critiques of SCMs have been written by Ogden (2003) and by Greve (2001). Some of the issues raised in these critiques are commented on here.

Ogden (2003) raises a number of concerns about the use of SCMs in health psychology. Her critique is based on 47 empirical studies published in four main health psychology journals over a four-year period and focuses on the HBM, PMT and TRA/TPB. Ajzen and Fishbein (2004) provide a strong rebuttal of each of the concerns raised. Ogden raises four issues which are briefly discussed here. First, she asks whether the theories are useful. She concludes that the models are indeed useful both from the perspective of researchers and '. . . to inform service development and the development of health-related interventions to promote health behaviors' (Ogden 2003: 425).

Second, she questions whether the theories can be tested. Her conclusion is that they cannot be disconfirmed. Ogden supports this conclusion by arguing that researchers do not conclude they have disconfirmed the theory under test when they find that one or more of the theory's antecedent variables do not predict the outcome measure or that the findings do not explain all or most of the variance in intentions or behaviour. Ajzen and Fishbein (2004) highlight that the logic of this argument is unsound; to conclude that a theory has been disconfirmed under such circumstances would not be consistent with the theories being tested. Taking the example of the TRA/TPB, numerous descriptions of the theory make clear that the extent to which each of the antecedent variables predicts intentions or behaviour is a function of the population and behaviour under study. For a specific behaviour and population one or more antecedents may indeed not be predictive, without disproving the theory. However, evidence disproving the theory would be obtained if none of the antecedent variables were predictive of intentions or behaviour. In this way the TRA/TPB could be disconfirmed.

Third, Ogden claims that the theories contain only analytic truths (as opposed to synthetic truths that can be known through testing) because the correlations observed between measured cognitions are likely to be attributable to overlap in the way the constructs are measured. She claims that this argument extends to measures of behaviour because these are often based on self-report. We would dispute this interpretation of the literature for two main reasons. First, it is not at all apparent that her explanation would account for the observed patterns of correlations among cognitions that are reported in the literature. Second, high levels of prediction of behaviour are also found with objective measures of behaviour that do not rely on self-report and thus cannot be biased in the way Ogden describes. For example, Armitage and Conner (2001), in their meta-analysis of the TPB, showed that intention and perceived behavioural control still accounted for an impressive 21 per cent of variance in behaviour when objectively measured.

Fourth, Ogden suggests that the application of the theories leads to the creation of cognitions rather than the measurement of such cognitions and this in turn influences behaviour. As Ajzen and Fishbein (2004) point out, this is a common concern in questionnaire and interview studies. However, the evidence to support the claim is lacking. For example, Ajzen *et al.* (2004) had participants complete questionnaires either before or after the opportunity to perform the behaviour. No evidence was found that behavioural performance was influenced by completing the questionnaire or that performing the behaviour influenced the completing of the questionnaire. Further empirical studies might usefully explore the impacts of questionnaire completion on cognitions, however we are not aware of data to support Ogden's claim.

Greve (2001) presents a more general critique of intention–behaviour theories and the TRA/TPB in particular. The main thrust of Greve's argument is that because actions are logically tied to intentions, this means that theories which include intentions, such as the TRA/TPB and PMT, cannot provide a scientifically compelling account of action. Greve argues that action cannot be defined without reference to the intention of the actor (i.e. that action presupposes an intention to act). This would specifically suggest that there is a necessary correlation between action and intention, and that empirical investigations of the size of this relationship are irrelevant. A failure to find a relationship between intention and action would, according to this view, be due to methodological and measurement biases. Such a position would make theories such as the TPB unfalsifiable. More generally, Greve's argument suggests that whenever the premises of a theory are logically related to the conclusions of the theory, then the theory is not scientifically compelling. A number of comments are worth making about both the specific and more general aspects of Greve's argument.

First, it is not clear that Greve's definition of intention or action would show a good match with the way in which intention or, the more general term, behaviour is defined in theories such as the TPB. Greve considers intention as a dichotomous variable, whereas intention is given a dimension of strength in theories such as the TPB. Behaviour also seems to encompass a broader range of observable actions than is used in Greve's definition. With such a broader definition there seems no logical reason to conclude that intentions must predict behaviour by definition.

Second, even if we accept Greve's claim that a behaviour or action pre-supposes an intention, this does not logically imply that an intention implies a corresponding action. ('If B then BI' does not imply 'If BI then B'.) Thus the relationship between intentions and action or behaviour remains an empirical question. The more general form of Greve's argument is also problematic in our view. A conclusion from Greve's general argument is that, to be scientific, premises of a theory must not be logically related to their conclusions. We do not believe this to be a sustainable position (see Hempel 1965).

Third, although Greve believes that there is a logically necessary con-nection between intention and action, extensive empirical evidence dis-confirms this. In particular, it is not easy to reconcile Greve's argument with a variety of studies showing that habit, stability of intentions and various other factors influence the extent to which intentions influence behaviours (see Cooke and Sheeran 2004). In addition, research on implementation intentions (Sheeran *et al.*, Chapter 7 in this volume) indicates that planning when, where and how one will perform a behaviour makes it more likely that one's intention will be enacted. This evidence suggests that the causal status of intentions is a more complicated issue than is implied by Greve's criticism.

Fourth, Greve (2001) argues that the TPB fails the Smedslund test. The test requires us to imagine the reverse empirical relation and ask if true would we then discard the theory. If the answer is no, then the test is failed, and this failure suggests that the theory is not falsifiable. Consider the study by Armitage and Conner (1999). According to Greve, if Armitage and Conner had found that as people's intention eat a low-fat diet increased, they actually were less likely to do so, then we would not believe the finding. According to Greve, this study fails the Smedslund test – no matter what was found, we would still believe the theory. However, closer examination suggests that this criticism is not well founded. In particular, Greve neglects the possibility that no correlation could have been found, in which case we would have less confidence in the TPB. If that finding had been replicated using a variety of operationalizations of the variables, we might be quite confident in rejecting the theory. Even in the extreme case described by Greve, if replicated in a sufficient variety of ways, the scientific community would come to agree that increasing intentions may decrease the probability of following a low-fat diet. Subsequent research attention would then be directed towards identifying the circumstances under which such counter-intentional behaviour occurs. On this basis it appears incor-rect to characterize the TPB as failing the Smedslund test.

In summary, recent critiques have raised a number of concerns over the application of SCMs to the prediction of health behaviour (Greve 2001; Ogden 2003). In particular, these critiques have focused on the conceptual basis of these models. However, it is not clear that these critiques form a useful basis for critical debate about the value of a social cognition approach. Nonetheless, we believe that such debate can be useful in identifying the general strengths and weaknesses of this approach. In addition, the individual models have been subjected to considerable critical analysis in the literature and many unresolved issues are detailed in other chapters in this book. We believe that such critiques are crucial for the continuing development of the models. Despite the success of the social cognition approach to the prediction of health behaviour there are still a range of issues for future work to address.

3 Changing health behaviour: future directions

3.1 The practicality of social cognition models

SCMs can also be used to inform the development of interventions to change health behaviour. Brawley (1993) argues that it is possible to assess the extent to which a model provides a sound framework for intervention design on the basis of its *practicality*. To have a high level of practicality a model must (a) have predictive utility, (b) describe the relationships between key constructs, (c) offer guidelines for the assessment of these constructs, (d) allow the translation of these constructs into operational manipulations and (e) provide the basis for detecting the reasons why an intervention succeeds or fails. Each of these factors will be considered in turn in relation to the major SCMs.

First, it is clear that many of the models have good predictive utility and, as such, provide a sound basis for developing interventions. For example, Armitage and Conner's (2001) meta-analysis of TPB studies revealed that both intention ($r_+ = 0.47$) and perceived behavioural control ($r_+ = 0.37$) had significant average correlations with future behaviour. These correlations represent medium to strong effect sizes (Cohen 1992). Similar results have been reported in relation to PMT (Milne *et al.* 2000) and the self-efficacy construct of SCT has attracted considerable empirical support (Luszczynska and Schwarzer, Chapter 4 in this volume). In contrast, the HBM (Harrison *et al.* 1992) and TTM (Herzog *et al.* 1999) have received less empirical support. Overall, considering the predictive utility of SCMs, it is clear that the TPB, PMT and SCT are likely to provide good frameworks for the development of effective interventions whereas the empirical basis for the practicality of the HBM and TTM is less well established.

Second, models should describe the relationships between key constructs. This requirement is easily satisfied by the TPB, PMT and SCT. For example, in the TPB attitude, subjective norm and perceived behavioural control are seen to predict intention which, in turn, is predictive of behaviour in conjunction with perceived behavioural control. In contrast, the HBM has been criticized for failing to detail the links between the model's variables

(Abraham and Sheeran, Chapter 2 in this volume) and Bridle *et al.* (2005) have argued that the TTM also requires greater model specification (see also Sutton, Chapter 6 in this volume). Overall, the TPB, PMT and SCT appear to provide sound frameworks for intervention design as they describe the relationships between key constructs, whereas the HBM and TTM require further model specification.

Third, a model should provide guidelines for the assessment of key constructs. Recommendations exist for the construction of both direct and indirect measures of attitude, subjective norm and perceived behavioural control within the TPB (Ajzen 1988; Conner and Sparks, Chapter 5 in this volume). In addition, there are clear guidelines for the measurement of self-efficacy (Bandura 1986; Luszczynska and Schwarzer, Chapter 4 in this volume). The TTM has also benefited from considerable work that has developed measures of stages of change, pros and cons, confidence and temptation, and the processes of change (Prochaska *et al.* 1992). In contrast, the psychometric rigour of many applications of the HBM has been questioned (Harrison *et al.* 1992). Finally, PMT fails to provide clear guidelines for the measurement of its constructs although recommendations for the development of reliable scales do exist (see Norman *et al.*, Chapter 3 in this volume). Overall, guidelines are available for the assessment of the key constructs of all the SCMs considered in this book, suggesting that they have high practicality according to this criterion. However, the TPB, SCT and the TTM stand out inasmuch as detailed guidelines have been provided by the models' authors (Ajzen 1988; Bandura 1986; Prochaska *et al.* 1992).

Fourth, it should be possible to translate a model's key constructs into operational manipulations, i.e. it should be possible to design interventions to change these variables. However, a common critique of the major SCMs is that while they can be used to identify the key beliefs for interventions to focus on, they provide few guidelines on how to change these beliefs. Given the cognitive nature of these models, most theory-based intervention studies use the presentation of persuasive messages to attempt to change beliefs (Hardeman *et al.* 2002). However, as Eagly and Chaiken (1993: 240) highlight in relation to the TPB, there is 'no formal guidance for choosing arguments to include in messages designed to influence a specific belief'. Instead, it is necessary to look to models of attitude change such as the elaboration likelihood model (ELM; Petty and Cacioppo 1986), which proposes that attitude change is dependent on message favourability and elaboration (for an example study, see Quine *et al.* 2001). An exception to this critique of SCMs is SCT. Bandura (1986) outlines various sources of self-efficacy that can be targeted to enhance self-efficacy. First, self-efficacy can be enhanced through personal mastery experience, e.g. splitting a target behaviour into various sub-behaviours so that mastery of each is achieved in turn. Second, self-efficacy can be enhanced through vicarious experience, i.e. from observing a person successfully perform the behaviour. Third, persuasive communications can be used, for example in leaflets, to enhance self-efficacy. Finally, physiological feedback compatible with successful performance of the behaviour can also be used to enhance self-efficacy.

Encouragingly, interventions encompassing the above suggestions have been found to increase the performance of health behaviour (see Luszc-zynska and Schwarzer, Chapter 4 in this volume). Other models also provide theory-based intervention techniques. For example, early work on the persuasive impact of fear appeals based on the fear-drive model (Hovland *et al.* 1953), a precursor of PMT, revealed that presenting a fear-inducing message followed by an action plan detailing how to deal with the threat increased the likelihood of performance of the recommended action (e.g. Leventhal *et al.* 1965). This work on action plans has been incorporated into the model of action phases (Heckhausen 1991). In particular, the formation of implementation intentions specifying when, where and how a behaviour is to be performed is a powerful volitional technique for ensuring that goal intentions are translated into behaviour (Gollwitzer 1993; Sheeran *et al.*, Chapter 7 in this volume).

Fifth, a model should provide a basis for detecting the reasons why an intervention succeeds or fails. It is clear that the major SCMs have the potential to provide such an account. For example, HBM-based interventions should produce changes in HBM cognitions which in turn lead to changes in behaviour. In other words, if an HBM-based intervention is successful in changing health behaviour, this effect should occur through (i.e. be mediated by) the beliefs that were targeted in the intervention. Such mediation effects are best tested through the use of regression analyses (Baron and Kenny 1986). Unfortunately, mediation analyses are rarely reported in the literature, although there are exceptions (e.g. O'Leary *et al.* 2000).

3.2 Evaluating theory-based interventions

The SCMs reviewed in this book satisfy many of the criteria put forward by Brawley (1993) for assessing the practicality of a model. As a result, they should provide a good basis for the development of interventions to change health behaviour. However, evidence for the utility of such interventions is mixed. Abraham and Sheeran (Chapter 2 in this volume) found evidence of health behaviour change in 13 out of the 17 HBM-based interventions they identified. In contrast, the few studies that have assessed the impact of PMT-based interventions on health behaviour have produced mixed results (Norman *et al.*, Chapter 3 in this volume). Hardeman *et al.* (2002) reported that TPB-based interventions had significant impacts on health behaviour in approximately two-thirds of studies, although the effect sizes were generally in the small to medium range. In relation to SCT, a number of interventions to enhance self-efficacy have been found to impact on health behaviour (Luszczynska and Schwarzer, Chapter 4 in this volume). Of the stage models reviewed in this volume, the TTM has attracted the most attention as a basis for intervention work. However, recent reviews have questioned the effectiveness of TTM-based interventions (e.g. Bridle *et al.* 2005). Intervention work on other stage models, such as the PAPM (Weinstein and Sandman 1992), has provided more encouraging results (see Sutton, Chapter 6 in this volume). Finally, evidence indicates that the formation of an implementation intention is an effective technique for translating intentions into action (Sheeran *et al.*, Chapter 7 in this volume).

There are various reasons for this mixed pattern of results, some of which relate to Brawley's (1993) criteria for assessing a model's practicality. For example, both the HBM and TTM have been found to have limited predictive utility and lack model specification. In addition, most of the models fail to specify how to manipulate key constructs. Most theory-based interventions simply use the presentation of persuasive messages to attempt to change beliefs and behaviour. However, there are a range of behaviour change techniques that could be utilized. Hardeman *et al.* (2000) identified 19 such techniques in behaviour change programmes to prevent weight gain that were classified according to the four 'fundamental intervention activities' identified by Kalichman and Hospers (1997). First is instruction in which individuals are provided with explanations and rationales for adopting the target behaviour (i.e. persuasive messages). Second is modelling in which a credible model is seen to perform the target behaviour successfully. Third is practice, or mastery experience, which may be achieved through the use of role-plays. Fourth is feedback in which practitioners and peers provide support and encouragement to reinforce behaviour change.

A number of reviews have noted that many theory-based intervention studies are poorly designed (Hardeman *et al.* 2002; Michie and Abraham 2004; Bridle *et al.* 2005). The literature reveals a range of limitations both in the design (i.e. a lack of randomized controlled trials, appropriate control groups, blinding of participants, intervention details, measurement of potential mediators, long-term follow-ups) and analysis (i.e. a lack of 'intention to treat' analyses, mediation analysis) of theory-based interventions. These factors undermine the quality of research evaluating the effectiveness of theory-based interventions and may, in part, account for many of the non-significant findings that have been reported in the literature. Michie and Abraham (2004) have therefore called for increased theoretical and methodological rigour in the design and evaluation of interventions in order to accelerate the development of effective theory-based interventions. In particular, they highlight Oakley *et al.*'s (1995) recommendations that evaluations of interventions should (a) include randomly allocated or matched control groups, (b) report pre- and post-test intervention data, (c) report 'intention to treat' analyses or control for differential attrition in the intervention and control groups, and (d) report analyses for all outcome variables targeted by the intervention. In addition, Michie and Abraham (2004) recommend that (e) the description of interventions should be sufficiently detailed to enable replication, (f) experimental examinations of specific intervention techniques, both in isolation and combination, should be conducted to identify those techniques that are critical to intervention effectiveness, and (g) measures of the theory-based determinants of behaviour should be taken to allow (h) mediation analyses to identify the underlying mechanisms responsible for any behaviour change.

3.3 The diffusion of interventions

Theory-based interventions have the potential to make a significant impact on people's health behaviour and, in turn, their health. However, there are additional steps that need to be taken to ensure that successful theory-based interventions are used by health professionals. Clearly, having a strong body of published research that speaks to the effectiveness of theory-based interventions is essential in this regard (Oldenburg *et al.* 1999). However, the mere availability of relevant research findings does not in itself guarantee that successful interventions are used in practice. Instead, other factors, such as formalized institutional support and training for health professionals, need to be in place to ensure the successful transfer of research knowledge into health practice. Unfortunately, as Johnson *et al.* (1996: S5) conclude, 'the gap between knowledge generation and knowledge use or application remains problematic'. While there is a considerable research base on the social cognitive determinants of health behaviour and, to a lesser extent, theory-based interventions, there is a paucity of research into methods for ensuring the wider dissemination and uptake of successful interventions (see Oldenburg *et al.* 1999). Greater attention is therefore needed on ways in which intervention work can be successfully diffused. One promising approach has been proposed by a group of US and Dutch health promotion researchers (Bartholomew *et al.* 2001; Kok *et al.* 2004) who describe the process of *intervention mapping* – a protocol for developing health promotion programmes – in which a number of steps are outlined to ensure the appropriate development, evaluation, and diffusion of theory- and evidence-based health promotion programmes. Similarly, Rogers (1995) has also provided an account of the processes underlying the effective diffusion and implementation of innovations that could be used to aid the dissemination and uptake of successful interventions. Without such work, the full potential of a social cognitive approach for improving people's health is unlikely to be realized.

4 Concluding comment

An adequate social cognitive account of health behaviour should be able to predict health behaviour *and* account for, and promote, health behaviour change (Fishbein 1997). The main SCMs of health behaviour have been found to provide strong predictions of health-related intentions and, to a lesser extent, behaviour. It is clear that further work is needed on the variables that are important in the volitional (i.e. post-intentional) phases of health behaviour. Over recent years there has been an increase in the use of SCMs to develop interventions to change health behaviour. However, evidence for the effectiveness of these interventions is mixed. As highlighted in this chapter, there are many important questions for future work to address before the full potential of a social cognition approach to prediction, and promotion, of health behaviour is realized. These questions represent a challenging, and exciting, agenda for future research on SCMs and health behaviour.

References

Abelson, R.P. (1981) Psychological status of the script concept, *American Psychologist*, **36**, 715–29.

Abraham, C., Norman, P. and Conner, M. (2000) Towards a psychology of health-related behaviour change. In P. Norman, C. Abraham and M. Conner (eds) *Understanding and Changing Health Behaviour: From Health Beliefs to Self-Regulation*. Amsterdam: Harwood, 242–369.

Abraham, C.S., Sheeran, P., Abrams, D. and Spears, R. (1994) Exploring teenagers' adaptive and maladaptive thinking in relation to the threat of HIV infection, *Psychology and Health*, **9**, 253–72.

Ajzen, I. (1987) Attitudes, traits and actions: dispositional prediction of behavior in personality and social psychology. In L. Berkowitz (ed.) *Advances in Experimental Social Psychology*, Vol. 20. New York: Academic Press, 1–64.

Ajzen, I. (1988) *Attitudes, Personality and Behavior*. Milton Keynes: Open University Press.

Ajzen, I. (1991) The theory of planned behavior, *Organizational Behavior and Human Decision Processes*, **50**, 179–211.

Ajzen, I. (2002) Residual effects of past on later behavior: habituation and reasoned action perspectives, *Personality and Social Psychology Review*, **6**, 107–22.

Ajzen, I., Brown, T.C. and Carvajal, F. (2004) Explaining the discrepancy between intentions and actions: the case of hypothetical bias in contingent evaluation, *Personality and Social Psychology Bulletin*, **30**, 431–4.

Ajzen, I. and Fishbein, M. (2004) Questions raised by a reasoned action approach: reply on Ogden (2003), *Health Psychology*, **23**, 431–4.

Albarracin, D., Johnson, B. T., Fishbein, M. and Muellerleile, P. A. (2001) Theories of reasoned action and planned behavior as models of condom use: a meta-analysis, *Psychological Bulletin*, **127**, 142–61.

Apostolopoulos, Y., Sonmez, S. and Yu, C.H. (2003) HIV-risk behaviours of American spring break vacationers: a case of situational disinhibition?, *International Journal of STD and AIDS*, **13**, 733–43.

Armitage, C. J. and Conner, M. (1999) Distinguishing perceptions of control from self-efficacy: predicting consumption of a low-fat diet using the theory of planned behavior, *Journal of Applied Social Psychology*, **29**, 72–90.

Armitage, C. J. and Conner, M. (2000) Social cognition models and health behaviour: a structured review, *Psychology and Health*, **15**, 173–89.

Armitage, C. J. and Conner, M. (2001) Efficacy of a minimal intervention to reduce fat intake, *Social Science and Medicine*, **52**, 1517–24.

Aspinwall, L.G., Kemeny, M.E., Taylor, S.E., Schneider, S.G. and Dudley, J.P. (1991) Psychosocial predictors of gay men's AIDS risk-reduction behavior, *Health Psychology*, **10**, 432–44.

Bagozzi, R.P. (1992) The self-regulation of attitudes, intentions, and behavior, *Social Psychology Quarterly*, **55**, 178–204.

Bagozzi, R.P. and Edwards, E.A. (1998) Goal setting and goal pursuit in the regulation of body weight, *Psychology and Health*, **13**, 593–621.

Bagozzi, R.P. and Kimmel, S.K. (1995) A comparison of leading theories for the prediction of goal-directed behaviours, *British Journal of Social Psychology*, 34, 437–61.

Bandura, A. (1986) *Social Foundations of Thought and Action: A Cognitive Social Theory*. Englewood Cliffs, NJ: Prentice-Hall.

Bargh, J.A. (1997) The automaticity of everyday life. In R.S. Wyer, Jr (ed.) *The Automaticity of Everyday Life: Advances in Social Cognition*, Vol. 10. Mahwah, NJ: Erlbaum, 1–61.

Bargh, J.A. and Chartrand, T.L. (1999) The unbearable automaticity of being, *American Psychologist*, 54, 462–79.

Bargh, J.A., Chen, M. and Burrows, L. (1996) Automaticity of social behavior: direct effects of trait construct and stereotype activation on action, *Journal of Personality and Social Psychology*, 71, 230–44.

Baron, R.M. and Kenny, D.A. (1986) The moderator–mediator distinction in social psychological research: conceptual, strategic, and statistical considerations, *Journal of Personality and Social Psychology*, 51, 1173–82.

Bartholomew, L.K., Parcel, G.S., Kok, G. and Gottlieb, N. (2001) *Intervention Mapping: A Process for Designing Theory- and Evidence-based Health Education Programs*. Mayfield, CA: Mountain View.

Baumeister, R. and Leary, M. R. (1995) The need to belong: desire for interpersonal attachments as a fundamental human motivation, *Psychological Bulletin*, 117, 497–529.

Belanger, D., Godin, G., Alary, M. and Bernard, P.M. (2002) Factors explaining the intention to use condoms among injecting drug users participating in a needle-exchange program, *Journal of Applied Social Psychology*, 32, 1047–63.

Bellg, A.J. (2003) Maintenance of health behaviour change in preventive cardiology: internalisation and self-regulation of new behaviour, *Behaviour Modification*, 27, 103–31.

Ben-Ahron, V., White, D. and Phillips, K. (1995) Encouraging drinking at safe limits on single occasions: the potential contribution of protection motivation theory, *Alcohol and Alcoholism*, 30, 633–9.

Bentler, P. and Speckhart, G. (1979) Models of attitude–behavior relations, *Psychological Review*, 86, 542–6.

Bermudez, J. (1999) Personality and health protective behavior, *European Journal of Personality*, 13, 83–103.

Blanton, H., Gibbons, F.X., Gerrard, M., Conger, K.J. and Smith, G.E. (1997) Role of family and peers in the development of prototypes associated with substance use, *Journal of Applied Family Psychology*, 11, 271–88.

Blanton, H., Van den Eijnden, R.J.J.M., Buunk, B.P., Gibbons, F.X., Gerrard, M. and Bakker, A. (2001) Accentuate the negative: social images in the prediction and promotion of condom use, *Journal of Applied Social Psychology*, 31, 274–95.

Boyd, B. and Wandersman, A. (1991) Predicting undergraduate condom use with the Fishbein and Ajzen and the Triandis attitude–behavior models: implications for public health interventions, *Journal of Applied Social Psychology*, 21, 1810–30.

Brawley, L.R. (1993) The practicality of using social psychological theories for exercise and health research and intervention, *Journal of Applied Sport Psychology*, 5, 99–115.

Bridle, C., Riemsma, R. P., Pattenden, J., Sowden, A. J., Mather, L., Watt, I. S. and Walker, A. (2005) Systematic review of the effectiveness of health interventions based on the transtheoretical model, *Psychology and Health*, in press.

Brooks-Gunn, J. and Furstenberg, F.F. (1989) Adolescent sexual behavior, *American Psychologist*, **44**, 249–57.

Caron, F., Godin, G., Otis, J. and Lambert, L.D. (2004) Evaluation of a theoretically based AIDS/STD peer education program on postponing sexual intercourse and on condom use among adolescents attending high school, *Health Education Research*, **19**, 185–97.

Caron, F., Otis, J. and Pilote, F. (1998) Evaluation of an AIDS/STD peer education program on multiethnic adolescents attending an urban high school in Quebec Canada, *Journal of HIV/AIDS Education and Prevention for Adolescents and Children*, **2**, 31–53.

Carver, C.S. and Scheier, M. (1990) Principles of self-regulation: action and emotion. In E.T. Higgins and R.Sorrentino (eds) *Handbook of Motivation and Cognition: Foundations of Social Behavior*, Vol. 2. New York: Guilford Press, 645–72.

Chatzisarantis, N.L.D., Biddle, S.J.H. and Meek, G.A. (1997) A self-determination theory approach to the study of intentions and the intention–behaviour relationship in children's physical activity, *British Journal of Health Psychology*, **2**, 343–60.

Cialdini, R.B., Kallgren, C.A. and Reno, R.R. (1991) A focus theory of normative conduct: a theoretical refinement and re-evaluation of the role of norms in human behaviour. In M. P. Zanna (ed), *Advances in Experimental Social Psychology*, Vol. 24. San Diego, CA: Academic Press, 201–34.

Cohen, E.S. and Fromme, K. (2002) Differential determinants of young adult substance use and high risk sexual behavior, *Journal of Applied Social Psychology*, **32**, 1124–50.

Cohen, J. (1992) A power primer, *Psychological Bulletin*, **112**, 155–9.

Conner, M. and Abraham, C. (2001) Conscientiousness and the theory of planned behavior: toward a more complete model of the antecedents of intentions and behavior, *Personality and Social Psychology Bulletin*, **27**, 1547–61.

Conner, M. and Armitage, C. (1998) Extending the theory of planned behavior: a review and avenues for further research, *Journal of Applied Social Psychology*, **28**, 1429–64.

Conner, M. and Armitage, C.J. (2002) *The Social Psychology of Food*. Buckingham: Open University Press.

Conner, M. and McMillan, B. (1999) Interaction effects in the theory of planned behaviour: studying cannabis use, *British Journal of Social Psychology*, **38**, 195–222.

Conner, M. and Norman, P. (1996) Body weight and shape control: examining component behaviours, *Appetite*, **27**, 135–50.

Conner, M., Norman, P. and Bell, R. (2002) The theory of planned behavior and healthy eating, *Health Psychology*, **21**, 194–201.

Cooke, R. and Sheeran, P. (2004) Moderation of cognition–intention and cognition–behaviour relations: a meta-analysis of properties of variables from the theory of planned behaviour, *British Journal of Social Psychology*, **43**, 159–86.

Courneya, K.S., Bobick, T.M. and Schinke, R.J. (1999) Does the theory of planned behavior mediate the relation between personality and exercise behavior?, *Basic and Applied Social Psychology*, **21**, 317–24.

Cummings, K.M., Jette, A.M. and Brock, B.M. (1979) Psychological determinants of immunization behaviour in a Swine Influenza campaign, *Medical Care*, **17**, 639–49.

Curry, S.J. and McBride, C.M. (1994) Relapse prevention for smoking cessations:

review and evaluation of concepts and interventions, *Annual Review of Public Health*, 15, 345–66.

Dasgupta, N., McGhee, D.E., Greenwald, A.G. and Banaji, M.R. (2000) Automatic preference for white Americans: eliminating the familiarity explanation, *Journal of Experimental Social Psychology*, 36, 316–28.

Deci, E. L. (1975) *Intrinsic Motivation*. New York: Plenum.

Deci, E. L., Koestner, R. and Ryan, R. M. (1999) A meta-analytic review of experiments examining the effects of extrinsic rewards on intrinsic motivation, *Psychological Bulletin*, 125, 627–68.

Deci, E.L. and Ryan, R.M. (1985) *Intrinsic Motivation and Self-determination in Human Behavior*. New York: Plenum.

Dunn, L., Ross, B., Caines, T. and Howorth, P. (1998) A school-bases HIV/AIDS prevention education program, *Canadian Journal of Human Sexuality*, 7, 339–45.

Dzewaltowski, D.A., Noble, J.M. and Shaw, J.M. (1990) Physical activity participation: social cognitive theory versus the theories of reasoned action and planned behavior, *Journal of Sport and Exercise Psychology*, 12, 388–405.

Eagly, A.H. and Chaiken, S. (1993) *The Psychology of Attitudes*. Fort Worth, TX: Harcourt Brace Jovanovich.

Eagly, A.H. and Chaiken, S. (1998) Attitude structure and function. In D.T. Gilbert, S.T. Fiske, and G. Lindzey (eds) *The Handbook of Social Psychology*, 4th edn, Vol. 1. New York: McGraw-Hill, 269–322.

Eysenck, H.J. (ed.) (1981) *A Model for Personality*. Berlin: Springer-Verlag.

Fazio, R.H. (1990) Multiple processes by which attitudes guide behavior: the MODE model as an integrative framework. In M.P. Zanna (ed.) *Advances in Experimental Social Psychology*, Vol. 23. New York: Academic Press, 75–109.

Fazio, R.H., Jackson, J.R., Dunton, B.C. and Williams, C.J. (1995) Variability in automatic activation as an unobstrusive measure of racial attitudes: a bona-fide pipeline, *Journal of Personality and Social Psychology*, 69, 1013–27.

Fazio, R.H. and Olson, M.A. (2003) Implicit measures in social cognition research: their meaning and use, *Annual Review of Psychology*, 54, 297–327.

Fishbein, M. (1993) Introduction. In D.J. Terry, C. Gallois and M. McCamish (eds) *The Theory of Reasoned Action: Its Application to AIDS-preventive Behaviour*. Oxford: Pergamon, xv–xxv.

Fishbein, M. (1997) Predicting, understanding, and changing socially relevant behaviors: lessons learned. In C. McGarty and A.S. Haslam (eds) *The Message of Social Psychology*. Oxford: Blackwell, 77–101.

Floyd, D.L., Prentice-Dunn, S. and Rogers, R.W. (2000) A meta-analysis of research on protection motivation theory, *Journal of Applied Social Psychology*, 30, 407–29.

Gagnon, M.P. and Godin, G. (2000) The impact of new antiretroviral treatments on college students' intention to use a condom with a new sexual partner, *AIDS Education and Prevention*, 12, 239–51.

Gerrard, M., Gibbons, F.X., Benthin, A.C. and Hessling, R.M. (1996) A longitudinal study of the reciprocal nature of risk behaviors and cognitions in adolescents: what you do shapes what you think, and vice versa, *Health Psychology*, 15, 344–54.

Gerrard, M., Gibbons, F.X. and Bushman, B.J. (1996) Relation between perceived vulnerability to HIV and precautionary sexual behavior, *Psychological Bulletin*, 119, 390–409.

Gerrard, M., Gibbons, F.X., Reis-Bergan, M., Trudeau, L., Vande Lune, L.S. and

Buunk, B.C. (2002) Inhibitory effects of drinker and nondrinker prototypes on adolescent alcohol consumption, *Health Psychology*, **21**, 601–9.

Gibbons, F.X. and Gerrard, M. (1995) Predicting young adults' health risk behavior, *Journal of Personality and Social Psychology*, **69**, 505–17.

Gibbons, F.X. and Gerrard, M. (1997) Health images and their effects on health behaviour. In B.P. Buunk and F.X. Gibbons (eds) *Health, Coping and Well-being: Perspectives from Social Comparison Theory*. Hillsdale: Lawrence Erlbaum, 63–94.

Gibbons, F.X., Gerrard, M., Blanton, H. and Russell, D.W. (1998a) Reasoned action and social reaction: willingness and intention as independent predictors of health risk, *Journal of Personality and Social Psychology*, **74**, 1164–80.

Gibbons, F.X., Gerrard, M., Ouellette, J.A. and Burzette, R. (1998b) Cognitive antecedents to adolescent health risk: discriminating between behavioral intention and behavioral willingness, *Psychology and Health*, **13**, 319–39.

Godin, G. and Gionet, N.J. (1991) Determinants of an intention to exercise of electric power commissions' employees, *Ergonomics*, **34**, 1221–30.

Gollwitzer, P.M. (1993) Goal achievement: the role of intentions. In W. Stroebe and M. Hewstone (eds) *European Review of Social Psychology*, Vol. 4. Chichester: Wiley, 141–85.

Greenfield, S., Kaplan, S.H., Ware, J.E., Yano, E.M. and Frank, H.J.L. (1988) Patients' participation in medical care: effects on blood sugar control and quality of life in diabetes, *Journal of General Internal Medicine*, **3**, 448–57.

Greenwald, A.G. and Farnham, S.D. (2000) Using the implicit association test to measure self-esteem and self-concept, *Journal of Personality and Social Psychology*, **79**, 1022–38.

Greenwald, A.G., McGhee, D.E. and Schwartz, J.K.L. (1998) Measuring individual differences in implicit cognition: the implicit association test, *Journal of Personality and Social Psychology*, **74**, 1464–80.

Greenwald, A. G. and Nosek, B. A. (2001) Health of the implicit association test at age 3, *Zeitschrift für Experimentelle Psychologie*, **48**, 85–93.

Greve, W. (2001) Traps and gaps in action explanation: theoretical problems of a psychology of human action, *Psychological Bulletin*, **108**, 435–51.

Grolnick, W. S. and Ryan, R. M. (1989) Parent styles associated with children's self-regulation and competence in school, *Journal of Educational Psychology*, **81**, 143–54.

Hardeman, W., Griffin, S., Johnston, M., Kinmouth, A.L. and Warehman, N.J. (2000) Interventions to prevent weight gain: a systematic review of psychological models and behaviour change methods, *International Journal of Obesity*, **24**, 131–43.

Hardeman, W., Johnston, M., Johnston, D., Bonetti, D., Wareham, N.J. and Kinmouth, A. L. (2002) Application of the theory of planned behaviour in behaviour change interventions: a systematic review, *Psychology and Health*, **17**, 123–58.

Harris, P. and Middleton, W. (1994) The illusion of control and optimism about health: on being less at risk but no more in control than others, *British Journal of Social Psychology*, **33**, 369–86.

Harrison, J.A., Mullen, P.D. and Green, L.W. (1992) A meta-analysis of studies of the health belief model with adults, *Health Education Research*, **7**, 107–16.

Harter, S. (1978) Effectance motivation reconsidered: toward a developmental model, *Human Development*, **1**, 661–9.

Heckhausen, H. (1991) *Motivation and Action*. Berlin: Springer-Verlag.

Heckhausen, H. and Beckmann, J. (1990) Intentional action and action slips, *Psychological Review*, **97**, 36–48.

Helweg-Larsen, M. and Shepperd, J.A. (2001) Do moderators of the optimistic bias affect personal or target risk estimates: a review of the literature, *Personality and Social Psychology Review*, **1**, 74–95.

Hempel, C. G. (1965) *Aspects of Scientific Explanation and Other Essays in the Philosophy of Science*. New York: The Free Press.

Herzog, T. A., Abrams, D. B., Emmons, K. M., Linnan, L. and Shadel, W. G. (1999) Do processes of change predict smoking stage movements? A prospective analysis of the transtheoretical model, *Health Psychology*, **18**, 369–75.

Higgins, E. T., Kruglanski, A. W. and Pierro, A. (2003) Regulatory mode: locomotion and assessment as distinct orientations, *Advances in Experimental Social Psychology*, **35**, 293–344.

Hodgkins, S. and Orbell, S. (1998) Can protection motivation theory predict behaviour? A longitudinal study exploring the role of previous behaviour, *Psychology and Health*, **13**, 237–50.

Hovland, C., Janis, I.L. and Kelley, H. (1953) *Communication and Persuasion*. New Haven, CT: Yale University Press.

Jeffery, R.W., French, S.A. and Rothman, A.J. (1999) Stages of change as a predictor of success in weight control in adult women, *Health Psychology*, **18**, 543–46.

Johnson, J.L., Green, L.W., Frankish, C.J., MacLean, D.R. and Stachenko, S. (1996) A dissemination research agenda to strengthen health promotion and disease prevention, *Canadian Journal of Public Health*, **87**, S5–S10.

Joseph, J.G., Montgomery, S.B., Emmons, C.A., Kirscht, J.P., Kessler, R.C., Ostrow, D.G. *et al.* (1987) Perceived risk of AIDS: assessing the behavioral and psychosocial consequences in a cohort of gay men, *Journal of Applied Social Psychology*, **17**, 231–50.

Kahle, L.R. and Beatty, S.E. (1987) The task situation and habit in the attitude–behavior relationship: a social adaptation view, *Journal of Social Behavior and Personality*, **2**, 218–32.

Kalichman, S.C. and Hospers, H.J. (1997) Efficacy of behavioral-skills enhancement HIV risk-reduction interventions in community settings, *AIDS*, **11**, S191–S199.

Karpinski, A. and Hilton, J.L. (2001) Attitudes and the implicit association test, *Journal of Personality and Social Psychology*, **81**, 774–8.

Kendzierski, D. (1990) Decision making versus decision implementation: an action control approach to exercise adoption and adherence, *Journal of Applied Social Psychology*, **20**, 27–45.

King, C.M., Rothman, A.J. and Jeffery, R.W. (2002) The challenge study: theory-based interventions for smoking and weight-loss, *Health Education Research*, **17**, 522–30.

Knapp, D.N. (1988) Behavioral management techniques and exercise promotion. In R.K. Dishman (ed) *Exercise Promotion: Its Impact on Public Health*. Champaign, IL: Human Kinetics, 203–55.

Kok, G.J., De Vries, H., Mudde, A.N. and Strecher, V.J. (1991) Planned health education and the role of self-efficacy: Dutch research, *Health Education Research*, **6**, 231–8.

Kok, G., Schaalma, H., Ruiter, R.A.C., Van Empelen, P. and Brug, J. (2004) Intervention mapping: a protocol for applying health psychology theory to prevention programmes, *Journal of Health Psychology*, **9**, 85–98.

Kruglanski, A.W., Thompson, E.P., Higgins, E.T., Atash, M.N., Pierro, A., Shah, J.H. and Spiegel, S. (2000) To 'do the right thing' or to 'just do it': locomotion and assessment as distinct self-regulatory imperatives, *Journal of Personality and Social Psychology*, 79, 793–815.

Kuhl, J. (1985) Volitional mediators of cognition–behavior consistency: self-regulatory processes and action versus state orientation. In J. Kuhl and J. Beckman (eds) *Action Control: From Cognition to Behavior*. New York: Springer, 101–28.

Laitakari, J., Vuori, I. and Oja, P. (1996) Is long-term maintenance of health-related physical activity possible? An analysis of concepts and evidence, *Health Education Research*, 11, 463–77.

Lauver, D.R., Henriques, J.B., Settersten, L. and Bumann, M.C. (2003) Psychosocial variables, external barriers, and stage of mammography adoption, *Health Psychology*, 22, 649–53.

Leventhal, H., Singer, R. and Jones, S. (1965) Effects of fear and specificity of recommendation upon attitudes and behavior, *Journal of Personality and Social Psychology*, 2, 313–21.

Liska, A.E. (1984) A critical examination of the causal structure of the Fishbein/Ajzen attitude-behavior model, *Social Psychology Quarterly*, 47, 61–74.

Locke, E.A. and Latham, G.P. (1990) *A Theory of Goal Setting and Task Performance*. Englewood Cliffs, NJ: Prentice Hall.

McAuley, E. (1993) Self-efficacy and the maintenance of exercise participation in older adults, *Journal of Behavioral Medicine*, 16, 103–13.

Macrae, C.N. and Johnston, L. (1998) Help, I need somebody: automatic action and inaction, *Social Cognition*, 16, 400–17.

McCrae, R.R. and Costa, P.T. Jr (1987) Validation of the five-factor model of personality across instruments and observers, *Journal of Personality and Social Psychology*, 54, 81–90.

McCrae, R.R. and Costa, P.T. Jr (1990) *Personality in Adulthood* (2nd edition). New York: Guilford Press.

Maison, D., Greenwald, A. G. and Bruin, R. (2001) The implicit association test as a measure of implicit consumer attitudes, *Polish Psychological Bulletin*, 2, 61–79.

Manstead, A. S. R. (2000) The role of moral norm in the attitude–behavior relation. In D. J. Terry and M. A. Hogg (eds) *Attitudes, Behavior, and Social Context*. Mahwah, NJ: Lawrence Erlbaum Associates, 11–30.

Marcus, B.H. and Simkin, L.R. (1994) The transtheoretical model: applications to exercise behaviour, *Medical Science in Sport and Exercise*, 26, 1400–4.

Marlatt, G.A. and Gordon, J. (eds) (1985) *Relapse Prevention: Maintenance Strategies in Addictive Behavior Change*. New York: Guilford Press.

Marsh, K.L., Johnson, B.T., Scott-Sheldon, L.A.J. and Smith-McLallen, A. (submitted) *Implicit Versus Explicit Attitudes: Predicting Behaviour over Time*.

Marshall, G.N., Wortman, C.B., Vickers, R.R., Kusulas, J.W. and Hervig, L.K. (1994) The five-factor model of personality as a framework for personality-health research, *Journal of Personality and Social Psychology*, 67, 278–86.

Michie, S. and Abraham, C. (2004) Interventions to change health behaviours: evidence-based or evidence-inspired?, *Psychology and Health*, 19, 29–49.

Milne, S., Sheeran, P. and Orbell, S. (2000) Prediction and intervention in health-related behavior: a meta-analytic review of protection motivation theory, *Journal of Applied Social Psychology*, 30, 106–43.

Murgraff, V., White, D. and Phillips, K. (1999) An application of protection motivation theory to riskier single-occasion drinking, *Psychology and Health*, 14, 339–50.

Nadler, A. and Fisher, J.D. (1992) Volitional personal change in an interpersonal perspective, in Y. Klat, J. Fisher, J. Chinsky and A. Nadler (eds) *Initiating Self-*

change: Social Psychological and Clinical Perspectives. New York: Springer-Verlag, 213–30.

Norman, P. and Brain, K. (2005) An application of an extended health belief model to the prediction of breast self-examination among women with a family history of breast cancer, *British Journal of Health Psychology*, **10**, 1–16.

Norman, P. and Conner, M. (1996) Predicting health check attendance among prior attenders and non-attenders: the role of prior behaviour in the theory of planned behaviour, *Journal of Applied Social Psychology*, **26**, 1010–26.

Norman, P., Conner, M. and Bell, R. (1999) The theory of planned behavior and smoking cessation, *Health Psychology*, **18**, 89–94.

Norman, P., Searle, A., Harrad, R. and Vedhara, K. (2003) Predicting adherence to eye patching in children with amblyopia: an application of protection motivation theory, *British Journal of Health Psychology*, **8**, 67–82.

Norman, P., Sheeran, P. and Orbell, S. (2003) Does state versus action orientation moderate the intention–behavior relationship?, *Journal of Applied Social Psychology*, **33**, 536–53.

Nowalk, M.P., Zimmerman, R.K., Shen, S.H., Jewell, I.K. and Raymund, M. (2004) Barriers to pneumococcal and influenza vaccination in older community-dwelling adults (2000–2001), *Journal of the American Geriatrics Society*, **52**, 25–30.

Oakley, A., Fullerton, D., Holland, J., Arnold, S., Francedawson, M., Kelly, P. and McGrelliss, S. (1995) Sexual health education interventions for young people: a methodological review, *British Medical Journal*, **310**, 158–62.

O'Brien, T.B. and DeLongis, A. (1996) The interactional context of problem-, emotion-, and relationship-focused coping: the role of the big five personality factors, *Journal of Personality*, **64**, 775–813.

Ogden, J. (2003) Some problems with social cognition models: a pragmatic and conceptual analysis, *Health Psychology*, **22**, 424–8.

O'Gorman, R., Perugini, M. and Conner, M. (2004) Predictive validity of implicit attitude measures: an application to sweets consumption. Paper presented at the BPS Social Psychology Section Annual Conference, University of Liverpool, 1–3 September 2003.

Oldenburg, B.F., Sallis, J.E., Ffrench, M.L. and Owen, N. (1999) Health promotion research and the diffusion and institutionalization of interventions, *Health Education Research*, **14**, 121–30.

Oldridge, N. (1988) Cardiac rehabilitation exercise program: compliance and compliance enhancing strategies, *Sports Medicine*, **6**, 42–55.

O'Leary, A., Maibach, E., Ambrose, T.K., Jemmot III, J.B. and Celentano, D.D. (2000) Social cognitive predictors of sexual risk behavior change among STD clinic patients, *AIDS and Behavior*, **4**, 309–16.

Orbell, S. and Sheeran, P. (1998) 'Inclined abstainers': a problem for predicting health-related behaviour, *British Journal of Social Psychology*, **37**, 151–65.

Orleans, C.T. (2000) Promoting maintenance of health behaviour change: recommendations for the next generation of research and practice, *Health Psychology*, **19**, 76–83.

Ouellette, J. and Wood, W. (1998) Habit and intention in everyday life: the multiple processes by which past behavior predicts future behavior, *Psychological Bulletin*, **124**, 54–74.

Perri, M.G., Nezu, A.M., Mc.Kelvey, W.F., Shermer, R.L., Renjilian, D.A. and Viegener, B.J. (2001) Relapse prevention training and problem solving therapy in the long-term management of obesity, *Journal of Consulting and Clinical Psychology*, **69**, 722–6.

Perugini, M. (in press) The interaction between implicit and explicit attitudes, *British Journal of Social Psychology*.

Petty, R.E. and Cacioppo, J.T. (1986) *Communication and Persuasion: Central and Peripheral Routes of Attitude Change*. New York: Springer Verlag.

Pierro, A., Mannetti, L., Higgins, E.T. and Kruglanski, A.W. (2002) Moderating role of regulatory mode on relationships between theory of planned behavior variables. Unpublished manuscript.

Povey, R., Conner, M., Sparks, P., James, R. and Shepherd, R. (1999) The theory of planned behaviour and healthy eating: examining additive and moderating effects of social influence variables, *Psychology and Health*, 14, 991–1006.

Prochaska, J.O., DiClemente, C.C. and Norcross, J.C. (1992) In search of how people change: applications to addictive behaviors, *American Psychologist*, 47, 1102–14.

Quine, L., Rutter, D. R. and Arnold, L. (2001) Persuading school-age cyclists to use safety helmets: effectiveness of an intervention based on the theory of planned behaviour, *British Journal of Health Psychology*, 6, 327–45.

Rhodes, K.E. and Courneya, K.S. (2003) Relationships between personality, an extended theory of planned behaviour model and exercise behaviour, *British Journal of Health Psychology*, 8, 19–36.

Rhodes, K.E., Courneya, K.S. and Jones, L.W. (2003) Translating exercise intentions into behavior: personality and social cognitive correlates, *Journal of Health Psychology*, 8, 447–58.

Rivis, A. and Sheeran, P. (2003) Descriptive norms as an additional predictor in the theory of planned behaviour: a meta-analysis, *Current Psychology*, 22, 218–33.

Roefs, A. and Janssen, A. (2002) Implicit and explicit attitudes toward high-fat foods in obesity, *Journal of Abnormal Psychology*, 111, 517–21.

Rogers, E.M. (1995) *Diffusion of Innovations* (4th edition). New York: Free Press.

Rogers, R. W. (1983) Cognitive and physiological processes in fear appeals and attitude change: a revised theory of protection motivation. In J. T. Cacioppo and R. E. Petty (eds) *Social Psychophysiology: a Source Book*. New York: Guilford Press, 153–76.

Ronis, D.L., Yates, J.F. and Kirscht, J.P. (1989) Attitudes, decisions and habits as determinants of repeated behaviour. In A.R. Pratkanis, S.J. Breckler and A.G. Greenwald (eds) *Attitude Structure and Function*. Hillsdale, NJ: Erlbaum, 213–39.

Rothman, A.J. (2000) Toward a theory-based analysis of behavioral maintenance, *Health Psychology*, 19, 64–9.

Rutter, D.R. and Quine, L. (eds) (2002) *Changing Health Behaviour*. Buckingham: Open University Press.

Ryan, R. M. (1982) Control and information in the intrapersonal sphere: an extension of cognitive evaluation theory, *Journal of Personality and Social Psychology*, 43, 450–61.

Ryan, R.M. and Deci, E.L. (2000) Self-determination theory and the facilitation of intrinsic motivation, social development, and well-being, *American Psychologist*, 55, 68–78.

Ryan, R. M. and Grolnick, W. S. (1986) Origins and pawns in the classroom: self-report and projective assessments of individual differences in children's perceptions, *Journal of Personality and Social Psychology*, 50, 550–8.

Ryan, R. M., Stiller, J. and Lynch, J. H. (1994) Representations of relationships to teachers, parents, and friends as predictors of academic motivation and self-esteem, *Journal of Early Adolescence*, 14, 226–49.

Sarver, V.T., Jr (1983) Ajzen and Fishbein's 'theory of reasoned action': a critical assessment, *Journal for the Theory of Social Behaviour*, 13, 155–63.

Schwartz, M.D., Taylor, K.L., Willard, K.S., Siegel, J.E., Lamdan, R.M. and Moran, K. (1999) Distress, personality, and mammography utilization among women with a family history of breast cancer, *Health Psychology*, 18, 327–32.

Schwarzer, R. (1992) Self-efficacy in the adoption and maintenance of health behaviors: theoretical approaches and a new model. In R. Schwarzer (ed.) *Self-efficacy: Thought Control of Action*. London: Hemisphere, 217–43.

Schwarzer, R. (1998) Optimism, goals and threats: how to conceptualise self-regulatory processes in the adoption and maintenance of health behaviors, *Psychology and Health*, 13, 759–66.

Schwarzer, R. and Renner, B. (2000) Social-cognitive predictors of health behavior: action self-efficacy and coping self-efficacy, *Health Psychology*, 19, 487–95.

Sears, S.R. and Stanton, A.L. (2001) Expectancy-value constructs and expectance violation as predictors of exercise adherence in previously sedentary women, *Health Psychology*, 20, 326–33.

Seibold, D.R. and Roper, R.E. (1979) Psychosocial determinants of health care intentions: test of the Triandis and Fishbein models. In D. Nimmo (ed.) *Communication Yearbook 3*. New Brunswick, NJ: Transaction Books, 625–43.

Senécal, C., Nouwen, A. and White, D. (2000) Motivation and dietary self-care in adults with diabetes: are self-efficacy and autonomous self-regulation complementary to competing constructs?, *Health Psychology*, 19, 452–7.

Seydel, E., Taal, E. and Wiegman, O. (1990) Risk-appraisal, outcome and self-efficacy expectancies: cognitive factors in preventive behaviour related to cancer, *Psychology and Health*, 4, 99–109.

Shankar, A., Conner, M. and Jones, F. (2004) Psychosocial predictors of maintenance of health behaviours. Unpublished manuscript, School of Psychology, University of Leeds.

Shannon, B., Bagby, R., Wang, M.Q. and McElroy, C. (1992) Self-efficacy: a contributor to the explanation of eating behavior, *Health Education Research*, 5, 395–407.

Sheeran, P. (2002) Intention–behavior relations: a conceptual and empirical review. In W. Stroebe and M. Hewstone (eds) *European Review of Social Psychology*, Vol. 12. Chichester: Wiley, 1–36.

Sheeran, P., Conner, M. and Norman, P. (2001) Can the theory of planned behavior explain patterns of behavior change?, *Health Psychology*, 20, 12–19.

Sheppard, B. H., Hartwick, J. and Warshaw, P. R. (1988) The theory of reasoned action: a meta-analysis of past research with recommendations for modifications and future research, *Journal of Consumer Research*, 15, 325–343.

Sherwood, N.E. and Jeffery, R.W. (2000) The behavioral determinants of exercise: implications for physical activity interventions, *Annual Review of Nutrition*, 20, 21–44.

Siegler, I.C., Feaganes, J.R. and Rimer, B.K. (1995) Predictors of adoption of mammography in women under age 50, *Health Psychology*, 14, 274–8.

Simmons, R.G. and Blyth, D.A. (1987) *Moving into Adolescence: The Impact of Pubertal Change and School Context*. New York: Aldine.

Stacy, A.W., Newcomb, M.D. and Ames, S.L. (2000) Implicit cognition and HIV risk behaviour, *Journal of Behavioral Medicine*, 23, 475–99.

Stephens, R.S., Roffman, R.A. and Simpson, E.E. (1994) Treating adult marijuana dependence: a test of the relapse prevention model, *Journal of Consulting and Clinical Psychology*, 62, 92–9.

Strack, F. and Deutsch, R. (2004) Reflective and impulsive determinants of social behaviour, *Personality and Social Psychology Review*, **8**, 220–47.

Swanson, J.E., Rudman, L.A. and Greenwald, A.G. (2001) Using the implicit association test to investigate attitude–behavior consistency for stigmatized behavior, *Cognition and Emotion*, **15**, 207–30.

Syrjala, A.M., Knuuttila, M.L. and Syrjala, L.K. (2001) Self-efficacy perceptions in oral health behaviour, *Acta Odontologica Scandinavica*, **59**, 1–6.

Thornton, B., Gibbons, F.X. and Gerrard, M. (2002) Risk perception and prototype perception: independent processes predicting risk behavior, *Journal of Personality and Social Psychology*, **28**, 986–99.

Trafimow, D. and Wyer, R.S. (1993) Cognitive representation of mundane social events, *Journal of Personality and Social Psychology*, **64**, 365–76.

Triandis, H. C. (1977) *Interpersonal Behavior*. Monterey, CA: Brooks-Cole.

Triandis, H. C. (1980) Values, attitudes and interpersonal behavior. In M. M. Page (ed) *Nebraska Symposium on Motivation 1979*. Lincoln: University of Nebraska Press, 195–259.

Vallerand, R. J. (1997) Toward a hierarchical model of intrinsic and extrinsic motivation. In M. P. Zanna (ed) *Advances in Experimental Social Psychology*, Vol. 29. San Diego, CA: Academic Press, 271–360.

Van den Putte, H. (1991) On the theory of reasoned action. Unpublished doctoral dissertation, University of Amsterdam.

Van der Pligt, J. and De Vries, N.K. (1998) Expectancy-value models of health behaviour: the role of salience and anticipated affect, *Psychology and Health*, **13**, 289–305.

Van der Velde, W. and Hooykaas, C. (1996) Conditional versus unconditional risk estimates in models of AIDS-related risk behaviour, *Psychology and Health*, **12**, 87–100.

Vansteenkiste, M., Simons, J., Soenens. B. and Lens, W. (2004) How to become a persevering exerciser? Providing a clear, future intrinsic goal in an autonomy-supportive way, *Journal of Sport and Exercise Psychology*, **26**, 232–49.

Verplanken, B. and Aarts, H. (1999) Habit, attitude and planned behaviour: is habit an empty construct or an interesting case of automaticity?, *European Review of Social Psychology*, **10**, 101–34.

Verplanken, B., Aarts, H., van Knippenberg, A. and van Knippenberg, C. (1994) Attitude versus general habit: antecedents of travel mode choice, *Journal of Applied Social Psychology*, **24**, 285–300.

Verplanken, B. and Orbell, S. (2003) Reflections on past behavior: a self-report index of habit strength, *Journal of Applied Social Psychology*, **33**, 1313–30.

Verplanken, B., Aarts, H., van Knippenberg, A. and Moonen, A. (1998) Habit versus planned behaviour: a field experiment, *British Journal of Social Psychology*, **37**, 111–28.

Watson, D. and Hubbard, B. (1996) Adaptational style and dispositional structure: coping in the context of the five-factor model, *Journal of Personality*, **64**, 737–74.

Wegner, D.M. and Wheatley, T. (1999) Apparent mental causation: sources of the experience of will, *American Psychologist*, **54**, 480–92.

Weinstein, N.D. (1983) Reducing unrealistic optimism about illness susceptibility, *Health Psychology*, **2**, 11–20.

Weinstein, N.D. (1984) Why it won't happen to me: perceptions of risk factors and illness susceptibility, *Health Psychology*, **3**, 431–57.

Weinstein, N.D. (1987) Unrealistic optimism about susceptibility to health problems: conclusions from a community-wide sample, *Journal of Behavioural Medicine*, **10**, 481–99.

Weinstein, N.D. (1988) The precaution adoption process, *Health Psychology*, **7**, 355–86.

Weinstein, N.D. and Klein, W. (1995) Resistance of personal risk perceptions to debiasing interventions, *Health Psychology*, **14**, 132–40.

Weinstein, N.D. and Klein, W. (1996) Unrealistic optimism: present and future, *Journal of Social and Clinical Psychology*, **15**, 1–8.

Weinstein, N.D. Lyon, J.E., Sandman, P.M. and Cuite, C.L. (1998) Experimental eidence for stages of health behavior adoption: the precaution adoption process model applied to home radon testing, *Health Psychology*, **17**, 445–53.

Weinstein, N.D. and Nicolich, M. (1989) Correct and incorrect interpretations of correlations between risk perceptions and risk behaviors, *Health Psychology*, **12**, 235–45.

Weinstein, N. D. and Sandman, P. M. (1992) A model of the precaution adoption process: evidence from home radon testing, *Health Psychology*, **11**, 170–80.

Wiers, R.W., van Woerden, N., Smulders, F.T.Y. and de Jong, P.J. (2002) Implicit and explicit alcohol-related cognitions in heavy and light drinkers, *Journal of Abnormal Psychology*, **111**, 648–58.

Williams, G. C., Freedman, Z. R. and Deci, E. L. (1998a) Supporting autonomy to motivate glucose control in patients with diabetes, *Diabetes Care*, **21**, 1644–51.

Williams, G.C., Gagné, M., Ryan, R.M. and Deci, E.L. (2002) Facilitating autonomous motivation for smoking cessation, *Health Psychology*, **21**, 40–50.

Williams, G.C., Grow, V.M., Freedman, Z.R., Ryan, R.M. and Deci, E.L. (1996) Motivational predictors of weight loss and weight-loss maintenance, *Journal of Personality and Social Psychology*, **70**, 115–26.

Williams, G.C., McGregor, H.A., Zeldman, A., Freedman, Z.R. and Deci, E.L. (2004) Testing a self-determination theory process model for promoting glycemic control through diabetes self-management, *Health Psychology*, **23**, 58–66.

Williams, G.C., Rodin, G.C., Ryan, R.M., Grolnick, W.S. and Deci, E.L. (1998b) Autonomous regulation and long-term medication adherence in medical outpatients, *Health Psychology*, **17**, 269–76.

Wilson, T. D., Lindsey, S. and Schooler, T. (2000) A model of dual attitudes, *Psychological Review*, **107**, 101–26.

Wing, R.R., Marcus, M.D., Epstein, L.H. and Jawad, A. (1991) A 'family-based' approach to the treatment of obese Type II diabetic patients, *Journal of Consulting and Clinical Psychology*, **59**, 156–62.

INDEX

Aarts, H. 295–7, 299, 302
Abraham, C. 42, 212, 213, 279, 291, 324, 325, 327
Abraham, C.S. 91, 95, 101, 103, 120, 265
action control theory 326
action phases model 13
action-outcome expectancies, and social cognitive theory 11
action-outcome-efficacy 9
addictive behaviours, and SCT (social cognitive theory) 135, 141–3
Agnew, C. 186, 187
Aho, W.R. 37
AIDS/HIV *see* HIV-preventive behaviours
Ajzen, I. 143, 170, 171, 172, 173, 175, 176, 178, 180, 184, 185, 186, 187, 189–90, 191, 192, 193–4, 195, 196, 197–8, 199, 200, 201, 207, 208, 211
    on past behaviour 341, 342, 343–4
    and PMT (protection motivation theory) 96
alcohol consumption
    and harm reduction self-efficacy 145
    and implementation intentions 290, 293–4
    and past behaviour 341

and PMT (protection motivation theory) 88, 89–90, 95, 97
and SCT (social cognitive theory) 142–3, 157
and the TPB (theory of planned behaviour) 183
and the TTM (trans-theoretical model of change) 228
alcoholism treatment, and the HBM (health belief model) 37
amotivation, and SDT (self-determination theory) 336
amputation, and SCT (social cognitive theory) 136
anticipated regret, and the TPB (theory of planned behaviour) 193
Armitage, C.J. 172, 178, 179, 184, 187, 191, 192, 194, 195, 198, 202, 291, 299, 353
Aspinwall, L.G. 98, 329
autonomous motivation, and SDT (self-determination theory) 337

Bagozzi, R.P. 184, 185, 186, 334–5
Bandura, A. 9, 10, 42, 61, 116, 257
    and SCT (social cognitive theory) 127–8, 129, 130, 132, 133, 137, 143, 146, 147, 158

THE SOCIAL PSYCHOLOGY OF EXERCISE AND SPORT

Martin Hagger and Nikos Chatzisarantis

This new textbook examines the role that social psychology has in the explanation of exercise and sport behaviour. It devotes considerable attention to key social psychological issues within the two disciplines; health-related exercise behaviour and the behaviour of competitive sport participants and the spectators of elite sport.

Rather than presenting a broad, superficial overview of diverse areas in exercise and sport, the book focuses on a range of selected topics and provides a comprehensive, in-depth and analytical coverage using social psychology as a framework. It thoroughly examines how social psychological research and intervention has contributed to the understanding of key topics in exercise and sport behaviour including:

- The social psychology of exercise and health
- Social cognitive theories of exercise behaviour
- Exercise and the physical self
- Eating disorders in exercise and sport
- Emotion and mood in athletes
- Social psychology and motivation in sport
- Group processes in sport
- Aggression and crowd violence

The Social Psychology of Exercise and Sport is key reading for undergraduate and postgraduate students on social or sport psychology courses and on health-related or sports science courses. Illustrated throughout with practical guidelines for researchers and practitioners, it is also a valuable resource for professionals interested in understanding and changing the behaviour of exercise participants and athletes.

Contents: *Preface – Introduction –* **Part 1: The social psychology of exercise** *– Social psychology, exercise, and health – Social cognitive theories of exercise behaviour – From exercise intention to behaviour and beyond – Exercise and the physical self –* **Part 2: The social psychology of sport** *– Social psychology and motivation in sport – Athletes are emotional, too – Group processes in sport – Aggression and crowd violence – Conclusions – Index.*

272pp   0 335 21618 8 (Paperback)   0 335 21619 6 (Hardback)

EMBODIMENT

Clinical, Critical & Cultural Perspectives

Malcolm MacLachlan

This book is for students of psychology, medicine, nursing and other health sciences. It lucidly illustrates why neither a simplistic mind-body dichotomy, nor the parallelism of the biopsychosocial model, sufficiently captures people's experience of *being a body*. Such experience is most salient when the body is in some way distressed, diseased, disordered, disabled or dismembered. Adding to the intriguing sociological and philosophical literature on embodiment, the book illustrates how such a seemingly abstract term has tremendous clinical significance to many people's experience.

Drawing a parallel with recent exciting work on neural plasticity, *Embodiment* illustrates how we are now in an age of 'body plasticity'; where our body boundaries are becoming increasingly ambiguous, allowing us more 'degrees of freedom' and offering more opportunities than ever before to overcome physical limitations. The book draws on research from diverse areas including health and clinical psychology, neuroscience, medicine, nursing, anthropology, philosophy and sociology: it is a key resource for students of these disciplines.

Contents: *Body Plasticity – Sensing Self – Somatic Complaints – Body Sculpturing – Illusory Body Experiences – Enabling Technologies – Forms of Embodiment.*

July 2004 c.192pp   0 335 20959 9 Paperback c.£16.99
0 335 20960 2 Hardback c.£50.00

HEALTH PSYCHOLOGY: A TEXTBOOK

Third Edition

Jane Ogden

Praise for this edition:

"This third edition...provides a clear, comprehensive and up-to-date over-view of a wide range of research and theory...it clearly deserves to maintain its place as the number one choice of health psychology textbook." John Weinman, King's College, London

Health Psychology: A Textbook has made a major contribution to the teaching and study of this rapidly expanding discipline. Maintaining its strong review of theory and research, the third edition has been substantially revised to provide increased coverage of the biological aspects of health and illness. This book now provides the most accessible and comprehensive guide to the field.

The new two-colour layout has been designed with students in mind, including clear illustrations, boxed discussion points, and specific research boxes. Many new features have been incorporated into this edition to further aid students and teachers, including:

- Additional, entirely new chapter on stress; now two chapters address this key topic
- Expanded and improved section on psychoneuroimmunology (PNI)
- Expanded chapter on pain
- New section on the consequences of coronary heart disease (CHD) and rehabilitation of CHD patients
- New chapter on eating behaviour
- New coverage of problems associated with social cognition models

Health Psychology: A Textbook is essential reading for all students and researchers of health psychology and for students of medicine, nursing and allied health courses.

Contents: Detailed table of contents – List of figures and table – Preface to third edition – Technology to enhance learning and teaching – Acknowledgements – An Introduction to Health Psychology – Health Beliefs – Illness Cognitions – Doctor-patient communication and the role of health professionals' health beliefs – Smoking and alcohol use – Eating behaviour – Exercise – Sex – Screening – Stress – Stress and illness – Pain – Placebos and the interrelationship between beliefs, behaviour and health – HIV and cancer: psychology throughout the course of illness (1) – Obesity and coronary heart disease: psychology throughout the course of illness (2) – Measuring health status: from mortality rates to quality of life – The assumptions of health psychology – Methodology glossary – References – Index.

352pp 0 335 21471 1 (Paperback) 0 335 21487 8 (Hardback)

THE PSYCHOLOGY OF APPEARANCE

Nichola Rumsey and Diana Harcourt

Appearance related concerns and distress are experienced by a significant proportion of people with visible disfigurements, and are also reaching 'epidemic proportions' in the general population. Coverage includes:

- A comprehensive summary and critical evaluation of research and understanding concerning the psychology of appearance
- A historical review of research to date
- A review of the methodological challenges for researchers in this area
- An overview of current understanding of appearance-related concerns and distress in the general population and amongst those with visible disfigurements

This book explores the psychosocial factors which are protective and those which exacerbate distress. Furthermore, it reviews current interventions, and offers a vision of a comprehensive approach to support and intervention in the future. It provides essential reading for undergraduate and postgraduate students of psychology, health professionals caring for the broad range of patient populations with disfiguring conditions, health psychologists, health care and social policy makers, and those interested in the evaluation of appearance.

Contents: Preface – Historical overview of appearance-related research – Methodological considerations – The psychology of appearance – The psychology of visible difference (disfigurement) – Predicting resilience and distress in relation to appearance – Current methods of support and interventions – Looking forward: A comprehensive approach to support and intervention – Current dilemmas and the future of appearance research – Index.

192pp   0 335 21276 X (Paperback)   0 335 21277 8 (Hardback)

RISK COMMUNICATION AND HEALTH PSYCHOLOGY

Dianne Berry

This is the first book to clearly assess the increasingly important area of communication of risk in the health sector. We are moving away from the days when paternalistic doctors managed healthcare without involving patients in decision making. With the current emphasis on patient empowerment and shared decision making, patients want and need reliable, comprehensive and understandable information about their conditions and treatment. In order to make informed decisions, the people concerned must understand the risks and benefits associated with possible treatments. But the challenge for health professionals is how best to communicate this complex medical information to diverse audiences.

The book examines:

- Risk: defining and explaining how the term is used by different disciplines, how its meanings have changed over time and how the general public understand it
- Health communication and the effects on health behaviours
- Effective risk communication to individuals and the wider public; effectiveness of patient information leaflets, and strategies for improving oral and written health communications
- The cognitive and emotional issues at stake for patients in understanding risk and health information
- The use of new technologies in risk and health communication
- Ethical issues, and the future of risk communication

Using examples from disciplines including psychology, sociology, health, medicine, pharmacy, statistics and business and management, this book is key reading for students who need to understand the effect of risk in health psychology as well as for health professionals interested in doctor-patient communication, informed consent and patient welfare.

Contents: Preface – An Introduction to Risk Communication in Health – Defining and Explaining Risk – Communicating Probabilistic Information – Understanding and Influencing People's health Behaviours – Communicating Information about Health and Treatment – Patient Information Leaflets and the Provision of Written Information – Other Risk Scales and Tools for Aiding Understanding of Health Related Information – Conclusions and Future Challenges – References.

June 2004 c.192pp   0 335 21321 0 Paperback c.£18.99
                    0 335 21352 9 Hardback c.£55.00